*PLAY with
a PURPOSE*

Harper's School and Public Health Education,
Physical Education, and Recreation Series

Under the Editorship of DELBERT OBERTEUFFER

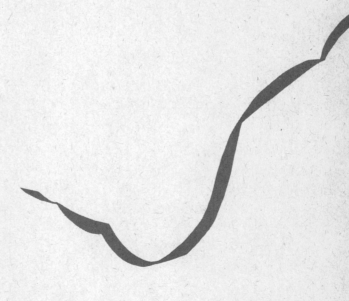

PLAY with a PURPOSE

Elementary School Physical Education

SECOND EDITION

Kindergarten Through Grade Eight

MARIAN H. ANDERSON
Professor Emeritus
University of California, Santa Barbara

MARGARET E. ELLIOT
State University College at Brockport, New York

JEANNE LA BERGE
Montecito Union Elementary School, Santa Barbara

HARPER & ROW, PUBLISHERS
New York, Evanston, San Francisco, London

Play with a Purpose: Elementary School Physical Education,
Second Edition.

Copyright © 1966, 1972 by Marian H. Anderson, Margaret E. Elliot,
and Jeanne LaBerge.

Standard Book Number: 06-040276-8
Library of Congress Catalog Card Number: 72-165028

CONTENTS

PART III   APPENDIX

PREFACE TO
THE SECOND EDITION

The second edition of *Play with a Purpose* represents continuing efforts to present movement activities that are soundly based on research and that reflect logical continuity. Evaluation of new information, incorporated with that of proven worth, results in program designs that provide the most meaningful experiences for children.

Research in sensorimotor and perceptual-motor development has provided guidelines for activity throughout the revision, particularly in Chapters 1, 5, 6, and 10. The manner in which a child orders his environment dictates his movement patterns and determines his successes. New activities are included that are designed to sharpen perception of individual movement, enhance control in movement, and elicit thoughtful responses to movement problems. All of these factors are encompassed in the term *movement education,* which depicts an exciting kind of learning environment for children.

Realignment of material in several chapters was accomplished to carry through this theme of individual movement development prior to the introduction of activities utilizing objects and implements. As in the first edition, material is presented in such a way that great flexibility in instructional approaches is possible: Movement skills are identified and described in several different contexts, including sport units; opportunities for competitive play are suggested; team games involving high-level skill and strategy are included. If the primary objective of the program is individual participation in activity, without regard for a competitive element, then the first section of each activity chart may be used to suggest sequences. The extent of group or team involvement desired will determine the emphasis on games included in the sport units. A program that is dedicated to individual interests and needs will probably include elements of each.

Some material has been consolidated into other chapters, some placed in the Appendix, particularly information dealing with facilities, equipment, and supplies. In addition to the theory in Part II, the reader will find pertinent theory and rationale at the beginning of each activity chapter. The intent is to bring each area into sharper focus and to align related subject matter. Purposes for each activity area have been restated for greater clarity and easier assessment of objectives. It is recommended that the rules to the various games be reviewed because many have been adapted to provide more activity for each individual.

The child remains as the primary focus in this second edition. If he achieves success and satisfaction through movement experiences and if he comes to the realization of his own capability in movement through participating in activities as presented here, then *Play with a Purpose* will have accomplished its end.

Marian H. Anderson
Margaret E. Elliot
Jeanne LaBerge

Santa Barbara, California
September 1971

PREFACE TO
THE FIRST EDITION

Education, in any subject area, should be a meaningful experience, stimulating and immediately rewarding while creating enthusiasm for further knowledge. No longer is it presumed necessary to approach a subject with morbid determination. If an exciting atmosphere of learning is maintained, the children will be excited to learn.

Play with a Purpose is a planned program of physical education that will be appealing to children because of its structure, variety, and suitability to their interests. Purposeful activity is inherently pleasurable and educative. Play is "play" if the experiences are satisfying and fun.

The main factors that contribute to enjoyment are having adequate skills, being reasonably active, and being accepted by the group. Engaging in activities which present challenges, having opportunities to be creative, and participating in the planning are among other factors which contribute to enjoyment. Play can be "drudgery" for a child if any of these factors are absent. Between the two extremes of play and drudgery is work. Work can be satisfying and children may work at their play because their work and play are often considered synonymous. If the experiences are satisfying, the children will work harder, play harder, and derive more benefit from the activity.

There is a natural sequence in the learning of motor skills. In the school years the learning of each new skill is easier, faster, and more satisfying if it progresses logically. Although there is a wide range of individual differences at the various grade levels, each child will achieve a fair level of skill if given sufficient opportunity.

The material presented herein is designed to aid the teacher in planning balanced units of instruction to meet the needs of boys and girls. The Suggested Grade Placement Charts at the beginning of each new type of activity will help to determine the activities most suitable for each grade level although they are by no means meant as rigid assignments. It will be found, rather, that there is a flow of instructional activities which both children and teachers will find stimulating.

The activities in Part I are organized in terms of motor skills. Section One presents a progression of "Activities Based on Movement Skills." This section is also concerned with the development of what have been termed

* Marion R. Broer: *Efficiency of Human Movement,* W. B. Saunders Company, Philadelphia, 1966, pp. 25–32.

the "prerequisites of efficient movement."* This includes the development of such factors as balance, coordination, agility, flexibility, strength, and endurance.

Section Two, "Activities Based on Ball Skills," is concerned with Movement Skills along with the additional skills of handling an object such as a beanbag, ball, bat, or racket. This brings into play progression in throwing, catching, kicking, and batting.

Section Three, "Activities Based on Dance Skills," parallels the development of the Movement Skills in Section One but adds accompaniment. This section also includes Folk Dance, Circle Mixers, and Square Dance.

The reasoning behind the organization of activities is to be found in Part II. The titles of the chapters are indicative of their contents; moreover, they are designed to aid those responsible for the establishment of a sound program.

The material in the book may be used by the children as well as the teacher. The children may assist in the selection and presentation of activities, increase their own skills by viewing the illustrations and reading the descriptions, and learn more about their own posture through the visual aids. Some well-skilled players may become interested in teaching and helping in a positive way rather than criticizing the lesser-skilled.

It is hoped that the presentation of material will help to instill in all children a love for activity, a desire to improve skills, a respect for sportsmanship, and a recognition of the values of fitness for work and play.

Marian H. Anderson
Margaret E. Elliot
Jeanne LaBerge

Santa Barbara, California
March 1966

ACKNOWLEDGMENTS

The authors express appreciation to the administrators and teachers of the Santa Barbara City and County Schools for their cooperation and to the children for their enthusiastic reactions to our requests.

We are also indebted to Dr. A. Jean Ayres, Associate Professor of Special Education, University of Southern California, and Mrs. Patricia Wilbarger, Registered Occupational Therapist. It was a privilege to work under their guidance in the Title III Project on Sensorimotor Dysfunction in Primary School Children.

We wish to give special recognition to the major contributors who worked with us in preparing material as indicated:

M. Marilyn Flint, University of California, Santa Barbara: revision of Chapter 4, "Body Alignment; Developmental Exercises."

C. James Anderson, formerly of La Colina Junior High School, Santa Barbara: resource person in the area of skill performance and the understanding of the adolescent boy.

Elizabeth Sehon Eidam, formerly of the University of California, Santa Barbara: contributor to Chapter 10, "Dance: Exploration and Creativity."

James A. Bottoms, illustrator: skill drawings.

H. Maxine Lagura, kindergarten teacher: drawings for Stunts and Tumbling.

John Glover, Wilfred Swalling, Edward Ellison, Tim Putz, and David Wagnor: photographers.

A particular note of appreciation is extended Emma Lou O'Brien and Patricia Sparrow for their invaluable assistance in the section on creative rhythms. The authors also wish to thank Jan Fritzen for her expert help with the volleyball unit, and M. S. Kelliher for the development of touch football diagrams and strategy.

A special thanks to the typists, Frances MacMillan and Eunice Balkwill, who were ever-pleasant and willing to do the impossible.

ACTIVITIES

The principle element of Part I is, of course, activity—developmental, educative activity. There is a definite pattern of progression from self-control to object-control designed to give each child a rewarding experience in motor skills. There is variety among the activities to tempt the interests of all students, and there are individual and small group games in which different skills are isolated for greater practice while offering the challenge of a competitive situation. Moreover, there is breadth of presentation through the grades from the "I" centered, simply organized primary program through the team-centered games involving strategy and great skill at the upper grade level. The section on dance moves from the initial experiences in creative activities to the participation in group dances of progressively more difficult composition.

It is recommended that the reader review the Preface and the material in Part II for a better understanding of the purpose of the book and the best use that may be made of it. Progression in each area has been carefully planned because random selection of games might negate their effectiveness in the overall pattern of development.

The activities have been presented in Part I because they are the prime function of the book. The theories behind these activities are to be found in the concluding chapters that substantiate, so to speak, the preceding material. Children may know the physical education period by different titles, but they almost always think of it in terms of *play*. Throughout Part I the reader will find *purposes* for the activities; hence the title, *Play with a Purpose*.

The purposes as presented with each type of activity should serve as guidelines. Each teacher will have many more specific purposes, reflecting the needs of his particular group.

The presentation in Chapter 14 will aid in the overall planning of the physical education program. It is suggested that instruction be presented in terms of units rather than by arbitrary selection. Thus blocks of time may be established for particular skills in each of the three sections: movement skills, ball skills, and dance skills. This will provide time for concentrated instruction, for reinforcement of learning, and will encourage exploration and creativity within a particular unit.

The Suggested Grade Placement Charts are the means through which progression is shown. They are designed to assist the teacher in the selection of activities and as a quick reference. It is recognized that there is a wide variation in interests and abilities not only within the same grade level in a particular school or community, but also within a single class. The charts will help in determining the ability level of the children and in the planning of a meaningful program of skill development.

At the beginning of each chapter will be found an overview of the content. This is followed by the previously mentioned Suggested Grade Placement Charts. Comments on the teaching of the activities and the purposes of the particular units of instruction are presented. The purposes may be used in discussions with the children for motivation, planning, and evaluation. Skill analyses are included in appropriate chapters for use in the presentation of new material and to aid in correcting faulty performance.

It is satisfying indeed to hear children comment, "That was fun!" at the conclusion of an activity period. This kind of response can be a daily occurrence if the children are reasonably active, have sufficient time to practice new skills following instruction, and are given a varied program. This book is dedicated to those aims.

SECTION ONE
ACTIVITIES BASED ON
MOVEMENT SKILLS

CHAPTER 1
MOVEMENT EXPLORATION

BODY AWARENESS

BODY CONTROL

MOTOR PLANNING

EFFICIENT MOVEMENT

FIG. 1.1. How far can you leap?

Observing a group of children engrossed in solving a problem in movement can be a most pleasurable and exciting experience. They may be attempting to balance or travel in some unique way, trying to discover their range of motion, or to see what happens when they spin themselves around. The excitement of discovery is pervasive; expressions of pride, achievement, and confidence are seen on every face. This is individualized learning in its most positive sense. Each child is allowed to respond according to his perception of the problem, selecting and utilizing information from past experiences to solve each new problem, making judgments as to the effectiveness of the solution. In so doing, he increases the ability to discriminate appropriate responses—thus increasing his intellectual understanding of movement. Equally as important, he advances in knowledge and understanding *as he is ready to do so*.

Contrast this kind of learning environment with a situation in which children are told to move or stand just so, to await turns, to succeed—perhaps. The unfortunate aspect of this type of program is that a child may be thrust into a performance or competitive role for which he is not suited. He has little opportunity to initiate his own movements and is performing according to some superimposed timetable that has little consideration for individual readiness.

Because so many traditional games are based on the success-or-failure principle, some poorly skilled children never really know the excitement of success. Such being the case we must guarantee initial success for *all* children so they will approach new situations eagerly and without fear. For *many* reasons movement exploration is considered the hallmark of programs that enables each child to realize his movement potential in his own fashion and according to his own timetable of readiness.

The material in this chapter has been organized in sequential components that are considered essential to successful physical performance. A child must be *aware* of himself. With this knowledge he is better able to know his position in space, and to *control* his movement. Such control is achieved through thoughtful response to movement problems, which is *motor planning*. With a rich movement vocabulary and understanding, the groundwork has been laid for *efficient* movement.

These are not only foundation skills, they are adjuncts of any motor learning situation. They are brought into special focus to emphasize their importance, and to suggest ways of presenting them to children. As in most classifications, there is overlapping in terms of purpose; however, activities are presented in the section of major emphasis.

Chapter 2 provides a natural sequel for these components and should be used in close coordination to provide ever more stimulating challenges to eager learners. In the activities described in Chapters 1 and 2, the child moves in his own way and at his own tempo. In Chapter 10, accompaniment is added to provide a guide for rhythm and ease of movement, reinforcement of concepts and patterns, and ever greater opportunities for creativity.

In movement exploration it is important that the teacher recognize the attempts of *every* child, no matter how minute, in his initial attempts at free movement. Sometimes a great deal of encouragement is needed to get him started but once under way his self-consciousness will soon be forgotten. Although the teacher should not dictate the movement, it is helpful if he offers suggestions during initial lessens, so that children can have some idea of what is expected. Examples of such suggestions are included in the chapter. Sometimes these examples may be used after the children have experimented in order to provide additional experiences, to fill in possible gaps, or to evoke further exploration. Verbal cues enhance a child's performance.

A Suggested Grade Placement Chart is not included in this chapter since most of the activities may be used at any grade level. The main differences lie in the amount of time spent, the presentation and motivation of the material, and the quality of movement. At primary level an entire period may be devoted to certain aspects, while in the intermediate and upper grades the same material may be used for an entire lesson, or it may provide only the warm-up activity at the beginning of a period. At primary level the motivation may be in terms of dramatization and "Who can . . . ?" while at the other grade levels the motivation may be in terms of sport skills, or there may be greater emphasis on "How can . . . ?" and "Why?" With small children success in doing the activity is stressed; with the older group emphasis is placed on efficiency and ease of movement along with a greater variety of "other ways."

Throughout the grades the total involvement of each child is stressed. The activities are not taught through imitation or rote memory. Rather, each child's thoughtful response is unique as he explores the infinite number of ways of working out a problem.

To initiate the movement exploration program start at the beginning—body awareness—which is the child's perception of his physical self. As the children progress through the suggested activities it will be obvious to the observer which ones may need additional work in a particular area. Through an interchange of ideas, children will demonstrate their level of understanding, so that clarification or generalizations may be brought out at that moment.

Actually it is entirely possible to develop numerous lessons simply by posing one movement problem and then using the children's reactions as stimuli for additional problems. In this way, the teaching is truly occurring at the child's level and is a most rewarding kind of experience.

The method of presenting such a lesson may vary somewhat, but the following teaching hints suggested by Bette Jean Logsdon are appropriate:

1. State problems in such a way as to bring about numerous responses from every child to most of the problems.

2. As the children move, give them subproblems that will enhance their movement.

3. Move about the room as you pose the subproblem.

4. Repeat some of the subproblems several times, particularly if the nature of the activity results in noise.

5. Watch how the children move; your observations should suggest meaningful subproblems to pose to them as they move.

6. Be concerned about the quality of movement exemplified by the responses of the children.

7. Use group and individual praise unsparingly, but be sincere.

8. Develop a single idea or movement concept to a fair degree before changing the idea of the movement.

9. Take the time necessary to teach the understanding of—and the appreciation for—the concepts being taught.

10. Avoid the type of demonstration that produces stereotyping movement.

11. Keep moments of inactivity at a minimum by giving complete problems that get the children from one part of the lesson to another.

12. Gain and maintain control of the children by teaching a response to the signal to stop and start activity, whether the signal is a sound from an instrument such as a dance drum or the spoken word.

13. Develop an awareness of the necessity for listening to further instruction as they move.

14. Do not be afraid of trying to teach it. Remember that everyone who has taught basic movement was a neophyte at it at some time.[1]

PURPOSES

The purposes of this area are very broad since the children who participate in it will be gaining many different kinds of experiences. (54)

The movement exploration program is intended to accomplish the following:

—to explore, and to experiment with, the infinite possibilities in movement;
—to provide success oriented activities;
—to increase body awareness, balance, and coordination;

[1]Bette Jean Logsdon, Ohio State University. Presentation at National Convention of the American Association of Health, Physical Education and Recreation.

—to encourage creativity in movement;

—to be aware of, and to improve the quality of, movement;

—to increase confidence in the individual's ability to handle movement problems successfully;

—to enhance social interaction through small and large group cooperation;

—to increase awareness of personal space and surrounding space;

—to recognize the need for consideration of safety for oneself and for others;

BODY AWARENESS

Body awareness is perception of the physical self: size; knowledge of body parts and their relationship to each other; ability to bend, stretch, twist or turn; the feelings derived from being in varied positions. This awareness is crucial to a child's understanding of his movement potential. It may be likened to an internal security system in that each child comes to know his physical boundaries and is secure in knowing that he is capable of performing a *variety* of movements. The confidence gained with this attitude encourages the child to continue exploring movement, providing him an enriched foundation upon which to build more sophisticated movement patterns.

At the outset it is best for the child to work in a lying position as he discovers where he is and how he can move. He then progresses up the ladder of difficulty during which time more and more demands are made in adjusting to the pull of gravity until the standing, bipedal position is reached. In this way, the natural sequence of a child's development is used to help him strengthen the foundation so greatly needed in his continuing development.

Note: Throughout this chapter, records are suggested for immediate repetition of activities and further reinforcement of patterns and concepts. See Chapter 10 for additional information about percussion instruments and records. When providing special equipment for one lesson such as hoops or streamers, plan several activities in which special equipment may be used.

PRONE POSITION (ON STOMACH)

1. Wiggle Worm. "Can you be a Wiggle Worm and move forward? . . . backward? . . . to one side? . . . to the other side?" Provide various surfaces over which to move such as floor, carpet, mat.

2. Commando Crawl. "Can you be a Commando and keep very close to the floor and move forward?" Provide *two* sets of markers (such as blocks or milk cartons with a yardstick across the top). Place one set at each end of an established distance and crawl *under*.

3. Swimming. "Who can swim?" "Can you use both arms at the same time? . . . one arm and then the other as in a crawl?" "Can you use your feet at the same time?"

4. Drying off. "Can you lie on the towel and get all parts of your body dry?" (Towel may be real or imaginary—preferably real.) "Did you remember to dry your back?"

5. Caterpillar—Cocoon—Butterfly. Dramatize the sequence. Allow children to respond in their own way at their own tempo.

Record: "Creepy . . . The Crawly Caterpillar" YPR 10005.

PIVOT-PRONE POSITION

(Back slightly arched with arms extended forward and upward, legs extended and off the floor, knees straight; Fig. 2.47A)

Note: If it is difficult for a child to assume the proper position of the legs, rub the back of the knees to give the feeling of straight knees and rub the back of the thighs to help him be aware of the muscles needed to lift the leg.

1. "Who can hold this position while counting to 5?" For progression on succeeding days count to 10 . . . to 20 . . . to 30. Hands and feet should be held *slightly* off the floor. The back should have a *slight*, not a pronounced curve.

2. "Can you be an airplane and fly around?" (Remain in pivot prone position.)

Records for airplanes and jets: Adventures in Rhythms, Ruth White; *Rhythm Time #1,* Bowmar; Phoebe James AED 3.

3. "Can you be a bird and glide through the air?" (Stress rocking from side to side.)

Records: Adventures in Rhythm, Ruth White; Phoebe James AED 4.

4. "Can you be a Top and spin around in this position?" "How fast can you spin? How slowly?" "Can you spin in the other direction?" (This is a critical point for the development of the nonpreferred side.)

Record: "Nothing To Do," YPR 10012.

5. See activities using Scooter Boards, Chapter 2.

SUPINE POSITION (LYING ON BACK)

1. Identification. "Touch your knees, touch your toes, touch your shoulders, head, and toes." Repeat, calling the instructions quickly and in any sequence. Add other parts of the body. Have children listen carefully and respond correctly to touching shoulder or shoulders, knee or knees.

2. Moving arms and legs. Starting position: legs and arms extended, arms against the body (Angels in the Snow). (47)

   a. Move feet apart as far as possible, keeping knees stiff; move back to starting position. Press heels to the floor for increased awareness of position (bilateral action.)

   b. Move arms along the floor until hands meet above head, keeping elbows stiff. Press hands and wrists against the floor as hands are moved. Clap hands over head and clap hands against sides for increased awareness. (Assist children who are unable to move arms smoothly and equally well on both sides.)

   c. Move feet apart and move arms over head at same time; clap hands over head, then clap hands at sides and click heels together. (Check and assist those children unable to perform smoothly with both hands and feet moving at same time.)

   d. Move only one leg. (May need to assist by first touching and then pointing to the leg for unilateral action.) "Can you move this leg without moving the other one?" (Observe possible overflow—moving both sides when attempting to move only one.) Repeat with other leg.

   e. Move *only* one arm; repeat with other arm.

   f. Move R arm and R leg and stretch as far as possible to the side; repeat with L arm and L leg; repeat with both arms and legs.

   g. Stretch lengthwise. Stretch R arm up and R leg down—point fingers and toes. Repeat with L arm and L leg.

   h. Repeat g. working in opposition, stretch one arm and the opposite leg, and then the other arm and leg.

   i. Combine stretching lengthwise (both arms and both feet) followed by complete collapse and relaxation. Check various children for relaxation. Play game of "Spaghetti." Speak to a child—then raise one or both of his hands, arms, knees or feet. Shake gently and then drop. Does it remain tense and upright or does it fall relaxed like a piece of wet spaghetti. Repeat with other children.

   j. Introduce variations in speed. Move fast—then slowly (slow motion). Move to the accompaniment of percussion instruments, music, or with children counting. Explore other possible movements.

3. Check for excess tension.

Have each child tighten the muscles of his face, make a face—then release quickly ("Relax!").

Tighten fingers and arm and shoulder muscles—relax!

Tighten hip and trunk muscles—relax!

Tighten leg muscles—relax!

Tighten toe and foot muscles—relax!

Breathe in deeply, tightening *all* the muscles from head to toe—hold—then relax forcing all the air out of the lungs. Remain completely relaxed and return to normal breathing.

Listen to your breathing. (If necessary, shift into a more relaxed position.)

4. Toe Peek. Lie on back with knees straight and arms at sides, "Keep your heels on the floor and raise your head until you can see your toes . . . wiggle your toes." Return to position, then repeat.

5. Knees to head.
   a. "Pull one knee up and touch your forehead . . . other knee."
   b. "Can you pull both knees up at the same time and rock from side to side?" "How far can you rock to the side without falling over?"
6. Paddle Boat (lying on back with knees bent and feet flat on floor). "Can you push your boat with your feet and scoot backward along the floor?" Have children who are pushing with both feet together (bilateral action) demonstrate. Have children using reciprocal action (such as walking) demonstrate. May have a towel or a large piece of cardboard under the back. May move over a smooth floor, a textured carpet.
7. Work on peripheral vision.
   a. Keep head stationary on the floor with arms extended toward ceiling, palms together. Keep eyes focused on a point straight above head on ceiling. Keeping eyes on ceiling, pull extended arms apart. "How far apart can you move your hands and still see them?" "Without moving head, and moving *eyes only*, look from one extended hand to the other." Repeat all several times.
   b. Place a red marker on each side of the room. Keep head stationary and move eyes only. Look at marker on one side of room; look at marker on opposite side of room. Repeat.
8. Crab Walk. (Fig. 2.16) Keep trunk in as straight a line as possible. "In how many different directions can you move?" (forward, backward, one side, other side, diagonal, circle)

ROLL

1. Use head lead.
   a. Review Toe Peek.
   b. In supine position bend right arm and touch right shoulder with hand. Extend opposite arm overhead. Start looking at toes, then look toward right side of room—roll in that direction. Continuing to lead with eyes and head, continue the roll in the same direction. Reverse position of arms and return to starting position. (If using Follow-the-Leader Formation down a mat, have child lie with head toward opposite wall for his second turn.)
   c. Explore various positions of the arms when executing a roll.
   d. Roll over various surfaces: rug, floor, mat, turf.
   e. Roll under a rope. Hold a rope a foot or so off the ground. Roll under the rope. Roll toward the right side; roll toward the left side.
   f. Roll down Incline Mat of foam and across a regular mat.
2. After a child has established firmly his ability to use a head lead, other leads may be explored. Use hip lead, shoulder lead, lead with feet.

HANDS AND KNEES POSITION

1. "Can you arch your back like a mad cat?" Relax, then arch again. (Fig. 4.3)
   "Can you balance on 3 points?" (such as 2 hands and 1 knee.) "Can you balance on a different 3 points? . . . 2 points? . . . different 2 points? . . . 3 points with one arm or leg extended? . . . a different arm or leg extended?" "In which position is it easiest to balance?" "Why?"
   "Can you put your right hand on your hip, look over your right shoulder, and balance on 3 points? . . . 2 points?" (4)
   Repeat with left hand on hip looking over left shoulder.
2. Move hands then knees. "Can you go forward by moving first both hands and then both knees?"
3. Move in a cross pattern. "Can you move like a dog?" "Can you move like a lame dog?" (Fig. 2.8) Change the lame foot . . . one front leg lame . . . other front leg lame.
   "How fast can you move on all fours?" "How slowly can you move—slow motion?" "Can you move backward? . . . to the side? . . . to the other side?"
   Crawl through a hoop held upright on floor by partner. "Can you crawl forward? . . . backward? . . . one side first? . . . other side first?" Exchange roles.

HANDS AND FEET POSITION

1. "Can you move like a bunny? . . . like a frog? . . . like a seal?" (Fig. 2.17) Knees may be between elbows for bunny, outside of elbows for frog. (Fig. 2.6)

2. "Can you be an old fashioned Coffee Grinder?" (Fig. 2.18) Put one hand down, then the other. "Can you move backward?"

SITTING POSITION

1. Check for tenseness. "Sit *tall*" (head up, chest up, shoulders down and relaxed), then relax and slump down. Return to a tall position. Hunch shoulders, then relax for awareness of tension. Play riding on a bouncy bus (shoulders bouncing up and down). "Can you collapse your body and push all the air out of your lungs, then roll up *slowly* to a *tall* position and fill your lungs with air?" Repeat. (Repeat at various times during the day.)

Discourage sitting with weight on inner border of knees with lower leg extended diagonally backward—results in undue pressure on the ligaments that are needed to protect the knee joint. Guard against children assuming this position at any time, including Story Time, Listening Time, and while playing sitting games.

2. Increase concepts of the structure of the body and resulting range of movement. (56)

   a. Toes. "How far can you move only your toes?" Say, *"Push-pull-push-pull. . . ."*

   b. Hold your ankles. "How far can you push and pull your foot when holding your ankle?" (Flex knees.) "Can you move your foot in another direction?" (Circular pattern: one way; other way.)

   c. Hold one knee. "How far can you *push* and *pull* your lower leg?" Repeat with other knee. (Hinge joint moves forward and backward *only*. Show a metal door hinge and the plane of movement.) Illustrate hyperextended knees, a position that results in inefficient movement and a harmful position. See Fig. 4.2 for possible effect of hyperextended (locked) knees on body alignment. For repetition and elaboration of activities a to c., use the record *At the Beach,* Barlin, LE 108.

   d. Sit in a crossed leg, tailor sitting position and hold your hips. "How far forward and backward can you move *keeping your head and trunk in a straight line?*" Lead down with the chest. Stand and explore circular movements at each hip joint. "When you balance on one foot, in how many different directions can you make the other leg go?" Illustrate ball and socket joint (may use a ball and cupped hand). Illustrate a rotation. Repeat the activity.

   e. Sit down and rotate trunk.

   f. Repeat preceding activities, using fingers, wrist, elbow, and shoulder joints. Show similarity to joints at toes, ankles, knees, and hips.
      Record: A Visit To My Little Friend, YPR 10005, "Thumbs Keep Moving."

   g. Hold your waist. Explore possible movement forward and backward —at *waist*, not hips; bend from side to side.

   h. Hold your neck. Explore possible movement: *bend* forward and backward; *bend* from side to side; *rotate* head to right, to left.

   i. Perform stunt, Human Ball (see Fig. 2.31).

KNEELING POSITION

1. "Can you be a Weather Vane in a big wind?" (trunk rotation; kinesthetic perception of one or both arms in straight line out of shoulders)

2. Be an airplane. You may use sound effects for added enjoyment.

3. Swing arms forward and backward: arms *together,* one arm, other arm; then swing arms in *opposition.*

STANDING POSITION

See Fig. 4.2 for understanding of proper alignment and use of visual aids.

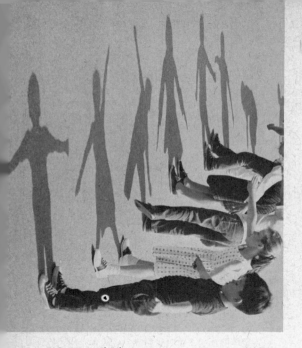

FIG. 1.2A. Shadow pictures—using straight lines.

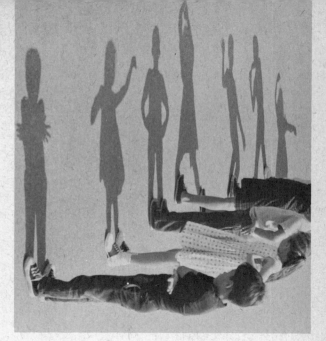

FIG. 1.2B. Using curved lines.

FIG. 1.2C. Working in groups of three.

Use Shadow Pictures (visual image) to reinforce kinesthetic perception of body parts. (Figs. 1.2A, B, and C)

1. "How tall can you stand?" "How high can you reach?" "How small can you be?"

2. "How thin can you be?" "How fat?"

3. "How many angles can you make with your body?" "How round can you make it?"

4. "What can you be, making straight lines?" (Fig. 1.2A—second figure is an airplane.) "What can you be, making curved lines?" (Fig. 1.2B—second figure is a teapot.) "What can you be when working in sets of 3?" (Fig. 1.2C)

5. Be letters of the alphabet.

6. Identification. Use one hand to: "Touch your knee, your ankle, shoulder, . . ." Use both hands: "Touch your ankles, shoulders, elbows, . . ." Mix the calls: "Touch your shoulders, arm. . . ." Use a specific hand and cross the midline of the body: "Touch your left hip with your right hand, your right ear with your left hand. . . ."

Record: Happy Times, "Touch Your Head, Shoulders, Knees and Toes," Educational Dance Recordings.

7. Use of Streamers (2-inch crepe paper streamers 4–6 feet long.) Cradle the streamer lightly in the palms of both hands. Toss it up in the air and have it land on various parts of the body. Ask questions such as "Can you make it land on your elbow? . . . knee? . . . back?" "On what other places can you make it land?"

8. Awareness of lower extremities and down space. (Use a double sheet of newspaper to crumple up tightly for a ball.) "Can you move this ball around with the inside of your feet? . . . outside? . . . with your toes?" "Can you pick the ball up with both feet and balance while you count to 5, 10, 20, 30?" "Can you rock from side to side?" "Can you pass the ball to a partner with your feet?"

What else can you do with the ball, using your feet? (Kick it forward with toes, backward with heel, to the side with the inside of foot, to other side with outside of foot, diagonally, move in a circle, move in a slalom pattern around three markers.) In each activity use one foot and then the other. (The paper balls may be dropped into a carton for future use.)

9. Follow sequence of "Games Stressing Response to Visual and Auditory Cues," Chapter 5. Check for suggested grade levels.

10. *Records: The Little Puppet,* CRG 1060; *Flappy and Floppy,* Barlin, LE 106. Show marionettes for motivation (Fig. 10.4).

BODY CONTROL[2]

As soon as a growing child becomes mobile, the major part of his waking hours are spent in learning to *control* his movements for the achievement of some goal. He learns to adapt to gravitational force as he strives for the upright stance, and begins to integrate the use of all his limbs as he moves through space. In so doing, he becomes aware of his position in space

[2]See Films, "Audio-Visual Materials—Section One": "Movement Exploration"; "The Basis of Movement"; "Elementary Physical Education Skills —Balance Skills—Basic Movement Skills"; "Learning Through Movement."

and the relative location of objects in his environment. Various patterns of locomotion emerge as he continues to explore his surroundings. Other factors relative to movement, such as balance, coordination, flexibility, strength, and endurance are incorporated in his experience.

The activities described in this section are designed to enhance a child's understanding of his position in space and his ability to move through space.

For repetition and reinforcement of the experiences in this section, present activities from Chapter 10, "Introductory Experiences in Movement."

SPATIAL AWARENESS[3] (VARIATIONS IN DIRECTIONS, LEVELS, AND SIZE)

Note: Material in this section, numbers 3 to 6, is especially important for grades 4 to 8 and may be presented on a basketball court for added motivation. Follow up with activities in Chapter 3.

1. Find own space (personal space). "Find a space away from everyone else. Reach out as far as you can and turn around slowly—down low, out to the sides, up high." "Now, how fast can you turn?"

2. Use of Hoops (objective measurement of personal space). Position hoops as equidistantly as possible over the available space, allowing one hoop to two children. One child sits inside and one outside the hoop.

The partner inside the hoop picks it up and holds it at arm's length moving about the area. "Who can walk around without touching anyone or anything? . . . tiptoe walk? . . . tiptoe run? . . . move in other ways?" Return to place and exchange positions with partner. (Activity provides stationary as well as moving objects in space.)

3. Use of large painted circle with an object in the center (includes work on peripheral vision). Use a colorful object such as an orange yarn ball or red marker.

   a. Each child stands in the middle of his own space on the circle (as

[3]Barsch divides space into six fields of space (front, back, up, down, side, side) and four zones of space (near space, mid-space, remote space, and far space). (7)

much space on one side of him as on the other). Children sit down, focus eyes on center object, and extend arms forward toward object with palms of hands together. Keeping eyes on center object and arms extended, separate hands. "How far can you move your hands and still be able to see them?" Repeat activity.

b. Stand, face counterclockwise, and place left hand on hip. Point elbow and focus eyes on center object. On signal, walk forward. Each child should keep to the middle of his own space. Call "Freeze" occasionally and readjust space (equal space in front and in back). Turn and face clockwise placing right hand on hip. Repeat activity going in this new direction.

c. Repeat preceding activity but create need for greater adjustments in space. Call "Freeze," then move one child from one position in the circle to another. Later have two children move, and then three or more of them.

d. Repeat preceding activity but do not call "Freeze." Indicate that certain children are to change positions as all children move around the circle.

4. Use of two concentric circles with object in center. (62) (Appropriate for second or third grade and up.) One-third of the children face in one direction making inner circle. Remaining two-thirds of group face in opposite direction on outside circle.

Stress focusing eyes on center object and remaining in the middle of one's own space while moving. Create the need to adjust space by tapping a child who is in the outside circle and have him move to the inside one. For initial experiences, "Freeze" when the positions of one or more children are moved; later on, have them adjust positions as they move.

5. Move and Freeze. Children find own space, well distributed over the available space. Each child moves around the area keeping in the middle of the space around him. "Freeze" on command and readjust position in order to keep all the available space fairly well covered. Move in a variety of ways: locomotor patterns such as gallop, skip; dramatizations such as a big elephant, a small pony. May add percussion instruments or music and "Freeze" when the accompaniment stops—then readjust spacing.

6. Move (stressing variations in direction). When having a child move, as in locomotor activities, increase his awareness of the "surrounding" space by having him move in a variety of directions: forward, front space; backward, back space; to the side, space on the right, and space on the left; diagonally forward right, forward left; diagonally back right, back left; and move in a circle returning to original position.

Examples of stunts to be used with variations in directions: Crab Walk, Kangaroo Jump.

Examples of locomotor activities: Jump or hop forward, backward, to one side, to other side, diagonal turning.

See "Variations in Directions," Chapter 10.

7. Variations in Levels. (Fig. 1.3) Provide experiences where the children move at a low level, or high level, or at a level in between. "How high can you skip?" "Can you slide keeping closer to the ground?" Provide experiences in changing levels, such as a Merry-Go-Round. *Records: Rhythm Time #1*, Bowmar; *Rhythm-Time Records*, Album 2, Sehon and O'Brien.

8. Variations in Size. Move in a small circle, a medium-sized circle, and a large circle. Find different sizes of circles, squares, and rectangles painted on the floor or on the black top. Perform various locomotor patterns while moving on the painted lines. Count the number of steps around the circles. Which is the largest, smallest? Count the number of steps on the sides of a rectangle and on the ends. Walk a square. How is it different from the rectangle? Make two triangles out of one square. Count the number of steps on the diagonal across a square.

Play with various sizes of yarn, plastic, and utility balls. Which ball is largest? . . . smallest?

FIG. 1.3. Variations in levels.

When using streamers, start with a very small circle and make it larger and larger. Reverse the procedure.

Increase awareness of such variations by being a small zoo animal and a large jungle animal; a baby animal and a full grown one. *Record:* "Baby Bear—Mother Bear—Father Bear" *Rhythm Time #2*, Bowmar.

VARIATIONS IN TEMPO, FORCE, MOOD

1. Tempo. Provide experiences in which the children may move slowly, normal speed, and move quickly. (Keep in mind safety and appropriateness of the activity.) Some activities may be learned while moving slowly; then speed may be increased gradually as the children gain the ability to control their bodies. However, activities such as hopping require more control to perform slowly.

Provide flash cards with the written words of slow (slowly), normal, fast, quick (quickly).

Records: Adventures in Rhythms, "Music for Engines that Accelerate," Ruth White; Merry-Go-Round.

See variations in tempo, force, and mood, Chapter 10.

2. Force. Variations in force may be provided in many ways: pushing or pulling something heavy that may be real or imaginary, stamping while walking and then tiptoeing for contrast, running flat footed with a heavy, noisy run, and then taking a light and efficient run on the balls of the feet. The children may gallop like big heavy horses, then like small circus ponies; they may walk like giants, and then tiptoe like boys and girls do on Halloween.

Become familiar with words such as strong-weak, heavy-light, loud-soft.

3. Mood. In many of the activities, variations in mood may be experienced through dramatizations. How sad, happy, angry, tired, gay, proud, or funny are a few examples of word pictures that provide cues for exciting variations in movement. Such variations usually result in total body

involvement and provide yet another way of giving children experiences in gross motor activity.

The children may suggest words that depict their feelings and then show what the word means.

Record: Balloons, Barlin, LE 104.

NONLOCOMOTOR PATTERNS (STATIONARY BASE)

Children may be asked to find own space and *sit* in the middle of it.

1. "V" Sit. (Fig. 4.3)
    a. "Bend knees, and then lean back until feet are off the floor." "Hold this position while *you* count to 5, . . . 10, . . . 15, . . . 20, . . . 30."
    b. "Can you use your hands and spin around in a circle? . . . The other way?" (Go to the *right* . . . to the *left.*)
    c. "How fast can you spin?" "How slowly can you move?—slow motion without stopping?"
2. Stretcher. Place hands on the floor behind the body. Keeping legs and arms straight, pull the hips off the floor and raise the body to a straight line. Return to sitting position.
3. Balance on one or more parts of the body. See "Body Awareness" "Hands and Knees Position."
4. "How small a circle can you be? . . . how large?" "Can you make another circle with a different part of your body?" "How many circles can you make at one time?"
5. "What letters of the alphabet can you be? . . . by yourself? . . . with a partner?" May use shadow pictures for added interest and to reinforce kinesthetic perception of position in space. (Figs. 1.2A, B, and C)
6. "What numerals can you be?" "In groups of three, how many sets can you make?"
7. Use visual cues. Show geometric figures and have children reproduce them, alone or with a partner: rectangle, square, triangle, diamond.
8. Use streamers (2-inch strips of colorful crepe paper 4–6 feet long). Stress large movements, gross motor movements.
    a. Hold the end of the streamer in both hands (bilateral action).
        (1) Make a circle.
        (2) Make a small circle and gradually make it larger. When it is as large as possible, start making it smaller.
        (3) Make other geometric shapes with the streamer.
        (4) Make a figure eight with the streamer.
        (5) What other ways?
    b. Hold the end of the streamer in one hand.
        (1) Repeat the preceding activities. Change to the other hand and try them.
        (2) With *left foot forward,* swing *right* hand forward and back like a pendulum and make a big half circle; repeat on other side with right foot forward.
        (3) What other ways?
    c. Hold one streamer in each hand (different color such as red in right hand, blue in left hand).
        (1) Make a circle on each side of the body at the same time . . . forward . . . backward.
        (2) Try making the circles in front of the body.
        (3) What other ways?
    d. Toss a streamer up in the air.
        (1) Catch it just before it touches the floor—with right hand, left hand. Catch it with your foot—first right, then left. Catch it with other parts of your body.
        (2) Move the same as the streamer moves as it falls to the floor (variations in levels). Position your body in the same "shape" as the streamer.
9. Standing on one foot.
    a. Crane stand. Stand erect on one foot with other foot placed against leg. Can you stand in this position for 30 seconds. Change feet. Close eyes and stand on one foot, other foot. Can you stand in this position for 10 seconds? . . .

20 seconds? Try it while keeping the knee of the supporting foot straight, then slightly bent.
   b. Swan position. Stand on one foot and bend body forward. In what position do your arms help you most to keep your balance? Change feet.
   c. Stand on one foot and extend the other foot forward (reverse Swan Position). In what other directions can you extend this foot? Repeat, standing on other foot.
   d. Stand on one foot and make a circle with the other foot, then shake it. Change supporting foot and repeat. What can you do to achieve better balance? (Bend knee of supporting foot to lower center of gravity; extend arms low to the side for more stability.) What other patterns can you make with one foot?
10. Present "Beginning Stunts (Individual and Partner)." See Chapter 2.
11. Use Hoops. See Chapter 2.

LOCOMOTOR PATTERNS (MOVING BASE)

Note: The following locomotor patterns provide a perfect setting to reinforce the concept of one's personal space—the space that one can reach all the way around—as well as surrounding space—the space that one can see immediately in front, and with peripheral vision. In addition, the child can increase his awareness of space in front, in back, and to the sides by moving in these various directions. He can also experience, through movement, the concept of geometric figures, such as circles, squares, rectangles. He can be aware of *up* and *down* space by moving up and down and moving on different levels through space.

The following activities also provide a myriad of opportunities to move quickly, slowly, or at a normal speed, to work hard or with little effort, and to dramatize one's feelings by showing variations in mood.

The locomotor patterns are divided into two groups: the first group, that has one sound and is done in an even rhythm; and the second group, that has two sounds and is done in an uneven rhythm. For "Mechanics," "Common Faults," and other "Learning Experiences," see the last section in this chapter, "Efficient Movement." Being aware of common faults and knowing good mechanics assist the teacher in posing problems and giving pertinent verbal cues.

ONE SOUND (EVEN RHYTHM)

1. Walk.
   a. Walk *tall,* then walk on tiptoe—taller.
   b. Walk backward. Walk backward without looking (awareness of back space).
   c. March. Have a Circus Parade. Walk like a clown.
   d. Mechanical walks (jerky movements): robots, toy soldiers or dolls, marionettes.
      For variations in tempo, "wind up" the mechanical toys and then let them run down. Work with a partner.
   e. Crooked Man Walk. Encourage crossing one foot over the other—crossing the mid-line of the body.
   f. Giant walk. Walk like a big gorilla.
   g. Elephant walk (change of tempo). Keep head up to see where going (visual guidance). Move in unison with a partner, two elephants in line . . . three in line.
   h. *Record:* "Walking Straight and Tall," *Rhythm-Time Records,* Album 1, Sehon and O'Brien.
2. Run.
   a. Tiptoe walk, tiptoe run—on balls of feet. (A so-called "tiptoe run" may also elicit a safer response in a limited area.)
   b. Run heavily, then run as quietly as possible.
   c. Run with knees held high, then run kicking feet out behind.
   d. Run in a large circle—incline weight slightly toward the center of the circle, as in running the bases in kickball or softball.
   e. Run slowly backward, incline weight *forward.* "Can you run

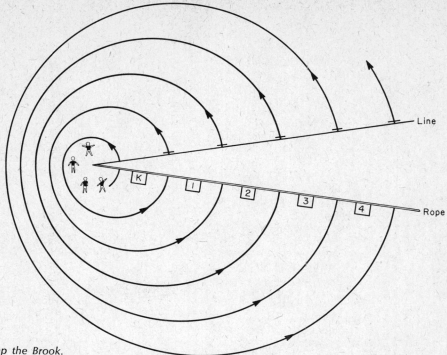

FIG. 1.4. Jump the Brook.

slowly *backward* without looking back?"

  f. Run forward and stop on sound of whistle. Adjust spacing. Repeat action. (Provide adequate space.) Run, stop, change directions. Use a *large* area. Check spacing to avoid collisions.

Have a different signal for each of the following activities: a walk, a jog, a run. Change activity according to the signal. May start with one whistle for walk, two for jog, and three for run. Later use a more difficult set of signals.

3. Leap (an extended run). (Fig. 1.1)

  a. Start with a slow run. Take an increasingly longer stride until leaping. Keep an even stride and an even rhythm (not a step with one foot and a leap on the other).

  b. Leap like a deer going over a fence, like a gazelle.

  c. Jump the Brook (leap). (Fig. 1.4) Place a rope in a position diagonal to a line, depicting a gradually widening brook. Place markers (milk cartons), at equal distances, along the rope. Markers may have "K" kindergarten, and numbers 1, 2, 3, and 4, for the first, second, third, and fourth grades.

In Follow-the-Leader Formation, children leap across the shortest distance. They run around the end of the "brook" and into position for the second distance, the third, and then the fourth. Get across without stepping into the "brook."

  d. Side Leap. Stand astride a line, rope, or one side of a hoop. Rock from side to side putting weight on one foot, then the other. Continue rocking but gradually get off the ground; leap from side to side. (Check ease with which children shift weight: easily and quickly; accomplished, but with difficulty; or unable to accomplish it.)

4. Jump (two feet, bilateral action).

  a. Jump in place. Bend knees and push off the floor; "give" as you land, bending ankles, knees, and hips.

b. Jump moving forward, backward. In how many other directions can you jump?

c. Use a hoop with a partner. Stand on opposite sides of hoop and hold it waist high. Jump in place. Stand with side to hoop and jump forward, backward, to the side.

d. The Top. All children face one wall (or in one direction). Take small jumps turning in place. Be a robot, a rag doll. "Which is more comfortable?" With a jump, make a quarter turn and face a different wall. Repeat three times to return to starting position. Take quarter jumps in the other direction. Experiment to determine the best position of feet when landing, and best use of arms. Make half turns in one direction, and then the opposite direction. When ready, make three quarter turns; then make full turns. Turn to the right, to the left.

e. With weight supported on hands and feet, and keeping hands in place, move feet backward and forward with small jumps. Keep knees bent.

f. Kangaroo Jump. (Fig. 2.11)

g. Practice jump rope rhythm: jump-bounce, jump-bounce . . . take a big jump and follow it with a small bounce. Jump like a Raggedy Andy or a Raggedy Ann, . . . like a robot. Alternate activities.

h. Use a line. Explore various ways and patterns of jumping over the line and back.

i. Use hoops. (Chapter 2)

j. Jump over a rope. Rope on the ground: jump forward, backward, to the side, with a turn. Rope a few inches off the ground: jump forward, jump with a turn.

k. Jump as the ball bounces. Bounce a ball low, medium, high (children simulate the bounce of the ball with jumps). Bounce the ball high and let it rebound until it rolls off by itself (children follow the pattern of the ball).

l. Play Jump the Brook—using a jump rather than a leap. (See Fig. 1.4.)

5. Hop (one foot, unilateral action). Practice maintaining balance while standing on one foot, on the other foot. Try with supporting knee stiff, with supporting knee slightly bent (lower center of gravity).

a. Hop on one foot, other foot. Push off and land on same foot.

b. Use a hoop with a partner. Stand on opposite side and hold hoop waist high. Hop in place on one foot, on other foot. Face in opposite directions. Hop forward, backward. Change feet.

c. Hop moving forward, backward. In how many different directions can you hop?

d. Take five hops forward. Count as you hop. Use other foot. Repeat action taking three hops, . . . two hops, . . . only one without losing balance.

e. Use hoops or jump ropes on the ground. (See "Hoops," Chapter 2.) How many different ways can you hop in and out of the hoop (or over the rope)? (Forward, backward, to side, with a turn . . . ?) Learn the written words, "in," "out," and "over."

f. Play Hopscotch. See Chapter 2.

g. Work out an Indian Dance using step-hops. A drum could provide the accompaniment. May use a line, a circle, and/or Follow-the-Leader formation.

TWO SOUNDS (UNEVEN RHYTHM)

1. Slide. Children tend to slide with knees straight. Encourage them to "get closer to the ground," and "keep head up so you can see." (Visual guidance.)

a. Face toward the center of the area. Move to the side without crossing one foot over the other. May start with a slow "step-close-step-close . . ." to the side, then increase speed to "slide and slide and . . ." (long-short-long-short). Move in the opposite direction.

b. Identify the sides, then slide to the *right,* to the *left.*

c. Count the slides—count "one and two and three and. . . ." Take seven slides and then a step in one direction, return to place with seven slides and a step. Continue action (the extra step allows for a smooth change of direction).

d. Slide, keeping closer to the ground (bend ankles, knees, and hips and keep head up). Change directions.

e. Slide on a painted straight line. Change directions. Slide on a painted line of a circle, square, rectangle. Change directions. Face out and repeat the action.

f. Slide around the outside of a hoop . . . inside. Change directions.

2. Gallop.

a. Face forward around the circle. Repeat the pattern of the slide. Move forward keeping one foot ahead of the other. Move forward keeping other foot forward. Face opposite direction. Move forward with one foot leading, then with the other foot.

b. "How high can you gallop?"

c. Gallop slowly without touching anything or anyone . . . gallop fast.

d. Gallop like a circus pony, a show horse, a work horse.

3. Skip.

a. Review galloping with one foot leading, and then the other foot leading.

b. Walk, even rhythm, then go into a bouncy walk getting slightly off the floor and moving into an uneven rhythm, "skip-and-skip-and-. . . ."

c. Hold an imaginary large ball in front of the body. March with knees high, like a drum major or marjorette (even rhythm). Hit the imaginary ball with each knee as you march. Hit the ball harder and harder (raising the knee higher and higher) until opposite foot is pulled off the floor (moving into uneven skip rhythm). *Record: The Toy Tree,* "Beachball" Barlin LE 107.

d. Hop. Call "and change" after several hops. Decrease number of hops between calls until children are skipping.

e. "Can you show me a happy, relaxed skip?"

f. "How high can you skip? . . . low?"

g. In how many different directions can you skip? (Forward, backward, to one side, to the other side, in circle, or diagonal.) "What do you have to do to keep your balance when you skip backward?" (Put weight forward—lean forward.)

h. "How loudly can you skip? . . how quietly?"

i. "Can you skip in place?" "Can you skip turning in place?" "Can you turn the other way?" "Can you skip to the side? . . . to the other side?"

j. *Record:* "Skipping We Go" *Rhythm-Time Records,* Album 2, Sehon and O'Brien.

COMBINATIONS OF PATTERNS

INFORMAL GROUP

1. Call the skills; have the children move from one skill into another. "Walk-tiptoe-run-leap." "Walk-gallop-skip." "Walk-jump-hop."

2. Play *Freeze.* As the teacher calls the skill, he points to indicate the direction in which to travel. For a signal to stop quickly, call "Freeze" or use a percussion instrument. Children then listen for the call of the next pattern. Point in the new direction and use the name of the next pattern as the starting signal. Use variations in tempo and levels. Teacher may occasionally call for a stunt.

Variation: Players who do not stop immediately are placed in a second group. After a short time, start the game again with all the children in one group.

SINGLE LINE OF PLAYERS

Children stand side by side behind one line facing the opposite line. (Children should have adequate spacing for running to and returning from the opposite line.) Go to the opposite line or goal, touch it, and hurry back to place. (Turn and hurry *straight* back to place. Demonstrate what is meant by *straight* back to place.)

1. Colors. Call, such as, "Run to the opposite line if you are wearing *blue*." Repeat calling various colors until all children have reached opposite line.

Use different colored flash cards. As each color card is held up, children wearing that color go to the opposite line and remain there. Determine the mode of travel before flashing the cards (such as a gallop, dog run, skip, or elephant walk). Continue until all children have reached the opposite line. Change the mode of travel and sequence of colors, and repeat action back to the original line.

2. Clothes. Call, such as, "*Jump* to the opposite line and *stay there* if you are wearing a *skirt; . . .* if wearing a *shirt!*" (auditory discrimination).

3. Numbers; Birds; Animals. Number off by threes (or give the name of a different bird or animal to each child in sets of 3). Call, such as, "Skip to the opposite line *and back* if your number is *2!*" When group returns to the line, the call may be, "Gallop over and back if your number is *3!*"

TWO LINES OF PLAYERS

Use opposite goal line. (Fig. 1.5) One-half the class stands behind one line and

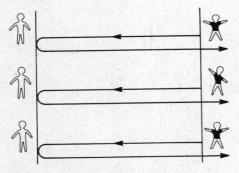

FIG. 1.5. Use opposite goal line.

the other half stands behind the opposite line 40 to 60 feet away. Players in one line perform, then players in the opposite line perform. Work on success and enjoyment rather than speed.

1. Who can skip to the opposite line, touch the line and skip back? Leap? Gallop? Slide without crossing one foot over the other? Who can hop to the line, changing feet as needed, and run back? Jump to the line keeping feet together as if tied, then run back?

2. Who can run to the opposite line, touch it, and return across the starting line? Who can make two round trips? Stress agility, fast change of directions. What is the fastest way you can make your turn? Experiment. May stop with forward foot over the line, bend knee of other leg, pivot, and face in new direction; touch line with hand and push off.

Use center line. (Fig. 1.6) Place a center line midway between the two lines of players. (May substitute a long jump rope on ground.)

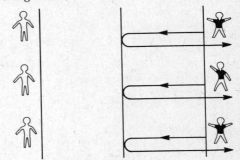

FIG. 1.6. Use center line.

1. Who can take the fewest jumps to get across the center line? Fewest leaps?

2. With side to the center line, slide to the center and back to place. Who can slide to the line, step over the line with one foot, and slide back to place without crossing one foot over the other or turning around?

3. Go up to the line and experiment in jumping back and forth over the line in different ways. ("Mary, would you show us your way? Let's all try her way." "John, show us what you were doing. Let's see how many can do it the way John showed us.") Experiment in hopping, leaping, bouncing, turning while moving back and forth. Hop over and back; leap over, turn, and leap back; jump over, bounce once,

jump back, bounce once (jump rope rhythm); jump over the line turning in the air; hop over the line turning in the air.

4. Go up to the line, leap over turning in the air, run backward a few steps. Repeat back to place.

5. How can you get over the line on both hands and both feet? One hand and both feet? One hand and one foot? Watch spacing for safety.

6. What other ways can you go over the line?

GROUPS OF PLAYERS IN LINES

Form lines with about six children standing side by side facing one long rope. One line at a time moves forward, performs the activity, then continues around either end of the rope returning to the starting position. Keep good spacing. Use stretch rope. Teach children not to release rope while it is stretched.

1. Rope on the ground. Example: Run and jump over the rope. Other ways?

2. Rope held slightly off the ground. Examples: Run and leap over the rope; stop at rope, jump over rope with both feet at same time; log roll or roll in tuck position under the rope. (Experiment with collapsing—complete relaxation, melting into the ground—then followed by continuation of the flow of movement into a log roll or roll in tuck position—knees flexed.)

3. Rope held more than head high. (Fig. 1.7) Stand directly under the rope and jump up hitting the rope with the top of the head. "Who can jump up and then land without making a sound?" "What can you do to jump higher?"

FOLLOW THE LEADER FORMATION

Use one long rope. Children move forward parallel to a long rope which is on the ground or held low. Leader performs an activity moving back and forth over the rope, others follow. Leader then goes to the end of the line. The second player becomes leader and changes the activity.

Use two long ropes. With ropes held low, jump over the first rope and crawl under the second one. Other ways?

PARTNER FORMATION

Use various locomotor patterns.
Examples: Skip with a partner. What

FIG. 1.7. How high can you jump? Can you push against the ground?

different ways can you skip with a partner? Skip forward, backward, in circles, to the side, around partner.

Join right hands, left hands, inside hands; link elbows.

How can you move with both hands joined?

Examples: Move forward, backward, to the side, in circles; take a given number of sliding steps in one direction, repeat in opposite direction. Stand with side to a line, slide to the line and back.

Move up and down in opposition—like a seesaw.

Direct the movements of partner through joined hands. Exchange roles.

Follow the movements of partner without hands joined. In slow, sustained movements, move exactly as partner—as if looking in a mirror.

SMALL GROUPS

1. Follow-the-Leader and Change. Children follow the leader, doing the same activity as the leader. When the teacher blows the whistle, the leader goes to the end of the line. The second player in line becomes leader and changes the activity. Subsequent leaders may not repeat any previous activity. Demonstrate with one group. Children should learn to balance the amount of energy expended and do some strenuous as well as some slow activities. (When introducing this game, do not allow forward rolls.) Leaders need to be careful not to interfere with, or break through, another group.

2. Slalom Race (moving forward). (Fig. 1.8) Members of the group space them-

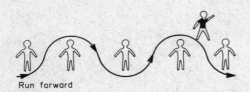
Run forward

FIG. 1.8. Slalom Race—moving forward.

selves 4 to 6 feet apart in single-file formation facing forward. The last player in line weaves his way forward and stops 4 to 6 feet ahead of the front of the line. After the first player reaches the second or third person, the next player starts from the end of the line. Each end player moves forward in turn.

Variation: Slalom Race-sliding to the side. (Fig. 1.9) Members of the group space

Slide to side

FIG. 1.9. Slalom Race—sliding to the side.

themselves 4 to 6 feet apart in single-line formation with six to eight players across. (Fig. 1.9) Using a slide step, a player at one end of the line weaves his way sideward and stops 4 to 6 feet ahead of the opposite end of the line. When the first player reaches the second or third person, the next player starts.

3. Follow-the-Leader and Last Man Up (intermediate and upper grades). The children run at an even pace, not too fast. Without changing the speed of the group as a whole, the last man increases his speed, runs to the head of the line, and becomes the leader. As he reaches the head of the line, the last player starts moving forward to become the leader.

MOTOR PLANNING

Motor planning may be considered as a *thoughtful* response to a posed question or situation. In this case the child must consciously determine a course of action, select the most appropriate movement pattern, and continually monitor his progress. This kind of experience is contrasted with the situation in which a child calls upon a previously learned motor pattern with an automatic response.

The stimuli are continually changing in this situation so that the child must be constantly alert to changing demands for decisions. This kind of activity is invaluable in helping children to think about movement and, as a result, to make intelligent decisions in response to problems.

EXAMPLES OF ONE KIND OF PROBLEM SOLVING

"Can you move around the area without stepping on any lines?"

"Can you move around the area without traveling in a straight line?"

"Can you travel around the area leading with your hand? . . . elbow? . . . shoulder? . . . hip? . . . knees?"

"Can you move around balancing on two hands and one foot? . . . two feet and one hand? . . . one foot and one hand?"

"Who can walk on the heel of one foot and the toe of the other foot?"

"Who can walk crossing one foot over the other with each step? . . . one foot behind the other with each step?"

"Step one foot across in front, then step to the side; take the next step in back and then to the side." (Grapevine step) "Can you do it quickly?"

"Put your toes together with heels out. Moving to one side only, touch heels together, then toes, then heels . . . Go in opposite direction." (Weight is on one heel and opposite toes as child moves.) "How fast can you move without breaking pattern?"

"Walk with one side of your body stiff and the other side limp. Reverse the sides."

"Move backward in a gallop . . . to the side with a skip."

"How could you balance having seven parts of your body touching the floor? . . . 2 parts? . . . 9 parts? . . . 1 part other than one foot? . . . 13 parts?"

Make geometric shapes, letters of the alphabet, numerals. Work alone; work with a partner.

Use Chinese Jump Ropes (circular stretch ropes shown in Fig. 2.52).

1. "Get inside a Chinese Jump Rope and make a triangle with your rope . . . a square, a rectangle, other shapes."

2. Work with a partner. One player gets inside the rope, and then the other player takes over possession of the rope without touching his partner. Partner takes rope back in a different way.

MOVING IN RELATION TO ONE OR MORE OBJECTS

MOVE IN RELATION TO MARKED LINES

1. Circles, squares, rectangles, triangles.

a. Walk forward, backward, slide to one side, to other side.

b. Jump, hop, skip.

c. Change activity at each corner. Count number of steps from one corner to the next. Compare results.

d. Find and move on small, medium-sized, large figures.

2. Ladder; hopscotch patterns. (Paint a ladder as well as hopscotch patterns on the playground.) (61)

a. Step into each square without touching a line. Repeat using plastic stilts. (Fig. 2.46)

b. Step, jump, or hop into every other square (2's); every third square (3's).

c. Walk, slide, skip in various ways on the lines at the sides.

MOVE IN RELATION TO SMALL EQUIPMENT

1. Set up a pathway by placing individual or long ropes, parallel to each other, 12 to 18 inches apart. Leave a space between each pair.

a. Children move down between the ropes. For example: walk, tiptoe, tiptoe run.

b. Change the activity at the beginning of each pair of ropes. For example,

(1) hop on one foot between first two ropes,

(2) hop on other foot between second two ropes;

(1) crawl,

(2) go on hands and feet;

(1) Rabbit Hop,

(2) Frog Hop (may use cards with written words).

2. Place about six individual jump ropes parallel and at irregular intervals. In Follow-the-Leader Formation children step into each of the spaces formed by the ropes.

a. Walk through several times without touching the ropes.

b. Progress to a tiptoe walk, a run, jumping, hopping.

c. Have children select the mode of travel.

d. Have each child select a different way on each of his turns.

3. Place a long or stretch rope on the floor (or draw a line) in serpentine-like fashion.

    a. Face the rope and slide along one side of it. When reaching the end, continue around the other side of the rope and back to starting position.

    b. With back to the rope, repeat the action of (a).

    c. Jump along the rope going on one side for a few jumps, and then jump over it and continue on the other side.

4. Place a long rope straight out on the floor (or use a line).

    a. Jump over the rope, bounce once, jump back over the rope, and bounce once. Continue the length of the rope.

    b. Advance along the rope leaping from side to side.

    c. Run alongside the rope, leap over the rope with the foot closest to it (scissor jump). Continue on around to starting position.

    d. Advance along the rope by hopping on the foot *away* from the rope. Step across the rope and hop on the other foot, foot *away* from the rope.

    e. Moving forward along the rope, take a few steps and then leap over the rope with the *closer* foot; take two steps and then leap back over the rope with the *closer* foot (this involves leaping with *one* foot, then the *other*). Repeat taking running steps.

Repeat all with rope raised a few inches off the ground.

5. Provide one individual jump rope for one or two children.

    a. Place rope on the floor. Repeat some of the previous activities and discover other things to do.

    b. Make various geometric shapes or forms with the rope and perform different activities in, out, along or around the rope.

6. Place 3 or more markers in line, 4–6 feet apart, as in a Slalom Relay. (Fig. 3.3)

    a. Walk to the right of the first marker, the left of the second, and around the last marker. Weave in and out again on the return trip.

    b. Jump over the first two markers and go around the last one.

    c. Repeat, moving in different ways: locomotor patterns, stunts, dramatizations of animals. . . .

    d. Go a different way than the player ahead of you.

7. Place hoops on the floor in a line or in a zigzag pattern. "How many different ways can you move from hoop to hoop without touching any of them?" (May use white side walls for tires. See Fig. 2.46.)

8. Use foot prints and hand prints. Cut a number of right (one color) and left (another color) foot and hand prints out of nonskid material such as rubber stair tread or matting.

    a. Make a "trail" for the children to follow under, over, and around obstacles in the room.

    b. Let one child make a trail for others to follow.

    c. Begin to stress use of proper hand and/or foot. Reinforce right or left by color coding the child's hand and foot to correspond to the print color.

    d. Repeat foot print trails using plastic stilts. (Fig. 2.46)

9. Use streamers (2-inch crepe paper, 4–6 feet long). (Fig. 10.1)

    a. With one streamer, have each child experiment with "writing" his name.

    b. Play Keep It Up. Bat the streamer into the air and see how long you can keep it in the air with consecutive hits.

    c. Shoot for Basket. Toss the streamer into the air, make a hoop with your arms, and have the streamer go through the hoop.

    d. Football Kick. Drop the streamer, kick, and then catch it.

MOVE IN RELATION TO A PARTNER

1. Review "Beginning Stunts (Partners)," Chapter 2.

2. Use Chinese Jump Ropes.

3. Use Hoops, see "Small Equipment," Chapter 2.

4. Follow the sequence of "Games Stressing Response to Visual and Auditory Cues" in Chapter 5. Check Suggested Grade Placement for games.

5. Partner activities involving resistance.
   a. Foot Pedaling. Sit facing partner with legs extended and the bottom of *heels* and soles of feet in contact with partner's. One player pushes while partner resists slightly. Push with both feet at once, then try pushing alternately with feet as in pedaling.
   b. Same as (a), except push with entire leg. Sit slightly closer together.
   c. Stunts, Chapter 2. Chinese Get Up, Wheelbarrow, Rocking Stunt.
   d. Strong Man. Push against a partner. (Fig. 4.4) May practice individually by pushing upper arms against the floor.
   e. Tug of War. (Fig. 4.4)

RESPOND TO VISUAL CUES

1. Follow the Pictures. Distribute pictures of animals around the area. Establish a prearranged direction of travel, or place an arrow with each picture to indicate the direction in which to go. Children follow the arrows and move from place to place like the animal pictured. (Acquaint children with the various directions to which an arrow may point.)

2. Follow the Signs. Same as Follow the Pictures except that signs are distributed around the play area with words such as skip, jump, walk, hop, and gallop. (Pictures of boys or girls doing the activity may be used first. The pictures may be placed on one side of a card with the word on the other side.)

3. The Maze. (Fig. 1.10) (Children find their way out of the maze by following the signposts, or directions, correctly. Activity includes locomotor patterns, number recognition, and reading skills.)

Equipment needed: Two small jump ropes, cards with instructions, or instructions marked on black top with chalk.

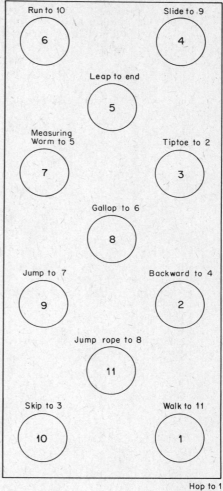

FIG. 1.10. The Maze.

Mark the play area as in diagram.

Players stand in file formation behind first station. The object of the game is to follow the written directions correctly from the first to the last station. If a mistake is made (such as galloping when he is supposed to be skipping), the child starts over again. No more than two players may be at one number at the same time. (Have one child return jump ropes from Station 8 to Station 11.)

RESPOND TO AUDITORY CUES

1. Combine a Movement Pattern with a Stunt. The signal can be the word "Freeze," or a percussion instrument may be used as a signal. The following activities are examples.

   a. Gallop ——— (signal), squat, and mule kick.
   b. Slide ——— (signal), change directions.
   c. Skip ——— (signal), bounce three times.
   d. Hop ——— (signal), turn in place, hopping.
   e. Jump ——— (signal), jump into the air turning as far as possible (the Top).
   f. Run ——— (signal), take a step and a hop, and throw overhand.
   g. Run ——— (signal), field a ball rolling on the ground, and then throw overhand.

2. Respond to Word Pictures.

   a. Use poems. Example: "I Have a Little Shadow," by Robert Louis Stevenson. This poem may be used as a culmination of a lesson on Shadow Pictures.
      See "Activity Songs and Poems," Chapter 10.
   b. Use selections from Do You Move As I Do. (8)
   c. Use selections from Hailstones and Halibut Bones, colors as motivation. (44)

3. Respond to sound effects, percussion instruments, and music.

   a. Produce sound effects. Respond in appropriate ways.
   b. Respond to percussion instruments, piano music, records. See Chapter 10.

SEQUENCING

1. Explore a pattern of steps.
   Take a run-run-leap-run-run-leap. . . .
   Take a hop-hop-jump, hop-hop-jump. . . . Hop on same foot. Alternate hopping foot: left-left-both, right-right-both.
   Take a leap-leap-jump, leap-leap-jump. . . .

Take a hop-step-jump, hop-step-jump. . . . (Triple jump.)

2. Try a hopscotch pattern.

3. What other steps can you put together?

EFFICIENT MOVEMENT

The first section in this chapter, activities for "Body Awareness," started with balance and coordination in a prone position and progressed developmentally until standing balance was reached; the following section on "Body Control" included many locomotor experiences for dynamic balance and coordination; "Motor Planning" provided even more challenging activities in that the child had to think and plan his responses—sometimes in an inverted position. With this background of experience the child should now be able to understand and cope with "Efficient Movement."

Efficient movement is considered smooth and coordinated, without excess tension or motion. Efficient movement also involves the expenditure of only the amount of energy needed to accomplish the task at hand; it should, therefore, result in a slower onset of fatigue.

Underlying the ability to perform the basic patterns identified in this section are certain factors termed by Broer as "prerequisites to efficient movement." (9) They include, in part: balance, timing, and muscular control; coordination; as well as such physical prerequisites as endurance, flexibility, and strength. Development of these factors occurs through participation in a wide variety of activities; such achievement is critical to truly efficient movement.

To achieve efficiency it is most helpful to understand the concept of the movement pattern, the mechanical analysis, and its appropriate use. To achieve understanding, the teacher may assist the child in learning to verbalize the movement, discuss how it is performed, and why it is used. The child who has this understanding will better appreciate movement, will tend to be more successful and adaptive, and will thrive on increasingly complex demands for movement responses.

COMPONENTS OF EFFICIENT MOVEMENT

BALANCE

Balance is a many-faceted thing, and there is a great deal yet to be learned. It appears that the skill of balance is specific; consequently, children need to perform a variety of *different* balance activities that make increasingly more challenging demands. These are presented throughout the chapter. Subsequent chapters, especially Chapters 2 and 3, provide even greater challenges in terms of dynamic balance and coordination, factors closely related.

According to Ismail and Gruber,

. . . the correlational and factor analytic study of relationships between coordination and balance abilities on the one hand and academic and intellectual achievement on the other would suggest that these two areas of learning are closely related. It would seem to follow that if advancement in one area can be brought about, a similar advance in the second area could be anticipated. . . . (33)

Balance involves four sensory modalities. In initial experiences, information from these four *different* sources is sent to the brain, integrated, and incorporated with past experiences. Such multisensory integration plays an important role in a child's development. (6) The sensory modalities involved in maintaining balance include:

1. Tactual System. This modality is responsible in part for receiving information through the pressure exerted on the soles of the feet indicating body sway while in an upright position. (Children are made more aware of such sensory input by working barefoot.)

2. Kinesthetic Sense. The kinesthetic sense involves the proprioceptors located in the muscles, tendons, and joints. The proprioceptors provide information as to movement and position in space. (Contrasting the uncertain movements of a small child with the sophisticated and precise movements of an Olympic gymnast or professional baseball outfielder gives an indication of the important part kinesthetic sense plays).

3. Visual Sense. The eyes provide information as to a point of reference in maintaining balance. The visual apparatus also effects the posturing mechanism. (Performing the Crane Stand, standing on one foot with eyes open and then with eyes closed, points out the importance of the eyes in maintaining balance.)

4. Vestibular. This is a most complicated system and—like balance as a whole—there is a great deal still to be learned. The vestibular organs are located in the inner ear and include the three semicircular canals. The vestibular system is concerned with the position and movement of the head and eyes, as well as the movements and balance of the body and the extremities through space. It appears that the *adjusting* to a changing center of gravity (the process) may be as important—if not more so—as the product. (Warm-ups, especially at the primary level, should include experiences that stimulate the vestibular system such as spinning or rocking in a pivot-prone or "V" Sit position or in a standing position. The Top and other turning, jumping, and landing activities may be used.)

The following fundamentals contribute to the *maintenance* of balance. (Children may be asked to think of examples of the following fundamentals that are used to increase balance in objects around them.)

Widen the Base of Support. 1. Side-to-side balance: take side-stride position with feet about shoulder distance apart.

2. Forward-and-back balance: take forward-stride position. The position is taken in the direction of the oncoming object.

3. Combination of both side-to-side and forward-and-back balance (Ready Position, Fig. 6.13): spread feet apart with one foot slightly ahead of the other—ready for oncoming force from *any* direction; ready to move in any direction.

Lower the Center of Gravity. The center of gravity is approximately at hip level. Bend knees, ankles, and hips to lower body weight and increase stability. Get "closer to the ground" (lowering center of gravity).

Adjust Weight to Shifting Positions. Keep knees in a slightly flexed position in order to lower center of gravity and be in position to adjust weight easily and quickly. When weight is moved in any direction, bend knee and shift foot position in the new direction—keep the center of gravity over the base of support.

Eye Focus. As a rule of thumb, eye focus should be ahead of the participant. For progression on pieces of balance equipment, eye focus may be directed downward for initial experiences, then shifted to eye level. When running, eye focus should be forward not downward.

Arms Held in Low Position to the Sides. Raise arms slightly to the side to provide for greater stability and, at the same time, to maintain a low center of gravity.

Increase Friction at Base of Support. Appropriate shoes in terms of the surface and the activity are a necessity. Working without shoes should be encouraged in appropriate situations to allow for greater tactile input.

COORDINATION

Coordination is the interaction of the body and body parts in achieving the purpose of a movement. This includes the accuracy, ease, and efficiency of the performance; and it involves good balance, proper sequential timing, and smooth interaction of the various muscle groups.

Control of the body's center of gravity over the base of support is essential to a smooth, coordinated transfer from one position to another. The kinesthetic perception that one has for the body and its parts during the performance of movement activities affects the quality of the performance.

The skills of running and dodging, turning and running, and stopping and starting quickly are presented in a wide variety of informal activities and elementary games. In Chapters 6 to 9 these same skills, along with greater emphasis on hand-eye and foot-eye coordination, are presented through activities using a ball. The skills are reinforced through progressions ranging from the beginning activities of manipulating an object to the highly organized team sports. Coordination is developed through repeated and thoughtful performance.

ALERTNESS AND ATTENTION

Children need the ability to react immediately—to a starting signal, to a change in game situation, to a sudden awareness of an oncoming opponent, or a threat to safety. If a child is to fully develop his ability to react to a situation, he must first develop a keen alertness to varied stimuli. He must be keyed up, as it were, in anticipation of a signal or a change in situation. According to a study by Hodgkins, the greatest improvement in reaction time occurs between the ages of 6 and 12 in both boys and girls. (27)

REDUCTION OF EXCESS TENSION

Tension is necessary to accomplish the objective of the movement. Excess tension speeds the onset of fatigue and reduces efficiency and ease of performance. Relaxation procedures should be taught to those children who show signs of excess tension.

FLEXIBILITY

Flexibility is defined as a wide range of movements in the joints of the body. Very young children are generally very flexible; as they mature, and as strength increases, an imbalance of musculature, inhibiting flexibility, sometimes occurs. Exercises and activities that stretch these muscles will aid in maintaining a wide range of movement. Increasing flexibility is a major concern in nonlocomotor activities.

A child may throw or kick a longer distance if he is flexible, since he is then able to increase the range of the preparatory movement (the wind-up) as well as the follow through (gradually decreasing the speed of movement necessary at point of contact or release of a ball). Flexibility is especially important in creative dance, gymnastics, and stunts and tumbling.

STRENGTH

Strength is needed in the efficient performance of most activities. Insufficient strength causes lack of ability and interest in participation. Inadequate strength to forcibly flex and extend the joint may be the difference between success and failure in activities such as running, changing directions, making a throw, or kicking the ball.

ENDURANCE

Endurance is important in one's ability to adjust to stress. Strenuous activity increases heart efficiency, improves circulation and respiration. Endurance improves the capacity for strenuous activity in work or play, increases the efficiency and ease of performnace, and improves the capacity to recover quickly after such activity. Endurance is an important factor in physical fitness and provides a margin of safety in cases of emergency when unusually strenuous demands are made.

NONLOCOMOTOR PATTERNS (STATIONARY BASE)

BEND-STRETCH; PUSH-PULL; SWING-SWAY

Mechanics

Controlled action of muscle groups are used to perform movements such as bending and stretching, pushing and pulling, or swinging and swaying. Gravity and momentum may also influence the movement.

Common faults

Lack of muscle strength.

Inability to relax certain groups of muscles thus limiting the expected range of movement.

Presence of fatty tissue or overdeveloped muscles limiting range of movement in areas such as the shoulders and hips.

Excess tension in performing a task, whether holding a pencil for writing, or throwing or catching a ball.

Inability to move only the segments of the body needed to perform a task.

Learning experiences

Review concepts of the mechanics of the joint structures and the range of movement in the joints. See "Body Awareness," "Sitting Position."

Activities: bend knees, and then push off the ground to jump, and "give" as you land with the pull of gravity; jump as high as possible, land as quietly as possible (on balls of feet, and bending ankles, knees, and hips); blast-off in a Space Capsule; be a Jack-in-the-Box. Roll a ball with two hands (push), stop or catch the ball (pull).

Stunts: Chinese Get-Up; Squat Thrust.

Work Activity: Push-Pull, Chapter 4.

Identify movement patterns in "Sport Skills." (The following activities may be included as part of the warm-ups to give the kinesthetic perception of a skill.)

1. What sport skills use *bending* and *stretching*? (All skills.) Why? (For greater force, better balance, more accuracy). Examples: Volleyball Overhead Pass, Fig. 8.25; Standing Broad Jump, Fig. 9.9; Ready Position, Fig. 6 13; Guarding, Fig. 8.7; Shooting for Goal, Fig. 8.4.

Show illustrations of the starting position, action, and follow through of skills. (May use an opaque projector to show skill pictures from Chapters 6, 7, 8, and 9, or to enlarge and reproduce the pictures.) Analyze the skills and discuss the mechanics and common faults. Experiment and determine similarities in skills.

2. What sport skills use a *pushing* action? (Basketball: chest pass and chest shot for goal, Fig. 8.3; one-hand push shot for goal, Fig. 8.4.)

Which foot is forward in a chest shot? (Either foot because both hands are used in the shot, Fig. 8.3.) Which foot is forward in a one-hand push shot? (Same hand and foot, exception to the rule of opposition, Fig. 8.4.) Experiment.

3. What sport skills use a *pulling* action? (Catching a ball. Fig. 6.25.) Why do you pull it in? (To break the force and slow down the momentum of the ball so that it will not bounce out of your hands as if it were hitting a wall.)

When should you pull the ball in a *great* distance? (A ball coming fast, a thrown ball, and a kicked ball.) Practice with different types of balls at various speeds.

4. What sport skills use a *swinging* action, a *pendular* swing? (Underhand pattern: rolling, Fig. 6.15; bowling a ball, Fig. 6.15; one-hand underhand throw, Fig. 6.23;

serving a volleyball, Fig. 8.24; two-hand underhand throw, Fig. 8.5; kicking a ball, Fig. 7.1.)

With left foot forward, use one arm in a pendular swing forward and backward. Can you make a half circle, shoulder high in back and shoulder high in front? Use the other arm. Which is more comfortable?

With right foot forward, repeat the action with one arm, then the other. Which is more comfortable? (Note: Discover or reinforce the principle of opposition.)

With weight supported on one foot, swing the other foot forward and backward in a fairly wide arc. As in punting the ball, try bending and then forcibly extending the knee as the foot swings forward to kick. Repeat all, with weight supported on other foot. What can you do to achieve better balance? (Adjust to the center of gravity; upper body forward when leg is extended back; upper body back when leg is extended forward; bend supporting knee, lowering the center of gravity. Use arms for increased stability. (Fig. 7.1 contacting a kickball; Fig. 7.25 punting the football.)

TURN-TWIST (ROTATE)

Mechanics

One segment of the body rotating on its axis, such as the ankle, trunk, neck, forearm.

Common faults

Lack of the kinesthetic awareness of how to twist, turn, or rotate.

Moving the entire body to adjust to a task rather than turning, twisting, or rotating one segment. Examples: a child moving his entire body rather than rotating his trunk to accomplish a given task while sitting at his desk; the total movement of a child learning to turn a knob.

Learning experiences

Make a circle with one foot (ankle rotation). Rotate the foot in the other direction. Repeat with other foot. Repeat with both feet.

While sitting, turn your body as far as possible to the right, to the left. Repeat the action but put arms out to the side. Keep arms exactly shoulder high and in direct line with the body. (Check for kinesthetic perception of this position.)

In standing position, perform a sport skill that uses body rotation. (One-Hand Overhand Throw, Fig. 6.29. Striking: with hand, as in Handball; with paddle, as in Paddle Tennis, Fig. 6.33; with bat, as in Softball, Fig. 9.1 and 9.16; and with racket, as in Tennis.) How wide a range of movement can you use in each of these patterns? Use a forward stride and face forward for overhand throw; stand in a ready position with side to imaginary oncoming ball for strike pattern.

Rotate forearms and hands inward, toward each other. Rotate outward.

What common tasks use this action? (Turning a door knob; opening a screw-top lid.) Can you do these tasks with either hand?

What sport skills use inward rotation of the forearms and hands? (Basketball: Chest Pass; Chest Shot for Goal, Fig. 8.3.) Experiment.

Rotate head. Look to the right, to the left. Repeat, leading with your eyes.

LOCOMOTOR PATTERNS (MOVING BASE)

Note: For additional learning experiences, see "Body Control," "Locomotor Patterns."

WALK

Mechanics

Even rhythm (one sound). Call, "Step step. . . ."

Maintain good balanced alignment with a feeling of lift and extension. "Pull up chest," "Stand tall," "Smile."

Maintain a relaxed and easy walk without excess tension. "Drop shoulders."

Walk from heel to toe with feet parallel, and approximately 1 or 2 inches apart. Use good ankle and foot action.

Common faults

Toeing out (duck walk), toeing in (pigeon-toed walk).

Poor ankle and foot action, allowing foot to pivot outward and pushing only from the big toe and side of foot (clown walk).

Pushing off rear foot too vertically, causing the body to bounce.

Lack of controlled movement, allowing body to jar at moment of heel contact.

Allowing hips to sway (rhumba walk).

Poor body alignment, round shoulders, and forward head (gorilla walk).

Shoulders or hips not level.

Vigorous swing of arms.

Swinging only one arm (may indicate poor use of one side of body).

Excess tension with stiff arms and hunched shoulders (mechanical walk).

Learning experiences

See Fig. 4.2 for segmental alignment showing five main weight centers.

Walk *"tall."* Pull chest *up* with shoulders relaxed.

Have children walk, then call "Freeze." Check position of feet (whether toeing in, out, or pointing forward).

Walk with exaggerated faulty patterns as presented under "Common Faults." Follow these poor patterns immediately with correct mechanics.

Walk with a book on the head.

Walk toward a mirror.

Practice correct mechanics of walking under the critical eye of a partner.

Use shadow pictures.

Conduct posture contests: standing posture, posture when walking.

RUN (FIG. 1.11)

Mechanics

One sound (even rhythm)

Run on the balls of the feet, not flat-footed.

Maintain good body alignment, with a forward inclination beginning at the ankle, not at the hips or waist (degree of inclination is determined by the speed—the faster the run, the more the body leans).

Hold head high with the eyes to the front, and lift with the chest in such a way as to give a feeling of leading with the chest.

Bend elbows and hold near the sides; maintain a natural forward and backward swing of arms in opposition to legs.

Point toes forward (or slightly inward).

Lift knees higher in the run than in the walk; legs swing through at the hips reaching forward for a long stride; back leg ex-

FIG. 1.11. How fast can you run?

tends with a strong push-off from ball of foot and toes.

Make first contact with the ball of foot, which is directly under the body's center of gravity—never beyond it.

Reduce jar of landing and any vertical bobbing by good foot, ankle, and knee action, and by pushing-off at the correct angle.

Note: For Standing Start and Racing Start, see "Activities in Track and Field," Chapter 9.

Common faults

Running flatfooted. (Listen for a slapping sound.)

Keeping an upright position or running with body weight held back.

Arms held away from the sides.

Arms swinging from side to side rather than forward and back.

Toeing out.

Not using good foot, ankle, and knee action.

In a race or game, failure to run *across* the finish line or goal at full speed. Need to *overrun* the line for best time in races and for safety in games.

Learning experiences

Start with a tiptoe walk, then move into a tiptoe run—running on balls of feet. When moving in a limited space, use the words "tiptoe run" to indicate a controlled, rather than an all-out, run.

Take a noisy run (flatfooted); then run as quietly as possible (on balls of feet).

Run in a large circle (incline weight slightly toward center of circle). Repeat running the bases of kickball or softball diamond.

Practice "starts" on signal.

Run with three or four runners for competition.

Have races and relays—short distances for speed, longer distances for strength and endurance.

RUN WITH QUICK CHANGE OF DIRECTION (FIGS. 1.5, 1.12, AND 3.27A B)

Mechanics

Extend forward foot for strong restraining force; a quick jump helps break forward momentum.

Bend rear knee and flex ankles and hips to lower center of gravity and shift weight, flexing all joints toward new direction.

Pivot on forward foot and turn body toward the new direction *keeping weight low.*

Extend arms out and low for balance (and to maintain low center of gravity).

Common faults

Failure to extend forward foot and bend rear knee.

Keeping knees straight and body in an upright position.

Keeping feet too close together.

Failure to use arms for balance.

Turning around rather than pivoting on forward foot.

Learning experiences

Run forward at a fast pace. At sound of whistle reverse direction and repeat action. (Allow adequate spacing.)

Review activities for "Two Lines of Players." Experiment to find the fastest way to "turn and run."

Shuttle Race. (Fig. 1.12) One-half of the group stands on one goal line and the other half stands on the opposite goal line 30 feet away. Groups participate alternately.

On signal, players in group one run to the opposite line, touch the ground beyond the line, turn and run back, touch the ground beyond their own line, and then go across and back once more. Finish by overrunning the starting line.

Repeat activity with opposite group.

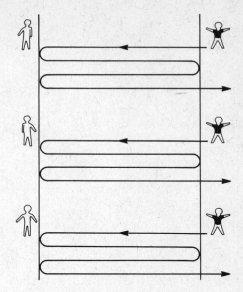

FIG. 1.12. Shuttle Race.

For safety provide adequate spacing between runners, and caution players to run across the area and back in a straight line.

Play games such as Fire Engine and Steal the Bacon that involve "turn and run." Play games involving the skill of dodging, such as Red Rover and Capture the Flag, Chapter 3.

LEAP

Mechanics

One sound (even rhythm).

An extended run. Both feet are off the ground at one time. Leap from one foot to the other in an even stride and an even rhythm. (Fig. 1.1)

Common faults

Failure to push off the ground for height and distance.

Failure to "give" when landing to prevent jarring the body; failure to land on balls of the feet.

Uneven stride and rhythm—leaping on one foot while taking a step or running with the other.

Learning experiences

Start with a walk and gradually increase the stride into a leap.

Call the rhythm, "leap, leap, leap . . ." and/or use a staccato percussion instrument for accompaniment to reinforce the even rhythm.

See "Body Control" for "Locomotor Patterns," 3c. Jump the Brook, and 3d. Side Leap.

JUMP (BILATERAL ACTION)

Mechanics

Take off and land on both feet. "Push off the ground." "Get closer to the ground, then *push!*"

Bend ankles, knees, and hips starting in a half-crouched position permitting these joints to flex in order to extend forcibly to overcome gravity.

Teach landing (jumping in reverse); absorb the force of gravity by landing on the fatty part of the balls of the feet, and bending ankles, knees, and hips. "Give" with all the joints to prevent jarring the body.

For better balance widen the base of support, feet apart, and extend arms low to the side for increased stability.

On a vertical jump, all force is directed upward. Swing arms back on the preparatory movement, and swing arms forward-upward on the push-off.

On a horizontal jump forward or *backward,* incline the body forward.

Note: For Broad Jump, see "Activities in Track and Field," Chapter 9.

Common faults

Failure to use both feet and both sides of the body, together.

Failure to crouch in preparatory movement, or tendency to crouch too deeply.

Failure to use the arms with proper timing—forward swing *with* the push-off.

Failure to extend joints forcefully.

Failure to "give," absorb the jar when landing.

Failure to land with feet apart, keeping weight slightly forward, and using arms for increased stabilization.

Learning experiences

Bounce up and down several times letting the body relax with each landing like a Raggedy Ann or Raggedy Andy. Try landing once or twice keeping knees stiff as a Toy Soldier's, then repeat, landing as a Rag Doll.

Jump down from objects of varying heights, landing on the balls of feet with feet apart and exaggerating the bending of ankles, knees, and hips. Keep weight slightly forward. See "Boxes" and "Incline Mats and Boards," Chapter 2.

For better understanding in terms of balance, land with feet together and then land with feet apart. Land with hands held tightly at sides; for contrast, hold arms relaxed and low out to sides.

Stress landing lightly, quietly. Have children listen as they land. They may land loudly, and then quietly, to recognize the difference. (Flatfooted, then on balls of the feet.)

"In how many different directions can you jump?"

Be a Jack-in-the-Box saying, "Down, down, down—push *up!*"

Blast-off saying, "Three, 2, 1—Blast off!"

Reinforce the concept by saying and reading the words, "Down-Up" with proper inflexion.

Work in sets of three. Practice a basketball Jump Ball. (Fig. 8.14)

Practice Jump and Reach and Rebound in Basketball; see Chapter 8.

HOP (UNILATERAL ACTION)

Mechanics

Take off and land on same foot.

Push off the ground as in the jump.

Land lightly on the ball of the foot, and absorb the force of landing as in the jump.

Maintain balance by keeping the support knee slightly flexed (lower the center of gravity). Use arms for balance as in jumping.

Common faults

Attempting to leap rather than hop.

Failing to keep "closer to the ground," lowering the center of gravity, for better balance.

Failing to use *both* arms in a low position to increase stability.

Moving too fast to counteract lack of balance.

Failing to land "quietly"—"giving" to

prevent jarring the body, and to achieve better balance.

Learning experiences

Hold both hands with a friend. Take turns hopping on one foot and then the other (there is a tendency to hop only on preferred foot).

Review holding a hoop with a partner: hop in unison.

Use variations in directions while hopping.

Take five, then four, three, two, and only one hop—without losing balance. Repeat on other foot. Count aloud.

Use hoops or jump ropes on the ground. "How many different ways can you hop in and out of the hoop (or over a rope)?"

Mark the floor or use nonskid foot patterns to indicate the path for hopping. Have children set up patterns to follow. (Stress using one foot and then the other.)

Hop on command: Right foot . . . left foot . . . left foot moving forward . . . right foot moving backward . . . right foot in a circle.

Hop in the squares of a ladder painted on the blacktop; play Hopscotch.

SLIDE (LATERAL ACTION)

Mechanics

Uneven rhythm (two sounds).

Move to the side without crossing one foot over the other.

Rapid step-close to the side. Call, "Slide and slide and . . ." (long-short, long-short).

Bend knees, get closer to the ground— lower center of gravity to achieve better balance and better head position (head held as in pivot-prone position).

Explore the best position for arms.

Move in a smooth, sliding-gliding manner.

Common faults

Crossing one foot over the other.

Failure to bend knees resulting in a stiff, awkward position, and lack of balance to change directions quickly and with ease.

Facing to the side, rather than facing forward and moving to the side.

Moving in a slow, even step-close, rather than a rapid, uneven pace.

Learning experiences

Slide in one direction; slide in the opposite direction. (Develop use of both sides of the body.)

First grade and up: Identify right and left sides. On command slide to the *right*, slide to the *left*.

Slide in a straight line or in a large circle changing directions on the command "Change. . . . Change!" (For safety allow adequate spacing on each side of each child—staggered formation.)

Take seven slides and then a step to the right; return to place with seven slides and a step. Repeat.

Take seven slides and a step to right, and then left; take three slides and a step to right, then left, then one, and change.

Practice Agility Slide Step (coordination and balance). (Fig. 8.15) Practice, then perform against time.

GALLOP

Mechanics

Same as a slide except that the direction is forward rather than to the side. Face forward around the circle. Repeat the pattern of the slide but move forward keeping one foot ahead of the other.

Uneven rhythm (two sounds). Call, "Gallop and gallop and . . ." (long-short, long-short).

A gallop is usually done with a choppy up-and-down movement while a slide is done smoothly.

Common faults

Keeping feet too far apart (trying to use a wide base to compensate for lack of balance).

Inability to keep one foot slightly ahead of the other.

Learning experiences

Slide to the side; make a quarter turn and gallop forward (same foot leading).

Gallop with one foot leading; change and lead with the other foot. (Develop both sides of the body.) For first grade and up, call the lead foot. Lead with *right* foot, lead with *left* foot.

Gallop in a circle counterclockwise using a left foot lead (foot toward center);

gallop clockwise with a right foot lead (as a trained horse in a ring).

SKIP

Mechanics

Uneven rhythm (two sounds). Call, "Skip and skip and . . ." (long-short, long-short, . . .)

Common faults

Skipping on one foot and taking only a step on the other.

Failure to alternate lead foot on each skip.

Failure to lift feet off the floor.

Learning experiences

See "Body Control" for "Locomotor Patterns," "Two Sounds," No. 3. Skip.

CHAPTER 2
STUNTS AND TUMBLING, SMALL EQUIPMENT, AND APPARATUS

FIG. 2.1. Exploring activities using small equipment.

If some freedom of word usage is acceptable in an introduction, then it is permissible to say that this is the most daring chapter in the book.

A cursory inspection of the apparatus area of a playground might lead the casual observer to believe that all children naturally know how to progress on the traveling rings or turn circles on the horizontal bar. Actually, many children have to be taken through the various steps carefully because of their fear of new activities or because they are unable to orient themselves in an inverted position.

The time spent on material included in this chapter is time well spent in leading children to discover the endless varieties of activities of which they are capable. As much courage and daring are required by the novice in tumbling as by the seasoned gymnast on flying rings. The expressions on the faces of children just learning how to run through a turning rope are priceless portraits of excited anticipation and achievement.

While one of the primary objectives of team sports is to develop a strong feeling for group endeavor, in individual activities self-reliance and initiative are among the primary aims. A child is able to proceed at his own pace in exploring the activities in this chapter without undue pressure from his peers. The challenge offered is a personal one, and each child is free to respond in his own way. Many of the activities may be done spontaneously since there is no need for large numbers of children.

Particular attention should be given to the order of progression in all of the activities. Each of the new skills is based upon knowledge of a previous skill and therefore should be presented in sequence. If the class has had previous instruction in these areas, a quick review of the simpler activities will help to prepare them for more advanced ones.

The material in this chapter is ideal for small group instruction and practice as described in "Station Teaching." Children enjoy the opportunity to have frequent turns and to rotate among several activities.

PURPOSES

Children derive different levels of satisfaction from working on stunts and tumbling, apparatus, and small equipment. The perceptive teacher will recognize these differences and plan accordingly, keeping the following purposes in mind:

—to provide activities that increase confidence in body control in inverted, horizontal, vertical, and rotatory positions;

—to increase body awareness, balance, coordination, and control by working with and on various objects;

—to plan progression and provide instruction that result in activities that are safe, satisfying, and fun;

—to increase awareness of limits in terms of fatigue;

—to encourage innovation and diversity of thinking through independent activity with small equipment;

—to develop the ability to plan a sequence of movements into a comprehensive routine.

STUNTS AND TUMBLING

The challenges in stunts and tumbling are among the most exciting of all those inherent in physical activity. It requires great courage and daring to place oneself in an upside-down position or to be suspended in mid-air. Body control is a requisite to any of these activities; consequently this unit is best presented after children have had a background in the activities as presented in Chapter 1.

The stunts can be introduced effectively while the class is arranged in a large single or double circle. Although the basic action for each stunt is described in this section, much enjoyment will be added by having the children create some of the activities. Such stunts as Bear Walk, Bird Walk, and Camel Walk may be introduced by having the children express their own ideas about them. *Several* children, not merely one, may be asked to show how they would perform the stunt. The activity may then be repeated, with a greater number of

STUNTS AND TUMBLING

SUGGESTED GRADE PLACEMENT CHART[a]

BEGINNING STUNTS—INDIVIDUAL, 40–43

Stunt	K	1	2	3	4	5	6	7	8
1. Raggedy Ann—Andy	x	x	·	·					
2. Bear Walk	x	x	x	·					
3. Bird Walk	x	x	x	·					
4. Camel Walk	x	x	x	·					
5. Elevator	x	x	x	·	·				
6. Frog Jump	x	x	x	·	·				
7. Rabbit Jump	x	x	x	·	·				
8. Heel-Toe Walk	x	x	x	·	·				
9. Tightrope Walker	x	x	x	·	·				
10. Toe to Head	x	x	x	x	x	·	·	·	
11. The Top	—	x	x	x	x	x	x	x	x
12. Bouncing Ball	—	x	x	·					
13. Rooster Hop	—	x	x	x	·	·			
14. Lame Dog Run	—	x	x	x	·				
15. Crane Dive	—	x	x	x	·	·			
16. Butterfly Clap	—	x	x	x	x	x	·	·	·
17. Crane Stand	—	x	x	x	x	x	·	·	
18. Kangaroo Jump	—	x	x	x					
19. Mule Kick	—	x	x	x	·				
20. Measuring Worm	—	x	x	x	·				
21. Corkscrew	—	x	x	x					
22. Grapevine	—	x	x	x	x	x			
23. Jitterbug Snap	—	x	x	x	x	·			
24. Turk Stand	—	x	x	x	x	x	·	·	
25. Crab Walk		—	x	x	·		·		·
26. Seal Walk		—	x	x	·		·		·
27. Coffee Grinder		—	x	x	x	x	·	·	

BEGINNING STUNTS—PARTNER, 43–46

Stunt	K	1	2	3	4	5	6	7	8
1. Wring the Dishrag	—	x	x	·	·				
2. Double Walk	—	x	x	·		·			
3. Twister	—	x	x	x	·		·		
4. Rocking Stunt	—	x	x	x	·		·		
5. Scooter	—	x	x	·		·			
6. Archway	—	x	x	x	·		·		·
7. Chinese Get-up	—	x	x	x	x	·		·	
8. Rooster Fight		—	x	x	x	·		·	
9. Leapfrog		—	x	x	x	·		·	
10. Wheelbarrow		—	x	x	x	·		·	
11. Back-to-Back Push		—	x	x	x	·		·	
12. Horizontal Stand				—	x	x	x	x	x
13. Partner Handstand					—	x	x	x	x

ideas to explore. The teacher may suggest "another" way, that proposed in the text.

In order to elicit a variety of responses and to present even greater challenges, ask such question as: "Who can walk like a bear . . . jump like a kangaroo . . . amble like a camel?"; "In how many different directions can you move?" (Crab Walk); "What can you do to have better balance?" (Tightrope Walker, The Top, Crane Dive);

SUGGESTED GRADE PLACEMENT CHART (Continued)

INTERMEDIATE STUNTS, 46–47	K	1	2	3	4	5	6	7	8
1. Heel Click			–	x	x	x	x	·	·
2. Heel Slap			–	x	x	x	x	·	·
3. Squat Thrust				–	x	x	·	·	
4. Thread the Needle				–	x	x	·		
5. Rise and Shine				–	x	x	x	·	·
6. Clown Trick				–	x	x	x	x	x
7. Human Ball				–	x	x	x	·	·
8. Robot					–	x	x	x	·
9. Knee Jump					–	x	x	x	·
10. Front Lean Variations						–	x	x	x

BEGINNING TUMBLING, 47–49	K	1	2	3	4	5	6	7	8
1. The Fall	–	x	x	x	x	x	·	·	
2. Log Roll	–	x	x	x	x	·	·	·	·
3. Squash			–	x	x	x	x	·	
4. Forward Roll			–	x	x	x	x	·	·
5. Backward Roll				–	x	x	x	·	·
6. Tripod				–	x	x	·	·	
7. Forward-to-Backward Roll					–	x	x	x	
8. Tip-up					–	x	x	·	·
9. Double Forward Roll						–	x	x	x

GROUP STUNTS—PYRAMIDS, 49–50	K	1	2	3	4	5	6	7	8
1. Sideward Rolls and Leap					–	x	x	x	x
2. Merry-go-round					–	x	x	x	x
3. Spread-Eagle Handstand						–	x	x	x
4. Handstand Archway						–	x	x	x
5. Monkey Roll						–	x	x	x
6. Squash Pyramid						–	x	x	x

— = May introduce activity x = Depth in instruction • = May continue activity

ªSuggested Grade Placement provides a starting point in the selection of material for the beginning teacher. For beginning and experienced teachers, the charts indicate progression and serve as a quick reference to activities.

"After balancing on one foot, can you keep your balance if you stand on your other foot?" (Toe to Head, Rooster Hop, Crane Dive); "Can you run as a dog would run? What would you do if you hurt one leg? The other leg?"; "How quickly can you change from going one direction to the other?" (Coffee Grinder).

For some stunts, one student may be selected to demonstrate, after which all children attempt the stunt. Sufficient time should be allowed for practice so that each stunt is done well before proceeding to the next. As a means of group control the class should be instructed to sit down when a signal is given so that the next stunt can be presented.

Turf is a very satisfactory surface for performing stunts, although a floor will suffice. Some of the stunts may even be performed on blacktop.

Tumbling is an activity that requires individual instruction. By dividing the class into small groups and assigning each to a different area of activity, the teacher can instruct a few children at a time on a rotation basis. Protective mats of some sort are necessary during initial instruction. Once proficiency is achieved, some of the items may be performed on turf. If commercially made mats are not available, cot mattresses or chaise longue pads may be substituted.

Safety is a most important factor to consider in stunts and tumbling. Children must be instructed *never* to interfere with, or distract, a performer. A child who is recovering from an illness should probably be excused from tumbling until he has returned to complete health.

The child who is overweight or unduly apprehensive should not be forced to perform. He may be given a choice of performing or not, without pressure from the teacher, with the understanding that when he feels able to do so he may inform the teacher of his willingness to try.

The technique of "spotting" is essential to a sound tumbling program. The spotter acts as an assistant to the performer by standing close by and guiding him through the activity, but touching him only if he loses his balance. He may help to break a fall, as from a headstand, but he should never attempt to catch a performer. Children can and should be trained in the art of spotting for one another.

The items listed are presented in approximate order of difficulty. Most children should be able to perform the stunts suggested for their grade level, plus, all items listed for previous grades. However, simple stunts should be thoroughly learned before more difficult ones are attempted.

BEGINNING STUNTS (INDIVIDUAL)

1. Raggedy Ann and Raggedy Andy. Walk like a rag doll with very relaxed head, body, and arms.

2. Bear Walk. (Fig. 2.2) Assume all-fours position. Walk forward slowly, rolling from side to side, moving right arm and leg, then left arm and leg. Sound effects are encouraged.

FIG. 2.2. Bear Walk.

3. Bird Walk. (Fig. 2.3) Bend knees *slightly*, place hands near the floor.
Walk forward, lifting the feet well off the floor, moving the head up and down at the same time.

FIG. 2.3. Bird Walk.

4. Camel Walk. (Fig. 2.4) Cross hands behind back and grasp opposite elbows. Bend forward, keeping head high, and walk with a lumbering gait.

FIG. 2.4. Camel Walk.

5. Elevator. (Fig. 2.5) Stoop slowly to a three-quarter squat position and return

slowly to an upright, standing position. Keep the body and head erect throughout. Arms remain at the side. (Partner may "push a button" on top of participant's head.)

FIG. 2.5. Elevator.

6. Frog Jump. (Fig. 2.6) From a squat position move forward by alternately reaching forward and taking the weight of the body on the hands and then taking a small jump forward with both feet. Spread the knees and bring them up *out-side* the arms.

FIG. 2.6. Frog Jump.

7. Rabbit Jump. Same as Frog Jump except that the knees are kept together, being drawn up *between* the arms.

8. Heel-Toe Walk. Walk forward, touching heel to toe on each step. Speed may be increased with practice.

9. Tightrope Walker. Walk on a line without stepping off or losing balance. May use balance beam. Extend arms sideward for balance.

10. Toe to Head. Standing on one foot, grasp other foot with both hands in front of the body and raise the foot upward as the head is bent down. Touch toe to head. Repeat with other foot.

11. The Top. Can best be described as doing a full turn in the air. Progression: Start with quarter-turns, then half-turns, then full turns. Bend knees to start, fling arms in the desired direction to add mo-

mentum. Land with knees bent and feet apart.

12. Bouncing Ball. The leader bounces a ball at varying heights, first low and then high. Students imitate the bounce by bending knees or jumping high in the air, attempting to maintain a rhythm with the ball.

13. Rooster Hop. (Fig. 2.7) In standing position, place L foot behind the R knee and grasp the L foot with the R hand. Hop forward, backward, sideways. Repeat, using other foot and hand.

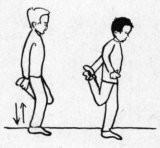

FIG. 2.7. Rooster Hop.

14. Lame Dog Run. (Fig. 2.8) Run forward on two hands and one foot. Keep the other foot off the ground. Change supporting foot.

FIG. 2.8. Lame Dog Run.

15. Crane Dive. (Fig. 2.9) Standing on one foot with opposite leg extended backward bend forward as far as possible without losing balance. Arms should be at sides. Repeat, standing on other foot.

FIG. 2.9. Crane Dive.

16. Butterfly Clap. Jump up and clap the hands over the head before landing. Repeat and add to the number of claps each time. Run a short distance, jump high into the air, and clap hands as many times as possible before landing.

17. Crane Stand. (Fig 2.10) In standing position, place one foot behind opposite knee and maintain balance for 30 seconds. Extend arms sideward for balance. Repeat, standing on other foot. Repeat with eyes closed. Hold for 10 seconds.

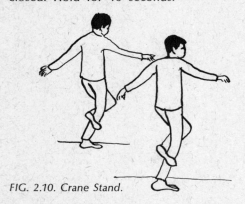

FIG. 2.10. Crane Stand.

18. Kangaroo Jump. (Fig. 2.11) Place a beanbag or a number 6 or 7 ball between the knees. Jump forward without dropping the object. (Wonderful relay!)

FIG. 2.11. Kangaroo Jump.

19. Mule Kick. (Fig. 2.12) Start with weight on hands and feet. Kick legs into the air, maintaining all weight on the hands. (Note: This is a prelude to a handstand, so students should be encouraged to kick high without going straight up.) Be

sure there is sufficient space between students to avoid collisions. Should be performed on turf for safety.

FIG. 2.12. Mule Kick.

20. Measuring Worm. (Fig. 2.13) Assume an all-fours position, weight on hands and feet, body arched, and knees straight. Walk the hands forward as far as possible, keeping the knees straight. Walk the feet up to the hands without bending the knees. Continue in this manner, stressing that first *only* hands move, and that then *only* feet move. May count, "Hands—two—three—four; feet—two—three—four." Use 6 counts for upper grades.

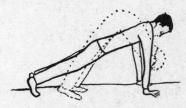

FIG. 2.13. Measuring Worm.

21. Corkscrew. (Fig. 2.14) With feet slightly apart, reach right hand across in front of the body, around behind the left knee, between legs, and touch the right toes. (Note: Heels may be lifted off the floor.)

FIG. 2.14. Corkscrew.

22. Grapevine. (Fig. 2.15) Stand with heels together, toes pointing slightly outward. Place palms of hands together, "dive" down between the knees, one hand going around each ankle, and join fingertips together in front of ankles. (A quite flexible student can clasp hands!)

FIG. 2.15. Grapevine.

23. Jitterbug Snap. Run a short distance and leap, taking off on one foot and landing on the other. While in the air snap the fingers. Continue, alternating leap and run.

24. Turk Stand. In standing position, fold arms on chest, cross legs at ankles. Sit down slowly. Without uncrossing the hands or feet, stand upright. (Encourage children to lean forward so that weight is directly over the feet.)

25. Crab Walk. (Fig. 2.16) Start in sitting position with knees bent, feet close to hips, hands on floor behind back. Raise the hips so that weight is supported on hands and feet. Keeping body in a straight line, walk forward, backward, sideways, diagonally, or in circles.

FIG. 2.16. Crab Walk.

26. Seal Walk. (Fig. 2.17) Start by lying face down on the grass. Place hands on ground under shoulders and push up so that weight is maintained on hands, fingers pointing out sideways. Walk forward on hands, allowing feet to drag, toes pointed backward. (Not advisable for overweight children.)

FIG. 2.17. Seal Walk.

27. Coffee Grinder. (Fig. 2.18) Start in sitting position, legs extended, hands on floor behind hips. Roll to one side, supporting weight on one hand and foot, with body in a straight line. Pivot around supporting arm, taking small steps with feet and maintaining body in a straight line. Repeat, supporting weight on other hand and foot. Try changing directions quickly and taking small, fast steps.

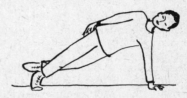

FIG. 2.18. Coffee Grinder.

BEGINNING STUNTS (PARTNERS)

Note: Children should be paired off by approximate size and weight.

1. Wring the Dishrag. (Fig. 2.19) Partners join both hands. Turn completely around by swinging hands up and over head, continuing around to starting position. Hands should remain joined throughout.

FIG. 2.19. Wring the Dishrag.

2. Double Walk. (Fig. 2.20) Partners face each other, one child standing on the

other's feet. Grasp each other's upper arms. Keeping this position, the one whose feet are on the bottom walks forward.

FIG. 2.20. Double Walk.

3. Twister. (Fig. 2.21) Partners join right hands. One student swings his right leg over the joined hands, then the other swings his left leg over so that both are now straddling their joined hands. The first continues to turn by swinging his left leg over, then the partner swings his right leg over, bringing them back to their original position.

FIG. 2.21. Twister.

4. Rocking Stunt. (Fig. 2.22) Partners sit facing each other with feet forward so that each sits on the toes of the other's feet. Each grasps the other's elbows. To rock, one leans backward and raises his feet while the other rises to a semistanding position. Reverse to continue the rocking. This stunt is most successful when it is repeated rhythmically. Stress sitting on the partner's toes, not the feet or ankles.

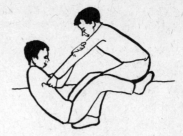

FIG. 2.22. Rocking Stunt.

5. Scooter. The starting position is the same as for the Rocking Stunt, No. 4. First child "scoots" backward, the other keeps his feet in contact with his partner's body. Then the other child "scoots" forward by lifting slightly off the ground and bending his knees. Continue and then reverse the direction.

6. Archway. (Fig. 2.23) Partners lie down, head to head, about a foot apart. Raise the feet, hips, and back, bracing the back with the hands. Touch the feet against the partner's feet. Keep the legs straight, together, and point the toes.

FIG. 2.23. Archway.

7. Chinese Get-up. (Fig. 2.24) Partners stand back to back with elbows locked. They slowly lower to a sitting position, extending the legs to the front. Drawing the feet close to the hips, they attempt to stand by pushing against one another and the ground without the use of hands.

8. Rooster Fight. Assume position described under Rooster Hop. Each player pushes with his *shoulder* against opponent's (partner's) shoulder in an attempt to cause opponent to lose his balance or release hand grip. (May attempt to push opponent out of a 4-to-6-foot circle.)

FIG. 2.24. Chinese Get-up.

9. Leapfrog. (Fig.2.25) One student gets into a squat position, weight on hands and feet and head tucked close to the knees. The partner leaps over his back, legs spread wide while going over. Try the same leaps, with the squatter increasing height of back. As the height is increased, the jumper may touch the squatter's upper back for balance, but may not put his full weight on his hands. Stress placing hands on the upper back, not on the small of the back.

FIG. 2.25. Leapfrog.

10. Wheelbarrow. (Fig. 2.26) One child bends over so that his weight is supported on his hands and feet. The partner steps between his feet and grasps his *knees*, lifting them to about waist height. He then walks his partner a short distance before they exchange positions. Stress that the player on his hands sets the pace. (Not recommended for overweight children.)

11. Back-to-Back Push. Partners fold arms

on chest, stand squarely back to back. On signal, they push against one another, attempting to force the partner to move forward. (Children must be warned against stepping aside quickly to cause a fall.)

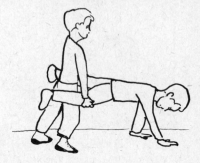

FIG. 2.26. Wheelbarrow.

12. Horizontal Stand. (Fig. 2.27) One student lies on his back with knees bent and feet flat on the floor. Top student faces the other's knees, legs straddling the head. Bottom person grasps top one's shins. Top one leans forward and places hands on the other's knees, arms straight. Bottom one lifts top one's legs as the top one shifts the weight to the hands on the bottom one's knees. Top one should keep his head up, body horizontal, and arms straight.

FIG. 2.27. Horizontal Stand.

13. Partner Handstand. (Fig. 2.28) Partners face each other about 4 feet apart. One places his hands on the ground and slowly brings his feet up over his head, one foot at a time. The other student grasps his ankles to steady him.

FIG. 2.28. Partner Handstand.

INTERMEDIATE STUNTS

1. Heel Click. Jump into the air, click heels together before landing with feet slightly apart, knees bent. Try clicking heels twice, following the same instructions.

2. Heel Slap. (Fig. 2.29) Start by bouncing lightly, then in rhythm raise one foot to the side (knee bent) and slap the heel with the hand. Repeat on opposite side. When proficient, try to slap both heels simultaneously, maintaining the rhythm.

FIG. 2.29. Heel Slap.

3. Squat Thrust, (Fig. 2.30) or the Rocket. Squat down, placing hands on floor between knees. Taking body weight on the hands, jump, extending legs backward until the body is in a straight line. Weight is then on hands and feet. Jump back to squat position, and return to standing position.

4. Thread the Needle. In standing position, clasp hands in front of the body and step through, first with one leg and then

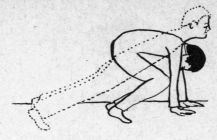

FIG. 2.30. Squat Thrust.

with the other. Repeat, returning to original position.

5. Rise and Shine. Lie flat on the back, hands clasped behind head. Get to feet without using hands, elbows, or knees; or by crossing legs.

6. Clown Trick. Lie on the floor face up. Place a small object (block, pebble) on the forehead. Get up to full standing position and return to lying position without dropping or touching the object.

7. Human Ball. (Fig. 2.31) Sit with knees bent to the chest and feet flat on floor. Put palms of the hands together and bring down between the knees. Separate hands, each going behind the calf of a leg and locking in front of legs. Roll over to one knee, shoulder, back, shoulder, then other knee. Sit up again. (If student rolls too slowly, he will have difficulty going all the way around—rock to one side then roll to the other side.)

FIG. 2.31. Human Ball.

8. Robot. (Fig. 2.32) Start with one leg raised backward and opposite arm raised forward. Swing the leg forward and the

arm backward, continuing for a stated number of counts. Change the alternate arm and leg and repeat. (Who can combine the two without breaking the rhythm? Example: "Swing—two—three—and change —swing—two—three—and change. . . .")

FIG. 2.32. *Robot.*

9. Knee Jump. (Fig. 2.33) Start in kneeling position with toes pointing backward rather than curled under. Swing arms upward and jump to a standing position. Stress jumping upward, not rocking backward.

FIG. 2.33. *Knee Jump.*

10. Front Lean Variations. Start with the body in a reclining position, face down, weight on hands and feet (like Seal Walk). Spring upward from the hands, slap chest; spring and clap hands; spring from toes, clicking heels.

BEGINNING TUMBLING

When introducing tumbling, have the students sit around the tumbling mats, both to observe and to avoid scuffling. Safety factors are most important in this unit and must be understood clearly by the students. Horseplay cannot be tolerated—complete attention must be devoted to the task at hand. It is possible to use cot mattresses, chaise longue pads, or heavy blankets when tumbling mats are not available.

1. The Fall. (Fig. 2.34) Stand with side to the mat, arms folded on chest. Bend knees slightly, "melt" into the mat by landing on the *outside* of the knee, side of hip, and shoulder. (These are the parts of the body best able to withstand the force of landing.) The child should be taught that there is greater safety in landing in this manner, and that the danger of broken arms is reduced considerably if the arms are kept out of the way.

FIG. 2.34. *The Fall.*

2. Log Roll. Lie across end of mat, arms extended overhead, palms touching. Roll to opposite end of mat, keeping the body in a straight line. Once learned, the Log Roll may be performed on any suitable surface.

Note: The Fall and Log Roll can be presented as a unit, since rolling is a desirable method of reducing the force of impact.

3. Squash. Assume an all-fours position. Extend arms forward and legs backward simultaneously, to finish in a prone position. Keep the head up and relax while falling to avoid jarring the body.

4. Forward Roll. (Fig. 2.35) Squat down with toes on edge of mat, hands on mat just inside the knees with fingers pointing forward. Tuck the chin down on the chest (this is very important), push off with the feet while maintaining weight on the hands. Land on back of shoulders and rounded back, rolling up onto feet. (To gain forward momentum, rock back before rocking forward.)

FIG. 2.35. Instruction in Forward Roll.

To return to a standing position, slap the hands on the shins, which provides the momentum to complete the roll.

Note: Some children will need to be reminded to keep the chin tucked down. Their tendency will be to "dive" into the mat. Stress landing on back of shoulders and rounded back.

5. Backward Roll. (Figs. 2.36A, 2.36B) Stand with back to mat. Squat down, heels

FIG. 2.36A. Backward Roll.

FIG. 2.36B. Backward Roll—down incline mat.

on edge of mat, chin tucked down on chest. Start by rocking forward on hands (away from the mat), then push off with hands, keeping back rounded, rolling up onto shoulder. Reach upward with the hands, placing them alongside the head and pushing against the mat to relieve the neck of body weight. Roll onto the toes, then to a standing position. Stress using the hands to relieve the neck of body weight. Best taught on incline mat.

6. Tripod. (Fig. 2.37) Start by tracing a fairly large triangle on the mat, with a base of at least shoulder width. Place the hairline of the head at the apex, the hands on the other corners, fingers pointing forward. Raise the hips as high as possible by walking the feet toward the hands. Place one knee on top of one elbow, and then the other knee on the other elbow. Hold this position for several seconds and then come down by reversing the procedure.

FIG. 2.37. Tripod.

Note: Students should be instructed to place the front of the head (at the hairline) on the mat; otherwise they will go into a forward roll.

7. Forward-to-Backward Roll. (Fig. 2.38) Do a forward roll as described previously, but start by crossing legs at the ankles so that the performer ends up squatting with legs crossed. Pivot while in the squat posi-

FIG. 2.38. Forward-to-Backward Roll.

tion so that the legs are uncrossed and do a backward roll ending up on the feet.

8. Tip-up. (Fig. 2.39) Squat with the knees spread, bring arms between the knees, place the hands on mat in front of the feet. Hands should be shoulder width apart, fingers spread facing forward. Transfer weight to the hands, place bent elbows into the bend at knees. Lean forward with head raised until the feet are lifted from the floor. Hold for five counts.

FIG. 2.39. Tip-up.

9. Double Forward Roll. (Fig. 2.40) One student lies on the mat facing up, the other student stands straddling the first one's head and facing his feet. They grasp each other's ankles. Roll begins with the one on top doing a forward roll, the one on the bottom being carried up by the momentum. Continue the roll in that direction. Stress tucking the head down and landing on the shoulders and upper back.

FIG. 2.40. Double Forward Roll.

GROUP STUNTS—PYRAMIDS

Teaching suggestions

As the students gain proficiency in the various stunts and tumbling activities, they may want to make a formal presentation of their achievements. This can be done by selecting certain of the items already presented and combining them in a logical sequence. The stunts may be assembled with low stunts to either side and the higher ones in the middle, thus creating a pyramid effect. Other symmetric designs may also be developed. Following is a list of group stunts that create interesting effects for presentation.

1. Sideward Rolls and Leap. (Fig. 2.41) Divide group in half, each half of the group standing in single file formation facing each end of the mat. On signal children at one end start log rolling down the mat. At the same time, children in the other line leap over the approaching rollers. Upon reaching the end of the mat, each "leaper" becomes a "roller" and vice versa.

FIG. 2.41. Sideward Rolls and Leap.

2. Merry-go-round. (Fig. 2.42) Work in groups of six or eight. Number the students off by twos. All stand in a circle grasping each other's wrists. Odd numbers sit with knees straight and feet together in the center of the circle. On signal all

FIG. 2.42. Merry-go-round.

even numbers take a step outward and all odd numbers raise hips until bodies are in an inclined position with body in a straight line. Even numbers move around the circle and odd numbers pivot on heels.

3. Spread-Eagle Handstand. (Fig. 2.43) An odd number of students stand at the back of the mat facing forward in line formation, approximately 3 feet apart. Even-numbered students, on a signal, place their hands on the mat and kick up into a handstand. Odd-numbered students grasp the left ankle of the person on the right and the right ankle of the person on the left. Dismount by odd-numbered students slowly lowering the even-numbered students to the mat, where they do a forward roll and stand.

FIG. 2.43. Spread-Eagle Handstand.

4. Handstand Archway. (Fig. 2.44) Work in groups of three, with any number of groups participating. Nos. 1 and 3

FIG. 2.44. Handstand Archway.

should be of the same size, No. 2 stronger than 1 and 3. No. 2 stands in the middle, 1 and 3 face each other. On signal, 1 and 3 kick up into a handstand and No. 2 catches their feet to balance the handstand. To descend, 1 and 3 flex hips and drop to mat.

5. Monkey Roll. (Fig. 2.45) Work in groups of three. All start in all-fours position, 3 feet between each, all facing the same direction. Center person drops and rolls to the right, right person dives over to the center and rolls to the left, left person then dives to the center and rolls right. Continue this shuttle process for three or four complete series.

FIG. 2.45. Monkey Roll.

6. Squash Pyramid. Work in groups of three or six. The strongest students should be bases and the lightest students should be on top. Using six students as an example: three "bases" drop to an all-fours position, with hands and knees touching, backs straight. The next two straddle the "bases'" backs, with one knee over the *hips* and hand over the *shoulder* of two "bases." Top person mounts gently, keeping weight forward, putting one knee and hand on *hip* and *shoulder* of one student and the other knee and hand on the other student. On signal all squash to the mat (see the Squash under "Beginning Tumbling"). Do not attempt this stunt until the Squash has been properly learned.

SMALL EQUIPMENT, JUMP ROPE, HOPSCOTCH

SUGGESTED GRADE PLACEMENT CHART

SMALL EQUIPMENT, 51–61	K	1	2	3	4	5	6	7–8
Scooter Boards	x	x	x	x	·	·	·	
Barrels; Boxes; Incline Mats and Boards; Ladders	x	x	x	·	·			
Hoops	−	x	x	x	x	·	·	
White Sidewalls for Tires; Small Airplane Tires	−	x	x	x	x	·	·	
Wands (Sticks)				−	x	x	x	·
Balance Beam (Walking Board)	x	x	x	x	x	x	·	·
Square Balance Board	−	x	x	x	x	x	·	
Stilts (Plastic)	x	x	x					
Bounce Board (Jump Board)	x	x	x	x				
Stegel	x	x	x	x	x	x	x	x
Obstacle Courses	−	−	x	x	x	x	x	x
Station Teaching		−	x	x	x	x	x	x
JUMP ROPE, 61–64								
Long Rope	x	x	x	x	x	x	x	·
Individual Ropes	−	x	x	x	x	x	x	·
Two Ropes				−	x	x	x	·
Verses		−	x	x	x	x		
Chinese Jump Rope				−	x	x	x	x
HOPSCOTCH, 64–67	−	x	x	x	x	·	·	

− = May introduce activity   x = Depth in instruction   • = May continue activity

SMALL EQUIPMENT (FIG. 2.46)

There is a wealth of equipment that can be assembled inexpensively and that will give children many hours of pleasurable, constructive activity. Through the use of the materials listed, children may sharpen their inventiveness while improving balance, coordination, and general body control.

During the introduction to small equipment, demonstrate one or two uses for each of the items and then let the children explore further activities on their own. Dividing the class into small groups will give each child sufficient time to become

FIG. 2.46. Small Equipment. Front row: Hoops; white side walls for tires; stretch rope; square balance board. Center: Triple balance beam (support blocks not shown). Back row: Bounce board; wands; 7-foot ladder mounted on saw horse; plastic stilts; balance beams, 4- and 2-inch widths.

familiar with one object before rotating to another. Some of the objects lend themselves to use by two or three players at one time.

A facility for storage convenient to the play area is important to frequent use of this equipment. Some of the equipment may be obtained without charge, such as discarded tires of the sort used on small planes. Other equipment may be constructed for less cost than outright purchase, such as hoops made of flexible plastic pipe. See the Appendix for lists of equipment, descriptions for the construction of some of the materials, and sources of selected pieces of equipment.

SCOOTER BOARDS

Scooter Boards provide excellent activity for bilateral and reciprocal action as well as the development of muscle tone and strength. According to recent research, the impact of some of the following activities may be even greater. (6) Jean Ayres[1] has found that certain types of scooter board activities enhance sensorimotor development for the children with deficits in postural and bilateral integration as well as in the ability to motor plan. (63) Such factors are essential in the development of efficient movement.

SAFETY

1. Scooter Boards are used only in a lying, sitting, or kneeling position, *never* standing.
2. When through with the scooter board, put in a safe place with wheels up.

INDIVIDUAL ACTIVITIES

1. Pivot-Prone Position. (Fig. 2.47A)
Note: If child has difficulty attaining this position, it sometimes helps to have him carry a box on his head, and/or feet, that is large enough so that it must be lifted to get it off the floor. Legs should be straight, with no bent knees. See description of Pivot-Prone Position under "Body Awareness," Chapter 1.
   a. Move forward—work both arms

[1]Dr. A. Jean Ayres, Associate Professor, Special Education, University of Southern California.

together, bilateral action; work arms alternately, reciprocal action.
   b. Move backward—arms working together; work arms alternately.
   c. Spin-turn in place to the right, to the left. "How fast can you spin one way? The other way?" (Fig. 2.47A)
   d. Obstacle Course. Follow the course without touching any object.
      (1) Move around three markers in slalom fashion. Repeat with eyes closed (visual memory). (Fig. 2.47B)
      (2) Move forward through a maze: around markers, boxes, chairs; under tables, benches. Repeat with eyes closed.
      (3) Follow rope trails—serpentine fashion.
      (4) Create own Obstacle Course.
   e. Marks on floor. (Masking tape X or chalk spot.)
      (1) Move toward mark. Place right hand on mark and pivot around it. Repeat with left hand.
      (2) Move toward mark. Stop when scooter board is over it and then pivot first to right and then to left.
      (3) Repeat (1) and (2) with eyes closed or with a large paper bag over head to occlude vision and reinforce tactile and kinesthetic input.

SMALL GROUP ACTIVITIES

Note: All individual and relay activities may also be done in small groups.
1. Follow-the-Leader.
2. Do As I Do. Use one board for two to four children in relay formation. One child performs an activity, other children take turns repeating the activity.
3. Do As I Do and Add Something (sequencing). Player No. 1 does one thing; No. 2 repeats and adds something; No. 3 repeats one and two, then adds another. Continue. After a miss, regroup and start again.
4. Follow the Sound (auditory cues).

FIG. 2.47A. Scooter board activities: spinning in good pivot-prone position.

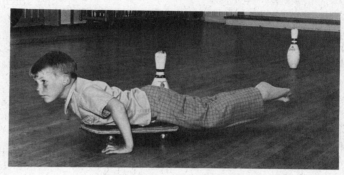

FIG. 2.47B. Obstacle Course or Slalom Relay.

Place a large paper bag over participant's head. Partner moves around ringing a bell (or making some other sound) while player on scooter follows the sound.

For additional enjoyment, the teacher may make yet another sound such as a sharp whistle. When heard, the participants spin around. Watch to see that there is proper spacing to spin in safety.

RELAYS USING SCOOTER BOARDS

Note: Use relays mainly for practice in skill and speed. Competition may be included as a special treat at the end of the given time.

1. File Formation. If possible, use two scooters for each line so the next player in line can be ready to start when tagged.

   a. Move forward around a marker and back
      (1) work arms together;
      (2) work arms alternately;
      (3) lie supine and use legs only.
   b. Move backward until scooter crosses a line, touch line with

hand, then return moving forward.

   c. Hoop held upright on opposite line. Last player in each relay team holds the hoop. In pivot-prone position move backward and put legs through hoop. Return to starting line moving forward. (Leader replaces last player in holding the hoop.)
   d. Farmer and Crow Relay (see Chapter 3, Relays).
   e. Slalom Relay (see Chapter 3, Relays, and Fig. 2.47B).
   f. Move forward to the line; spin around three times, then return.
   g. Propel self to the middle of the area. Push off and coast to the end.
   h. Auditory Race. One child at goal line holds a sound maker (different sound for each team). Participant places paper bag over head and travels to the sound, trades places with other child who rides scooter board to next player in group and then goes to the end of the line.

2. Shuttle Formation. (Use two scooters for each team.)

 a. Travel to center, grasp right hands, swing around and back to place. Repeat using left hands. (Allow for adequate spacing between lines.)

 b. Backward to center, touch soles of feet, circle around, and return to own line. If additional stimulus is needed follow a taped line.

BARRELS; BOXES; INCLINE MATS AND BOARDS; LADDERS

BARRELS

Crawl through the tunnel: moving first hands then feet; hand and opposite leg; hand and leg on the same side.

Crawl inside and make the barrel roll (barrel can be lined with sponge rubber or carpeting). (4) Mark a given distance. Child rolls straight to the mark and back again (motor planning).

BOXES

According to Espenschade and Eckert,

the first stage in jumping is considered to be the exaggerated step down from a higher level to a lower one so that the onset of jumping and descending stairs has the same origin and, of course, the same occurrence in time. (20)

With this in mind many opportunities should be provided for young children to step or jump down off boxes of increasingly greater heights. Success in such a progression may alleviate, at least in part, fear of reasonable heights. The words "up" and "down" may be verbalized as the child ascends and descends boxes, foam equipment of varied shapes, and steps.

INCLINE MATS AND BOARDS

Incline mats (Fig. 2.36B)

Incline Mats made of foam are soft, fun to use, and remove some of the fear from initial experiences in rolling and tumbling.

Incline boards

One end of the Incline Board is placed on a sawhorse and the other end rests on the ground. For safety, check constantly to be sure that the cleats of the board are securely anchored over the sawhorse.

Activities

Explore various ways of going *up* the incline and getting off the high end such as: going up on hands and knees, hands and feet, walking, running, other ways . . . ; getting down by turning around going feet first, stepping down without turning, jumping down, other ways. . . . "How quietly can you land?" (When jumping, land quietly on the balls of the feet and go into an exaggerated crouch position in order to break the force of gravity.) For Incline Boards start with a sawhorse 1 foot, then 2 feet, and finally 3 feet high.

Activities for Incline mat

Explore various ways of moving *down* the Incline Mat such as: Commando Crawl, hands and knees, hands and feet, walking. Place a flat mat at the end of the incline to extend the area of activity.

Explore various ways of rolling down the Incline Mat.

Log Roll, with head toward one side of the mat, head toward opposite side.

Forward Roll. See Chapter 2, "Beginning Tumbling" for instructions and safety.

Backward Roll. See Chapter 2, "Beginning Tumbling" for instructions and safety.

Slide in Pivot-Prone Position. Run up to and slide down the mat.

LADDERS (FIG. 2.46)

Safety: Check end of Ladder constantly to be sure that the cleats are securely anchored over the sawhorse.

Ladder on ground. Walk in the spaces; walk on the rungs; if ladder is heavy enough, walk on the rails.

Ladder with one end on sawhorse. Crawl up the ladder; walk up ladder on hands and feet; walk up in standing position. Assistance should be available if required by the child. Discuss balance (knees slightly flexed to lower center of gravity; weight slightly forward; arms extended low to the side for added stability).

Progression: Use 1-foot, then 2-foot sawhorse.

HOOPS

See Appendix for method of construction; films: 59.1, 61.

The following material presents examples of activities in specific areas. In the first section activities are planned in terms of Body Awareness and Body Control. In the remaining sections, motor planning is the major concern. Ample time should also be allowed for children to explore other possibilities, create activities, and share the results with peers.

HOOP ON THE GROUND
(CHILD'S PERSONAL SPACE)

1. What can you tell me about your hoop? (Color, texture, shape, size, etc. May guess, then measure the circumference and diameter.)

2. Sit in the center of your hoop. Now can you leave it and find it again?

3. Do As I Do (visual cues). Children follow the movements of the leader in and around their own hoops.

Examples: Crawl around the hoop with one hand and knee inside, and other hand and knee outside, the hoop.

May start in large group with one leader; divide into small groups with several leaders; then work in partners.

4. Do As I Say (auditory cues). Use such instructions as "Place your knees and one hand inside and one hand outside your hoop."

May work in large group, then in small groups.

5. Number concepts and balance. Examples: "Balance three parts of your body on the floor inside your hoop. Add five parts. Take away seven parts." Culmination: "How many parts can you touch on the floor inside your hoop?"

6. Locomotor Patterns.

Walk around the *inside* of your hoop . . . *outside* your hoop.

Gallop around with the foot *closer* to the hoop leading. Change direction and lead foot.

Slide around *facing* the hoop . . . with your *back* to the hoop, continuing in the *same direction*.

How many different ways can you jump in and out of your hoop? (Forward, backward, to the side, with a turn. . . .)

Stand with one foot inside and one foot outside the hoop. Rock side to side. (Evalu-

ation of balance.) Push off with increasing force until doing a side leap.

Leap into the hoop and then out on the opposite side. Repeat in the other direction.

Others? (Exploring activities—see Fig. 2.50.)

MOVING THE HOOP
WHILE REMAINING IN OWN SPACE

1. Pick up hoop with one hand, pass it to other hand, put it down.

2. Pass hoop around the body transferring it from hand to hand while remaining in place.

3. Hold hoop in two hands, step into it and bring it overhead.

4. Hold hoop overhead, turn it around with fingers, then drop it down over body.

5. Stand the hoop on edge: crawl through . . . step through . . . go through head first . . . feet first . . . walk around it . . . jump in and out while holding it.

6. Pick up hoop with feet, raise overhead.

7. Scoot out of hoop, pick it up, and put it around you. Repeat several times moving away from, and back to, place.

8. Work with a partner. Hold hoop, walk in a circle . . . hop together . . . jump together.

9. Beginning jump rope—step through each time.

Use hoop as a jump rope: rock hoop forward and back jumping each time; turn hoop as a jump rope and use jump rope step pattern, "*Jump*-bounce, *Jump*-bounce. . . ."

MOVING THE HOOP WHILE MOVING AROUND

1. Roll the hoop without touching anyone or anything.

2. Roll the hoop, allow it to fall, jump in before it stops moving.

3. Roll the hoop, run through while it is rolling. How many times can you run through before it goes down?

4. Roll the hoop, run around in front, catch it with one hand . . . other hand.

5. Spin the hoop on one arm . . . other arm. Can you move the hoop from one arm to the other while spinning it?

6. Toss the hoop into the air. Catch

it with both hands . . . one hand . . . other hand.

7. Spin hoop on leg, neck, elbow.

8. Put reverse spin on hoop so that it rolls back to you. Jump over it.

9. Use hoop as jump rope and travel around the area.

RELAYS USING HOOPS (FILE FORMATION)

1. Roll the hoop to a line and back.

2. Run to the line, jump the hoop (as in jump rope) three times, run back.

3. Spin the hoop on one arm while going to the line, on the other arm while returning.

4. Roll the hoop to a teammate standing on the opposite line. Take his place as he carries the hoop back and gives it to the next player.

5. Toss the hoop three times while going to the line, carry it back.
Variation: toss with one hand, catch with the other.

6. Dizzy Izzy Relay. Carry the hoop to the opposite line. Put forehead on upright hoop and turn yourself around three times. Return.

OTHER WAYS

(Exploration and creativity as individuals, with partners, or in small groups)

WHITE SIDEWALLS FOR TIRES; SMALL AIRPLANE TIRES

White sidewalls may be purchased in 12, 13, 14, and 15 inch sizes from stores handling automobile accessories. The side walls are flat, safe, easy to handle, and can be stored. (They also make good targets.)

1. Follow-the-Leader Formation (using sidewalls).
Sidewalls touching in zigzag position. Run up, step into each one . . . hop . . . jump.
Sidewalls in wide zigzag position. Run, stepping into each one; jump in and out of each one; leap from side to side. (Fig. 2.50)
Sidewalls spaced 4 to 6 feet apart in a straight line. Slalom Race: Weave in and out around them.

2. Roll the airplane tire.

3. Straddle-jump the tire. (Fig. 2.1)

4. Driving Relay (file formation). Roll a tire to and around a marker and back.

5. Slalom Relay (with tires). Use three players or markers spaced 12 to 15 feet apart. The "driver" weaves in and out between the players on the way out and back. The "driver" then takes the place of a player as the turn is completed as driver. Encourage players serving as markers not to move unless *absolutely* necessary!

6. Work with a Partner.
Roll the tire and pass it back and forth between the two players.
Tug-of-War. One partner on each side of a line. Grip the tire and pull partner across a line. (May use a space 4–6 feet wide.)

7. Work in 3's.
One player rolls the tire, center player straddle jumps it and exchanges places with the roller. Third player stops the tire and rolls it back changing places with center player. (Fig. 2.1) Continue in shuttle fashion.

8. Encourage the students to develop their own games.

WANDS (STICKS)

Emphasize the proper use of wands-sticks for safety.

Wands 1 inch x 40 inches are made commercially. Broom handles or ½ inch doweling may substitute.

1. Imitation of Movements. In large group, small group, or with partners, one person leads while the others follow the movements: in front, in back, one side, other side, diagonal; low, high, medium; under, over; both hands working together, hands working in opposition.

   a. Mirror the movements, go in the same direction as the facing leader (if leader goes to left the follower goes in the same direction, which is to his right).

   b. Do the same as leader (if leader goes to his right, follower goes to *his* right).

   c. Go in opposition (if leader goes down, follower goes up; if leader moves to one side, follower moves to opposite side—as they face).

2. Step over the stick; change from front to back over head.

3. Balance stick on ground. Turn once around and grasp stick before it drops to ground.

4. Balance stick on one finger, palm of hand, back of hand, chin, right elbow, left elbow. . . .

5. Use for posture. Stand in forward-stride position. Hold stick overhead and grasp ends with reverse grasp. Pull stick down behind back *pulling shoulder blades together*. Return to position overhead. Repeat several times.

6. If stick is heavy enough and without splinters, turn stick in opponent's hands. Grasp stick firmly alternating with hands of opponent. Each opponent tries to rotate the stick forward.

7. Explore and create other activities.

BALANCE BEAM (WALKING BOARD)

The walking board "provides experiences that will aid the child in the development of dynamic balance and contribute to the learning of laterality and directionality." (36) Use a 2 x 4-inch board 6 to 12 feet long and 6 to 24 inches off the floor. Preferably, it should be adjustable so that the 4-inch surface can be used for beginners, the 2-inch surface used as the children gain control, and the 4-inch surface can be used for the more advanced balance stunts.

A Triple Balance Beam may be used for practice or in testing balance (51) Use three beams 8 feet in length: first beam 2½ inches in width and marked off in feet, 1 to 8; second beam 1½ inches and marked off 9 to 16; third beam ½ inch and marked off 17 to 24. (Fig. 2.48) See Appendix for a description of the construction of a Triple Balance Beam.

The object of the activity is to walk as far as possible without losing balance. Shoes should be removed for test. Participant starts at the one foot mark on the 2½-inch surface and walks across the beam. He steps off the end of the beam and repeats the activity across the 1½-inch beam. The participant scores his last successful step. If he steps off the beam at 17 feet, his score will be 16. Twenty-four is a perfect score. When testing, allow two trials and record the better score.

The following material presents a progression of activities. However, children should be encouraged to explore other possibilities and create their own activities.

Walk forward

1. Slide. With one foot always in front, slide along.

2. Alternate Feet (touching). Walk with toe touching heel, alternate foot ahead.

3. Alternate Feet (not touching). (Fig. 2.48) Feet do not touch each other. (Do not allow the child to run as he will avoid the necessity for balance.)

4. Eye Focus off Board. Same as No. 3,

FIG. 2.48. How far can you walk without stepping off? Look at your number. Can you start again and go farther? (Boards of decreasing width used.)

but focus on the end of the board or on an object in the distance.

5. Carry Wand. Carry a wand or broomstick in both hands, hands spread apart.

6. Carry Objects. Carry a light object in one hand and a heavy object in the other. Repeat with the objects in the opposite hands.

Slide sideways (Fig. 3.6)

With side toward the end of the board, slide along slowly. Do not cross feet. Travel first with the right foot leading and then with the left foot leading.

Walk backward

Walk backward, alternating feet. Encourge children not to look back.

Combinations

1. Forward and Sideways. Walk to center, turn, and move sideways.

2. Forward, Turn, Forward. Walk to center, turn, and walk to starting position.

3. Forward, Stoop, Forward. Walk to center, stoop, pick up an object placed on the board, and walk to the end. (As the child's skill increases, have him pick up an object from the floor and walk to the end.)

4. Forward, Bounce. Walk to the center, bounce twice, walk to the end. (May bounce twice, and turn to go back to starting position.)

Note: Use 4-inch side of board for Nos. 5–8.

5. Hop. Take small hops on one foot at least halfway across. Later on, change supporting foot at the center and continue across.

6. Leg Extension. Walk to the center, bend at the waist, and put hands on the board. Extend one leg back horizontally, recover, and walk on to the end.

7. Arms and Leg Extension. Same as No. 6 except that the arms are extended back.

8. "V" Sit. Walk to center, sit on the board, place hands on board behind hips, raise feet and straighten legs, and then extend arms to the side and hold. Recover, stand, and walk to the end.

Safety

1. First child should be halfway across the board before the next child starts.

2. Children should not interfere with one another.

3. Make sure that the board is securely braced so that it will not slip.

4. If metal bar is used, cover it with a nonskid surfacing.

BOXES

Use for creative play.
Climb up and jump down.
Make steps with boxes. Climb up and jump down.
Combine with other equipment. Automobile Tire: Jump off box and land in automobile tire (white sidewall or hoop).

SQUARE BALANCE BOARD (48) (FIG. 2.49)

Balance on equipment. Vary eye focus: look down; look forward.
Balance and rock: rock side to side; rock forward and back.
Balance and stoop to pick up an object off floor.
Balance an object on head.
Balance and bounce a ball: single bounce, consecutive bounces.
Play catch with partner.
Throw ball at targets.
Explore and create other activities.

FIG. 2.49. Square balance board, showing the larger balance posts that may be used for initial experiences.

STILTS (FIG. 2.46)

(Plastic: 3 inches high with 5-inch base. See Appendix for further information.)

Plastic stilts are kept in contact with the feet by plastic ropes that pass through the stilt and are held in the hands. Walking on these stilts provides yet another experience in balance and hand-foot coordination.

1. Walk forward, backward, to one side, to the other side, in a circle.
2. Walk forward and backward on a straight line or on a circle.
3. Walk forward and backward stepping into each square, such as those that appear in diagrams for Hopscotch and Ladder.
4. Follow Obstacle Courses, such as a slalom pattern, or trails of foot prints. See "Motor Planning," "Move in Relation to Small Equipment," No 8.
5. Other activities?

BOUNCE BOARD
(JUMP BOARD; FIG. 2.46)

MOUNT AT THE CENTER

1. Jump. Each child in turn mounts the board then takes consecutive jumps. The teacher assists with balance if needed.
2. Increase number of jumps. On first turn jump once, on second turn jump 2 times. Continue up to 5 or 10 jumps. Count aloud as you jump.
3. Jump while bouncing a ball. Stand in center section on Jump Board and bounce a ball as you jump.
4. Jump while catching and tossing a ball. Work with partner. While jumping, partner tosses the ball. Catch the ball and toss it back while jumping. Exchange roles.
5. Jump while alternating feet together, feet apart. Verbalize, "Together, apart, together. . . ."
6. Turning Jump. Take small jumps, turning once around to the right, and once around to the left.
7. Jump with arm movements. Take jumps in place while changing position of arms.

MOUNT AT THE END

1. Jumps moving forward. Take small jumps forward across the board, with assistance as needed.
2. Jump in specific area. Mark off the length of the jump board into equal sections.

a. Jump once in first section, step into next section and jump once. Continue on across the board. On second turn jump twice in each section. Continue up to five jumps in each section.
b. Jump once in each section continuously across the board. Next turn, jump two times in each section. Continue up to five turns. Count number of jumps aloud.
c. Making consecutive jumps, jump once in first section, two times in second section. Increase by one jump in each section.

3. Jump to the side. Take small jumps to the right as you travel across the board. On the next turn, face opposite direction and take small jumps to the left.
4. Jump forward and backward. Take two small jumps forward and one backward across the board.

STEGEL

For activities on the Stegel, see the guide by Frank E. Isola, *ABC's of the Stegel*, 89 Orinda Way, #6, Orinda, California: Educational Consulting Service, 1970.

Films showing activities on the Stegel are listed under Bradley Wright Films with the "Audio-Visual Materials—Section One," at the end of Chapter 5.

For manufacturers of the Stegel, see "Sources of Special Equipment" in the Appendix.

OBSTACLE COURSES

Use all types of equipment. Some pieces of equipment may be made or they may be purchased.

Have a group of children set the pattern for the layout of the obstacle course. Suggested layouts may be drawn to scale in the classroom by each child and the work integrated with other subject areas.

Obstacle courses may be very simple and used even at kindergarten level as a follow-the-leader activity, or they may be set up to be very challenging to upper grade children. Obstacle courses may include some of the following activities: hang and travel on horizontal ladder;

travel on parallel bars; dodging, as in Slalom Race (objects may be offset to involve more dodging); *walking* on the balance beam; crawling through a barrel or rolling under a rope; jumping over a milk carton, low rope, or low hurdle; agility run using blocks or touching the lines used for the run; jumping rope in place or while traveling in a circle; locomotor skills other than running, for part of the distance; and stepping into automobile tires or hoops in a zigzag pattern.

For safety, check that each activity as set up in the course is safe for participation; that there is sufficient overrun area at the finish line; and that the course is not tòo long or too strenuous for the children involved.

OBSTACLE COURSE EXAMPLE

Note: Second child starts as first child reaches the end of the horizontal ladder.

1. Horizontal ladder. Hand-over-hand travel.

2. Three poles on three pairs of blocks, spaced approximately 6 feet apart. Jump over as hurdles.

3. Six tires. Step into tires—alternate feet.

4. Low horizontal bar. Jump up to inclining position—forward hip circle over low bar. (Stress changing grip.)

5. Milk cartons. Run to the right of the first one, left of the second, completely around the third.

6. Board across two sawhorses. Crawl under.

7. Balance beam. *Walk* forward.

8. Tetherball pole. Grasp the pole—swing completely around.

9. Run across finish line.

STATION TEACHING

Small equipment may be used in Station Teaching. Children may explore activities at the various stations (Fig. 2.50). With review activities at several stations and one *new* station, the teacher may remain at the *new* one. The teacher presents safety and gives basic instructions as each group rotates to the *new* station.

When the activities are review ones, children may be organized into groups based on skill level. The teacher may rotate along with one or two groups. A card at each station may list activities in order of difficulty. Well-skilled groups may

FIG. 2.50. Exploring activities at various stations.

perform more advanced activities on certain equipment, while lesser skilled groups work at their own levels.

JUMP ROPE

Instructing children in how to jump rope may seem like a waste of valuable class time. There are, however, many students who apparently have never experienced this activity—primarily boys. As motivation for boys, stress that boxers as well as basketball and tennis players use rope jumping to strengthen the legs and develop footwork.

Rope jumping is rhythmic and takes courage and timing to be successful. Children receive a great deal of satisfaction as they succeed in performing new patterns. In its many forms, jumping rope can be interesting and challenging from the first grade upward, and it provides excellent activity.

For very young children, the teacher may fasten one end of the rope to a fence and work with a small group. (The rhythm and skill may be demonstrated to all the children before the jump rope is actually used.)

When introducing this unit, it is helpful to add other activities to insure more participation. For example, in follow-the-leader formation jump the rope and then travel around a designated course using various locomotor skills before returning for the next turn to jump.

As children learn to turn the rope in good rhythm, they may work alone in groups of four to six children. A child may automatically become a turner of the rope after he has completed his jumps. Changing turners without stopping the rope or breaking the rhythm adds additional challenge. Demonstrate new activities with one group, then have all groups participate.

A few samples of the many available verses are presented in this section. Allow time for the children to create their own stunts and verses. The verses may be developed during a creative writing period. Interesting patterns with jump ropes lend themselves to program presentations.

SKILLS OF ROPE JUMPING

Big jump, followed by a bounce. Call, "*Jump*-bounce, *jump*-bounce."

LONG ROPE

1. Rope on the Ground. Run up, jump over (both feet), continue on.
2. Rope Held off the Ground (about 6 inches). Run up, jump over, continue on.
3. Rope Swinging Back and Forth (low water). Leap over as the rope swings *toward* the player.
4. Stand In and Jump. (Fig. 12.2.) Stand beside the rope that is on the ground. As it is turned, try to jump up to 5; up to 10.
5. Stand In, Jump, Run out.
6. Run Through—Front Door (rope turning toward player). *Start* to run as rope is moving down to strike the ground; chase the rope.
7. Run in—(front door), Jump, Run out (opposite side).
8. Follow-the-Leader.
9. Jump with Stunts. Touch the ground, turn around, hop, heel-toe, clap hands (in front of body, in back, under knee). Create other stunts and combinations of stunts.
10. "Hot Pepper." Jump with rope turning as rapidly as possible. Use single jumps, no bounce.
11. Run in Back Door (rope turning away from player). *Start* to run as rope strikes the ground and is moving up. Be ready to jump over rope as it turns again.
12. Work with a Partner. Exchange places. Do stunts in unison.
13. Pattern of 4's, 3's. Run, jump four times, run out *as* next player runs in and jumps four. Take end of rope as turner, as jumps are completed. Later try changing on three. Take a series: each player changes on five, then on four, on three, on two. Work in groups of four.

Create other tricks: as individual; with partner; in small groups.

14. Jump the Shot. Tie a beanbag to the end of an individual rope. Turner stands in the center and twirls the rope around close to the ground. Turner may whirl around or he may shift the rope from one hand to the other to keep the rope in motion. Vary the height according to the skill of the jumpers. Jumpers may run in and out.

INDIVIDUAL ROPES

Note: Use hoops for activities 1 through 4, then repeat with ropes.

1. Single Jumps (first attempts). Hold the rope so that the middle part of it is resting on the ground in front of the feet. Jump over the rope, swing it over the head from behind, let it rest on the ground to be jumped again. Gradually increase the pace until there is no hesitation between turning and jumping.

2. Continuous Jumps. Try to increase the number of continuous jumps before a mistake is made. Count number of jumps.

3. Traveling Jumps. Move from one spot to another while jumping the rope. This can be done with a jump, gallop, skip, or run.

4. Reverse Jump. Turn the jump rope backward.

5. Variations in Jumps. Hop on one foot; skip; cut step rocking forward and backward; cut step swinging free foot forward; jump fast omitting the bounce ("Hot Pepper"). Create patterns to music.

6. Jump, Turn Rope at Side, Jump. Jump the rope, put both hands together at the side and turn rope, jump the rope. Continue sequence.

7. Crossed-Arm Jump. While jumping, cross the arms over the chest so that the hands hold the rope on opposite sides. Jump in that position and then uncross the arms on the next jump. (Stress that arms should be *extended* out beyond body and must *remain crossed* until rope completes the circle.) Turn rope backward and cross arms.

Create other tricks as an individual.

8. Jump with Partner. One player turns the rope, partner runs in; partners turn rope with outside hand, may run out and in again while turning the rope.

Create other tricks with partners.

TWO ROPES

1. Four Turners. (Fig. 2.51A) Each turner stands in the corner of an imaginary square. Two ropes cross in center of square. Start the top rope turning, then turn the bottom rope in the same direction and at the same time. Jump with usual jump-bounce. Keep ropes same length.

2. Double Dutch. (Fig. 2.51B)
   a. Turn ropes inward. Two turners stretch the two ropes out, measuring them for equal lengths, then move forward until ropes touch the ground. Standing in a side-stride position and holding arms apart, start one rope turning inward, then the other (like an egg beater). Turn in *even* rhythm or ropes will tangle. *Start* to run in when one rope is high and the other is on the ground; run in and jump over oncoming rope. The jump pattern is the same as for "Hot Pepper," with no bounce. Run all the way into center of ropes and *start jumping immediately.* Experiment with approach from position beside turner and from position opposite center of rope.
   b. Turn ropes outward. Stress turning ropes in even rhythm. Some children may find b easier to perform than a. Run in as back rope hits the ground.

3. Long Rope and Individual Rope. (Fig. 2.51C) Player with a single rope jumps at center of long rope. Have jumper stand in and start jumping the long rope, then start turning and jumping the individual rope.

Create other tricks.

VERSES

Blue bells, cockle shells
[*swing rope back and forth on ground*].
Evie ivie overs
[*turn rope*].

Teddy bear, teddy bear, turn around;
Teddy bear, teddy bear, touch the ground;
Teddy bear, teddy bear, show your shoe;
Teddy bear, teddy bear, that will do.

House for rent, inquire within,
When I move out, let [name] move in.

Mabel, Mabel, set the table;
Don't forget the
Red . . . Hot . . . Pepper
[*turn double time*].

FIG. 2.51A. Four Turners.

Mother, Mother I am ill;
Call the doctor over the hill.
In came the doctor [one player],
In came the nurse [another player],
In came the lady with the alligator purse
    [third player].
Measles, said the doctor;
Mumps, said the nurse;
Nothing, said the lady with the alligator purse.
Out went the doctor [first player]
Out went the nurse [second player]
Out went the lady with the alligator purse
    [third player].

Partners:

    Changing bedrooms, No. 1;
[Partners exchange places with four jumps]
    Changing bedrooms, No. 2;
    Changing bedrooms, No. 3;
    Changing bedrooms, all out free
[run out].

CHINESE JUMP ROPE (ORIGIN UNKNOWN)

Equipment (Fig. 2.52)

A loop of rubber bands or elastic. Use elastic rope, the elastic used in dressmaking, long rubber band, or a series of small rubber bands looped or tied together in a continuous chain; or use plastic rope for each end (around holders' ankles) with rubber bands or elastic in section for jumping. The entire loop is from 6 to 10 feet in circumference.

FIG. 2.51B. Double Dutch.

FIG. 2.51C. Long rope and individual rope.

FIG. 2.52. Chinese Jump Rope.

Players

Same as in jumping with a long rope, two players hold the rope while one or two other players jump. Players holding the rope place it behind their ankles with feet approximately shoulder distance apart.[2]

Changing positions

When a player misses or makes an error, players rotate. When the first player has his turn again, he starts from the stunt he missed.

Activity

1. Jumper stands outside the ropes with side toward the ropes.
   a. Lift foot next to the rope and touch toe down between the ropes; return to starting position. Repeat three times.
   b. Hook foot under the closer rope, draw it over the top of rope on the far side and touch the toe to the ground; return to starting position.
   c. Repeat a and b two more times.
   d. Jump between ropes; jump and land on both ropes; jump out on

[2]With rope placed in this position, children may create step patterns or practice the basic steps of the Philippine Bamboo Dance, Tinikling. Several children may participate at one time with each rope.

the other side. Repeat the sequence from a to d with other foot and return to starting position. (Face same direction throughout the stunt.)

2. Holders move rope up to calves of the legs. Repeat all activities in No. 1.

3. Holders move rope up to knees. Repeat all activities in No. 1.

4. Holders return rope down to ankles. Repeat all activities in No. 1, but with each action, hop on the outside foot. Continue using the hop with Nos. 2 and 3.

Note: Encourage children to develop their own stunts as their skills increase.

5. Two examples of more difficult activities are as follows:
   a. When going from one side of the rope to the other, jumper picks up the first rope with the foot and touches the ground on the far side over the second rope, then inserts his other foot next to the one already in the center between the two ropes. He jumps up and makes a half-turn in the air. Repeat turn two more times. To finish the stunt the player leaps into the air, releases the ropes, and lands straddling both ropes facing one of the holders.
   b. Work with a partner. Two players jump at the same time.

HOPSCOTCH

The game of hopscotch is as old as civilization itself. Its beginnings have been traced back to Greek myths; and in the old forum in Rome, one can still see the hopscotch diagrams that were scratched in the pavement. (21)

The games of hopscotch are as varied as a child's imagination allows. Sometimes a marker is used to designate a player's spot in the game. The marker is called by such names as tor, loger, potsie, and pally-ully. Even the method of moving from one box to another may vary from a simple step or hop to a fancy dance movement. The children can and will develop their own unique hopscotch game; and it will increase in its complexity as the children strive for new challenges to parallel their skill development.

The following samples of hopscotch diagrams are suitable for a playground. They have purposely been kept clear of numbers (except for Hopscotch No. II) or words in or around the squares. This allows for more varied use by the children.

The rule of thumb for dimensions is to make the squares from 12 to 18 inches each, and the lines dividing them not more than 1½ inches wide.

SNAIL (FIG. 2.53)

Basic rules

1. Each child has a marker (stone, bobby pin, chain, paper clip, twig) that he places in the outermost square.

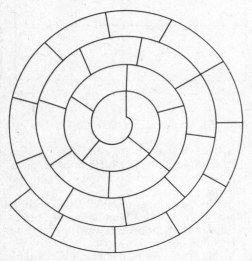

FIG. 2.53. Snail.

2. Each child, in turn, attempts to hop in every square not occupied by a marker. He hops to the center and out again.

3. If he goes in and out again without a miss, he places his marker in the second square and waits for his next turn. If he misses, his marker remains in the same square.

4. The winner is the child who moves his marker all the way in and out of the diagram first.

Rules for losing a turn

1. Stepping on a line.
2. Touching the ground with any part of the body other than the hopping foot. (Exception: Upon reaching the center of the diagram, player may stand on both feet to rest before starting his return trip.)
3. Hopping into a square occupied by an opponent's marker.

Variation

Use no markers. If successful in going in and coming out without stepping on a line, place initials in any one square. This square becomes that child's private resting spot and no one else can hop in it or rest there.

HOPSCOTCH NO. I (FIG. 2.54)

Basic rules

1. Each player places a marker in the first square.

2. The first player hops into each single square, and places one foot in each of the two parallel squares simultaneously.

3. Upon reaching the end of the diagram, he turns around and hops back to the last free square before reaching the one occupied by his own marker.

4. Standing on one foot, he reaches forward and picks up his own marker without touching a line or any other marker.

5. He then hops over the square that contains the other markers, and out of the diagram.

6. The same player tosses his marker into the next square after the one it previously occupied. If the marker reaches player continues. If not, the marker stays in the square but the player gives up his turn. the square and does not fall on a line, the

Rules for losing a turn

1. Stepping on any line.
2. Hopping into a square occupied by a marker.
3. Touching the ground with any part of the body other than the foot on which the player is hopping. (Exception: Putting one foot in each parallel square).
4. Touching another marker when attempting to pick up his own marker.
5. Tossing the marker into the wrong square, or having it fall on a line.

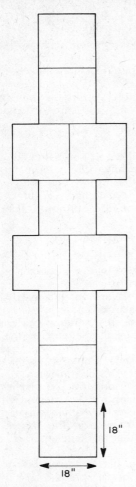

FIG. 2.54. Hopscotch No. I.

When the player reaches the last square with his marker, he picks it up, carries it to the first square, places it on the back of his hand, and attempts to hop in all the squares up and back without dropping the marker or stepping on a line. If successful, he plays as before but starts at the other end. The player who gets back first to the first square with his marker wins.

HOPSCOTCH NO. II (FIG. 2.55)

Basic rules

1. Each child starts with a marker in his hand.

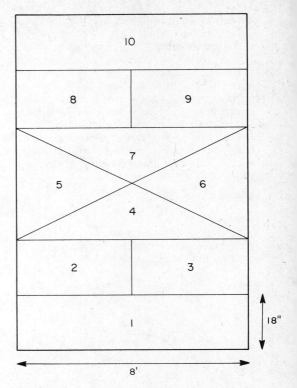

FIG. 2.55. Hopscotch No. II.

2. First player starts by tossing the marker into square No. 1. He hops in, picks up the marker, and hops back out of the square.

3. He then tosses to No. 2, hops into 1, jumps into 2 and 3 simultaneously, picks up the marker, hops backward into 1, and then hops out.

4. He continues in this manner, hopping into the single numbers and straddling the numbers that are opposite each other (2 and 3, 5 and 6, 8 and 9), picking up the marker, then hopping and jumping backward through the squares.

Rules for losing a turn

1. Stepping on any line.

2. Tossing the marker into the wrong square or having it fall on a line.

LADDER (FIG. 2.56)

The "Ladder" rungs are made narrow to force the children to hop sideways up and

1'

8'

FIG. 2.56. Ladder.

back. This helps to develop coordination and balance as well as strength. Encourage the children to use alternate feet, the right foot to hop up and the left foot to hop back. As many as 20 children can be participating at one time in this game.

Basic rules

1. Hop in each space going up and back.
2. Hop in every other space going up and back.
3. Continue, adding one more space each time a successful trip is made in going up and back.
4. When able to skip four spaces between each hop, change to a jump between the spaces.
5. Continue until a winner has been determined. The winner is the player who can skip the most spaces without missing.

Rules on misses

1. Stepping on a line.
2. Losing balance and touching the ground with any part of body except the hopping foot.
3. Penalty for a miss: Player returns to beginning of diagram and starts again at the point at which he missed.

Teaching hint

Have children go up the right side of the ladder and back down the left side. This will permit many children to participate at the same time.

APPARATUS

Apparatus can be either an expensive nuisance or a significant tool in motor learning. When used as an integral part of total physical development, its value and uses are unlimited. Too often one can see a myriad of primary children going over, under, and through apparatus during free play periods; and that same type of equipment standing idle when intermediate or upper grade children are on the playground. This equipment should and can be used with the same excitement by older children *if* they are given appropriate challenges. It is hoped that the activities and ideas to follow will provide further challenges to children of all ages.

When a new stunt is introduced, a rotation system is very effective. The class is divided into several small groups, and while the teacher is instructing one group, the others can be occupied with other equipment. The whistle signal indicates rotation, and a new group works with the teacher. If a child has difficulty overcoming the fear of a new stunt, encourage him to try, and then allow him to repeat a familiar stunt on the same piece of equipment. Many times adults set standards that a child is not ready to handle. This may result in an accident. Under no circumstances should a teacher "lift" a child completely through a stunt. He may assist him, but not do it for him.

The progression listed for each piece of equipment starts with the very basic activ-

APPARATUS

SUGGESTED GRADE PLACEMENT CHART

JUNGLE GYM, 69–71

	K	1	2	3	4	5	6	7	8
1. Through the Cave	x	x	•						
2. Circular Travel	x	x	x	•					
3. Over the Top	–	x	x	x	•				
4. Single Knee Lift		–	x	x	x	•			
5. Double Knee Lift			–	x	x	x	•		
6. Knee Hang and Drop				–	x	x	x	•	
7. Single Leg Lift					–	x	x	x	•
8. Double Leg Lift						–	x	x	x

HORIZONTAL LADDER, 71–72

	K	1	2	3	4	5	6	7	8
1. Hang and Return	x	x	x	•	•	•	•	•	•
2. Hang and Drop	x	x	x	•	•	•	•	•	•
3. Side Travel	x	x	x	x	•	•	•	•	•
4. Forward Travel (Grip Side Bars)	x	x	x	x	•	•	•	•	•
5. Two Hands on Each Rung	–	x	x	x	x	•	•	•	•
6. One Hand on Each Rung	–	x	x	x	x	•	•	•	•
7. Skip One Rung				–	x	x	x	•	•
8. Skip Two Rungs				–	x	x	x	x	x
9. Backward Travel (Grip Side Bars)				–	x	x	x	x	x
10. Backward Travel (Rung to Rung)				–	–	x	x	x	x
11. Circle Travel (Rung to Rung)					–	x	x	x	x
12. Circle Travel (Down Side)					–	x	x	x	x

RINGS, 72–73

	K	1	2	3	4	5	6	7	8
1. Hang and Swing	x	x	x	•	•	•	•	•	•
2. Sustained Pull-up		x	x	x	x	•	•	•	•
3. Ring Travel		–	x	x	x	x	•	•	•
4. Sustained Pull-up and Swing			–	x	x	x	x	x	•
5. Circle Travel				–	x	x	x	x	x
Note: For rings installed in line									
6. Ring Hang and Swing				–	x	x	x	x	x
7. Ring Sit				–	x	x	x	x	x
8. Skin the Cat					–	x	x	x	x
9. Inverted Arch						–	x	x	x

ities and moves to the more advanced stunts. Instruction in safety is an integral part of the instruction in each activity. Find where the children are in the progression and then move on from there. Also include repetition of previously learned activities.

The best insurance against accidents lies in good instruction in activities and safety, *constant* supervision, and a safe surface covering under each piece of apparatus. (See Appendix.)

In the list of recommended apparatus, teeter-totters and moving apparatus such as merry-go-rounds, are not included; they

SUGGESTED GRADE PLACEMENT CHART (Continued)

	K	1	2	3	4	5	6	7	8
HORIZONTAL BAR—CHEST HEIGHT, 73									
1. Swing Under	x	x	x	•	•	•			
2. Sloth Hang	x	x	x	•	•	•			
3. Hip Mount	–	x	x	x	•		•	•	•
4. Front Hip Circle		–	x	x	x	•		•	•
5. Knee Hang	–	x	x	•	•	•			
6. Knee Swing		–	x	x	x	•		•	•
7. Skin the Cat			–	x	x	x	•	•	•
8. Bird Nest			–	x	x	x	•	•	•
9. Single Knee Mount				–	x	x	x	•	•
10. Single Knee Circle Backward					–	x	x	x	•
11. Single Knee Circle Forward					–	x	x	x	•
12. Double Leg Circle						–	x	x	x
HORIZONTAL BAR—JUMP AND REACH HEIGHT, 73–74									
1. Swing and Drop				–	x	x	x	•	•
2. Chin-ups				–	x	x	x	x	x
3. Knee Raise				–	x	x	x	•	•
4. Swinging Turn						–	x	x	x
PARALLEL BARS—JUMP AND REACH HEIGHT, 74									
1. Hang, Side Travel	x	x	x	•		•		•	•
2. Hang, Travel with Hands on Both Sides	x	x	x	x		•		•	•
PARALLEL BARS—BELOW SHOULDER HEIGHT, 74–75									
3. Arm Extension—Hold					–	x	x	•	•
4. Hand Walk Forward					–	x	x	x	x
5. Hand Walk Backward						–	x	x	x
6. Extend Arms and Swing						–	x	x	x
7. Straddle Travel						–	x	x	x
8. Hammock Hang						–	x	x	x
CLIMBING ROPES AND POLES, 75									
1. Chinning				–	x	x	x	x	x
2. Standing to Lying				–	x	x	x	x	x
3. Lying to Standing					–	x	x	x	x
4. Climbing					–	x	x	x	x
5. Climbing with Leg Lock					–	x	x	x	x

– = May introduce activity   x = Depth in instruction   • = May continue activity

have little to offer toward gross muscular development.

JUNGLE GYM (FIGS. 2.57, 2.58, AND 2.59)

This piece of equipment is called by such names as jungle gym, climbing tree, or climbing dome, and is seen in many shapes. The jungle gym satisfies in part the urge to climb, and helps to develop strength, balance, coordination, and flexibility.

1. Through the Cave. Crawl under the bars from one side to the other. Continue

FIG. 2.57. Is it the Matterhorn, a rocket ship, a lookout tower?

FIG. 2.58. Sand placed under the jungle gym.

in the cave "higher up the mountain" (second level, third level, etc.).

2. Circular Travel. Travel around the outside edge of the equipment. Start at the lowest level and then move higher.

3. Over the Top. Start on one side. Travel up, over, and down the other side.

4. Single Knee Lift. Face out and grasp a horizontal bar. Hang high enough so that the feet do not touch the ground. Lift one knee to the chest and then *slowly* lower it. Alternate knee lifts as many times as possible.

5. Double Knee Lift. Same as No. 4 but

FIG. 2.59. Permanent rubber matting installed under Geodesic Dome.

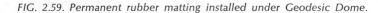

lift both knees to the chest and then slowly lower them. Do as many times as possible.

6. Knee Hang and Drop. *Caution:* Test the bar height in relation to the height of the child first. There must be at least three horizontal bars, one above the other. The child must be able to hang from the third bar with his knees touching or below the lowest bar.

Sit on the second bar facing in; grasp the third bar with both hands, shoulder width apart, palms away from the body with fingers on top and thumbs underneath. Slowly bring the knees up one at a time, and hook them over the third bar between the hands. Lower the body to an inverted knee hang. Grasp the bottom bar with both hands, then release the knees and drop to the ground, landing with bent hips, knees, and ankles, arms straight with elbows "locked."

7. Single Leg Lift. Grasp a horizontal bar, facing out, high enough so that the feet do not touch the ground. Lift one leg to a right-angle position in relation to the body. Lower the leg slowly. Lift the other leg in the same manner. Repeat. (Preliminary practice: Raise bent knee, extend leg, lower the leg slowly.)

8. Double Leg Lift. Same as single leg lift except both legs are raised and lowered at the same time. (Preliminary practice: Same as in No. 7, using both legs.)

Safety

Always insist on an overlapping grip— fingers on one side of the bar, thumbs on the other.

Never allow a child to hang by one arm or leg, nor allow him to *stand* without grasping bar with at least one hand.

Do not pull, tease, or touch another child.

HORIZONTAL LADDER (FIG. 2.60)

1. Hang and Return. Hang from first rung, palms away from face and thumbs under the rung, return to mounting step.

2. Hang and Drop. Hang from second rung as in No. 1, then drop to the ground. Land on balls of feet, and bend knees, ankles, and hips, keeping weight forward.

FIG. 2.60. Horizontal ladder. Can you swing in unison?

3. Side Travel. Both hands on one side of rail. Inch along, hands never crossing over each other. Repeat activity, moving along other side.

4. Forward Travel (Grip Side Bars). With one hand on each side, travel with side-to-side swing.

5. Two Hands on Each Rung. With two hands on first rung, swing forward, back, then forward, and move one hand at a time to the next rung. Travel as far as possible.

6. One Hand on Each Rung (Fig. 2.60) With one hand on each of the first two rungs, travel across the ladder alternating hands.

7. Skip One Rung. Skip every other rung.

8. Skip Two Rungs. If the child can reach far enough, skip two rungs. One hand *must* be kept on *one* rung at all times.

9. Backward Travel (Grip Side Bars). Grip the rail on each side of the ladder and travel backward.

10. Backward Travel (Rung to Rung).

11. Circle Travel (Rung to Rung). Alternate turns, first forward, then backward, the length of the ladder.

12. Circle Travel—(Down Side). Travel down side, making a half-turn forward each time.

Safety

All travel in the same direction.

Second child starts when the first has reached the middle of the ladder. (Paint the half way mark of the ladder yellow to control spacing of children.)

No climbing on top of the ladder.

Do not pull, tease, or touch another child hanging from the ladder.

Keep away from under the ladder.

RINGS

1. Hang and Swing. Jump up, grasp ring with both hands, hang and swing. Drop at the top of the backswing, landing on toes and bending ankles, knees, and hips, with weight forward.

2. Sustained Pull-up. Grasp ring with palms facing participant. Raise up until the chin is level with the ring. Hold as long as possible. With one child on each ring, teacher may count seconds to determine which student can stay up the longest.

3. Ring Travel. Grasp ring with both hands. Swing body to gain momentum, then transfer one hand to next ring. Continue around. The arms are used to pump by bending first one arm and then the other.

4. Sustained Pull-up and Swing. Grasp ring with palms facing participant. Pull ring back as far as possible, jump *straight* up in the air, and pull ring to body, chin resting on hands. Hold for one complete swing. Increase number of swings as strength increases. (This is an excellent trunk, shoulder, and arm exercise.)

Gradual conditioning is necessary to avoid excessive muscle soreness.

On circular rings, stand with back to center pole, jump *straight* up, and rest the chin on the hands. This will reduce the possibility of collision with the center pole.

5. Circle Travel. Turn circles occasionally while progressing around the rings.

Note: The following activities are exclusively for rings installed in a straight line.

6. Ring Hang and Swing. Grasp two rings, bring legs up between arms, slide legs into rings, hang upside down in rings, and swing by the knees.

7. Ring Sit. Grasp two rings, one in each hand, bring legs up between arms, slide feet into rings, and climb up to sitting position. Reverse to descend.

8. Skin the Cat. (Fig. 2.61) Grasp two rings, bring legs up between the arms, extend legs downward, then return to a straight hang.

9. Inverted Arch. Grasp two rings, bring legs up between arms, extend the legs upward along the chain, and arch the back.

FIG. 2.61. Horizontal bar: Skin the Cat; Hip Circle; Sustained Chin-up.

Safety

If used for travel, children should be at least four rings apart. It may be suitable to have the rule that second child does not start until first child is halfway around or halfway across the rings. (Paint middle ring yellow.)

Stop the rings from swinging after dismount.

Waiting line should be well away from rings.

Travel only in one direction.

No standing in the rings.

Children should never grasp the top of the ring to hang—always the bottom edge.

Install one low ring from which children of different heights may start without the use of hazardous boards, rocks, or benches.

HORIZONTAL BAR—CHEST HEIGHT

1. Swing Under. Reach forward, grasp bar with palms away from the body, swing under the bar, and land on the far side.

2. Sloth Hang. Grasp the bar with one palm facing and one palm away from the face, kick up and hook the feet over the bar, one on each side of the bar. Hang in upside-down position.

3. Hip Mount. With palms facing away from the body, grasp bar with both hands shoulder distance apart. Jump up to a full extension, with the hips touching the bar and elbows locked. Dismount by pushing the body away from the bar. Do not remove hands until the stunt has been completed.

4. Front Hip Circle. (Fig. 2.61) Use the hip mount to get on the bar. Change the grip so that the thumbs are on top and fingers are underneath the bar. Turn a forward circle on the bar and land.

5. Knee Hang. Grip the bar, hang, then bring the knees up to hook over the bar (both on same side). Release the hand grip and hang by the knees. Recover by reversing the process.

6. Knee Swing. Same as No. 5 except when in knee hang position, swing backward and forward a few times.

7. Skin the Cat. (Fig. 2.61) Grasp bar with palms away from the body. Hang and bring the legs up between the arms; extend the legs down until they almost touch the ground. Reverse the action and then stand.

8. Bird Nest. Grasp bar with palms away from the body, hang. Bring legs up through the arms until the toes touch the bar. Bring the body through the arms and lower the trunk to an arched position, the toes still gripping the bar. Reverse procedure to dismount.

9. Single Knee Mount. Hang from the bar with palms away from the body. Hook one knee over the bar between the arms. Swing the free leg downward. Pull with the arms and swing the body to a support position on top of the bar. Reverse to dismount.

10. Single Knee Circle Backward. Use a single knee mount to obtain the position on top of the bar. Slide the knee back until it is touching the bar, and hook the foot under the free leg. Thrust the head and shoulders backward to execute the circle as many times as possible. To stop on top, pull strongly with the arms and bring head and shoulders forward.

11. Single Knee Circle Forward. Same as the single knee circle backward except that the hands should be reversed so that the thumbs are on top of the bar. The free leg moves under the bar first and the head is thrust forward.

12. Double Leg Circle. Start in a sitting position on the bar, hands close to hips and palms away from the body. Raise the body slightly and thrust the knees against the bar as the head and shoulders lead on a backward circle downward. Stop at the top of the bar by pulling strongly with the arms and moving the knees slightly away from the bar.

HORIZONTAL BAR—JUMP AND REACH HEIGHT (SLIGHTLY HIGHER THAN A CHILD CAN REACH)

Child's feet should be off the ground, but without a long drop to the ground. (Fig. 2.61)

1. Swing and Drop. Jump up and grasp the bar with palms away from the body. Swing and drop, releasing the grip at the *top* of the backswing. Land on balls of feet

and bend ankles, knees, and hips, keeping weight slightly forward.

2. Chin-ups. (Fig. 2.61) Grasp the bar with palms facing the body. Pull the body up so that the chin is level with the bar. Slowly drop down to full extension and then pull up again.

3. Knee Raise. Grasp the bar with palms away from the body, hang, raise one knee to the chest, lower, then raise the other knee to the chest. Continue. (For strengthening abdominal muscles.)

4. Swinging Turn. Jump up to a hang on the right side of the bar, palms away from the body. Swing backward and forward. At the top of the forward swing, release the right hand and bring the right arm in front of the body, executing a half-turn pivoting on the left hand. Grasp the bar again with the right hand. The left palm is now facing the body. On a forward swing again, release the left hand, bring it across the body, and regrasp the bar.

5. Most of the stunts on the chest-height bar may be performed on the bar at jump-and-reach height when skill and confidence are gained.

Safety—for both horizontal bars

Only one child on the bar at a time. Others wait for turns a safe distance from the bar behind a waiting line.

Make sure that the bar is securely bolted or cemented in the floor or ground.

Use plenty of mats or proper surface covering material under *and around* the equipment.

Keep the bar clean of rust by using emory paper or steel wool to rub the bar.

Always have the child grasp the bar with the thumb opposite the fingers (locked grip).

It is advisable to have the children work on the bar for short periods of time as friction can cause blisters.

The child should use a bar at appropriate height for safety: a high bar he can jump for and reach, or a low bar approximately chest high.

Children should not attempt to lift one another up on the bar.

Hands should not be removed from the bar until the stunt is completed.

Never allow a child to stand on the bar.

If a child sits on top of the bar, he should sit in a straddle position (unless in preparation for a stunt).

PARALLEL BARS—JUMP AND REACH HEIGHT

1. Hang, Side Travel. Both hands on one side, inch along as one hand and then the other slides sideward.

2. Hang, Travel with Hands on Both Sides. With one hand on either side, travel with lateral swing. Travel forward, travel backward.

PARALLEL BARS—BELOW SHOULDER HEIGHT

3. Arm Extension—Hold. With one hand on either side, jump to full extension above the bars (elbows locked), hold for 10 seconds.

4. Hand Walk Forward. Begin like No. 3. Hand-walk forward, taking small "steps" with the hands.

5. Hand Walk Backward. Begin like No. 3. Hand-Walk backward.

6. Extend Arms and Swing. With one hand on either bar, jump to full extension of arms and then swing. (Supervise carefully.)

7. Straddle Travel. With one hand on either bar, jump to full extension of arms. Swing legs back and forth. Swing legs forward and hook each knee over a bar. Bring hands forward in front of the knees. Put weight on hands and raise hips, snapping legs together behind the body, swinging forward and once again hooking knees over each bar. Continue to end of bars. Do the reverse and travel backward.

8. Hammock Hang. Grasp bars with hands and hang with back to opposite end of bar. Turn over backward, bringing feet over the head. Place the toes on the bars; slide feet toward far end and arch the back. Reverse to standing.

Safety

Always be in a position to break safely the fall of a child if he should slip. Reach *under* the bars to spot a performer.

Do not allow a child to do Hand Walk

FIG. 2.62. The challenge of climbing a rope.

Forward or Backward before Arm Extension Hold is mastered.

One child on the equipment at a time.

For last group of activities, make sure that bars are *below* shoulder height in case a child should drop down between the bars.

CLIMBING ROPES AND POLES (Fig. 2.62)

Rope and pole climbing can be an exciting challenge to children. At the same time it is especially good for building up the chest, shoulder, and arm muscles. Provide proper safe surfacing under this equipment. Use 3-inch manila rope and anchor it securely to an overhead support. Knotting the rope at the bottom keeps it from fraying. (One continuous rope with extra play at the bottom may be used.) Check attachment at top of rope frequently.

1. Chinning. With legs in a vertical or horizontal position, grasp the rope or pole up high. Pull the body up with the arms alone until the chin touches the top of the hands, lower slowly and repeat.

2. Standing to Lying. Stand about 2 feet from the rope or pole. Grasp it and lower the body to the ground, using a hand-under-hand alternating grip. Do not move the feet.

3. Lying to Standing. Reverse the instructions in No. 2. Start on the ground and work up to a standing position using the arms only.

4. Climbing. Grasp rope or pole and climb upward three or four strokes (one hand over the other). Return to stand. Stress: Keep elbows slightly flexed throughout the climb for more efficient movement.

5. Climbing with Leg Lock. Climb by first reaching up high. Pull the body up until in a bent arm position with rope between the legs. Bring the rope around behind one leg and then over the instep. Step on top of the foot and rope with the other foot. (Fig. 2.62) Again pull with the arms and repeat the action. (For efficient movement, reach up with elbow slightly flexed; do not fully extend arm.) Go as high as possible. Return to ground alternating hand under hand; do not slide.

Safety

Be sure the children learn to climb down a rope. Sliding down will burn the hands and legs.

Limit the amount of time on this piece of equipment. It is a very tiring activity.

One person on a rope or pole at a time.

Keep away from the base of the rope when another child is performing.

Ropes should be used for climbing, not swinging.

RELAYS

CIRCLE GAMES

LINE GAMES

OTHER FORMATIONS

FIG. 3.1. Dodging, broken field running.

When the announcement is made that the time has arrived for "games," there is a general surge of excitement in the classroom. The type of game is not too important to children, so long as running and chasing are involved.

These games have particular appeal for children because of their individualistic nature. The challenge of pitting oneself against an adversary contains all the excitement and daring of the most dangerous occupation. The anticipation of being selected taxes a 7-year-old's patience to the very limit, for he is sure *he* will be successful in meeting the challenge. An older child may be able to contain himself in more sophisticated fashion, but he is just as eager to be on his way.

The concepts of team play and loyalty are also introduced here. The relays, particularly, provide the transition from *I* to *We* games, in which individual endeavor contributes to team success. This cooperation is vital to the enjoyment of games encountered at higher grade levels.

In each of the divisions of the chapter, only those games are included that insure activity for (or at least involve) the greatest number of players possible. There is little logic or value in having a child wait an entire period for *one* turn when games are available in which everyone has many opportunities to participate.

Relays are presented to add a dimension of competition in the reinforcement (utilization) of skills introduced in Chapters 1 and 2. They involve repetition and elaboration of the basic locomotor patterns; relating to a partner or objects; or going over, under, or around small equipment.

Relays have been developed to increase skill in balance and coordination, and the ability to dodge, such as Dodging Relay, Countdown, and the use of the slalom formation. These relays may be included in a unit on dodging along with games such as Pom Pom Pullaway, Touchdown, and Capture the Flag. The skill of turning and running used in the relays of Farmer and Crow and Rescue Relay may be repeated in the games such as Fire Engine and Steal the Bacon.

Circle games are appropriate for initial experiences in the lower grades; the children seem to appreciate the structural security of this kind of formation. Once they become accustomed to the functions of runner and chaser, they seem eager to expand the limits of their play area to include the whole playground.

Line games provide this larger area in which children exhibit a wonderful freedom and great excitement at the "thrill of the chase." Activities to increase awareness of peripheral vision and surrounding space such as suggested in Chapter 1, are an important adjunct to success in Line Games. When running, one not only has to be aware of the direction in which he is going (eye focus), he also needs to be aware of runners and taggers approaching from the sides (in his peripheral vision). He needs to "run to daylight," run where no one is.

In selecting a game for the day, the teacher will be concerned with several factors: whether each child has sufficient turns, that good sportsmanship is in evidence, that the game fits into the overall objectives of the activity program, and that the class members will have benefited from their time on the playground.

If a game has been selected in which only a few children are active at one time, it is better to have several games going concurrently. If the game requires that all children be active constantly, a second, more slowly-paced, game should be chosen. (For "Suggestions for Presenting New Activities," see Chapter 14.)

Very little, if any, equipment is needed to play the relays and games included here. It was stated previously that children need to be able to control themselves before attempting to control objects. This chapter provides yet another step toward that end.

PURPOSES

Games present a different structure in which children can utilize individual movement skills in an exciting setting. Here they are provided opportunities:

ELEMENTARY GAMES
SUGGESTED GRADE PLACEMENT CHART

	K	1	2	3	4	5	6	7–8
SKILLS, 79	x	x	x	x	x	x	x	•
RELAYS, 80–87								
File Relay		—	x	x	x	x	x	
Slalom Relay		—	x	x	x	x	x	x
Locomotor Relays		—	x	x	x	x	x	
Stunt Relays		—	x	x	x	x	x	x
Farmer and Crow Relay			x	x	x	x	•	
Number Relay			x	x	x	•		
Posture Relay			x	x	x	x	•	
Human Obstacle Relay			x	x	x	•		
Rescue Relay			x	x	x	•		
Three Way Relay				x	x	x	•	
Jump Rope Relay				x	x	x	x	•
Jack Rabbit Relay					x	x	x	x
Dodging Relay					x	x	x	x
Countdown				x	x	x	x	•
Sack Relay					x	x	x	x
Three-Legged Race					x	x	x	x
CIRCLE GAMES, 87–93								
Circle Freeze	x	x	x					
Number Change	x	x	x					
Cut the Pie	x	x	x	x				
Easter Bunny	—	x	x					
Find a Number		x	x					
Magic Carpet, Chapter 5		x	x	x	•			
Bear in the Trap		x	x	x				
Snap the Trap		x	x	x				
Squirrel in Trees			x	x				
Forest Lookout			x	x	•			
Back to Back			x	x	x	•		
Two Deep and Change			x	x	x	x	x	x
Circle Tag			x	x	x	x	x	x
LINE GAMES, 93–100								
Scat	x	x	x					
Fire Engine	x	x	x					
Cowboys and Indians		x	x	x				
Red, White, and Blue		x	x	x	x			
Pom Pom Pullaway		x	x	x	x	•	•	
Midnight			x	x	x			
Red Rover			x	x	x	x	•	
Steal the Bacon			x	x	x	x	x	x
Touchdown				x	x	x	x	x
Blue and White				—	x	x	x	x
Crows and Cranes				—	x	x	x	x
Exchange Tag				x	x			
Here We Come!				x	x	x		
Hand Slap					x	x	x	x
OTHER FORMATIONS, 100–104								
Freeze, Chapter 1	x	x	x					
Queen Bee		x	x					
Tag Games			x	x	x	x	x	•
Third Man Tag				x	x	x	x	x
Last Couple Out					x	x	x	x
Gold Rush					x	x	x	x
Capture the Flag					—	x	x	x

— = May introduce activity   x = Depth in instruction   • = May continue activity

—to participate in structured situations in which the various movement skills are employed;

—to increase awareness of surrounding space in game situations;

—to increase ability to use appropriate movement patterns automatically in ever changing situations;

—to understand the organization and rules of the various elementary games;

—to learn to work together and to develop strategy;

—to learn to control movement for safe participation and for the safety of others;

—to participate as an individual with the aim of contributing to group success.

SKILLS

READY-TO-RUN POSITION

One foot forward, knees bent with weight slightly forward.

Learning experiences: Relays, Line Games.

RUNNING

For mechanics and learning experiences, see Chapter 1, "Efficient Movement," "Locomotor Patterns."

TAGGING

"Touch-Tag." Tag, do not push.

Learning experiences: Most of the Line Games, some Circle Games.

TURNING AND RUNNING

For mechanics and learning experiences, see Chapter 1, "Efficient Movement," "Locomotor Patterns," "Run with Quick Change of Direction."

Learning experiences: Farmer and Crow Relay (Agility Race), Two Deep and Change, Fire Engine, Steal the Bacon, Crows and Cranes.

DODGING

(See Figs. 3.1, 8.1, and 8.15; for ready position see Fig. 6.13.)

Feet apart, knees bent, weight forward; take small sliding steps to one side, then to other side. Be ready to change directions quickly and accelerate rapidly.

Learning experiences: Work on peripheral vision, Slide Step—Balance and Coordination (see Figs. 8.1 and 8.15), Dodging Relay, Countdown, Pom Pom Pullaway, Touchdown.

STARTING ON SIGNAL

Ready-to-run position with one foot forward, knees bent, weight slightly forward. Push off quickly.

Learning experiences: Relays, Scat, Cowboys and Indians, Steal the Bacon, Hand Slap.

STOPPING ON SIGNAL

Bend knees in forward stride position to absorb forward momentum. Shift weight back.

Learning experiences: Run—then stop on signal, Circle Freeze, Freeze.

OVERRUNNING (FINISH LINE, FIRST BASE, GOAL LINE)

Do not slow down until the line or base has been crossed. Children tend to respond literally to the instructions, "Run *to* the goal line"; instruction should emphasize running *across* the line or base.

Learning experiences: Practice overrunning the line of a race or relay; first base on a softball diamond; the goal line in Line Games.

SAFETY

PROVIDE A LARGE ENOUGH AREA FOR NUMBER OF CHILDREN IN RELATION TO THE GAME

When children are running in a straight line, see that they are more than double elbow distance apart. (With elbows extended out to side, no elbows touch.)

When all the children are going to run at the same time and dodge an opponent, use more than double *arm's* distance apart.

When turning and running, teach "turn and run position," and stress running *straight* to the goal line.

PROVIDE A SAFE SURFACE

No benches, holes, faucets, posts, extra balls, or other hazards in the area.

No running on wet turf or on blacktop with pools of water.

PROVIDE A MARGIN OF SAFETY AROUND THE BOUNDARY LINES

Have at least a 20-foot margin of safety for overrunning goal lines.

Caution children not to run into any fence, steps, or other obstruction that might be beyond the 20-foot margin.

No tetherball posts, basketball standards, benches, or extra balls near the side lines of the area in case a child runs out of bounds.

PROVIDE SUFFICIENT SPACE BETWEEN RELAY LINES

Allow 8 to 10 feet between relay lines when using locomotor skills. (All players should return to the end of the line, not stop and stand around the finish line.)

Allow 10 to 15 feet between relay lines when throwing and catching, depending upon the accuracy of throws and the hardness of the ball.

AVOID INTERFERING WITH OTHER ACTIVITIES ON PLAY AREA

Establish games so that kicked or batted balls, overthrows, or children overrunning boundaries do not interfere with other games or with apparatus.

TEACH SAFETY WITH EACH ACTIVITY

During the walk-through, present safety precautions needed to start a new game. Add other safety rules during the game.

Stress not falling down (purposely) and becoming a hazard. (For repeated violation, a child may be asked to observe.)

Stress *overrunning* goal line, not slowing down in running area and getting hit or knocked down by tagger. (Tagger is running at top speed.)

RELAYS

The activities in Chapters 1 and 2 allow children to move at their own tempo and in their own way; now a premium is placed on speed. For this reason it is important to allow time for the children to become acquainted with the new challenges before encouraging all out speed.

1. Practice the skill in relay formation. This allows time for demonstration by one group, experimentation by all groups, coaching, and becoming acquainted with the task at hand.

2. Work for accuracy in the activity.

3. Work for speed to determine how fast each group can perform. The major emphasis should be on numbers 1 and 2. Lack of knowledge and skill under the stress of competition results in aggravated peer relationships.

Practice the relay for a given period of time rather than "once through." This can be easily accomplished by having the children practice until a signal is given by the teacher. At this time the child at the front of the line becomes the leader. When working on speed, have each group go through the relay *two* times and then sit down in the original order to determine the winner. Going through the relay twice provides more turns to perform; sitting down helps to determine the winning team and aids in class control.

The starting signal during competition should be a clear three part command: "Ready" (pause) "Set" (pause) "Go!" (or short, sharp whistle sound).

For maximum participation, the class should be divided into teams that have no more than six or seven players. For safety, allow 8 to 10 feet between relay lines when performing locomotor patterns; 10 to 15 feet when throwing and catching a ball.

Relays provide high motivation not only for the reinforcement of basic movement skills, but sport skills as well. They are an ever-popular activity for children in all grades, and the variety is endless.

FILE RELAY (FIG. 3.2)

Players of each team stand in file formation behind starting line. First player of each line runs to opposite line, returns, touches hand of next player, and goes to the end of his line. Continue action.

Team that finishes first with players in original position wins.

Teaching hints

1. To provide for more participation in a short period of time, have each team go through the relay two times. The team that finishes first, after each player has had two turns, wins.

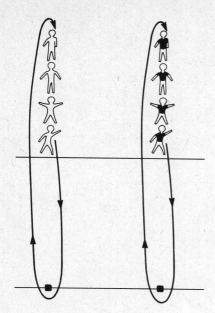

FIG. 3.2. File Relay.

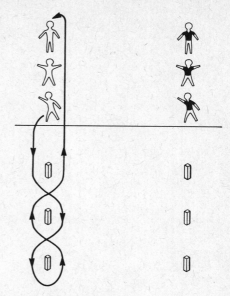

FIG. 3.3. Slalom Relay.

2. To be sure that each child goes the entire distance each time: (a) Have each child touch the opposite line with hand before returning. (b) Place an object for players of each team to run around before returning. (Use milk cartons, quart plastic detergent containers, chalk erasers, or beanbags.) (c) Have each runner carry a beanbag or chalk eraser, touch the opposite line with the beanbag or eraser, then return and hand the object to the next player.

3. Stress that players wait *behind* the starting line until hand is touched (or until beanbag or chalk eraser is received).

SLALOM RELAY (FIG. 3.3)

Players of each team stand in file formation behind the starting line. Place three objects equidistant apart and directly in front of each file of players.

On signal the first player travels to the right of the first object, left of the second, around the third, then weaves back to the starting line and tags off the next player. Continue the action. Team finishing first wins.

Teaching hints

Stress that every one must go to the right of the first object, then proceed in a zigzag pattern.

Variations

1. Offset the three objects and increase the zigzag pattern.

2. Use players for objects. End player should stand on a marked line to assure that each team travels the same distance.

LOCOMOTOR RELAYS

Skills

Run, hop, jump, leap, gallop, skip.

Formations

File Relay, Slalom Relay. (See Figs. 3.2 and 3.3.)

Relay

First player goes up and touches a line or goes around one or more objects, then returns to place and tags off the next player. Continue action. Go through relay two times. Team finishing first wins.

Variation

Using file relay formation, run backward to opposite line, then run forward on return trip. Hop or jump backward, then forward. Stress keeping weight forward when moving backward.

STUNT RELAYS

Stunts

Examples: Rooster Hop, Dog Run, Frog Jump, Heel-Toe Walk, Kangaroo Jump (carrying a ball between knees). (See "Stunts," Chapter 2.)

Formation

File Relay.

Relay

Perform the stunt while going to touch opposite line, *run* back to place and tag off next player. Continue as in Locomotor Relays.

Variation

Run to opposite line, perform the stunt, run back to place, and tag off next player. Stunts: Turk Stand, Mule Kick.

FARMER AND CROW RELAY
(AGILITY RACE; FIG. 3.4)

Equipment

Two beanbags or blocks for each line.

Formation

Players in file relay formation with two beanbags in front of starting line, and a circle (or line) 30 feet away.

Relay

First player in line (Farmer) picks up one object, takes it down, and *places* it in the circle; comes back for the second object, takes it down, and places it in circle; runs back and tags next player.

When tagged, the second player (Crow) retrieves the objects one at a time. This continues, Farmer "planting" and Crow "digging up," until all have had a turn. First group to finish wins.

Stress *placing* the beanbag in circle, not tossing or throwing it.

NUMBER RELAY (FIG. 3.5)

Equipment

One chalk eraser, milk carton, or other substitute for each team.

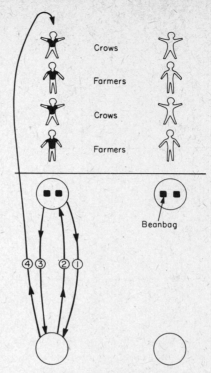

FIG. 3.4. Farmer and Crow Relay.

Formation

The children stand in line formation by teams behind the same line and face their chalk eraser 40 to 60 feet away. Number the children in each group.

Relay

The teacher or a leader calls a number. The player with that number runs around the chalk eraser, or substitute, and back across the starting line. The player crossing the line first wins a point for his team.

Keep score for each team. At the end of the playing period, the team with the greatest number of points wins.

Teaching hint

Place the chalk eraser or substitute directly opposite the center of each group.

POSTURE RELAY

Equipment

Two chalk erasers or blocks of wood for each team.

Teacher

Formation

Each team stands behind a line in file formation facing another line 40 to 60 feet away.

Relay

The first child in each team places the eraser on his head and attempts to walk to the opposite line and back without touching or dropping the eraser. If he drops it or touches it, he must return to the line he just left, put it back on his head, and continue. Second child stands ready to move with object on head. Each child takes a turn. First team to finish wins.

Teaching hints

1. Keep the teams small so that each child does not have too long to wait for a turn.

2. For primary grades, have child continue after replacing a block on his head rather than return to the line.

3. Having two objects for each team speeds up the relay.

HUMAN OBSTACLE RELAY (FIG. 3.6)

Formation

Runners in each relay stand in file relay formation. Place three players equidistant apart in front of each relay line. First player crouches down into a ball with back to line of runners; second player (boy) stands in stride position; third player stands *on* a *line.*

Relay

Leapfrog over the first player, crawl through the legs of the second player, and make one complete turn around the last

FIG. 3.6. Human Obstacle Relay: over, under, and around.

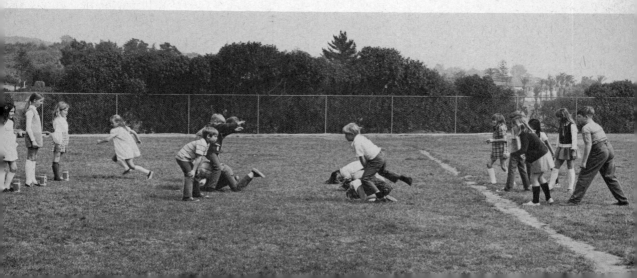

player. Run back and touch off next runner. First group to finish wins.

Repeat relay, then rotate players with first three players in line becoming "obstacles" and former "obstacles" going to the end of own line.

Teaching hint

For the leapfrog, have the runner place hands on *shoulders* of crouched player, then stride-jump over.

Stress practice and avoid contact with second and third players at all times.

Variation

Use other obstacles, such as milk cartons or substitute, to jump over or run around; tires to step into in a zigzag pattern; low hurdles to jump over; long ropes held low to jump over or roll under.

RESCUE RELAY (FIG. 3.7)

Formation

Each team stands in file formation, with a leader 40 to 60 feet away from his team.

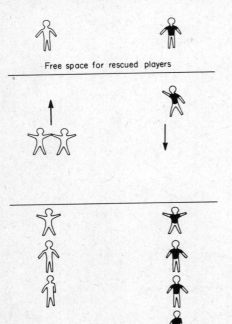

Free space for rescued players

FIG. 3.7. Rescue Relay—in progress.

Relay

On signal the leader runs to the first child in his team, grasps his hand, and runs with him back to the leader's line. The leader stays there and the child he "rescued" goes back to get the next child. This continues until all children are with the leader on the opposite line. The first team to rescue all its players wins.

Teaching hints

1. Do not allow the child waiting to be rescued to travel over his line until the rescuer grasps his hand.

2. Neither player may release his hand from the other's until both players have crossed the leader's line.

3. For safety, allow free space at finish line for rescued players.

THREE-WAY RELAY

Formation

Teams stand in file formation behind one line facing a line 40 to 60 feet away.

Relay

The teacher announces three methods of travel to the opposite line and back (e.g., run, jump, skip). The children decide in what order they will use the three ways. Repeat, using each method in turn, until all players have had a turn. The team finishing first wins.

Teaching hints

1. After playing the relay several times, have the teams select (in secret) the methods of travel they will use. The addition of an element of surprise will add to the spirit of the relay. It may be necessary to eliminate running as one of the choices in this case.

2. A waiting player may not cross the starting line until tagged.

3. Encourage the children to select unusual ways to travel.

JUMP ROPE RELAY

Equipment

One individual jump rope for each team.

Formation

File formation behind one line facing another line 40 to 60 feet away.

Relay

On signal the first person in each line jumps rope to the opposite line and runs back carrying the rope in one hand. He *hands* the rope to the next child, then goes to the end of the line. First team to finish wins.

Teaching hint

As the children become more proficient at jumping, have them jump both up and back.

JACK RABBIT RELAY (FIG. 3.8)

Equipment

One individual jump rope for each team.

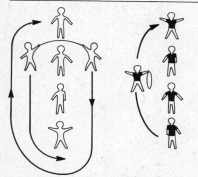

FIG. 3.8. *Jack Rabbit Relay—in progress.*

Formation

File formation. There should be at least 10 feet between relay teams, and each team member stands an arm's distance behind the player in front of him. The first person on each team holds the two ends of the jump rope in his hands.

Relay

On signal the first player in each line turns, hands one end of the rope to the player behind him; the two of them face the end of the file, one on each side, and race to the end. As the jump rope goes down the file, each player jumps the rope. When the two players reach the end of the line, the leader stays there; the second person in line goes back to the front, hands one end of the rope to the person now at the front of the file, and those two

race down the line. This continues until the leader is back at the front of the line *after* having gone down the line with the *last player*. The first group to have *all* players back in original positions wins.

Safety

Have the players practice this relay before they compete against each other. Stress that all players must be alert at all times. Insist that players keep an arm's distance apart throughout relay.

DODGING RELAY (FIG. 3.9)

Equipment

Three markers (milk cartons or substitutes) for each relay team.

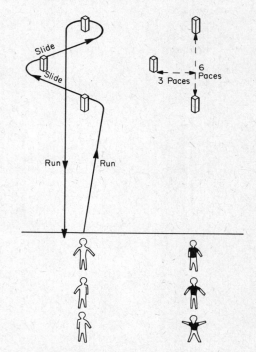

FIG. 3.9. *Dodging Relay.*

Formation

File relay formation. Place one marker directly in front of each team about 30 feet away. Place the second marker 3 paces beyond and 3 paces to the left of the first marker. Place the third marker in line with the first marker and 6 paces beyond it.

The relay

First player in each line runs to the right of the first marker, slides to left past the second marker, slides right behind second marker and, in front of the third marker, runs on around third marker and returns to touch off next teammate in line. (See diagram.) The teammate repeats the action, following the same path. Continue until each player has had two turns. The team that is first to return, and is sitting down in original position, wins.

Teaching hints

1. Stress that each player keeps facing *forward* and changes lead foot as he changes directions; do not cross one foot over the other.
2. Practice before playing for speed.

Variations

1. Use five staggered markers.
2. Run the entire distance.

COUNTDOWN (FIG 3.10)

Formation

Shuttle relay formation. Each group has the opposite group as opponents. Players behind one goal line represent missiles; players behind the opposite line represent interceptors. Provide each group with a lane 30 to 40 feet in width, to allow for dodging.

The game

Start play with a countdown: "Three—two—one—fire." On the signal "fire," the first missile and the first interceptor in each group run forward. The object of the game is for the missiles to reach the opposite goal line without being tagged by the interceptors. (Opponents in each group must keep within their own lane.) Whether tagged or not, each player goes to the end of the opposite line and the player at the head of each line starts to run (without a countdown).

Continue play with the missiles becoming interceptors and interceptors missiles, until each player returns to his original

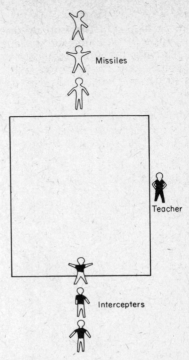

FIG. 3.10. Countdown.

position. Score 1 point for each successful missile run, player not tagged. The team with the greatest number of points wins. Rotate teams to face new opponents and repeat.

Teaching hint

If any players take too long to go across the area, give a 5-count countdown to make the move. Failure to move across the area by the count of 5 results in no score.

SACK RELAY

Equipment

Gunny sack for each team participating.

Formation

Shuttle formation; team divided in half with an area of approximately 30 feet between the two halves.

Relay

The first member of each team is provided with a gunny sack, which he holds in his hands until the signal to start is given. On signal he puts both feet into the sack and jumps to the opposite line, where he steps out of the sack and hands it to the next player. That player repeats the action. The team that is back in its starting position first wins.

Safety

1. Do not play on blacktop.
2. Players must pull sack on completely before starting to jump.

THREE-LEGGED RACE

Equipment

Wide band of material, towel, or flour sack—one for each two children.

Formation

Partner relay formation. Line up facing a goal line approximately 40 to 60 feet away.

Race

The partners tie the towel securely around their inside legs when standing side by side on the starting line. On signal they race toward the opposite line. First couple to get to the goal line without falling down or untying the towel wins. Announce the winners and repeat the action.

Safety

1. Cord or rope should not be used to tie the players' legs together as it causes rope burns.
2. Allow a few minutes of practice to work on balance, rhythm, and coordination.

CIRCLE GAMES

CIRCLE FREEZE (FIG. 3.11)

Formation

Players stand in a single circle facing counterclockwise. IT stands outside the circle, facing clockwise.

The game

Players move around the circle using a locomotor skill called by the teacher. When the teacher calls "Freeze," circle players stop and IT tags a player. Tagged player

FIG. 3.11. Circle Freeze.

turns and chases IT once around the circle and back to place.

If IT gets once around the circle and back to the vacant place before being tagged, he is safe and the chaser becomes IT. If tagged, IT must go to the center of the circle for one turn of the game. Chaser always becomes IT.

Safety

Allow sufficient space between players.

Teaching hints

1. Have IT tag a player near him after "Freeze" is called.
2. Have children next to vacant space raise hands to indicate "home."
3. Occasionally have circle players perform a stunt such as Crane Stand or Turk Stand, while IT is being chased.
4. Reverse the direction of the circle players occasionally.
5. Have IT call out the activity for circle players.
6. Occasionally substitute a stunt such as Measuring Worm or Frog Hop for the locomotor skill.

NUMBER CHANGE (FIG. 3.12)

Equipment

Chalk. Place a number in front of each player: 1, 2, 3; 1, 2, 3; . . . (Numbers may

FIG. 3.12. Number Change.

be printed on 3 x 3-inch squares of colored poster board for repeated and easier use.)

The game

One player stands in the center.

Teacher may call, "Ones." All "Ones" exchange places; extra player tries to get a number at the same time. Player without a number goes to the center. Repeat, calling "Twos" or "Threes."

Call two numbers at once. Players may change numbers.

Call, "All change."

Teaching hints

1. Encourage children to try to get a number each time rather than going to the center.

2. Later on, use greater numbers: 4, 5, 6; 7, 8, 9.

CUT THE PIE (FIG. 3.13)

Adaptations

Good Morning, Merry Christmas, Happy New Year, Happy Easter—use when meeting.

Formation

Players stand in a circle, hands joined.

The game

Pie Cutter, in center, places palms together and says, "I am going to cut a ——— pie" (naming a kind of pie), at the same time bringing his hands down on the joined hands of two players.

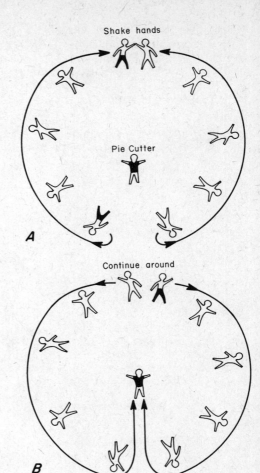

FIG. 3.13. Cut the Pie.

The two players run in opposite directions around the circle and stop to shake hands when they meet. They continue on to the vacant place and into the center of the circle to tag the Pie Cutter's hand. (Fig. 3.13B) The first player to tag him becomes the new Pie Cutter.

The remaining two players return to the circle.

Safety

1. Cut pie gently.
2. Stop to shake hands.
3. Tag the nearest outstretched hand of Pie Cutter. (See diagram.)

Teaching hint

Divide the class in half and have two games.

EASTER BUNNY

Note: Use for a change of pace after vigorous activity.

Equipment

One colorful cardboard Easter egg or substitute.

Formation

Open area or a marked circle. Each player stands facing into the circle with hands cupped behind his back (making a nest). One player (the Bunny) stands outside the circle holding the Easter egg.

The game

The Bunny runs around the outside of the circle. He puts the Easter egg into the nest (hands) of one of the players. The player receiving the Easter egg runs after the Bunny and tries to tag him before he can go once around the circle and back to place. If the Bunny is tagged, he has to go into the Easter Basket (the center of the circle) for one turn of the game. If not tagged, he remains in place on the circle. The player with the Easter egg becomes the new Bunny.

Teaching hints

1. The Bunny should place the Easter egg on his *first* trip around the circle.

2. When a player leaves his place to chase the Bunny, have the players on both sides of the vacant spot face and raise hands to identify the spot for the runners.

3. Divide group into two or more games.

FIND A NUMBER (FIG. 3.14)

Equipment

Chalk or set of cards with numbers 1, 2, 3.

The game

Players stand in a single circle, each standing behind a number. The teacher calls out a locomotor skill and gives a starting signal. Children travel counter-

FIG. 3.14. *Find a Number.*

clockwise around the circle until the teacher calls, "Find a number."

When all children are in position, the teacher calls, "Number Ones, raise your hands," "Number Twos, raise your hands," "Number Threes." (Each time call the numbers in a different order.)

Repeat the game, calling a different locomotor skill.

Teaching hint

If the class is using flash cards in the classroom for addition and subtraction, use the flash cards so that children have to add or subtract in order to identify their own numbers.

MAGIC CARPET

See Index.

BEAR IN THE TRAP (FIG. 3.15)

Adaptation

Turkey in the Pen.

Formation

Players stand in a single circle, hands joined, with a Bear standing in the center.

The game

Bear tries to break through or dodge under the hands. When he does so, all players chase him as he runs around within a predetermined area. The first player to

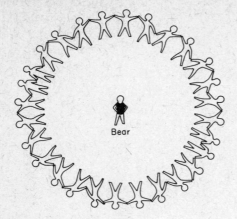

FIG. 3.15. Bear in the Trap.

tag him becomes the new Bear, and the game begins again.

Safety

1. Encourage the Bear to use strategy rather than force in breaking through the circle.

2. Tag without pushing or grabbing.

3. Children should be cautioned to run carefully to avoid collisions.

Teaching hints

1. Before starting game, point out the boundaries of the forest within which the Bear must run.

2. Blow the whistle immediately when the Bear is tagged, for players to return quickly and form a new circle.

3. Stop the game if the Bear or players run out of bounds, or if the Bear cannot be tagged fairly quickly.

4. Have two Bears and have them run in opposite directions.

5. Game should not be repeated too often at one time.

SNAP THE TRAP (FIG. 3.16)

Formation

Double circle formation, inner circle ("Trap") going one way, and the outer circle ("Mice") going the other. (Boys form one circle, girls the other.)

The game

Players move forward in the direction they are facing until the teacher calls,

"Mousetrap—ready!" Players in the inner circle immediately face the center and join hands, arms held high. Outer circle of players weave in and out (like "Go In and Out the Window"), all moving in the same direction.

When the teacher calls, "Snap," the inner circle players lower their arms to trap the mice inside. All players trapped inside the circle join the inner circle.

Repeat again from the beginning until most of the mice have been trapped, then have children exchange roles.

FIG. 3.16. Snap the Trap.

Teaching hint

1. Children enjoy playing boys against girls in this game, and it is easier to remember initial positions.

2. Caution to lower hands carefully.

SQUIRREL IN TREES (FIG. 3.17)

Formation

Children stand in very large circle formation. Count off by threes and have players 1 and 3 join hands around player No. 2, the squirrel in the tree. (Take positions as they count.) Have one or two extra players.

FIG. 3.17. Squirrel in Trees.

The game

As leader calls, "Change," all the squirrels run to another tree. Extra players also attempt to find a tree. (All squirrels must change trees.) Any squirrel left without a home exchanges places quickly with a tree-player. After a period of time, have all the squirrels exchange places with a tree-player who has not had a turn as a squirrel. After another period of time, exchange places again, giving all players a turn to run.

Teaching hints

1. Tree-players raise their hands and admit *any* squirrel into their tree.

2. Stress safety when entering the tree. On a close play commend a child who stops when another player reaches the tree just ahead of him.

FOREST LOOKOUT (FIG. 3.18)

Formation

Players stand in a double circle with one player, the Forest Lookout, in the center. Players on the inside circle face into the circle and stand in a stride position as trees. Players on the outside circle face counterclockwise.

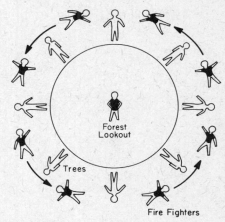

FIG. 3.18. Forest Lookout.

The game

Forest Lookout starts clapping hands and calls, "Fire on the mountain! Run, run, run!" Outside circle of players, the fire fighters, run around the circle. When Forest Lookout stops clapping his hands and stands in front of a "tree," all the fire fighters step in front of a tree. Player left without a tree becomes the Forest Lookout. Circle players then exchange roles. The trees step back to the outside circle and become fire fighters; they face counterclockwise and get ready to run. The new trees "plant their roots" on the inside circle.

Stress

Only the players on the outside circle run; those on the inside circle have planted their roots and cannot move. No child is the Forest Lookout more than once during the game. If the same child is caught without a tree a second time, he chooses someone to take his place.

Teaching hint

Use different locomotor skills. Example: "Fire on the mountain! Skip—skip—skip."

BACK TO BACK (FIG. 3.19)

Formation

Children take a partner and scatter around the outside of a large circle. Partners join hands back to back. One child is in the center of the circle.

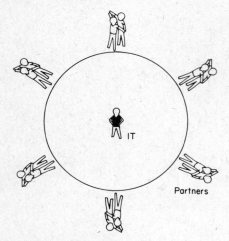

FIG. 3.19. Back to Back.

The game

When the teacher calls, "Change," players run to another partner and join hands back to back. Extra player also gets a partner. (Take a new partner each time and stand outside the marked circle.) Player without partner goes to the center of the circle. Repeat the game. At the end of the playing time, identify all the players who were able to get a partner every time.

Teaching hint

Stress that the player in the center of the circle is not IT and should be accepted as partner. (Circle players tend to avoid the player in the center.)

TWO DEEP AND CHANGE (FIG. 3.20)

Formation

Single circle facing the center. One runner and one chaser are outside the circle.

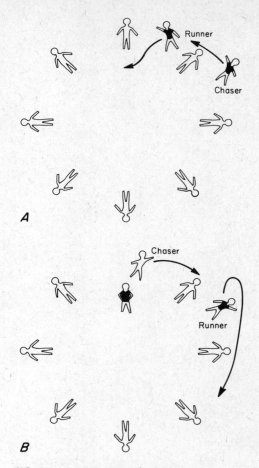

FIG. 3.20. Two Deep and Change.

The game

The runner and chaser run around the outside of the circle. The runner stops in front of a circle player to be safe from being tagged, thus forcing the player behind him to become the chaser. Immediately, the original chaser becomes the runner and turns and runs in the opposite direction. If a runner is tagged before he stops in front of a circle player, he immediately becomes the chaser.

Teaching hints

1. Have the children walk through the game before starting the play, until they clearly understand the change of direction

when a runner stops in front of a circle player.

2. Stress that the runner should cut in quickly and not run too long.

3. If a runner cuts in front of a circle player, he *must* stop. (No one runs across the center of the circle or away from the circle.)

CIRCLE TAG (FIG. 3.21)

Formation

In a single circle formation, number players 1, 2, 3.

FIG. 3.21. Circle Tag.

The game

The leader calls one of the numbers. Players with that number turn and run in a *clockwise* direction once around the outside of the circle.

While running, each player tries to tag the runner ahead of him. If tagged, the runner goes quickly to the center of the circle, where he remains until all numbers are called. Repeat the game, calling each number.

Count the number of 1's, 2's, and 3's that occupy the center of the circle. Players then return to their original places in the circle and the game is repeated.

Safety

Tag without pushing or grabbing. All run in same direction. Lean toward the center when running in a circle.

When introducing the game, call a number and have players with that number

step out of the circle and face clockwise. Then give the signal, "Go," to start running.

Teaching hints

1. Vary the locomotor skill for greater interest.

2. Call two numbers at the same time.

Variations

1. Players run until whistle is blown, then stop and return to place.

2. On whistle, players change direction; when whistle is blown twice, players stop and return to place. (Upper grades.)

LINE GAMES

SCAT (FIG. 3.22)

Formation

Children stand behind one goal line facing Clown. (See diagram.)

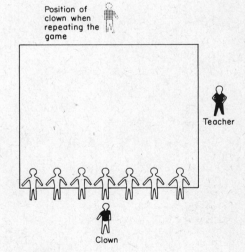

FIG. 3.22. Scat.

The game

The Clown performs "tricks," which the players imitate. When Clown calls the magic word, "Scat," all children turn and run *straight* to opposite goal line.

First child to cross opposite goal line becomes the new Clown. (If he has already had a turn, he should select someone to take his place.)

Teaching hints

1. When introducing the game, stress that children run to the opposite line each time.

2. Do not allow one Clown to perform too long before calling, "Scat."

3. Teacher should position herself to determine the winner each time, or the Clown may remain in position and judge the winner when group returns to his goal line. Clown then rejoins the group.

FIRE ENGINE (FIG. 3.23)

Adaptation

Shore Patrol (speedboats, sailboats, cutters); Peter Rabbit (easter eggs—three colors); Bird Catcher (hawk and birds).

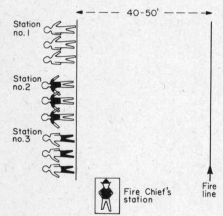

FIG. 3.23. Fire Engine.

Formation

One child is chosen to be the Fire Chief and stands at one side line. The other players are divided into three groups, each of which is given a number: 1, 2, or 3. These groups stand behind the goal line.

The game

The Fire Chief gives an alarm, crying, "Fire! Fire! Station No. 2!" The group called runs to the opposite goal line and back across the starting line. The first player to cross the starting line is the new Chief. The new Fire Chief stands at the side line and calls another fire station.

If the chief should call, "Fire! Fire!

General alarm!" all groups run to the opposite goal line and back.

Safety

1. Stress running *straight* to the opposite line and *straight* back.

2. Check spacing between children. Children should be more than two elbows' distance apart (elbows extended to sides).

Variation

1. Use a triangle. Fire Chief strikes the triangle once, twice, or three times to call a fire station. If he makes a circular motion inside the triangle striking all three sides, it is a "General alarm."

2. Use own method of giving the alarm, such as clapping, stamping, or jumping the given number of times.

COWBOYS AND INDIANS (FIG. 3.24)

Formation

Rectangle with end lines as goal lines. Mark a waiting line parallel to and 5 feet from each end line.

Divide the group into two equal teams. One team stands behind one goal line (Cowboys) and other team stands behind opposite goal line (Indians).

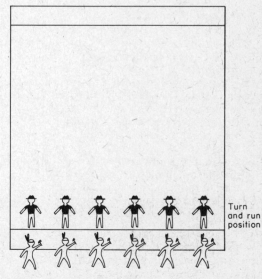

FIG. 3.24. Cowboys and Indians.

The game

Cowboys face away from the rectangle with eyes closed. Indians creep up behind Cowboys and stand in a turn-and-run position at the waiting line. Teacher gives the signal, "Here come the Indians!" Indians run back across own goal line. Cowboys turn and chase. Indians tagged before crossing own goal line join opposing team.

Repeat the game with the Indians closing eyes and Cowboys creeping up to opposite waiting line. Teacher gives signal, "Here come the Cowboys!"

After a period of time, identify the winners (players who were *not* tagged). Have all players return to original group and start the game again with the Cowboys creeping up first.

RED, WHITE, AND BLUE (FIG. 3.25)

Adaptations

Animal Catcher. Children select names of animals. A Lion is IT, the small circle is the Lion's Den, and the field is a jungle. The animals have homes on the edge of the jungle.

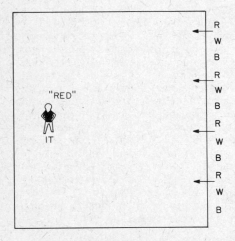

FIG. 3.25. Red, White, and Blue.

Easter Basket. Players are Easter eggs such as yellow, blue, and green. Peter Rabbit is IT and plays in the cabbage patch. The small circle is Peter Rabbit's Easter Basket.

Fish Catcher. Children are three different kinds of fish. A Whale is IT and lives in the middle of the ocean.

Number Catcher. Players are numbered 1, 2, 3.

Halloween Witch. The three groups are Owls, Black Cats, and Ghosts. A Witch is IT and lives in the forest.

Formation

Two goal lines are drawn 80 feet apart. Players are counted off as Red, White, or Blue down the line of players. One player, IT, stands in the center of the area.

The game

IT calls a color, such as "Red!" All players with that name run to the opposite line and remain there. The other colors are called in turn until all players are on the opposite goal line. IT tries to tag runners as they cross the center area.

Repeat, returning to original line. Players tagged assist IT. Last player to be tagged is IT for the next game.

POM POM PULLAWAY

Formation

Two goal lines are drawn on the play area about 80 feet apart. All the players stand behind one goal line.

The game

One child stands in the center of the area and calls, "Pom Pom Pullaway! If you don't run, I'll pull you away!" All the players run to the opposite goal. The player in the center tags as many children as possible. Those tagged become his helpers, and the game continues. The last child tagged is the winner and becomes the caller for the next game.

Safety

Provide very wide area for dodging.

Variation

When caller says, ". . . . if you don't skip . . . . . ," the players must skip to the opposite goal. The caller, too, must use the same skill. Use various locomotor skills.

MIDNIGHT (FIG. 3.26)

Formation

Large rectangle with the goal line (Sheepfold) on one side of the rectangle, and the Fox's Den behind the opposite line. One player (the Fox) stands in the Fox's Den and all the other players (the Sheep) stand behind the goal line.

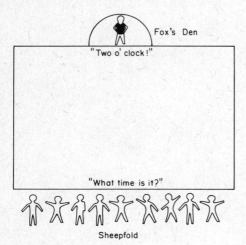

FIG. 3.26. Midnight.

The game

The Sheep walk toward the Fox and ask the Fox, "What time is it?" The Fox answers, "Three o'clock," "Six-thirty . . ." The Sheep keep walking closer each time they ask the time. Each reply of the Fox is closer to twelve o'clock midnight, but he cannot leave his Den until he says the word, "Midnight." When the Fox calls, "Midnight," the Sheep turn and run back home, and the Fox tries to tag them. Anyone tagged before crossing the goal line joins the Fox in his Den.

Only the Fox can answer the question, "What time is it?" but all his helpers can tag the Sheep when he calls out "Midnight." After a period of time, count the Sheep not tagged and repeat the game with a new Fox chosen from players not tagged.

Teaching hints

All children move toward the Fox each time the question is asked. (This is a good game to help with verbalizing the times of the day and night.)

Safety

All the Sheep are spread out in *one single* line. All players move forward together rather than having some aggressive children too far in front and some timid children too far behind the group. When "turning and running," no child should be *behind* another player.

RED ROVER

Adaptation

Color Tag. IT calls the name of a color such as blue. All children wearing any blue run to the opposite goal line. All center players try to tag the runners. Caller continues and names other colors until all children have been called.

Formation

A large rectangle with the long side lines as goal lines. Players spread out double arm's distance apart behind one goal line. Select one child to be IT and stand in the center of the area.

The game

IT calls, "Red Rover, Red Rover, let (name) come over." The player named tries to run across to the opposite goal line without being tagged. If he is successful in getting across without being tagged, *all* the remaining players also run across the area. If he is tagged, he goes to the center area and becomes the caller.

All the players in the center area chase when all the players on the goal line run, but *only* the *caller* chases when *one* player is called. (After leaving the goal line, players may not return and be safe.) Play continues.

The last player to be tagged becomes IT for the next game.

Teaching hints

1. Allow enough width in the play area for the children to run and dodge safely.
2. Have IT stand far enough away from the goal line to allow a player to start running.
3. Only one person, the caller, chases the player called by name.

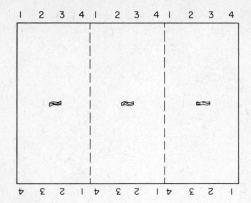

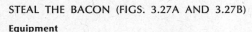

FIG. 3.27A. Steal the Bacon.

FIG. 3.27B. Steal the Bacon.
Encourage players to employ finesse in dodging. →

STEAL THE BACON (FIGS. 3.27A AND 3.27B)

Equipment

One beanbag or chalk eraser for each group.

Formation

Class is divided into two teams with one team standing behind each goal line. Divide players on *each team* into groups of four. Number players 1 to 4, with No. 1's standing diagonally opposite each other, and place a beanbag equidistant between opposite groups of fours. (See diagram.) Teacher calls a number. All players with number called run forward and try to pick up the beanbag and return across own goal line without being tagged by opposing player.

Scoring

Score 1 point for each player on a team who is successful in returning across own goal line with the beanbag without being tagged.

Teaching hints

1. Encourage finesse in outmaneuvering opponent when securing the beanbag. (A player may not stand and hold a hand over his opponent.)
2. If players are slow in picking up a beanbag, count slowly to 5. Call "No score" if beanbag has not been picked up by the count of 5.
3. After game has been learned, call two numbers at one time.
4. Include addition, subtraction, multiplication, and division when calling the number ($2 + 2 - 1$, 2×2, $6 \times 6 \div 9$).
5. Provide around 60 feet between opposing lines.

Safety

Provide sufficient width for each group. Stress staying within own lane. (If lanes are not marked, place a marker on the goal line between each group of four.)

TOUCHDOWN (FIG. 3.28)

Equipment

Pebble, piece of chalk, or marble.

Formation

A *very large* rectangle with long side lines as goal lines, 60 or more feet apart. The players are divided into two teams. Each team stands behind one goal line.

The game

One team goes into a huddle, and the members decide which player is to carry the ball (pebble, chalk, marble) across the opponents' goal line. (All players come out of huddle with fists closed as if carrying

FIG. 3.28. Touchdown.

the object, and line up the entire length of the goal line.)

When the whistle blows, each player of the team holds his hands as if he were carrying the object and runs to the opponents' goal line. The opponents run forward and attempt to tag the players as they meet. When a player is tagged, he has to *stop immediately* and open both hands. If the player who is carrying the object can reach the opponents' goal line without being tagged, he calls "Touchdown," and scores 6 points for his team. If player with the object is tagged, no score is made. Award the object to opposing team and repeat the game.

The team scoring the most points (touchdowns) during the playing time is the winner.

Safety

Provide an extra wide area for children to run and dodge safely. Encourage the use of previously learned dodging skills.

Caution children against running headlong toward opponents. Stress the use of peripheral vision.

Teaching hint

Stress that each child *stops immediately* and opens hands when tagged.

BLUE AND WHITE (FIG. 3.29)

Equipment

One cardboard disk with one color on each side.

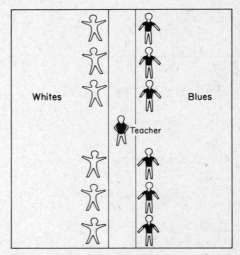

FIG. 3.29. Blue and White.

Formation

Players are divided into two teams and stand in turn-and-run position 6 to 8 feet apart at center field.

The game

Assign the color blue to one team and the color white to opposing team. Teacher tosses the disk into the air. If it lands with the blue color up, the Blues run and the Whites give chase. If the white side comes up, the Whites run and the Blues give chase. Players tagged go onto other team. At the end of a short period of time, have players who have not been tagged raise their hands. These players are the winners. All players then return to original team and game is repeated.

Teaching hints

1. Colors on disk may be adapted to the season: red and green; green and

white; black and orange (black cats and pumpkins).

2. Keep sufficient space between teams while disk is being tossed. When introducing the game, provide a wider distance.

CROWS AND CRANES

Adaptations

Ghosts and Goblins; Chiapas and Chihuahua (states in Mexico).

The game

Game is similar to Blue and White except the players start from goal lines and, on signal, walk forward. When groups are fairly close, teacher calls "Cr-cr-crows" or "Cr-cr-cranes."

If Crows are called, Cranes chase and tag. If Cranes are called, Crows chase and tag. Players tagged go onto other team.

Players who were not tagged win.

EXCHANGE TAG (FIG. 3.30)

Equipment

Write a number in front of each player as in diagram.

Formation

Two lines of players divided into groups

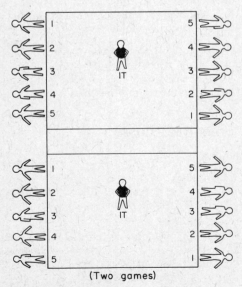

(Two games)

FIG. 3.30. Exchange Tag.

with one player, IT, in the center of each group.

The game

IT calls a number. Players with that number try to exchange places without being tagged by IT. If a player is tagged, he becomes IT, and IT takes his number. If IT is unable to tag anyone within two tries, he exchanges places with a player.

Variation

Each player may hold a small number card. When a player is tagged, he gives his card to IT.

Teaching hints

1. Teacher may call numbers to assure everyone a turn.

2. Have eight or ten players in each group (four to five players on a side).

Safety

Keep within own area when running. Provide sufficient width for running and dodging within each area.

HERE WE COME
(NEW ORLEANS, NEW YORK, TRADES)

Formation (same as Fig. 3.24)

Large rectangle with a goal line at each *end*. Parallel to the goal lines and 5 feet from each goal line is a waiting line the width of the rectangle. Divide the players into two equal groups. One group is behind one goal line and the second group is behind the opposite goal line.

The game

Group 1 decides upon a trade, some type of work. The players then spread out across the area and go to the opposite waiting line. As they move, the following conversation takes place:

Group 1: "Here we come!"
Group 2: "Where from?"
Group 1: "New York" (or the name of some other city or town).
Group 2: "What's your trade?"
Group 1: "Lemonade."
Group 2: "Show us some."

Group 1 then acts out the trade decided

upon by the players. Group 2 tries to guess the name of the trade. If it is not guessed quickly, give the initials of the trade. When the trade is guessed correctly, group 1 turns and runs back to own goal line. Group 2 chases and tries to tag as many players as possible. Any players tagged become members of group 2. The game is repeated with group 2 returning to own goal line and deciding upon a trade. They then go to the opposite waiting line and act out the trade.

The winners are the players who were able to reach the goal line without being tagged throughout the game. After a period of time, identify the winners; have all players return to original team, and repeat the game.

Teaching hints

1. When acting out the trade, have the visiting group line up in a turn-and-run position with one foot on or near the waiting line and side toward the waiting line.

2. If the trade is too difficult to guess, even with initials, allow the guessing group to ask questions about the trade which may be answered with "Yes" or "No."

HAND SLAP (FIG. 3.31)

Formation

Two goal lines 60 to 75 feet apart. Divide the players into two equal groups with one group standing behind each goal line.

The game

Four players of one group advance toward the opposite line of players. Each player on the opposite line extends his arms forward and holds out both hands with palms up. Each visiting player draws his hand across the palm of first one and then the other hand of an opponent. He may then move to another player and repeat the action. When he not only draws his hand across the palm but also quickly slaps the bottom of a hand, it is the signal to chase. The visiting player turns and runs back across his own goal line, and the opponent who has been slapped

FIG. 3.31. Hand Slap.

chases. Score one point for each player tagged before crossing own goal line.

Repeat the game with the chasers becoming the visiting players. Team with most points wins.

Teaching hints

1. Stress that visiting player stands in a turn-and-run position while he draws his hand across opponent's hand (in order to be in position to run).

2. Encourage children to slap a hand quickly and not delay the game.

3. For safety, have all visiting players start hand action at same time.

4. After a given period of time, have all players who have had a turn put hands down until *everyone* has had a turn.

OTHER FORMATIONS

FREEZE

See Index.

QUEEN BEE (FIG. 3.32)

Formation

Appoint one Queen Bee for each game. All other players stand beside a beanbag (or substitute, such as a 3 x 3-inch poster board square or a marked X), which represents a flower.

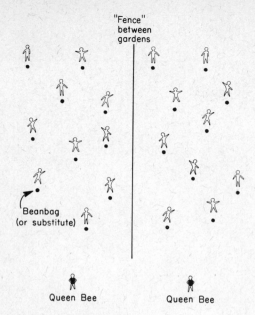

FIG. 3.32. Queen Bee—
formation for two games.

The game

The two Queen Bees fly around their *own* gardens tapping each bee on the shoulder. Players tapped join in line and follow the leader. When the teacher gives a signal, all the bees and the Queen Bee fly back to a flower. One player is left without a flower.

Queen Bee selects another player standing by a beanbag to take her place and the game is repeated. Vary the locomotor skill.

Stress that each Queen Bee flies only in own garden. (See diagram.)

At the end of the game have children who reached a flower *every time* raise their hands. Commend them.

TAG GAMES

Formation

Children scatter over a large area within designated boundaries.

The game

One player is IT. He runs and tries to tag another player. When another player is tagged, he becomes IT. See various types of tag and methods of immunity to keep from being tagged.

Limit the number of times each player may use his immunity while one player is IT. May limit the number to two or three times.

Simple Tag—No immunity.

Wood Tag—Touch wood.

Line Tag—Stand on a line.

Squat Tag—Assume a squat position.

Skunk Tag—With arm under knee, hold nose with thumb and forefinger.

Nose and Toe Tag—Hold nose and hold toe.

Hindu Tag—Have forehead and both knees touching ground.

Japanese Tag—When tagged, IT must hold the spot tagged.

Cross Tag—IT starts by chasing one player. He chases the runner until another player crosses between him and the runner. IT must then chase only the player who crossed off the runner.

Freeze Tag—Player tagged must remain in "freeze" position until tagged by a free player.

THIRD MAN TAG (FIG. 3.33)

Formation

Couples scattered over a fairly large area. Partners face same direction with inside elbows joined, outside hand on hip. Have two extra players, a runner and a chaser. Chaser is IT.

FIG. 3.33. Third Man Tag.

The game

IT chases the runner. To be safe, the runner links elbows with any player. This forces the "third man" to disengage himself. The *third man immediately becomes IT, the chaser.* The former IT immediately becomes the runner. He turns and runs to link elbows with another player, for safety. If tagged before linking elbows, he immediately becomes IT again and chases the player who tagged him.

After a period of time, have all players who have not had a turn to run raise their hands. Have each *partner* of these players keep hand on hip; other players drop outside hand to side until everyone has had a turn.

Teaching hint

Play this game after having played Two Deep and Change. Both games have the same basic pattern.

LAST COUPLE OUT (FIG. 3.34)

Formation

Couples stand in line facing an open area. IT stands in front of the group with his back to them.

FIG. 3.34. *Last Couple Out—formation for two games.*

The game

IT calls, "Last couple out," without turning or otherwise looking behind him. The last couple separates, runs forward, and attempts to join hands in front of IT, before IT can tag either player.

If a player is tagged by IT, he becomes his partner; the other player becomes IT. The couple returns to the *head* of the line after running. (Players must run in front of IT to join hands.)

Teaching hint

Play two games at one time. Players in each game face and run in opposite directions. (See diagram.)

GOLD RUSH (FIG. 3.35)

Equipment

Eight (to twelve) beanbags; identifying team bands for one team.

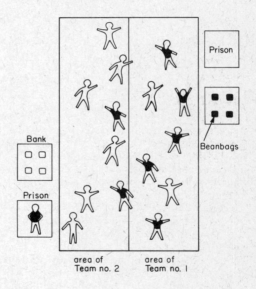

Formation

Very large rectangle with the long side lines as goal lines. Place four (to six) beanbags behind the center of each goal line, in "the bank." Adjacent to the bank, draw a prison.

Divide the players into two teams. Players of one team wear the identifying bands. They stand on one side of the center line facing the players of the other team on opposite side of the line.

The game

On signal players of both teams attempt to run through opponents' area and cross their goal line without being tagged. If successful, a player may take a bag of gold (beanbag) back to his own goal line without liability of being tagged if he *returns outside* the boundary lines. (He may be tagged if he *returns inside* the boundary lines.) If a player is tagged before *reaching* opponents' goal line he goes to prison. (See diagram.)

If there are prisoners, a player getting across opponents' goal line safely must return a prisoner rather than a beanbag. The prisoner who has been in prison the longest is rescued first. (Prisoners stand in order of being tagged.) The first team to steal all the opponents' gold (beanbags) and rescue all prisoners wins.

Teaching hint

Provide sufficient width in area for running and dodging.

CAPTURE THE FLAG (FIG. 3.36)

Equipment

Two beanbags, chalk erasers, or pieces of material; identifying team bands for one team.

Formation

Very large rectangle with long side lines as end lines. Draw a center line lengthwise of the area, and a flag circle and prison for each team. (See diagram.)

Divide the group into two teams. Each team scatters over own half of play area, with one player to guard the prison and one player to guard the flag.

Object of the game

To capture the opponents' flag and *return to own* play area without being tagged. The team wins when it captures the opponents' flag and returns it to own area, and no member of the team is in prison. (The winning team must also have own flag.)

The game

Players run into opponents' area to capture the flag. A player tagged while in op-

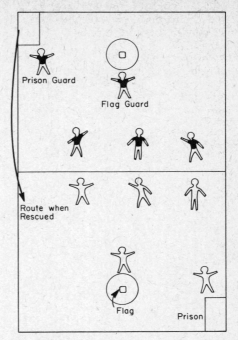

FIG. 3.36. Capture the Flag.

ponents' area becomes a prisoner and goes to opponents' prison.

A prisoner may be rescued by a player either reaching the prison or tagging the prisoner. He and the prisoner return to their own area without being tagged, but *must go out of bounds* when *returning* to own area.

Prisoners may make a chain of players by joining hands. The chain extends outside of prison, but one prisoner must have one foot inside the prison. Prisoners stand in the order they go to prison with the player who has been in prison the longest at the head of the chain.

Opponents' flag may be captured at any time and placed in circle with own flag. (Only a player in the act of capturing the flag is allowed to enter the flag circle. The guard and his teammates cannot step into the circle.)

Optional rules

1. Decide whether flag should be returned to flag circle or dropped to the

ground where player was tagged, when a player is tagged before reaching own area with flag.

2. "Prison Break." Prisoners may grab the prison guard and pull him into prison. If this occurs, all the prisoners "break prison" and run through opponents' area to own area. Prisoners may be tagged by opponents.

Teaching hints

1. Allow a *very* wide area in which children have an opportunity to run and dodge to avoid being tagged.

2. If one game goes on too long and some children remain in prison too long, declare a winner (team with fewest prisoners) and start a new game.

3. Check that all players are actively engaged in the game.

CHAPTER 4

BODY ALIGNMENT AND DEVELOPMENTAL EXERCISES

BODY ALIGNMENT

MECHANICS OF POSTURE

DEVELOPMENTAL EXERCISES—GRADES 4–8

PHYSICAL PERFORMANCE TESTS

FIG. 4.1. Vertical Line Reference Test: Checking body alignment.

The elementary school teacher is in a strategic position to discover and to help prevent the development of faulty posture. Through daily contact he is able to observe and appraise the posture habits of the active and the sedentary child. The teacher need not be highly trained nor skilled in posture evaluation. Rather, he needs to be sensitive to normal and abnormal postures by understanding individual variations in body structure, and by accepting temporary changes in posture patterns which may stem from fluctuating mental or physical states.

The teacher can prevent and help eliminate minor problems of malposture: by providing opportunities that encourage the use of good posture habits; by eliminating situations that exaggerate faulty positions; and by encouraging active participation in a physical activity program designed for total development and fitness.

Since the activity period does not always provide for such aspects of development as endurance, strength, and flexibility, two sections of exercises have been included. The first, Exercises for Improving Posture, is provided for those children in whom a particular muscle weakness is apparent or in whom an imbalance of strength has developed. The child could be assigned to perform the exercises either at home or as a part of the regular warm-up routine.

The second section of exercises has value in that every area of the body is involved in each series. Major emphasis is placed upon endurance activity because of its importance in total fitness. Interest in performing these exercises can be maintained by increasing the challenge of the activity: extend the number of repetitions, the length of time, or the distance.

These exercises are recommended for grades 4–8, rather than for all grade levels. Primary grade children will benefit from participating in activities such as those presented in Chapters 1, 2, and 3.

Performance tests are also presented in this chapter. It is possible to measure such factors as speed, agility, strength, and endurance. These tests may be presented through group participation; later individual tests may be administered and scored.

In the chapters on sport units, skill tests appropriate to each unit are presented.

PURPOSES

The awareness of individual posture patterns sometimes needs to be brought into sharper focus, since there is a tendency for teachers to become involved in what students are doing rather than how they look as they stand or move. The material in this chapter is an important facet of the instructional program, and is designed for the following purposes:

—to increase awareness of good body alignment;

—to strive toward good posture, which contributes to an attitude of self-confidence and poise;

—to develop good posture habits to reduce the possibility of physical difficulties for the present as well as later on in life;

—to present information regarding factors that influence posture: genetic, environmental, emotional, physical;

—to present guidelines for selection and presentation of activities conducive to good postural development;

—to present a means through which posture may be evaluated;

—to provide knowledge and understanding as to the purposes and values of the exercise series, and to the practice of good posture;

—to provide vigorous exercises for improved circulation and respiration, for increased endurance and slower onset of fatigue.

BODY ALIGNMENT

DEFINITION OF POSTURE

Posture is the manner in which one stands, moves, and performs his daily activities. Sitting and standing may be termed static posture, while movement activities are dynamic. Posture is generally rated as excellent, good, or poor and is judged by determining the relationship of the various body parts to each other, a procedure referred to as segmental alignment. Five blocks of wood stacked one on top of another and held together with two rubber bands represent the human body and its five main weight centers: the head, thorax (chest and shoulders), pelvis, knees, and feet. (Fig. 4.2) When each block or segment is placed directly one above the other, the structure typifies a strong, sturdy, well-balanced column. However, should one block deviate to one side away from the midline, the balance of the column is threatened. Not until a compensatory weight adjustment is made by one of the other blocks moving in the opposite direction will balance be restored. This zigzag alignment, although balanced, is less attractive and certainly less efficient. The muscles and ligaments are put on a stretch, weight stresses are unevenly placed on joint structures, and, because of the precarious alignment, the muscles are required to work continuously to maintain the position. Figure 4.2 shows the superimposing of the body over the column of blocks:

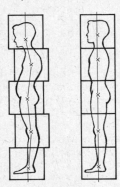

FIG. 4.2. Segmental alignment showing five main weight centers; improper alignment, proper alignment.

the figure on the left typifies faulty alignment and the figure on the right represents good alignment. Such a device as a jointed wooden model will also demonstrate the body in good and poor alignment.

The way one stands is reflected in all other body movements. For example, if one stands with his feet pointed outward, he undoubtedly will run in a like manner. Consequently, a measurement of the sta-

tionary posture will give some degree of accuracy in general posture determination.

CAUSES OF POOR POSTURE

Many factors contribute to faulty posture. Some of the most important ones are presented.

MENTAL IMAGE

A child's concept of himself affects his appearance. The child imitates his real-life idol or favorite television character or a person he admires such as his father, mother, an older brother, or a teacher. This may change from day to day or week to week. For example, he tires of being a tough and rugged cowboy after a day or so and prefers to be a pirate with a peg leg instead. In some cases the child plays a part too long. As a result, the pattern becomes habitual with the child.

LACK OF MUSCLE STRENGTH

Malnutrition, fatigue, illness, or inactivity may contribute to weakness. Flint and Diehl found a high and significant relationship between the strength of the trunk muscles and posture. (22) The less the strength of the abdominal and back muscles and the greater the imbalance of strength between them, the greater the postural deviations of the trunk region.

LACK OF FLEXIBILITY

The aforementioned study also determined that the greater the flexibility of the hip and lumbar region, the less the tendency for sway-back. However, a highly flexible body may be unstable. Emphasis should be placed not on exercises that concentrate on flexibility alone, but rather on an exercise series that is designed for body flexibility, strength, and endurance.

FAULTY CUES

The phrase, "Stand (or sit) *tall*," is preferred to other posture cues. Such cues as "Tuck your seat under," "Throw your shoulders back," "Stand straight," are cue phrases that may possibly eliminate the problem at hand but often cause other serious postural problems. Performing the action suggested by the phrase, "Tuck your seat under," reduces the normal lumbar curve, causing a condition of flat back and flexion of the knees. "Throwing one's shoulders back" or standing straight in an exaggerated position, creates considerable tension and tends to form a sway-back condition.

CONGENITAL AND ACQUIRED STRUCTURAL DEFORMITIES

A shortened lower extremity that has resulted from an injury or from malfunction of the growth center in the bone will cause a weight displacement to one side. A wedge-shaped vertebra will cause the vertebral column to lean to the side of the wedge, causing the more severe types of postural deviations of the spinal column such as hunchback and scoliosis. Paralysis, muscle weakness, scar tissue, fractures, and unilateral growth are other factors that contribute to posture faults.

INHERITED BONY STRUCTURE

This cannot be overlooked as one of the most important contributing factors to postural variations. These factors cannot be changed. A horizontally placed sacrum, for example, makes the buttocks protrude and the back appear to have an increased curve in the lumbar region. In reality the curve may be perfectly normal for that person. A congenitally rigid flatfoot is strong and normal for the person who has it. If acquired, the condition becomes a postural problem.

PSYCHOLOGICAL FACTORS

As a rule, all people of all ages look the way they feel—their emotions are portrayed in their appearance. The type of posture one has is often characteristic of one's mental and emotional state. Insecurity, fear, depression, and unhappiness are often characterized by flexion or stooping of the body, with hesitancy in movement. On the other hand, attitudes of joy and security are generally characterized by elevation or extension of the body, with sureness in movement.

HABITS OF POSITION

Faulty habits of position contribute to permanent changes in body alignment. Standing on one leg causes the knee to hyperextend, the ankle to roll in, and the tibia (shinbone) to bow or twist from the constant unilateral pressure. Standing with arms crossed and resting on the supporting shelf of the abdomen, standing with one knee braced against the other, sitting on one leg, or sitting for long periods without back support are other faulty positions that put unnecessary strain on joints and encourage the development of undesirable postures.

EVALUATION PROCEDURES

The chief purpose in appraising the posture of schoolchildren is to identify those pupils who deviate sufficiently from the standard to need help. The earlier in life this discovery is made, the greater the probability for correction. Corrective procedures should be begun before faulty movement patterns become habitual to the child or before the bony structure conforms to the pressures of poorly balanced posture. Once an exaggerated posture fault is discovered, it then becomes the responsibility of the teacher to seek professional aid for its correction by referring the case to the school nurse or school physician and to the parents.

The more complicated objective measures used by professional people in determining the extent and type of postural faults would be both burdensome and unnecessary for the elementary school teacher. A simple subjective appraisal of each child's standing and moving posture is all that is necessary. This appraisal may be made during informal situations where the teacher observes the child in his various postural patterns on the playground and in the classroom. It can be done in a more formal way by setting aside a special day or days for the careful scrutiny of each child by the teacher, or by the teacher and nurse, or by several teachers. By applying both the formal and informal procedures, a more accurate overall posture description of the child may be obtained.

The following procedure has been found to be effective and can be done in a very short time with a certain amount of objectivity. It is recommended that children be encouraged to bring shorts or trunks for Posture Day. (See Posture Evaluation Charts)

VERTICAL LINE REFERENCE TEST (FIG. 4.1)

A weighted line is hung from an overhead support such as a door frame or a bar or standard, and is just long enough for the weight to touch the floor. The child stands behind the line in a relaxed, natural position. The teacher, by using the vertical line as a reference, can then observe the following points from both the side view and the back view.

Side view

The child stands sideways to the line so that the bob or weight falls slightly in front of the ankle bone.

1. General Alignment. As one reads upward from the ankle, the following guide points should be situated one above the other so that a vertical line will pass through the center of each point: the knee just behind the knee cap; the center of the hip joint; the center of the shoulder joint; and the ear lobe.
   a. The body should give the appearance of extended control without tension or rigidity.
   b. The curves of the body are moderate and the five main segments—head, thorax, pelvis, knees, and feet—are balanced evenly one above the other. There should be no backward or forward lean of the upper trunk.
2. Upper Back and Head.
   a. Curvature of back should be mild with no pronounced apex along the thoracic curve.
   b. Shoulder blades should not protrude outward or be drawn to the sides of the rib cage away from the vertebrae.
   c. The arms should hang loosely at the sides, with palms directed in toward the body rather than facing backward.
   d. The outline of the anterior chest wall should be slightly convex or vertical rather than sunken or concave.
   e. The head is held comfortably back over the shoulders with chin horizontal. The line of the back of the neck should not project diagonally forward and upward.
   f. Shoulders should be neither shrugged and tense nor "thrown back" in a stiff, exaggerated position. They should be relaxed and low. Correction of round shoulders is not done by forcing them back. As one stands or sits tall, the shoulders, if relaxed, will fall into their correct relative position.
3. Lower Back, Abdomen and Pelvis.
   a. Lumbar curve should be mild. If the curve appears extreme, the accompanying deviations of forward pelvic tilt, relaxed abdomen, and hyperextended knees (backward knees) will usually be present. A condition of compensatory backward lean of the trunk may give the illusion of lordosis. If the curve is reduced or flat, there may be a possibility of a weak, poorly supported back.
   b. The abdomen should be flat or only mildly rounded. A definite indentation of the abdominal wall at the level of the waist should be present. The wall should not be sagging or relaxed or excessively rotund. It is natural for children below the age of 7 to have a round abdominal wall.
   c. A line falling vertically downward from the sternum (breastbone) should fall clear of the lower abdomen.
   d. The pelvis should tilt neither forward nor backward but rather should be placed squarely beneath the trunk.
4. Knees.
   a. Knees should be directly below the hip joint in an "easy" position.
   b. Knees should be neither flexed forward nor thrown back in hyperextension.

Back and/or front view

Child stands with his back to the line so that the weight on the line hits exactly between the feet.

1. General Appearance. As one reads upward from the feet, the line should pass between the knees, through the cleft in the buttocks, through the center of the vertebrae and back of head.

2. Head, Shoulders, Back and Hips.

    a. The head should not tilt to either side.

    b. The shoulders should be level. (If not level, the *high* shoulder is lowered.) The scapulae should be of equal distance from the spinal column and should not protrude.

    c. The hips should be level and one hip should not be more prominent than the other.

    d. Scoliosis determination.

        (1) The spinous processes of the vertebral column should be in vertical alignment with no lateral deviation. To determine this, it may be necessary to mark the spinous processes.

        (2) The musculature running vertically along the side of the vertebrae should be approximately of the same density on both sides.

        (3) The shape of the rib cage should be the same on each side.

        (4) The distance between the arms and body at waist level should be the same on each side.

3. Knees and Feet.

    a. Knees should not be bowed, knocked, or rolled inward.

    b. Lower legs should not bow outward.

    c. Feet should be parallel pointing neither outward nor inward.

    d. The inner border of the feet and ankles should not roll inward (pronation).

    e. The heel cords (Achilles' tendons) should be parallel and vertical, and not turn inward toward each other.

    f. A longitudinal arch should be present and observable along the inner border of the foot.

    g. The forepart of the foot should not be spread and flattened.

    h. The toes should be straight without any deviation, such as hammer toes.

COMMON POSTURE FAULTS

Note: The following terms describe certain postural deviations which may be noted during evaluation.

SIDE VIEW APPRAISAL OF BODY ALIGNMENT

Forward Head. Head projects forward. The line of the neck is directed diagonally forward and upward from the shoulders.

Round Shoulders. The scapulae (shoulder blades) are spread apart, chest shows a mild to marked concavity, the arms are rolled inward toward the body with the palms facing backward.

Winged Scapula. Inner or vertebral borders of the scapula project backward and outward away from the rib cage.

Kyphosis (hunchback). Exaggeration or increase in the normal amount of convexity in the upper region of the spine. Generally it accompanies round shoulders.

Lordosis (sway-back). Exaggeration or increase in the normal amount of concavity in the lower region of the back.

Relaxed Abdomen. Protruding abdominal wall without an indentation at the waist level.

Forward Pelvic Tilt. The pelvis should be squarely under the trunk so that the crest of the ilium (top of the hip bone) does not slope downward and forward.

Compensatory Backward Lean. The upper trunk leans backward from the hips and overhangs the pelvis.

Hyperextended Knees or Backward Knees. The knees have a backward curve.

BACK VIEW APPRAISAL OF BODY ALIGNMENT

Head Tilt. Affects proper alignment and may indicate a visual problem.

High Shoulder. One shoulder will not be on the same horizontal line as the other. (Fig. 4.1)

High Hip. One hip will be higher and slightly more prominent than the other.

Scoliosis. A lateral curvature of the spine. This curvature may include the total vertebral column or may be found only in the thoracic or in the lumbar region. A high hip and shoulder on opposite sides may be the first obvious signs of a beginning curvature of the spine.

Knock-Knees. Knees touch, with a definite angulation of the thighs toward the midline of body. The lower legs will be directed outward.

Bowlegs. Knees are bowed outward. The bowing begins in the thigh region.

Tibial Torsion. Twisting of the tibia (shinbone). The lower legs bow outward. The bowing begins below the knees. Knees turn inward and ankles are pronated.

Pronation. Ankles roll inward. When viewed from the back, the heel cords (Achilles' tendons) form an inward curve, as does the inner side of the ankle.

Acquired Flattened Longitudinal Arches (flatfeet). Reduced arch on the inner border of the central part of the foot.

Eversion (duck walk). Toes are pointed outward.

Inversion (pigeon-toed). Toes are pointed inward.

TOE DEFORMITIES

Hallux Valgus (bunions). Large toe points toward other toes rather than straight forward.

Hammer Toes. Toes are held in a constant gripping position.

Corns. Callused and rubbed areas indicating too much pressure from poorly fitting shoes.

PROCEDURES FOR IMPROVING POSTURE

1. Eliminate causative factors.
   a. Consult with parents and the school nurse or physician to understand any physical and/or emotional problems which may exist.
   b. Encourage parents and school district to purchase furniture that will adjust to the size of each child.
   c. Place blocks of wood under the feet of children whose feet do not touch the floor when sitting, in order to eliminate back strain and undesirable sitting habits.
2. Provide activities that contribute to general body development. Encourage good and efficient use of the body. Eliminate activites that encourage and exaggerate faulty movement patterns. For example:
   a. Activities that require the children to sit for long periods of time without back support (sitting on floor or stools) may provoke the development of a thoracic kyphosis and round shoulders.
   b. Games and exercises that put excessive strain on joints may cause irreparable damage. The following are some common exercises that should be eliminated from all exercise programs. (23)
      (1) Full squat positions, such as the "Duck Walk" and deep knee bends, put undue stress on the knee joints. Squat Thrust (or "Burpee") may be used without harmful effects if the weight is placed on the hands as the body is lowered.
      (2) Toe-touching exercises from a standing position, such as the "Windmill," accomplish nothing as far as strength development or flexibility are concerned. The movement itself is of little or no value and places considerable strain on the lower back and promotes knee hyperextension.
      (3) Forward flexion of the trunk from the long sitting position and touching the toes. If the trunk is not held in easy extension, with the bend at the *hip* rather than the waist, an exaggerated curve of the upper back results, causing a roundness or hunching of the back. The movement is performed by directing the *chest* toward the knees rather than the head toward the knees. Hands should be placed on the hips to circumvent round shoulders.
      (4) Straight-leg raises from the back-lying position and sit-ups with legs extended are exercises that place undue strain on the lumbar region (midsection of back). The move-

ment is performed by the hip flexors rather than by the abdominal muscles. The abdominal musculature functions to stabilize the trunk and prevent the lower back from hyperextending. If there is limited strength in the abdominals, however, the lower back will be forced into hyperextension, causing a compressional force of considerable magnitude on the spine.

c. Children should learn to use correct joint mechanics when performing all their daily activities. The movements should be taught and practiced continuously until they become habitual. (Refer to section on "Mechanics of Posture.")

d. Games and activities should stimulate habits or feelings for correct body position. Experiences should be provided for the practice and maintenance of good posture. Correct and accurate posture cues should be used when necessary without nagging and antagonizing the child.

e. Discourage such faulty posture habits as sitting or standing on one leg, sitting with head tilted to one side, standing with knees back (hyperextended) and shoulders hunched.

3. Select exercises that help to accomplish the following:

a. Strengthening of muscles. Emphasis is placed on exercises that strengthen the weakened muscles that are on the convex side of a curve. (For example, in a condition of round shoulders and kyphosis, the muscles of the back and shoulders are generally the ones that are weak.) Exercises that are designed to strengthen the total body should be a part of the program, including such activities as running, climbing, and jumping. (See "Resistance Exercises for Upper Back.")

b. Flexibility. Exercises that stretch the muscles on the concave side of the curve should be provided. (For example, the chest muscles may be tight in a condition of round shoulders and kyphosis.) Activities and exercises should help to maintain a balance in strength and flexibility between muscle groups on either side of the curve.

c. Kinesthetic feel for the correct position. Exercises, impressions, and study experiences should help develop a feeling or an awareness of good alignment without unnecessary tension. If a child has a high shoulder, he can determine faulty position by looking in a mirror, or by having the teacher touch that shoulder. He then attempts to correct the faulty position by lowering the high shoulder, and then concentrating on the feeling of the new position.

d. Release of Tension Exercises and experiences help the child consciously to hold a good position without excessive tension. The position of standing "like a soldier" is generally one of extreme tension. Instruction in relaxation can provide an awareness of excess tension.

EXERCISES FOR IMPROVING POSTURE

ABDOMINAL EXERCISES (TO TIGHTEN ABDOMINAL MUSCLES AND REDUCE PROTRUDING ABDOMEN AND SWAY-BACK)

"V" sit (Fig. 4.3)

1. Sit with knees bent, feet flat on floor. Place hands on floor behind hips, raise feet and straighten legs, then extend arms toward feet and hold. The body forms a "V"; arms are used for balance.

2. Assume the "V" position. Bend and straighten the legs, maintaining balance on the sacrum (back of hips). This exercise requires more muscular exertion than No. 1, and should be presented second in order.

FIG. 4.3. Abdominal exercises: "V" Sit; Mad Cat.

Mad cat (Fig. 4.3)

Begin on hands and knees. Tighten lower abdominal muscles and at the same time arch the back like a mad cat. Hold for a count of 5; relax without letting the body sag, and then repeat.

Basket hang

Hanging suspended from a bar or ring, draw the knees to the chest so the lower back is curled. Hold position for a count of 5; lower the legs until straight and then repeat.

Curl–down

See "Developmental Exercises," "Series Two."

Curl–down with twist

Begin in sitting position, with knees bent, feet flat on floor. Twist trunk to right and lower to the floor. Curl up and touch left shoulder to the outside of the right knee. Twist trunk to left and lower to the floor. Curl up and touch right shoulder to the outside of the left knee. Repeat several times, alternating each time.

Isometric contraction

This is an exercise in which certain muscles are tightened and held for increasing lengths of time. Any muscle may be exercised in this manner. An example of this procedure is shown in the following exercise for lower abdominals: Lie on back with knees bent, feet flat on floor.

Tighten lower abdominal muscles and at the same time push the small of the back against the floor. Hold for 10 counts; relax and repeat several times. The count is gradually increased up to a minute, over a period of time. The upper abdominal muscles (just below the rib cage) should be relaxed so that normal breathing is not interrupted.

EXERCISES FOR THE BACK
(TO AID IN STRENGTHENING BACK MUSCLES AND MAINTAINING GOOD BODY ALIGNMENT)

Body extension

Begin in standing position, sitting, or lying on the back. This exercise is merely a forceful stretch of the body to its maximum length and holding. The pelvis should be held stationary by tightening the abdominal and buttock muscles.

Modified swan

Lie face down on floor with arms extended out to the side at shoulder level. Bend elbows, making a reverse T position. Head, chest, and arms are raised a *few inches* from the floor. Chin is kept tucked and eyes directed toward the floor. Back has only a slight arch.

Tug of war with partner

Many different objects may be used safely for this activity such as automobile or airplane tires; broomstick handles or lengths of 2-inch doweling; knotted towels. Jump ropes should ordinarily not be used because of their thinness and the need to maintain control of these ropes for jumping.

Activities such as climbing, hanging, reaching, and jumping are additional activities that use and strengthen the back and abdominal muscles.

EXERCISES FOR UPPER BACK AND NECK

Shoulder stretch

These exercises will stretch the chest muscles, which, if overdeveloped, tend to cause a round-shouldered condition.

1. Sitting Indian style, stretch tall, raise arms shoulder high, bend elbows, and point fingers toward ceiling, palms facing forward. Keep chin horizontal, head back, tighten abdominal and buttock muscles to stabilize the pelvis, and slowly draw elbows and backs of hands backward as far as possible.

2. Using a wand or towel, clasp one end in each hand and extend arms overhead. Draw down behind head and back to stretch pectoral (chest) muscles. Stabilize pelvis by tightening abdominal and buttock muscles.

Resistance exercises

To strengthen upper back and shoulder muscles, reduce round shoulders and hunchback (kyphosis).

1. Against a pulley: Face pulley, arms shoulder high. Draw one or both arms back against progressively increased resistance. Pelvis and back must be stabilized by tightening abdominal and buttock muscles.

2. Against a partner (Fig. 4.4): Stand in forward-stride position, arms shoulder high and elbows bent. Partner stands behind the performer in a stride position, and offers resistance by placing his hands against the performer's elbows. Performer pushes against the hands with his elbows. Repeat several times and then exchange places.

Resistance for this exercise may be acquired by assuming a back-lying position, with knees bent and arms resting on floor in a reverse T position. Press hard against floor with elbows.

3. Tug of War (Fig. 4.4): Performer sits

FIG. 4.4. Partner resistance exercises: Tug of War; arm push for shoulder strength.

with legs crossed, arms raised, and elbows bent. Partner stands right behind him in side-stride position. Partners hook fingers and performer pulls down and back against resistance. Standing partner must keep his back straight, bending only the knees if necessary.

Arm circling

See "Developmental Exercises," "Series Four."

NECK EXERCISES

These should include experiences in developing a kinesthetic feel for correct head position and for strengthening upper back muscles. (1) Walk with an object on the head. (2) Push back of head against a resistance such as a mat. (3) Put a towel against the back of the head. Grasp each end and then pull forward as the head pushes backward. Keep chin level.

EXERCISES FOR STRENGTHENING MUSCLES OF THE THIGHS
(TO IMPROVE STANDING AND WALKING POSTURE AND FOR EFFICIENT MOVEMENT)

Partial knee bend

See "Developmental Exercises," "Series One."

Chair sit

Stand with back flat against a wall. Bend knees and slide down to a half-sit position. Hold for 30 seconds; gradually increase the time required until the complete exercise is done in 2 minutes.

Progressive resistance exercise

Sit on a table or chair with knees hanging over edge, total length of thighs supported. Slowly straighten and lower the lower leg against a progressive but controlled increase of resistance. A partner may provide the resistance, or a weighted boot may be used.

Stair step

Place one foot on a step or bench. Step up with the other foot, and then lower the first foot to the floor. Continue stepping up and down for an increasing length of time in a continuous rhythm. Change the leading foot after one or two minutes. Progressively increase the length of time exercise is continued.

Running, jumping, hiking, climbing, and bicycle riding are other activities which use the quadriceps muscles of the thigh.

EXERCISES FOR FOOT (TO STRENGHTEN MUSCLES OF THE FOOT, CORRECT FLATFOOT AND PRONATION)

Foot circle

Slowly rotate the feet so that the toe of each foot circles in and upward toward the opposite knee.

Toe gripping

Pick up a pencil or marbles from the floor by grasping them with the toes.

Place a towel on the floor and wad it up under the arch by gripping the towel with the toes and pulling toward the heels.

Long arch peek

Sit on the floor, legs extended. Roll the feet so that the soles of the feet touch. Return to starting position and repeat several times.

Walking

Walk along a line, first with the toes pointing inward (pigeon-toed), then outward (duck walk), then with toes pointing straight ahead.

Walk on outer border of feet with toes curled under.

MECHANICS OF POSTURE

STATIC POSTURE

STANDING POSITION

Mechanics

Toes point forward; knees easy; tall position with moderate curves in lower and upper back; shoulders relaxed; head back with chin level (head over shoulders); over-all position of standing tall without tension.

Common faults

Toeing out; locked knees (knees hyperextended); standing on one leg; protruding abdomen and hollow back; round shoulders and flat chest; forward head.

Learning experiences

1. Practice standing tall in front of a mirror.
2. Stand in front of a mirror. Close eyes and assume balanced position. Open eyes and evaluate standing position. Make corrections. Relax, and then repeat.
3. Take vertical line test.
4. Be evaluated by teacher.
5. Be evaluated by classmate.

SITTING-LISTENING POSITION

Mechanics

Feet resting flat on the floor (or box placed under feet); knees in a right-angle position with no pressure at back of knee from chair; buttocks pushed against back of chair; upper back against back of chair (support just below the shoulder blades); shoulders relaxed; head back with chin level (head over shoulders); over-all position of sitting tall without tension.

SITTING WORK POSITION

Mechanics

Lean forward, bending from the hips with head and trunk in good alignment. Elbows should be close to waist level when placed on table, shoulders relaxed.

Common faults—listening position

Sitting on one foot; feet dangling; legs wrapped around chair or one leg wrapped

POSTURE EVALUATION CHART—STATIC POSTURE

NAME ....
  Age .... Height .... Weight ....
Key to Score
  Not present 0   Moderate 2   R = Right
  Slight   1   Severe   3   L = Left

Side View Date				
General Alignment & Balance				
Body Lean (bkw or fwd)				
Compensatory Back Lean (overhang)				
Fatigue Slump				
Forward Head				
Round Shoulders				
Winged Scapula				
Kyphosis (hunched back)				
Lordosis (sway-back)				
Flat Back (no lumbar curve)				
Relaxed Abdomen				
Pelvic Tilt — Forward				
Pelvic Tilt — Back				
Hyperflexed Knees				
Hyperextended Knees				
Back View				
Head Tilt				
Shoulder — High				
Shoulder — Shrugged				
Abducted (spread) Scapula				
Hip High or Prominent				
Trunk List (lean or twist to one side)				
Scoliosis (curvature of spine)				
Bowlegs				
Knock-Knees				
Tibial Torsion				
Pronation				
Flattened Longitudinal Arch				
Eversion (toeing out)				
Inversion (toeing in)				
Toe Deformity				
Comments and results				

POSTURE EVALUATION CHART—DYNAMIC POSTURE

NAME ....

Key

Excellent	0	Fair	2
Good	1	Poor	3

Walking Posture	Date			Date		
General Alignment & Balance			**Lifting**			
Foot Mechanics			Muscle Control			
Heel Contact			Alignment			
Foot Flexibility			Object Control			
Pivot Push-off (rolling foot outward on ball of foot for push-off)			**Carrying & Holding**			
			Object Control			
			Body Adjustment			
Predominance of Weight			**Pushing & Pulling**			
Carried on One Foot						
Rhythm of Gait			**Stair Climbing**			
Length of Stride						
Free Swing of Leg from Hip			**Throwing**			
Lateral Hip Sway						
Exaggerated Arm Swing (one or both)			**Catching**			
Exaggerated Bounce			**Reaching**			
Eversion (toeing out)						
Inversion (toeing in)						
Running			**Strength**			
Body Lean			Abdominal			
Foot Mechanics (contact and push-off)			Back			
			Upper Legs			
Arm Swing			Arms			
Rhythm			Grip			
Jumping			**Flexibility**			
			Back			
Landing			Hamstrings (back of thighs)			
			Pectorals (chest)			
Sitting						
Up and Down			Achilles' Tendon (heel cords)			
Stationary						

around the other; pressure against back of knee from chair or from crossed knees; sitting on spine; round shoulders, excess tension in shoulders and neck, with shoulders hunched; forward head.

Common faults—work position

Rounded back and shoulders; elbows resting on too high a table with shoulders hunched; forward head; eyes too close to the work.

SITTING ON THE FLOOR

Mechanics

Sit with legs crossed, Indian style, bend forward from hips; sit on knees with weight resting on heels.

Common faults

Sitting with shoulders hunched.

Sitting on legs with lower legs extended diagonally backward. Extreme stress on inner border of knees.

Learning experiences
(for correct position when sitting)

1. Practice sitting on all types of chairs, on the floor, bench, stool, at a table.
2. Watch demonstrations.
3. Practice under critical eye of partner.
4. Analyze stress resulting from incorrect positions.

WORK ACTIVITIES

PUSHING AND PULLING

Mechanics

Stand close to the object with feet in a forward stride position.

Bend the knees and hips and lean into object, pushing with both hands. Elbows are flexed and back is straight with body inclined forward. (In pulling, the body leans away from object.)

Push with back foot and use the strong leg and hip muscles, not solely the arms and shoulders.

Apply the force in the direction in which the object is to be moved.

Apply the force through the center of weight of the object or as near to it as correct body position will permit.

Common faults

Pushing with arm and back muscles instead of stronger leg and hip muscles.

Pushing against the edge of an object rather than through its center of gravity.

Leaning forward from the waist rather than the ankles, which reduces the amount of force.

Learning experiences

Push and pull against a partner who resists your force by applying the same mechanical principles described above.

Push and pull against objects of varying sizes and shapes.

Apply principles to various household equipment, such as pushing a broom, raising and lowering a window, opening and closing drawers, and moving furniture.

LIFTING

Mechanics

Whenever possible, divide a heavy load into lighter loads.

Stand close to the object to be lifted so that the force will be directed vertically rather than at a diagonal angle.

Have one foot in advance of the other with weight distributed over the feet.

Lower the body by bending at the *hips, knees,* and *ankles.* The back is held in good alignment and inclined *slightly* forward. The depth of the stoop is regulated by the weight and height of the object. The heavier the object, the lower one will stoop in order to get under its center of gravity.

Grasp the object firmly and as near to its center as possible. Hands should be placed below and on either side of the object's center of gravity if it is very heavy.

Draw the object as close to the body as possible so that its weight will be centered over the base of support and near the body's center of gravity.

Keep the weight evenly distributed between the feet, and raise the body and the object by using the large leg muscles rather than the back muscles. Lift is slow and steady if the object is heavy. Keep the object as near to the body as possible and over the base of support throughout the total lift.

Common faults

Bending forward at waist without bending knees.

Failure to bring the object in close to the body so that its weight becomes part of the body weight.

Failure to pick up an object under its center of gravity or on either side of its center so that weight is balanced.

CARRYING

Mechanics

Maintain good body alignment. Do not protrude abdomen or hip to help support the object.

Keep the load as close to the body as possible—the closer the load is kept over the center of gravity, and the more directly over the base of support, the less the expenditure of energy and the less the strain on the joints. The ideal place for supporting the load would be either on the head or shoulders.

When unable to keep the object over the body base, hold it as close to the body as possible. The body then compensates for the additional weight by moving as a unit from the ankles in the direction opposite to the added weight. By extending the opposite arm sideways a certain counterbalance is created.

Adjust rate of walk to the load.

Common faults

Not keeping the object near the central line of the body, over the base of support.

Making compensatory adjustment for the weight by thrusting the hip or abdomen out to make a carrying shelf.

Not holding the object near its center of gravity.

Learning experiences for lifting and carrying

Pick up a long pole, first by the end and then in the middle.

Practice lifting and carrying objects of various weights and sizes and in different ways.

Apply principles of lifting and carrying to objects that are used in daily activities.

DEVELOPMENTAL EXERCISES—GRADES 4–8

The following exercise series have been developed for the convenience of teachers and as an interesting challenge for children. Each series is complete in itself, and may be used for a period of two or three weeks. Once the four series have been introduced, they may be repeated time and again with gradually increased repetitions, or with extended time, speed, or distance as additional incentives. Children always seem eager to challenge the record; a class performance chart with a running account of the number of repetitions may be maintained. This serves to keep interest high and provides goals for improved performance.

These series are meant to be used *in conjunction with* the activity program. A routine can be established in which the children spend the first few minutes of the period in developmental exercises before engaging in the selected program for the day. It will be found that a positive attitude toward exercises can be maintained if they are presented in this manner, rather than used as the only activity or as a disciplinary measure.

All the exercises in one series should be performed in continuous order, one exercise immediately following the other without rest.

SERIES ONE

TORTOISE AND HARE (RUNNING IN PLACE)

Starting position

Stand tall with weight on the balls of the feet.

Activity

Call, "Tortoise!" at which time everyone jogs slowly in place.

Call, "Hare!" to initiate a very fast run in place, lifting the knees high on each step. Alternate the calls several times, and gradually increase the length of time between calls.

Stress

Running on the toes at all times.

PARTIAL KNEE BEND

Starting position

Stand tall with arms outstretched at sides, toes pointing straight ahead. Keep the trunk erect throughout the exercise.

Activity

Slowly bend knees until the body is in a partial squat position. Count: "One—two—three—four."

Slowly return to a tall standing position. Count: "One—two—three—four."

Repeat five times; gradually increase the number of repetitions.

Stress

1. Keep the buttocks tucked under and the trunk erect.

2. Do *not* go down into a full squat position (this can be harmful to the knees over a period of time).

PUSH-UPS (MODIFIED)

Starting position

Weight on hands and knees, arms straight and body held in an inclined straight line from knee to shoulder. Place hands directly under shoulders with fingers pointing forward.

Activity (Fig. 4.5)

Bend elbows until chest touches ground. Count: "One!" Push up to starting position. Count: "Two!"

Repeat five times; gradually increase the number of repetitions to 25.

Girls should be encouraged to progress to regular push-ups.

Stress

1. Keep the body straight throughout the exercise, without any bending or sagging at the hips.

2. The chest must touch the ground on each push up.

3. The elbows in bending should point backward rather than out to the sides.

PUSH-UPS (REGULAR)

Starting position

Weight on hands and toes, body in straight line from heel to head. Fingers should point forward.

Activity (Fig. 4.5)

Bend elbows until chest touches ground. Count: "One!" Push up to starting position. Count: "Two!"

Repeat five times; gradually increase the number of repetitions to 15.

Stress

1. Keep part of the body weight on the hands while touching the chest to the ground.

2. Keep the body straight and without bending or sagging at the hips throughout the exercise.

3. The elbows in bending should point backward rather than out to the sides.

TOE PEEK

Starting position

Lie flat on back with arms at sides.

FIG. 4.5. Knee Push-up; Curl-down; Push-up.

Activity

Raise the head and shoulders and peek at the toes. Count: "One—two!"

Return to starting position. Count: "Three—four!"

Repeat 10 times; gradually increase repetitions to 25.

Stress

Do not use the elbows to help in lifting the shoulders from the ground. Control the movement up *and* down.

WING SPREAD

Starting position

Sit Indian style, with elbows raised to shoulder level and fingertips touching in front of the chest.

Activity

Keeping the arms bent, draw the elbows backward as far as possible. Count: "One!"

Return to starting position. Count: "Two!"

Again draw the elbows backward, this time straightening the arms during the movement so that the hands are reaching backward.

Count: "Three!"

Return to starting position. Count: "Four!"

Stress

1. Keep the arms on a level with the shoulders throughout the exercise.

2. Keep the head up in good alignment with trunk and keep the back as straight as possible.

TORTOISE AND HARE

Starting position

See description at beginning of this series.

Activity

Alternate fast and slow running in place several times, ending with an extended slow run to taper off following the entire series.

SERIES TWO

JUMPING JACK

Starting position

Stand tall with feet together, arms at sides.

Activity

Jump up, clap hands overhead, land with the feet in a side stride position. Count: "One!"

Jump again and return to starting position. Count: "Two!"

Repeat 10 times; gradually increase repetitions to 25.

Count the number of jumping jacks done in 30 seconds. Gradually increase to 45 seconds, then to one minute.

Note: The Treadmill exercise may be substituted for the Jumping Jack or Running in Place in any of the exercise series. For the Treadmill, begin in a racing start position on hands and knees. Keep hands on the floor and begin running in place. Bring knees well forward. Gradually increase speed in running. Gradually increase time running at top speed. May run, rest, then run again while building up endurance.

Stress

1. Land lightly on balls of the feet and give with the knees (bounce) with each jump.

2. Keep knees in line with toes; do not let the knees bend in toward each other.

3. Arms should be extended high overhead when clapping.

4. Keep head in good alignment with the trunk.

CURL-DOWNS

Starting position

Sit with *knees bent,* feet flat on ground, fingers touching sides of neck.

Activity

Slowly uncurl (back first, then shoulders) until the lower back touches the ground. Count: "One—two—three—four." Curl up to the starting position and stretch tall. Count: "One—two—three—four."

Do five repetitions the first week; gradually increase the number by fives up to 25.

Stress

1. Keep the back rounded throughout the exercise.
2. Keep knees bent.
3. Exercise is controlled and rhythmical.

CHEST DOWN—CHEST UP

Starting position

Sit with legs extended to the front and hands on hips.

Activity

Bend forward *from the hips,* bringing the chest as close to the knees as possible while keeping the back in easy extension and the head in alignment with the back. Count: "One—two!"

Rock backward and place hands on ground behind hips, raising hips so that weight is supported on hands and heels without arch or sag. Count: "Three—four!"

Repeat entire exercise five times; gradually increase repetitions to 10.

SUSTAINED CHIN-UP

Starting position

Stand facing a tall bar or ring. Grasp the bar with the palms toward the face.

Activity

Pull up until the chin just touches the bar. Hold this position for 10 seconds.

Drop down to rest the arms for a short interval and then repeat.

Gradually increase the length of time of each chin-up.

Alternate activity with a partner

One person lies flat on the ground. The partner stands over him with feet on either side of the rib cage. The partners grasp wrists; the lower person bends his elbows and pulls himself upward until the torso is off the ground. Hold position for 10 seconds before returning to starting position.

Partners exchange assignments.

Stress

1. The standing participant must keep his back straight throughout the exercise.

If necessary, he may bend his knees while grasping wrists with his partner.

2. His partner maintains a straight line from heel to head throughout the exercise.

ENDURANCE RUN (LONG DISTANCE)

Starting position

Start the run slowly; run on the balls of the feet; arms should be relaxed and elbows slightly bent.

Activity

Run around a predetermined course, keeping an even, slow pace. At the beginning of the year or after a vacation period limit the distance of the course to approximately 150 yards. As endurance is developed, increase the distance to 300–400 yards, and/or increase the speed of the run.

Stress

Walking is permissible to "catch the breath"; however, the children should be encouraged to run as much of the distance as possible to develop endurance.

SERIES THREE

JUMPING JACKS (VARIATIONS)

Starting position

See description in Series Two.

Activity

1. Jump up and land in side-stride position, clapping hands over head. Return to starting position. Count: "One—two!" Jump and land in forward-stride position, clapping hands over head. Return to starting position. Count: "Three—four!"

Repeat 10 times, alternating the foot placed forward. Perform the exercise for 30 seconds, increase to 45 seconds, and then to one minute.

2. Jump up and land in side-stride position, clapping hands overhead. Return to starting position. Count: "One—two!" Jump and kick one leg to the front, reaching under that leg to clap the hands. Return to starting position. Count: "Three—four!" Jump and kick the other leg to the front, reaching under that leg to clap the hands. Return to starting position. Count: "Five—six!"

Repeat the entire exercise 10 times.

Stress

Land lightly on the balls of the feet and give with the knees (bounce) with each jump. Keep knees in line with toes; do not let the knees point inward.

FORWARD LUNGE

Starting position

Stand with feet together, arms at sides.

Activity

Take an extra long step forward with one foot, allowing the other foot to turn out slightly. Keep trunk erect. Count: "One!"

Slowly bend the front knee until the back leg almost touches the ground. Count: "Two—three—four!"

Slowly return to a standing position. Count: "Five—six!"

Repeat with opposite foot forward.

Stress

1. Do not bounce down or up; this is slow, sustained movement.
2. Step far enough forward to accomplish a stretch in the hips.
3. Point forward foot straight forward and bend knee directly over foot.

HAND PUSH-PULL

Starting position

Sit Indian style, palms of hands together, fingers pointing upward, elbows out so that the forearms are parallel to the ground.

Activity

Push the hands together as tightly as possible. Count: "One—two—three—four!"

Hook the fingers together and pull the elbows backward as far as possible, keeping head up. Count: "One—two—three—four!"

Repeat the entire exercise 10 times.

Stress

Keep the elbows raised to shoulder level throughout the exercise.

SITTING RELAY

Starting position

Arrange the class in file relay lines, and have the students sit down with knees bent, feet slightly apart. Provide an object for each line.

Activity

First person in line lies down slowly and passes the object back to the next in line, remaining in the lying position. When the last person in line receives the object he lies down, touches the object to the ground behind his head, and then slowly sits up to pass it forward again. As each succeeding person receives the object he sits up to pass it on. Repeat the entire relay four times.

Stress

This is not a relay for speed; the team finishing *last* is the winner. The object must be in constant motion throughout the relay. The movement is done in a slow, controlled manner.

FOOT PASS

Starting position

From the previous exercise, rearrange the relay lines into circles, students sitting with legs extended toward the center of the circle. Provide a ball for each circle.

Activity

Pass the ball from one student to the next by picking it up between the feet and depositing it at the feet of the next. Continue until the ball has made five complete circuits of the circle.

Stress

Use of the feet alone to move the ball. The hands may be placed on the ground behind the hips for support.

ENDURANCE WIND SPRINT

Starting position

See description of Endurance Run in Series Two.

Activity

Begin the run by jogging slowly around the course.

On a whistle signal, run at top speed. On a second signal, slow down to a jog. Continue the run, alternating the jog and sprint. (A suggested ratio would be 30 seconds of jogging to 10 seconds of sprinting.)

Stress

Run lightly on the toes, arms relaxed but slightly bent.

SERIES FOUR

TORTOISE AND HARE BOUNCE

Starting position

See description in Series One.

Activity

Jog slowly in place when "Tortoise" is called. Run rapidly in place when "Hare" is called, lifting the knee high on each step.

When "Tortoise" is called again, bounce on one foot and then the other. Another time, bounce on both feet.

Continue alternating the calls for 2 minutes.

PULL-UPS

Starting position

Stand beneath a horizontal bar that is at least arm's length above the head. Grasp the bar with the palms of the hands toward the face.

Activity

Pull up until the chin is even with the bar and then return to the starting position. Do not allow the feet to touch the ground once the exercise is begun. Repeat five times; gradually increase the number of repetitions.

Stress

Do not involve the legs in this exercise, by kicking or swinging, to add impetus to the arm movement.

CURL-DOWNS WITH TWIST

Starting position

Sit with *knees bent,* feet flat on ground, hands clasped behind head, right shoulder touching left knee.

Activity

Curl down toward lying position until the right shoulder just touches the ground.

Curl up and touch the *left* shoulder to the *right* knee. Curl down and touch the left shoulder to the ground..

Curl up again and touch the *right* shoulder to the *left* knee.

Continue alternating from side to side 10 times; gradually increase the number to 25 repetitions.

Stress

If the right shoulder touches the ground, the *left* shoulder touches the right knee on the curl up. The opposite is true if the left shoulder touches the ground.

FOOT SLAP

Starting position

Sit facing a partner, knees bent and feet flat on the floor.

Activity

Recite the rhyme "Peas, Porridge Hot," clapping with the feet rather than the hands. The clapping pattern is as follows: slap both feet on the ground, slap soles of feet together, slap partner's right foot; slap the ground, slap soles of feet together, slap partner's left foot; slap the ground, slap soles of feet together, slap partner's right and then left foot; slap ground, slap soles together, slap partner's two feet.

Repeat three times.

Stress

Touch the soles of the feet together rather than the ankles.

ARM CIRCLES

Starting position

Sit Indian style, back straight, arms extended to the sides on a level with the shoulders.

Activity

Describe small circles with the arms, revolving them *backward*.

Gradually increase the size of the circles to the greatest possible size, and then reduce the circle to a small movement. Allow one minute for this exercise.

Stress

1. Move the arms *backward* in describing the circles.

2. Keep the back straight and the head directly over the shoulders throughout the exercise.

ENDURANCE UP AND DOWN (THE YO-YO)

Starting position

Lie down on one side, arms folded across the chest.

Activity

In 30 seconds' time, count the number of times each performer can rise to a tall standing position and then return to lying on the side. The count is made each time the lying position is reached. Arms may be used to push off.

Stress

1. Come to a full standing position each time.

2. Move as rapidly as possible through each cycle.

PHYSICAL PERFORMANCE TESTS—GRADES 4–8 (12, 43)

In order to acquaint the children with the tests, each item may be introduced through mass participation. After this experience, the tests may be administered more quickly and scored more accurately when taken by the individual. Test items may be repeated frequently during the time allotted to exercises, stunts and tumbling, and free movement.

Adequate progressions in distances, timing, and number of repetitions should be included in the physical education program before actual testing begins. Such progressions could be incorporated into the daily warm-up activities. Participants should also have appropriate warm-ups before going all-out for a test.

PURPOSES

Measurement of performance is done by children informally as they challenge one another. It is equally important to evaluate by some formal standard, in order to accomplish the following purposes:

—to determine each child's level of performance so that proper programming can be facilitated;

—to provide standards by which each child can measure his own performance and set his own goals for improvement;

—to increase understanding of the components of efficient movement and how they can be measured and improved;

—to understand and practice progression in terms of work load; increasing gradually—distance, time, and number of repetitions.

CURL-DOWNS (FIG. 4.5)

Equipment

Turf or mat.

Starting position

The contestant starts in a sitting position with knees bent, feet flat on the floor, and arms folded in front of chest. For a stronger exercise, fingers may be placed on the sides of the neck.

Activity

The contestant tightens his abdominal muscles and rolls down until his lower back touches the mat. Without resting he returns to the sitting position. This constitutes one Curl-down. The back should be kept in a curled position throughout the activity, and the movement performed in a slow controlled manner.

Rules

Back is kept in a curled position. No resting between Curl-downs. Arms are kept close to the chest (or fingers kept in contact with the neck). The number of repetitions should be increased gradually up to 15 or 20. This activity should not be performed against time.

Safety

Build up to the test by performing curl-downs during exercise period. The value of doing "as many as possible" is questionable, possibly harmful, especially without proper progression.

KNEE PUSH-UPS (FIG. 4.5)

Equipment

Turf or mat.

Starting position

Kneel on turf. Walk forward on hands while bending knees and raising feet. Place hands directly under shoulders, arms straight. Body is *straight from head to knees,* with weight supported on hands and knees.

Activity

Bend the arms and lower the body. Touch the chest, *only* the chest, and quickly push up again until arms are straight. Repeat activity.

Rules

No resting is permitted between push-ups.

For push-up to count, student must:

1. Keep body in straight line from head to knees.
2. Touch the chest and *only* the chest to floor.
3. Push up to a full extension of the arms.

Scoring

Count each correctly performed down-and-up movement.

Safety

During the exercise period, gradually increase the number of knee push-ups performed. Students should not try to do as many as possible the first few times.

Perform Knee Push-ups, then progress to Push-ups.

Variation: Push-up (Fig. 4.5)

Contestant supports body weight on hands and toes. Keep body in straight alignment from head to heels throughout the test.

AGILITY SLIDE STEP

See Basketball Skill Tests, Chapter 8.

SUSTAINED CHIN-UP (RINGS OR HORIZONTAL BAR)

Equipment

Rings or horizontal bar; stop watch optional.

Activity

Grip one ring in both hands, palms of hands toward face. Pull up until chin is level with hands and hold as long as possible. Breathe easily.

With one child at each ring, count off the seconds to determine how long each child can hold, and who can hold for the longest period of time. When counting without a stop watch, call, "One thousand one, one thousand two. . . ."

STANDING BROAD JUMP

Equipment

Turf or mats; measuring tape extended along jumping area or marked distances on mat.

Starting position

The contestant stands with feet several inches apart, with toes just back of the take-off line and pointed straight forward.

Activity

Crouch and swing arms back. Swing arms forward and jump off both feet. Jump as far as possible, landing on both feet. (Fig. 9.9)

In preparation, arms should be swung back and forth with knee bending, but feet must not creep forward over starting line.

Rules

Feet must not touch take-off line. Allow three fair trials. Mark first trial, then take the next jump. Measure the longest jump. Measure from the take-off line to the heel (or the nearest point on the turf touched by any part of the body).

Scoring

Record the distance of the longest jump in feet and inches to the nearest inch.

Practice

Use one single line or two opposite goal lines. Children may take one jump or a given number of jumps to determine who can jump the greatest distance.

PULL-UPS

Equipment

Horizontal bar, approximately 1½ inches in diameter, which should be fixed to prevent rotation. The horizontal bar should permit the contestant to hang so that his arms and legs are fully extended and his feet are a few inches above the floor.

Starting position

Grasp the bar with the palms of hands toward the face.

Activity

Pull body up by the arms until the chin is placed over the horizontal bar. Lower the body to a full hang as in the starting position. Repeat the activity as many times as possible.

Rules

Allow one trial unless the teacher believes that the contestant did not have a fair opportunity.

Pull must not be a snap movement.

Knees must not be raised. Kicking the legs is not permitted.

The body must not swing (partner may stop the swing by extending arm across the front of contestant's thighs).

Scoring

Record the number of correctly executed pull-ups. Score one complete pull-up each time the student places his chin over the horizontal bar.

Practice

Start with Sustained Chin-ups.

Note: Due to the small percentage of potential strength at elementary level and varying body builds, scores may be low.

50-YARD DASH

Equipment

A 50-yard straight running surface; one or two stop watches; starting line and finish line.

Starting position

Contestant stands behind the starting line. He may use either a standing start, in a ready position with one foot forward, or a start from a crouch position. (See "Track and Field Events," Chapter 9.)

The timer takes a position at the finish line in order to judge the exact time at which the contestant crosses the line.

Activity

The starter calls, "On your mark—get set—go!" The word "go" is accompanied by a downward sweep of the starter's arm as a signal to the timer. The contestant runs and crosses the finish line. (*Overrun* the finish line.)

Scoring

Record the lapsed time between the starter's signal and the instant the contestant crosses the finish line. Record the time in seconds to the nearest tenth.

Safety

Precede test with reasonable warm-up.

Practice

Children stand in lines with four to six players across. Run the dash. It may or may not be timed. Stress running as fast as possible across the finish line; do not start to slow up until across the line.

SOFTBALL THROW FOR DISTANCE

Equipment

Three softballs, 12-inch; tape measure; two markers (milk cartons).

Two lines drawn parallel and 6 feet apart mark the starting zone. To facilitate measurement, additional lines may be drawn parallel to the restraining line and 10 feet apart as far down the throwing area as most balls will land. Measure throwing distance from nearest 10-foot line to spot on which ball lands.

Starting position

Contestant grips the ball in his fingers and stands several feet behind the restraining line, but within the starting zone. (Fig. 9.15)

Activity

Moving forward, the contestant throws the ball overhand as far as he can. Contestant may not cross the restraining line. One fielder places a marker on the spot where the ball lands. *Fielder's* partner recovers the ball.

Contestant throws the second ball. Fielder marks the new spot if the throwing distance is greater. Partner recovers second ball. Repeat for third throw.

Measure the longest throw to the nearest foot. Measurement is taken at right angles to restraining line.

Rules

Throw must be overhand. Disqualify throw if contestant steps over restraining line.

Scoring

Record the distance of the longest throw. Record score to the nearest foot.

Safety

Precede throws with reasonable warm-up.

Practice

Players stand in shuttle formation behind opposite goal lines farther apart than any of the players can throw.

Give one ball to each leader behind one goal line. The leader throws as far as he can toward his teammate in opposite line. (The thrower then goes to the end of his *own* line.)

Teammate in opposite line recovers the ball *after one or more bounces,* returns to his own goal line, and throws the ball back to the next player in the opposite line (then goes to the end of his own line). Group players by ability.

SHUTTLE RUN

Equipment

Two blocks of wood, 2 x 2 x 4 inches (beanbags or chalk erasers may be used) and stop watch. Mark two parallel lines 30 feet apart (volleyball court may be appropriate width). Place the blocks of wood behind one of the lines.

Starting position

Contestant stands behind the line opposite the blocks in a ready-to-run position.

Activity

On the signal "On your mark—get set—go!" the contestant runs to the blocks, picks up one, returns, and *places* it be-

hind the starting line. (He does not throw or drop it.) He returns and picks up the second block and *carries* it back *across* the starting line (*overrunning* the starting line with the block in hand).

Rules

Allow two trials. Disqualify any trial in which block is thrown or dropped.

Scoring

Record the better of the two trials in seconds to the nearest tenth.

Practice

Use two goal lines 30 feet apart with one-half of the contestants on each line. Players in one line run across the area, touch the ground *beyond* the line, return to the starting line and touch the ground *beyond* the starting line, go back to the opposite line, touch the ground beyond the line, and return running *across* the starting line.

JOG-RUN (440 YARDS)

Equipment

Stop watch; running area with starting line and finish line.

Starting position

Contestant stands behind starting line in ready-to-run position.

Activity

On the signal "On your mark—get set—go!" the contestant starts jogging the 440 yard distance (walking only if necessary).

Rules

Walking is permitted, but the object is to cover the distance in the shortest time possible.

Scoring

Record the time in minutes and seconds.

Practice

Run (jog) in informal formation as warm-up for activity period. Increase distance gradually.

CHAPTER 5
ACTIVITIES FOR LIMITED INDOOR AREAS

GAMES STRESSING RESPONSE TO VISUAL AND AUDITORY CUES

CLASSROOM GAMES

ACTIVITIES FROM OTHER CHAPTERS

BIBLIOGRAPHY AND AUDIO-VISUAL MATERIALS—SECTION ONE

SELECTED REFERENCES: ACTIVITIES FOR THE HANDICAPPED

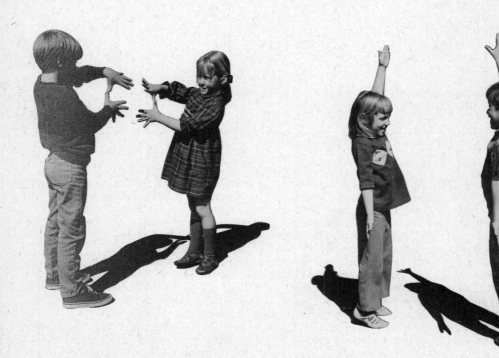

FIG. 5.1. Do As I Do (Mirror Image).

ACTIVITIES FOR LIMITED INDOOR AREAS

SUGGESTED GRADE PLACEMENT CHART	K	1	2	3	4	5	6	7–8
GAMES STRESSING RESPONSE TO VISUAL AND AUDITORY CUES, 131–132								
Do As I Do (Mirror Image)	x	x	x					
Do As I Say	x	x	x	x				
Simon Says		x	x	x	•	•	•	
Ducks Fly		—	x	x	x	x	•	
Do As I Say, Not As I Do			x	x	x	x	x	•
Do As I Do (Right and Left Differentiation)			x	x	x	x	x	•
Do As I Do, but in Opposition				x	x	x	x	•
Do As I Do, but One Beat Later					x	x	x	•
CLASSROOM GAMES, 133–136								
Hide in Sight		—	x	x	•			
Magic Carpet	—	x	x	x	•			
Down and Up Relay		—	x	x	x	x	•	
Posture Tag (King and Queen)			—	x	x	x	•	
Poor Pussycat (Poor Turkey)			—	x	x	x	•	
Seven Up			—	x	x	•		
Finding Uranium			—	x	x	•		
Bicycle Race			—	x	x	•		
Blackboard Relays			—	x	x	x	x	•
Automobile Race				—	x	x	x	
Missing Persons				—	x	x	•	
Spelling Bee				—	—	x	x	x
F.B.I.					—	x	x	•
Paper, Rock, Scissors			x	x	x	x		
Tic Tac Toe (Human)				—		x	x	•
Buzz						x	x	x

— = May introduce activity   x = Depth in instruction   • = May continue activity

There are days during the school year when outdoor activities are not practical, due to inclement weather or disrupted schedules. At these times the teacher must have much ingenuity and patience to keep his restless charges in hand. Some schools are fortunate in having gymnasiums, so that the restrictions are not too great. However, when classrooms must double as activity rooms, there are limits to the amount and type of movement possible. The material selected for this chapter is felt to be entirely suited to limited indoor areas.

The sequence of games at the beginning of the chapter provides a focus for response to visual and auditory cues. Here the child is given a specific visual or auditory stimulus that he must then translate into appropriate movement. This kind of experience is reinforced through many of the classroom games in the subsequent section.

There are certain exercises that lend themselves well to limited space. Chapter 4 presents many that may be accommodated in the classroom. Discussion periods concerning good and poor posture may be held, culminating in tests for good body alignment while standing and walking.

Being indoors, records may provide accompaniment for exercises and for some of the games described at the beginning of this chapter. Children enjoy performing to the rhythm of music, especially when contemporary records that have popular appeal for children—such as the various folk and rock groups—are used.

Creative dance activities and Folk and Square Dances can be managed in the classroom or multipurpose room as well as many of the activities in "Movement Exploration." Upper-grade students might enjoy creating pantomime acts and presenting them to their classmates. Stories being studied during the reading period can be acted out.

Since the expenditure of energy in movement must necessarily be reduced in the classroom or limited area, the amount of the children's *involvement* should be increased, if at all possible. Assigning teams by rows is one way of insuring a greater number of turns per player. Pushing chairs or desks against the walls or combining rows will increase the amount of space available for activity.

Indoor target games may be played safely with yarn balls, deflated utility balls, or large sponges. A variety of plastic equipment may also be used in limited indoor areas. For tag games, a speed limit consisting of a fast walk should be imposed. All sharp objects should be put away, and furniture with sharp corners should be removed from the activity area. If this is not possible, assign a student to stand in front of the object to protect the players. Instruct waiting children to avoid interfering with those moving about.

Start most relays with the last child in the row instead of the first. He completes the activity, then touches the child in the seat in front of him as he passes on his return trip. To control speed and avoid pushing when children must meet in a narrow area, have them stop to shake hands before passing.

PURPOSES

Limited space does not necessarily preclude activity, but it may require some ingenuity and adaptation to conduct such a program in a reduced area. Meaningful activities can be planned that accomplish the following:

—provide challenging activities appropriate to the space available;
—provide opportunities for the enhancement of body awareness, and kinesthetic, visual, and auditory perception;
—increase knowledge and appreciation of movement and its underlying principles through discussion and experimentation;
—demonstrate methods of adapting equipment and activities to limited space;
—develop judgment relative to safe practices in a limited area.

GAMES STRESSING RESPONSE TO VISUAL AND AUDITORY CUES

Activities in this section provide experiences in visual and auditory perception and involve body awareness and kinesthetic perception (knowledge of position in space). The performer is required to attend to a particular stimulus, sometimes screening out extraneous cues, sometimes responding in a delayed fashion or from memory. These are fun activities for children; they are important learning experiences as well, since visual and auditory perception are critical to higher order learning.

DO AS I DO (MIRROR IMAGE; FIG. 5.1)

Formation

Children stand about the room with more than an arm's distance of space around them (own space). A leader stands at the front of the room.

The game

The leader assumes a position or performs an activity. All the children imitate the movement. The leader continues for a given period of time, then chooses someone to take his place. The game is repeated.

Play the game in a large group, in small groups (several leaders) and, finally, with partners. Exchange roles frequently (everyone a leader).

Teaching hints

Children tend to repeat what others have done. Encourage various types of activity such as the following:

1. Balancing and turning: each leader should include one activity that requires adjusting to a changing center of gravity.

2. Bilateral action, moving both hands or both feet together.

3. Unilateral action, moving one arm, one leg.

4. Crossing midline such as: touch left knee with right hand and right knee with left hand.

5. Nonlocomotor movements such as: bend forward, to the right, to the left; crouch, then push off and jump up; reach high—climb a ladder, reach low; push and pull; swing and sway; twist and turn—rotate a leg, trunk, forearm, head.

DO AS I SAY (AUDITORY CUES)

Same as Do As I Do, except that cues are verbal.

Start game with eyes open, then play with followers closing their eyes. (Children will be unable to watch others for cues. Check various children's ability to follow auditory cues and/or to perform the activity.)

SIMON SAYS (AUDITORY CUES)

Same as Do As I Do except that cues are verbal and leader starts by saying, "Simon Says, . . ." If "Simon Says" to do the activity the children respond; if a leader calls the activity without "Simon Says," children should not perform.

After a period of time, ask how many players had no misses; how many had only one miss?

Variations

(Children should not be eliminated. Those who miss need the activity the most.) Score minus points. Each player scores one point against himself each time he misses. Players with *fewest* points win.

May have all children start with 5 points and lose 1 point for each miss. Children with *most* points win.

Play game with followers keeping eyes open then play game with them keeping eyes closed.

DUCKS FLY (AUDITORY CUES)

Same as Do As I Do with the following exceptions: The leader calls out the activity of any animal by saying, for example, "horses run," "dogs bark," or "ducks swim." The players imitate the movement or sound, either in place or around the room. If the leader calls an activity that the animal cannot do by saying "chickens swim" or "ducks bark," the players do not move. See "Simon Says" for various ways of handling misses.

DO AS I SAY, NOT AS I DO (AUDITORY CUES)

Same as Do As I Do except that the leader calls one movement, but performs a different one. Followers must do what the leader *says* to do, not what he actually performs. See "Simon Says" for various ways of handling misses.

DO AS I DO (RIGHT AND LEFT DIFFERENTIATION)

Same as Do As I Do except that followers use same arm or leg in a particular position. If leader places right arm out to the side, followers also place right arms out to the side (appears opposite).

DO AS I DO, BUT IN OPPOSITION (62)

Same as Do As I Do except that the group responds in the opposite way: if leader goes up, group does the same activity but goes down; if leader reaches to his right, the group reaches to the right (opposite direction when facing); if leader moves forcefully, group responds gently.

DO AS I DO, BUT ONE BEAT LATER (62) (VISUAL MEMORY; SEQUENCING)

Same as Do As I Do except that while the leader makes the first movement, the group observes; after the leader makes the second movement, the group assumes the first. Continue with the group performing all the movements, but performing one movement after the leader does it.

For progression try moving two beats later than the leader.

CLASSROOM GAMES

HIDE IN SIGHT

Equipment

One small object that is not duplicated in the room.

Formation

All players but one sit in their seats.

The game

Select one player to "hide" the object somewhere in the room where it can be seen without anything being moved (Hide in Sight). Each remaining player puts an arm on the desk and places his head in the crook of his elbow, with his eyes closed. As soon as the object is hidden, the other players are told to move around the room to look for the object. When a player sees the object, he continues around the room and then returns to his seat without giving away the hiding place. When he returns to his seat, he says, "I spy." After most of the players have seen the object and taken their seats, the first player to say "I spy" gets the object. He becomes the new leader, and the game is repeated.

Teaching hint

The player hiding the object should continue walking around the room after hiding it, to avoid giving away the area in which the object was placed.

MAGIC CARPET

Equipment

Music or a percussion instrument may be substituted for clapping hands.

Formation

A pathway in the classroom around which the players may walk, tiptoe, or skip. Mark four magic carpets (3 feet long) equidistant apart.

The game

While the leader claps his hands in a normal walking tempo, all players walk around the circle. When the leader stops clapping and calls, "Freeze," all players freeze in place. Anyone standing on a magic carpet is eliminated and takes his seat (or sits in center of circle). The procedure is then repeated. After repeating the game a few times, count the number of children remaining on the circle. These are the winners. Have all the players return to the circle and start the game again.

Teaching hints

1. Children should stop immediately when the leader stops clapping and calls, "Freeze." (Instead of calling "Freeze," the leader may finish with a loud clap or heavy beat on a percussion instrument.)

2. Since children are eliminated from the game, start a new one frequently.

3. Vary the accompaniment. Provide slow, normal, and fast tempos as well as even and uneven rhythms.

DOWN AND UP RELAY

Equipment

One beanbag (or chalk eraser) for each team.

Formation

File formation, with one beanbag on the floor in front of each team.

The game

On signal first player in each line picks up the beanbag, reaches overhead, and drops it straight down behind him. Remaining players repeat the action. Last player picks up the beanbag, runs to the front of his line, and drops it back over his head. The team finishing first wins.

POSTURE TAG (KING AND QUEEN)

Equipment

Two chalk erasers.

Formation

Children sit in their seats. Two players, a boy and a girl, are active and each one balances an eraser on his head.

The game

The object of the game is for the boy to tag the girl without the eraser falling off his head. When the girl is tagged, or if either player drops his eraser, each player selects someone to take his place.

Teaching hint

Divide the room in half and have two games going at the same time.

POOR PUSSYCAT (POOR TURKEY)

The game

A player is chosen to be the Pussycat. He stands or sits in front of a player, meowing and making faces, trying to make the player laugh. In the meantime, the player must pat the Pussycat on the shoulder three times and repeat "Poor Pussycat" three times without laughing. If the player laughs, he must sit down. The Pussycat moves on to the next player and tries to get him to laugh.

Teaching hint

Commend children who are able to keep from laughing and choose one of them to be the new Pussycat.

SEVEN UP

Formation

Seven players stand side by side facing the class. All other players are seated at their desks.

The game

The teacher or a student leader says, "Heads down and thumbs up." Each player puts his head down in the crook of his bent elbow and holds up one thumb. The seven players each tag *one* thumb. A player tagged puts his thumb down. The seven players return to the front of the room. The leader then says, "Heads up and seven up." The seven players tagged stand and, in turn, try to guess who tagged them. A player guessing correctly takes his place as one of the seven players and the one who tagged him sits down. Players guessing incorrectly sit down. Repeat the game.

FINDING URANIUM (11)

Equipment

Small pebble or stone.

The game

One child is chosen to be IT and leaves the room. The class agrees on a hiding place for a small pebble, which represents the uranium ore. When IT comes into the room, the other children imitate a Geiger counter by making a ticking noise with their tongues. The speed of the "Geiger counter" is increased as IT gets closer to the uranium. When he is far away, the tick is very slow and barely audible. The point of the game is to develop the hearing sense of IT so that he can find the uranium when the "Geiger counter" reaches its highest speed. When IT finds the uranium, he chooses someone to take his place and the game is repeated.

Teaching hint

For more excitement, divide the class into two teams and time the child who is hunting. The teams participate alternately and the one with the lowest time score at the end of the game period wins.

BICYCLE RACE

Formation

Each child stands between two desks. He places a hand on each desk.

The game

On signal the children imitate riding a bicycle, supporting themselves on their hands. The child who rides the longest time without letting his feet touch the floor is the winner in his row. Have all the winners compete to see who is the class champion.

BLACKBOARD RELAYS

Formation

Assign equal numbers of students to each row. Have all rows equidistant from the blackboard. On signal the *last player* in each row goes to the blackboard, writes, then returns to his seat. As he returns and passes the player in the seat ahead of him, that player goes to the board. Continue the action.

1. Addition Relay. Each player writes a number in a column on the board. Last player totals the column. (Numbers may not be in any prearranged order.)
2. Geometric Relay. First player draws a geometric figure; each player adds one

line to make a picture. Class discusses each picture.

3. Theme Drawing Relay. Each player adds one line or object to make a seasonal picture (Halloween pumpkin, Christmas tree, Easter bunny).

4. Social Studies Relay. Each player adds a letter that spells the name of a President, a state, or a river. Last player may have to add all the final letters.

AUTOMOBILE RACE

Equipment

One object for each row of players.

Formation

File formation, with an equal number of players in each row.

The game

Each row of players chooses the name of an automobile. The last player in each row is given an object to carry. On signal he gets up and walks quickly around his row. When he gets back to his seat, he passes the object to the next player in front of him. The game continues until everyone has had a turn. The row finishing first has won the automobile race.

MISSING PERSONS

Formation

The class is divided into two equal teams. Players sit at their desks with an area dividing the two teams.

The game

A child from each team leaves the room. The teacher, or a student leader, chooses one child from each team to hide out of sight. Players on each team then change seats on their *own* side. As soon as they have mixed themselves up, the leader calls the first two children back in the room, and they attempt to find the missing person from their own team. No one from either team may say a word or make any gesture until one of the two children guesses correctly. Score 1 point for the team with the first correct guess. The team with the greatest number of points at the end of the playing period wins.

SPELLING BEE

Equipment

Alphabet cards (two or more sets). Each set has all letters of the alphabet plus duplicates of the vowels and a few blank cards. Mix up the letters and drop them on the floor in a pile in front of each team (about 5 to 8 feet away).

Formation

Divide the class into as many teams as there are sets of cards. Each team lines up in file formation behind a restraining line.

The game

The teacher, or a student leader, calls out a number indicating the number of letters in his word—say, "Six." Immediately each team counts off down its line until it gets to its sixth player. When the leader calls out, "My word is 'camper,'" the six players run up to their set of cards and hunt for the letters. As each one finds a letter, the players arrange themselves in correct order so that the leader can read the word. The word must be spelled correctly for the team to score. The first team to do so gets a point. As soon as the score has been made, the six players go to the end of their line. Repeat the action with a new word. At the end of the playing period, the team with the most points wins.

Teaching hints

1. The blank cards in the alphabet sets may be used only when a necessary duplicate letter is not already within the set.

2. Do not allow the teams to arrange their piles of letters in any special order.

F.B.I.

Formation

Divide the players into two equal groups. Each player stands in line some distance from and facing a partner in the opposite group.

The game

Each player in group 1 takes a good look at the appearance of his partner in group 2. Group 1 then turns and faces in the opposite direction. Each player in group 2 changes something about his personal appearance (pushes up a sleeve, removes a piece of jewelry, puts belt on backward). Group 1 then faces group 2. Starting at one end of the line, each player in group 1 has one turn to guess what his partner has changed. Score 1 point for each correct guess. Repeat the game, with group 2 guessing. The team with the most points at the end of the playing period wins.

PAPER, ROCK, SCISSORS

Formation

Four teams stand in line formation—two teams to a side, each facing another team. Designate one end as the head of the line for each team.

The game

Each team member selects an item, either rock, paper, or scissors. The leader or teacher then says, "One—two—three—show!" On command, players show either paper (flat hand), rock (doubled fist), or scissors (two fingers extended). Players hold hand positions until scores are counted and tallied on the board.

Scoring

Paper covers rock, rock breaks scissors, and scissors cuts paper. The leader at the head of each team walks down his line scoring a point for each player who is successful against his directly opposite opponent. He then goes to the board and records the total number of points. After doing this, he goes to the end of his line and the game begins again with a new leader. Team with the most points at the end of the playing time wins.

TIC TAC TOE (HUMAN)

Equipment

Nine chairs.

Formation

Place the nine chairs in three rows of three chairs each. Have the boys stand in one line, the girls in another.

The game

The object is to get three girls (or three boys) sitting three in a row, straight or diagonally across the rows of chairs. Girls and boys alternate turns sitting down until there is a winner or until all seats are occupied. Repeat the game, changing the team having the first turn. Score 1 point each time one group wins.

Stress

All players must be absolutely quiet while each player selects a seat.

BUZZ

Formation

The players stand in a semicircle around the classroom.

The game

The teacher or the players decide upon the number that they are going to use. Any time that number, or a multiple of it, comes up, players must substitute the word "buzz." The play starts with the person at the head of the line saying, "One." Assuming that the chosen number is 7, the play continues as follows: Each succeeding player gives the next number in numerical order: 2–3–4–5–6–buzz–8–9. . . . "Buzz" was substituted for 7 because 7 was the chosen number. Fourteen is "buzz," 17 is "one-buzz," and 77 is "buzz-buzz." A player who fails to say "buzz" when he should or says it at the wrong time must sit down. End the game at 100. All children return to the semicircle, and the game is repeated.

Teaching hints

1. Have the eliminated children help listen for errors by others.
2. Game may be played using only multiples of a number, not the number itself.

ACTIVITIES FROM OTHER CHAPTERS

The following types of activities, with minor adaptations, may be used in the classroom very successfully. Incorporating these activities with games from this chapter would provide a varied program even in a limited area.

FIG. 5.2. Bouncing the ball to music is challenging and fun.

FIG. 5.3. Accompaniment for classroom activities. Ready for the downbeat.

FIG. 5.4. Creating rhythmic patterns with Lummi Sticks.

Chapter 1: "Body Awareness"; "Motor Planning" (Follow-the-Leader Formation); "Efficient Movement."

Chapter 2: "Individual Stunts"; "Small Equipment."

Chapter 4: "Body Alignment"; "Exercises for Improving Posture" (to music); Mechanics and Evaluation of Static Posture, including Posture Evaluation Chart; "Developmental Exercises" (to music); "Physical Performance Tests."

Chapter 6: "Manipulating an Object—Exploration and Creativity" (to music, Fig. 5.2); "Station Teaching: Target Activities" (Fig. 6.6).

Chapter 7: Crab Walk Soccer (Fig. 7.14).

Chapter 10: "Creative Activities." With limited space some children may play percussion instruments; exchange roles (Fig. 5.3).

Chapter 11: "Folk Singing Games"; "Folk Dances"; "Folk Dance Steps"; "Square Dances." Create rhythmic patterns using Lummi Sticks, Kalaau or Maori Sticks (Fig. 5.4). See "Dances Around the World," Pacific Islands.

BIBLIOGRAPHY—SECTION ONE

1. American Association of Health, Physical Education and Recreation. *AAHPER Youth Fitness Test Manual,* rev. ed., 1201 Sixteenth Street, N.W., Washington, D.C.: American Association of Health, Physical Education and Recreation, 1965.

2. American Association of Health, Physical Education and Recreation. *How We Do It Game Book,* rev. ed. 1201 Sixteenth Street, N.W., Washington, D.C.: American Association of Health, Physical Education and Recreation, 1964.

3. American Association of Health, Physical Education and Recreation. *Perceptual-Motor Foundations: A Multidisciplinary Concern,* Highlights and major addresses presented at the AAHPER-sponsored Perceptual-Motor Symposium, 1201 Sixteenth Street, N.W., Washington, D.C.: American Association of Health, Physical Education and Recreation, 1969.

4. Ayres, A. Jean. "Activities for Children" (Unpublished manuscript). By permission of Dr. Ayres.

5. Ayres, A. Jean. *Perceptual-Motor Dysfunction in Children,* Monograph, 1539 Shenandoah Ave., Cincinnati, Ohio: The Greater Cincinnati District, Ohio Occupational Therapy Association, 1964.

6. Ayres, A. Jean. "Sensory Integrative Processes and Neuropsychological Learn-

ing Disabilities," Jerome Hellmuth (ed.), *Learning Disorders,* Vol. 3, Seattle, Washington: Special Child Publications, Inc., 1968, pp. 41–58.

7. Barsch, Roy H. *Achieving Perceptual Motor Efficiency; A Space Oriented Approach to Learning,* Seattle Sequin School, Inc., 71 Columbia Street, Seattle, Washington: Special Child Publications, 1967, pp. 73–77.

8. Borten, Helen. *Do You Move As I Do?,* New York: Abelard-Schuman, 1963.

9. Broer, Marion R. *Efficiency of Human Movement,* 2nd ed., Philadelphia: W. B. Saunders Company, 1966, pp. 25–32.

10. *Ibid.,* pp. 46, 47.

11. Bucher, C. A., and E. M. Reade. *Physical Education and Health in the Elementary School,* New York: The Macmillan Company, 1971, p. 375. (See basic rules for "Finding Uranium.")

12. California State Department of Education. *The Physical Performance Test for California,* 721 Capitol Mall, Sacramento, California: Department of Education, 1971.

13. Clark, Carol E., Consultant, Physical Education, Los Angeles County Schools. "An Action Research Program, A Program for Children."

14. Cratty, Bryant J. *Developmental Sequences of Perceptual-Motor Tasks,* Freeport, L.I., New York: Educational Activities, Inc., 1967.

15. Cratty, Bryant J. *Movement, Perception and Thought, The Use of Total Body Movement as a Learning Modality,* Palo Alto, California: Peek Publications, 1969.

16. Davies, Evelyn A. *The Elementary School Child and His Posture Patterns,* New York: Appleton-Century-Crofts, Inc., 1958.

17. Diem, Liselott. *Who Can . . . ,* Frankfort Am Main, Germany: Wilhelm Limpert-Publisher, 1957.

18. Drury, Blanche J. *Posture and Figure Control Through Physical Education,* rev. ed., Palo Alto, California: National Press, 1966.

19. Edwards, Jerry. *Inclement Weather Activities,* New York: Arco Publishing Company, Inc., 1961.

20. Espenschade, Anna S. and Helen M. Eckert. *Motor Development,* Columbus, Ohio: Charles E. Merrill Books, Inc., 1967, p. 115.

21. Evans, Patricia. *Hopscotch,* 308 Clement Street, San Francisco 18, California; The Porpoise Bookshop, 1955.

22. Flint, M. Marilyn, and Bobbie Diehl. "Influence of Abdominal Strength, Back-Extensor Strength, Trunk Strength, Balance Upon Antero-Posterior Alignment of Elementary School Girls," *Research Quarterly* 32:4 (December 1961).

23. Flint, M. Marilyn. "Selecting Exercises," *Journal of Health, Physical Education, and Recreation* 35:2 (February 1964).

24. Getman, G. N., Elmer R. Kane, Marvin R. Halgren, and Gordon W. McKee. *Developing Learning Readiness—A Visual Motor Tactile Skills Program,* San Francisco: Webster Division, McGraw-Hill Book Co., 1968.

25. Hackett, Layne C., and Robert G. Jenson. *A Guide to Movement Exploration,* Palto Alto, California: Peek Publications, 1966.

26. Halsey, Elizabeth, and Lorena Porter. *Physical Education for Children,* rev. ed., New York: Holt, Rinehart and Winston, Inc., 1963, Chapter 10.

27. Hodgkins, Jean. "Reaction Time and Speed of Movement in Males and Females of Various Ages," *The Research Quarterly* 34:342 (October 1963).

28. Horne, Virginia Lee. *Stunts and Tumbling for Girls,* New York: The Ronald Press Company, 1943.

29. Hueser, I., and G. Spohn. *Come On, Join In,* Physical Education Supply Associates, P. O. Box 292, Trumbull, Connecticut, 1963.

30. Hunt, Sarah Ethridge, and Ethel Cain. *Games and Sports the World Around,* 3rd ed., New York: The Ronald Press, 1964.

31. Hunter, Madeline. *Theory into Practice: Retention, Reinforcement, and Motivation,* El Segundo, California: T.I.P. Publications, 1967.

32. International Council on Health, Physical Education, and Recreation. *ICHPER Book of Worldwide Games and Dances,* 1201 Sixteenth St., N.W., Washington, D.C.: NEA Publications-Sales, 1967.

33. Ismail, A. H., and J. J. Gruber. *Motor Aptitude and Intellectual Performance, Integrated Development,* Columbus, Ohio: Charles E. Merrill Books, Inc., 1967, p. 191.

34. Kephart, Newell C. *Learning Disability: An Educational Adventure,* West Lafayette, Indiana: Kappa Delta Pi Press, 1968.

35. Kephart, Newell C. "Perceptual-Motor Aspects of Learning Disabilities," *Exceptional Children* 30:201–206 (December 1964).

36. Kephart, Newell C. *The Slow Learner in the Classroom,* Columbus, Ohio: Charles E. Merrill Books, Inc., 1960, p. 217.

37. Knickerbocker, Barbara M. "A Central Approach to the Development of Spatial and Temporal Concepts," Jerome Hellmuth (ed.), *Learning Disorders,* Vol. 3, Seattle, Washington: Special Child Publications, Inc., 1968, pp. 481–521.

38. Latchaw, Marjorie, and Glen Egstrom. *Human Movement With Concepts Applied to Children's Movement Activities,* Englewood Cliffs, N.J.: Prentice-Hall, Inc., 1969.

39. Lowman, Charles Leroy, and Carl Haven Young. *Postural Fitness; Significance and Variance,* Philadelphia: Lea and Febiger, 1960.

40. Metheny, Eleanor. *Body Dynamics,* New York: McGraw-Hill Book Company, Inc., 1952.

41. Mosston, Muska. *Developmental Movement,* Columbus, Ohio: Charles E. Merrill Books, Inc., 1965.

42. Mosston, Muska. *Teaching Physical Education: From Command to Discovery,* Columbus, Ohio: Charles E. Merrill Books, Inc., 1966.

43. *New York State Physical Fitness Test For Boys and Girls Grades 4–12,* Albany, New York: The University of the State of New York, The State Education Department, 1958.

44. O'Neill, Mary. *Hailstones and Halibut Bones, Adventures in Color,* Garden City, New York: Doubleday and Company, Inc., 1961. Illustrated by Leonard Weisgand.

45. Prentup, Frank B. *Skipping the Rope,* Boulder, Colorado: Pruett Press, Inc., 1963.

46. Provaznik, Marie, and Norma B. Zabka. *Gymnastic Activities With Hand Apparatus for Girls and Boys,* Minneapolis, Minn.: Burgess Publishing Company, 1965.

47. Radler, D. H., with Newell C. Kephart. *Success Through Play,* New York: Harper & Row, Inc. Reprinted with permission of Harper & Row, Publishers. Copyright © 1960. Adapted from pp. 71–75.

48. *Ibid.,* pp. 81–83.

49. Ryser, Otto E. *A Teacher's Manual for Tumbling and Apparatus Stunts,* 5th rev. ed., Dubuque, Iowa: William C. Brown Company, Publishers, 1968.

50. Schlein, Miriam. *Shapes,* New York: William R. Scott, Inc., 1952.

51. Skubic, Vera, and Marian H. Anderson. "The Interrelationship of Perceptual-Motor Achievement to Academic Achievement and Intelligence of Fourth Grade Children," *Journal of Learning Disabilities* 3:413–420 (August 1970).

52. Swanson, William L. "The Scope of Vision Training," *Journal of the California Optometric Association* (June-July 1969), pp. 234–235.

53. Steinhaus, Arthur H. "Your Muscles See More Than Your Eyes," *Journal of Health, Physical Education, Recreation* 37:38–39 (September 1966).

54. Sweeney, Robert T., *Selected Readings in Movement Education,* Reading, Massachusetts: Addison-Wesley Publishing Company, 1970. See "Movement Exploration" and "Movement Education."

55. Valett, Robert E. *The Remediation of Learning Disabilities: A Handbook of Psychoeducational Resource Programs,* Palo Alto, California: Fearon Publishers, 1967.

AUDIO-VISUAL MATERIALS—SECTION ONE

CHARTS

56. F. A. Owen Publishing Co.
Dansville, New York, 14437.
The Human Body 10 charts, 20 x 28 inches—color. "The Body; The Skeleton; The Muscles; The Nerves; The Brain; Circulation; Respiration; Digestion; The Glands; The Senses." By Shaw, Sprague, and Palmer.

FILMS

57. Aims Instructional Media Services, Inc.
Physical Education Basic Skills—in slow motion. "Softball—Tumbling—Soccer" "Football—Basketball—Apparatus." (See Audio-Visual Materials—Section II.)

58. Bradley Wright Films
309 North Duane Avenue, San Gabriel, California, 91775
1. *Anyone Can,* Learning Through Motor Development. "Rope Skills" (other than jumping), "Ball Handling," "The Stegel," "The Trampoline." Consultant: Frank Isola.
". . . techniques for directly *involving* atypical children in motor skills which enhance learning and improve self-image." May be used for all children.
Four films in one: 16mm color/sound—27 minutes. Sale.
2. *Up and Over*—exploring on the Stegel.[1]
Consultants: O. William Blake and Frank Isola.
Demonstrates progressions in the use of the Stegel, a versatile piece of equipment for the following natural activities: balancing, climbing, crawling, hanging, swinging, jumping, and vaulting.
16 mm color, 20 minutes. Sale/preview.

59. Documentary Films
3217 Trout Gulch Road, Aptos, California.
1. *Movement Exploration*
Robert G. Jenson and Layne S. Hackett.
For teachers, kindergarten to grade eight.
Activities include: Locomotor Activities, Ball Handling, Hula Hoops, Spatial Awareness, Jump ropes, Apparatus stations.
16 mm Sound/color, 800 feet—22 minutes. Sale/rental.
2. *Fun With Parachutes*
Consultants: O. William Blake, Evelyn M. Taix, and Frank E. Isola.
". . . a visual presentation of selected parachute activities that will add a

[1]Isola, Frank E. *ABCs of the Stegel, A Guide for a Physical Education Program* (89 Orinda Way, #6, Orinda, California: Educational Consulting Service, 1970).

new exciting dimension to all levels of the Physical Education Program. . . ."
16 mm Sound/color—11 minutes. Sale/rental.

60. Ealing Film—Loops
2225 Massachusetts Ave., Cambridge, Massachusetts, 02140.
The Basis of Movement—6 loops.
"Moving in Many Directions," "Movements: Large and Small," "The Force of
Movement," "The Flow of Movement," "Moving at Different Levels," "Move-
ments: Fast and Slow." Hayes Kruger and Gay Amato.
For children of kindergarten through third grade.
Cartridged Super 8 loops films, color, 3 minutes, 30 seconds each. Sale—
individually or in sets.

61. Filmfair Communications
10946 Ventura Boulevard, Studio City, California, 91604
Elementary Physical Education Skills
Directed by Gabor Nagy; supervised by Craig Cunningham.
"Balance Skills," Basic Movement Skills."
May be shown along with participation in activities in Chapters 1 and 2.
"Apparatus Skills," "Ball Skills."
Four Films: 16 mm color, 9–11 minutes each. Sale/preview individually or in
sets.

62. S-L Productions
5126 Hartwick Street, Los Angeles, California, 90041.
Learning Through Movement
Paul and Ann Barlin
The film provides a wealth of approaches to movement.
Children grades one to six are totally involved.
Appropriate for viewing by all teachers and by children grades 3 to 6.
16 mm b/w—32 minutes. Sale-rental/preview.

63. University of Southern California, School of Performing Arts
Film Distribution, Cinema Division
Los Angeles, California 90007
"Therapeutic Activity for Perceptual Motor Dysfunction."
"Clinical Observation of Dysfunction in Postural and Bilateral Integration."
Dr. A. Jean Ayres, Associate Professor of Education,
University of Southern California.
16 mm Sound b/w. Rental.

64. National Instructional Television Center
Box A, Bloomington, Indiana, 47401.
Ready? Set . . . Go!
"Jumping and Landing," Lesson 7.
"Twisting and Turning," Lesson 14.
"Manipulating a Ball with Specific Body Parts: Feet," Lesson 28.
Films from Television Series, see Television.
16 mm sound. Sale—individually or in sets.

TELEVISION

65. National Instructional Television Center
Box A, Bloomington, Indiana, 47401.
Ready? Set . . . Go!
Consultants: Bette J. Logsdon and Kate R. Barrett.
Production station WHA-TV University of Wisconsin.
Television teacher: Mrs. Jane Young.

Thirty-20 minute student lessons and four teacher in-service lessons.

A sequential elementary physical education series of television lessons with actual instruction for children. Includes teacher in-service tapes, and a teacher's guide that aids in follow-up lessons with the children.

The series focuses on the development of a movement foundation and predominantly utilizes the problem-solving method.

SELECTED REFERENCES: ACTIVITIES FOR THE HANDICAPPED

1. Clark, H. Harrison, and David H. Clarke. *Developmental and Adapted Physical Education*, Englewood Cliffs, New Jersey: Prentice-Hall, Inc., 1963.
2. Buell, Charles E. *Physical Education for Blind Children*, Springfield, Illinois: Charles C. Thomas, Publisher, 1966.
3. Daniels, Arthur S., and Evelyn A. Davies. *Adapted Physical Education*, 2nd ed., New York: Harper & Row, Publishers, 1965.
4. Hunt, Valerie. *Recreation for the Handicapped*, Englewood Cliffs, New Jersey: Prentice-Hall, Inc., 1955.
5. Kelly, Ellen Davis. *Adapted and Corrective Physical Education*, 4th ed., New York: The Ronald Press Company, 1965.
6. Mathews, Donald K. *The Science of Physical Education for Handicapped Children*, New York: Harper & Row, Publishers, 1965.
7. Pomeroy, Janet. *Recreation for the Physically Handicapped*, New York: The Macmillan Company, 1964.
8. Rathbone, Josephine L., and Valerie V. Hunt. *Corrective Physical Education*, Philadelphia: W. B. Saunders & Co., 1965.
9. Wheeler, Ruth H., and Agnes M. Hooley. *Physical Education for the Handicapped*, Philadelphia: Lea and Febiger, 1969.

CHAPTER 6
BALL SKILLS AND ACTIVITIES

MANIPULATING AN OBJECT (EXPLORATION AND CREATIVITY)

BALL SKILLS AND GAMES (EFFICIENT MOVEMENT)

FIG. 6.1. How many different ways can you toss the beanbag with your feet? Catch it!

BALL SKILLS AND ACTIVITIES

SUGGESTED GRADE PLACEMENT CHART[a]

MANIPULATING AN OBJECT (EXPLORATION AND CREATIVITY), 149–160	K	1	2	3	4	5	6	7–8
Identification	x	x	·	·				
Individual Participation	x	x	x	x	x	·		
Partner and Small Group Participation	x	x	x	x	x	·	·	
Station Teaching								
Station Card Examples			x	x	x	x	x	·
Relay Formations (Using an Object)								
Teacher and Class	—	x	x	x	·			
File Relay		x	x	x	x	·	·	·
File Relay with Leader		—	x	x	x	·	·	·
Shuttle Relay		—	x	x	x	x	·	·
Zigzag Relay				x	x	x	x	·
Partner Relay					x	x	x	x

BALL SKILLS AND GAMES (EFFICIENT MOVEMENT), 160–179	K	1	2	3	4	5	6	7–8
Ball Skills (Basic 3's)			x	x	x	x	x	x	x
Rolling and Fielding								
Circle Roll Ball	x	x	x					
Line Roll Ball		x	x	x				
Rolling the Ball (Shuttle Relay)		—	x	x	·			
Boundary Ball		—	x	x	·			
Line Call Ball			—	x	·			
Sink the Ship			—	x	x			
Shoot the Circle				x	x	·		
Bouncing and Catching								
Bounce and Catch (Shuttle Relay)		x	x	x				
Going Through School		x	x	x	·	·		
Chinese Ball (File Relay)		x	x	·				
Dribble the Ball (File Relay)		—	x	x	x	·		
Seven Down			—	x	x	·		
Chinese Handball			—	x	x		·	

A ball is a wonderful tool for children to use. It can be bowled, thrown, batted, or kicked at targets that are stationary, moving, upright, or flat. Sometimes the object is to contact the ball, at other times contact is to be avoided. Whatever the object or name of the game, children are forever eager to accept the challenge presented by, simply, a ball.

Activities in this chapter provide excellent training in hand-eye coordination in a myriad of interesting and exciting ways. The skill patterns may be bilateral, as in making a two-hand underhand toss or in

SUGGESTED GRADE PLACEMENT CHART (Continued)

	K	1	2	3	4	5	6	7–8
Tossing, Throwing Underhand, and Catching								
Teacher and Class	x	x	x	x	x			
Throw and Catch (Shuttle Relay)		x	x	x	x	•		
Race the Ball		x	x	x	x	x	x	•
Complete the Circuit		x	x	x	x	•	•	
Dodge Ball		—	x	x	x	•	•	
The Target		—	x	x	•	•		
Over the Line			—	x	x	•		
Stop Ball			x	x	•			
Throwing Overhand and Catching								
Stride-Jump Ball				—	x	x		
Zigzag Line–Up Ball			x	x	x	•	•	
Guard the Castle			x	x	•			
Shoot the Rapids				—	x	x	•	
Battle Ball				—	x	x	B	B
Striking (Sidearm Pattern)								
Striking with Hands								
Batting Ball To Ground and To Wall		x	x	x	•	•		
Two Squares		x	x	x	•			
Four Squares			—	x	x	x	•	
Tetherball			—	x	x	x	x	•
Handball								
Beginning			x	x	x	•		
Advanced					—	x	x	x
Striking with a Paddle								
Informal Activities				—	—	x	x	x
Paddle Tennis						—	x	x
Striking with a Racket (Official Guide)								
Short-Handled Tennis Racket						—	x	x
Regulation Tennis Racket						—	—	x
Striking with a Bat (Chapter 9)								
Hitting Off a Batting Tee				—	x	x	x	x
Hitting a Pitched Ball					—	x	x	x

— = May introduce activity   x = Depth in instruction   • = May continue activity   B = Boys

[a]Suggested Grade Placement provides a starting point in the selection of material for the beginning teacher. For beginning and experienced teachers, the charts indicate progression and serve as a quick reference to activities.

catching. They may be unilateral as in a one-hand throw. Far-point, near-point focus, as well as tracking, are also involved when throwing and catching. In addition children may be made aware of various textures by using such equipment as yarn, fleece, and plastic balls, along with a wide variety of rubber balls. The equipment may be small, medium, or large.

The development of a solid foundation of skills is pertinent not only to enjoyment of the moment but to adult pastimes as well.

The skills presented herein begin with

the most rudimentary forms of throwing and catching, and progress through activities that require a high degree of skill. The games are listed in order of difficulty to reinforce the learning of basic movement patterns of throwing, catching, and kicking. These very same movement patterns are used in the most sophisticated of team sports—a point that should be emphasized frequently. The principle of the application of force to an object is as applicable to a beanbag as it is to a baseball. Likewise, reduction of the force of an object is as important in kickball as in football.

Particular attention should be given to the description of basic skills. They are based upon sound mechanical principles that insure the proper application of force and the attainment of accuracy and balance. An athlete is often admired for his apparently effortless performance; analysis of his action would demonstrate his mastery of these very same basic skills.

The variety of games incorporate the skills in different ways; sometimes speed is the major factor, at other times distance or accuracy are more important.

Whatever the objective, children will approach the more advanced, more demanding games with greater confidence if the foundation is carefully prepared, and if they have reasonable assurance that they can control a ball, whatever its shape, with consistency.

PURPOSES

The ability to control a ball well is an important skill for most children. Those who are poorly skilled in this area tend to avoid such activity if at all possible. The material presented in this chapter is carefully designed to encourage *all* children to develop skill in controlling an object, and includes the following purposes:

—to present activities requiring the manipulation of objects for basic understanding of object control;
—to integrate body control with object control;
—to increase hand-eye coordination;
—to provide many opportunities for visual

tracking; far-point near-point focus; and a greater awareness of space;
—to describe proper performance of basic skills to increase understanding of the principles involved;
—to present activities that utilize basic ball skills in game situations.

GLOSSARY OF TERMS

Accuracy. Hitting the target. Accurate timing and the application of the proper amount of *force* to hit the target: the ball does not go too high or too low. Controlling the *direction* of the ball: the ball does not go to the left or to the right of the target.

Balance. The control of one's position in relation to his center of gravity in order to move efficiently.

Force. When throwing, the speed or power imparted to the ball.

Opposition. Stepping out with foot opposite throwing hand. If throwing with right hand, step out with left foot; if throwing with left hand, step out with right foot.

EFFICIENT MOVEMENT (USING AN OBJECT)

Note: Review "Efficient Movement," Chapter 1.

ABILITY TO EXERT FORCE IN MOVEMENT

Muscular strength, proper sequential timing of movements, and momentum are embodied in the ability to exert force in movement or obtain distance in a skill such as throwing or kicking.

The need for strength is self-evident. Proper sequential timing of movements involves the ability of the child to bring into play, *at the proper moment,* each element of the skill. "Step *as* you throw" is one example. In the overhand throw proper sequential timing would also include body rotation, movement of the arm, wrist, and fingers, transfer of weight, release of the ball, and the follow-through. (See "Principles of Levers" in next section of text.)

Momentum is developed by increasing the distance through which the body parts move in a preparatory movement: the backswing in the underhand throw; rotation away from the throw and reaching way back in preparation for throwing overhand; or the arm circle when starting to shoot for a basket. This momentum must be maintained throughout the total movement to assure maximum force.

The force of the movement is increased by increasing the speed at which the body part moves; the forward movement of the arm in the overhand throw for distance may be likened to a ballistic movement. Force is also augmented and the speed of the movement increased by including such activities as: transferring the weight from the back to the forward foot and stepping *as* you throw; rotating the body; and extending or flexing the joints forcibly (full extension of the body and throwing arm, snapping the wrist, and flicking the fingers).

The follow-through *after* the object has been released or contacted is an important part of the total action. If the movement is stopped at the point the object is released, the "brakes" have been applied too soon, the speed of the movement has been reduced, and less momentum is imparted to the object. Stopping the forward motion in this manner also causes excess tension and possible injury to the joints. The follow-through should complete the natural arc of the movement, losing momentum gradually.

PRINCIPLES OF LEVERS IN THROWING[1]

Note: This is an excellent lesson to introduce the overhand throw. Begin by discussing different examples of levers such as automobile jacks and crowbars, pointing out that increased leverage exerts more force. Arrange the class in two lines about 6 feet apart. As each lever is added, have one line move backward a few steps.

First position

Hold a beanbag or ball in one hand; immobilize everything except the wrist of that hand by holding the forearm with the opposite hand. Toss the ball to the partner, using only the wrist to supply force. (May use a variety of balls appro-

[1]See Appendix for children's books on mechanical principles.

priate for an overhand throw—from a yarn ball to a football.)

Second position

Immobilize the upper arm against the body, and use only the forearm (elbow and wrist) to supply force in the throw.

Third position

The whole arm (shoulder, elbow, wrist) is used at this time; feet should be together, trunk should not be allowed to twist (rotate).

Fourth Position

Add trunk rotation, so that the throwing motion is initiated at the hips, then shoulder, then elbow, and finally the wrist is snapped as the ball is released. (If children continue to have difficulty in throwing, or if they lack power, have them repeat this step several times until a good sequence of motion is attained. Stress that the elbow leads as the arm starts forward (see Fig. 6.29).

Fifth position

The entire body is used. In the wind-up the trunk rotates away from the throw as the arm is drawn back. Weight is shifted back, and then forward onto the foot opposite the throwing arm in a stepping motion. The trunk rotates in the direction of the throw, followed by the shoulder, elbow, and wrist. Allow the arm to follow through naturally across the body with arm extended and wrist flexed (see Fig. 6.29). Stress that the elbow must be kept high and away from the body as the throw is made.

MANIPULATING AN OBJECT (EXPLORATION AND CREATIVITY)

The possibilities for activity using an object are endless and only a few can be presented here. All kinds of materials should be used such as yarn balls, fleece balls, wadded newspaper balls, beanbags, tennis and sponge rubber balls, scoops, deck tennis rings (quoits), and utility balls. (Figs. 6.2 and 6.3) These materials provide initial experiences in manipulating an object. Each has unique properties that allow

FIG. 6.2. Ball equipment. Front row: *Plastic scoops, ½ gallon, with assorted sizes and weights of balls; yarn balls; plywood paddles; softball base target for bowling. Middle row: Milk carton targets for bowling. Assorted sizes* of playground balls in plastic bag (small mesh); *white side wall target and bean bags; launcher.* Back row: *Box of 15 milk carton markers; rebound net; small rebound net; pateca.*

for concentration on specific skills while eliminating undesirable activity: beanbags do not roll away when learning to throw; yarn, fleece and wadded newspaper balls have little bounce, are easier to catch, and can be used safely indoors; No. 6 and 7 balls are small enough to hold comfortably when learning to toss and catch.

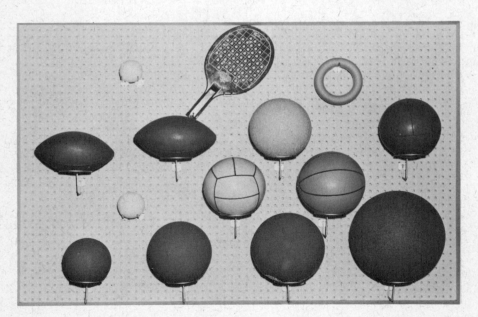

FIG. 6.3. Ball equipment. Bottom row: *utility balls (left to right) No. 7, 8½, 10, 13;* second row: *12-inch softball, volleyball, intermediate basketball;* third row: *No. 6 football, No. 7 football, No. 8 kickball (deluxe utility), soccerball;* top row: *10-inch softball, paddle tennis paddle, deck tennis ring.*

Scoops and old tennis balls may be obtained free. (See Appendix for directions to make yarn balls and scoops, and for lists of equipment.)

IDENTIFICATION

Initial exploration should begin with questions and activities for identification of the various properties of the equipment.

While sitting in a circle, pass the object around the group for the children to see, handle, and feel. Ask for descriptions of the object.

"This object is. . . ." (Soft, light, warm, squashy, heavy, small, bumpy . . . larger than . . . smaller than . . . green, blue, red. . . .)

Ask what they could do with it. "I could roll it, throw it, catch it . . ."

The following activities involving handing and receiving would logically follow such inquiry.

1. *Object Passing.* Sitting (or standing) in a circle, pass objects of various sizes and textures around the circle, such as yarn balls, bean bags, tennis and sponge rubber balls, as well as various sizes of utility balls. Alternate large and small objects, soft and hard objects.

At the end of a given period of time, ask players who passed the objects without dropping them to raise their hands.

Stress *handing* an object, then turning with hands ready for the next object.

2. *Chase the Animal.* Sit (or stand) in a circle. Start one object, such as a yarn ball, around the circle and follow it with a second object, such as a bean bag or utility ball. See if the second object can catch up with the first one before it gets back to the starting point.

May use three objects. Start a beanbag (mouse), followed by a yarn ball (cat), followed by a larger ball (dog).

3. *Hot Potato.* (Fig. 6.4) Stand in a circle; divide the circle in half with an equal number of players in each group.

The teacher starts the game by handing one ball to a member of each team. Players pass the ball quickly around their half of the circle to the last player of the group, the Captain. Captain raises the

ball overhead. (1) See which group can pass the ball without dropping it. (2) See which group can pass it faster.

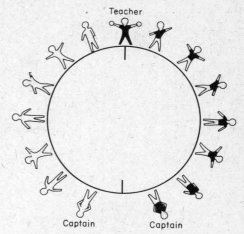

FIG. 6.4. Hot Potato.

After receiving the ball, Captains take the balls to the teacher and step into their own halves of the circle (beside the teacher). Repeat the game.

4. *Overhead Relay* (file formation). Pass the ball overhead to each player until the ball reaches the end of the line. Last player carries the ball to the head of the line. Continue until all children have had a turn. Each player must handle the ball; it cannot be thrown. If it is dropped, the ball is started from the place it was dropped.

   a. See which group can pass the ball with the fewest misses.
   b. See which group can pass it the fastest and finish first.

Variations: Under-Relay. Hand the ball back between legs; roll the ball back (not necessary for each player to touch the ball). Over-Under Relay. First player passes the ball overhead, second player hands ball back between legs. Continue alternating the pattern. (Always start the ball overhead at the head of the line.)

INDIVIDUAL PARTICIPATION

Now the children are ready to explore possibilities for activity as an individual—each with his own object.

FIG. 6.5B. Children showing outcomes of working with a partner: centering a "football" and throwing a forward pass; overhead toss; underhand throw (two groups working together); Keep Away (group with extra player).

FIG. 6.5A. Ball monitor bringing out No. 7 balls.

FIG. 6.5C. Returning equipment.

The No.'s 6 and 7 utility balls are inexpensive and are very versatile. A sack of these balls in combination with beanbags and the other types of balls provides a great deal of activity and allows each child many opportunities to learn by doing, to experiment, and to create. (Figs. 6.5A, B, and C)

1. Toss object up and then catch it; gradually toss or throw it higher. (Rub the padded part of fingers, top segment, to get a "feel" of the part used in catching a ball.)

2. Toss object up, clap hands as many times as possible, and catch it "with your fingers." (See No. 1.)

3. Put object on toes, toss it up, and catch it with hands.

4. Reach back between legs and throw the object overhead, then catch it.

5. Bounce the ball while in a sitting position with feet astride . . . kneeling position . . . standing position . . . kneeling and then sitting again (for better control, for tracking, hand-eye coordination, variations in force, and for balance). Bounce the ball three times in each position; five times.

6. In sitting, kneeling, then standing, kneeling, and sitting positions, bounce the ball in front, on right side, on left side (body rotation, awareness and identification of space on the right and on the left).

7. In standing position, try consecutive bounces. "How many consecutive bounces can you make today?"

One, Two, Three, O'Leary: after every three consecutive bounces, throw one leg over the ball. "Can you throw the other leg over the ball?"

8. Roll the ball out, run out, and field own ball.

9. Toss ball up, catch the ball without making *any* noise. (On the catch, reach up and then *pull* the ball down. Increase the distance through which the ball is carried *down* in order to break the momentum of the ball. Go into a semicrouching position.)

10. Roll, toss, or throw the ball at a target.

11. Keep the object circling around the body from one hand to the other touching the body all the way and then without letting it touch the body.

12. Hold the object in one hand out to the side. Toss it over the head and catch it on the other side with the other hand. Repeat back to the opposite side.

13. Keep the ball bouncing continuously while you go into a sitting position; lying position; and return to standing position.

14. Throw the object overhand as far as possible. Run and get it.

15. Sit down, balance object on toes, and go into a "V" Sit Position. (Legs extended forward-upward, body tilted back slightly. Use arms to assist with stability in balance. See Fig. 4.3.)

16. In what other ways can you toss or throw the object? (Nonpreferred hand, bottom of both feet, with ankle, elbow, back of one hand—other hand.)

17. "How many different ways can you toss the beanbag with your feet?" "Catch it!" (Fig. 6.1)

18. "What other tricks can you do?"

PARTNER AND SMALL GROUP PARTICIPATION (FIG. 6.5B)

Further learning can take place when a child works with another child or a small group of children. Leading questions should continue to be asked to encourage greater understanding of object control in simple games.

ROLLING AND STOPPING
(TWO-HAND UNDERHAND; BILATERAL ACTION)

1. Roll the ball to a partner. Sitting on the floor with legs astride, roll the ball back and forth to a partner. Say, "Push," using both hands evenly and following through. When stopping the ball, say, "Pull," make a pillow of your hands, "give in." Look at the target, partner, when rolling the ball. When receiving it, focus on the ball (far-point) and track it, keep eyes on it *all the way into both hands* (near-point).

2. Roll the ball along a line. "Can you keep the ball on the line all the way to your partner?" (Use both hands evenly.)

3. Roll the ball at a target. Place a marker, block, or beanbag between the partners. Roll the ball and hit the target.

4. Repeat activities in a standing position (Fig. 6.14)

TOSSING AND CATCHING
(TWO-HAND UNDERHAND; BILATERAL ACTION)

1. Toss the object to a partner.
Stress "push" and "pull."
Count the number of catches made without a miss.
"What tricks can you do?" Example: Turn back to partner and toss the object back overhead (awareness of back space).

2. Toss the object *up* and catch, then throw it to partner.

3. Partner throws the object underhand;

receiver claps his hands as many times as possible before catching it.

4. Scoop Ball. (Fig. 6.2) Use gallon Scoops. Hold Scoop with both hands and toss the object to partner. Catch object returned by partner. Practice, then increase the distance of the toss gradually. Use various weights and sizes of objects: plastic, tennis, sponge rubber, fleece, or yarn ball.

ROLLING THE BALL (ONE-HAND UNDERHAND; UNILATERAL ACTION; FIG. 6.15)

1. Roll the ball to a partner. Stand with opposite foot forward from throwing hand. *"Reach back"* then *"roll"* the ball forward and *"point"* to the partner (follow through). "Can you get close to the ground so that the ball will roll smoothly along the ground?" (not bounce)

2. Roll the ball along a line. "Can you keep the ball on the line all the way to your partner?" Gradually increase the distance. (Point the hand along the line.)

3. Roll the ball at a target.

Place a target between the partners.

TOSSING, THROWING
(ONE-HAND UNDERHAND; UNILATERAL ACTION)

1. Toss the ball to a partner. Practice. Count number of catches without a miss.

2. Start close together. Take one step backward with each successful catch.

3. One player tosses the ball while partner makes a target: Makes a circle with both hands; makes a circle at side with one hand; makes a circle at other side; holds a target such as a hoop or white side wall. Others?

4. Throw the ball under one leg. "What other tricks can you do?"

5. Toss the object *up* (one hand), and pull it *down* (two hands). *"Look* the object into your hands when catching."

6. Scoop Ball. Use gallon or half-gallon scoops. Hold the Scoop with one hand and toss the object to a partner. Catch the object returned by partner. Practice. May increase the distance of the toss gradually. Try putting Scoop in *other* hand for tossing and catching. Use various sizes and weights of objects.

7. Toss the object into a Rebound Net.

(See Fig. 6.2.) Toss with one hand, with the other hand. Increase distance gradually.

8. Triangle Catch. Work in 3's spaced equidistant apart. Toss the object clockwise in a triangular pattern. Stress keeping the eyes on the ball. Track the ball from left to right when it is tossed on opposite side of triangle. Practice. Later on, keep head in place and move eyes only as object is tossed.

9. Exchange Dodge Ball. Work in 3's or small group. (Fig. 6.6) Two players stand 12 to 15 feet apart. A third player

FIG. 6.6. Exchange Dodge Ball.

stands between them. The two end players throw a yarn, fleece, or No. 7 ball underhand and attempt to hit the center player, below the waist. If he is hit, he exchanges places with player who hit him. If the ball drops in the center area, the end player on whose side it dropped recovers the ball and returns to place.

Stress standing in a forward stride position with correct foot forward. Later stress stepping *as* you throw.

After playing a short time, ask children who have not had a turn in the center to raise hands. Have them exchange places with center players.

For preliminary practice, throw underhand and catch the ball with a partner in two-line formation; then take one couple out of each three and place in center positions for Exchange Dodge Ball.

THROWING (ONE-HAND OVERHAND;
UNILATERAL ACTION)

1. Beanbag Overhand Throw. (Fig. 6.7)

One beanbag for two players. Players line up on a line in partners, one behind the other.

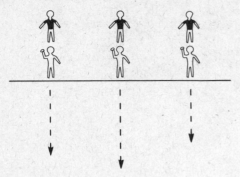

FIG. 6.7. *Beanbag Overhand Throw.*

Give one beanbag to each player in front line. Players throw the beanbag overhand as far as possible. On signal they all run out and stand astride their own beanbag. Recognize good throws; then have each child run back to the line with his beanbag.

After three turns, give the beanbag to partner and exchange places. (Grip beanbag in fingers; do not hold corner of beanbag and "sail" it.)

2. *Keep Away in 3's.* A center player tries to intercept the ball being thrown back and forth by the other two players. If successful, he exchanges places with nearest opponent.

ONE OR MORE SKILL PATTERNS

1. Teacher and Class Formation. The players in the circle or on a line return the ball in the same manner they receive it, such as rolling the ball with one hand, two-hand underhand toss, one-hand overhand throw.

2. Keep two objects going, throwing and catching underhand. Keep a rhythm in throwing and catching.

3. How many different ways can you throw the object to your partner?

4. Use as a basketball. One player makes a circle (basket) with his hands and arms. Partner uses a one-hand push shot, two-hand chest shot, or a two-hand underhand free throw and attempts to make a "basket."

5. Use as a football. (Fig. 6.5B) One player centers the ball back between legs; partner receives ball and throws a "forward pass" to partner running "downfield!"

6. Use strike pattern. One player puts the ball in play by bouncing it, then batting it against the wall. Partner returns the ball to the wall after one bounce. "How many consecutive hits can you and your partner make?"

7. Use as a volleyball. Partners count the number of consecutive times they can bat the ball up into the air. Each player may take two consecutive hits, one to control the ball and one to return it. Stress keeping *palms* of hands pointing *upward*. Bat the ball with finger tips, making no sound. Keep the ball going high on each hit.

8. Sequencing. Select two skills, throw to partner (or in small groups) alternating the skills.

Select three skills and throw in proper sequence. Example: One hand roll, one hand underhand, one hand overhand. Later use a more difficult sequence.

"Who can follow a sequence of four?"

STATION TEACHING (FIG. 6.8)

Note: The preceding material lends itself to Station Teaching. Once the children learn the procedure for Station Teaching the benefits and enjoyment are great. Such organization allows each child to work at his own level of proficiency and provides freedom as well as the opportunity to develop self-discipline. Station Teaching also establishes an effective setting for creativity.

With the children organized in small groups, one leader may be responsible for taking out, setting up, and returning the equipment for one station. The leader may be given a card with the list of equipment and a diagram of the activity on one side, and the directions for the activity on the other side. To allow for progression, insert distances on the cards in pencil. Practice in establishing distances may

FIG. 6.8. Station Teaching: Reinforcing the underhand patterns—all activities are intrinsically motivating.

be a special lesson in Math with the use of yard sticks and measuring tapes. The lesson could also include practice in pacing off given distances.

For additional Stations using ball skills, check the various activities in this chapter, as well as the Skill Tests and Small Group Games in Chapters 7, 8, and 9. Examples of *station cards* follow.

YARN BALLS (BEANBAGS; UTILITY BALLS)

Equipment

One box with Yarn Balls.

Directions

1. What can you do working by your·self?
2. What can you do working with a partner?
3. What can you do working in sets of three?
4. What can you do working in sets of four?

(Class *may* work as individuals one day, with partners the next, in threes or fours another day.)

MILK CARTON TARGET

Equipment

Two milk cartons; one No. 6 Utility Ball

Distance

10 feet (15, 20).

Directions

Can you roll the ball and hit the two targets that are lying down end to end?

Can you hit one target that is lying down?

Can you hit one target that is standing up?

COLOR TARGET

(Use the end of a large cardboard carton and paint three half circles of different colors with numbers 5-3-1 from the center color out. Target may be seasonal such as a purple Easter Bunny made of construction paper with a tail of cotton for the target.)

Equipment

One color target; one yarn ball or No. 6 ball.

Directions

Roll the ball at the target. Take two turns from each distance: 5 feet; 10 feet. Partner returns the ball. Add the numbers hit on each turn.

How many points can you make?

CLOWN TARGET (FIG. 6.8)

Clown may be painted on a large cardboard such as the cover for shipping a 3 x 6-foot folding table. Clown stands in stride position with cardboard cut out for ball to roll through the tunnel. A large mouth cut out provides a target for beanbag toss. The Clown may be made of wood; available commercially.

Equipment

One Clown Target; one ball.

Directions

Take five turns. Score one point for each time the ball goes through the tunnel.

What do you have to remember to have the ball *roll*, not *bounce*, through the tunnel between the legs of the Clown?

BOWLING (FIG. 6.8)

Equipment

One 11 x 8½-inch piece of construction paper, cardboard, or oilcloth (mark paper at center front, and back left and right corners); one No. 6 ball; three milk carton targets.

Directions

Place one milk carton on each mark on the paper. Can you bowl the ball and knock all three targets down at one time? (Make a strike.)

Can you bowl the ball again and knock down the other targets? (Make a spare.)

Where should you aim on the first hit? (Between center and right-hand marker if right handed.)

What causes the ball to go to the left? What causes the ball to go to the right? What causes the ball to bounce?

BOUNCE THE BALL

Equipment

One No. 7 ball for each player (three slalom markers optional).

Directions

How many bounces can you make without missing?

How many bounces with right hand? How many bounces with left hand? How many bounces pushing with one hand then the other hand?

Can you move while you bounce the ball?

Can you bounce the ball and move through a slalom course? Push the ball with right hand when moving to the right, push the ball with left hand when moving to the left.

Can you bounce the ball without looking directly at it? (See it in your peripheral vision.)

Take a partner. Bounce the ball in a given pattern behind his back. Partner listens, then tries to repeat the bounce pattern. Partner listens with eyes open, later with eyes closed. Exchange roles.

Note: Auditory sequencing. See "Rhythmic Patterns," Chapter 10.

BEANBAG TOSS (FIG. 6.8)

Equipment

One box (marked circle or white sidewall of tire, see Fig. 6.2); three beanbags.

Distance

5 feet.

Directions

How many beanbags can you toss into the box? (Liners are good if using circle.)

SCOOP BALL (FIG 6.8)

Equipment

One scoop for each player; one ball for two players (plastic, yarn, fleece or tennis ball).

Directions

Stand close to your partner. Place the ball in your scoop and then toss the ball to your partner. Practice.

Take one small step *backward* each time you catch the ball.

Take one small step *forward* each time you miss the ball.

DECK TENNIS RING

Equipment

One deck tennis ring (quoit); two, three, or four players.

Directions

Toss and catch the ring, underhand toss only. Use opposition when tossing and catching underhand.

Use same foot forward as throwing hand when serving. (See Fig. 8.38. Exception to rule of opposition.)

REBOUND NET

Equipment

One rebound net; one beanbag (or No. 6 or No. 7 ball).

Directions

Throw with one hand, catch with two hands. Stand close to the target. Take one step backward with each successful catch. Take one step forward with each miss. Repeat throwing with other hand. (Check foot position for opposition.)

Measure the distance of your longest throw with a successful catch.

Variation

Use established lines from which to throw. Practice, then count number of successful catches out of *two* trials from each line (three or five trials).

LAUNCHER (FIG. 6.2)

Equipment

One launcher; four beanbags or substitute.

Directions

Place one beanbag at end of the board. Stamp on opposite end of board with sufficient force to send the beanbag into the air. Catch the beanbag. Practice with one beanbag, then two, then three, then four at one time.

The game

Take two turns with one beanbag, two turns with two beanbags, two turns with three, then two turns with four. Count 1 point for each beanbag caught.

SMALL REBOUND NET (HELD IN HANDS, FIG. 6.2)

Equipment

One small rebound net; one beanbag.

Directions

Place beanbag in net and toss the beanbag into the air. Keep eyes on the beanbag as it goes *up* and *down*.

How many times can you toss the beanbag into the air without missing? Score one point for each consecutive toss.

How high can you toss the beanbag?

Questions

How can your eyes help you to make more points?

How can your knees help?

How can your feet help?

OVERHAND THROW

Equipment

One No. 6 or No. 7 ball; wall with a line marked 3 feet from the ground.

Directions

Stand with both feet behind a throwing line 25 feet from the wall. Take one step forward over the line as you throw the ball overhand. Throw the ball so that it hits above the marked line on the wall. Catch the ball after it bounces once. Take five trials.

Score one point for each throw which hits the wall above the line and is caught after one bounce.

Questions

With which foot should you step over the line? Why?

What can you do to add force, more power, to your throw?

What can you do to prevent the ball from bouncing out of your hands when catching?

RELAY FORMATIONS (Using an Object)

Note: The greatest values of the following formations lie in the variety of ways in which the children may participate, and the assurance that each child has an equal opportunity for turns. Unfortunately when children hear the word "relay," they immediately associate it with speed, throwing *skill* to the wind. Speed may be an ultimate goal. However, success in practice and accuracy, rather than speed, commands the major emphasis.

For better control and greater ease in determining winners, have children sit down in original positions to indicate that they have finished.

TEACHER AND CLASS

Players of each group stand on a line side by side. "Teacher" or leader stands facing the group. Starting at the head of the line, the leader throws the ball to each player and each player returns the ball. After all the children have had one turn, the leader tosses the ball to the first player, who becomes the new leader. The previous leader retires to the end of the line. Continue the action until players have returned to original positions. Play for practice and accuracy. Later play for speed. Leader then stands behind a *marked* line to assure throws of equal distance.

Variations

1. Team that has the fewest misses after a given period of time wins.

2. Play literally as Teacher and Class. The teacher stands in front of the group, and passes the ball to each child in an irregular pattern, keeping everyone alert. As the teacher passes the ball, he coaches and gives suggestions to each child as he throws or catches the ball. Sometimes throws are repeated to one child for immediate practice and better performance. The teacher may vary the throws so that the children have to return the ball with the same type of throw they received. (Before tossing the ball to a child, have him rub the padded part of his fingers together to increase awareness for catching with fingers—not palms.)

FILE RELAY (FIG. 3.2)

Players of each team stand in file formation behind starting line and first player holds a ball. First player of each line runs to opposite line with the ball. He turns and throws the ball to the next player and goes to the end of his line. Continue action until players are in their original positions.

FILE RELAY WITH LEADER (FIG. 6.9)

Players of each team stand in file formation behind one line. Leader of each team stands behind opposite line facing own team. (Ball may start with first person in line or with the leader.) If leader starts the ball, he rolls, bounces, or throws the ball underhand to the first player in line. First player in line returns the ball and goes to the end of his line. Continue the action.

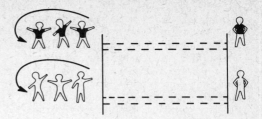

FIG. 6.9. *File Relay with Leader.*

To avoid overthrows into a line of players when using an *overhand* throw, the leader may return the ball to the line by rolling or throwing it underhand. Line players throw overhand. Change leaders after each relay.

SHUTTLE RELAY (FIG. 6.10)

Going to the end of opposite line. Good activity.

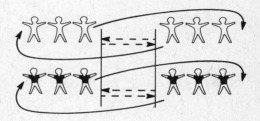

FIG. 6.10. *Shuttle Relay.*

Each team is divided in half. One-half the players stand in file formation behind one line, and face the other half of the same team standing in file formation behind the opposite line.

The first player in one line rolls, bounces, or throws a ball underhand to his teammate at the head of the opposite line and goes to the end of the opposite line. Player receiving the ball returns it and runs to the end of the opposite line. Play continues until each player returns to *original* position (has two turns). When going through the relay two times, each player has *four* turns.

ZIGZAG RELAY (FIG. 6.11)

Divide players of *each team* in half. Half the players stand behind one line facing teammates, who stand behind opposite line. Ball starts at one end and follows a zigzag path down the two lines of players. When the ball reaches the other end of the line, the last player *returns* it to the *same* teammate and starts the ball back in a zigzag path to the head of the line. Play for practice, accuracy and later, for speed.

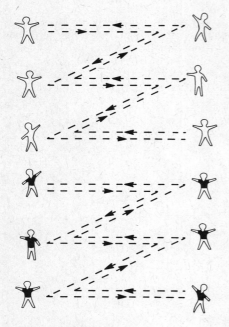

FIG. 6.11. Zigzag Relay.

Stress that the last player in line *returns* the ball to the same player from whom he received it (or the teammate will miss a turn).

PARTNER RELAY (FIG. 7.16)

For dribbling and passing a soccerball or basketball.

Each team stands in a double line, in partners. Partners stand about 2 paces apart. First player dribbles a soccerball a short distance, then passes it to his partner; partner dribbles the ball, then passes it back. Continue action until *ball* crosses opposite line, then return to place using

same pattern. Next couple continues the action.

Stress "leading" partner with pass; do not pass directly to (or behind) him.

Variations with basketball

1. Pass and catch. (Fig. 6.12) Pass and then run to receive the ball. Stress "leading" partner and not traveling (taking steps) with basketball in hand.

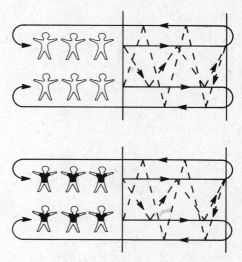

FIG. 6.12. Partner Relay.

2. Dribble the basketball with one hand for a short distance, then pass to partner. Stress "leading" partner with pass, aiming slightly ahead of him. Stress not traveling with basketball in hand.

BALL SKILLS AND GAMES (EFFICIENT MOVEMENT)

BALL SKILLS, BASIC 3's

Note: Post in classroom.

READY POSITION (FIG. 6.13)

1. Place feet shoulder distance apart, one foot slightly ahead of the other.
2. Bend ankles, knees, and hips; take a slight crouch position.
3. Keep body relaxed with weight over balls of feet; bounce on balls of feet.

FIG. 6.13. Ready position: to field a ball, to dodge, or to chase.

FIG. 6.14. Rolling the Ball—two hands. Bend the knees; keep head up.

THROWING (UNDERHAND PATTERN, FIG 6.23; OVERHAND PATTERN, FIG. 6.29)

1. Keep eyes on the target.
2. Step forward with foot away from the throwing hand; step forward *as* you throw.
3. Reach out toward target—follow through naturally.

CATCHING (PULLING MOVEMENT; FIGS. 6.25A AND B)

1. Keep eyes on the ball *all the way to the hands*.
2. *Reach out* with palms of hands toward the ball, fingers easy and pointing up or down, not toward ball.
3. *Pull* it in; *give in* with the ball.

FIELDING A GROUND BALL (FIG. 6.16)

1. With one foot forward, bend knees and keep hips down, head up, and eyes on the ball.
2. *Reach out* with palms of hands facing toward the ball.
3. *Pull* it in.

ROLLING AND FIELDING A GROUND BALL

ROLLING THE BALL—TWO HANDS (UNDERHAND PATTERN; FIG. 6.14)

Place feet in stride position, knees bent, head up—for balance, accuracy.

Holding the ball in both hands, reach back between the legs to increase the range of movement.

Roll the ball and reach, point to target—for accuracy, force.

Roll the ball equally with both hands—for accuracy.

ROLLING THE BALL—ONE HAND (UNDERHAND PATTERN; FIG. 6.15)

Place one foot slightly forward, *knees bent*—for balance and to release ball close to the ground (prevent ball from bouncing).

Hold the ball in front of body.

Keep eyes on the target—for accuracy.

Reach back with the ball. (Flex wrist to hold ball if necessary. See Fig. 6.24.)

Step forward with foot away from throwing hand *as* you roll the ball—for

FIG. 6.15. Rolling the Ball—one hand. Bend the knees; take a long step; keep the ball close to the ground.

opposition, balance, accuracy, force. Release the ball close to the ground.

FIELDING A GROUND BALL (FIG. 6.16)

Take a forward stride position toward oncoming ball.

FIG. 6.16. Fielding a ground ball. Keep eyes on the ball; reach out with palms facing the ball.

Bend knees, keep hips down and head up—for balance, accuracy.

Keep eyes on the ball, *all the way to the hands.*

Keep *palms* of hands facing *forward* toward the ball, with fingers relaxed and pointed *down*—for safety, accuracy.

Pull the ball in; "give" with the ball—to break the force.

Descriptions of various learning experiences follow.

CIRCLE ROLL BALL (FIG. 6.17)

Equipment

Two utility balls, three milk cartons or substitutes (milk cartons may be numbered 1, 2, 3).

FIG. 6.17. Circle Roll Ball.

Formation

Single circle with milk cartons placed in the center of the circle.

The game

Players roll the ball at the milk cartons. If a player is successful in knocking one or more cartons down, he has the privilege of setting them up. He then returns to his place on the circle and sits down. (Players remain standing until successful in hitting a target.)

Teaching hints

1. When presenting the game, explain and at the same time demonstrate. Use one ball until the rules are understood. Later introduce one or two additional balls.

2. After playing Circle Roll Ball in one large group, play Line Roll Ball, a small group game.

LINE ROLL BALL (FIG. 6.18)

Equipment

One ball and one target (milk carton or plastic container) for each group. Place milk carton on side lengthwise.

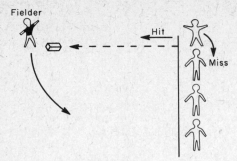

FIG. 6.18. Line Roll Ball.

Formation

Each group stands in line formation behind one line. Place a target 15 to 25 feet away from the line, opposite the first player in each group. A fielder stands behind each target to recover the ball.

The game

First player in each line rolls the ball at his target. If he hits the target, he has the privilege of setting it up again and becoming fielder. Fielder recovers the ball, rolls it to the next player, then goes to the end of the line (in his own group).

If a player misses the target, he steps back and goes to the end of his own line. (Fielder remains behind target.)

Teaching hint

Stress main points in skill, rolling the ball one-hand underhand.

ROLLING THE BALL—SHUTTLE RELAY

Equipment

One ball for each group of six players.

Formation

Shuttle Relay with three players behind each line.

Relay

First player rolls the ball to his teammate in opposite line, then goes to the end of opposite line. Teammate rolls the ball back to next player and then runs to the end of opposite line.

Play continues until all players have *returned to original positions.* Team returning to starting positions first wins.

BOUNDARY BALL (FIG. 6.19)

Equipment

Use one or two utility balls for each game.

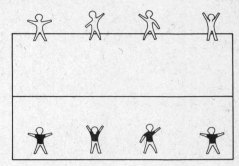

FIG. 6.19. Boundary Ball.

Formation

Rectangle with center line drawn lengthwise. Children line up in two groups with one group on each side of the area. Players stand immediately in front of their own boundary or goal line.

The game

Players try to roll the ball over the opponents' goal line. Ball is thrown from the place it is caught. The ball must bounce at least once before crossing the goal line. Score 1 point each time the ball goes across opponents' line.

Variations

1. Child recovering the ball may run up to the center line with the ball and then roll it.
2. Introduce a second ball.

LINE CALL BALL (FIG. 6.20)

Equipment

One ball for each group.

Formation

Players of each group toe the starting line. Leader stands behind a line 40 to 60 feet away. Draw a fielding line 10 to 15 feet from the line of players.

The game

The leader calls out a player's name *as he rolls the ball toward the group. If that player stops the ball without fumbling it before it crosses the fielding line, he becomes leader. If he does not stop the ball, he returns to place and the leader calls another name.

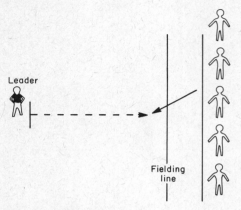

FIG. 6.20. Line Call Ball.

Teaching hints

1. Encourage the leader to roll the ball so that it may be stopped, not too hard or too fast.

2. Encourage player called to move quickly to stop the ball.

3. Be sure the leader calls the name *as* he rolls the ball.

4. Divide the class into small groups and have several games going at one time.

5. Player receiving the ball must stop it without fumbling.

6. Adjust the distance to the fielding line and the distance the ball is rolled to ability of the children.

SINK THE SHIP (FIG. 6.21)

Equipment

Two utility balls, two beanbags, and one milk carton (or substitute) for each group.

Formation

Teams line up on opposite sides of a rectangle. An object (milk carton, bowling pin) is placed in the center as a target. Place a ball (on a beanbag) in front of each line. (See diagram.)

The game

On signal the first player in each line runs to the ball and bowls it at the target. If he knocks over the target, he sets it up, returns the ball, and then goes to the end of his line. If neither player hits the target, each player runs and bowls his *own* ball from the spot where he *recovers* it. Continue until target is hit. Score 1 point for each successful hit. Team with highest score wins.

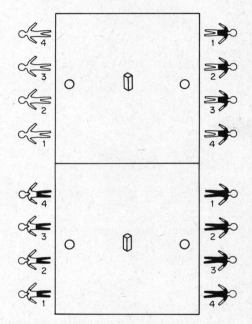

FIG. 6.21. Sink the Ship—formation for two games.

Note: Players standing on goal line stop the ball for all contestants.

Variation

Number the players. Teacher calls a number. Children with the number called roll the ball.

Teaching hint

For more turns have several games. Have children in each game give own starting signal, in unison, "On your mark—get set—go!"

SHOOT THE CIRCLE (FIG. 6.22)

Equipment

One utility ball.

Formation

Two teams of equal number line up facing each other 30 to 60 feet apart. Draw a circle about 3 feet in diameter equidistant between the lines. Adjust the distance and size of circle to the abilities of the players. Number the players start-in from opposite ends of the lines as in the diagram.

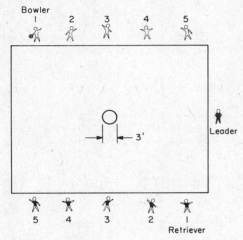

FIG. 6.22. Shoot the Circle.

The game

Player No. 1 of one team attempts to bowl the ball through the circle. As soon as the ball touches the edge of the circle, the teacher or leader claps his hands or blows a whistle to signal a fair roll. On the signal, the bowler runs forward to tag the circle with one or both feet; player No. 1 on the opposite team immediately runs out to retrieve the ball. The bowler attempts to return to his position before his opponent can hit him with the ball. Player retrieving the ball may chase the bowler and then throw, or stand in place and throw to hit below the waist. If the bowler is not hit, he scores a point for his team.

Outs are scored by hitting a bowler below the waist with the ball, or failing to bowl the ball into the circle. When one team makes three outs, the opposite team gains possession of the ball and play continues.

Rotation

After each turn *both* No. 1 players go to the end of the line and all other players move up one position.

BOUNCING THE BALL AND CATCHING OFF A BOUNCE

BOUNCING THE BALL (TWO HANDS; ONE HAND)

Two hands. Hold the ball in the fingers of both hands. Push the ball to the ground with *fingers;* extend wrists and arms—for accuracy, force.

One Hand. Push the ball to the ground with fingers and use good wrist action—for accuracy, force.

Keep eyes on the ball—for greater accuracy.

CATCHING OFF A BOUNCE

Keep eyes on the ball.

Using both hands together, catch ball in fingers for accuracy.

Pull the ball *up; give* with the ball—to break the force.

Descriptions of various learning experiences follow.

BOUNCE AND CATCH (SHUTTLE RELAY)

Equipment

One ball for each group.

Formation

Shuttle Relay.

The game

Same as Rolling the Ball (Shuttle Relay), except that the players bounce the ball to opposite line. (Decrease the distance between lines.) Ball should contact the ground closer to receiver than to player bouncing it.

GOING THROUGH SCHOOL

Equipment

One ball for each circle.

Formation

Divide the class into several circles, one ball for each circle.

The game

On signal the first player bounces the ball to himself once (first grade) and then passes it to the next player. When the first player receives the ball again, he bounces it twice (second grade) and passes it on. Circle that completes the sixth grade first wins.

For greater challenge, go all the way through the twelfth grade.

CHINESE BALL (FILE RELAY)

Equipment

No. 8 or 8½ utility ball, a wall.

Formation

File Relay formation with four to six players on a team.

The game

The first child bounces a ball against the wall. No. 2 runs forward and tries to catch it on the first bounce. If he catches it, he scores a point. No. 2 throws the ball and No. 3 runs to catch it. As each child throws it, the next one tries to catch it. The team that has the most successful catches at the end of a given amount of time wins.

Have each team call out own cumulative score as it is made: "One—two—three . . ."

DRIBBLE THE BALL (FILE RELAY)

Equipment

One ball for each group.

Formation

File Relay formation.

Relay

Dribble (consecutive bounces) the ball up and across the opposite line. Throw the ball back to next player and go to the end of the line. Group finishing first wins.

Teaching hint

Stress pushing the ball with fingers.

SEVEN DOWN

Equipment

One utility or volleyball for each station, a total of seven balls.

Teaching the game

The object of this game is to see who can progress the farthest, performing the most difficult stunt, by the time the play period has ended.

Provide seven teaching stations along a wall, with one ball for each station. The children start at station No. 7 and attempt to perform the skill taught there. If unsuccessful, they go to the end of the line and await their turn to try again. If successful, they move to station No. 6, where the teacher instructs the first child on that skill. From then on, the child successful in completing that activity must teach it to the next child in line before he can go on to the next station. This procedure is followed at all stations. In this way the teacher instructs only once at each station and devotes his time to helping children having difficulty with any particular skill.

After this initial instructional period, the game can be used as an independent activity during instruction in another area. Two to six children play the game at one station, using one ball.

Stations

No. 7. Toss the ball against the wall and catch it before it bounces—seven times.

No. 6. Toss the ball against the wall, let it bounce once, catch it—six times.

No. 5. Five continuous bounces, pushing the ball with the fingers each time, and catching it after the fifth bounce.

No. 4. Bounce the ball, bat it with an open hand against the wall, catch it before it again touches the ground—four times.

No. 3. Bat the ball against the wall three times in succession without catching or holding the ball between hits. (Fingers should point up, palms facing the wall.)

No. 2. Toss the ball under one leg, let it hit the wall, bounce once, and then catch it. Repeat tossing the ball under the other leg.

No. 1. Toss the ball against the wall, turn around, catch the ball after it has bounced once.

Variations

As the children's skill increases, they will be able to progress to No. 1 rather quickly and will want additional restrictions to add to the difficulty of each station.

Examples: Clap once with each turn; clap twice with each turn; use nondominant hand.

Have children develop own progression. Have them write up and number each activity on a separate card for others to perform.

CHINESE HANDBALL

Equipment

One No. 7 or 8½ utility ball, or No. 8 kickball; a wall or handball backboard.

Formation

Four players stand in file formation facing a wall. Other players stand behind waiting line.

The game

First player throws the ball to the ground causing it to bounce against the wall and rebound into the court. The second player catches the ball *after one bounce*. If he catches the ball, play continues and action is repeated. If he misses the ball, he goes to the end of the waiting line and first player in waiting line enters the game.

Misses

Player goes to waiting line.
1. Failure to bounce the ball against the wall after it hits the ground.
2. Failure to catch the ball after one bounce on the rebound from the wall.

Teachings hints

Stress that no "baby hits" are allowed, which purposely cause the ball to hit near the base of the wall and roll back.

Variation

1. First player throws the ball directly to the wall with overhand throw. Second player recovers the ball after first bounce.

2. O-U-T. Two to six players, without extra players on waiting line. On a first miss a player receives an "O"; on his second miss, he receives a "U"; on his third miss, he receives a "T." Player (or players) with the fewest misses when one player is "out" wins the game. Start a new game.

3. Draw a line on the ground 6 feet from the wall and parallel to it. It is a miss if the ball does not rebound across the 6-foot line.

TOSSING AND THROWING (Underhand) AND CATCHING A FLY BALL

TOSSING UNDERHAND (TWO HAND)

Stand with feet apart and eyes on the target—for balance, accuracy.

Hold the ball in two hands against the body, knees bent—for balance.

Toss the ball and *reach*, point to the target—for accuracy.

Extend knees *as* you toss—for force.

THROWING UNDERHAND (ONE HAND, FIG. 6.23; PROGRESSION, FIGS. 6.24A and 6.24B)

Place one foot slightly forward, knees bent (lower center of gravity)—for balance.

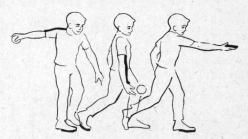

FIG. 6.23. One-Hand Underhand Throw. Use opposition; follow through with palm up.

Hold ball in front of body.

Keep eyes on the target—for accuracy.

Reach back with the ball. (Flex wrist to hold ball if necessary. See Fig. 6.24A)

Step forward with foot away from throwing hand—for balance, accuracy, force, opposition.

Step *as* you throw.

Reach, *point to target*—for greater accuracy, force. (There is a tendency to reach *across* the body.)

FIG. 6.24A. Progression:
second grader with No. 7 ball.

FIG. 6.24B. Fourth grader
with 12-inch softball.

FIG. 6.24C. Sixth grader
with No. 6 football.

FIG. 6.24D. Eighth grader
with 10-inch softball.

FIG. 6.25A.
Catching a Fly Ball:
Keep your eyes
on it—reach!

FIG. 6.25B.
As it touches your
fingers—pull!

Keep palm *up.* (There is a tendency to rotate forearm inward which decreases accuracy.)

CATCHING A FLY BALL (FIGS. 6.25A AND B)

Stand with one foot forward, in direction of oncoming ball—for balance, and for longer distance through which to expend the force of the ball.

Keep your eyes *on the ball all the way to the hands* ("*Look* the ball into the hands.")—for accuracy.

Reach out, fingers easy—in order to provide a longer distance to expend the force of the ball.

Palms of hands face the ball, fingers pointing up or down, not toward the ball —to catch the ball and to avoid injuring fingers.

Pull it in, continuing the flight of the ball. "*Give in*" with it as the ball touches the fingers—to decrease the speed of the ball, and to be able to hold onto it, not have it bounce out of hand. (Do not make a wall of your hands, make a pillow. Ball bounces off a wall; a pillow "gives" and breaks the force.)

Catch ball in padded fingers rather than solid palm of hand to prevent ball from bouncing out of hand.

Use both hands together—bilateral action. Failure to coordinate the two hands may cause player to drop the ball.

Descriptions of various learning experiences follow.

TEACHER AND CLASS

Formation

Divide class into several small groups, one ball for each group. One player becomes teacher and stands in front of his group, 5 to 20 feet away.

The game

Teacher passes the ball to each player in turn. He then goes to the end of the line while a new teacher steps out from the head of the line.

Teaching hints

Vary the type of pass used; encourage stepping out with opposite foot. Increase distance between teacher and class gradually.

THROWING AND CATCHING (SHUTTLE RELAY)

Equipment

One ball or beanbag for each group of six players.

Formation

Shuttle Relay formation with three players behind opposite lines.

Relay

First player tosses or throws the ball underhand to his teammate in opposite line and runs to the end of the opposite line. Teammate tosses the ball back to next player and runs to the end of opposite line. Play continues until all players have *returned to original positions*. Team returning to starting positions first wins.

RACE THE BALL (FIG. 6.26)

Equipment

A volleyball or No. 8½ utility ball.

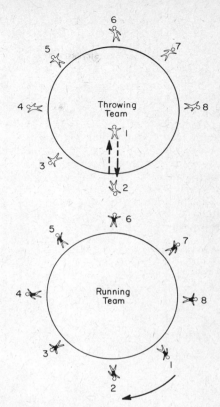

FIG. 6.26. Race the Ball.

Formation

Two (or multiples of two) circles with an equal number of players on each circle. Each circle must be the same size.

Number the players in both circles. It is important that each child remembers either his number or place in line.

The game

At the beginning of the game, one circle represents the throwing team and the other circle the running team. On signal, No. 1 of the throwing team goes to the center of his circle and starts passing the ball around (e.g., to No. 2, who tosses it back to him, then to No. 3, who tosses it back to him). As soon as he passes the ball completely around the circle, everyone on his team calls, "Stop!" While the throwing team is passing the ball, No. 1 of the running team runs around the outside of his circle and tags No. 2, who runs around. This continues until the throwing team yells "Stop!" The running team counts up the number of runs completed before "stop" was called.

It is then time to exchange activities. The running team throws and the throwing team runs. The running team must remember who was the last player to run so that the *next* child in line starts the running when it is again their turn. When they are the throwing team, No. 1 is in the center the first time, No. 2 is in the center the second time.

Team with the highest score after each team has an equal number of turns to throw the ball wins.

COMPLETE THE CIRCUIT (FIG. 6.27)

Equipment

One ball.

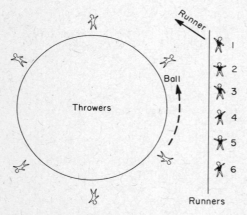

FIG. 6.27. Complete the Circuit.

Formation

One team stands outside a large marked circle; the other team stands in a line at least 2 paces from the circle.

The game

At the signal the ball is passed from player to player around the circle; it must make as many round trips as there are players in the opponents' line. At the same time the first player in the line runs around the circle, touches off the second runner,

runs to the end of the line, and so on until all have run.

A player who fumbles the ball must recover it and return to position before passing it on to next player.

Scoring

The team that finishes first wins.

Teams exchange positions and repeat.

Teaching hints

1. Vary the type of pass for greater variety in skill.

2. Increase the distance between the circle and line of players to allow for more running.

DODGE BALL

Equipment

Two No. 8½ utility balls, a large marked circle.

Formation

Form a circle, then count off by twos with No. 1's going into the center of circle *as they count.* (Children should not change places in the circle while counting.)

The game

Circle players throw the ball, *underhand throw* only, and try to hit center players below the waist. Center players step out to the circle when legally hit with the ball.

Play for one or two minutes with one ball, then introduce the second ball. Play for one or two minutes with two balls, declare as winners those left inside the circle, and exchange sides. When exchanging sides, have center players stoop down while players on the circle space themselves evenly.

Repeat the same game procedure with the second group.

Safety

Use an underhand throw. (If a child repeatedly uses an overhand throw, ask him to observe. Have him rejoin the group later.)

Use only the lightweight rubber utility balls.

Player throwing the ball should step into the circle with *one* foot. (Step *as you* throw.) If thrower has both feet inside the circle, throw does not count.

If the ball goes away from the circle, only *one* player (the closest) runs to recover the ball.

Avoid dangerous hitting: throwing too hard, hitting too high, or knocking the feet out from under a player.

THE TARGET

Equipment

One or two No. 8½ utility balls.

Formation

Ten to 12 players in a single circle facing the center. One player, the target, stands in the center, inside a smaller circle about 3 feet in diameter.

The game

The players try to hit the center player with the utility ball. If the player in the center is hit below the waist or gets both his feet outside the smaller circle, the thrower becomes the target. The use of two balls makes this game more interesting.

OVER THE LINE

Equipment

No. 7 or 8½ utility ball.

Formation

Two teams scattered in their own halves of a rectangular playing field with a center dividing line. Number the children on each team.

The game

The object of the game is to throw the ball high into the air, causing it to land in the opposing team's area. If the other team catches the ball, they get a point. If they drop it or it bounces before being touched, the throwing side gets a point. Regardless of the one who catches the ball, No. 1 of the receiving team throws the ball high in the air back to the other team. If a thrown ball lands outside the playing field, the receiving team gets a point. Play until all players have had a turn to throw the ball at least once.

(Players on each team throw the ball in numerical order.)

Teams call cumulative score as each point is made.

STOP BALL (FIG. 6.28)

Equipment

One utility ball, volleyball, or kickball for each group.

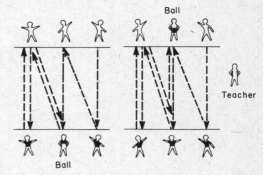

FIG. 6.28. Stop Ball.

Formation

The children are divided into teams of five or six players. Each team stands in a line facing an opposing team. The distance between the two teams depends upon the skill of the players.

The game

The teacher, or a student leader, stands with his back to the lines of teams and calls out, "Go." On signal the team with the ball throws it across to the other team, who in turn throws it back again. They continue throwing the ball back and forth down the line and back again until the teacher calls, "Stop." The team caught with the ball loses and the opposing team gets a point. Continue until the end of the playing period or until one team has reached a predetermined number of points.

Teaching hints

1. Vary the types of throws (overhand, underhand, chest pass, bounce pass) to add interest to the game and provide more skill development.

2. Divide the class into four equal teams and play the game twice. Winners play winners and losers play losers.

THROWING (OVERHAND) AND CATCHING A FLY BALL

THROWING (ONE-HAND OVERHAND; FIG. 6.29)

Note: Introduce this skill through "Principles of Levers."

FIG. 6.29. One-Hand Overhand Throw. *Reach back; step as you throw. Note the wrist action in the follow-through.*

Stand in forward stride, step position, with left foot forward (if right handed)—which allows body to rotate, and for opposition.

Keep eyes on the target—for accuracy.

Rotate the body away from the throw and pull the right hand way back (left shoulder points to the target)—for force (wide range of movement).

Start rotating the body into the throw. Step *as* you throw (transfer weight to forward foot)—for force, balance, accuracy.

Bring arm forward forcibly, with elbow leading. Continue through the arc and snap forearm and wrist forward—for force, sequential use of levers, ballistic movement.

Follow through to the target; complete the natural arc of the throw, finishing with wrist flexed—for additional force (wide range of movement and efficient use of levers), accuracy, balance.

CATCHING A FLY BALL

See preceding section.

Descriptions of various learning experiences follow.

STRIDE-JUMP BALL

Equipment

No. 7 or 8½ utility ball; a wall or handball backboard.

Formation

Three players, numbered 1 to 3, stand in file formation behind a line 6 feet from the wall and parallel to it. These players keep the same order until one of them misses. Remaining players stand behind the waiting line.

The game

First player throws the ball against the wall with an overhand throw. (Ball must rebound across 6-foot line.) Second player stride-jumps over the ball as the ball bounces. Third player catches the ball after one or two bounces.

Repeat the action with player No. 3 as thrower, No. 1 as jumper, and No. 2 as catcher; repeat the game with player No. 2 as thrower, No. 3 as jumper, and No. 1 as catcher. Continue play. (*Note:* The three players rotate the action in order, 1-2-3.)

Misses

Player goes to waiting line.

1. Failure to throw the ball against the wall and have it rebound (not bounce before crossing) over the 6-foot line.

2. Touching the ball or failing to stride-jump the ball as it bounces.

3. Failure to catch the ball after one or two bounces.

Variation

With three players, play O-U-T as described under Chinese Handball.

ZIGZAG LINE-UP BALL (FIG. 6.30)

Equipment

One ball for each group (No. 8½ utility ball, No. 8 kickball or football).

Formation

Two or more teams with half the players of each team behind one line, facing *team-mates* behind opposite line. Each player toes the line.

The game

Players in each group pass the ball back and forth in a zigzag pattern down the line and back, within their own group.

On the whistle the player with the ball holds the ball and the other players in his group line up behind him. As the players line up, the ball is handed overhead from player to player. The last player in line runs up to the head of his line and calls, "Stop!" The first group to call, "Stop," wins.

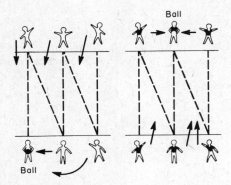

FIG. 6.30. Zigzag Line-up Ball.

Each player returns to his position and the game is repeated. Score 1 point each time a team finishes first.

Teaching hints

Each player must hand the ball when passing it overhead; it cannot be thrown. If ball is dropped, it is started again at the point it was dropped.

Variations

1. Vary the types of passes used between the two lines: underhand, overhand, chest pass, bounce pass, rolling the ball, forward pass with football.

2. Vary the passing down the single line after whistle is blown: overhead, under, over and under; stand side to side to hand and receive.

GUARD THE CASTLE

Equipment

One or two No. 8½ utility balls, one milk carton or substitute.

Formation

Ten to 12 players stand in a single circle. One player stands in the center, guarding the castle (a milk carton).

The game

A player in the circle throws a ball, trying to knock over the castle. The player in the center guards the castle with his hands, feet, and body so that the castle will not be hit. When the castle is knocked over, the player who threw the ball becomes the guard.

After the game is learned, the use of two balls increases the interest and excitement.

SHOOT THE RAPIDS (FIG. 6.31)

Equipment

No. 7 utility balls. If possible, provide one ball for every fourth child.

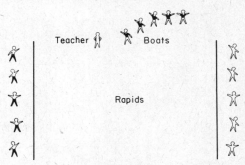

FIG. 6.31. Shoot the Rapids.

Formation

Divide the class into three teams. Two teams stand on the side lines and the other team lines up behind the teacher on the end line. The children on the side lines hold "rocks" (No. 7 balls) that they throw across the "rapids." The teacher is the "dam" that holds the "boats" from going down the "rapids" until everyone is ready.

The game

When the teacher drops his arm, the team behind him attempts to "shoot the rapids" without getting "sunk." If they are touched below the waist by a ball, they retire behind one of the teams. (They recover any balls that get by the players.) If the runners do not get touched, they circle around the teams and "shoot the rapids" again. As the children become tired, the teacher raises his arm to stop them for a rest. Another team then takes its turn, and the game starts over, with the previous runners taking places on one side line. Then the third team takes its turn.

If time permits, the winners from each team can compete while all other players on the side lines throw the balls. Another way of determining a winner is to set a given number of times to "shoot the rapids." The team with the most players left wins.

Safety

1. Use No. 7 utility balls.
2. Stress hitting below the waist.

BATTLE BALL[2] (FIG. 6.32)

Equipment

One utility ball (ball must be *lightweight*). A second ball can be added when the children understand the game.

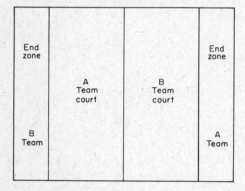

FIG. 6.32. Battle Ball.

Formation

A basketball court or similar area. Divide the main area by a center line and mark off a 3-foot end zone at each end of the court. Two teams of equal number stand in their own halves of the main court area. (At the beginning of the game there is no one in either end zone.)

The game

The object of the game is to put the entire opposing team in their own end zone. This is done by throwing the ball at a member of the opposite team. If he is hit by the ball below the waist, he must go into his own end zone (at *opposite end* of court). However, if he catches the ball before it touches the ground, he is not out and has the added privilege of calling the name of an opposing player, who must then go into his end zone. Once in the end zone, players continue to participate by throwing the balls at their opponents in a cross fire. If a ball hits the ground before touching any player, it is considered a "dead" ball and can be picked up and thrown at opponent.

Teaching hints

This game is best played as a boys' or girls' game; however, if the skill level is comparable it may be played coeducationally. Encourage fast, accurate throws. Any player attempting to hit an opponent above the waist should be sent into his end zone. Use a *lightweight* ball, a utility ball.

STRIKING (Sidearm Pattern; Figs. 6.33A and B)

See Figs. 9.1 and 9.16 for using a bat.

Stand in a ready position with *side* in direction the ball is to go—for balance, accuracy.

Reach *way* back parallel to the ground, rotating the body away from the ball.

Start rotating the body toward the ball and contact it in line with front foot (Fig. 6.33B)—for force, accuracy. Arm should be in an extended (reach) position rather than flexed (tight) position as ball is contacted.

Keep eyes on the ball *all the way to contact* with hand, paddle, bat, or racket.

Follow through forward *through* the ball, and transfer weight to forward foot—for force, accuracy, balance.

STRIKING WITH HANDS (LEARNING EXPERIENCES)

Note: Activities are provided to give a variety of experiences in contacting the ball with hand, and for keeping the eyes on the ball *all the way to contact.*

BATTING BALL TO GROUND—TO WALL

Equipment

Sponge-rubber ball, No. 6, 7, or 8½ utility ball, or volleyball.

[2]Contributed by Carol Clark, Consultant of Physical Education, Los Angeles County Schools, Los Angeles, California.

FIG. 6.33A. Paddle Tennis serve

FIG. 6.33B. Paddle Tennis return.

The game

Practice making consecutive bounces to the ground. How many times can you bounce the ball without missing?

Practice making consecutive bounces to the wall. Return the ball to the wall after one bounce. How many times can you hit the ball against the wall without missing?

Work with a partner hitting the ball alternately.

TWO SQUARES (FIG. 6.34)

Equipment

One volleyball or utility ball, for four to eight children.

Formation

Divide the class into even numbers of teams with two to four players on each team. Each team lines up in file formation behind its end line, as shown in the diagram. The first child stands just inside that end line facing an opponent.

The game

Object of the game is to see if team members can continue playing longer than the members of the other team. The game starts with the first player on one team tossing the ball over the line causing it to bounce within the opponents' square. The opponent must catch the ball after the first bounce or he is out. Play continues

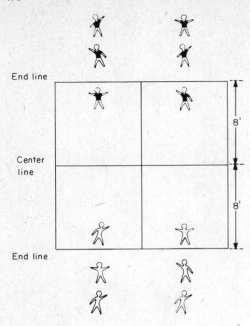

End line

Center line

End line

8'

8'

(Two games)

FIG. 6.34. Two Squares.

with a player going to the end of his line when he makes an out; all others in the line move up one place.

Outs

1. Not catching a ball after first bounce.
2. Catching the ball before it bounces.
3. Causing the ball to hit the ground before it goes over the line.
4. Causing the ball to touch a line.
5. Ball bouncing outside the square.

If player is able to stay in his square (is not put out) until all members of the other team have played against him, he automatically rotates to the end of his line.

Variation

Play the rules of Four Squares, but with two players.

FOUR SQUARES (FIG. 6.35)

Equipment

Utility ball, volleyball, or No. 8 kickball.

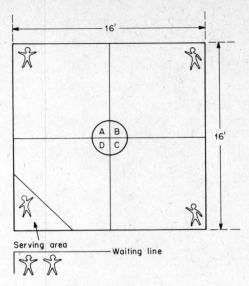

Serving area   Waiting line

FIG. 6.35. Four Squares.

Formation

One player stands in each of the four 8 x 8-foot squares, with the waiting group standing behind waiting line near square D.

The game

Player D stands behind the serving line and serves the ball by batting it off a bounce into any one of the other three squares. The player in the square into which the ball was served must bat the ball into another square after the ball has bounced once. Play continues until a foul is made. A player committing a foul goes to the end of the waiting line, and players below the one making the foul move up one square. (If only four persons are playing the person making a foul moves to square D and everyone below him moves one square toward A.) The object of the game is to advance to square A and stay there as long as possible.

Fouls

1. Not returning the ball to another square after one bounce.
2. Causing the ball to go out of bounds.
3. Causing the ball to touch a line.
4. Getting hit with the ball or contacting

it with any part of the body except the hands and forearms.

5. Holding or throwing the ball.

6. Hitting the ball with a closed fist.

7. Hitting the ball into the center circle.

TETHERBALL (FIG. 6.36)

Equipment

Tetherball, rope 7½ feet long (unless tied to a permanent chain at the top of the pole), and a pole 10 feet long with a painted line 5 feet from the ground.

Playing area

Twenty-foot circle divided in half.

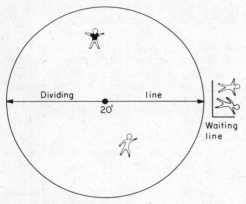

FIG. 6.36. Tetherball.

The game

One player stands in each half of the circle. The game is started by a third child straddling the dividing line and holding the ball so that the rope is taut. He releases the ball, hitting it against the pole. The ball will deflect into one of the two playing areas. The child in that area is allowed the choice of either the "side and way" (direction) or "serve." The other player is allowed the choice the first child rejects.

The object of the game is to wind the rope up above the 5-foot mark until the ball touches the pole. Once the ball is in play it must be batted, not caught, held, or thrown. Any time a foul occurs, the other player gains possession of the ball and puts it in play by batting it completely around the pole.

If there are only two children playing, the loser of the game serves first in the next game. If there are children waiting in line, the new child gets to choose "side and way" or "serve."

Fouls

1. Touching the ball with any part of the body other than the hand or forearm.

2. Holding, catching, or throwing the ball.

3. Stepping on or over the dividing line.

4. Touching the rope or pole during play.

5. Playing the ball outside the court.

6. Hitting the ball more than once before it goes into the opponents' territory.

Rotation

With players on a waiting line, the winner of a game plays the next player in the line (one bonus game for the winner). If the same player wins again, both players retire to the end of the waiting line.

HANDBALL (FIG. 6.37)

Equipment

Sponge-rubber ball, volleyball, or utility ball; handball court.

Formation

The active players stand behind the service line; remaining players stand on one side boundary line. (See diagram.)

The game

Handball may be played as a singles game (one against one), as doubles (two against two), or as a revolving game in which a losing player merely goes to the end of the line. In the latter game as many as eight players may engage in play at the same time.

BEGINNING HANDBALL

Players number off in consecutive order. Player No. 1 serves the ball by batting it against the ground, causing the ball to rebound against the wall and back into the play area. Player No. 2 bats the ball in like fashion after one bounce so that it again rebounds from the wall. Play continues until a player misses the ball or causes it to go out of bounds. When this occurs, that player becomes the one with the last number and takes his place accordingly. All other players move up one position. When play resumes, the next player in order serves the ball.

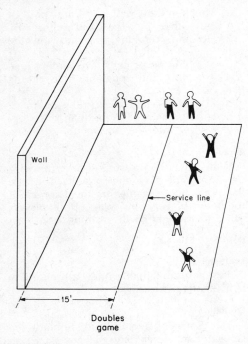

FIG. 6.37. Handball court.

The object is to become player No. 1 and retain that position as long as possible.

Violations

1. Failing to bat the ball after one bounce.
2. Interfering with the next player's attempt to play the ball.
3. Causing the ball to go outside the court. (Liners are good.)
4. Batting the ball in such a way that it fails to rebound into the play area.

Penalty

Player committing violation must go to last position or be replaced from a waiting line.

ADVANCED HANDBALL

In this more advanced game the ball is served out of the hand and against the wall without bouncing. Either an underhand or overhand serve may be used. A service line is drawn on the court 15 feet from and parallel to the wall.

Singles

Player No. 1, the server, bats the ball against the wall from behind the service line. Player No. 2, the receiver, bats the ball after one bounce with one or both hands, causing it to hit the wall and bounce within the court. Play continues until a player either misses the ball or causes it to go out of bounds.

Scoring

If the receiver commits a violation, the server gets a point. If the server misses the ball, he loses his serve and the receiver becomes server.

Eleven points constitute a game.

Doubles

The rules are similar to those of the singles game, with the following additions:

1. Serving and receiving teams alternate hitting the ball; however, it is not required that each player must hit the ball in turn.
2. Serving order is established as follows: Player No. 1 on team A, player 1 and then 2 on team B, player 2 on team A. This serving order remains constant throughout the game.
3. Only the *serving* team may score points.
4. Eleven points constitute a game.

STRIKING WITH A PADDLE (FIGS. 6.33A AND B) (LEARNING EXPERIENCES)

Note: For paddles, see Figs. 6.2, 6.3.

Informal activities

Individual, with partner, in groups of 4.

Equipment

Paddle tennis paddle for each player; one sponge-rubber ball, tennis ball, or No. 6 utility ball for each player.

Activities

(Grip: Hold the paddle with handle toward you and paddle vertical to the ground. Shake hands with paddle—"Hand shake grip.")

In each activity, try to increase the number of consecutive hits.

1. Practice bouncing the ball consecutively to the ground. How many bounces can you make without missing?

2. Repeat bouncing the ball up into the air.

3. Repeat bouncing the ball against a wall. Return the ball to the wall after one bounce.

4. Work with a partner. Hit the ball over a net 3 feet in height. Hit the ball on the volley *or* after one bounce.

5. Repeat No. 4 working in groups of four. With two players on each side of the net, hit the ball back and forth over the net. How many hits can you make without missing?

PADDLE TENNIS (FIGS. 633A, B AND 6.38)

Equipment

Four paddles, sponge-rubber or tennis ball, net 3 feet in height. Junior court, for players up to 16 years. (See diagram.)

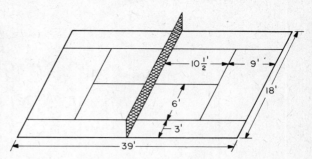

FIG. 6.38. Paddle Tennis court.

The game

Play as in tennis. The rule on the serve may be adapted to allow serving the ball either in the air or on the bounce.

STRIKING WITH A RACKET (LEARNING EXPERIENCES)

Using a short handled tennis racket.
Using a regulation tennis racket.
See "Official Tennis Guide."

STRIKING WITH A BAT (LEARNING EXPERIENCES)

Hitting off a Batting Tee, Fig. 9.1
Hitting a pitched ball, Fig. 9.16.
See Chapter 9, "Activities Using a Softball."

CHAPTER 7

KICKBALL, SOCCERBALL, AND FOOTBALL SPORT UNITS

ACTIVITIES USING A KICKBALL

ACTIVITIES USING A SOCCERBALL

ACTIVITIES USING A FOOTBALL

FIG. 7.1. Contacting the ball. Contact the ball with the top of the kicking foot. Note the position of the left foot in relation to the ball. *Physical Education Teaching Guide for Kindergarten and Grades 1–2,* Publication No. 472, p. 25, 1957. Courtesy Los Angeles City Schools.

The fall of any year is ushered in not only by the new crispness in the air, but also by the sight of footballs spiraling toward the sky. Suddenly winter arrives; it is time for basketball and volleyball. Softballs and bats arrive with the spring thaw, along with the running and jumping of track and field events.

The seasons for these sports are felt as keenly in the elementary school as on high school or college playing fields. With proper consideration for young capabilities, these sports should receive a goodly share of the instruction offered during physical activity periods. It must be remembered, however, that elementary-school-age children do not have the development to play the team games as they are officially written. The nets must be lowered, the playing fields shortened, and the equipment be smaller and lighter if the students are to benefit from exposure to these games.

Since a high degree of skill is essential to the success of various seasonal sports, it will be necessary to spend a great deal of time working on fundamentals. This "skill drill" can be made interesting and challenging by having the children develop or create related activities, and by having them use the many relays and small group games listed in each unit. These are designed to build knowledge gradually in the skills, rules, and strategy necessary to each team game. By limiting the complexity of a game for a time, both as to rules and position of players, the children will learn more easily and with more enjoyment.

Some sports, such as volleyball and softball, do not contribute to all the desired aims of the program. If the objective of improving physical fitness is to be met, some part of the activity program must be devoted to general conditioning. This can be accomplished by introducing various series of exercises, related warm-ups, or including an endurance run as a part of the warm-up procedure. Achieving a balance of activities will meet the objectives and provide the children with a worthwhile program of activities.

When introducing a team game for the first time, it is often helpful if the initial presentation is made in the classroom. Using the chalkboard, (1) diagram the play area and position of players; (2) using the diagram, point out the object of the game; and (3) present the rules and safety necessary to *start* the game. At this point limit the number of questions. Once on the field, place the teams in position and conduct a walk-through of the game, stressing pertinent rules. With the use of this procedure, there will be fewer questions and less confusion, and the children will understand the structure of the game more quickly. Additional rules as well as safety measures can then be presented as the situations arise. For relays and small group games, the skills may be presented or reviewed in the classroom, while the new game or relay could be demonstrated on the area and main points stressed.

By alternating periods of skill practice and playing the game, the children will improve rapidly to the point of surprising proficiency. This is as it should be.

PURPOSES

It is fitting that there is such a variety of team games available for children to play, since they certainly do enjoy the challenge of a new game or the satisfaction of a familiar game well played. All of the units in this chapter are related to kicking skills in some manner, and are included to accomplish the following:

—to present a variety of activities that are suitable to the performance levels of the players: for success; for satisfaction;
—to utilize the various kicking and catching skills in structured game situations;
—to respect the rules for *safety* established in each game;
—to develop progressively more complex *skills* and increased *control* in kicking activities;
—to appreciate the necessity of *rules* in games, and learn to accept the decisions of officials automatically;
—to understand, create, and apply *strategies* inherent in the various games;
—to learn to control and utilize the unique qualities of a football.

ACTIVITIES USING A KICKBALL

SUGGESTED GRADE PLACEMENT CHART

	1	2	3	4	5	6	7	8
KICKBALL SKILLS, 183–184	x	x	x	x	x	G		
RELAYS AND SMALL GROUP GAMES, 184–186								
Informal Activities—Working with a Partner	x	x	x	x	x	x	G	G
Bowling and Fielding (Shuttle Relay)	x	x	x	x	•			
Bowling and Fielding (File Relay with Leader)	x	x	x	x	•			
Underhand Throwing and Catching (Shuttle Relay)	x	x	x	x	•	•		
Overhand Throwing and Catching (File Relay with Leader)	x	x	x	x	x	•	G	G
Zigzag Line-up Ball		x	x	x				
Kick, Catch, and Carry		x	x	x	x	•	•	•
Diamond Relay		x	x	x	x	G	G	
SKILL TESTS, 187–188								
Bowling (Accuracy)	x	x	x	x				
Underhand Throw (Accuracy)		x	x	x	x			
Overhand Throw (Accuracy)			x	x	x	x	•	•
Kicking (Accuracy)			x	x	x	x	x	x
Base Running (Speed)			x	x	x	x	x	x
TEAM GAMES, 188–194								
Line-up Kickball	—	x	x	•				
Variation: Throw ball into field	—	x	x	•				
Danish Rounders		x	x	x	•			
Variation: Throw ball into field		x	x	x				
Bases on Balls I—with Stationary Ball		x	•					
Bases on Balls II—with Bowled Ball and Rotation			x	x	•			
Pin Kickball			x	x				
Home Run or Out—Kickball			x	x	x	•		
Variations: Beatball; Three-Team		—	x	x				
Kickball		—	x	x	G			
Kickball Work-up		—	x	x	G			
Three-Team Kickball			x	x	G			
Variation: Three-Team Home Run or Out		—	x	x	G			

— = May introduce activity   • = May continue activity
x = Depth in instruction   G = Girls, B = Boys

ACTIVITIES USING A KICKBALL

Kickball is an ever-popular game for children, full of the excitement of major league baseball, but with skills appropriate to the level of elementary-school-age players. Most of the ball skills are used, as well as kicking and running, making it an all-inclusive type of activity. Its only drawback, but an important one, is the lack of activity for certain players. If there are many fielders, some may never have an opportunity to catch a ball; a poorly skilled kicker may never run beyond first base.

If this game is to meet the requirement

of maximum participation for *all* students, certain modifications are indicated. First, provide sufficient small group practice for the development of throwing, catching, and kicking skills. Second, adjust the size of teams so that all players have equal opportunity to handle the ball, and so that certain players are not "lost" in the field. Third, introduce automatic rotation so that all children get to play all positions during a game period.

If adjacent diamonds are available, organize two games for greater activity. Otherwise, limit the number of players on a team to eight or nine and have the remaining children work on skills in small groups, rotating them into the game. Two games of Work-up, in which each player is limited to a maximum of two runs, also provide for more activity and for automatic rotation.

For safety, all fielders should remain at least 25 feet away from the kicker. Also, the kicker must be instructed not to cross home plate until he has kicked the ball. The practice of throwing the ball at the runner to put him out often leads to spills, and is not in the best interests of the game.

The rules of kickball are the same as those for softball except for the rules concerned with putting the ball in play, bowling, and kicking. A review of softball rules and the explanatory diagrams in Chapter 9 would increase the understanding of the "Kickball Unit."

GLOSSARY OF TERMS

Catching and Fielding. Although used interchangeably, catching is a term used for receiving a thrown ball. Fielding is mainly used for receiving a kicked or batted ball—receiving a ball "in the field."

Tagging the Base. Touching the base with foot while holding the ball in hand. (This is used for a force-out, it is not necessary to tag the base runner to put him out.) (Fig. 9.24)

SAFETY

AS KICKER

Learn to contact the ball with the top of kicking foot.

Learn to keep eyes on the ball and to contact it at the bottom of the kicking arc, with other foot beside or slightly behind the ball (not kick over the top of ball and lose balance). (Fig. 7.1)

Develop the habit of waiting until ball reaches home plate before kicking it. (Kick from a position *on*, in line with, or *behind* home plate rather than running up on the ball and endangering the safety of the bowler and fielders.)

Learn to remain in the designated safe place for kicking team while waiting turn.

AS BASEMAN OR FIELDER

Learn how to catch a kicked ball without injury.

Learn to stay at least 25 to 30 feet away from the kicker.

Learn fielding positions and stay off the base and the base lines when there is no play on the base runner.

For a force-out, learn to touch the *front edge* of the base with one foot, thus preventing a collision with oncoming base runner. (Fig. 9.24)

Learn playing positions and cover appropriate area when on fielding team.

Learn to call "Mine" when in a better position than a teammate to field a ball.

For times when two teammates rush to catch a ball, learn to call the name of the player in the best position to make the catch.

KICKBALL SKILLS

LIST OF KICKBALL SKILLS

Bowling, Fig. 6.15.
Underhand throwing, one hand, Fig. 6.23.
Overhand throwing, one hand, Fig. 6.29.
Catching thrown ball, Figs. 6.25A and B.
Kicking.
Fielding a kicked ball.
Base running.

ANALYSIS OF KICKBALL SKILLS

KICKING—STATIONARY OR BOWLED BALL

Starting position

Keep eyes on the ball.
Starting with kicking foot, take two steps

forward, right-left. (If left-footed, step left-right.)

As second step is taken, flex right knee. With second step, step into position to kick. Extend the right knee forcibly.

Execution

Contact the ball with the top of kicking foot. (Time the approach steps and the kick so that the supporting foot is about opposite the point of contact. See Fig. 7.1)

Keep eyes on the ball as the ball contacts the foot.

Follow through with right leg continuing the forward upward movement with the toe pointed.

Take steps and follow through in the direction the ball is to go.

Common faults and coaching hints

1. Too many approach steps.
   Limit approach steps to a maximum of four.
2. Lack of force.
   Stress flexing the right knee and extending the knee forcibly. Add momentum through the continuous movement of approach steps, kick, and follow-through.
3. Contacting the ball with end of toes.
   Stress pointing toe and contacting the ball with the top of the foot.
4. Kicking over the top of the ball and losing balance.
   Stress keeping eyes on the ball.
   Stress contacting the ball at the bottom of the kicking arc. Left foot is to the left of the point of contact with ball. (Fig. 7.1)
5. Contacting the ball *after crossing* home plate (or a kicking line).
   Stress timing. Take approach steps so that supporting foot is beside, on, or behind home plate when ball is kicked. (For safety of bowler.)
6. Lack of balance.
   When approaching and contacting the ball, keep body weight forward. Use arms to aid in maintaining balance.
   On follow-through extend body and maintain balance over supporting foot.

FIELDING A KICKED BALL

Starting position

Place feet in a comfortable stride position with one foot forward.

Keep eyes on the ball.

Reach out, raising arms forward with elbows slightly bent and held comfortably close together.

Relax hands and hold them slightly above shoulder level, palms up, fingers spread, and little fingers almost touching.

Execution

Start hands and arms in downward direction *before* ball contacts hands.

Give with *hands* and *arms,* and bend ankles, knees, and hips as ball contacts fingers.

Guide ball in to body.

Trap ball with hands, forearms, and body.

Give with body down to a crouch position.

Common faults and coaching hints

1. Failure to keep eye on the ball.
   Stress keeping eyes on the ball *all the way to hands.*
2. Fear of the force of the ball.
   Stress breaking the force of the ball.
   Reach out; start hands and arms in downward direction before ball contacts hands; give with hands and arms, and bend ankles, knees, and hips.

RELAYS AND SMALL GROUP GAMES—USING A KICKBALL

Note: See description of skills for points to stress while presenting activities. For bowling, throwing, and catching, and for relay formations, see Chapter 6.

INFORMAL ACTIVITIES—WORKING WITH A PARTNER

Equipment

No. 7, No. 8½ utility ball, No. 8 kickball.

Skills

Bowling, underhand and overhand throwing, catching.

1. Roll the ball and field ground ball.
2. Roll the ball at a target (milk carton

or plastic container). Partner recovers and returns the ball. He then sets up milk carton. One player takes three trials, then exchanges places with partner.

3. Throw underhand and catch. Start close together and move back gradually. "How far apart can you go without missing?" After a miss, return to starting distance and repeat the action.

4. Throw overhand and catch. Follow the same procedure as for No. 3.

BOWLING AND FIELDING (SHUTTLE RELAY)

Equipment

One No. 8½ utility ball or No. 8 kickball for each group.

Relay

Shuttle Relay formation.

First player in each line rolls the ball to his teammate in the opposite line and goes to the end of the opposite line. Teammate fields the ball and rolls it back to next player in line and goes to end of the opposite line. Continue the action.

1. Practice for a given period of time. Evaluate and repeat practice.

2. Play for accuracy. Score 1 point *against* a team each time a player has to move his feet to field the ball. Team with *lowest* score wins.

BOWLING AND FIELDING (FILE RELAY WITH LEADER)

See Line Roll Ball.

UNDERHAND THROWING AND CATCHING (SHUTTLE RELAY)

Equipment

One ball for each team.

Relay

First player with the ball throws it underhand to his teammate in opposite line, then goes to the end of the opposite line. Teammate catches the ball and throws it back with an underhand throw to next player in line, and goes to the end of the opposite line. Continue the action.

1. Practice for a period of time. Ask how many were able to throw the ball straight. Evaluate and repeat practice.

2. Play for speed. Team finishing first wins. If children can follow the directions, go through the relay two times with each player finishing in his *original* position, after *four* turns.

OVERHAND THROWING AND CATCHING (FILE RELAY WITH LEADER)

Equipment

One ball for each team.

Relay

First player in each line throws the ball with an overhand throw to his leader, then goes to the end of his *own* line. Leader catches the ball and *rolls* it back to the next player. Continue the action.

1. Practice for a period of time. Evaluate and change leaders. Have the leader in each line go to the end of his line, and the first player in each line take the leader's position. Repeat the activity.

2. Play for speed. Go through the relay twice. Team wins that finishes first. Change leaders and repeat.

ZIGZAG LINE-UP BALL

See Fig. 6.30.

KICK, CATCH, AND CARRY (USING STATIONARY BALL; FIG. 7.2)

Equipment

One kickball and one beanbag for each group.

Directions

File formation with a fielder. Place a kickball on a beanbag in front of each line of players.

Player No. 1 kicks the ball to the fielder and immediately runs out to take the fielder's place. The fielder fields the ball, runs in carrying the ball, and places it on the beanbag in position for the next kicker. Fielder then goes to the end of the line.

Safety

Provide a safe distance between squads, for safety in case of poorly directed kicks.

DIAMOND RELAY (BASE RUNNING; FIG. 7.3)

Equipment

Four beanbags or balls.

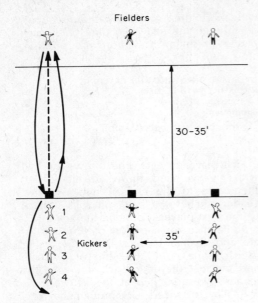

FIG. 7.2. Kick, Catch, and Carry.

Directions

Squads of no more than five players line up as shown in the diagram.

On signal the first runner at each base runs completely around the diamond, hands the ball to the next runner in his line, and then retires to the end of that line. Game continues until all players have run. First squad to finish wins.

Safety

Players awaiting turns should stand *inside* the base to give runners sufficient room.

One runner passing another must run to the outside.

Teaching hints

1. Have all players line up facing their respective bases in order to be ready to run.

2. Players completing their turns should sit down in line to indicate they have finished.

3. Have No. 1 players walk through the relay first for better understanding of the procedure.

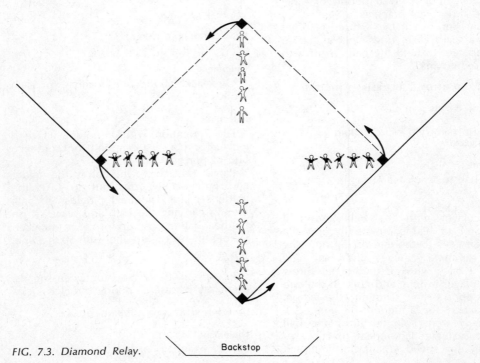

FIG. 7.3. Diamond Relay.

SKILL TESTS—USING A KICKBALL

BOWLING (ACCURACY)

Equipment

One ball, one target (home plate, a base, two milk cartons on side and end to end, or marked lines 17 inches apart at the base of a wall).

Action

Contestant stands on a line 25 feet from the target and bowls the ball at the target. He should step forward over the line with *one* foot *as* he bowls. Contestant has five trials.

Scoring

Score 1 point for each successful hit.

UNDERHAND THROW (ACCURACY; FIG. 7.4)

Equipment

One ball, 5-foot circle drawn on a wall. The lower edge of the circle is 1 foot from the ground.

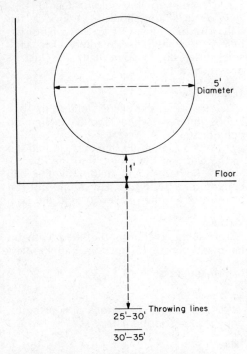

FIG. 7.4. Skill Test: Underhand Throw; Overhand Throw.

Action

Contestant stands on a line 25 to 30 feet from the target and throws the ball underhand at the target. He should step forward over the line with *one* foot *as* he throws. Contestant has five trials.

Scoring

Score 1 point each time the ball hits inside or on the 5-foot circle. (Liners are good.)

OVERHAND THROW (ACCURACY; FIG. 7.4)

Same as Underhand Throw (Accuracy), with following exceptions:

1. Contestant stands on a line 30 to 35 feet from the target.
2. Contestant throws overhand.

KICKING (ACCURACY; FIG. 7.5)

Equipment

One ball, two markers (two milk cartons or substitutes), beanbag (optional). Place the two markers on a line 18 feet apart. Place the ball on a kicking line, or on a beanbag, 20 to 35 feet away from the mid-point between the two markers.

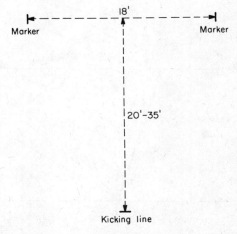

FIG. 7.5. Skill Test: Kicking for Accuracy.

Action

Contestant kicks the ball over the line between the two markers. Contestant has five trials.

Scoring

Score 1 point for each time the ball is kicked between the two markers.

BASE RUNNING (SPEED)

See "Skill Tests for Softball," Chapter 9.

TEAM GAMES—USING A KICKBALL

LINE-UP KICKBALL

Equipment

Kickball, two milk cartons or substitutes for bases, one beanbag or marked home plate.

Skills

Kicking, fielding kicked ball, running.

Play area and position of players (Fig. 7.6)

Open area with restraining line, 25 to 30 feet from home plate. Two markers may be substituted for the marked restraining line. (See diagram) Place a first base diagonally to the right of home plate. Distance to base depends upon ability of players. Place another marker in third base position to be used *only* to determine fair and foul balls.

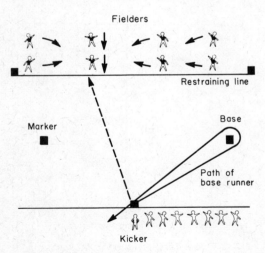

FIG. 7.6. *Line-up Kickball.*

The fielders stand in two lines across the field. The front line of fielders must stand behind the restraining line. The kickers stand in a line behind and to the right of home plate.

Object of the game

To kick the ball into the field, run *around* the first base, and return across home plate before *all* the fielders line up behind the player fielding the ball.

The game

Place the ball on the beanbag or the marked home plate. Kicker kicks the ball into the field and runs around the first base and back across home plate. Player fielding the ball stands *at the spot* he fields the ball while remaining fielders run to line up behind him.

Scoring

If the fielding team lines up first, score 1 point for the fielding team. If the kicker returns to home plate first, score 1 point for the kicking team. (When a fly ball is caught, the kicker is out immediately. Score 1 point for the fielding team.)

Two trials are allowed to kick a fair ball. The ball must not go out of bounds before reaching the markers. Exchange sides after all (or one half) the kickers have a turn to kick.

Teaching hints

1. Stress that the player fielding the ball *stands in place* while teammates line up behind him.

2. When lining up, fielders should go to the end and not crowd into the line.

3. A fielder should field only the ball coming directly to him. He should not run in front of another player to field the ball.

Variation

Throw the ball into the field with an overhand throw to put the ball in play.

DANISH ROUNDERS

Equipment

Kickball, two milk cartons or substitutes, one beanbag (optional).

Skills

Kicking, fielding kicked ball, running, passing ball overhead.

Play area and position of players (Fig. 7.7)

Open area with a restraining line 25 to 30 feet from home plate. Place a milk carton (or substitute) on each side line for determining fair and foul balls. (Imaginary line between two milk cartons may be substituted for restraining line.)

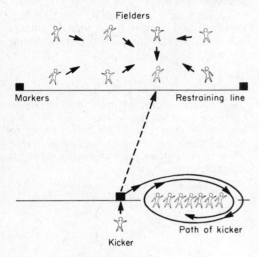

FIG. 7.7. Danish Rounders.

The fielders stand in two lines across the field. The front line of fielders must stand behind the restraining line. The kickers stand in line behind and to the right of home plate and face toward home plate.

Object of the game

To kick the ball into the field and run around teammates as many times as possible before being put out.

The game

Place the ball on the beanbag or the marked home plate. Kicker kicks the ball into the field and runs around his teammates. The team counts each time the kicker *completes* a run around the team. The kicker's team calls out, "One—two—three. . . ."

The player fielding the ball *stands at the spot* he fields the ball while the other fielders run to line up behind him. He immediately starts passing the ball back over his head. Each player in line receives the ball and passes it back overhead. The last player in line runs with the ball to the front of the line and calls, "Danish Rounders," thus putting the kicker out. (Fly ball caught puts kicker out immediately.)

Scoring

Score 1 point for each time the kicker runs *completely* around his own team.

Two trials are allowed to kick a fair ball. The ball must not go out of bounds before reaching the fair ball markers.

Allow one-half of the team to kick, then exchange sides while one-half of the other team kicks. Exchange two more times in order to give each player a turn.

Rotation

The front and back lines of fielders exchange places each time the team goes out to the field.

Safety

Fielders must stand at least 25 to 30 feet away from the kicker, behind the restraining line.

Teaching hints

1. Kicking team should not count until the kicker reaches the head of the line each time. See also "Teaching Hints" for Line-up Kickball.

2. May have boys in front line in field while boys kick, girls in front line while girls kick.

3. Discourage fielders from *trying* to be last in line.

Variations

1. Throw the ball into the field with an overhand throw to put the ball in play.

2. Use a football. Punt the ball or throw a forward pass into the field to put the ball in play.

Methods of passing the ball down the line of fielders include: (a) each fielder hiking the ball back between his legs; (b) each fielder turning and handing off the ball to the next fielder; (c) first fielder hiking the ball back between his legs, second player receiving the ball and then turning and handing off to the next fielder.

Players alternate the action to the end of the line.

3. Use a volleyball or a No. 8½ utility ball. Serve the volleyball out-of-hand into the field to put the ball in play.

BASES ON BALLS I—WITH STATIONARY BALL

Equipment

Kickball, three bases, and home plate with an extra home plate or base, one beanbag (optional).

Skills

Kicking, fielding kicked ball, base running.

Play area and position of players (Fig. 7.8)

Kickball diamond, three bases, and two home plates with a marked area outside the diamond 25 feet from home plate and 15 feet from first base line. (See diagram.)

Players on fielding team scatter in the field beyond an imaginary line from first to second to third base. Kicking team stands behind backstop with the next kicker at the right end of the backstop (first base end).

Object of the game

To score points by kicking the ball into the field and to run to as many bases as possible, in correct order, before being put out.

The game

Place the ball on home plate (on beanbag). Kicker kicks the ball into the field and runs to as many bases as possible before being put out. When *returning* to home plate he crosses the *extra* home plate or base. (See path of base runner on diagram.)

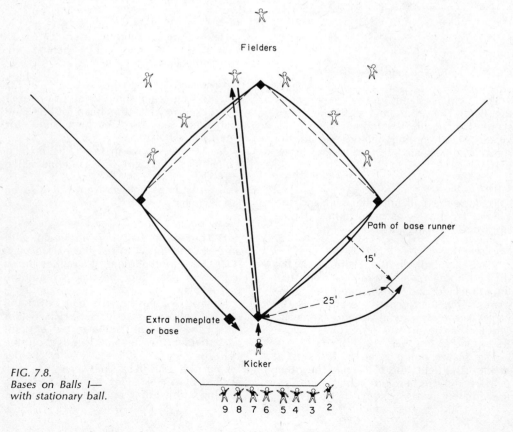

FIG. 7.8.
*Bases on Balls I—
with stationary ball.*

Player fielding the ball runs with the ball and carries it *across* the *regular* home plate, thus putting the base runner out.

The fielder then places the ball on home plate and goes to the marked area behind the first base line. After all the fielders have had a turn to *field* the ball and are lined up on the side line, exchange sides. Kickers go to the field; fielders line up behind home plate.

Scoring

Kicker scores 1 point for each base he touches before being put out, 1 point for reaching first base, 2 points for reaching second base, 3 points for reaching third base, and 4 points for a home run. On a fly ball caught, kicker is out. The team with the most points after all the players have had a turn to kick wins. (If number of players is uneven, have one player kick twice.)

Safety

Provide the extra home plate or base to prevent collisions on close plays at home plate. The base runner coming from third base should veer to the right; the fielder running in with the ball should veer to the left. Explain and demonstrate. When learning the game, call to the base runner to cross the extra home plate.

Teaching hint

Have fielders respace themselves as teammates become fewer in number. When only one player remains in the field, he should stand near second base to be in good position to field the ball.

BASES ON BALLS II—
WITH BOWLED BALL AND ROTATION (FIG. 7.9)

Same as Bases on Balls I, with the following exceptions:

1. Players are placed on the diamond as in kickball. If more than nine players

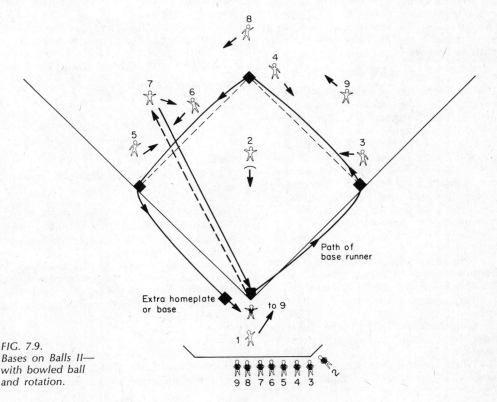

FIG. 7.9.
Bases on Balls II— with bowled ball and rotation.

on a team, increase the number of fielders and space the fielders evenly across the outfield.

2. Bowler (pitcher) bowls the ball to the kicker.

The game

Bowler bowls the ball. Kicker kicks the ball into the field and immediately runs to first base, second base, third base, and *extra* home plate. He runs to as many bases as he can reach before being put out.

The player fielding the ball runs with it and crosses the *regular* home plate, thus putting the base runner out.

Scoring

Score 1 point for each base the runner touches before the fielder crosses home plate with the ball: 1 point for reaching first base, 2 points for reaching second base, and so on. The team with the most points after all the players have had a turn to kick wins. (If teams are uneven, have one player kick twice.)

Kicker is out automatically: (1) on a fly ball caught, or (2) if he kicks the ball *before* it reaches home plate.

Rotation

Fielders rotate as in work-up and move one position after each out is scored: Catcher goes to right field; right fielder, No. 9 moves to center field; 8 to 7, 7 to 6, and so on. (See diagram.) Rotate quickly. (Check on correct fielding position of each player.) Bowler should not bowl the ball until fielders have rotated. The player fielding the ball and running to home plate returns immediately to the field and then rotates one position.

Teaching hints

1. One player should not run in front of another player to field the ball.
2. Check the kicker and call him out if he *crosses* home plate before contacting the ball.
3. Bowler should not bowl the ball until fielders have rotated. Encourage fielders to rotate quickly.
4. When learning the game, have the fielder who runs in with the ball tag home

plate, return to his fielding position, and *then* rotate.

Safety

See "Safety" as presented in Bases on Balls I.

Variations

1. Use a football. The *ball is given to the kicker by the catcher.* The kicker may either punt the ball or throw a forward pass into the field. (Forward pass must go at least 25 feet, or distance to the pitcher, before touching ground; no bunts—baby kicks.) Kicker must not advance across home plate in the act of kicking or passing the ball; take approach steps *behind* home plate.

After putting kicker out, fielder with the ball tosses it to the *new* catcher (player moving in from the pitching position). Catcher *holds* the ball until the fielders rotate, *then* gives the ball to the kicker. Stress not kicking until fielders have completed rotation.

2. Use a softball, and bat the ball off a batting tee. Catcher places the ball on the batting tee *after* players have rotated.

3. Use a softball and bat a pitched ball.

PIN KICKBALL (13)

Equipment

Kickball, four milk cartons numbered 1 to 4, two bases and home plate.

Skills

Kicking, fielding a kicked ball, bowling, running.

Play area and position of players (Fig. 7.10)

Kickball diamond. Four milk cartons numbered 1 to 4 are placed in the outfield. (See diagram.)

Players are placed on the diamond as in kickball. If more than nine players are on a team, increase the number of fielders and space the fielders evenly across the outfield.

Object of the game

To kick the ball into the field and to knock down (with hand) as many milk cartons as possible before being put out.

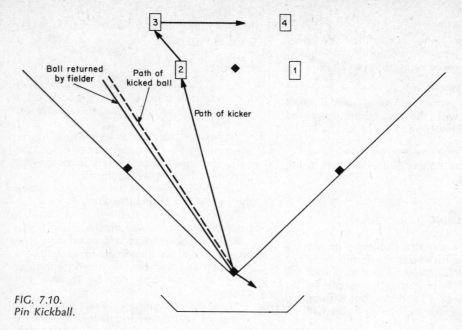

FIG. 7.10.
Pin Kickball.

The game

Bowler bowls the ball. Kicker kicks the ball, runs into the field, and hits down as many milk cartons as possible before being put out.

The player fielding the ball runs with it and crosses home plate, thus putting the kicker out.

Scoring

Kicker scores the number of points indicated on each milk carton he knocks down. (If he knocks down two cartons marked 2 and 3, he scores 5 points.)

Kicker is out automatically: (1) on a fly ball caught, or (2) if he kicks the ball *before* it reaches home plate.

Rotation

Fielders rotate one place after each kicker has a turn. Catcher goes to right field, right fielder moves to center field, etc. See rotation as indicated on diagram for Bases on Balls II (Fig. 7.9). Rotate quickly. Check on correct fielding position of each player.

Safety

Bowler should not bowl the ball until fielders have rotated.

Teaching hints

1. Stress knocking the pins down with hand.

2. Kicker should assist in setting pins up again. Set them up at the same spot.

HOME RUN OR OUT—KICKBALL

Rules are the same as for Home Run or Out—Softball (Fig. 9.21), with the exceptions presented under the following rules of kickball. (Use three-team formation.)

Variation

Beatball. Put the ball in play at home plate by throwing the kickball or a No. 7 utility ball into the field.

KICKBALL

Rules are the same as for softball (Fig. 9.22), with the following exceptions:

1. Bowler bowls the ball to the kicker, who kicks it into the field.

2. Kicker is out if he crosses home plate *before* he kicks the ball. (Take approach steps *behind* home plate.)

3. Fielders may *not throw* the ball at a base runner to put him out. ("Throwing them out" is a common, unsafe practice.)

KICKBALL WORK-UP

Rules the same as Softball Work-up (Fig. 9.26), with the exceptions presented under the preceding rules of kickball.

THREE-TEAM KICKBALL

Rules the same as Three-Team Softball (Fig. 9.27), with the exceptions presented under the preceding rules of kickball.

Variation: three-team home run or out

Play Home Run or Out—Kickball, using three teams.

ACTIVITIES USING A SOCCERBALL

There is a distinct challenge in playing a ball game in which the hands may not be used. Such a game is soccer, one of the most active field games being played today. Closely akin to soccer, but with added elements of football and basketball, is speedball.

A good deal of coaching will be necessary in the beginning to keep students from picking up or catching a soccerball. Once this is understood, they will enjoy seeing the many different ways a ball can be controlled with the feet and body alone. The relays and small group games will provide the children with many opportunities to practice this art, and may be used as games as well as drill.

Because elementary school children tend to bunch up around the ball, it is best to have them play the team games in which positions are well controlled, such as End Zone Soccer or End Zone Speedball. Beginning in the sixth grade, when players realize the value of team play, the official game may be introduced. Since speedball uses additional ball skills, and since the hands may be used, it would be wiser to introduce it following soccer rather than preceding it.

Provide a safe game situation in terms of the activity, the number of participants, and the area. It is also advisable to separate boys and girls for most of the activities in this unit, since boys tend to kick harder, play a more aggressive game, and monopolize the ball. Furthermore, girls will have greater opportunity to develop skills when playing separately.

GLOSSARY OF TERMS

Aerial Ball. In speedball a thrown ball that has not touched the ground, or a ball that is raised into the air *directly* off the foot.

"Breaking" for the Ball. Moving to receive the ball (in order to advance the ball more quickly and attempt to prevent opponent from intercepting it).

Dribble the Ball—with Feet. Advancing the ball with consecutive taps.

Ground Ball. A ball that is rolling, bouncing, or stationary on the ground.

Kick-up. Converting a ground ball into an aerial ball in speedball. In speedball a ground ball may be contacted with feet only; an aerial ball may be thrown and caught.

"Leading" Teammate. Passing the ball ahead of teammate (in order to advance the ball more quickly and attempt to prevent opponent from intercepting it).

Trapping the Ball. Stopping the ball with foot, with inside of leg, or with front of both legs.

SAFETY

Control and advance the ball with respect for one's own safety and the safety of others—kicks should not be too hard or too high.

Control own movement for own safety and the safety of others.

SOCCER AND SPEEDBALL SKILLS

LIST OF SOCCER SKILLS

Dribbling the ball with feet.
Passing the ball with feet, "leading" teammate.
Kicking ground ball.
Blocking a kicked ball with body.
Trapping the ball.
Punting (punting the football; Fig. 7.25).
Spatial awareness, see Chapter 1, "Body Control."

LIST OF SPEEDBALL SKILLS

Soccer skills
Basketball skills (See Chapter 8.)

ACTIVITIES USING A SOCCERBALL
(Kickball may be substituted.)

SUGGESTED GRADE PLACEMENT CHART

	3	4	5	6	7	8
SOCCER AND SPEEDBALL SKILLS, 194–197	x	x	x	x	x	x
RELAYS AND SMALL GROUP GAMES, 197–203						
Square Soccer	–	x	x	G		
Circle Soccer	–	x	x	G		
Bombardment	–	x	x	G		
Crab Walk Soccer			x	x	x	x
Dribble and Kick (Shuttle Relay)	–	x	x	x	x	x
Variation: Dribble the Ball, Kick, Trap		–	x	x	x	x
Dribble and Kick (Slalom Relay)	–	x	x	x	x	x
Variation: Dribble the Ball, Kick, Trap		–	x	x	x	x
Dribble and Pass (Partner Relay)			x	x	x	x
Dribble the Ball and Pass (Drill)			x	x	x	x
Variation: Dribble and Pass Against a Defensive Player			x	x	x	x
Break, Catch, and Pass (Drill)		–	x	x	x	x
Variation: Break, Catch, and Pass Against a Defensive Player			x	x	x	x
Kick, Catch, and Carry	x	x	x	•	•	•
Danish Rounders	x	x	•			
Bases on Balls II	x	x	•			
Punt Back (Variation)		x	x	x	x	x
SKILL TESTS, 203–204						
Punt for Distance		x	x	x	x	x
Kick for Accuracy	x	x	x	x	x	x
Slalom Dribble and Kick for Goal			x	x	x	x
TEAM GAMES (USING SKILLS OF SOCCER), 204–209						
Prisoners' Ball (Variation)	x	x	x			
Punt Back (Variation)		x	x	x	x	x
Soccer Kickball			x	x	x	
End Zone Soccer			x	x	x	
Zone Soccer			–	x	x	x
Seven- or Nine-Player Soccer			–	x	x	x
Eleven-Player Soccer					x	x
TEAM GAMES (USING SKILLS OF SPEEDBALL), 209–211						
Speedball Rules and Skills				x	x	x
Touchdown—Keep Away			x	x	x	x
Soccer Kickball (with Speedball Variations)			x	x	x	x
End Zone Speedball				x	x	
Zone Speedball				x	x	x
Seven- or Nine-Player Speedball				x	x	x
Eleven-Player Speedball					x	x

— = May introduce activity   x = Depth in instruction   • = May continue activity   G = Girls

Passing the ball with hands, "leading" teammate.

"Breaking" to receive a pass.

Catching a pass.

Guarding.

Pivoting.

Skills of speedball only

Kick-up to self.

Kick-up to teammate.

Catching a kicked ball (aerial ball).

ANALYSIS OF SOCCER AND SPEEDBALL SKILLS

DRIBBLING THE BALL WITH FEET

Starting position

Running on toes, move into position to intercept the path of the ball.

Keep eyes on ball, but use peripheral vision to check position of other players.

Execution

Rotate leg outward in order to contact the ball with inside of foot.

Tap the ball below its center lightly and alternately with each foot, keeping it 10 or 12 inches in front of the feet.

Take several short running steps between each contact with the ball. Develop rhythm in running and tapping.

Common faults and coaching hints

1. Kicking the ball too hard rather than tapping it.
   Turn the foot outward to contact the ball with the inside of the foot. Take shorter running steps.
2. Raising the foot too high so that it rolls over the top of the ball.
   Lift the foot just enough to clear the ground; tap the ball below its center.
3. Losing the ball to an opponent through lack of control.
   Keep the ball close to the feet; use peripheral vision to note position of opponents and alter course when indicated.

PASSING THE BALL WITH FEET

Starting position

Keep the ball under control and close to the feet. Note position of the receiver and whether moving or stationary.

Turn slightly toward the receiver.

Execution

Increase the backswing of the kicking foot and contact the ball with more force than for dribbling; follow through in the direction of the kick.

If the receiver is moving, direct the ball ahead of him so that it is not necessary to slacken pace in order to gain control of the ball.

Common faults and coaching hints

1. Lack of control in passing the ball.
   Use just enough force to kick the ball to receiver. Use the side of the foot to contact the ball.
2. Kicking the ball behind a moving receiver.
   Practice passing the ball to a point several running steps in front of the receiver.

KICKING GROUND BALL

Starting position

Keep eyes on the ball.

Face the direction in which the ball will travel.

Execution

Swing kicking foot back with knee bent and toes pointed downward.

Swing leg forcibly and contact ball *below* its center with the top of foot.

Follow through in the direction of the kick.

Common faults and coaching hints

1. Kicking over the top of the ball.
   Keep eyes on the ball; point toes downward to contact ball with top of foot. Stand close to the ball on the supporting foot. (See Fig. 7.1.)
2. Lack of distance in the kick.
   Increase the backswing; swing the kicking foot forcibly.
3. Lack of direction in the kick.
   Stand squarely behind the ball, facing the desired direction of the kick.

TRAPPING THE BALL

Starting position

Get in line with the oncoming ball.

Shift weight onto one foot.

Execution

Raise the nonsupporting foot, heel extended *downward*. As the ball contacts the sole, drop the toes down onto the ball. Do not step onto the ball.

Keep the knee of the supporting leg bent slightly for better balance.

Common faults and coaching hints

1. Kicking the ball rather than trapping it.
   Keep the heel down and toes pointed upward until the ball contacts the foot, then drop the toes down on the ball.
2. Allowing the ball to roll by the trapping foot.
   Keep eyes on the ball and get in line with the oncoming ball.
3. Putting weight on the ball.
   Maintain weight on supporting foot.

BLOCKING A KICKED BALL WITH BODY

Starting position

Get in line with the flight of the ball; keep eyes on ball.

Execution

Break the force of the ball by jumping back as it contacts the body.

Then block the rebound by raising the knee over the ball and pushing downward. The ball is then in position to be played by the feet.

Common faults and coaching hints

1. Failure to reduce the force of the ball, causing it to bounce away.
   Cushion the force of the ball by jumping backward just as the ball contacts the body.
2. Safety.
   Girls should fold arms over the chest for added protection when blocking a ball.

KICK-UP TO SELF WITH ROLLING BALL

Starting position

Get in line with the oncoming ball.
Keep eyes on the ball.

Execution

With weight on one foot, bend knee of supporting leg and extend other foot forward. Point toes forward and press them against the ground.

As the ball rolls onto the foot, bend knee upward and outward, turning toes up sharply.

Bend forward to receive the ball.

Common faults and coaching hints

1. Allowing the ball to roll off the side of the foot.
   Get in line with the oncoming ball; press toes against the ground. Lift the foot sharply as the ball rolls onto the instep.
2. Kicking rather than lifting the ball.
   Get into position and keep toes pointed down.

KICK-UP TO TEAMMATE WITH STATIONARY BALL

Starting position

Stand facing intended receiver, toes of one foot under the ball, knees bent.

Execution

Lift ball to teammate by scooping the ball upward with the toes and instep, extending knee forcibly.

Adjust force of the lift to the distance.

Common faults and coaching hints

1. Failure to lift the ball off the ground.
   Press toes of the lifting foot against the ground; scoop ball up against the instep and extend the knee forcibly toward the receiver.
2. Lack of accuracy.
   Follow through to the target.
   Practice lifting ball to receiver; vary the distance.

RELAYS AND SMALL GROUP GAMES USING A SOCCERBALL

Note: See description of skills for points to stress while presenting activities.

For relay formations, see Chapter 6.

Activities for Spatial Awareness, Chapter 1.

SQUARE SOCCER

Equipment

Kickball or soccerball.

Skills

Kicking, trapping, blocking.

Play area and position of players (Fig. 7.11)

Square area with an imaginary line diagonally across the area. The four sides of the square are the goal lines.

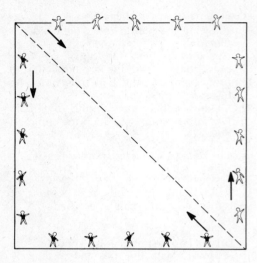

Arrows indicate rotation

FIG. 7.11. Square Soccer.

Place players of one team at the goal lines on two adjacent sides of the square, with players of the other team evenly spaced at the goal lines on the opposite two adjacent sides.

Object of the game

To score points by kicking the ball across the opponents' goal line lower than waist height.

The game

One player kicks the ball from his own goal line, attempting to kick it over the opponents' goal line below waist height. Opponents kick the ball back across the center area. They may trap the ball before kicking it. Players stay on or within a step in front of own goal line except to retrieve the ball.

If the ball stops in the center area, one player from the team on whose half of the square it stopped recovers the ball. He passes it with his feet to a teammate on the goal line.

If the ball goes across the goal line, the player on whose right it passed retrieves the ball and sends it back to a teammate.

Fouls

1. Touching the ball with hands.
2. Kicking the ball over opponents' goal line higher than waist height.
3. Dangerous kicking, kicking too hard.

Scoring

Score 1 point for each kick that goes across the opponents' goal line below waist height. Score 1 point for each foul made by an opponent.

Rotation

After each score, rotate one place to the right. (See arrows on diagram.)

Teaching hints

1. Stress keeping the ball low and not kicking too hard.
2. The end player on a team should not be allowed to kick the ball over the opponents' goal line at the corner adjacent to his own position.

CIRCLE SOCCER

Play the same as Square Soccer with the following exceptions:

Players remain in the double circle, between the two circle lines, except to retrieve the ball. (Fig. 7.12)

The outside circle is the goal line. Score 1 point for opponents each time the ball is kicked across the outside circle.

BOMBARDMENT

Equipment

Kickball or soccerball, eight markers (milk cartons or plastic detergent containers), four of one color and four of another color.

Skills

Kicking, trapping, blocking.

Play area and position of players (Fig. 7.13)

Rectangle with eight markers, four dark-colored markers (green) for one team and four light-colored (white) for the other team. Place markers alternately, one green, one white.

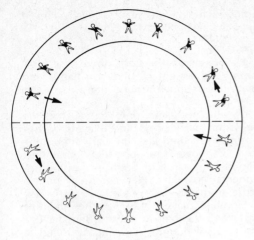

Arrows indicate rotation

FIG. 7.12. Circle Soccer.

Number players. Place players along the kicking line and side line with one player on each half of each side line. Each team covers one-half of the rectangle. (See diagram.)

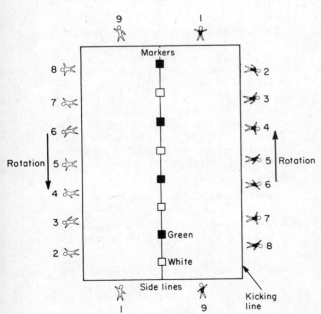

FIG. 7.13. Bombardment.

Object of the game

For the green team to kick the ball and knock down the green markers and the white team to kick the ball and knock down the white markers. The team that knocks down all its own markers first wins.

The game

A player on one team kicks the ball from behind his own kicking line and attempts to knock down one of his team's markers in the center area.

The ball is then kicked back by a player on the opposing team from behind his kicking line. He attempts to knock down one of his own team's markers. (Kickers must keep one foot on or behind kicking line.)

If a player accidentally knocks down an opponent's marker, the marker remains down and scores for the opponent.

Each side-line player tries to prevent the ball from going out of bounds on his half of the side lines, and kicks the ball to his own kickers. He also recovers any balls which stop in his quarter of the playing area.

Fouls

1. Touching ball with hands while ball is in play.
2. Stepping *across* kicking line into center area when contacting ball.
3. Kicking the ball higher than waist height.
4. Side-line player attempting to knock down a center marker.
5. Dangerous kicking, kicking too hard.

Penalty for a foul

Ball is dead and is awarded to the opposing team. If a marker is knocked down on a foul, the marker is set up again, and play is resumed.

Ball is dead

1. On a foul.
2. When it is kicked over a boundary line and away from the rectangle. If kicked away over the side lines, the appropriate side-line player recovers the ball and rolls it (with his hands) to his teammates on the kicking line. If kicked away over the kicking line, the player on whose right it

passed recovers the ball and rolls it back to his kicking line.

Rotation

At the end of each game (all pins for one team knocked down) rotate two places to the right within own team.

CRAB WALK SOCCER (FIG. 7.14)

Equipment

Kickball or soccerball.

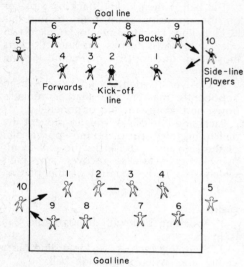

FIG. 7.14. Crab Walk Soccer.

Skill

Kicking the ball while in crab walk position.

Play area and position of players (Fig. 7.14)

Small area with short kick-off line placed in the center of each half of the area.

Each team is composed of forwards, backs, and side-line players numbered 1 to 10. (See diagram) Forwards: 1—2—3—4; backs: 6—7—8—9; side-line players: 5 and 10.

Object of the game and scoring

To score points by kicking the ball over the opponents' goal line. (Ball must roll or bounce over the goal line.) Score 1 point each time the ball is legally kicked over the goal line.

The game

Players sit on the floor, then raise hips, supporting weight of body on hands and feet. Players move around the area in this position.

To start the game, one "back" kicks the ball from the kick-off line. Players on opposing team then kick the ball, attempting to kick it over the opponents' goal line. The ball must roll or bounce over the opponents' goal line. Play continues until a score is made.

Side-line players *stand* at the side line and keep the ball in play. When the ball goes out of bounds, it is quickly rolled to the closest teammate.

Rotation

After a score, players of both teams rotate one position, 10 to 1, 1 to 2, 2 to 3, and so on. (See arrows on diagram.)

DRIBBLE THE BALL AND KICK (SHUTTLE RELAY)

Equipment

One kickball or soccerball for each team.

Relay

With players in shuttle formation, the first player in each team dribbles the ball across the area, passes it to his teammate in opposite line, and then goes to the end of the line. Player No. 2 repeats the action, passing to player No. 3. Continue play. No one may touch the ball with hands.

1. Practice for a given period of time.
2. Play for speed. Team wins that is first to sit down in *original* position after two times through the relay, *four* turns for each player.

Variation: dribble the ball, kick, trap

Player receiving the ball traps the ball before starting the dribble. Player failing to trap the ball must return to the line and start to dribble the ball again.

DRIBBLE THE BALL AND KICK (SLALOM RELAY; FIG. 7.15)

Equipment

One kickball or soccerball for each team.

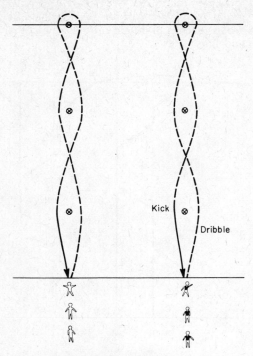

FIG. 7.15. Dribble the Ball and Kick—Slalom Relay.

Relay

Three players stand in file formation behind the starting line. Three teammates stand at 20-foot intervals with the end player standing on the end line.

The first contestant in each line dribbles the ball to the right of the first player and to the left of the second player. He continues to weave in and out around each player. When the contestant returns and is passing the first player in line again, he kicks the ball to the second contestant. The first contestant goes to the end of the line while the second contestant repeats the action.

Fouls

1. Touching the ball with the hands.
2. Failure to weave around each player-marker.
3. On the *return* trip, kicking the ball *before* reaching the first player-marker.
4. Player-marker moving his feet during the relay or interfering with the ball or a contestant.

Penalty for foul

Contestant returns to the starting line and begins again.

1. Practice for a period of time. Then have contestants exchange places with teammates acting as markers.
2. Play for speed. The team wins that is first to sit down in file formation behind the starting line after each player has had two turns. Repeat the relay and then exchange positions with teammates serving as markers.

Variation: dribble the ball, kick, trap

Player receiving the ball traps the ball before starting the dribble. Player failing to trap the ball must return to the line and start to dribble the ball again.

DRIBBLE THE BALL AND PASS (PARTNER RELAY; FIG. 7.16)

Equipment

One kickball or soccerball for each team.

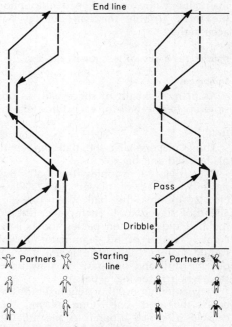

FIG. 7.16. Dribble the Ball and Pass—Partner Relay.

Relay

Teams line up in partner formation. Partners stand "passing" distance apart.

First couple on each team runs forward, with one partner dribbling the ball. He then passes the ball, passing it ahead of his partner ("leading" his partner). The partner dribbles the ball, then passes it back to the first player, again leading the partner.

Partners continue to dribble and pass the ball until the ball crosses the end line. They turn and continue the action back to the starting line. As they approach the starting line they pass the ball to the next couple.

1. Practice for a given period of time. Evaluate and repeat practice.

2. Play for speed. Team that finishes first after each couple has two turns wins.

Safety

Teams should be a safe distance apart.

Teaching hints

Stress passing ahead of partner and maintaining the same speed throughout the relay. Dribble the ball quickly, pass accurately.

DRIBBLE THE BALL AND PASS (DRILL; FIG. 7.17)

Equipment

As many kickballs or soccerballs as possible up to one ball for each three players.

Drill

Three players take the ball the length of the field and back.

Player No. 1 dribbles the ball, then passes it ahead of player No. 2. Player No. 2 dribbles the ball, then passes it ahead of player No. 3. Each player dribbles the ball quickly, then passes the ball accurately ahead of his teammate. (Players should maintain the same speed throughout the drill and not have to slow up or stop when receiving a pass.)

Players continue the action until they cross the end line. One player then dribbles the ball around to the adjacent area and the three players continue the drill back to the starting line. Second

group of players start as soon as the first group reaches mid-field on the way to the end line.

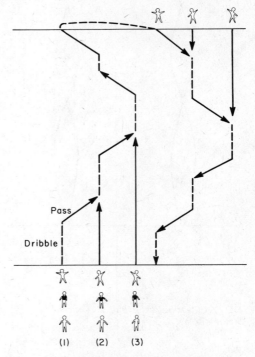

FIG. 7.17. Dribble the Ball and Pass—Drill.

Variation: dribble the ball and pass against a defensive player

Repeat the Dribble the Ball and Pass Drill with two players going through the drill while player No. 3 acts as a defensive player. Player No. 3 tries to intercept the ball before the partners, players 1 and 2, reach the end line.

Repeat the action with player No. 3 attempting to intercept the ball before the partners reach the starting line.

Rotation

Repeat the drill with player No. 2 as defensive player. Repeat the drill with player No. 1 as defensive player.

Scoring

Score 1 point for each successful interception.

**BREAK, CATCH, AND PASS
(DRILL FOR SPEEDBALL SKILL, AERIAL BALL)**

Equipment

As many kickballs or soccerballs as possible up to one ball for each three players.

Relay

Play as Dribble the Ball and Pass Drill except that the players throw and catch the ball and must stop when they receive the ball.

Players No. 2 and No. 3 run forward. Player No. 1 passes slightly ahead of player No. 2, "leading" him with the pass. Player No. 2 "breaks" for the spot to receive the ball, catches it, and stops. (Taking more than a two-step stop when running is a violation.) Action is repeated with player No. 2 passing to No. 3. Continue action out to and across the end line. Move on to adjacent area and repeat activity back to the starting line.

Second group of players begins play as soon as the first group reaches mid-field on the way to the end line.

**Variation: break, catch, and pass
against a defensive player**

Players Nos. 1 and 2 pass and catch the ball as partners. Player No. 3 becomes the defensive man and attempts to intercept the ball. See Variation for Dribble the Ball and Pass.

KICK, CATCH, AND CARRY

See Fig. 7.2.

Skills

Place-kicking, catching.

DANISH ROUNDERS

See Fig. 7.7.

Skills

Place-kicking, catching.

BASES ON BALLS II

See Fig. 7.9.

Skills

Kicking and catching.

PUNT BACK, VARIATION

See Punt Back, use soccerball.

SKILL TESTS—USING A SOCCERBALL

PUNT FOR DISTANCE (FIG. 7.18)

Equipment

Two kickballs or soccerballs. Draw three lines and divide the field into three areas: area 1 between kicking line and second line; area 2 between second and third lines; area 3 beyond third line.

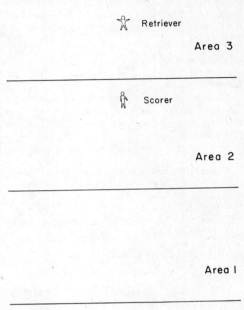

FIG. 7.18. Punt for distance.

Action

Take the test in groups of three players: contestant, a scorer, and a retriever. Contestant stands approach steps' distance behind the kicking line. Scorer and retriever take positions in the field.

Contestant punts one ball into the field. Scorer notes the spot the ball touched the ground and retriever recovers the ball. Contestant punts the second ball. Scorer notes the spot the ball touched the ground and retriever recovers the second ball.

Scoring

Score 1 point for a ball landing in the first area, 3 points for a ball landing in the second area, and 5 points for a ball landing in the third area. Record the total score for the two punts.

Rotation

Players rotate, the retriever running in with the soccerballs and becoming contestant; contestant moves to the fielding area as scorer; and scorer becomes retriever.

KICK FOR ACCURACY

Equipment

One kickball or soccerball, two markers 12 feet apart, with a short kicking line 24 feet from the target. Place the ball on the kicking line.

Action

Kicker attempts to kick the ball between the markers lower than waist height.

Scoring

Score the number of successful kicks out of three trials.

SLALOM DRIBBLE AND KICK FOR GOAL

Equipment

One kickball or soccerball, stop watch, five markers. Place three markers 20, 40, and 60 feet, respectively, from the starting line. Place two goal markers 12 feet apart on the starting line.

Action

On signal "On your mark—get set—go!" contestant starts to dribble the ball. He goes to the right of the first marker and weaves down and back around each object. When he reaches the first marker on his *return* trip, he kicks the ball over the starting line between the markers representing the goal. The ball must travel below waist height.

Scoring

Score the elapsed time from the starting signal until the *ball* crosses the starting line between the goal markers. Record the score in seconds to the nearest tenth. If

the kicked ball fails to go between the goal markers below waist height, allow one more trial.

TEAM GAMES—USING SKILLS OF SOCCER

PRISONERS' BALL

See Prisoners' Ball, variation.

PUNT BACK

See Punt Back, variation.

SOCCER KICKBALL

Equipment

Kickball, five markers or three markers and a restraining line. (Use milk cartons or plastic detergent containers for markers.)

Skills

Kicking a stationary ground ball, blocking, trapping, dribbling the ball with feet, kicking for goal, running to base and back.

Play area and position of players (Fig. 7.19)

Large rectangle with the goal line at one end. Draw a semicircle with an 18-foot *radius* at the center of the goal line, forming the penalty area. Place two markers 12 feet apart at the center of the goal line for the goal. Place two markers on the side lines 35 feet from the goal line. Place a base marker on the right side line. Distance to the base depends upon the ability of the children.

Place one team in the field, with three rows of players covering the area from the restraining line to the end line. Players on the other team are kickers, with No. 1 in kicking position, No. 2 in ready position to kick ("on deck"), and the remaining kickers standing behind the goal line to the *right* of the semicircle.

Object of the game

To kick the ball into the field, then run around the base and back across the goal line between the goal markers without being put out.

The game

Place the ball on the goal line in the center of the goal. The kicker kicks the ball into the field, runs out *around* the base marker, returns and crosses the goal line between the goal markers.

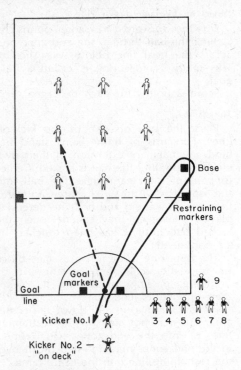

FIG. 7.19. Soccer Kickball.

The fielder receiving the ball blocks, traps, dribbles, kicks, or passes it. Fielders advance the ball toward the penalty area, the semicircle, and attempt to kick the ball *across* the penalty area and over the goal line between the two goal markers. The ball must touch the ground at least once inside the penalty area. (The ball must bounce or roll over the goal line.) *At least three fielders* must play the ball before it goes over the goal line.

Scoring

Score one run if the kicker crosses the goal line ahead of the ball. If the ball is kicked across the goal line ahead of the kicker, the kicker is out . (The succeeding kicker, the kicker "on deck," should recover the ball on the kick for goal and place the ball in position for his own kick.

Fielders should return to positions behind restraining line quickly.)

Fouls and fielders

1. Using hands (playing, striking, or moving the ball with the hands or arms).
2. Stepping on or into the penalty area. Exception: If the ball stops within the penalty area, a fielder may enter and kick the ball out to a teammate.
3. Less than three fielders playing the ball before it crosses the goal line.
4. Ball not touching the ground at least once inside the penalty area on a kick for goal.
5. Crossing the restraining line before the kicker kicks the ball.

Penalty for foul on fielders

Kicker scores a run.

Fouls when running to base

1. If kicker interferes with the ball in the field, he is out.
2. If kicker fails to run *around* his base, he must go back and circle the base before returning to the goal line.

Out of bounds

1. A kicked ball that lands on an outside boundary line is out of bounds.
2. A ball going out of bounds before reaching the restraining line is out.
Note: A ball that *lands* inside the rectangle beyond the restraining line and then rolls out of bounds is good. A ball touched by a fielder before the ball touches the ground is good even if the fielder is standing on the line or out of bounds.

Exchanging sides

1. When learning the game, give each player on the kicking team a turn to kick, then exchange sides.
2. When it is a review game, the teams may exchange sides after three outs or after the entire team has a turn to kick, whichever occurs first.

Rotation

Rotate fielders by rows (1) after one third of kickers have kicked, or (2) after a team returns to the field.

Teaching hints

1. Stress that the kicker should not kick the ball until fielders are in position behind restraining line, and that fielders should return to positions quickly.

2. In a gymnasium use a slightly deflated kickball or soccerball.

3. Beanbag may be used to hold ball for kicker.

4. For advanced players: (a) decrease distance between goal markers, (b) increase size of penalty area, and/or (c) *increase* width of goal area to 18 feet and have the succeeding kicker, the kicker "on deck," act as goalkeeper. Goalkeeper attempts to block the ball and keep it from crossing the goal line.

5. In blocking a ball at chest height, a girl should fold arms across chest as a means of protection. A foul is not called if the arms are not raised from this position to meet the ball.

END ZONE SOCCER

Equipment

Kickball or soccerball; identifying team bands or pinnies for one team.

Skills

Skills of soccer.

Play area and position of players (Fig. 7.20)

A very large rectangle with a restraining line 15 feet inside and parallel to each goal line. On each half of the rectangle mark a short kick-off line.

Place three players, forwards, from each team in the center area. One player from each team stands on either side line. Remaining players of each team are goal-

keepers. Goalkeepers are stationed inside and across the end zone area.

Object of the game and scoring

For the forwards to score points by kicking the ball through the end zone and across the goal line below waist height. This method of scoring is called a field goal.

Score 2 points for each field goal.

The game

Place the ball on one of the kick-off lines. Forwards of both teams stand behind an imaginary extension of their own kick-off line until the ball is kicked. Center forward of one team kicks the ball into the opponents' area. All three forwards then run downfield and become defensive players. However, they cannot touch the kicked ball until it has been touched by an opponent.

The opposing three forwards may block or trap the ball, then advance it by dribbling, passing, or kicking it toward their opponents' end zone.

Forwards move up and down the center area, but may not step on the restraining lines or into the end zones. Goalkeepers in the end zones may not step on or over the restraining line into the center area.

Forwards attempt to kick the ball from the center area across the back line of the end zone, the goal line. The ball must cross the goal line below waist height.

Fouls

1. Using hands (playing, striking, or moving the ball with the hand or arm).

2. Causing ball to go out of bounds over the side lines.

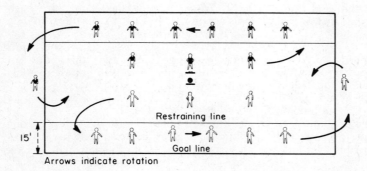

Restraining line

Goal line

15'

Arrows indicate rotation

FIG. 7.20. End Zone Soccer.

3. When kicking for goal, kicking the ball higher than waist height.

4. Forwards stepping on a restraining line or into an end zone.

5. Goalkeepers stepping on or over the restraining line into the center area to prevent a score.

6. Pushing, tripping, kicking, striking, jumping at, or holding an opponent.

7. Failure to follow rules for a free kick.

8. Dangerous kicking, kicking the ball too hard and endangering another player; endangering another player while kicking a bouncing ball or a ball on the fly.

Penalty for fouls

Free kick is awarded to an opponent at the spot the foul was committed. Exceptions: (1) If ball goes over goal line higher than waist height, defensive player takes the free kick from the restraining line. (2) Score 2 points for opposing team if a goalkeeper commits a foul while attempting to prevent the ball from crossing the end zone or the goal line. See foul No. 5.

Free kick

Place the ball on the ground at the spot of the foul. All players except the kicker must be at least 5 yards away from the ball. The ball must move at least the distance of its circumference before it is played by another player. The kicker may not contact the ball again until it has been played by another player. A goal may not be made *directly* from a free kick. Award a free kick to opponents if rules for free kick are not followed.

Out of bounds

One player from each team covers one side-line area prior to becoming a forward. (See diagram.) The side-line players move up and down the side line opposite the ball. If the ball goes out of bounds, he stops it and places it at the point the ball crossed the side line. He also calls the name of the team *not* causing the ball to go out of bounds (not touching it last).

Rotation

After each score (or after a period of two or three minutes), players rotate. Goalkeepers move to the right, one player becomes right side-line player and three players become forwards (includes previous side-line player). Forwards enter left side of end zone. (See arrows on diagram.)

Play after rotation: If a field goal has been scored, the team scored against shall have a choice of kicking off or receiving the ball to start the game again. If a field goal has not been scored, the kick-off is taken by the alternate team from the previous kick-off.

ZONE SOCCER

Equipment

Kickball or soccerball; identifying team bands or pinnies for one team, four goal markers.

Skills

Skills of soccer.

Play area and position of players (Fig. 7.21)

Large rectangle with a center line across the field. On each half of the field, mark a short kick-off line midway between the center line and goal line. Draw a semicircle, penalty area, with an 18-foot radius

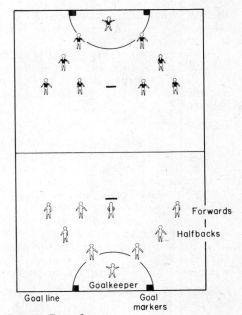

FIG. 7.21. Zone Soccer.

at the center of the goal line. Place two goal markers at the intersection of the semicircle and goal line.

Each team consists of four forwards (left forward, two center forwards, and right forward), four halfbacks (left halfback, two center halfbacks, right halfback), and a goalkeeper.

Object of the game and scoring

For forwards to score points by kicking the ball across the goal line lower than waist height. This method of scoring is called a field goal.

Score 2 points for a field goal. Score 1 point for a penalty kick.

The game

On the kick-off, forwards space themselves across the field behind their own kick-off line. Halfbacks cover the area behind the forwards, and the goalkeeper stands in front of the goal.

After the kick-off, both lines of forwards *must* cross the center line and play in opponents' half of the field. Left and right halfbacks *may* cross the center line. Their zone extends approximately to opponents' kick-off line. Center halfbacks remain in their own half of field and do not cross the center line. Goalkeepers remain within their own penalty area.

Forwards attempt to advance the ball by dribbling, passing, and kicking the ball downfield. Then they attempt to kick the ball across the goal line below waist height.

Fouls

1. Using hands (playing, striking, or moving the ball with the hand or arm).
2. Pushing, tripping, kicking, striking, jumping at, or holding an opponent.
3. When kicking for goal, kicking ball higher than waist height.
4. Failure to follow rules for free kick.
5. Dangerous kicking, kicking the ball too hard and endangering another player, endangering another player while kicking a bouncing ball, or a ball on the fly.

Penalty for fouls

Free kick is awarded to a halfback of the opposing team at the spot the foul was committed. (Exception: For a foul committed by the defensive team inside the penalty area the opponents are awarded a penalty kick.)

Free kick

Place the ball on the ground at the spot of the foul. All players except the kicker must stand at least 5 yards away from the ball. The ball must travel at least the distance of its circumference. The kicker must not contact the ball again until it has been played by another player.

A goal may not be made *directly* from a free kick.

Award a free kick to the halfback of the opposing team if rules for a free kick are not followed.

Penalty kick

For a foul committed by the defensive team inside the penalty area, award a penalty kick to the opposing team. Place the ball on the semicircle directly in front of the mid-point of the goal. All players except the goalkeeper must be outside the penalty area. A player from the offensive team attempts to kick the ball across the goal line below waist height. If successful, score one point for the penalty kick. If unsuccessful, the ball is in play.

Out of bounds

When the ball goes out of bounds, a player of the opposite team to that which played it out shall take a one-hand underhand throw-in. Player stands out of bounds and all other players stand 5 yards away.

Roll-in

A roll-in is taken under the following circumstances: for an infringement of the rules by both teams; the ball going out of bounds off the feet or body of two players of opposing teams; or after a temporary suspension of the game not involving a foul or a goal. The umpire takes the ball and from a point 5 yards away from the spot the ball was declared dead, rolls the ball between two opponents. The two opponents stand facing opposite goal lines. Umpire blows his whistle when the ball leaves his hand. The two players may move to play the ball when the whistle blows. All other players must be at least 5 yards away until the ball has been played.

Rotation

After a score has been made (or after a given period of time), players rotate. Forwards move to halfback positions, one halfback to goalkeeper, three halfbacks and goalkeeper to forwards.

Teaching hints

During the game, check playing positions. Blow the whistle twice for all players to "freeze," stop immediately. Correct playing positions if necessary and resume play.

SEVEN-PLAYER SOCCER

Players: three forwards, three halfbacks, goalkeeper.

Use official rules in Soccer Guides for boys or girls.

NINE-PLAYER SOCCER

Players: five forwards, three halfbacks, goalkeeper.

Use official rules in Soccer Guides for boys or girls.

ELEVEN-PLAYER SOCCER (FIG. 7.22)

Players: five forwards, three halfbacks, two fullbacks, goalkeeper.

Use official rules in Soccer Guides for boys or girls.

TEAM GAMES—USING SKILLS OF SPEEDBALL

SPEEDBALL RULES AND SKILLS—BASIC ADDITIONS TO AND CHANGES FROM SOCCER RULES AND SKILLS (FIG. 7.23)

To start game

Take a "place kick" at center line. All players must stand at least 5 yards from the kicker and must stand on own side of halfway line (center line) until ball is kicked. Ball must be kicked diagonally or straight forward at least 27 inches from the kicker.

Advancing the ball downfield

1. Aerial Ball.
   a. A *thrown* ball that has not touched the ground, or a ball that has been raised into the air *directly* from a kick by one or both feet. This includes a punt, drop kick, and kick-up.
   b. An aerial ball may be thrown and caught, advancing the ball as in basketball; or it may be punted, drop-kicked, or dropped to the ground and played as a ground ball. A thrown ball which is missed

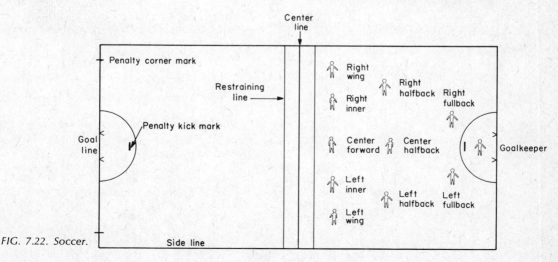

FIG. 7.22. Soccer.

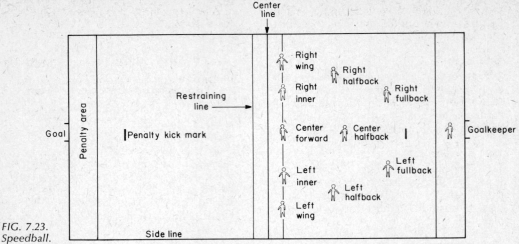

FIG. 7.23.
Speedball.

and falls to the ground is a ground ball and must be handled only with the feet.
2. Ground Ball.
   a. A ground ball is one that is rolling, bouncing, or stationary on the ground.
   b. A ground ball *must* be kicked, headed, or bounced off the body; it *may not* be played with the hands. A ground ball is played as in soccer.
3. Kick-up. A ball can be converted from a ground ball to an aerial ball by means of a kick-up. A kick-up to a teammate may be used on a free kick after a foul. See "Soccer and Speedball Skills" for a description of a kick-up.
4. Out of Bounds. Ball is awarded to opponent for a throw-in. The penalty is the same as for an out of bounds in basketball.

Scoring (adapted)
1. Field goal: 2 points.
2. Penalty kick: 1 point.
3. Touchdown: 2 points. A completion of a forward pass from outside the penalty area in the field of play and caught by a teammate who is back of the goal line extending from side line to side line, with the exception of the part between the goal posts, is a touchdown. In order to score, a player must be completely over the goal line when the ball is caught and must not be behind the goal line between the goal posts. (Penalty area is a zone 15 feet deep extending across the field in front of each goal line.)

Additional fouls—fouls involving aerial ball
1. Traveling with the ball: taking more than two steps while holding the ball following a run or more than one step at any other time.
2. Holding the ball: For more than 5 seconds inbounds if guarded, for more than 5 seconds on a free kick or out of bounds, or more than 10 seconds on a penalty kick.
3. Overguarding.

TOUCHDOWN—KEEP AWAY
See Touchdown—Keep Away, variation.

SOCCER KICKBALL WITH SPEEDBALL VARIATIONS
Play as Soccer Kickball with the following exceptions:
1. Kicked ball may be caught and passed as in speedball—an aerial ball.
2. Additional foul: traveling with ball, steps.
3. Kick-up may be used.
4. To score, the ball must be dribbled on the ground before kicking for goal.

END ZONE SPEEDBALL

Play as End Zone Soccer with the following exceptions:

1. Use rules for speedball, advancing the ball as either an aerial ball or ground ball. To score, the ball must be dribbled on the ground before kicking it into the end zone.

2. Out of bounds: Use a throw-in.

ZONE SPEEDBALL

Play as Zone Soccer, using speedball rules and skills.

SEVEN- OR NINE-PLAYER SPEEDBALL

Use official rules in Speedball Guides.

ELEVEN-PLAYER SPEEDBALL

Use official rules in Speedball Guides.

ACTIVITIES USING A FOOTBALL

As one of our most popular spectator sports, football has endeared itself to many because of the power and bruising contact so *vital* to its success. Football is not the most suitable game for elementary school children, since many are not ready to withstand its rigors. In addition, proper safety equipment is expensive, and a thorough knowledge of coaching is essential. Therefore, by removing the element of physical contact (which is a threat to many), and by offering many different group games using a football, the children will be able to develop skills in keeping with their abilities. And, while football is not considered a girls' game, they have a better appreciation of it if they learn to handle this strangely shaped ball successfully. However, games such as Field Ball and Touch Football are not co-educational games.

Much time will need to be spent in passing a football. Ideally, several footballs of the junior or intermediate size should be available for each class. The official size is too large for the majority of children in this age group. When most of the students can pass with fair accuracy, introduce a game such as Prisoners' Ball, Pass Back, or Base Football for the added excitement of a game situation.

It is recommended that the game of Field Ball be used as the "major" football game through the sixth grade. There is greater opportunity for passing and for activity in general than in either Touch or Flag Football, and personal contact is not allowed.

GLOSSARY OF TERMS

Centering or Hiking the Ball. Putting the ball in play by passing the ball back (usually back between the legs) to a teammate.

Down. One play of a game. From the time the ball is put in play until it is declared dead.

Drop Kick. Same as punt except the ball is kicked just as it touches the ground.

Lateral Pass. Passing the ball directly to the side or diagonally back from one player to another.

Off-side. The act of moving forward, before the football is centered or hiked, into a neutral area between the two teams. The neutral area extends the width of the field and is as wide as the ball is long.

Place-kick. Kicking a stationary ball off the ground. Football is placed on a kicking tee or it is held in place by a teammate.

Punt. Dropping the ball from the hands and kicking the ball before it touches the ground.

TOUCH FOOTBALL SKILLS

LIST OF TOUCH FOOTBALL SKILLS

Forward passing.
Catching a forward pass.
Punting.
Catching a punt (fielding a kicked ball). See "Analysis of Kickball Skills."
Carrying the ball.
Broken field running, Fig. 3.1.
Hiking (centering) the ball.
Handing off.
Blocking a player.
Lateral passing, two-hand underhand pass.
Place-kicking.

ACTIVITIES USING A FOOTBALL

SUGGESTED GRADE PLACEMENT CHART

	4	5	6	7	8
TOUCH FOOTBALL SKILLS, 212–216	B	x	x	B	B
RELAYS AND SMALL GROUP GAMES, 216–219					
Forward Pass and Catch—Zigzag Formation	B	x	x		
Run and Pass (File Relay)	B	x	x		
Hike Ball Relay (File Formation)	B	B	B		
Variations: Hand-Off Relay,	B	B	B		
Hike and Hand-Off Relay	B	B	B		
Hike, Run, and Catch (File Relay)	B	B	B	B	B
Variation: Add a defensive player		B	B	B	B
Hike, Pass, and Catch (Drill)	B	B	B	B	B
Variation: Add a defensive player		B	B	B	B
Hike, Pass, Catch, and Run (Drill)					
Triple File Formation		B	B	B	B
Slalom Relay (File Formation)	B	x	x	B	B
Punt and Run Back (File Relay with Leader)	B	x	x	B	B
Variations: Add a defensive player		x	x	B	B
Use a forward pass		x	x	B	B
SKILL TESTS, 219–220					
Forward Pass (Accuracy)	B	x	x	x	x
Centering (Accuracy)			B	B	B
Punt (Distance)	B	x	x	B	B
Slalom Run (Speed)			x	B	B
TEAM GAMES, 220–231					
Danish Rounders, Variation	x	•			
Bases on Balls II, Variation	x	•			
Punt and Catch	x	x			
Prisoners' Ball	x	x			
Punt Back	x	x	x	B	B
Base Football	x	x	x	•	
Variations: Home Run or Out	x	x	x	•	
Base Football Work-up	x	x	x	•	
Three-Team Base Football	x	x	x	•	
Variation: Three-Team Home Run or Out	x	x	x	•	
Field Ball		B	B	• B	• B
Variation: Use a Soccerball		G	G	G	G
Seven-Man Touch Football		– B	B	B	B
Nine-Man Touch Football			B	B	B
Flag Football		– B	B	B	B

— = May introduce activity x = Depth in instruction • = May continue activity
G = Girls, B = Boys

ANALYSIS OF TOUCH FOOTBALL SKILLS

FORWARD PASS

Starting position

Stand in forward-stride position, with foot opposite throwing arm in front.

Hold throwing hand at shoulder, cup the hand with thumb opposite the spread fingers. Slip the football into the hand so that the fingers can grip the lacing on the ball. Grip the ball slightly behind its center.

FIG. 7.24. Gripping the football for a forward pass.

Keep eyes on the target.

Execution

Keep the elbow reasonably high; draw the ball back past the ear, rotating the body away from the throw.

With the elbow leading, rotate the body back toward the target; whip the forearm and wrist forward; snap the wrist and roll the ball off the fingers.

Follow through naturally.

Complete action with weight on forward foot.

Common faults and coaching hints

1. Lack of force.

   Grip the ball between fingers and thumb, fingers on laces (*palm* the ball); rotate the body back away from the throw and then forward; lead with elbow, whip forearm and snap wrist forward (keep nose of ball pointing up slightly and toward the target); step *as* you throw; and follow through pointing to target.
2. Lack of accuracy.

   Step in direction of throw; keep nose of ball pointing up slightly and toward the target; follow through pointing to the target. When passing the ball to a receiver who is running (moving target), aim the ball *ahead and above* the receiver, "lead" the receiver.
3. Lack of spiral.

   Keep the nose of ball pointed up slightly; snap the wrist, roll the ball off the fingers. Do not try to spin the ball; throw naturally and it will spiral.

4. Short pass:

   Ball passes close to the ear with nose of ball slightly elevated and pointed toward target.
5. Long pass:

   Ball does not go as close to the ear. Step *as* you throw; step in the direction of the target.

CATCHING A FORWARD PASS

Facing the ball

Turn and face the passer.

Reach out for the ball.

Keep hands in view, *but eyes on the ball*.

Keep fingers spread and relaxed, thumbs pointing in (ball above waist), elbows slightly flexed.

Cushion force of the ball by catching the ball with fingers and continuing to give with it.

Pull it in.

Catching the ball over shoulder

Run in the direction of the flight of the ball.

Raise arms as ball approaches (not before). *Reach* out.

Have palms of hands turned toward the ball, fingers spread, thumbs wide apart and little fingers held close together. Hold elbows fairly close together.

Keep eyes on the ball until ball is caught. *As* ball contacts hands, bring it in toward the body.

Common faults and coaching hints

1. Failure to keep eyes on the ball until caught.
2. Failure to reach out for the ball—in order to "pull it in."
3. Fighting the ball, using hands for protection, holding hands out, and having ball bounce off hands.

   Start at short distances and learn to catch before attemping longer and harder throws.

   Stress *keeping eyes on the ball until it is caught; reach out;* catch ball *in fingers* and pull it in.
4. Reaching out for the ball too soon.

PUNTING—RIGHT-FOOTED KICKER (FIG. 7.25)

Starting position

Hold ball with left hand on left *side* near front of ball and place right hand on right *side* near back of ball.

FIG. 7.25. *Punting the football. Hold the ball at a slight angle; drop the ball; follow through forcibly.*

Point forward end of ball in a slightly diagonal fashion, with the point angled slightly down and slightly toward the left.

Keep eyes on the ball.

Execution

Take two steps forward in direction of target—step right, step left.

Drop ball from both hands as kicking leg comes forward forcibly with knee somewhat flexed.

Kicking leg swings through forcibly and knee extends sharply.

Contact ball about knee height with top of right foot (from big toe to outside ankle bone).

Keep head down and eyes on the ball as ball contacts foot.

Follow through with right leg continuing the forward and upward movement with the *toe pointed*.

Use arms for aid in balance.

Common faults and coaching hints

1. Working for distance before form and accuracy.
2. Holding the ball incorrectly.
3. Tossing rather than *dropping* the ball from the hands.
4. Failure to keep head down and eyes on the ball until ball is kicked.

5. Lack of force.
   Take two-step approach (step right, step left), swing kicking leg through forcibly, extend right knee sharply and follow through.
6. Lack of accuracy.
   Drop the ball and do not alter the position of the ball when hands are removed. Take preparatory steps and follow-through in direction the ball is to go. Keep the toe of kicking foot pointed down and in.
7. Safety.
   If the punted ball is not caught, keep head up until the ball bounces. The bounce of the elliptical football is unpredictable.

HIKING OR CENTERING THE BALL (FIG. 7.26)

Starting position

Crouch in a wide stride position with one foot ahead of the other.

Keeping the ball on the ground, grasp it as described for a forward pass. Use the other hand to steady the ball. (Grasp ball without picking it up or moving it.)

Beginners should look back between legs at the receiver while hiking the ball to increase accuracy.

Common faults and coaching hints

1. Picking the ball up or moving it.

FIG. 7.26. *Hiking or centering the football.*

FIG. 7.27. Hand-off.

2. Incorrect grip.
3. Lack of balance.

Execution

Pass the ball back and reach toward the target.

HAND-OFF (FIG. 7.27)

Starting position

Receiver holds one hand and forearm parallel to ground and low, and holds other hand and forearm parallel to ground and high, palms facing (low hand is toward the oncoming ball). Upper body is bent slightly forward.

Execution

Player with the ball pushes it into the mid-section of the receiver with a firm, but not hard, hand-off.

Hand off with the long axis of the ball parallel to the ground.

Receiver takes the ball in both hands.

He shifts it under right arm if running to the right and under left arm if running to the left.

Common faults and coaching hints

Tossing rather than handing the ball.

CARRYING THE FOOTBALL (FIG. 7.28)

Starting position

Tuck the ball under one arm.

Execution

Hold the hand over the nose of the ball with fingers and thumb spread; hold the other end of the ball in the crook of the elbow.

Hold the ball tightly and firmly against the body.

Common faults and coaching hints

Failure to grasp the ball correctly and fumbling the ball or having it knocked from the arm.

FIG. 7.28. Carrying the football.

BLOCKING AN OPPONENT (FIG. 7.29)

Starting position

Ready position. Have feet apart with one foot slightly ahead of the other for balance.

Bend ankles, knees, and hips, weight forward.

Execution

Place fists against body with elbows pointing out to the sides.

Position oneself between opponent and ball carrier.

Be ready to move in any direction. (It is illegal for blocker to leave his feet at any time.)

Common faults and coaching hints

Failure to keep fists close to body.

Failure to maintain balance in order to move with opponent.

FIG. 7.29. Blocking an opponent.

RELAYS AND SMALL GROUP GAMES USING A FOOTBALL

Note: See description of skills for points to stress while presenting activities.

For relay formations, see Chapter 6.

For broken field running use some of the Relays and Line Games, Chapter 3.

FORWARD PASS AND CATCH (ZIGZAG FORMATION)

Formation

Two lines of players facing. *One* line of players stands behind a marked line.

Activity

With no more than eight players in a group, forward pass the ball in a zigzag pattern down and back up the two lines of players. Start with a short distance and increase the distance as skill is increased.

RUN AND PASS (FILE RELAY)

Equipment

One football for each team.

Rélay

First player of each team runs to a line carrying the ball. He turns and throws a forward pass to the next player, then runs to the end of the line. Remaining players repeat the action.

1. Practice for a period of time. Evaluate and repeat.

2. Play for accuracy. Count the number of misses. Continue play until each player has had two turns. Team with *lowest* score wins.

3. When players are fairly accurate, play for speed. Team wins that sits down first after each player has had two turns.

HIKE BALL RELAY (FILE FORMATION)

Equipment

One football for each team.

Relay

In file relay formation all players face toward the front of the line. On signal the first player in each line hikes the ball back between his legs to the next player in line. Continue action to the end of the line. Last player in line runs to the front of the line with the ball and starts hiking it back again. Team wins that returns to starting position first and sits down.

Variation

Hike and Hand-off Relay. File formation: First player hikes the ball back between his legs. The second player receives the ball, pivots, and hands off the ball to the next player. Continue alternating the hike and the hand-off to the end of the line.

HIKE, RUN, AND CATCH (FILE RELAY)

Formation (Fig. 7.30)

Each team stands in file formation with player No. 2 standing 5 or 6 feet behind player No. 1. Allow safe distance between teams.

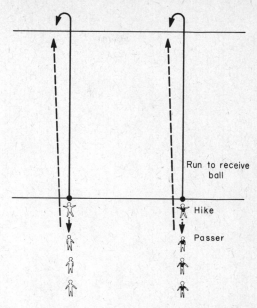

FIG. 7.30. *Hike, Run, and Catch—File Relay.*

Relay

First player in each line hikes the ball back between his legs to player No. 2 and runs downfield to turn and receive a forward pass from player No. 2 After catching or recovering the ball, player No. 1 passes it back to No. 2 and goes to the end of the line. Player No. 2 repeats the action with No. 3. Continue the action.

1. Play for a period of time. Evaluate and repeat practice.

2. Play for accuracy. Score 1 point for each pass completed over a given line, with each player having two turns, twice through the relay. Distance to the line depends upon the skills of the players.

HIKE, PASS, AND CATCH (DRILL)

Formation (Fig. 7.31)

Use a marked line for a scrimmage line. Player No. 1, the end, stands in a ready-to-run position at the scrimmage line. Player No. 2, the center, takes a position on the scrimmage line to the right of the end player. Player No. 3, the quarterback, stands 5 or 6 feet behind the center. Remaining three or four players line up in a single file behind the quarterback.

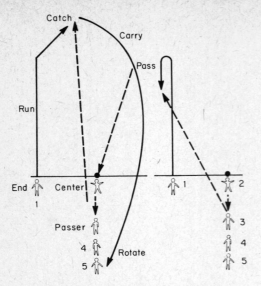

FIG. 7.31. Hike, Pass, and Catch—Drill.

Drill

The quarterback starts counting, "One —two—three—four—five." On a prearranged snap signal, such as "three," the center hikes the ball back to the quarterback and the end runs downfield. The quarterback throws a forward pass to the end. End returns the ball and tosses it to the next center player.

Rotation

Quarterback moves to center position, center to end, end to last position in line behind quarterback, and new leader in line becomes quarterback.

Variations

1. Work on different patterns for the end player to run, such as running downfield and cutting diagonally to the right, or running downfield and button-hooking directly back toward scrimmage line.

2. Have the end player take a position to the right of center as a right end.

3. Add a defensive player. Defensive player attempts to intercept forward pass thrown to end player. Both players must make a bona fide attempt to catch the ball and not interfere with opponent. (Penalty in Touch Football: pass interference.)

Rotation

The end becomes defensive player, defensive player returns the ball and goes to the end of the line behind quarterback.

HIKE, PASS, CATCH, AND RUN (DRILL, TRIPLE FILE FORMATION)

Formation (Fig. 7.32)

Players line up in three files. Files of players stand 10 to 12 feet apart behind a scrimmage line. Second player in center line stands 5 to 6 feet behind first player. Work in groups of four, two players from center line and one player from each outside line.

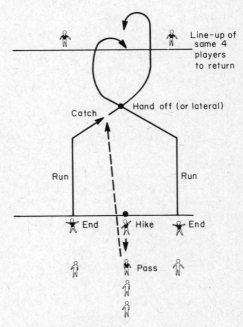

FIG. 7.32. Hike, Pass, Catch, and Run.

Drill

Center player on the scrimmage line hikes the ball back between his legs to the second player. At the same time, the two end players on the line of scrimmage run downfield. The second player in the center line, quarterback, receives the ball from the center and throws a forward pass to one of the end players. The end receiving the forward pass hands the ball to the other end as they cross and proceed downfield.

Center and quarterback follow the play downfield. The action is repeated back to the scrimmage line, with the ends as center and quarterback, and the center and quarterback as ends. Players then return to the end of the lines in original positions. Stress throwing the forward pass alternately to the end players.

SLALOM RELAY (FILE FORMATION)

Equipment

One football and three markers (milk cartons, or plastic containers) for each team. Players may be substituted for markers.

Skills

Running and dodging—carrying the ball.

Formation

Players stand in teams in file formation. Place three markers equidistant apart and in a file formation in front of each line of players. The last marker should be placed on a marked line. Three players from each team may be substituted for the markers.

Relay

The first player in each line, carrying the ball under his right arm, runs to the right of the first marker and the left of the second marker. He continues weaving out and back around the markers. He finishes by crossing in front of the next contestant, handing off the ball with his right hand and going to the end of his line. The remaining players repeat the action.

Runner may not touch markers. Player-markers may not touch or interfere with the runner or he has to return to the starting line and begin again.

Play for speed. Team wins that finishes first after each player has had two turns and is sitting down in original position.

PUNT AND RUN BACK (FILE RELAY WITH LEADER)

Note: Boys and girls play separately when punting the ball.

Formation

Each group stands in file formation behind one line. Leader stands behind an opposite line. For safety, provide at least 35 to 40 feet between groups.

Activity

First player in line on each team punts the ball to the fielder, then runs to become next fielder. Fielder catches or recovers the punt, runs it back to his line, hands off the ball to the next player, and then goes to the end of the line. (Stress carrying the ball correctly on the runback.)

1. Practice for a period of time. Evaluate and repeat.

2. Play for accuracy. Count number of successful catches completed over the fielders' line.

Variations

1. Add a defensive player. Play the same as described in Punt and Run Back except that the kicker becomes a defensive player immediately after kicking the ball. He runs out and tries to tag the fielder when the fielder returns the punts. (Limit the width of the area the fielder may run.) Fielder must be tagged with two hands below the waist.

Rotation: Defensive player (kicker) becomes fielder, and fielder goes to the end of the line.

    a. Practice for a period of time. Evaluate and repeat.

    b. Keep individual scores. Score 1 point for each successful punt return (fielder crossing kicking line within established limits without being tagged by the defensive player).

2. Use a forward pass (a) without a defensive player, (b) with a defensive player.

SKILL TESTS—USING A FOOTBALL

FORWARD PASS (ACCURACY)

Equipment

Football. On a wall, draw a circle 5 feet in diameter with the lowest point 1 foot from the ground. Mark a throwing line 25 feet from the target for fourth grade, 32 or 35 feet for fifth grade, 45 feet for sixth grade, 50 feet for seventh grade, and 55 feet for eighth grade. (See Fig. 7.4.)

Action

Contestant stands behind the throwing line and steps over the line with one foot as he throws the ball at the target. Take five trials.

Scoring

Score 1 point for each throw that lands inside or on the target. (Liners are good.) Partner stands near the target to keep score and to return the ball.

CENTERING (ACCURACY)

Equipment

Football. Use the target as described in "Forward Pass (Accuracy)." Draw a line across the center of the target, dividing it into an upper and lower half. Mark a throwing line 6 to 8 feet from the target.

Action

Place the ball on the throwing line. Contestant stands with back to the target. With the ball on the ground he reaches out, grips the ball and centers it back between his legs to hit the target. Take five trials.

Scoring

Score 1 point for each throw that lands inside or on the *lower half* of the target. (Liners are good). Do not pick up the ball before centering it. Partner stands near the target to keep the score and to return the ball.

PUNT (DISTANCE)

Equipment

One or two footballs, kicking line, markers or field with marked lines at 15 yards, 25 yards, and 40 yards, respectively, from the kicking line.

Action

Contestant stands approach steps away from the punting line. He takes approach steps and punts the ball into the field from behind the punting line. (It is a foul to cross the line before punting the ball.) Take two trials.

Scoring

Score 1 point for a ball landing between the first two markers; 3 points for a ball landing between the second and third marker; and 5 points for a ball landing beyond the last marker. Record the total number of points for the two trials. Work in groups of four, with one set of partners taking the test while another set of partners are fielders. One fielder checks the spot the ball lands and calls the score while the other fielder recovers the ball. When the two contestants complete the test, they exchange places with fielders.

SLALOM RUN (SPEED)

Equipment

Football, stop watch, starting line, three markers placed 20, 40, and 60 feet, respectively, from the starting line.

Action

On signal the contestant, carrying the football, runs to the right of the first marker, then weaves out and back around the markers and *overruns* the starting line.

Scoring

Score the lapsed time between the starting signal and the instant the contestant returns across starting line. Record time in seconds to the nearest tenth.

TEAM GAMES—USING A FOOTBALL

DANISH ROUNDERS

See Danish Rounders, variation.

BASES ON BALLS

See Bases on Balls II—with Rotation, variation.

PUNT AND CATCH

Equipment
Football.

Skills

Punting, catching a punted ball.

Play area and position of players (Fig. 7.33)

Large rectangle with a 35-foot neutral zone across the center of the field.

Place the players of each team in two

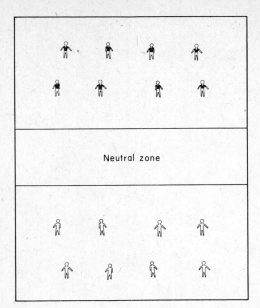

FIG. 7.33. Punt and Catch.

lines covering the area between the neutral area and their own goal line.

Object of the game

To punt the ball over the neutral area and to score points by having it land in opponents' area.

The game

A player on one team puts the ball in play by punting the ball from his own area, over the neutral zone, into opponents' area.

The opponent closest to the ball attempts to catch it. If the opponent catches the ball, he immediately punts the ball back over the neutral zone. If the opponent misses the ball and it touches the ground, the opponents score 1 point and call, "One!"

The ball is immediately put in play by the player recovering the ball. The game continues with the players punting the ball back and forth across the neutral zone.

Out of bounds

A ball is out of bounds if it *lands* on a line, in the neutral zone, or outside the opponents' playing area. If a player touches a ball and drops it while standing on a line or out of bounds, a point is scored for the opponents. A ball going out of bounds is put in play at the point it crossed the boundary line.

Scoring

Score 1 point each time a player punts a ball over the neutral zone that *lands* on the ground in the opponents' area. (A ball that is caught on the fly or which rolls or bounces into opponents' area does not score.) Each team keeps its own score and calls out its own cumulative score aloud as each point is made.

Rotation

1. Rotate by lines after one-half of the playing time. Front line goes to the back, back line moves up.

2. A team rotates each time the ball touches the ground in its own area. Rotate as in volleyball, starting with the front line moving to the right.

Variation

Use a soccerball.

PRISONERS' BALL—USING A FOOTBALL (FIG. 7.34)

Play the same as Punt and Catch with the following exceptions in rules:

1. The object of the game is to get as many opponents in prison as possible. The team with the most prisoners at the end of a given period of time wins. Prisoners then return to their own team and a new game is started.

2. Before punting the ball, the kicker calls the name of an opponent. *Any player* on the opposing team may catch the ball. However, if the ball is not caught by *any* of the opposing players, and if it *lands* inside the opponents' area, the player whose name was called goes across the neutral zone into the opponents' prison. (A ball landing on a line or in the neutral zone is out of bounds.)

3. To release a player from prison, a kicker may call, "Prisoner." If the punted ball lands in the opponents' area, the prisoner who has been in prison the longest period of time returns to his own team.

4. Play for a short period of time, declare the winner, have prisoners return to

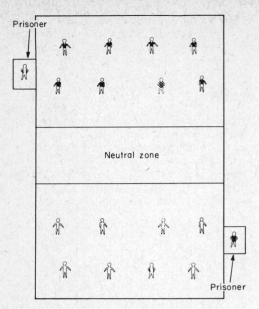

FIG. 7.34. Prisoners' Ball—using a neutral zone.

their own team, and then rotate by lines. Have the front line go to the back and the back line move to the front.

Teaching hints

1. Do not allow prisoners to remain in prison for too long a period. A game may be set at a maximum of 5 minutes.

2. When introducing the game, (a) stress that *any* player may catch the ball, not only the player whose name is called, and (b) wait until a player is in prison before presenting the rule on how to release prisoners.

Variation

Use a soccer ball.

PUNT BACK (THREE STEPS)

Equipment

Football.

Skills

Punting, catching a punt.

Play area and position of players (Fig. 7.35)

Large rectangle. The size of the rectangle depends upon the ability of the children to punt the football. Draw a short kick-off

line halfway between the center of the field and the goal line on each half of the area.

FIG. 7.35. Punt Back (Three Steps).

Start the game with players of each team in two lines covering the area between an imaginary extension of their own kick-off line and their own goal line.

Object of the game

To punt the ball and have it *land* behind the opponents' goal line.

The game

One player standing behind his own kick-off line punts the ball toward the opponents' goal line.

Any member of the opposing team attempts to catch the ball. If the ball is *not* caught before it touches the ground, the player recovering the ball punts back from the spot he recovered it. If the player catches the ball on the fly, he gets a bonus of three running steps before he punts the ball back.

Players of both teams move *up and down the entire length of the field* in order to be in the best position to catch the ball.

For safety, all opponents stand at least 30 feet away from the kicker. Teammates should not stand in front of the kicker.

After a ball has been punted, no matter how short the kick may be, the ball automatically becomes the opponents' ball and cannot be touched by the kicking team. The opponents take possession of the ball at the point it is caught, recovered, or goes out of bounds. If the ball goes over a side boundary line, the team receiving the punt puts the ball in play at the spot it crossed the line.

Ball crossing the goal line: A punt that *lands* in the area behind the opponents' goal line *on the fly* scores 1 point. The team scored against elects whether they wish to kick off or receive the ball. Ball is put in play at the kick-off line as at the start of the game.

Scoring

Score 1 point each time a player punts a ball that *lands* on the ground in the area behind the opponents' goal line. (If the ball is caught on the fly behind the goal line or if the ball *rolls* or *bounces* over the goal line, no score is made. The ball is carried to the goal line and punted back.)

Rotation

After either team scores, rotate by lines. The front line of players on each team moves to the back and the back line moves up to the front.

Teaching hints

1. Encourage the players to move up and down the field quickly in relation to the ball; to recover the ball quickly; and to put it in play quickly in order to have a good and exciting game.

2. When introducing the game, stress that players move up and down the entire length of the field.

3. Stress covering one's own area only and not fielding a ball going to another player.

4. To help avoid collisions when catching a punted ball, have players call, "Mine."

5. A football may bounce in any direction. For safety keep head up to avoid being hit in the face.

Variations

1. Pass Back. Use a forward pass with the football.
2. Punt Back. Use a soccer ball.

BASE FOOTBALL

Equipment

Football, three bases, and home plate.

Skills

Punting, catching a punted ball, forward passing, catching a forward pass, base running.

Play area and position of players (Fig. 7.36)

Softball diamond with 45-foot bases.

Position players as in softball. (See diagram.)

Object of the game

To score runs by punting or forward passing the ball into the field and running to first base, second base, third base, and home plate according to the rules of softball.

The game

Rules are the same as softball with the following exceptions:

1. Start the game by having the catcher give the ball to the kicker. (A player is in pitcher's position, but only for fielding the ball.) Kicker either punts the ball or throws a forward pass into the field, then runs the bases as in softball.

2. When a fielder returns the ball to the catcher or to the kicker to put the ball in play again, all base runners return to or remain on their bases. Base runner is out if he then leaves his base before the ball leaves the kicker's foot or hand.

3. Kicker is out:
   a. After two fouls balls.
   b. If he steps *across* home plate before the ball leaves his hand or foot. (Take approach steps behind home plate.)
   c. If the ball does not *land* beyond an imaginary restraining line from first to third base. (See diagram.) Fielders may not stand closer to home plate than the imaginary restraining line.

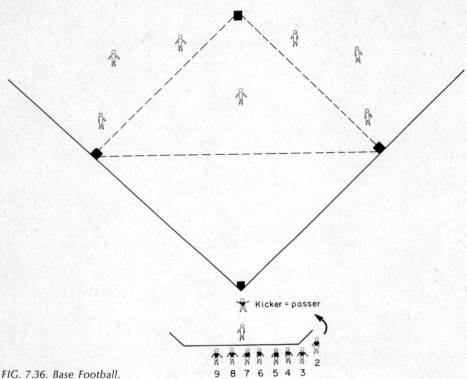

FIG. 7.36. Base Football.

Teaching hint

Encourage kickers to punt or pass the ball quickly and encourage fielders to return the ball to home plate quickly in order to have a faster and more interesting game.

Variations

Home Run or Out—Base Football.
See Home Run or Out—Softball, variation, Fig. 9.21.
Play Home Run or Out using three teams, Fig. 9.27.
Base Football Work-up.
See Softball Work-up, Fig. 9.26.
Use exceptions to rules as in Base Football.

Three-Team Base Football.
See Three-Team Softball, Fig. 9.27.
Use exceptions to rules as in Base Football.

FIELD BALL (12)

Equipment

Football.

Skills

Skills of football.

Play area and position of players (Fig. 7.37)

Large rectangle. End lines are goal lines. On each half of the play area, place a 2-foot kick-off line halfway between the goal line and the center of the field.

Goal line

Kicker

Starting line-up

Goal line

FIG. 7.37. Field Ball.

With a maximum of eight players on a team, start the game with the kicking team behind the kick-off line and evenly spaced across the width of the field. The receiving team starts the game with two or three lines of players evenly distributed in their own half of field.

Object of the game and scoring

To make a touchdown by running the ball across opponents' goal line without being tagged, or by catching a forward pass behind opponent's goal line.

Score 6 points for each touchdown.

The game

Start the game with a kick-off at the kick-off line. A kicker punts the ball to the opponents waiting on their own half of field. The kicking team may not advance until the punt *is caught,* or if not caught, until it is recovered. (If kick-off goes out of bounds, punt again.)

Receiving team catches or recovers the punt and then advances the ball downfield by running with it, passing it with forward or lateral passes, or using hand-offs. An unlimited number of passes, hand-offs or laterals, may be used on each down.

Opponents attempt to gain possession of the ball by tagging the ball carrier with two hands below the waist, or by intercepting or blocking a pass. If a pass is intercepted in the air, the team intercepting the pass becomes the offensive team and play continues.

The ball is declared dead and play stops when:

1. Ball carrier is tagged with two hands below the waist by an opponent.

2. The ball touches the ground except on a kickoff.

3. The ball or ball carrier goes out of bounds.

4. A foul is committed.

Note: Play is not stopped on an intercepted pass.

Putting the ball in play after the ball is declared dead: Award the ball to the opponents. Place the ball equidistant from the side lines and in line with the point at which the ball was declared dead. The new offensive team huddles while the captain designates a new center and receiver, and the type of play to be used. The center then stands over the ball while the *remaining players* line up *in the backfield* (see Fig. 7.38) spaced evenly across the field with the receiver behind the center. (Players on the new defensive team face their opponents from a line 4 paces away from the ball with players evenly spaced across the field.)

On signal the center hikes the ball to the designated backfield receiver. If the receiver fails to catch the hiked ball, the ball is hiked again. (No player on either team may run until the ball is caught by the receiver.)

Downs

The offensive team has one down on which to score. If the ball is declared dead before a touchdown is made, the ball is awarded to the opposing team.

Note: A play that starts by returning the kick-off or by intercepting a pass is not counted as a down. In either case, the team receiving the ball returns the ball as

FIG. 7.38. Field Ball: putting the ball in play.

far as possible and when play is stopped, maintains possession of the ball. The same team is allowed the allotted one down and puts the ball in play.

Putting the ball in play after a score: The team scored against receives a kick-off.

Fouls

Blocking, tripping, pushing, or holding an opponent.

Penalty for fouls

1. By offensive team—loss of the ball.
2. By defensive team—ball is advanced 8 paces from the spot of the foul and the down is taken again. (The ball may not be placed closer than 4 paces from the goal line on a foul.)

Length of game

Two periods—8 minutes each—constitute a game. At the end of the first period of play, squads exchange goals, and the ball is put in play with a kick-off by the team that received the ball at the start of the game.

Coaching hints

1. Stress that there is *no* body contact in this game.
2. Stress that all players are eligible to receive a pass and should break to an advantageous position to receive the ball. Check that *all* players are *used* in advancing the ball, not only the tallest or the more mature or the "best" players.
3. Remind players that the ball is dead if it touches the ground.

Variations

Use a soccerball—an excellent game for girls. Provide for separate games for girls and boys.

After the ball is declared dead, the center may face the backfield players. The center then tosses or throws the ball to the designated backfield player to put the ball in play.

SEVEN-MAN TOUCH FOOTBALL (12)

Equipment

Football.

Play area and position of players (Figs. 7.39 and 7.40)

Large rectangular field with a center line and an end zone.

Seven players on each team: left end, center, right end, quarterback, left half-back, fullback, and right half back. See diagram for starting positions.

Object of the game

To score a touchdown by running the ball over the goal line or completing a forward pass inside the end zone.

Scoring

1. Touchdown—6 points.
2. Points after touchdown:
   a. Running the ball over goal line—2 points.
   b. Completing a forward pass in end zone—2 points.
   c. Place–kick over crossbar and between the uprights or imaginary extension of uprights—1 point.

Note: Place ball 3 paces from the goal line on try for points after touchdown.

3. Safety—2 points for defensive team. *Offensive* player with the ball, touched when on or behind his own goal line; offensive team having a centered ball go into own end zone.
4. Field goal—3 points. Place–kick over crossbar and between the uprights or imaginary extension of uprights from field of play.

The game

To start the game:

Start the game with a kick-off, using a place–kick or a punt from the kick-off line.

If the kick-off is good, the receiver runs with the ball toward the opponents' goal line until he is touched by a player on the kicking team.

If the ball is fumbled while receiving the kick-off, play stops. The receiving team begins offensive play from that point.

Offensive team play:

1. After the runner who received the kick-off is touched, place the ball on the field at the exact location where the tagging took place. (If it is necessary, move the position of the ball 5 paces from the side lines.)

2. The offensive team now has four downs in which (a) to cross the center line or (b) to score a touchdown. (Start a new series of downs after a team crosses the center line.)

3. To execute any play, the *offensive* team must have at least three men on the scrimmage line when the play begins.

4. The scrimmage line should be thought of as a wall as thick as the ball, extending in both directions from the ball across the field. Any player who extends his body over the scrimmage line before the ball is centered will draw an off-side penalty for his team.

5. The offensive team may use any desired passing or running play, provided it contains the following requisites:
   a. At least three men on line of scrimmage.
   b. Center passes the ball backward through his legs to a backfield player at the start of the play.
   c. Backfield man receiving the ball from the center and giving it to another player: hands-off, laterals, or passes the ball at any point *behind* the *scrimmage* line.
   d. Only *one* forward pass play during any *one* play.
   e. On a forward pass, any player except the center may receive the pass. Center is not eligible.

6. When the ball exchanges hands and a team starts a new series of downs, players rotate. (Rotate in order to give all players an opportunity to play various positions. Continue player rotation on successive days.)

7. Punt play: A team may punt on any down providing that it first calls for punt formation. (Fig. 7.40) Neither squad may cross the scrimmage line until the *punt receiver* has caught or recovered the ball.

Dead ball: The ball is dead and play stops in the following situations:

1. Player running with the ball is legally touched.
2. Ball is thrown, kicked, or carried out of bounds.
3. On forward pass play, ball is not

Legend for diagrams

O	Offensive player
X	Defensive player
⊗	Offensive center
●	Point of a hand-off
=	Point of a fake
---→	Ball in flight
—→	Path of a player
—⊣	Path of a player with block
◐ ◑	First and second ball carriers

Normal offensive and defensive line-up
7 man game – single wing

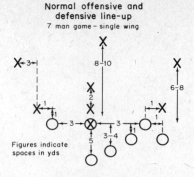

Figures indicate spaces in yds

An offensive formation
Double wing

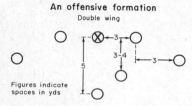

Figures indicate spaces in yds

FIG. 7.39. *Seven-Man Touch Football—Series I.* (Appreciation is expressed to M. S. Kelliher, University of California, Santa Barbara, for development of football series I, II, III.)

Offensive huddle

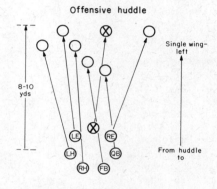

Single wing – left

From huddle to

8-10 yds

---

caught and falls to the ground. (Ball put in play at point from which it was centered on previous down.)

4. Ball is fumbled. On a fumble of a pass from center, during a running play, or on a lateral pass, the ball is dead at the spot it first touched the ground. It is put in play by the same team, unless the fumble occurred on the fourth down.

Defensive team play:

Within the limits already stated, the defensive team is unrestricted as to the distribution of its players on the field. See typical defensive positions in diagrams. The defensive team play is confined to the following actions:

1. A defensive player may touch an offensive ball carrier. The official touch is two hands placed on or below the waist of the ball carrier. After a touch is made, the "toucher" should bring his arms up distinctly above his head to indicate that a touch has occurred.

2. A defensive player may intercept a forward or a lateral pass in the air. When a player intercepts a pass, his team becomes the offensive team and he runs toward the opponents' goal.

3. Safety: If a defensive player touches an offensive ball carrier while behind the latter's own goal line, the *defensive* team scores a safety, 2 points. When this happens, the team that was scored on must put the ball in play with a punt or place-kick from the kick-off line.

4. Touchback:

a. If a ball punted by the offense goes over the defensive team's goal line without being touched by a defensive player, a touchback is ruled. The defensive team then puts the ball in play on its own

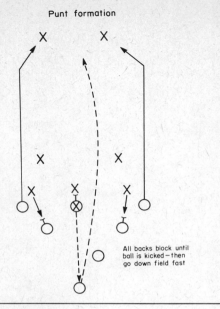

Punt formation

All backs block until
ball is kicked—then
go down field fast

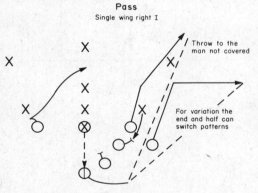

Pass
Single wing right I

Throw to the
man not covered

For variation the
end and half can
switch patterns

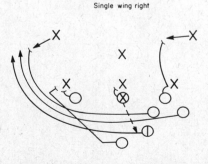

End run to left
Single wing right

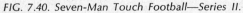

FIG. 7.40. Seven-Man Touch Football—Series II.

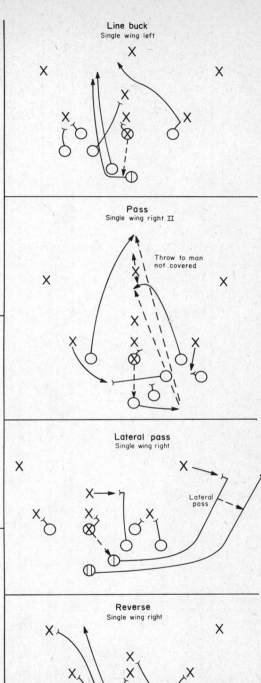

Line buck
Single wing left

Pass
Single wing right II

Throw to man
not covered

Lateral pass
Single wing right

Lateral
pass

Reverse
Single wing right

Hand-off

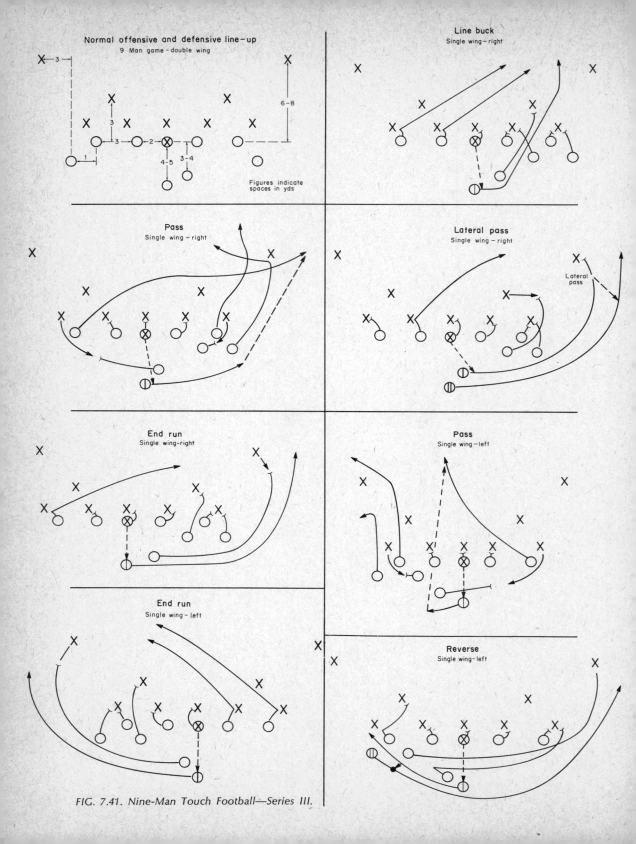

Normal offensive and defensive line-up
9 Man game - double wing

Figures indicate spaces in yds

Line buck
Single wing - right

Pass
Single wing - right

Lateral pass
Single wing - right

Lateral pass

End run
Single wing-right

Pass
Single wing - left

End run
Single wing - left

Reverse
Single wing - left

FIG. 7.41. Nine-Man Touch Football—Series III.

kick-off line, and begins a new series of downs.

b. If the kicked ball is touched or caught and fumbled by the receiving team *behind* the goal line, play stops. The receiving team then puts the ball in play from the kick-off line and begins a new series of downs.

Blocking:

In blocking at the line of scrimmage as well as in the open, no part of the blocker's body except his *feet shall be in contact with the ground throughout the block,* nor immediately before or after the block. Both feet must be on the ground at all times. Hold fists against body with elbows pointing out to sides. (See Blocking an Opponent, Fig. 7.29.) Breaking rules of blocking is a foul.

Fouls

1. Tripping, pushing, or holding.
2. Pushing or striking the ball carrier, unnecessary roughness.
3. Breaking rules of blocking.
4. Interfering with the pass receiver.

Penalty: pass is ruled completed.

Penalty for a foul

The team, offensive or defensive, is penalized half the distance to the goal line.

Violations

1. Offside.
2. Failure of ball carrier to stop immediately when touched.

Penalty for violation

Five-pace penalty toward own goal line. When the violation occurs within 5 paces of the goal line, the penalty is one-half the distance to the goal line. *On a penalty,* *the down remains the same.* The captain of the team fouled against may decline a penalty and take the play.

Length of game

Usually four equal periods not to exceed the regular instructional time, or two 8-minute periods.

Teaching hints

1. Stress blocking according to the rules.
2. Explain and stress player rotation. "We learn by doing," and it is fun to handle the ball. Rotation should also encourage each child to work on his skills.

NINE-MAN TOUCH FOOTBALL (FIG. 7.41)

Use the rules of "Seven-Man Touch Football," with nine players on a team. Five *offensive* players must be on the line of scrimmage for each play.

Players—linemen: left end, left guard, center, right guard, right end; backfield: quarterback, left halfback, fullback, right halfback.

FLAG FOOTBALL

Equipment

Football; two "flags" for each player, one "flag" hangs over each hip. (Plastic flag football belts with snap-on "flags" may be purchased. A large handkerchief with a knot tied 5 inches from the end may be pulled *up* to the knot under the player's belt.)

The game

Play the same as Seven- or Nine-Player Touch Football except for the method of "touching" a player. In Flag Football a ball carrier must stop when a flag is pulled from his belt. Flags may also be used when playing Field Ball.

CHAPTER 8

BASKETBALL AND VOLLEYBALL SPORT UNITS

ACTIVITIES USING A BASKETBALL

ACTIVITIES USING A VOLLEYBALL

FIG. 8.1. Practicing the Agility Slide-Step: basic skill in team and dual sports.

The onset of winter generally signals the end of field sports for a time. In regions where snow and rain are plentiful, the activity program is moved indoors; in other areas it is a matter of moving to weatherproof surfaces for the duration of the wet season. Basketball and volleyball are particularly suited to winter, since they both may be played in a gymnasium or on a hard outdoor surface.

Basketball can be a tremendously active game when the skill level is high. It is a frustrating game without the proper foundation of skills, or with an imbalance of skills among team members. Many activities are included in this unit that provide for development of specific skills, and that can be played competitively. In conjunction with skill development, intermediate grade children will especially enjoy the small group games because of their simplicity.

Volleyball is undergoing some rather exciting changes at present. The style of play has been improved a great deal, so that it has become a fast-moving, strategy-filled team sport. It was introduced at the 1964 Olympics for the first time, further identifying it as a game of stature. The excitement of the game can be realized at the elementary school level *if* the number of players on a team is kept to a maximum of nine, and *if* the students are allowed sufficient time for skill development. If only one court is available for play, one-half of a class could be assigned to one of the small group games for a period of time and then rotated into the volleyball game.

In both these court games the small group activities can serve as ends in themselves insofar as challenging and satisfying experiences for children are concerned. In some cases children are more comfortable with these games because they feel inadequate in the face of the complexities of the major games. An opportunity to improve skill and increase confidence should certainly be made available to these children.

PURPOSES

Limit the size of the play area and increase the speed with which players move, and a whole new dimension is introduced to team games. Court sports such as basketball and volleyball contain this dimension, and as a result offer yet another kind of movement challenge. The purposes of these two units are as follows:

—to insure the successful performance of each player through carefully planned skill progression;
—to provide activities that demand a high level of skill in movement control and ball control;
—to provide sufficient opportunities to develop accuracy and consistency in shooting for baskets or serving a volleyball;
—to further enhance awareness of spatial relationships in a relatively small playing area;
—to develop group cooperation leading to team success;
—to introduce a variety of games and related activities suitable to leisure time play.

ACTIVITIES USING A BASKETBALL

Basketball must be introduced slowly if best results are to be achieved. Players need to learn not to take steps with the ball, to control their movements in a small area, and to control the ball while passing or dribbling it. There are many small group games that are equally as satisfying as the game itself, and which insure greater participation. For example, the goal-shooting games and relays may occupy a large part of the basketball season. Only when the majority of students have developed fairly accurate skills should the formal game be played.

There should be at least four baskets available for one class if maximum participation is to be realized. Otherwise, the class should be divided into several groups, one group should be assigned to each available basket, and the remaining groups should be assigned to work on passing and dribbling skills (or on other activities) on a rotation basis.

The official size basketball is not suited

ACTIVITIES USING A BASKETBALL
(A kickball or soccerball may be substituted.)

SUGGESTED GRADE PLACEMENT CHART

	4	5	6	7	8
BASKETBALL SKILLS, 235–240	x	x	x	x	x
RELAYS AND SMALL GROUP GAMES, 240–247					
Activities for Spatial Awareness	x	x	x	x	x
Pass and Follow (Shuttle Relay)	x	x	x	x	x
Break, Pass, and Catch (Partner Relay)		x	x	x	x
Keep Away, Small Group Game	—	x	x	x	x
Shoot and Recover (File Relay)	x	x	x	x	x
Twenty-one (Team)	x	x	x	x	x
Thirteen (Individual)	x	x	x	x	x
Around the World (Individual)	x	x	x	x	x
Six Line Shoot (Individual)		x	x	x	x
Freeze O-U-T (Individual)		x	x	x	x
Shoot and Recover (Shuttle Relay)		x	x	x	x
Dribble and Pass (Shuttle Relay)	—	x	x	x	x
Dribble and Pass (Partner Relay)		x	x	x	x
Dribble and Shoot for Goal (File Relay)		x	x	x	x
Dribble and Shoot for Goal (Shuttle Relay)		x	x	x	x
Dribble and Shoot for Goal (Small Group Game)			x	x	x
Pivot, Pass and Follow (Drill)		x	x	x	x
Jump Ball (3's)		x	x	x	x
SKILL TESTS, 247–248					
Basketball Speed Pass	x	x	x	x	x
Shooting Field Goals	x	x	x	x	x
Shooting Free Throws	—	x	x	x	x
Agility Slide-Step	x	x	x	x	x
TEAM GAMES, 248–257					
Net Ball	x	•			
Prisoners' Ball	x	•			
Basket Race Ball	x	x	•		
Zigzag Basketball	x	x	x		
Six Zone Basketball	—	x	x		
Captain Ball		x	x		
Touchdown—Keep Away		x	x	x	x
Basketball—Half-Court		B	x	x	x
Basketball Court Diagram					

— = May introduce activity   • = May continue activity
x = Depth in instruction   B = Boys

to children in the fourth through sixth grades. Use the junior or intermediate basketball for this age group. If enough basketballs of this size are not available, a soccer or No. 8 kickball may be substituted.

It is best for boys to play on one court while girls play their game on another. Boys generally play a faster game in which a certain amount of roughness is inherent; and they seem to prefer throwing the ball to another boy. As a result girls have more turns when playing their own game and they can also develop their own strategy.

Players must be instructed to move continually on the court in order to be in position to receive the ball. Any player who shoots for a basket should follow his shot to be in position to get the possible rebound. Finally, since basketball is essentially a noncontact game, players must learn to be aware of spatial relationships with other players to help them avoid body contact.

GLOSSARY OF TERMS

Break for the Ball and Catch. Run to get away from guard. Break to the spot of the "lead pass." Catch on the run, not while standing still, or the ball will be intercepted by a guard. Stop immediately when ball is caught. A two-step stop is allowed when on the run; one step if not running.

Dribble the ball. A dribble is the act of bouncing a ball on the floor. A player may use either hand and may change hands, but it is a violation to use both hands at one time. A dribble ends when the player allows the ball to come to rest in one or both hands, directs it to another player, or loses control of it.

Field Goal. A field goal is a successful shot at the basket from the court, and scores 2 points.

Free Throw. A free throw is an unguarded shot at the basket from behind the free throw line, and scores 1 point if successful.

Foul. A foul is a more serious infringement of the rules than a violation and usually involves personal contact; one or two free throws are awarded the opponents

Jump Ball. A jump ball is one tossed up between two opponents. The two opponents stand in one of the three circles: free-throw circles, or center circle. A jump ball is taken to put the ball in play at the beginning of each quarter, after a tie ball, after a double violation, or after the free throws following a double foul.

Key. The lane and free-throw circle marked in front of each basket.

Lead Pass. Throw ball ahead of teammate.

Pass and Follow. Pass and move into position.

Pivot. A player with the ball steps once or more than once in any direction with the same foot; the other foot, the pivot foot, is kept at its initial point of contact with the floor.

Violation. An infringement of the rules *usually* involving the handling of the ball or footwork. A player on the opposing team is awarded the ball out of bounds on the side line opposite the spot the violation occurred. (A ball going out of bounds over the end line is thrown in from the spot behind the end line.)

BASKETBALL SKILLS

LIST OF BASKETBALL SKILLS

Passing and catching
  Chest pass.
  Bounce pass.
  Underhand pass, one-hand, underhand pattern, Fig. 6.23.
  Underhand pass, two-hand.
  Overhand pass (shoulder pass), one-hand, overhand pattern.
  Overhead pass, two-hand.
Shooting field goals and recovering ball from backboard (rebounds)
  Chest shot—for goal.
  One-hand push shot.
  Lay-up shot.
Shooting free throws
  Underhand free throw.
  One-hand push shot.
Related skills
  Spatial Awareness. See Chapter 1 "Body Control."
  Run-stop.
  Reverse turn.
  Pivot.
  Jump.
Other skills
  Dribbling the ball.
  Guarding.
  Jump ball. Figs. 8.14A and B.

ANALYSIS OF BASKETBALL SKILLS

CHEST PASS

Starting position

Grip the ball in *fingers* and *thumbs* with fingers spread and placed a little behind the center of the ball. (Fig. 8.2)

FIG. 8.2. Basketball Pass. Grip the ball with fingers and thumbs.

FIG. 8.3A. Chest Shot for Goal. Preparing to shoot, eyes on front rim of basket.

FIG. 8.3B. Note the complete extension of the body, arms, and fingers.

Bend elbows and hold the ball chest high.

Point elbows downward, not out to the side.

Execution

Extend arms forward with a snap, *stepping as you pass.*

Snap the ball through with wrists, and push the ball forward with *fingertips.*

Rotate the hands inward.

Reach for the target, weight on forward foot.

BOUNCE PASS

Perform the same as Chest Pass except that the ball is directed downward to hit the court at a spot more than half the distance to the receiver.

Common faults and coaching hints

1. Holding the ball in palms of hands.
   Stress gripping the ball in *fingers* and *thumbs,* fingers spread. (Fig. 8.2)
2. Not enough force.
   Point elbows downward, not out to the side.
   Step *as you pass.*
   Rotate hands inward *as you pass* and reach toward the target.
   Develop finger and wrist strength.
   Snap the ball through with wrists, and push the ball off with fingertips.

UNDERHAND PASS, TWO HANDS

Starting position

Keep eyes on the target.

Hold the ball at side of body and grip ball with fingers and thumbs, fingers spread and pointed diagonally back.

Execution

Swing the arms forward with a quick extension of the elbows and a forward snap of the wrists.

Step as you pass.

Follow through naturally, extending both arms forward and turning palms upward.

Weight on forward foot.

Common faults and coaching hints

Lack of force.

Grip ball with fingers and thumbs.

Cock wrists back, then snap wrists forward.
Step *as* you pass.
Reach, turning palms upward.

CHEST SHOT FOR GOAL (FIG. 8.3)

Starting position

Place the feet in a comfortable stride position with one foot slightly forward. (Fig. 8.3A)

Hold the ball at chest height with *fingers* and thumbs (do not palm the ball).

Hold the ball slightly behind its center. (Fig. 8.2)

Keep eyes on a front rim of the goal (or on a spot on the backboard for a banked shot).

Keep elbows bent and pointed downward.

Execution

As the ankles, knees, and hips are bent, make a small preparatory circular motion with the ball by pushing it out, down, and in to original position.

Continue motion by extending arms up forcibly. Snap the wrist and *rotate hands inward,* pushing ball with *fingertips.*

Step as you throw and push toward goal with legs, arms, and fingers.

Follow through naturally, extending the entire body and taking another step forward as the action is completed. (Fig. 8.3B)

Common faults and coaching hints

1. Lack of force—ability to reach basket.
   Bend ankles, knees, and hips—then extend legs and body forcibly.
   Make a small preparatory circular motion with ball.
   Step as you throw and *reach for the basket.* (Step forward with either foot—two-hand throw.)
   Hold ball in *fingers and thumbs;* rotate hands inward and push the ball off fingertips.
2. Lack of accuracy.
   Hold ball in front of body and push equally with both hands.
   Keep eyes on front rim of basket; or if shooting a banked shot, keep eyes on a spot on the backboard.
   Follow through to the target, reach.

FIG. 8.4A. One-hand Push Shot. Exception to the rule of opposition: right foot and right hand.

FIG. 8.4B. Reach for the basket, flicking the ball off the fingertips.

ONE-HAND PUSH SHOT[1] (FIG. 8.4)

Starting position

Place feet in a forward-stride position with *right* foot forward (exception to the rule of opposition). (Fig. 8.4A)

Keep eyes on front rim of basket (or spot on backboard for banked shot).

Shift ball to fingers of right hand with palm facing goal. Cock wrist back and balance ball with left hand.

Hold ball *in front of eyes,* with *right elbow pointing to the basket.*

Execution

Bend ankles, knees, and hips and at the same time make a preparatory circle with the ball—out, down, and in.

Continue motion, extending right arm upward and forward toward the basket. Snap the wrist forward, rolling the ball off the fingertips.

Extend knees and transfer weight to forward (right) foot.

[1]Skill is described for right-handed player.

Follow through naturally.

Reach for the basket and flick the wrist. (Wave at the basket.) (Fig. 8.4B)

Common faults and coaching hints

1. Trying to use this push shot from too great a distance from the basket. This is a push shot from in front of body, not a throw from outside the shoulder.
2. Placing wrong foot forward.

   Place *right* foot forward if *right*-handed; place *left* foot forward if *left*-handed (exception to rule of opposition).
3. Lack of accuracy.

   Hold ball in front of eyes with palm of hand facing basket. Look over the top of the ball at basket. *Point right elbow to the basket.*
4. Lack of force.

   Bend ankles, knees, and hips in preparation for the shot.

   At the same time make a preparatory circle with the ball—out, down, in, and then *up* (wider range of movement through which to gain momentum).

   Extend arm, wrist, and fingers forcibly and wave at the basket.

UNDERHAND FREE THROW (FIG. 8.5)

Starting position

Place the feet in a comfortable stride position; one foot may be slightly ahead of the other.

Extend arms forward, holding the ball with fingers and thumbs.

Sight front rim of goal over the ball. (Fig. 8.5A)

Execution

Bend knees, keeping back fairly straight up, not bent forward.

Keeping arms extended, bring ball down between knees and cock wrists back. (Bring ball down as knees bend.) (Fig. 8.5B)

Keep eyes on front rim of goal.

FIG. 8.5A. Underhand Free Throw. Pendular swing, with eyes focused on the front rim of the basket.

FIG. 8.5B. The wrists are cocked back at the bottom of the arc. Keep back fairly straight.

FIG. 8.5C. Snap the ball upward and follow through naturally.

Reverse the motion of the ball and swing the arms out and up in the same wide arc. (Fig. 8.5C)

At the same time, extend the knees, straighten the wrists, and rotate hands inward, palms up.

Follow through naturally to the goal in a fully extended position. (Fig. 8.3B)

Common faults and coaching hints

1. Failure to keep elbows straight throughout the entire shot.
2. Bending forward from the hips and taking eyes off basket.
3. Holding ball in palms of hands rather than with fingers and thumbs.

LAY-UP SHOT—ADVANCED (FIG. 8.6)

Starting position

Move toward the right side of the basket, either dribbling the ball or in preparation to receive a pass.

Execution

Take the ball in both hands and then shift it into position on the fingers of the right hand with palm facing basket. The left hand steadies the ball.

Take off in a high jump from the *left* foot. When ball is raised to eye level, remove the left hand and extend the right arm upward toward the basket. (Fig. 8.6)

Direct the ball against the backboard about 10 to 12 inches above the basket and about 2 inches to the right of the center line of the basket.

Keep eyes on the spot on the backboard where ball is to hit.

(When moving toward basket from the left side, take off in a high jump from the *right* foot and shoot for basket with left hand.)

Common faults and coaching hints

1. Failure to get sufficient height in the jump.
   Increase momentum during the approach and raise the *right* knee forcibly as the jump is made.
2. Ball rebounds over the top of the basket.
   Player should make the jump closer to the basket, and direct the ball softly against the backboard.

FIG. 8.6. Lay-up Shot. Take off on left foot when shooting right-handed. Jump for height, not distance.

3. Ball rolls off the opposite side of the basket.
   Player is aiming at a spot too close to the center line of the basket. Adjust point of aim.

DRIBBLING THE BALL

Starting position

Feet in stride position; head up so that opponents and and teammates can be kept in view.

Execution

Push the ball toward the floor with the *fingers,* using good wrist action. Reach for the ball as it rebounds from the floor, keeping the bounce fairly low.

Alternate hands may be used when dribbling the ball, but do not contact the ball with both hands simultaneously.

For speed in dribbling, direct the ball diagonally *forward* and *downward* to cover a greater distance.

Common faults and coaching hints

1. Lack of control in dribbling the ball.
   Use the fingers to bounce the ball for greater control and direction.
2. Pushing the ball too hard, causing it to bounce high in the air.
   Reduce the amount of force applied to the ball; reach for it with the fingers to keep the rebound below waist level.
3. Inability to travel while dribbling the ball.
   Direct the ball diagonally *forward* and *downward* so that it rebounds in the desired direction of travel.

GUARDING (FIG. 8.7)

Starting position

Feet in stride position for good balance and for quick movement in any direction.
Keep ball and opponents in view.

Execution

Guarding an opponent without the ball: Stay between opponent and the basket; be alert to move in any direction; take small sliding steps instead of crossing the feet; do not touch or tag opponent. Be aware of position of the ball.

Guarding an opponent with the ball: Do not stand too close to opponent or he may dodge around; hold one hand high to intercept a pass, the other down to increase size of the barrier; watch opponent's eyes for possible indications of his intentions.

Common faults and coaching hints

1. Failure to keep up with opponent.
   Keep weight on the balls of the feet with knees and hips bent. Take a stride position ready to move in any direction.
2. Allowing opponent to dodge around and make successful pass.
   Increase distance from opponent; keep arms outstretched; watch opponent's eyes.

RELAYS AND SMALL GROUP GAMES— USING A BASKETBALL

Note: See description of skills for points to stress while presenting the activities.
For relay formations, see Chapter 6.
Activities for Spatial Awareness, Chapter 1.

PASS AND FOLLOW (SHUTTLE RELAY)

Passes

Chest pass, bounce pass, one-hand underhand pass, one-hand overhand pass

FIG. 8.7. Guarding. Note ready position; balance to move in any direction.

(shoulder pass), two-hand underhand pass, two-hand overhead pass.

Formation

Shuttle formation with 12-to 15-foot distance to pass.

The relay

First player *steps forward* with one foot as·he passes the ball to his teammate. The first player then runs to the end of the opposite line. Teammate receiving the ball repeats the action and goes to the end of his opposite line.

Note: Players should step over the line with forward foot.

Stress

Step *as you throw,* then run (follow).

1. Play for a period of time and coach the skills. Evaluate and repeat the practice.

2. Play for speed. Team wins that finishes first after two times through the relay; each player passes the ball *four* times to get back to his original position.

BREAK, PASS AND CATCH (PARTNER RELAY)

Passes

Chest pass, bounce pass. Players explore use of other passes.

Formation

Each team lines up in couples. Partners stand 6 feet apart. For safety, space teams at least 12 feet apart.

Relay

One player of each couple runs forward. Partner passes the ball to a spot ahead of the runner. Runner catches the ball on the run and stops within two steps. Partners repeat the action down to and across end line, back to starting line. Ball is then passed to next couple and the first couple goes to the end of the line of players. Continue action.

Stress

Use lead pass. Partner should break to the spot to receive the ball. Partner should not have to turn back or stop before receiving the pass.

1. Play for a period of time and coach the skills. Evaluate and repeat practice.

2. Play for speed, two times through the relay.

KEEP AWAY (SMALL GROUP GAME)

Note: Explore use of various passes. Lead with the pass and break into a position to receive the ball.

Equipment

One ball, identifying color bands or pinnies for players of one team.

Play area and position of players

Rectangle.

Two teams, players scattered on the area, with opposing players matched fairly well in terms of height.

Object of the game

To complete five passes from one player to another without having the ball intercepted by other team or having it touch the ground.

The game

Award the ball to one player in center of area. Players pass the ball as in basketball. As a player catches the ball, all the members of the team call out, "One"; on the next successful pass call, "Two." If the ball is intercepted by a player on the opposing team, they start passing and counting.

If a player drops the ball or causes it to touch the ground, the ball automatically goes to the closest opponent. The opponent puts the ball in play at the spot it is recovered.

The team wins that makes five consecutive passes.

Award the ball to the opposing team and start playing again.

Violations

1. Traveling with the ball. Taking more than one step in any direction while in possession of the ball. (Two steps are allowed if the ball is received on the run.)

2. Holding the ball more than 5 seconds.

3. Causing the ball to go out of bounds.

4. Taking the ball away from another player.

Penalty for violations

Ball goes to an opponent out of bounds at the side line nearest the spot where the violation occurred.

Fouls

Personal contact with opponent.

Penalty for a foul—

Team with the ball: loss of the ball at the spot. Team not in possession of the ball: bonus of 2 passes added to opponents' score.

SHOOTING FOR GOAL (TEACHING HINT)

Use chest shot, one-hand push shot, and lay-up shot. When aiming for the basket, keep eyes on front rim and shoot the ball in a medium arc (Fig. 8.8). When banking a shot on the backboard, keep eyes on a spot above and to the right of the basket (if shooting from the right of basket).

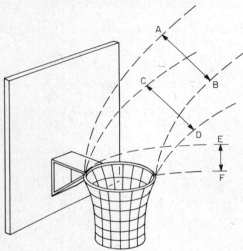

FIG. 8.8. Shooting for Goal. There is greater probability of success in a medium trajectory (C-D) than in a flat shot (E-F); too high an arc lacks accuracy (A-B).

Stress recovering ball before it touches the ground, and not taking steps while in possession of ball.

SHOOT AND RECOVER FOR ACCURACY (FILE RELAY; FIG. 8.9)

Formation

Each team stands in file formation 6 to 12 feet from the basket.

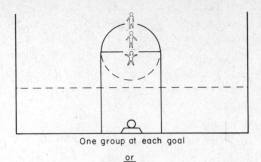

One group at each goal

or

Two groups at each goal

FIG. 8.9. Shoot and Recover—File Relay.

Relay

First player in each line shoots for the goal and attempts to recover the ball before it touches the ground. He takes a second shot from the spot where the ball is caught or recovered. He catches or recovers the ball again, passes it to the next player, and goes to the end of his line. Continue the action.

If a player recovers the ball directly under the basket, he may bounce ball once in order to get into a better position for his second shot. If he recovers the ball out of bounds, he may return to the boundary line and take one bounce into the court.

1. Play for a period of time and coach the skills. Evaluate and repeat the practice.

2. Play for accuracy. Score 2 points for each field goal. Each team calls out own cumulative score as field goals are made. Team with highest score at the end of a given period of time wins.

3. Increase the shooting distance and repeat, playing for accuracy.

Variation (for accuracy and speed)

Same as Shoot and Recover for Accuracy with the following exceptions: Each player has a maximum of three trials to make a field goal. As soon as a player makes a field goal or after he makes three unsuccessful trials, he passes the ball to the next player and goes to the end of his line.

1. Practice for a period of time and coach the skills. Evaluate and repeat the practice.

2. Play for accuracy and speed. Team wins that finishes first after going through the relay two times.

TWENTY-ONE (TEAM; FILE FORMATION)

Same as Shoot and Recover—for Accuracy with the following exceptions:

1. Team in file formation behind a line 8 to 12 feet from the goal.

2. If a player makes a field goal on his first trial, score 2 points.

3. If he catches the ball before it touches the ground, he gets a second (bonus) shot from the spot the ball is caught. Score 1 point for a successful second shot.

4. Teams call out own cumulative score as points are made.

5. Team making 21 points first wins.

Teaching hint

Stress that a second (bonus) shot is taken only if the ball is caught before it touches the ground after the first shot (whether goal is made or not).

THIRTEEN (INDIVIDUAL; FILE FORMATION)

Same as Twenty-one except each player calls out his own cumulative score. *Player* scoring 13 points first wins.

AROUND THE WORLD (INDIVIDUAL; SMALL GROUP GAME; FIG. 8.10)

Players stand in file formation behind station No. 1. Players number off and shoot in this order throughout the game. Player No. 1 shoots and recovers. If successful in making a field goal, he continues and shoots from station No. 2. When he misses, he goes to the end of the line at the station where he missed.

Players continue to shoot for goal in the order in which they are numbered, regardless of position on the area.

Player wins who is first successful in

making a goal from each station in the proper order.

Note: Players may use an underhand free throw from station No. 3.

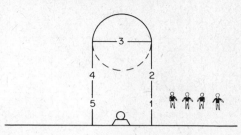

FIG. 8.10. *Around the World.*

Variations

1. Player wins who first advances to station No. 5 and back to station No. 1. (4–3–2–1).

2. Send players "home." A player successful in *making* a field goal at a station sends all other players at that station back to No. 1. If a player is returning from station No. 5, he is sent back to station No. 5 by any player who passes him going in the same direction.

3. "Take a chance." A player missing a field goal may "take a chance" by taking an extra shot. If successful when taking the extra shot, he advances to next station; if unsuccessful, he returns to station No. 1 and waits for next turn.

Teaching hints

Encourage players to recover the ball before it touches the ground. Encourage players to move quickly and to pass accurately.

SIX LINE SHOOT (INDIVIDUAL; SMALL GROUP GAME; FIG. 8.11)

Same as Around the World with the following exceptions: Two groups, each with a ball, play at one goal. Group 1 moves from station to station up one side (1 to 6), while group 2 moves from station to station up the other side (1 to 6). Player finishing at station No. 6 first wins. Groups exchange sides and repeat the game.

See Variations for Around the World.

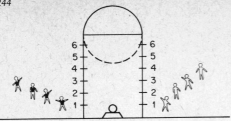

FIG. 8.11. Six-Line Shoot.

FREEZE O-U-T (INDIVIDUAL; SMALL GROUP GAME; FILE FORMATION)

Players stand in file formation in front of the goal. Player No. 1 shoots for goal from any place using any shot he chooses. He then goes to the end of the line.

If player No. 1 misses the goal, player No. 2 may change the place and the shot. If player No. 1 is successful in making the goal, player No. 2 must make a goal from the same place using the same type of shot. If player No. 2 is successful, player No. 3 must also make the shot.

If player No. 2 is unsuccessful, he gets one strike, an "O." Player No. 3 can then change the shot. Play continues, with a player getting a strike each time he fails to make a goal when the player preceding him makes the goal.

The player or players win who have no strikes (or the fewest strikes) when one player has three strikes: O-U-T. Start the game again, reversing the order of players.

SHOOT AND RECOVER (SHUTTLE RELAY; FIG. 8.12)

Formation

Place one team at each goal with half the players in file formation at one side of goal and other half of team in file formation at other side of goal. Adjust distance to goal to ability of children.

Relay

First player in one line shoots for a field goal. He then runs forward *behind* the goal and around to the end of the opposite line.

First player in other line recovers the ball before it touches the ground and passes it to the next player in the opposite line. After recovering the ball, the player goes to the end of the shooting line of players.

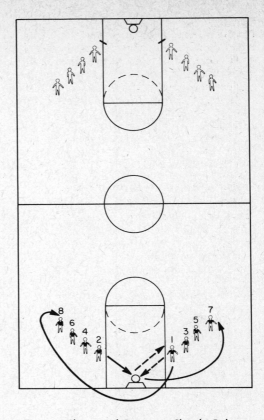

FIG. 8.12. Shoot and Recover—Shuttle Relay.

Play continues, with players shooting for field goals from one line and recovering the ball from the other line.

1. Practice for a given period of time. Evaluate and repeat practice.

2. Play for speed. Team making the most field goals in a given period of time wins. (Players at one basket compete against players at other baskets.)

Repeat the game and have the players shoot from the other line, on other side of basket.

Note: In competition, players at each basket should shoot from the same side of the basket and from the same distance.

RULES IN DRIBBLING THE BASKETBALL

Legal dribble

Giving impetus to the ball in consecutive bounces with one hand *or* the other.

Violations: Regaining control of the ball, then bouncing the ball to self or starting to dribble the ball a second time; contacting the ball with both hands at one time.

DRIBBLE THE BALL AND PASS (SHUTTLE RELAY)

This is the same as Pass and Follow (shuttle relay) except the lines are 20 to 30 feet apart.

1. First player dribbles the ball toward opposite line, then directs the ball to the next player with a bounce pass, using the one hand as in the dribble. Player in opposite line dribbles the ball back across the center area without taking the ball in both hands. Continue the action.

2. First player dribbles the ball toward opposite line. He then recovers the ball and passes it to the next player. Player receiving the ball catches it and then starts dribbling the ball back across the center area. Continue the action.

DRIBBLE THE BALL AND PASS (PARTNER RELAY)

Same as Break, Pass, and Catch (partner relay), except that each player dribbles the ball and then passes.

DRIBBLE THE BALL AND SHOOT FOR GOAL (FILE RELAY)

Each team stands in file formation 18 to 20 feet from the basket. Dribble the ball in and shoot for goal. Recover the ball, then dribble and pass it back to the next player. Continue the action.

1. Practice.

2. Play for accuracy and speed. Team calls out cumulative score after each successful field goal. Score 2 points for each field goal. Team with highest score after given period of time wins.

DRIBBLE THE BALL AND SHOOT FOR GOAL (SHUTTLE RELAY)

Same as Shoot and Recover (shuttle relay) with the following exceptions:

1. Shooting line of players stands 18 to 20 feet from the goal.

2. Each player in the shooting line dribbles in and shoots for goal.

3. Player recovering the ball dribbles and passes the ball back to next player in shooting line.

DRIBBLE THE BALL AND SHOOT FOR GOAL (SMALL GROUP GAME; FIG. 8.13)

Skills

Passing, catching, dribbling, shooting, and guarding.

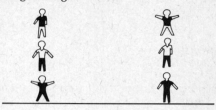

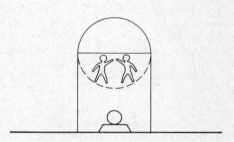

FIG. 8.13. Dribble the Ball and Shoot for Goal— Small Group Game.

Formation

Partner formation with partners standing in two lines 6 to 8 feet apart and behind the center line of the basketball court. One couple stands in front of the basket as guards.

Activity

First couple in line advances toward the goal, passing the ball back and forth, and attempts to make a basket while being guarded by the other couple. Play ends when a field goal is made, the ball is intercepted by the guards, or a violation or foul is committed.

Score 2 points for a field goal, or for a violation or foul committed by the guards.

Rotation

The two guards go to the end of the line of players, and the two forwards become guards. Continue action, with the next couple in line advancing the ball.

Couple with highest score after given period of time wins. (Each couple should have the same number of turns to shoot for basket.)

PIVOT, PASS, AND FOLLOW (DRILL)

Formation

Large circle formation. Players stand about 8 or 9 feet apart facing center of circle in ready position, knees bent and feet apart.

Drill

Use two balls, starting one ball on each side of the circle. Keeping left foot in place, each player *with the ball* pivots away from the circle. (Raise right foot, pivot away from the circle with a *half-*turn and step forward with right foot.) At the same time pass the ball to next player. Move to next player's position, face into the center of the circle, and be ready to receive the next ball.

Stress

Keep a wide stride position; keep one foot stationary; pivot away from the circle not into it; raise *right* foot and pivot back-

ward with a *one-half turn;* take a long step forward when passing the ball.

Repeat the drill passing in opposite direction. Raise *left* foot, turn backward with a *one-half turn;* and take a long *step forward as you pass.*

JUMP BALL (3'S; SMALL GROUP GAME; FIGS. 8.14A AND 8.14B)

Formation

Two contestants stand on opposite sides of a line. If right-handed, have right side toward line; if left-handed, left side toward line. Third player is the referee. Referee holds the ball in one or both hands between the two contestants and directly above the line.

Activity

Referee tosses the ball straight up and higher than either player can jump and reach. Contestants take a crouch position with arms free at the sides. Contestants spring upward and attempt to tap the ball as it descends from its highest point. Tap the ball with *fingers.*

Violations

1. Contacting the ball *before* it reaches highest point.

FIG. 8.14A. Jump Ball. Take crouch position, side to opponent, eyes on the ball.

FIG. 8.14B. Note the height of jump, with full extension of the body and fingertip control of the ball.

2. Failure to stay on own side of line.

3. Tapping the ball *more* than *twice*.

4. Playing the ball before it touches the ground (or is played by another player).

Foul

Contacting opponent.

Rotation

After three trials, players rotate.

Scoring

Score 1 point for each successful tapping of the ball without committing a violation or a foul.

Contestant wins who has the highest score after each contestant has had six trials. Repeat activity.

Stress

1. In order to spring high into the air, crouch; then forcibly extend feet, ankles, knees, and hips. At the same time swing arms forcibly upward.

2. Tap the ball with *fingers* in order to reach higher and to guide the ball more easily. Try tapping the ball in different directions.

3. Work on timing. Time the jump and contact the ball as high as possible after the ball has reached its *highest* point.

SKILL TESTS—USING A BASKETBALL

Note: One person with one stop watch could call the starting and stopping signal for all contestants taking a 30-second test.

BASKETBALL SPEED PASS—30 SECONDS (SPEED AND ACCURACY)

Equipment

One ball, stop watch, wall. Mark a line on the ground 6 feet from a smooth wall.

Action

The contestant throws (not bats) the ball against the wall and catches it on the rebound from the wall. He must keep both feet behind the line on the ground. Time the contestant for 30 seconds.

Scoring

Score the number of times the ball hits the wall in 30 seconds.

Work in partners, one contestant and one scorer (counter).

SHOOTING FIELD GOALS—30 SECONDS (ACCURACY AND SPEED)

Equipment

One ball, stop watch, goal. Mark a line on the ground 10 or 12 feet from the goal.

Action

The contestant stands at the 10- or 12-foot line. He shoots for a field goal, recovers the ball, and shoots from the spot where the ball was recovered. Time the contestant for 30 seconds.

Scoring

Score 2 points for each successful field goal in the 30 seconds.

Work in partners, one contestant and one scorer.

Note: If the ball is recovered directly under the basket, contestant may bounce ball once to get into a better position to shoot. If recovered out of bounds, contestant returns to boundary line and takes one bounce into the court.

Stress

Violation if contestant takes steps with the ball.

SHOOTING FREE THROWS (ACCURACY)

Equipment

One ball, one goal, one retriever-scorer. Draw a line 12 feet from the goal (or official distance for adults, 15 feet from goal).

Action

The contestant stands with both feet *behind* the line. He shoots at the goal for a free throw. Retriever-scorer recovers the ball and passes it back to the contestant. Contestant has five trials.

Scoring

Score 1 point for each successful free throw without a violation.

Violation

Stepping on or beyond the free-throw line before the ball has touched the ring or backboard or has entered the basket.

Players exchange positions and repeat the skill test.

AGILITY SLIDE-STEP (10) (SPEED; FIGS. 8.1 AND 8.15)

This is for balance and coordination.

Equipment

Stop watch, two lines 8 feet apart with a line down the center. (Half a four-square area may be used.)

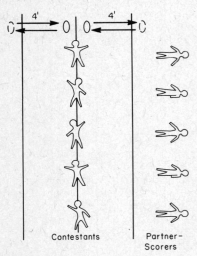

FIG. 8.15. Agility Slide Step.

Action

Contestants stand astride the center line facing forward. On signal "On your mark —get set—go!" contestants slide to the left, touching the left foot on the left line; then slide to the right, touching the right foot on the right line; then continue to left. (Contestants keep shoulders facing forward and *slide* from side to side. They may not cross one foot over the other.)

Time contestants for 10 seconds. On signal, contestants stop immediately.

Scoring

Score 1 point for each time a contestant steps on *one* of the side lines or the center line. (Four points for a complete trip across to left, center, to right, and back to center.) Continue counting for the ten seconds.

Test one-half the class, then the other half of the class. Work in partners, having contestants and scorers exchange places. Repeat the test.

TEAM GAMES—USING A BASKETBALL

A kickball or soccerball may be substituted.

NET BALL

Equipment

One ball, net 6½ feet in height (ball must rise to go over net). A volleyball may be used.

Skills

Throwing and catching.

Play area and position of players (Fig. 8.16)

Volleyball court with net 6½ feet in height. Place players of each team in three lines as in volleyball. Number as in diagram.

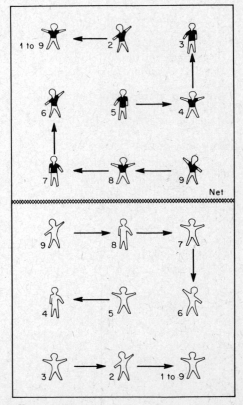

FIG. 8.16. Net Ball.

Object of the game

To throw the ball over the net and have it land on opponents' court.

The game

To start the game, a player on one side of the court throws the ball over the net into the opponents' court.

Any one of the opponents attempts to catch the ball. If the ball is caught, it is immediately thrown back over the net from the spot where it is caught, and play continues. However, if the ball lands on the court or is dropped, score 1 point for the throwing team. The team that missed the ball rotates immediately and then puts the ball in play by throwing it over the net from the spot where it is recovered.

Out of bounds

A ball *landing* outside the court is out of bounds. If a player catches a ball going out of bounds, the ball is considered in play. If he drops or only touches the ball, score 1 point for opponents.

Violations

1. Holding ball more than 5 seconds while ball is in play.
2. Traveling with the ball.

Penalty for violation

Loss of ball. Ball is thrown under the net to the opposing team.

Rotation

Rotate as in volleyball, starting with front line moving to the right. (See arrows on diagram.)

Scoring

Score 1 point for the throwing team if the ball lands on the opponents' court, if the ball is dropped, or if it is touched by a player before it lands out of bounds. (Ball landing on a boundary line is good and scores a point.) The team that reaches 15 points, with a 2-point advantage, wins. (Final score may be 15–13, 16–14, 17–15, but not 15–14.) Teams may call out their cumulative scores as they make each point.

Safety

The net should be high enough that the ball has to rise to go over the net. The ball should not be thrown straight over the net or down over the net.

Teaching hint

Introduce the basketball violations: holding the ball too long on court, traveling with the ball.

PRISONERS' BALL, VARIATION

Same as Prisoners' Ball, Fig. 8.34, except that the skills of *throwing* and catching are used.

BASKET RACE BALL (FIG. 8.17)

Equipment

One intermediate basketball, soccerball, or kickball (volleyball or No. 8½ utility ball for variation); basketball court.

Skills

Throwing, catching, pivoting and passing, shooting for goal, running the bases (serving volleyball for variation).

Play area and position of players

Basketball court. Mark three regular bases and a home base: first base on side line at mid-court; second, third, and home base on the side lines at the corners of the court. Exception: For safety allow a 20-foot overrun distance beyond home base. If area beyond home base is limited, place home base closer to mid-court to allow for a 20-foot overrun. Check path of base runner between second and third bases. Place bases in line with or slightly beyond goal post. Base runner runs outside of goal post.

Place fielding team as marked on the diagram, with player No. 1 on a shooting line 8 to 12 feet from the basket, No. 3 in the center circle, and No. 2 halfway between 1 and 3. Starting with No. 4, number fielders and place them in two lines in the back court (maximum of nine players on a team).

Object of the game

To throw the basketball over the center line into the court and run to first, second, third, and home base before player No. 1 of fielding team makes a basket.

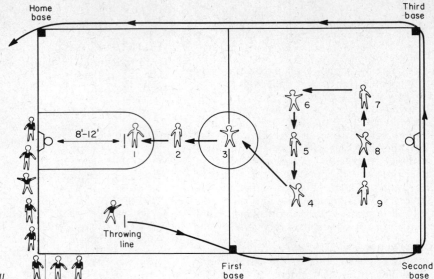

FIG. 8.17.
Basket Race Ball.

Scoring

Score 1 point for each successful run.

The game

First player stands at the throwing line and throws the ball over the center line within the court. The ball must *land* within the court. He then runs to first, second, third base, and across home base.

Fielder catching or recovering ball throws it to *another* fielder. The ball must then go to player No. 3, 3 to 2, 2 to 1. Player No. 1 attempts to make a basket. The first shot is from the shooting line. If basket is missed, succeeding shots are taken from the spot where the ball is recovered. (If ball is recovered directly under the basket, one bounce is allowed to get into a better position to shoot; if ball goes out of bounds, it is recovered, returned to the point where it crossed the boundary line, and the player takes one bounce into the court.)

If the base runner crosses home base before the basket is made, he scores one run. If basket is made first, base runner is out.

Rotation

After each thrower has had a turn, fielders rotate. Player No. 1, shooter, goes to last fielding position and all other players move up one place. The next thrower should not start his turn until fielders have completed the rotation.

Violations for fielding team

1. Traveling—taking more than one step while in possession of ball.

2. Fielders failing to make *at least one* pass to another fielder before throwing the ball to player No. 3.

3. Fielding team failing to pass the ball from player No. 3, then to No. 2, then to No. 1, who shoots for the goal.

Violations for throwing team

1. Failure to throw the ball over the center line so that it *lands* within the court. (Allow three trials.)

2. Failure to touch each base when running.

Penalty for violation

1. By fielding team—opponents score a run.

2. By throwing team—player is out.

Exchanging sides

Exchange sides after all players on the throwing team have had turns.

Teaching hints

1. For fielders, stress: quick passes; playing own area; rotating quickly.

2. For shooter, stress: recovering ball off backboard, do not let ball bounce; shooting from spot ball is recovered, not taking steps with the ball.

Variation

Serve a volleyball into the court to put ball in play.

ZIGZAG BASKETBALL

Equipment

Two balls.

Skills

Passing (and following), catching, shooting field goals, recovering ball from backboard, dribbling the ball.

Play area and position of players (Fig. 8.18)

Basketball court. On each half of the court, mark two parallel lines 12 to 15 feet apart lengthwise of the court. Start the lines 3 feet from the center line and stop 10 feet from the end line.

Players of one team are at one end of the court, with half the players behind one line facing teammates, and the other half of the players behind the opposite line. Players should be evenly spaced the length of the two lines. Place members of the opposing team in a like manner at the opposite end of the court.

Object of the game

To pass the ball down the two lines of players in a zigzag pattern to the last player, who scores points by making field goals.

The game

Each team has a ball. The first two players of each line stand on marks 3 feet from the center line, and the last two players stand on marks 10 feet from the end line.

On signal each team passes the ball in a zigzag pattern down the line of players. After each player passes the ball, he follows the pass and takes the place of the player to whom he passed, thus rotating

one position. Stress moving across the center area on side away from the basket. See diagram.

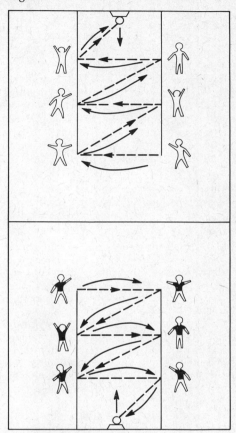

FIG. 8.18. *Zigzag Basketball.*

When the last player in line receives the ball, he shoots for the basket, recovers, and shoots from the spot where he recovered the ball. After recovering the ball from his second shot, he dribbles it down the center to the spot left vacant at the head of one of his lines.

Repeat the entire action until the leader returns to his original position and all players sit down, signaling the finish.

Scoring

Score 2 points for each field goal without a violation. The team calls out the cumulative score as each field goal is made. Award 2 bonus points for the team that finishes first.

Violations

1. Traveling with the ball.
2. Failure to shoot from the spot where the ball is recovered.

Exception: If the ball is recovered directly under the basket, a player bounces the ball once in order to get into a better position to shoot. If the ball is recovered out of bounds, player returns to the boundary line and takes one bounce into the court.

Penalty for violations

Basket, if made, does not count.

Teaching hints

1. In presenting the game the first time, explain and demonstrate the game with one team while the other team sits and observes from behind the center line. (Game is difficult to understand from a diagram.)

To place players, have the team line up in couples (two files). Have one file lead down one line and space themselves evenly the length of one line while the other half of the team leads down the other line. The two teams must have the same number of players.

2. For the first game use a chest pass. Later use other passes. See description of skills for coaching hints.

3. Stress: (a) Stand behind the line, step over the line with one foot as you pass, run to the next position keeping on side away from basket; (b) when shooting field goals, recover the ball before it touches the ground; (c) do not take steps with ball in hand (violation for steps).

Variations

1. Play until one team makes given number of points, such as 12, 16, or 20. Each team calls out cumulative score as points are made.

2. Play for a given period of time. Team with the most points wins.

SIX ZONE BASKETBALL

Equipment

One ball, color bands or pinnies to identify players of one team.

Skills

Passing, catching, shooting field goals, recovering ball from backboard, guarding —but from separate zones.

Play area and position of players (Fig. 8.19)

Basketball court. Divide court into six zones crosswise of court. Draw one line across the center of the court; draw another line 8 feet from a point *directly under the basket* and parallel to the end line; draw a third line halfway between the center line and 8-foot line. (The basket is usually projected onto the court. Measure the 8 feet from a point under the basket rather than from the end line.)

Place two or three players in each zone, with players from one team in every other zone, so that white guards are in one end zone, green forwards in next zone, white centers in third zone, and so on. (See diagram.) Note that *guards* are placed in zones under the basket.

Object of the game and scoring

To pass the ball down the court to the forwards in order to make field goals.

Score 2 points for each field goal; score 1 point for a free throw.

The game

Start the game with a jump ball. Two opposing players take a jump ball at center line and try to tap the ball back to own centers. Center players then pass the ball to their forwards, who shoot for the basket.

Violations

Definition: Infringement of rules *usually* involving ball handling and footwork.

1. Not passing the ball at least once *within* each zone.

2. Not passing to *each* zone when advancing the ball. (Guards must pass to centers.)

3. Not passing to own zone from out

of bounds, before advancing the ball down court.

4. Traveling with the ball. Taking more than one step in any direction while in possession of the ball in bounds.

5. Holding the ball more than 5 seconds.

6. Causing the ball to go out of bounds.

7. Carrying the ball into court from out of bounds.

8. Stepping *on* or over a line while in possession of the ball.

9. Stepping *on* or over a line when guarding a player with the ball or a player about to receive the ball. (Violation is not called if the goal or the pass is successful.)

10. Stepping on or over the free-throw line before the ball has touched the ring or backboard or has entered the basket.

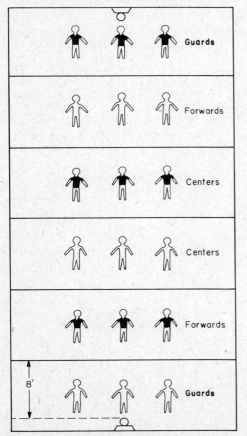

FIG. 8.19. Six Zone Basketball.

Penalty for violation

Ball goes to an opponent out of bounds at the side line nearest the spot where the violation occurred. (If ball goes out of bounds over the end line, the ball is put in play at the end line.)

Fouls

Definition: More serious infringement of rules, *usually* involving personal contact.

Personal contact with opponent.

Penalty for fouls

1. If player is not in the act of shooting for goal, one free throw is awarded.

2. If player is in the act of shooting for goal, two free throws are awarded. (However, if basket is made, only one free throw is allowed.)

To put the ball in play after a goal is made: Guard of opposing team takes the ball out of bounds behind the end line. He must pass the ball into his own zone, to one of his own guards.

Rotation

Divide playing time into three equal periods. Rotate at the end of each period. Forwards become guards, guards become centers, and centers become forwards.

Teaching hints

1. Encourage passing the ball quickly.

2. Encourage players to break for a more advantageous position on the court. Stress *moving* to receive the ball.

3. When presenting the game, introduce the definition of a violation. During the game, stop and explain various violations as they occur. This is a good game for identifying violations.

4. When placing players the first time, have the team with color bands or pinnies line up on one side line, and the other team line up on the opposite side line. Place guards from one team, then forwards from the other team. Alternate assignments and point out boundary lines for each zone *as* the players are placed.

5. When learning the rotation, have one team stoop down while the other team rotates.

CAPTAIN BALL

Equipment

One basketball.

Skills

Passing, catching, shooting field goals, guarding, dribbling the ball, jump ball.

Play area and position of players (Fig. 8.20)

Basketball court with 11 (or 7) circles, each 4 feet in diameter. (See diagram.)

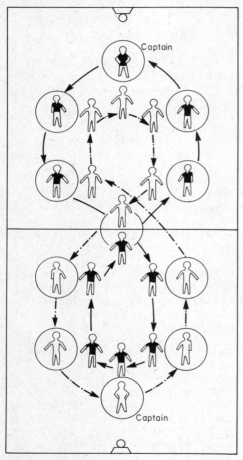

FIG. 8.20. Captain Ball.

Each team is composed of five forwards, five guards, and one center. Forwards occupy the circles on one-half the court, with the captain in the circle near the basket. Guards stand outside the circles on the other half of the court. The center player starts at the center circle on the guards' half of the court.

Object of the game and scoring

To pass the ball from the guards to the forwards to the captain, who shoots for the basket. Score 2 points for each basket.

The game

Start the game with a jump ball in the center circle. Guards (outside the circles) recover the ball, pass and dribble it to the center line. They then pass the ball to one of their forwards in a circle. Forwards. pass the ball to the captain, who shoots for a basket. Forwards *must* stay in circles.

If the goal is made, both teams rotate. (See arrows on diagram.) Game is started again with a jump ball at center circle. If the goal is missed, ball is recovered (usually by the guard) and play continues.

Violations

1. Stepping on or over a line: a circle line, center line, or boundary line.
2. Causing the ball to go out of bounds.
3. Traveling—taking steps with ball.
4. Holding the ball for more than 5 seconds.

Penalty for violation

Award the ball to closest opponent. (Ball is never awarded to the captain.)

Foul

Personal contact.

Penalty for a foul

One free throw if opponent is not shooting for a goal; two free throws if opponent is shooting for a goal and goal is missed. (One free throw if goal is made.)

Teaching hint

If a score is not made within a reasonable length of time, have players rotate.

Variation

Use seven circles, with three circles on each half of the court; use three forwards, three guards, and a center player.

TOUCHDOWN—KEEP AWAY

Equipment

One ball, color bands or pinnies to identify players of one team.

Skills

Passing (and following), breaking for the ball, and catching.

Play area and position of players (Fig. 8.21)

A rectangle the size of a large basketball court or larger. The two end lines of the rectangle serve as goal lines. Draw a 2-foot penalty throw line in the play area 12 feet from the mid-point of each goal line. Play with five to eight players on each team. Each player should be matched with an opponent of approximately the same height. Couples (two opponents) then scatter on the area.

Object of the game

To advance the ball, as in basketball, down to the goal line, and to make a touchdown by having a player inside the play area complete a pass to a teammate behind the goal line (end line).

The game

Start the game with a jump ball. Team receiving the ball advances it toward opponents' goal line.

If a player drops the ball or causes it to touch the ground, the ball *automatically* goes to the closest opponent. The opponent puts the ball in play at the spot where it is recovered.

Scoring

Score 2 points for a touchdown, a completed pass over the opponents' goal line. Score 1 point for a penalty pass.

Violations

1. Traveling with the ball. Taking more than one step in any direction while in possession of the ball. (Two steps are allowed at the end of a run or dribble.)
2. Holding the ball more than 5 seconds.
3. Causing the ball to go out of bounds.
4. Taking the ball away from another player.

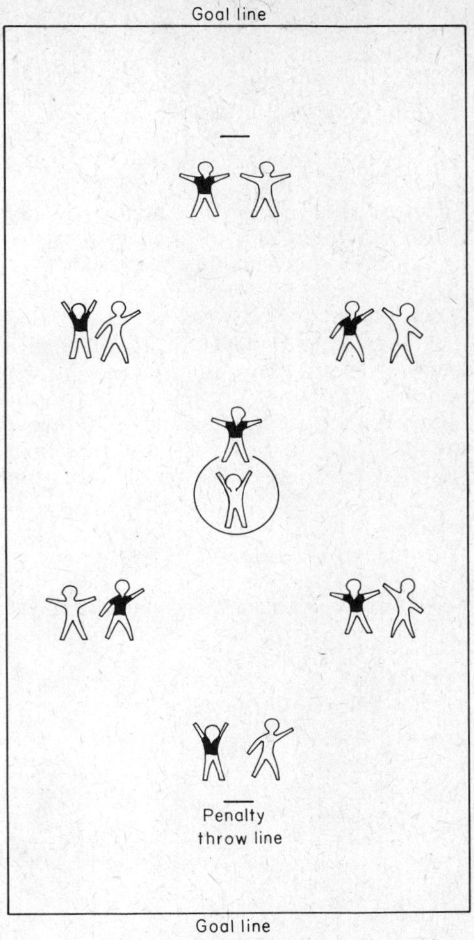

FIG. 8.21. Touchdown—Keep Away.

Penalty for violations

Ball goes to an opponent out of bounds at the side lines nearest the spot where the violation occurred.

Foul

Personal contact with opponent.

Penalty for fouls

Penalty throw. Opponent takes the ball at a line 12 feet from the center of the end line. Without being guarded he attempts to complete a pass to a teammate behind the goal line. (Receivers may be guarded.)

If successful in completing the pass, score 1 point.

Tie ball

Two players of opposing teams place one or both hands firmly on the ball at the same time; or a player places one or both hands firmly on a ball already held by an opponent. Put the ball in play with a jump ball between the two players.

Teaching hint

Stress that if a player drops the ball or causes it to touch the ground, the ball *automatically* goes to the closest opponent. An opposing player should recover the ball quickly and pass to a teammate from the spot where the ball is recovered.

Variation

Use a soccerball or kickball.

BASKETBALL—HALF COURT (USING SIDE-LINE PLAYERS)

Equipment

One ball, color bands or pinnies to identify players of one team.

Skills

Skills of basketball.

Play area and position of players (Fig. 8.22)

One-half a basketball court.

Players of one team line up according to height along one side line of the half-court, taller players toward the center line. Players of the opposing team line up in the same manner behind the opposite side line.

The three shortest players of each team move onto the court. Remaining players of one team space themselves evenly *behind* the side line and end line, from the center line to the basket on one side. Sideline players of opposing team space themselves in a like manner on opposite side and adjacent half of end line. (See diagram.)

Object of the game

To make points by shooting field goals and free throws.

Scoring

Field goals—2 points.
Free throws—1 point.

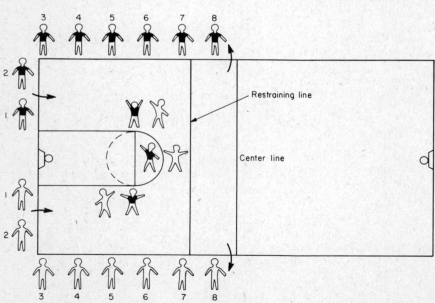

FIG. 8.22. Basketball—Half Court (using side-line players).

The game

Start the game with a jump ball at back of free-throw circle. Team gaining possession of the ball advances it toward the basket and shoots for goal.

Play as basketball with the following exceptions:

1. Both teams play for one goal.

2. When the ball is intercepted by the opposing team, the ball must be advanced out *beyond the back edge of the free-throw circle and* must be passed to a teammate on the side lines *before* members of the team may shoot for a basket.

Note: The team in possession of the ball may take successive shots at the basket.

3. After a field goal is made, or after a given period of time, players rotate. Players on court go to the side lines. They return near the center line while the three players nearest the basket move onto the court. (See arrows on diagram.)

4. End and side-line players serve three purposes:

  a. To keep the ball from going out of bounds. They throw the ball to own teammate on court.

  b. To assist teammates on court to advance the ball. Players on court should be *encouraged* to pass the ball to teammates on side lines. (Side-line players must return the ball to the court, not pass it down the side line.)

  c. To learn rules and strategy of basketball. (Explain violations and fouls as they happen.)

Teaching hints

1. If a score is not made in a reasonable amount of time, stop the game and have players rotate.

2. Use this game to identify fouls and violations.

Variation

Play Half-Court Basketball without side-line players. Game may be called Three on Three.

BASKETBALL (FIG. 8.23)

See Official Rules (4; 7).

FIG. 8.23. Basketball Court Diagram.

ACTIVITIES USING A VOLLEYBALL

In most sports the use of skill drills is considered drudgery that must be tolerated in order to arrive finally at the major game. The addition of a game element or competition into skill drills helps to alleviate the dullness, and can even inject some enjoyment into an otherwise dreary session.

In the volleyball skills, for instance, a great deal of excitement can be generated by challenging groups to see who can achieve the greatest number of digs, or to see which individual can score the greatest number of successive spikes against a wall. It is this kind of drill that will help children

ACTIVITIES USING A VOLLEYBALL

SUGGESTED GRADE PLACEMENT CHART

	2	3	4	5	6	7	8
VOLLEYBALL SKILL DRILLS, 263–264							
Agility Slide Step, Basketball Skill Test		—	x	x	x	x	x
Dig Pass (Double Forearm Pass)				—	x	x	x
Overhand Serve				—	x	x	x
Overhead Pass				—	x	x	x
Set-up				—	x	x	x
Spike					—	x	x
RELAYS AND SMALL GROUP GAMES WITHOUT NET, 264–267							
Sky Ball	—	x	x	·			
Keep It Up			—	x	x	x	·
Circle			—	x	x	x	·
Four Square			—	x	x	x	·
Above the Line			—	x	x	x	·
RELAYS AND SMALL GROUP GAMES WITH NET, 267–268							
Keep It Up—Over the Net			—	x	x	x	x
Volleyball—Doubles				—	x	x	x
Deck Tennis—Doubles					—	x	x
SKILL TESTS, 268–269							
Serve (Accuracy)				x	x	x	·
Volley (Accuracy)			—	x	x	x	·
Agility Slide Step, Basketball Skill Test		—	x	x	·	·	·
Jump and Reach, Chapter 9		—	x	x	x	·	·
TEAM GAMES WITHOUT NET, 269–270							
Danish Rounders	—	x	x	·			
Fist Ball	—	x	x	·			
Bat Dodge Ball	—	x	x	·			
Basket Race Ball			x	x	·		
TEAM GAMES WITH NET, 270–277							
Bullets		—	x	x	·		
Prisoners' Ball		—	x	x	·		
Finger Volleyball			—	x	x		
Bounce Volleyball			x	·			
Serve and Volley				x	x	·	
Volleyball				—	x	x	x
Deck Tennis—Team					x	x	x

— = May introduce activity   x = Depth in instruction   • = May continue activity

develop skills necessary for a successful game of volleyball.

The use of small groups for these activities cannot be stressed too much. A child can learn to handle a volleyball properly only if he has many opportunities to practice. This is not possible if the team is comprised of one-half of a class, especially if the child is the least bit hesitant about trying to hit the ball.

There are several modifications that may be incorporated during the initial game experience in volleyball. Although players should always try to hit the ball on the volley, one modification is to consider the ball in play even after one bounce. This will encourage more successful returns, and provide time for novice players to get into proper position to hit the ball. Much playing time is lost at the beginning of the season because students do not move quickly enough, and because time is wasted in recovering a dead ball and putting it in play. Hitting the ball either after a bounce or on the volley will liven the game considerably and provide more activity. When learning the game, the ball may be put in play by tossing or throwing it over the net. A tossed ball is easier to return than a ball that is served. Another modification is the provision for assistance on the serve. This may be necessary until all the players achieve sufficient strength and skill to serve the ball across the net. As skill increases, these rules may be rescinded.

If the number of volleyballs available is not sufficient for all the groups, then No. 7 or 8½ utility balls may be used quite effectively for drills. The important thing is that children be given an opportunity to play volleyball as it is meant to be played, with speed, finesse, and strategy.

GLOSSARY OF TERMS

Foot Fault. Stepping on or over the end line when serving the ball.

Illegal Control of Ball. Holding, lifting, or throwing in which the ball comes to rest momentarily in the hands; contacting the ball with any part of body below the waist; striking ball more than once in succession.

"Point." The call made by the official when the receiving team makes a fault; the same server continues to serve the ball.

Serve. Putting the ball in play.

Set Up. Batting the ball high into the air and close to the net in preparation for a spike by a teammate.

"Side Out." The call made by the official when the serving team makes a fault; opposing team rotates and then serves.

Spike. A net player jumping high into the air and batting the ball over the net in a downward path, usually hit with one hand. (Player may not reach over the net to contact ball.)

Volley. Contacting the ball before it touches the court or any other object.

VOLLEYBALL SKILLS[2]

LIST OF VOLLEYBALL SKILLS

Underhand serve.
Overhand serve (advanced).
Overhead pass.
Dig pass (double forearm pass).
Agility Slide-Step, Figs. 8.1 and 8.15.
Set-up.
Spike.
Block.

ANALYSIS OF VOLLEYBALL SKILLS

UNDERHAND SERVE (FIG. 8.24)

Note: The skills are described for a right-handed player.

Starting position

Place the feet in a forward-stride position, with left foot forward, knees slightly bent.

Hold the ball in front and to right of body.

Keep eyes on the back of the ball.

Bend fingers at second joint and place half-closed fist against underside of ball. (Fig. 8.24A)

Execution

Swing right arm directly backward as a pendulum with elbow straight.

Shift weight from front to back foot. (Fig. 8.24B)

Swing right arm forward as a pendulum.

Swing forcibly and bat the ball *off* the left hand, keeping wrist firm.

Keep eyes on back of ball.

Shift weight to forward foot. (Fig. 8.24C)

Follow throught naturally and completely.

---

[2]Grateful acknowledgment is made to Miss Jan Fritsen, Laguna Beach High School, Laguna Beach, California, for her valuable contribution to this material.

FIG. 8.24A. Underhand Serve. Measuring for pendulum swing.

FIG. 8.24B. Arm is drawn back in a wide range of movement, greater distance in which to develop momentum.

FIG. 8.24C. Ball is batted off the supporting hand with the heel of the other hand.

Reach forward with right hand and arm in direction ball is to go.

Straighten knees and extend body.

Common faults and coaching hints

1. Lack of force.

Bat ball with half-closed fist; use wide range of movement; swing through forcibly; transfer weight—step as you hit; follow through completely—reach. Move from partial crouch position to full extension.

2. Tossing ball with left hand.

Bat the ball *off* left hand.

3. Poor direction.

Follow through in direction ball is to go.

4. Not hitting ball high enough.

Contact underside of ball and bat ball *up.*

OVERHAND SERVE

Starting position

Take a forward-stride position, with the left side of body closer than the right side to the serving line.

Hold the ball in left hand.

Execution

Toss the ball 3 or 4 feet into the air in front of the right shoulder.

Draw the right hand back by the right ear, elbow raised to shoulder level (as if to throw a softball).

Keep eyes on the ball.

Cup the right hand, with the thumb tucked against the base of the index finger.

Contact the ball on a level with the top of the head. Contact the ball with the heel and outer sides of the hand.

Follow through naturally with the hand and arm, wrist flicking downward.

Common faults and teaching hints

1. Not watching ball.

Eyes should focus on ball from the start of the toss until it is contacted by the hitting hand.

2. Attempting to hit the ball too hard.

Stress accuracy and careful placement of the ball rather than speed at the beginning.

3. Wrist too relaxed on serve.

The hitting arm should be stiff from

elbow to fingertips at the moment of contact with the ball.

The wrist may bend naturally on the follow-through.

OVERHEAD PASS (FIG. 8.25)

Starting position

Take a forward-stride position, body slightly crouched. (Fig. 8.25A)

FIG. 8.25A.
Overhead Pass.

FIG. 8.25B.
Follow-through.

Place hands even with the forehead with thumbs about 1 inch apart, fingers tilted back and slightly curved, elbows away from body.

Execution

Contact the ball in front of the forehead with the fleshy pads of all the fingers.

Straighten the elbows and knees at the moment of contact.

Bat the ball sharply upward with good use of the fingers. (Ball must not be allowed to rest in the hands.)

Follow ball upward with hands and body as the wrists flick forward. (Note position of hands and fingers in Fig. 8.25B.)

Common faults and teaching hints

1. Contacting the ball with the palms.
   Keep fingers curled forward.
   Develop finger strength to increase confidence.

2. Hitting the ball forward into the net.
   Assume a crouch position, fingers *tilted back*, palms facing *upward*.
   Extend arms and body upward on contact with ball.

DIG PASS (DOUBLE FOREARM PASS; FIG. 8.26)

Note: The Dig Pass is intended for use with the arms in front or to either side of the body. The ball should always be directed in an upward arc.

Starting position

Place the feet in forward-stride position knees bent so that the body assumes a half-crouch position. The back is straight.

Place the back of one hand in the palm of the other; bring elbows close together so that a shelf is formed with the forearms.

Keep elbows close together and slightly away from the body.

Execution

Contact the ball with the fleshy part of both forearms.

Meet the ball with the arms and give slightly rather than swing at it. (Fig. 8.26)

FIG. 8.26. Dig Pass—Double Forearm Pass.

Straighten the knees and body slightly in an easy upward motion.

Direct the ball in an *upward arc* rather than *forward* or *over the net*.

Follow the ball upward naturally with the arms, and then separate them.

Keep the body in an upright position, ready to move quickly.

Common faults and teaching hints

1. Swinging at ball.
   Ball is *met* by the arms and directed upward.
2. Insufficient height.
   As the ball is contacted, the shelf formed by the forearms is raised to a position parallel to the floor.

SET-UP

Starting position

Take a forward-stride position.
Bend knees slightly, keep back straight.
Extend elbows outward at shoulder level, hands above forehead with thumbs and index fingers almost touching. Palms of hands face upward, fingers spread and slightly bent.
Watch the flight of the approaching ball closely in order to get in position *under* it.

Execution

Contact the ball with the fleshy pads of the fingers.
Extend the wrists, elbows, and knees upward with a snap at the moment of contact.
Extend fingers upward in follow-through; the body is erect.
Get into position to play the ball again if necessary.

Common faults and teaching hints

1. Improper position to set the ball.
   Setter stands with side to net and sets the ball to a spot close to the net, not to the hitter.
2. Lack of control in setting, causing the ball to land on the net or go into opposite court.
   Repeat drills of setting, especially No. 3 in the series of drills for Set-ups.
3. Not enough height in setting.
   Bend the knees to get under the ball; drive it upward with full extension of the body as well as good use of the arms, wrists, and fingers.

SPIKE

Starting position

Stand an arm's length from the net, feet in forward-stride position, with the left side of the body closer than the right side to the net.
Bend elbows and hold them close to the body, hands at waist level.
Bend knees and take a slight crouch position.
Turn head to watch the approach of the ball.

Execution

As the ball approaches a point 10 to 12 inches above the net, drop the arms and then thrust them upward.
Extend the body into a jump by straightening hips and knees, pushing forcefully off the floor with both feet.
Draw the hitting arm back with the cupped hand behind the ear, as in the overhand serve.
Raise elbow above shoulder level.
When the ball is 6 to 8 inches above the net, bring the hitting hand upward and forward, contacting the ball with the heel of the hand. The fingers snap downward at the moment of contact to direct the ball downward into the opposite court.
Bend knees in landing to maintain balance. Bring the hitting arm across the body in the follow-through to avoid contact with the net. Fold the other arm against the chest at the height of the jump.

Common faults and teaching hints

1. Missing the ball.
   Keep eyes on the ball from the moment of the jump. Improve timing through drill.
2. Hitting the ball after the peak of the jump.
   Delay the take-off a little longer.
3. Hitting the ball into the net.
   Extend the arm and reach for the ball. Hit the ball outward more than downward. Improve jumping ability to gain height.
4. Contacting the net after spiking.
   The follow-through of the hand and arm is directed across the chest. The set-up should be 18 to 24 inches from the net.

DRILLS—USING VOLLEYBALL OR NO. 8½ UTILITY BALL

DIG PASS (DOUBLE FOREARM PASS; FIG. 8.26)

1. Teacher and class formation. Teacher tosses the ball to the first player in line, who digs it back to him. After three turns, go on to the next player. The teacher goes to the end of the line after everyone has had a turn to dig, and the first player in line becomes the teacher. Stress accuracy.

2. Teacher and class formation. Play the same as No. 1 except that the teacher uses a chest pass rather than tossing it, aiming at a spot just above the knees.

3. File formation facing a wall. Standing 6 to 8 feet from the wall, the first player digs the ball, causing it to rebound from the wall so that he can play it again. Rotate after five hits. Strive for consecutive hits.

Play as a small group game by adding the total consecutive hits by each group to determine a winner.

OVERHAND SERVE

1. One ball for every two players. (No. 7 or No. 8½ utility ball may be used.) Players stand 10 feet apart and serve the ball to one another. Accuracy is essential to develop skill in placing a serve. The players take one step back and repeat the serve after two successful hits. Continue to back up until each player is standing on an end line of the volleyball court.

2. Partners stand 10 feet apart on either side of the volleyball net, serve the ball across the net. Step back after two successful serves.

3. Server stands 6 to 8 feet from the net. His partner stands on the end line in the opposite court. Exchange places after five hits. Increase distance from net on successive turns.

OVERHEAD PASS (FIG. 8.25)

1. Two-Line formation with six to eight players in each group. In ready position with hands above forehead, players toss the ball back and forth. Gradually lessen the amount of time that the ball rests in the hands until the players can pass accurately with the fingers. Stress catching the ball with the fingers rather than the palms.

2. Teacher and class formation. "Teacher" tosses the ball high into the air to each player in turn. The players pass the ball back to him, striving for finger contact and accuracy. Rotate so that each player has a turn as teacher.

3. Teacher and class formation. Same as No. 2 except that the "teacher" passes the ball rather than tossing it; the players pass the ball back to him. Stress finger control and accuracy.

SET-UP

1. The formation is similar to that of Basketball—Around the World. Marks are placed along the free-throw lanes on a basketball court. Player starts at No. 1 and sets the volleyball up so that it goes through or hits the rim of the basket. After each successful set he moves to the next mark. If unsuccessful, he must remain at that mark until a hit is made. Stress setting the ball into the air so that it drops down onto the basket.

2. One group stands in shuttle formation parallel to a wall. (The wall represents the net.) The leader of one line sets up the ball to the leader of the opposite line standing 6 to 8 feet away. The first leader then goes to the end of the opposite line. The second leader sets up the ball to the opposite player and then goes to end of the opposite line. Continue until all players have set the ball from both lines. The object of the drill is to set the ball as close as possible to the wall (which represents the net) without having the ball hit the wall.

3. Mark a square, 3 x 3 feet, on the court. Mark the square close to one side line and with one side directly under the net.

Players stand in file formation with leader. The file of players stands adjacent to the net and 8 to 10 feet from the square. The leader stands in front of the square and tosses the ball to the first player in line. He sets up the ball in a high arc so that it drops into the square. After three turns, player goes to the end of the line. The leader rotates after all players in line have had turns, and the drill is repeated with a new leader.

SPIKE

1. File formation with leader (setter). One player, the "setter," stands beside the net and tosses the ball so that it arcs 2 to 3 feet above the net. The "spiker" jumps and spikes the ball, causing it to go downward into the opposite court. The spiker has three turns and then goes to the end of the line. The setter retains his position until all players in line have had a turn, and then he rotates into the line of spikers.

2. Play the same as drill No. 1 except that the setter sets up the ball for the spiker rather than tossing it.

3. File formation facing a wall, four players in each group. The first player tosses the ball into the air and then spikes it so that it hits the floor 3 to 4 feet from the wall. As it rebounds from the wall he spikes the ball again, attempting to hit it several times consecutively. Rotate frequently so that all players have several turns.

4. Place a volleyball or other similar ball in a cloth bag and attach to it a rope 10 to 12 feet long. Rather than securing the rope to a pole, pass the free end of the rope through a basketball hoop so that the bag is suspended at arm's length above the player's head. One player should be assigned to hold the rope for quick adjustment to player's height.

The player jumps into the air and spikes the ball, driving it downward. He should be encouraged to contact the *top* of the ball for a proper hit. The flight of the ball will determine the effectiveness of the hit; a ball that swings outward indicates lack of height on the jump and insufficient reach with the spiking arm.

RELAYS AND SMALL GROUP GAMES— USING VOLLEYBALL, NO. 7 OR 8½ UTILITY BALL

Note: See description of skills for points to stress while presenting activities. For relay formations, see Chapter 6.

SKY BALL

Equipment

One No. 7 or 8½ utility ball for each group.

Skills

Tossing ball vertically, catching.

Play area and position of players (Fig. 8.27)

Open area free of hazards. Each group of players stands in a circle formation.

FIG. 8.27. Sky Ball.

Object of the game

To catch the ball, which has been thrown high into the air, before the ball touches the ground.

The game

One player stands in the center of the circle with the ball. He calls the name of another player in the group *as* he tosses the ball high into the air.

Player whose name is called tries to catch the ball before it touches the ground inside the circle. (Player tossing the ball steps out of the center of the circle immediately.)

Scoring

Score 1 point *against* a player each time he fails to catch the ball. The player with the *fewest* points after a given period of time wins.

Teaching hints

Stress: (1) calling the name *as* you toss the ball, (2) tossing the ball up and tossing it reasonably high, and (3) stepping out of circle immediately after tossing the ball to avoid interfering with the catch. For infringements, take the throw again.

KEEP IT UP—CIRCLE FORMATION

Equipment

One volleyball or No. 8½ utility ball for each group.

Skill

Volleyball volley.

Formation

Four to eight players in a circle; two or more circles of players. This game may be played on one-half a volleyball court and used as a warm-up preceding the game of volleyball.

Object of the game and scoring

To bat the ball into the air, not allowing it to touch the ground. The group wins that scores the highest number of *consecutive* hits without a foul, in a given period of time.

The game

On signal all groups start playing. One player in each group tosses the ball up to himself, then *bats* the ball *up* and toward another player across the circle.

Players continue to bat the ball *up* into the air and the *entire* group calls the number of each consecutive hit, "One—two—three—four. . . ." Play until a foul is made, then put the ball in play again and start counting from "One."

Fouls

1. Contacting ball more than once consecutively.
2. Contacting ball with any part of body below the waist.
3. Holding the ball (ball momentarily coming to rest in the hands of a player). Ball must be clearly batted.
4. Ball touching the ground or an object.

Winner

(1) Play for a period of time such as 3 or 4 minutes; group with highest number of consecutive hits without a foul wins, or (2) play for a given number of points, such as 15 or 21.

Teaching hints

1. Stress the importance of calling fouls on oneself, an important measure of sportsmanship. The purpose of the game is to learn some of the rules of volleyball as well as the skills.
2. Stress that ball must be clearly batted, not held even momentarily.
3. Stress batting ball at least 6 feet above head in order (a) to practice getting ball high enough to go over net, and (b) to give teammate time to get into a good position under the ball for an accurate hit.
4. Stress getting into position quickly to hit ball. Stress agility. Use small sliding steps to side, forward, or backward.
5. Have each group count the hits loud enough for all other groups to hear.

Variations

1. Bounce Keep It Up. Ball must bounce after each hit.
2. One Bounce or Volley the Ball. Players try to volley the ball, but if missed, the ball is in play after one bounce. If the ball is hit successfully after one bounce, the counting continues.
3. Partner Keep It Up. Play the same as Keep It Up—Circle Formation except that each group is composed of two players, partners. May use a No. 7 utility ball.
4. Partner Keep It Up—Over the Net. Same as No. 3 except for batting the ball over a net. May start with partners *tossing* ball back and forth over the net with *two-hand overhead* toss and catch. Catch ball in fingers only. Gradually work into batting the ball with fingers. (See "Drills.")

KEEP IT UP—FOUR SQUARE

Play the same as Keep It Up—Circle Formation, with the following exceptions:

Play area and position of players (Fig. 8.28)

Four-square court. Number players as in volleyball. Adapt positions to number of players participating.

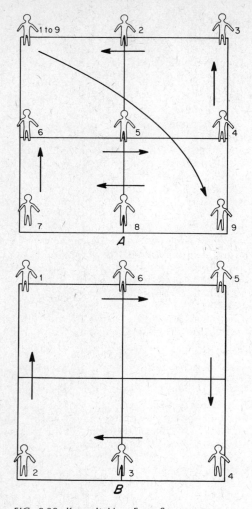

FIG. 8.28. Keep It Up—Four Square.

The game

Players rotate each time a foul is made.
1. With three lines of players use "S" rotation. (See arrows, Fig. 8.28, part A.)
2. With two lines of players use circle rotation. (See arrows, Fig. 8.28, part B.)

Teaching suggestions

Use this form of Keep It Up to teach rotation. May write the numbers for positions on Four Square diagram when introducing the game.

Stress rotating quickly, thus allowing more time to score.

KEEP IT UP—ABOVE THE LINE

Equipment

One No. 8½ utility ball or volleyball for each group. One backboard or wall with a line drawn parallel to and 7 feet from the ground.

Skill

Volleyball volley.

Play area and position of players (Fig. 8.29)

Open area in front of a backboard or wall. Players stand in file formation.

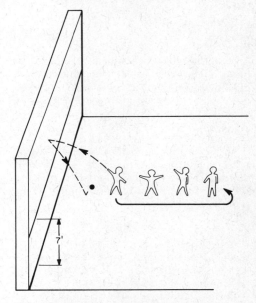

FIG. 8.29. Keep It Up—Above the Line.

Object of the game

To bat the ball up and have it hit the wall above the 7-foot line.

The game

First player in line puts the ball in play by tossing it up to himself, then batting it against the wall above the line. He immediately runs to the end of his line of players.

Second player plays the ball after one bounce and bats it *up* against the wall above the line. Play continues until a foul is made.

Fouls

1. Holding the ball.

2. Contacting the ball with any part of the body below the waist.

3. Failure to bat ball above the line.

4. Interference with play by another player.

5. Not complying with the rules of the game.

Variations

1. After the ball hits the backboard, each player bats the ball either before it touches the ground or after one bounce.

2. Each player bats the ball *only* on the volley. It is a foul if ball touches ground

3. As a group: Group that has the highest number of consecutive hits in a given period of time wins.

4. As an individual: Each time a player commits a foul, he gets a "strike." The players having the fewest strikes when one player gets three strikes win.

KEEP IT UP—OVER THE NET

Play the same as Keep It Up—Circle Formation with the following exceptions:

Play area and position of players

Each group is divided in half, with half the players on each side of the net, but all working together as *one team*.

The game

Players on one volleyball court compete against players on a separate court.

Count aloud each time the ball is batted *over the net*. However, ball should be batted more than once on each side of the net.

Players on both sides of the net rotate each time a foul is made, and counting starts again.

Group with the highest number of consecutive hits over the net wins.

Additional fouls

1. Touching the net.

2. Reaching over net to hit the ball.

3. Stepping *over* the center line.

Teaching hints

1. Encourage back lines of players to bat the ball up to front-line players to hit over the net.

2. Stress rotating quickly.

3. If situation arises, make a rule against two players batting the ball back and forth to each other over the net.

4. Rules may be modified to allow players to continue playing the ball after *one* bounce.

VOLLEYBALL—DOUBLES (FIG. 8.30)

The game is the same as volleyball with the following exceptions:

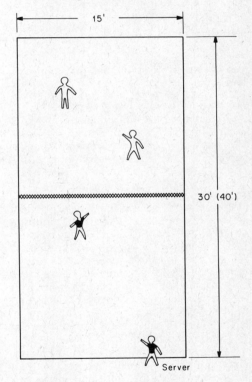

FIG. 8.30. Volleyball—Doubles.

Court

15 x 30–40 feet.

Players

Two (or three) players on each team. With three players, play two up at net and one player back; rotate clockwise.

DECK TENNIS—DOUBLES

Play the same as Deck Tennis—Team, Fig. 8.38, with the following exceptions:

Court

15 to 18 feet in width and 20 feet deep on each side of net.

Players

Two (or three) players on each team. *Note:* For Official Deck Tennis Rules, see *Recreational Games and Sports,* Division for Girls' and Women's Sports. (4)

SKILL TESTS—USING VOLLEYBALL OR NO. 8½ UTILITY BALL

SERVE (ACCURACY)

Equipment

One No. 8½ utility ball or volleyball, and volleyball net.

Play area and position of players (Fig. 8.31)

Volleyball court, volleyball net 6 feet 6 inches high.

Players stand in line formation behind serving line with one player in opposite court.

Action

Player stands behind the service line and serves three times. Player in opposite court allows ball to land, then recovers ball and rolls it back under the net to server. After the three serves, server rotates quickly to opposite court to recover the ball for the following player; player who *was* recovering the ball goes to the end of the serving line.

To serve ball successfully: (1) Server may not step on or over service line. (2) Ball may be served underhand or overhand. (3) Ball may not touch the net. (4) Ball must go over the net and land inside opposite court or on a boundary line.

Scoring

Score number of successful serves.

Safety

When two groups are using one court, servers of opposite teams should alternate putting ball in play and be careful not to serve when a player is recovering a ball.

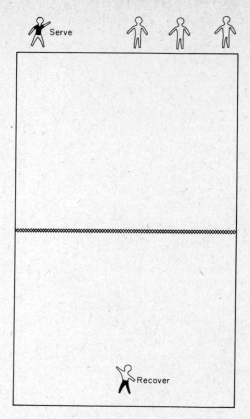

FIG. 8.31. Serve (accuracy).

VOLLEY (ACCURACY)

Equipment

One volleyball or No. 8½ utility ball.

Play area and position of players

An open area in front of a handball backboard or a wall with a line drawn parallel to, and 7 feet above, the ground. Contestant stands at any point in front of the wall.

Action

Player tosses the ball up to himself, then bats the ball against the wall above the line. He bats the ball on the volley and attempts to make ten consecutive successful volleys.

Fouls

1. Ball hitting below the line.

2. Holding the ball.

3. Hitting the ball more than once with each volley.

4. Contacting ball with any part of body below the waist.

Scoring

Score 1 point for each consecutive successful hit.

TEAM GAMES—USING VOLLEYBALL OR NO. 8½ UTILITY BALL

DANISH ROUNDERS—SERVING THE BALL

Play the same as Danish Rounders, Fig. 7.7, with following exceptions:

1. Use a volleyball or No. 8½ utility ball.

2. Serve the ball into the field to put the ball in play.

3. Fly ball caught is not an out.

FIST BALL

Play the same as Softball with the following exceptions:

1. Use a volleyball or No. 8½ utility ball.

2. Serve the ball into the field to put the ball in play.

3. In order to encourage long, high serves, a fly ball caught is not an out. Server runs to first base and base runners may advance.

4. When the ball is returned to the batter to put the ball in play, each base runner returns to his base and remains there until the ball is served.

BAT DODGE BALL

Equipment

One No. 7 or 8½ utility ball or volleyball, three markers (milk cartons, plastic containers).

Skills

Serving, fielding served ball, throwing and catching, running and dodging.

Play area and position of players (Fig. 8.32)

Large rectangle. One end line of the rectangle is the serving line. Draw a restraining line 25 to 30 feet from and parallel to the serving line (or place a marker on each side line 25 to 30 feet

from the serving line). Place a marker in the field at least 20 feet from the opposite end boundary line and equidistant from the side lines. (See diagram.)

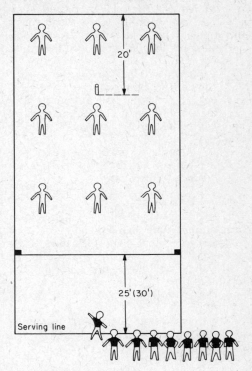

FIG. 8.32. Bat Dodge Ball.

The batting team stands 15 feet behind the serving line. Place the fielding team in two or three evenly-spaced rows between the restraining line and the end boundary line.

Object of the game

To score runs by serving the ball into the field, then running around the center marker and back over the serving line without being put out.

The game

First batter stands behind the serving line and serves the ball as far as possible into the field. He runs into the field and goes *around* the center marker (running and dodging as needed to avoid being hit with the ball) and then returns across the serving line.

A fielder gets the ball, then *stays* in *place* as he passes the ball in the direction of the runner. The ball is passed from player to player until close enough to hit the runner. The fielder must throw safely and must hit the runner below the waist.

Batter is out if he:
1. is hit with the ball below the waist
2. runs out of bounds
3. fails to serve the ball in bounds after two trials (Children in upper grades may be required to serve ball over restraining line.)

Note: In order to encourage good long and high serves, a fly ball caught does not put the base runner out.

Violations by fielders

1. Running *with* the ball. A fielder may turn around with ball in hand, but may not take more than two steps toward the runner.
2. Dangerous hitting—throwing the ball too hard.
3. Fielder holding the ball more than 5 seconds.

Note: Fielders remain behind restraining line until ball is served.

Penalty for violations

The runner is safe and a run is automatically scored. (Referee should blow the whistle and stop play immediately. He then calls the foul and declares a run.)

Scoring

Score 1 point for a successful run (or for a violation called on a fielder). The team with the most points in even innings wins.

Exchanging sides

(1) After each player on the batting team has a turn at bat *or* (2) after three outs, whichever occurs first.

Rotation

Rotate by lines after each inning; front line moves to the back and back lines move up one row.

Strategy

1. Pass the ball quickly in order to get short throws at the runner.
2. Fielders should move in *behind* the runner in order to recover the ball if runner is missed.

Teaching hints

1. Stress *not* running *with* the ball, limit the players to two steps.
2. Stress not throwing the ball too hard. After warning a player, ask a violator to step out of the game and watch how the ball should be thrown. Allow violator to return to game in due time.
3. If a fielder holds the ball, start counting, "One—two—three—four—five."
4. If two players throw the ball back and forth, make a rule that the ball may be thrown to a player and back again, but must then be thrown to a third player.
5. When introducing the game, may have half the batting team have a turn at bat and then exchange sides.

BASKET RACE BALL

See Variation of Basket Race Ball.

BULLETS

Equipment

Volleyball net, five or seven utility balls ranging in size from No. 7 to 13. (Do not use the No. 8 kickball.)

Skills

Throwing, catching.

Play area and position of players (Fig. 8.33)

Volleyball court with net height *6 feet 6 inches*. Divide players of each team into four equal groups. Players in group 1 stand equally spaced across the front third of court, group 2 across middle third, and group 3 across back third of court. Group 4 stands outside the court evenly spaced (to recover balls going out of bounds).

Object of the game

To throw all the balls quickly into the opponents' court in order to prevent having points scored against own team.

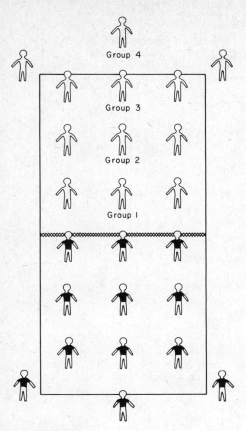

Group 4

Group 3

Group 2

Group I

FIG. 8.33. Bullets.

The game

Give four balls to one team and three balls to opposing team. (Use three and two distribution if using five balls.) On the whistle each player throws the ball across the net into opponent's court.

Players continue to catch and throw the balls over the net into opponents' court.

Balls going out of bounds are recovered quickly by teammates in group 4, who are stationed outside the court. After recovering a ball, a player in group 4 tosses the ball to a teammate on court, who immediately throws it over the net.

Play for 1 minute, then blow the whistle. Play stops *immediately.* (A ball in the air when the whistle blows is counted according to where it lands.) Count the

number of utility balls on each side of the net.

Scoring

Score 1 point *against* a team for each ball on its side of the net when the whistle blows. Score 1 point *against* a team for each violation. (Score points for violations *as* violations are made.)

Violations

1. Throwing a ball that lands outside opposite court before being touched by opponents in groups 1, 2, or 3. (A player in group 4 may catch the ball out of bounds and call the violation as he catches the ball.)
2. Player in group 4 throwing the ball over the net.
3. Dangerous throwing.

Rotation

After each period of 1 minute of play, groups rotate. Groups on court move back one line with group 3 moving out of bounds. Players in group 4 take position near the net.

Teaching suggestions

1. Keep the net height at 6 feet 6 inches to avoid straight hard throws. Ball should rise to go over net.
2. Stress covering own area.

Note: If court is located in an enclosed area, divide each team into three groups and place them *on* the court. A fourth group would not be needed to recover out-of-bounds balls.

PRISONERS' BALL

Equipment

Volleyball net 6 feet 6 inches in height, volleyball or No. 8½ utility ball.

Skills

Serving as in volleyball, catching.

Play area and postion of players (Fig. 8.34)

Volleyball court with a prison marked outside the back right-hand corner of each court. Place players on the court in two equal lines and number the players. (See diagram.)

Object of the game

To serve the ball over the net into the opponents' court so that the ball lands inside the court.

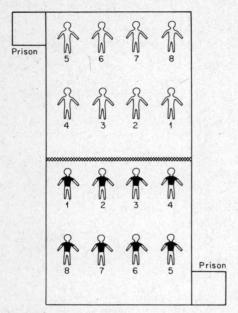

FIG. 8.34. Prisoners' Ball.

The game

One player serves the ball over the net from his position on the court. As he serves the ball he calls a number.

Any player on the opposite court may catch the ball. However, if *no one* catches the ball, the player whose number was called goes to the prison. If the ball is caught, the player catching the ball serves it immediately and calls an opponent's number *as* he serves. He serves the ball from the spot where he caught it (unless he is standing too close to the net, in which case he may step back to serve).

To release a player from prison, the server may call, "Prisoner," instead of calling a number. If an opponent does not catch the ball, the prisoner who has been in prison the longest period of time returns to his own court. If ball is caught, play continues.

Winning team

After a brief period of time, count the number of prisoners. Team having the greatest number of opponents in prison wins.

Additional rules

A ball landing on a boundary line (a "liner") is good.

If the ball is served out of bounds or does not go over the net, the player closest to the ball recovers it and serves.

Let ball

A ball touching the top of the net and landing in the opponents' court does not count. Recover the ball and serve.

Teaching hints

1. Stress returning the ball quickly; calling the number or name *as* you serve; placing the serve, serving the ball to an open spot.

2. Instruct in skills of serving and catching.

3. Players should not remain in prison too long. After a period of time count the prisoners, declare a winner, have prisoners return to own team and start another game.

Variations

1. Call the names of the opponents instead of calling them by numbers.

2. Throw the ball over the net instead of using a serve. Use the volleyball or No. 8½ utility ball.

FINGER VOLLEYBALL

Equipment

One volleyball or No. 8½ utility ball for each game.

Skills

Throwing, catching with fingers, passing the ball from one player to another.

Play area and position of players (Fig. 8.35)

Volleyball court; net placed 6 feet 6 inches high; either two or three rows of players on each side of the net with three players in each row.

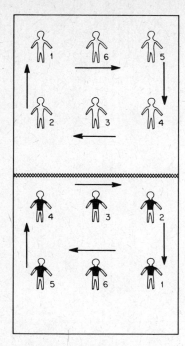

FIG. 8.35. Finger Volleyball.

Object of the game

To score points against the opponents through strategy and teamwork; to prepare for more advanced volleyball skills.

Scoring

Score 1 point each time the *serving* team (1) causes the opponents to miss the ball or (2) throws it out of bounds. Fifteen points with a 2-point lead constitute a game.

The game

The server stands behind his end line and *throws* the ball across the net, attempting to get it as close to the opposite end line as possible.

A player on the receiving team catches the ball with his fingers (rather than using the arms); he passes the ball to a second player on his team, who passes it to a third. The ball is sent over the net only after *three* passes have been made on a side.

The ball must be passed from one player to another in an *upward arc*, be-

ginning by holding the ball *in front of the forehead* and then pushing it upward with the fingers. The third player to touch the ball should always attempt to pass it to the opposite end line, making it all the more difficult for the opponents to make a successful play.

Fouls

1. Failure to have three players contact the ball before sending it over the net.
2. Catching the ball with the arms or cradling it against the body.
3. Passing the ball too low. (Ball must go at least as high as the net on each pass.)

Penalty for fouls

If the receiving team commits a foul, the serving team gains a point.

If the serving team fouls, the receiving team gains possession of the ball for service.

Rotation

Each time the receiving team gains the ball for service, the players rotate. (See diagram.)

BOUNCE VOLLEYBALL

Equipment

One volleyball or No. 8½ utility ball.

Skills

Volleying the ball after one bounce, passing the ball, moving quickly to get into position to play the ball.

Play area and position of players

Same as for Finger Volleyball.

Object of the game

To score points through strategy and teamwork by returning the ball over the net without committing a foul.

Scoring

Score 1 point for a team each time the opponents commit a foul.

The game

A player on one team tosses the ball over the net to start the game. After the ball bounces once, a player on the receiving team volleys it into the air, passing it to another player on his team. Players continue volleying the ball *after each bounce,* moving it into position close to the net so that it may be returned across the net. The ball may be contacted any number of times by one team before it is hit across the net.

Play continues until one team commits a foul. The opposing team is awarded a point, and the player holding the ball when play was stopped begins again by tossing the ball over the net.

Fouls

1. Failure to return the ball over the net.
2. Causing the ball to go out of bounds.
3. Allowing the ball to bounce more than once before playing it.
4. Hitting the ball twice in succession before another player touches it.
5. Not clearly batting the ball: holding or allowing it to rest momentarily in the hands; throwing the ball (except to put the ball in play).

Penalty for fouls

The team not committing the foul receives a point.

Rotation

Players rotate after every 2 or 3 minutes of play. (See arrows in diagram, Fig. 8.35, for rotation.)

Teaching hints

1. Play Bounce—Keep It Up as a lead up to this game.
2. Encourage players to move quickly to get into position to play the ball.
3. Ball should be contacted with the fingers rather than the palms of the hands. (Listen for the difference in sound between contacting the ball with the fingers and with the palms of the hands.)
4. Ball should be returned over the net by the front-row players, and hit to the back of the opponents' court.

SERVE AND VOLLEY

Equipment

Two volleyball nets and courts, two volleyballs or No. 8½ utility balls. (If only one court is available, rotate groups.)

Skills

Serve, assist serve (if needed), volley.

Play area and position of players (Fig. 8.36)

Volleyball court. Nine players on one court as in volleyball (Nos. 1–9); player No. 11 in serving position on opposite court; player No. 10 inside the same court.

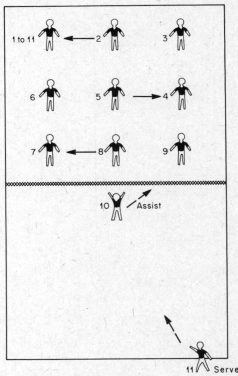

FIG. 8.36. Serve and Volley.

Object of the game

To score points by serving the ball over the net, keeping the ball up two or more times on opposite side of net, then returning the ball over the net.

The game

Server serves the ball over the net. Player No. 10 may "assist" (bat) the ball over if server fails to reach the net with the ball.

Players on opposite court volley or bat the ball up two or more times, then bat the ball back over the net. Server and "assist" player attempt to keep the ball up two or more times and then return it over the net again. Play continues until a foul is made. When a foul is committed, the ball is returned to a server in No. 11 position. Each server has two turns to serve. (Allow one additional trial for an unsuccessful serve.)

Scoring

Score 1 point each time the ball *is returned* over the net after two or more hits on a side, without a foul. Players on *one* volleyball court compete against players on another court.

Players making 15 points first, or most points in a given period of time, win the game.

Fouls

Same as volleyball with exceptions as described.

Rotation

Same as volleyball except that player No. 1 goes to position No. 11 in opposite court and serves; player No. 11 goes to position 10, and 10 to 9. (See diagram.)

Variation

When introducing the game, server may throw the ball over the net.

VOLLEYBALL[3]

Note: For beginning players, see "Adaptations." For warm-up, play Keep-It-Up.

Equipment

Volleyball net, volleyball or No. 8½ utility ball.

Skills

Serving, volleying, set-up, spike.

Play area and position of players (Fig. 8.37)

Volleyball court 25 x 50 feet; net height 6 feet 6 inches; center line directly under net crosswise of court. Keep the net tightly stretched by the four corners. (Official

---

[3]Permission to adapt Volleyball Rules granted by the Division Executive Council of the Division of Girls' and Women's Sports. For complete rules, see *Official Volleyball Guide* (4).

court 30 x 60 feet; net height for women 7 feet 4¼ inches at the center.)

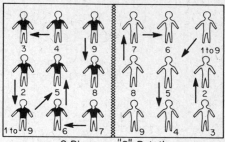

9 Players — "S" Rotation

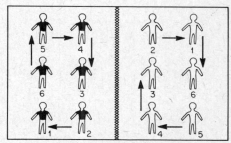

6 Players — Circle Rotation

FIG. 8.37. *Volleyball Rotation: nine players; six players.*

Place the players as shown in the diagram, with a maximum of nine players on a team.

Object of the game

To serve the ball over the net or to return the ball over the net into opponents' court in order to make points *or* to gain the serve. (Only the serving team makes points.)

Scoring

Point. Score 1 point for *serving* team if any player on *receiving* team commits a foul.

Side out. If any player on the *serving* team commits a foul, the team loses the serve and no points are scored. The new serving team rotates before putting ball in play.

Game score is 15 points with a 2-point advantage. To win, one team must be at least 2 points ahead of the opponent such as 15–13, 16–14, 19–17. (See "Additional Official Rules.")

The game

A player in the right back position serves the ball over the net from a point *behind* the end line. The receiving team attempts to return the ball back over the net by batting it before it touches the ground (on the volley). The ball continues in play back and forth over the net until a player commits a foul.

1. If any player on the receiving team commits a foul, call, "Point," for the serving team and the same server continues to serve.

2. If any player on the *serving* team commits a foul, the team loses the privilege of serving. Call, "Side out." The ball then goes to the receiving team. The receiving team rotates, and the new player in the right back position serves.

Fouls on the serve

1. Failure to serve the ball into opponents' court. (a) A ball landing on a boundary line is good. (b) A ball touched by an opponent is good, even if he is standing outside the court. (c) A ball touching the top of the net and *going into* opponents' court is a foul on the serve (good on a return).

2. Not clearly batting the ball, holding the ball even momentarily, or throwing the ball.

3. More than one assist on the serve. (Adapted rule allows one player to assist and bat the ball once if the ball does not go over the net on the serve.)

4. Foot fault. Server stepping on or over the service line during the act of serving.

Fouls on return

1. Not clearly batting the ball.

2. Contacting ball with any part of body below the waist.

3. Failure to return ball into opponents' court. See "Fouls on the Serve," No. 1.

4. Striking ball more than once consecutively.

5. Touching net with any part of the body except when ball is dead. If two opponents touch net at same time, take serve again.

6. Reaching over the net to contact the ball. Follow-through over the net is not a foul.

7. Stepping *over* the center line. Player may step on but not over the center line.

8. Interfering with the play or the ball if the ball is in play on opponents' side of net.

Teammates contacting ball simultaneously

Count as one hit. Either player may take the following play.

Double foul

Players on opposing teams commit a foul simultaneously or on the same play at the net. Repeat the play.

Adaptations

1. Ball may be hit *either* on the volley *or* after *one* bounce. (Players should try to bat the ball before it touches the ground.)

2. Throw the ball over the net to put it in play.

Additional official rules for players in grades 7 and 8

1. No assist on the service.

2. Only three players allowed to contact the ball before returning it over the net. (It is legal for player A to contact the ball, then player B, then player A to return the ball over the net. This is considered three players.)

3. Game score—official rule for women: A game is completed when (a) one team scores a total of 15 points, or (b) 8 minutes of actual playing time have elapsed. The winning team must have a 2-point advantage. (Play continues until one team is 2 points ahead.)

Teaching suggestions

1. Stress using a ready position and moving with small slides to side, forward, or backward to get into position to play the ball.

2. Stress using dig pass to return a low ball. See description of skills.

3. Stress keeping hands forehead high

for an overhead pass. See description of skills.

4. Stress passing ball up to the players in the front line before returning it over the net. Bat the ball *up* high enough to allow time for teammate to get into good position to play the ball.

5. Stress moving and getting into position to use *two* hands when returning the ball.

6. Server steps into court *immediately after* serving in order to cover his play area on the return.

7. Motivate good teamwork and covering own area.

8. Back line of players stand well inside the end line. (Only necessary to cover ball that will land inside the court.)

9. To save time, stress sending the ball *under* the net to the server.

10. Officiating: Referee stands on the same side of the net as server and changes side of the net with the serve. (It is easier for referee to determine the team putting the ball in play and whether to call, "Point" or "Side out.")

DECK TENNIS—TEAM (FIG. 8.38)

Play the same as volleyball with the following exceptions:

FIG. 8.38. *Deck Tennis—cross-body throw. Right foot is forward when throwing right-handed. Support the ring with fingers and thumb. Follow through in the direction the ring is to travel.*

Equipment

Deck tennis ring; net, height as in volleyball, 6 feet 6 inches.

Rules

Serve. Toss the ring over the net from behind the service line. Use an underhand throw. A short service line may be placed inside the court at right angles to the right side line 20 to 25 feet from the net.

Return the ring with a cross-body throw (Fig. 8.38) or regular one-hand underhand throw. (For underhand throw, the ring extends below the hand and is held with thumb and fingers. Use pendulum swing parallel to side of body—underhand pattern.)

Foul on serve

Failure to use an underhand throw.

Fouls on return

1. Failure to use an underhand throw; using a downward stroke.

2. Catching or throwing ring with both hands.

3. Changing ring from one hand to the other.

4. Failure to catch the ring and allowing it to travel over the hand onto the arm.

Variation

Play the game with nondominant hand only.

Teaching hints

1. Stress following through in the direction the ring is to go, pointing to the spot at completion of follow-through.

2. When catching, stress (a) keeping eyes on the ring *all the way to the hand,* (b) reaching out and pulling it in—*giving* with it.

3. When the ring is caught overhead, it may be returned from this position with an overhead return. With back or side of wrist toward the net, use a wrist snap up in order to have the ring *rise* from the hand.

CHAPTER 9
TRACK AND FIELD AND SOFTBALL
SPORT UNITS

ACTIVITIES IN TRACK AND FIELD

ACTIVITIES USING A SOFTBALL

BIBLIOGRAPHY AND AUDIO-VISUAL MATERIALS—SECTION TWO

FIG. 9.1. *Use the batting tee. Teach: correct stance at the plate, eyes on the ball, and level swing.*

The spring of every year is greeted with a surge of activity by all living things. The lethargy of winter is thrown off; young animals gambol, plants begin to bloom, and children run. It is as though the air were suddenly charged with some revitalizing agent that stimulates the young and rejuvenates their elders.

If educators are to capitalize on "teachable moments," this becomes the ideal time to introduce the unit on track and field. This is movement in its most natural form, wherein the body is the projectile that is thrust along, upward, or through space against the measure of the clock or tape. The individuality of the events—one against a measure—makes them especially appealing to children. If no watch or measured course is available, one child may very well challenge another to a race "from here to there" just for the fun of running.

Another mark of the advent of spring is the sudden appearance of gloves, mitts, and baseball caps. The pronouncement that spring training is under way for major league baseball players is signal enough to introduce a bat and ball to playgrounds and corner lots across the country. In terms of activity, neither baseball nor softball offers much in the way of vigorous exercise. The excitement comes with the crack of bat against ball, the suspense of watching a fly ball going deep into the field, and the spectacular diving or jumping catch. However, these are not routine occurrences; more often the batter is left standing at home plate or is called out at first base.

To meet the objective of maximum activity for all students, the softball unit presented here includes a goodly number of adapted games that *do* provide activity while still maintaining the excitement of the major game.

It would seem that both softball and track and field provide the fitting climax to a year filled with variety and purpose in developmental and enjoyable activity.

PURPOSES

Track and field activities capitalize on the natural movements of children; softball often requires much diligent practice to gain proficiency. Bearing these two observations in mind, the following purposes have been designed:

—to enhance the ability to run, jump, hurdle, and throw by providing instruction and understanding;

—to provide instruction in, and use of, the various softball skills;

—to understand and practice rules of safety;

—to promote cooperative play for team success;

—to demonstrate ways of utilizing isolated skills in game situations;

—to provide objective assessment of performance to measure improvement;

—to present opportunities for competition within various skill levels;

—to develop sufficient skill for recreational use.

ACTIVITIES IN TRACK AND FIELD

Track and field events include most of the natural movements that children enjoy in their daily activities. Leaping over bushes, or low hedges or one another, leads them to hurdle jumping; leaping over cracks in the sidewalk leads to the long jump; and jumping for an apple on a tree or a ball high in the air leads to the jump and reach.

To achieve the best possible performance, instruction in the proper technique is emphasized. Some children run well naturally; others need to be reminded to keep the elbows in or to run on the toes. Leg strength is an essential factor in both running and jumping; much time should be spent in conditioning the legs during the early days of the unit. Rather than starting with dashes, children should begin with endurance runs of increasing distances. These, coupled with conditioning exercises (Chapter 4), will lead to better performances and reduce the possibility of injury to muscles.

The three jumping events in which running is also a factor (long, triple, and high jump) should only be performed when a suitable landing surface is available. Sand may be used for the long jump

ACTIVITIES IN TRACK AND FIELD

SUGGESTED GRADE PLACEMENT CHART

TRACK EVENTS, 281–285	K	1	2	3	4	5	6	7	8
30-Yard Dash	—	x	x	x	•				
50-Yard Dash				—	x	x	x	x	x
75-Yard Dash								x	x
Jog—Run					—	x	x	x	x
220-Yard Relay—Pursuit					—	x	x	x	x
440-Yard Relay								x	x
200-Yard Relay—Shuttle					—	x	x	x	x
50-Yard Hurdles						—	x	x	x
FIELD EVENTS, 285–290									
Standing Broad Jump	—	x	x	x	x	x	x	x	x
Jump and Reach				—	x	x	x	x	x
Softball Throw for Distance				—	x	x	x	x	x
Long Jump								x	x
Triple Jump								B	B
Basketball Throw								x	x
High Jump								x	x

— = May introduce activity   • = May continue activity
x = Depth in instruction   B = Boys

and triple jump; shavings should be used in the high jump pit. The cost of installation is not prohibitive. Competent instruction and adequate supervision are also necessities in these events.

Increased communications systems around the world have brought such outstanding events as the Olympics and the Pan-American Games to the forefront of public attention. The participation of women in these programs is increasing yearly. It is fitting that girls should be encouraged to take part in track and field events. It has been shown that feminine grace has a place in tests of speed, height, or distance.

GLOSSARY OF TERMS[1]

Baton. A tube-like object of wood or cardboard, approximately a foot long, that is passed from one runner to another in a relay race.

[1]Used by permission of the Division Executive Council of the Division for Girls and Women's Sports. (4)

Break in the Pit. Mark made by the contestant when landing in the pit.

Clapboard. Two pieces of board connected by a hinge and used by the starter in place of a gun. (Fig. 9.2)

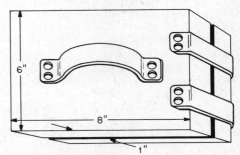

FIG. 9.2. Clapboard.

Clear the Watches. Setting the watches back to zero in order to be ready for the next race.

Crossbar. The bar over which the high jumpers jump.

Dead Heat. A race in which two or more runners cross the finish line at exactly the same time.

Finish Posts. Posts to which the finish tape or string is attached.

Gun Up. A warning signal to timers and judges that the starter has raised his arm and is about to start the race.

Heat. A preliminary round of a race, the winners of which participate in the semi-finals or finals.

High Jump Standards. Uprights that are used to hold the crossbar for the high jump.

Inside Lane. The lane on the inside of the track (the one closest to the infield), that is often referred to as the pole position.

Leg of a Relay. The distance that one member of a relay team must run.

Medley Relay. A relay race in which the members of the relay team run different distances.

Passing Zone. The area or particular distance in which the baton *must* be passed in a relay race.

Pit. The area in which a jumper lands. The pit is filled with sand or sawdust.

Preliminaries. In running events, it is a series of heats in the same event. Preliminaries are used when there are more competitors than there are lanes. In the throws, preliminaries consist of three throws per competitor. Competitors making the best scores are placed in the finals.

Pursuit Relay. A relay in which all runners run in the same direction.

Recall. The calling back of runners after a false start (one or more contestants starting before the gun is fired, jumping the gun).

Runway. The approach to the take-off board or scratch line for field events.

Sector Lines. Boundary lines within which a throw must land in order to score.

Shuttle Relay. A relay run on a straight-away with half of each relay team at opposite ends of a prescribed distance. The first runner runs straight across the area and tags off the next runner, who runs straight back to the starting line.

Staggered Start. The start of a race in which the competitors do not start on a straight line. The race is run around a curve.

Starting Board. See "Clapboard."

TRACK EVENTS

Note: See Chapter 1 for mechanics of running. See Appendix for equipment and supplies.

30-YARD DASH

Performance

The children start in forward stride position behind the starting line, eyes on the finish line, weight slightly forward. On the signal, "On your mark—get set—go!" push off with the rear foot. Run on the balls of the feet; run in a straight line; run *past* the finish line and then slow up.

Measurement

The dash can be a group race in which the first child across the line wins, or a timed race in which the contestant races against his previous score or against a school record.

Violations

1. Touching starting line. (Children sometimes slide front foot over the line while waiting for the signal.)
2. Starting before the signal, "Go."
3. Blocking another runner.

50-YARD DASH

See Chapter 4 for additional instructions.

Equipment

Stop watch, if race is to be timed; finish yarn; starting blocks, optional; starting gun or board (Fig. 9.2), optional.

Crouch start (Fig. 9.3)

1. "Go to your mark" position. (Fig. 9.3A) Back foot 4 to 6 inches behind the front foot. Arms straight down, elbows locked, fingers just behind the starting line —thumb and forefinger parallel to the line, fingers together. Kneel on the rear knee. Fix the eyes on a point 10 yards down the track. Balance weight on the hands and front foot, with some weight on the back foot and knee.
2. "Get set" position. (Fig. 9.3B) Rock forward until the hips are level with the shoulders. Weight is slightly forward on arms and front leg. Look forward.

FIG. 9.3A. "Go to your mark" position.

FIG. 9.3B. "Get set" position.

FIG. 9.3C. "Go!"

3. "Go!" (Fig. 9.3C) Push hard with the rear foot and forcefully extend the front leg. The rear knee then snaps upward toward the chest. Thrust the arm opposite the front leg forward and thrust the other arm backward and upward with the elbow pointed toward the sky.

Running the dash

1. First three or four steps. Overexaggerate the pumping action of the arms but do not allow the elbows to extend too far backward. Bring the knees high with short, chopping leg action. Gradually rise to correct running position and increase the size of each step until regular running pace is set.

2. During the dash. Keep the body weight slightly forward; relax neck and shoulders; focus eyes straight ahead, swing arms straight forward and backward; flex and extend legs from the hips; run on the balls of the feet; point toes forward and run in a straight line.

3. Finishing the dash. Lean as far forward as possible. Run at top speed *beyond* the finish line (or yarn); then slow to a jog and then to a walk. Do not sit down immediately after any race—walk slowly for a period of time.

Violations

1. Starting before the signal.
2. Crossing into another lane.

Variation

75-Yard Dash.

JOG—RUN

See Chapter 4, for additional instructions.

Equipment

Stop watch, marked 440-yard course with markers on corners if a square or rectangle is used.

Violations

1. Starting before the signal.
2. Cutting inside the line or markers.

220-YARD RELAY—PURSUIT

Equipment

Stop watch, if race is to be timed; starting board or gun; finish yarn; one baton for each team: ruler without metal edge; dowel, 1 inch by 1 foot; or cardboard tube.

Performance (Fig. 9.4)

Four runners on each team spaced 55 yards apart facing the finish line. The first runner holds the baton in his left hand. On signal the first runner races toward the second runner, who is watching his teammate's approach. No. 2 runner waits with the right arm extended back, palm up, fingers together, and thumb out. When runner No. 1 gets about 3 yards away, No. 2 starts to run—eyes forward. No. 1 places the baton into the hand of No. 2 and slows down to stop. (Fig. 9.5) No. 2 immediately transfers the baton to his left hand as he races toward No. 3. This passing procedure continues from 2 to 3 and 3 to 4. No. 4 runs with the baton across the finish line. Team finishing first wins.

Violations

1. Starting before the signal.
2. Running more than one leg of the race.
3. Throwing rather than passing the baton.
4. Dropping the baton.
5. Not staying in own lane, even after completing the pass.

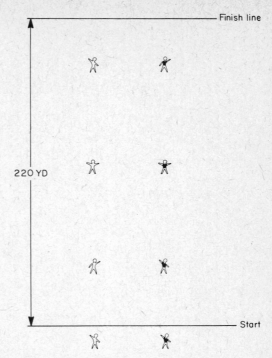

FIG. 9.4. 220-Yard Relay—Pursuit.

FIG. 9.5. Pursuit Relay—blind pass of baton.

Variation

440-Yard Relay with eight runners, each running 55 yards.

200-YARD RELAY—SHUTTLE

Equipment

One baton for each team; starting board or gun, optional; stop watch, if race is to be timed; two stakes, 5 feet high, for each team. Use two stakes for each team, one at each end of the area—50 yards apart.

Performance (Fig. 9.6)

Each team consists of four players standing in shuttle formation with two players at each end. The first runner holds the *end* of the baton in his *right* hand, vertically.

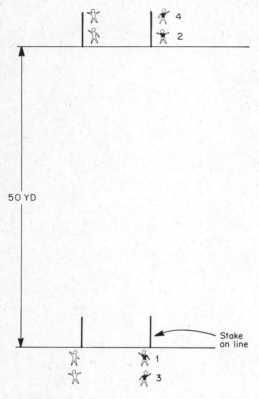

50 YD

Stake on line

FIG. 9.6. 200-Yard Relay—Shuttle.

On signal he runs toward the second runner, who waits with his right arm encircling the stake, palm facing the oncoming runner, fingers together, and thumb out. As the first runner passes the stake, he places the baton in his teammate's open hand. (Fig. 9.7) Immediately the second runner brings his right arm back around (not over) the stake and starts to run. The passing procedure is repeated with the second to third and third to final runner, who crosses the finish line, the original starting line.

Violations

1. Starting before the signal.
2. Dropping or throwing the baton.
3. After grasping the baton, reaching over the stake with the receiving hand, rather than around it.
4. Running into another lane.

50-YARD HURDLES

Equipment

Starting board or gun, optional; finishing yarn or line; four hurdles, 2½ feet high, for each lane.

Set up the hurdles with the first one 39 feet 4½ inches from the starting line, and the succeeding three hurdles 26 feet 3 inches apart.

Performance

The race is run as an ordinary 50-yard dash with the addition of the hurdles.

Progression (Fig. 9.8)

1. When learning to jump, have the performer first walk up to a hurdle, jump

FIG. 9.7. Shuttle Relay—baton pass around a stake.

beside it (not over), and continue on, doing the same at each hurdle. The lead leg is lifted straight forward from the hip and the toe points upward. The foot touches the ground close to the hurdle on the far side. The trailing leg swings over the hurdle, knee leading and toe turned out to avoid hitting the hurdle, then takes the next step. The arms swing naturally throughout the jump.

FIG. 9.8. Jumping a hurdle. Rotate trailing leg outward and pull toe upward to avoid contact with the hurdle.

2. The next step is to stretch a string between two hurdles placed side by side. Have the student repeat the jump over the string many times to gain confidence.

3. Start jumping the hurdles. Gradually increase the speed. Practice to improve performance. Keep the shoulders parallel to the hurdles. Land on the ball of the foot. Lean forward into the jump. Eye focus is down the entire length of the course and just above the hurdles.

The start of the race can be from a standing or crouched position, or from starting blocks. If starting blocks are used, the take-off foot (when jumping the hurdle) should be on the back block.

Violations

1. Starting before the signal.
2. Knocking down a hurdle (adapted).
3. Crossing into another lane.

Note: Hurdles should not be tied down and the hurdle race should never be run on blacktop.

FIELD EVENTS

Note: See Appendix for equipment and supplies.

STANDING BROAD JUMP

The standing broad jump may take place on dirt or turf.

Equipment

Dry, nonslip surface for take-off (a rubber softball base with rough surface may be used); steel tape; ruler or straight stick.

Performance (Fig. 9.9 A, B, and C)

See Chapter 4 for additional instructions.

Measurement

Attach the steel tape to the front edge of the take-off board. Measurement is taken from the front edge of the board to the closest point of contact made by the contestant. For ease in measurement, extend the tape 8 feet out from the board, parallel to the jumping area. When measuring, place the ruler perpendicular to the tape opposite the nearest spot touched by the jumper. In this way, the tape need not be moved after each jump.

Violations

1. Taking a preparatory step or jump.
2. Touching the ground in front of the board.
3. Not jumping from both feet.

JUMP AND REACH

See Chapter 1, "Efficient Movement," for mechanics of jumping and landing.

Equipment

Yardstick; chair or bench to facilitate measurement. For marking: Use chalk and chalk eraser, chalkboard 2 × 5 feet with bottom edge 5 feet from the ground; or use four or five magnets and a tin board approximately 2 × 5 feet with bottom edge 5 feet from the ground.

Performance (Fig. 9.10 A and B)

Child stands with his side to the wall and feet flat on the floor. He reaches up, holding the chalk between his thumb and index finger, and makes a mark on the board as high as he can reach. (If using a

FIG. 9.9A. Standing Broad Jump. Eye focus down course; arms drawn back for the forward swing; knees flexed for forward and upward thrust. (Take-off board is securely anchored to avoid slippage.)

FIG. 9.9B. Full extension of the body, ↓ with arms raised overhead.

← FIG. 9.9C. Land on balls of the feet and toes; keep body weight forward to avoid falling backward.

magnet, he sets it on the board.) He then jumps from a crouch position, stretching as high as possible, making his mark. Three trials are allowed.

Measurement

With the yardstick, measure from the standing mark to the highest jumping mark. Record the highest mark to the nearest ¼ inch.

Violations

1. Touching the wall while jumping upward.

2. Missing the board on the jump.

3. Not using a standing, two-footed jump.

SOFTBALL THROW FOR DISTANCE

Equipment

At least three softballs; two markers;

FIG. 9.10A. Jump and reach. Side to the wall with arm fully extended, mark.

FIG. 9.10B. Crouch, jump high, and mark. Land with knees bent.

two 100-foot tapes or area marked off in 10-foot sections.

Performance

Using an overhand throw, contestant has three trials. Record distance of longest throw.

See Chapter 6, "Principles of Levers," and Fig. 6.29. (See Fig. 9.15 for proper grip on the softball.)

Measurement

For ease in measurement, have the teacher or a child spot the place where the ball first touches the ground and place a marker at that spot. (If succeeding throws are of greater distance, additional markers are placed.) The best throw is measured and recorded. One or more children may serve as retrievers, stopping the ball after it has bounced at least once.

Violations

1. Stepping on or over the throwing line.

2. Throwing the ball outside the sector lines. (Contestants should throw the ball within the scoring lane, a lane not more than 10 yards in width.)

3. Not using the overhand throw.

LONG JUMP (RUNNING BROAD JUMP)

Equipment

Take-off board; jumping pit, 5 × 20 feet, with 3 inches of sand; steel tape; rake, to smooth the pit before each jump.

Performance

A good long-jumper must have both speed and spring in order to run the 80 to 150 feet to the board and then jump forward and upward for distance on the actual jump.

1. The run. First determine which foot is to be used for the take-off from the board. The runner must pace himself so that his run will end with this foot hitting the board. This can be done by starting on the take-off foot and running back the desired distance (far enough for that runner to gain sufficient speed for the jump without fatigue). Stop on the take-off foot, mark the spot, and then take the run and jump.

2. Take-off. The take-off foot should hit the board, knee bent, with knee and ankle ready to extend (explode!) *forward* and *upward*. Eyes focus beyond the edge of the pit. Arms are thrust in front of, and above, the head for extra lift. Chest should be high.

3. In the air. There are two traditional actions used while in the air. Teach both types and the student can choose the one most natural for him.

    a. Running in the air. Run with head up, chest out, arms forward and high, legs taking two or three running step motions.

    b. Hang. Thrust both legs forward in a semisitting position, head up and arms forward with hands higher than the head.

4. Landing. Bend elbows slightly to get a final thrust forward with the arms. The heels touch the pit first. At the moment of impact, thrust the arms back and drop

the head between the knees, causing the body to tip forward over the feet, in order to avoid falling back and scoring poorly.

Measurement

Measure perpendicularly from the front edge of the take-off board to the nearest break in the pit.

Violations

1. Stepping *over* edge of take-off board.
2. Taking off with two feet.

Safety

The long jump (running broad jump), triple jump (hop, step, and jump) and the high jump must be done in properly surfaced pits. If these pits are not available, do not allow the children to attempt these jumps.

Stress that each contestant check that the pit is clear before starting a jump; stress that the pit must be raked before each jump.

TRIPLE JUMP (HOP, STEP, AND JUMP FOR BOYS)

Equipment

Take-off board; jumping pit 5 × 30 feet, with 3 inches of sand; steel tape; rake, to smooth the pit before each jump.

Performance (Fig. 9.11)

(Teach the sequence from a standing start in order to promote timing. Later a running start may be used.) Take off from the board on one foot. Land on the *same* foot to complete the *hop*. Leap forward to *other* foot for *step*. Immediately take off from this foot for the *jump*. Land on both feet with body weight forward.

Each performer determines his own length of run in approaching the take-off board. Once determined, it should remain constant.

Measurement

Measure perpendicularly from the front edge of the take-off board to the nearest break in the pit.

Violations

1. Touching the ground directly in front of the board with the toes. (Toes may be curled over the edge.)

FIG. 9.11. Triple Jump. Hop . . . step . . . jump . . . land.

2. Taking a preparatory step or jump on or before reaching the take-off board.
3. Touching the free foot to the ground on either the hop or step.

BASKETBALL THROW

Equipment

Two or three basketballs, markers, steel tape. (Soccerballs may be used.)

Performance

There is no established ruling on the method of throw for this event. Elementary-school-age children could use a sidearm throw to good advantage. Starting with the side to the restraining line, hold the basketball with the throwing arm extended at shoulder height away from the restraining line, and the weight back on the foot closest to the ball. The other arm is pointed toward the field for balance. Take several slide steps toward the restraining line to establish momentum. When close to the line, the arm holding the ball swings forward in a horizontal arc as a forward step is taken with the back foot. The ball is released into the field.

The basketball throw is a good lead-up to the discus event.

Measurement

Contestant takes three trials from behind the restraining line. Measure the throws in the same way as for the softball throw, and score the farthest of the three throws.

Violations

1. Stepping on or over the restraining line while executing the throw.
2. Throwing outside the sector lines, which are 10 yards apart.

FIG. 9.12. Scissors Jump. The jumper clears the bar in a sitting position with legs straight.

HIGH JUMP

Equipment

Jump standards, bamboo crossbar, jumping area 8 × 14 feet, steel tape, rake to level area for jumper, shavings or hay piled 2 to 4 feet high.

Performance

The jumper starts as close to, or as far from, the bar as he wishes. He should start at least 4 or 5 strides from the bar. On the other hand, care should be taken that he does not run so far that his timing is affected.

The contestant approaches the front of bar from either side. The side approached and the distance run depend on the individual runner. Most right-footed jumpers will prefer to approach the bar from the left side at about a 45° angle.

In order to determine the point of take-off, the jumper should face the bar, stretch both arms forward, and touch the bar with the fingers. Mark the ground in front of the toes.

Beginning height of the bar for fourth through sixth grades should be at 1 foot 6 inches. Starting height for seventh and eighth graders should be 2 feet 6 inches.

Individual preference determines which method of jumping the contestant will use. The following methods are appropriate for elementary school.

1. Scissors Jump. (Fig. 9.12) The leg closest to the bar swings up and over the bar. At the same time the arms are thrown upward to gain more height. The outside leg follows the inside leg in a scissors-like movement. Do not bend the knees during flight. The jumper clears the bar in a sitting position landing on one foot and then the other, facing the same direction as at the beginning of the jump.

2. "Western-Straddle" Roll. (Fig. 9.13) Take off with the leg closest to the bar. The outside leg swings upward and over the bar and the inside leg is tucked under the outside leg at the knee in order to clear the bar. The jumper rolls over the bar, facing it at all times. This is accomplished by thrusting the outside arm up and across the body; at the same time the inside arm (the one closest to the bar) is thrust behind the back. Land facing the direction of the approach on both feet and maintain balance with outside arm.

Measurement

Record the greatest height cleared by the contestant. Measure with the steel tape from the ground to the upper edge of the center of the crossbar.

Violations

Knocking the bar off the standards. (If bar is knocked down on the approach, the take-off spot may be too close to the bar.

FIG. 9.13. "Western-Straddle" Roll. The outside arm has been thrust high in the air, and the inside leg has begun its upward extension. The jumper has failed to thrust his inside arm behind his back, which may tend to limit the height of his jump.

If the bar is knocked down on the descent, take-off may be too far from the bar.)

Three jumps to clear the bar are given at each height. A third miss at any one height disqualifies the contestant.

ACTIVITIES USING A SOFTBALL

Softball can be a most inactive game if batting is weak, or if the pitching is extremely good or poor. Fortunately, there are remedies for this inactivity. One is the use of a batting tee for novice players or for inexperienced players at the beginning of the season. It provides training in looking at the ball, increases confidence in hitting ability, and eliminates the necessity of accurate pitching. Once the batter gets the feeling of contacting the ball squarely and hitting through the ball, he is ready to face a pitcher. Many of the games included here provide for the use of the batting tee, which contributes greatly to initial enjoyment of the game. Pictures of major league baseball players using a batting tee provide excellent motivation.

Pitching is a matter of throwing at some point within a rectangular target. Targets may be easily marked on a wall or fence for practice during small group activities, so that when pitching is used in a game there is some measure of accuracy.

Catching or fielding a softball is a more familiar movement for children because of previous experience in games such as kickball. The size of the ball will present some difficulties, and its hardness may dissuade some players from handling it confidently. It is recommended that a super-soft softball be used for novice players until the correct techniques of catching are mastered.

The various skills of softball are particularly suited to small group activity. In fact, it is much more satisfying for children if the playing teams are kept small in size, with extra players engaged in skill development in an adjacent area rather than waiting interminably for a turn. In this way the skill level of the entire class will be considerably improved and there will be greater enthusiasm for the game.

There are several safety practices that must be recognized and followed by students if accidents are to be avoided. It would be well to review these at the beginning of the season, perhaps by posting a safety chart in the classroom. One or two items could be stressed each day when planning the activity and then repeated during evaluation.

ACTIVITIES USING A SOFTBALL

SUGGESTED GRADE PLACEMENT CHART

	3	4	5	6	7	8
SOFTBALL SKILLS, 293–294	—	x	x	x	x	x
RELAYS AND SMALL GROUP GAMES, 294–297						
Underhand Pitch and Catch (Relay)	—	x	x	x	x	
Overhand Throw and Catch (Relay)	—	x	x	x	x	
Fielding Ground Ball and Throwing Overhand (Relay)	—	x	x	x	x	
Striking—with Hand, Paddle, Bat, Racket Activities	x	x	x	x	x	x
Hit, Drop, and Overrun—Softball	—	x	•			
Two Grounders or a Fly	—	x	x	x	•	•
Variation: "200" to "500"		x	x	x	•	•
SKILL TESTS, 297–298						
Underhand Pitch (Accuracy)		x	x	x	x	x
Overhand Throw (Accuracy)		x	x	x	x	x
Softball Throw (Distance)		—	x	x	x	x
(Performance Tests, Ch. 4)						
Base Running (Speed)		x	x	x	x	x
TEAM GAMES, 298–306						
Line-up Tee Ball	—	x				
Bases on Balls II, Kickball Unit	—	x				
Home Run or Out—Softball		x	x	x	•	•
Variation: Beatball, Three-Team		x	x	x		
Softball		x	x	x	x	x
Variation: Tee Ball		x	x	x	•	•
Softball Work-up		x	x	x	x	x
Three-Team Softball			x	x	x	x
Variation: Three-Team Home Run or Out		x	x	x	•	•
Baseball—Using 10" or 9" Softball				B	B	B

— = May introduce activity   • = May continue activity
x = Depth in instruction   B = Boys

GLOSSARY OF TERMS[2]

Ball. Pitched ball which, in judgment of umpire, does not enter the strike zone (or which touches ground before reaching home plate), and which is not struck at by the batter.

Note: After four called balls, the batter is entitled to a walk to first base.

Bunt. A bunt is a legally hit ball not swung at but intentionally met with the bat and tapped lightly within the infield.

[2]Permission to adapt glossary of terms granted by the International Joint Rules Committee on Softball.

Note: After two strikes, a bunt that goes foul puts the batter out.

Dead Ball. Ball is not in play and is not considered in play again until the pitcher holds it in pitching position and the umpire has called, "Play ball."

Fair ball. (See Fig. 9.25.)

a. Settles, or is touched, on fair ground in infield (between home and first base or between home and third base).

b. First falls on fair ground in outfield (beyond first or third base).

c. Is on or over fair ground when bounding past the infield.

d. Touches first, second, or third base (or passes over a base).

e. While on or over fair ground touches the person or clothing of an umpire or a player.

Fly Ball. A fly ball is any ball batted into the air.

Force-Out. A force-out is an out that can be made when a base runner loses the right to the base occupied because the batter has become a base runner. (Force-out can also be made when a base runner fails to return to base in time after a caught fly ball.)

Foul Tip. A foul tip is a foul ball that touches the bat, goes directly back, and *is caught by the catcher.* The ball does not go higher than the batter's head.

Effect on batter: A foul tip is always a strike, and if it occurs on third strike, it puts the batter out.

Note: A foul fly which goes directly back to the catcher must go higher than the batter's head to be declared a fly ball. If caught, the batter is out.

Infield. The infield is that portion of the field that is included within the diamond made by the base lines.

Inning (complete inning). An inning is that portion of a game within which the teams alternate on offense and defense and in which there are three outs for each team.

Outfield. The outfield is that portion of the field beyond the infield (beyond an imaginary line from first to second to third base), and within the foul lines beyond first and third bases, and the boundaries of the grounds.

Overthrow. An overthrow is a play in which the ball is thrown from one player to another to retire a runner who has not reached, or is off, base, and goes into *foul* territory on a play at first, third, or home bases.

Effect on base runners: Base runner may advance one base on the overthrow—at his own risk.

Note: On such a throw that goes into *fair* territory, base runners may advance any number of bases—at own risk.

Passed Ball. A ball that is legally pitched and should have been held or controlled by the catcher with ordinary effort.

Note: Recommendation for elementary school: Base runners should not be allowed to score a run on a passed ball.

Strike Zone. The strike zone is that space over home plate that is between the batter's armpits and the top of his knees when the batter assumes his natural batting stance.

Called Strike. Strike called on the batter by the umpire when the batter fails to swing at the ball and, in the judgment of the umpire, the ball has entered the strike zone.

Walk. Batter is allowed to go to first base due to four pitched balls which, in judgment of umpire, did not enter the strike zone. Only base runners *forced* to advance due to the walk may advance one base.

SOFTBALL SAFETY

As batter

Learn to remain in the designated safe place for batters while waiting for a turn to bat. (Waiting batters emerge from *first* base side of backstop.)

Remember to swing bat only at home plate. Learn to drop the bat after hitting the ball; do not *throw* it.

Learn to hold the bat with trade-mark on top to prevent splitting it.

As fielder and baseman

Learn how to catch the ball without injury.

Learn fielding positions and stay off the base and the base lines when there is no play on the base runner.

On a force-out, learn to touch the edge of the base with one foot while catching the ball, thus preventing a collision with oncoming base runner. (See Fig. 9.24.)

Learn to play own area.

Learn to call, "Mine," when in a better position than a teammate to catch a ball.

When two teammates rush to catch the same ball, learn to call the name of the player in the best position to make the catch.

SOFTBALL SKILLS

LIST OF SOFTBALL SKILLS

Underhand pitch—underhand throw.

Overhand throw. See Chapter 6, "Principles of Levers," and Fig. 6.29.

Catching a thrown ball. Figs. 6.25A and B.

Batting:
    Batting off a batting tee, Fig. 9.1.
    Batting a pitched ball.

Fielding:
    Fly ball, Figs. 6.25A and B.
    Ground ball, Figs. 6.16 and 9.17.

Base running. See "Skill Tests."

ANALYSIS OF SOFTBALL SKILLS

UNDERHAND PITCH (FIGS 9.14 AND 6.23)

Starting position

Stand with both feet touching the pitching line.

Face home plate.

Grip the ball with fingers and thumb, fingers spread. Do not palm the ball.

Before pitching, hold the ball in both hands in front of the body.

Keep eyes on target.

Execution

Reach back with ball, rotating the body away from the target.

Step forward with the opposite foot *as* you throw (one step only).

FIG. 9.14. Underhand Pitch—starting position. Both feet touching the pitching line. Take one step forward as the pitch is delivered.

Reach, point to the target keeping palm up.

Common faults and teaching hints

1. Palming the ball.
   Grip the ball with fingers and thumb, fingers spread. (Fig. 9.15)
2. Lack of force.
   Swing arm in pendular swing with wide range of movement. Swing through forcibly and step *as* you throw.
3. Throwing ball too high.
   Release the ball while it is moving forward through the flat, bottom section of throwing arc, not on the upward swing.
4. Throwing ball to the side.
   Follow through to the target (point to

FIG. 9.15. Gripping the Ball. Grip the ball with fingers and thumb.

target) and keep the palm of the hand facing up.

BATTING[3] (FIG. 9.16)

Starting position

Grip bat 1 or 2 inches from the end with *right* hand above left.

FIG. 9.16. Batting. Stand in a ready position, elbows away from the body. Take a level swing with eyes on the ball. Drop the bat.

Face home plate with left side toward pitcher.

Stand with feet in easy *side*-stride position, with knees and hips bent.

Keeping knees bent, assume ready position by bending forward from the waist with weight over the balls of feet.

Keep left forearm parallel to the ground —"Look at your wristwatch." Keep right elbow away from body.

Reach back with the bat; rotate body slightly and shift weight to back foot.

Execution

Keep eyes on the ball *all the way to the bat.* Swing the bat with a *level swing.*

Take slide-step forward *as* you swing, and transfer weight to forward foot.

Drop the bat from left hand and start for first base.

Common faults and teaching hints

1. Poor position at home plate.
   Check starting position carefully.
2. Not keeping eyes on the ball *when contacting* the ball.

[3]Skill is described for right-handed player.

When coaching, watch batter's eyes as he contacts the ball. Is he looking at the pitcher, the field, *or at the ball?* (You cannot hit the ball if you are not looking at it.) Practice using batting tee. (Fig. 9.1)

3. Hitting down at the ball, chopping wood.
   Keep left forearm parallel with the ground. Swing into and through the ball, not *down* on it.
   For level swing, practice batting ball off the batting tee. (Fig. 9.1)
4. Lack of force.
   Reach back, then rotate body (hips) into the hit, and swing bat with force. Contact ball with power from legs, body, arms, and wrists. Keep firm grip on the bat at moment of contact.
5. Throwing the bat.
   At the beginning of the softball unit, especially with children starting softball, practice dropping the bat. Play Hit, Drop, and Overrun in order to get the feel and awareness of dropping the bat. If a bat is thrown, call the child back immediately for another turn to learn this safety skill. Later in the unit, call an "out" for throwing the bat. Appoint one player in each group to be responsible for keeping all batters behind the backstop or safety lines, except when at bat.

RELAYS AND SMALL GROUP GAMES— USING A SOFTBALL OR SOFTBALL AND BAT

Note: See description of skills for points to stress when presenting activities. For relay formations, see Chapter 6. Provide safe distances *between* relay lines.

UNDERHAND PITCH AND CATCH (ZIGZAG RELAY)

The relay

1. Play for practice, then evaluate the skills. Start at 20 to 25 feet.
2. Play for accuracy. Count the number of times ball is *not* caught. Team with fewest misses wins. Increase distance in relay to softball pitching distance.

OVERHAND THROW AND CATCH (ZIGZAG RELAY)

The relay

1. Play for practice, then evaluate the skills. Start at 25 to 30 feet. Stress how to catch as well as how to throw.

2. Play for accuracy as in Underhand Pitch and Catch. Increase distance to that between softball bases.

3. Play for speed. Team finishing and sitting down first wins.

FIELDING GROUND BALL AND THROWING OVERHAND (FILE RELAY WITH LEADER; FIG. 9.17)

The relay

Leader rolls the ball to his teammate in opposite line. Player receiving the ball catches and then returns it with an overhand throw. He then goes to the end of the line.

FIG. 9.17. *Fielding Ground Ball.*

1. Play for practice to learn the pattern of the relay and to learn the skills.

2. Play for accuracy. Count the number of misses when fielding the ground ball *and* receiving the thrown ball.

3. Play for speed. Team finishing and sitting down first wins.

STRIKING (USING HAND, PADDLE, BAT, RACKET)

See Chapter 6, "Striking (Sidearm Pattern)." Some children will benefit from reviewing the strike pattern in activities using the hand or paddle. Stress the similarities: ready-position with side to the oncoming ball; eyes on the ball all the way to contact; level swing.

HIT, DROP, AND OVERRUN—SOFTBALL

Equipment

Softball and bat; first and third bases, home plate. (Third base is used only to determine fair and foul balls.) Batting tee is optional; see variation.

Skills

In addition to batting and fielding, players learn to: *drop* the bat; play first base safely; overrun first base; rotate as in Work-up.

Formation (Fig. 9.18)

Two players at bat and a fielding team on a softball diamond as in Work-up. Number fielders as in diagram.

Object of the game

To make two successful runs to first base.

The game

Pitcher pitches the ball to the batter. The batter bats the ball into the field, *drops* the bat, and runs as fast as he can *across* first base. (He steps *on* the base as he runs across it.) Fielder recovering ball throws it to first base.

Whether the batter is safe at first base or not, he turns to the right and returns to batters' waiting position behind the backstop until his second turn (or returns behind the safety lines). After his second turn at bat, he automatically continues out to right fielder position and all other players rotate, 9 to 8, 8 to 7, and so on.

Scoring

Score one run for reaching first base successfully. There is a maximum of two runs each time at bat.

Outs

1. Throwing the bat a second time. (If a player accidentally throws the bat, give him another turn immediately to get the feel of *dropping* the bat.)

2. Fly ball caught.

3. First baseman receiving the ball and touching the base before the batter reaches first base. (See Fig. 9.24.)

4. Fielder tagging batter with the ball before the batter reaches first base.

5. Batter making two successful runs to first base.

Note: Batter is not out on strikes. He remains at bat until he hits a fair ball.

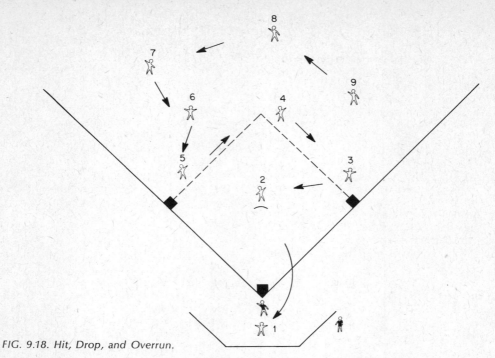

FIG. 9.18. Hit, Drop, and Overrun.

Teaching hints

1. Stress running as fast as possible and overrunning first base.

2. Stress correct way for baseman to cover first base. (See Fig. 9.24.)

3. Stress that batter must return to a safe position behind the backstop or behind safety lines while waiting for his second turn at bat.

Variation

Use a batting tee. This speeds up the game at beginning of softball unit.

TWO GROUNDERS OR A FLY

Equipment

Softball and bat; batting tee (optional in variations).

Skills

Batting and fielding a batted ball.

Formation

One batter with two to five fielders, open area.

Object of the game

For a fielder to catch *one* fly ball or to field *two* ground balls in order to become batter.

The game

Batter bats the ball off the batting tee into the field. (Fig. 9.1) (See Variations for other means of putting ball in play.) When a fielder is successful in catching one fly ball *or* fielding two balls that touch the ground, he becomes batter. The previous batter goes into the extreme right position in the field (right field when facing the field from batting position). With each new batter all scoring starts over again.

Variations

1. Use a pitcher and catcher. The pitcher pitches the ball to the batter, who hits it into the field. When a fielder has caught one fly ball or fielded two ground balls, he becomes *pitcher*. Pitcher becomes catcher, catcher becomes batter, and batter moves out to extreme right position in the field. (Pitcher should not interfere with, or try to catch, a batted ball.)

2. Batter tosses the ball up to himself and then hits it into the field.

3. Score an established number of points, 200 to 500. Use any variation of the game, but players rotate after scoring the prearranged number of points. Fly balls caught score 100 points; a ball fielded after one bounce scores 75 points; a ground ball (ball hitting ground more than once) scores 50 points; and any ball picked up after it stops rolling scores 25 points.

4. Hit the Bat. Play the game or play variation No. 1 with the following addition to the rules: A fielder goes up to bat (a) after catching a fly ball or (b) by hitting the bat. After hitting the ball, the batter places the bat on the ground with the long side toward the fielder. Fielder rolls the ball at the bat and attempts to hit it.

SKILL TESTS—USING A SOFTBALL

UNDERHAND PITCH (ACCURACY; FIG 9.19)

Equipment

One or two softballs; target on wall. The target is a rectangle 18 inches wide and 32 inches high, with lower edge 16 inches from the ground. This represents the strike zone, the area over home plate between the armpits and the knees of the batter.

Action

Contestant stands with both feet touching a line that is pitching distance away from the target. He holds the ball in front of his body and then takes *one* step forward *as* he pitches the ball underhand. Contestant has five (or ten) trials. Partner counts the score and retrieves the ball.

Scoring

Score 1 point for each time the ball hits the target. A ball hitting the line is good.

OVERHAND THROW (ACCURACY)

Perform the same as Underhand Throw with the following exceptions:

Target is a circle 5 feet in diameter, with the lower edge 1 foot from the ground.

Contestant stands with both feet *behind* a line 35 to 45 feet from the target (distance between bases). He steps over the line with his forward foot *as* he throws overhand.

SOFTBALL THROW (DISTANCE)

See "Performance Tests," Chapter 4.

BASE RUNNING (SPEED)

Equipment

Softball diamond with three bases and a home plate; stop watch.

FIG. 9.19. Underhand Pitch for Accuracy—working with a partner.

Action

Contestant stands in a ready-to-run position with back foot touching home plate. Starter-timer gives the signal, "On your mark—get set—go!" On signal the contestant runs the bases, touching each base and running across home plate.

Scoring

Record the lapsed time between the starter's signal and the instant the contestant's foot touches home plate at the finish. Record the time in seconds to the nearest tenth.

Teaching hints

Contestant attempts to touch each base with his left foot as he circles the bases. Lean in toward the diamond when rounding corners. Overrun home plate.

TEAM GAMES—USING A SOFTBALL AND BAT

LINE-UP TEE BALL

Equipment

One softball and bat, first and third bases, home plate, batting tee. (Third base is used only to determine fair and foul balls.)

Skills

Batting, fielding a batted ball.

Play area and position of players (Fig. 9.20)

Softball diamond with a first and third base and home plate. Place batting tee *outside* the *third* base line, 3 feet from home plate.

Batting team (five to seven players) stands behind the backstop with first batter at right end of backstop. Place fielding team (five to seven players) across the fielding area as in softball. (See diagram.)

Object of the game

To bat the ball off the batting tee into the field and run to first base and back across home plate without being put out.

The game

Batter bats the ball off the batting tee into the field, and then runs to first base and back across home plate.

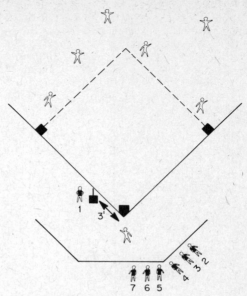

FIG. 9.20. Line-up Tee Ball.

Fielder receiving the batted ball *stands in the place* where ball is fielded. All other players run and line up behind him.

Scoring

1. If batter returns back across home plate first, batting team scores 1 point.
2. If fielders line up first, fielding team scores 1 point.
3. If a fielder catches a fly ball, fielders automatically score 1 point.

Play until each player on batting team has a turn at bat, then exchange sides. Team with most points after everyone has had a turn at bat wins.

Each team may call out the cumulative team score as points are made.

Teaching hints

1. Stress that player fielding the batted ball must remain on the spot he fielded the ball—other players run and line up behind him.
2. Stress safety in touching first base and turning to run back. It may be safer to run around a marker at the base. Adjust distance to base to ability of players.

3. Rotate positions when a team returns to the field.

Variation

As fielder receives the ball, he throws it to another player and then sits down, indicating that he has had a turn. Last fielder to receive the ball calls "Out." Increase the distance to first base.

BASES ON BALLS II

Rules are the same as in Bases on Balls II in "Kickball Unit," but use softball and bat. A batting tee may also be used.

HOME RUN OR OUT—SOFTBALL

Equipment

Softball and bat, three milk cartons, three bases and home plate, with an extra home plate or base. Batting tee is optional.

Skills

Batting, fielding a batted ball, pitching, throwing, catching a thrown ball, base running.

Play area and position of players (Fig. 9.21)

Softball diamond. Place one milk carton about 10 feet beyond each base. Distance depends upon the batting and throwing ability of the players. When using batting tee, place the tee *outside* the *third* base line 3 feet from home plate. Place *extra* home plate or base outside the batting tee. (See diagram.)

Place the players on the diamond as in softball.

Object of the game

To make a home run by running *outside* the milk cartons beyond first, second, and

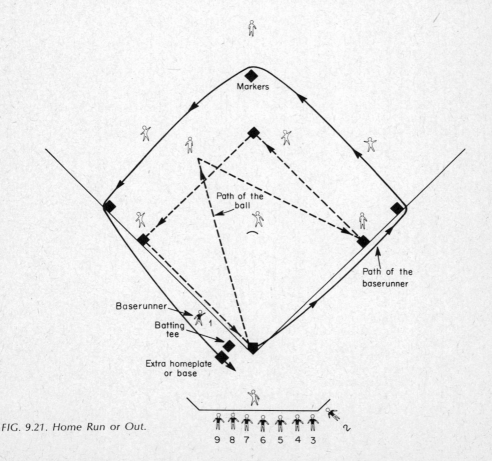

FIG. 9.21. *Home Run or Out.*

third bases and across the *extra* home plate or base before the ball completes the circuit around the bases, from first to second to third base, and then to home plate.

The game

The pitcher pitches the ball (or batter bats ball off batting tee). The batter bats the ball into the field and runs around the outside of each milk carton and across the *extra* home plate.

The player fielding the ball *must* throw it to first base. First baseman must touch first base with his foot while holding the ball in hand (tag up), then throw the ball to second. Second baseman tags up, then throws to third; third baseman tags up and throws to home plate. *(After tagging up,* the baseman should step off the base to make a better throw.)

Scoring

Score one run for each successful "home run."

Outs

(1) When the ball legally passes around the bases and the catcher tags home plate while in possession of the ball before the base runner reaches the extra home plate; (2) on a fly ball caught; (3) after three strikes.

Note: For a description of fair and foul balls, see Fig. 9.25.

Variations in base running

(Adjust the running distance of the base runner to the throwing abilities of the fielders.)

1. Have one set of bases and three milk cartons. The ball is thrown around the first set of bases. The base runner runs around the outside of milk cartons placed about 10 feet beyond each base.

2. Have two sets of bases. The ball is thrown around the inside set of bases. The base runner tags the second set of bases placed about 10 feet beyond the first set, and tags the extra home plate.

3. Base runner runs *outside the one set of bases.*

Exchanging sides

1. Play until each batter has had a turn to bat, then exchange sides.

2. Play for three outs or until each batter has had a turn to bat, whichever occurs first, then exchange sides.

Team with most runs at the end of completed innings wins.

Safety

To avoid collisions on close plays at home plate, the catcher should be *inside* the diamond reaching toward third base; base runner should run outside the diamond and touch the extra home plate. Explain and demonstrate.

Variations

1. Beatball. (a) Throw the ball into the field to put the ball in play. (b) Use a No. 7 utility ball.

2. Home Run or Out—Kickball. Use a kickball. The bowler (pitcher) bowls the ball to the kicker, who kicks the ball into the field. Additional rule: Kicker is out if he crosses home plate *before* he kicks the ball.

3. Home Run or Out—Base Football. Use a football. The ball is given to the kicker by the catcher. Kicker may either punt the ball or throw a forward pass into the field. Kicker must not advance *across* home plate in the act of kicking or passing the ball. A forward pass may not be thrown to the ground in front of home plate; it must be passed into the field.

Note: When using a football, it may be sufficiently challenging for the kicker to run *outside the bases* rather than any added distance around the milk cartons.

SOFTBALL[4]

Equipment

Softball and bat, three bases and home plate, catcher's mask.

Skills

Batting, fielding a batted ball, pitching, throwing, catching a thrown ball, base running.

[4]Used by permission of the International Joint Rules Committee on Softball.

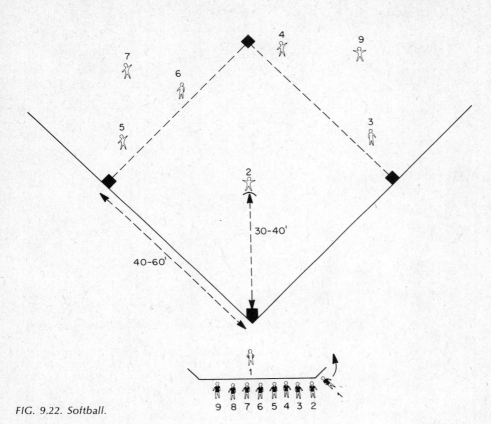

FIG. 9.22. Softball.

Play area and position of players (Fig. 9.22)

Softball diamond.

An official team consists of nine players: (1) catcher, (2) pitcher, (3) first baseman, (4) second baseman, (5) third baseman, (6) shortstop, (7) left fielder, (8) center fielder, (9) right fielder. (See diagram for fielding positions.) Batting team stands behind backstop with first batter at right end (end toward first base). If no backstop, batting team may stand behind marked lines 25 feet from home plate and 15 feet from *first* base line. (For ease in rotation, players are numbered consecutively rather than pitcher No. 1 and catcher No. 2 as in baseball.)

Object of the game

To bat the ball into fair territory and run to first base. Batter continues to run if he can reach succeeding bases safely.

The batting teams remain at bat until three outs are made. After three outs, teams exchange sides. A turn at bat for each team *completes* one inning.

Scoring

Score 1 point for each successful run. Team with most runs at end of completed innings wins.

Note: If the team second at bat has scored more runs than the first team at bat, the score is that of the incomplete

Red Team			Blue Team		
Inning	Runs	Outs	Inning	Runs	Outs
1			1		
2			2		
3			3		
4			4		
5			5		
6			6		
7			7		

FIG. 9.23A. Simplified score card.

	INNINGS								INNINGS						
Players	1	2	3	4	5	6	7	Players	1	2	3	4	5	6	7
Susie	①	①	/					Mary Jane	◆	/					
Tom	◆	◆	③					Tony	◆	③					
Bill	◆	②						Paul	①		◆				
Joan	◆	◆						Julie	◆		◆				
Ralph	⌐	/						Sharon	⌐		◆				
Ann	②	③						Louise	②		◆				
Jean	/		①					Lila	③						
Marian	③		②					Harry		①					
Dick		◆	>					Kathy		②					
Running score	1 2 3 4 5 6 7 8							Running score	1 2 3 4 5 6 7 8						
	9 10 11 12 13 14 15 16								9 10 11 12 13 14 15 16						
	17 18 19 20 21 22 23 24								17 18 19 20 21 22 23 24						

Legend:
①②③ Number of Outs
▢ End of inning
◆ Home run

Bases traveled:
/ One base
> Two bases
⌐ Three bases
◆ Completed run

FIG. 9.23B. Score card with legend.

inning. See suggestion for score card. (Figs. 9.23A and B)

Outs for the batter

1. Fair or foul fly ball caught.
2. Three strikes.
3. Throwing the bat (adapted rule).
4. Touching his own batted ball *while in fair territory*. (If batter is hit with his own batted ball while standing in the batter's box, before *starting* to first base, batter is considered to be in *foul* territory and a foul ball is called.)

Outs for the base runner

1. A force-out. (When the baseman receives the ball, he may tag the base since it is not necessary to tag the base runner on a force-out.) (Fig. 9.24) (a) Ball reaches first base before the batter. (b) Ball reaches any base before the base runner if the preceding bases are occupied and base runner must advance.
2. On a fly ball caught, if the base runner leaves his base before the ball is caught and the ball reaches the base be-

fore the base runner returns. (Base runner may remain on his base until the fly ball is caught or he may return to his base and tag up after the fly ball is caught. He may then *legally advance* to the next base, but with liability of being put out. After the fly ball is caught, he may tag his base and then try to advance on either a *fair* or a *foul fly* ball caught.)

FIG. 9.24. Covering first base. Touch the edge of the base and reach out toward the oncoming ball.

3. Being tagged by the ball in possession of a fielder when base runner is not touch-

ing the base. (Exception: overrunning *first* base after batting the ball. Base runner then turns back and returns to first base. However, if he starts toward second base, he may be tagged out.)

4. Leaving his base before the ball leaves the pitcher's hand.

5. Running more than 3 feet from a direct line between bases *to avoid being tagged*.

6. Being hit directly by a batted ball while in fair territory when not touching a base.

7. Passing a base runner ahead of him.

8. Failing to touch each base.

Fair balls

To be fair, a batted ball must *settle* fair in the infield (between the first and third base lines, from home plate to first or third base); or *land* fair in the outfield (beyond first and third base between extended first and third base lines). (Fig. 9.25)

If a batted ball is in fair territory and is touched by a fielder, it is fair no matter where it rolls; if ball is in foul territory and touched by fielder, it is a foul ball. A batted ball hitting or passing over first or third base is fair.

Overthrows

Base runners may run *one* additional base with liability of being put out if the ball is thrown to a base and goes into *foul* territory. (If the ball goes into *fair* terri-

tory, the base runner may go any number of bases, with liability of being put out.)

Runs do NOT *score* if the third out of the inning is a result of: (a) the batter being put out before legally touching first base; (b) a base runner being forced out due to the batter becoming a base runner; (c) a base runner leaving base before the pitcher releases the ball to the batter.

Variation

Tee Ball. Bat the ball off a batting tee. Place the batting tee *outside* the *third* base line, at least 3 feet from home plate, and outside the path of the base runner.

SOFTBALL WORK-UP

Equipment

Softball and bat, three bases and home plate. A batting tee is optional.

Skills

Batting, fielding a batted ball, pitching, throwing, catching a thrown ball, base running.

Play area and position of players (Fig. 9.26)

Softball diamond.

Fielders: (1) catcher, (2) pitcher, (3) first baseman, (4) second baseman, (5) third baseman, (6) shortstop, (7) left fielder, (8) center fielder, (9) right fielder. (See diagram for fielding positions.) Place *four* batters behind backstop.

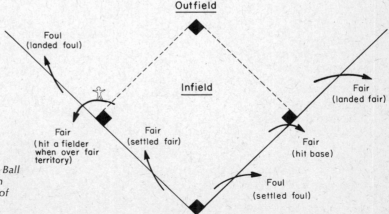

FIG. 9.25. Fair and foul balls. Ball lands at the beginning of each arrow and stops at the point of the arrow.

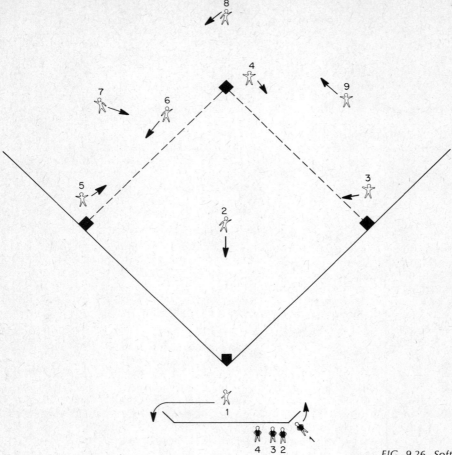

FIG. 9.26. Softball Work-up.

Object of the game

To make two runs.

The game

Play the same as softball with the following exceptions:

1. After a player makes an out, he goes to right field and all fielders rotate one position, 9 to 8, 8 to 7, and so on. (See diagram.)

2. After a batter makes *two* runs, he automatically goes to right field and gives another player a turn to bat. Players rotate.

3. On a fly ball caught, batter goes to right field and players rotate.

4. For safety, waiting batters emerge from *first* base side of backstop.

Variations

1. Kickball Work-up. Use a kickball. Follow rule adaptations as in Kickball.

2. Base Football Work-up. Use a football. Punt or forward pass to put the ball in play. For further rules see Base Football.

3. Fist Ball Work-up. Use a volleyball or a No. 8½ utility ball. Serve the ball out-of-hand. Rule adaptation: fly ball caught is not out.

THREE-TEAM SOFTBALL (FIG. 9.27)

Rules are the same as for Softball except that the players are divided into three instead of two team. Each team is composed of five (or four) players.

Five players are at bat; five players are

FIG. 9.27. Three-Team Softball.

in the infield: catcher, pitcher, first base-man, second baseman, third baseman; and five players are in the outfield: shortstop, left fielder, center fielder, right fielder, and a short fielder between first and second bases.

After three outs, batting team goes to the outfield; team in outfield moves to the infield; team in infield goes up to bat. After the next three outs, teams rotate again. After all three team have made three outs, one inning has been completed.

Optional rule: After *each out*, infield team rotates within own team. The catcher goes to third base, third baseman to sec-ond base, and so on. The team in the out-field also rotates within own team. The shortstop goes to short fielder, short fielder moves back to right field, and so on.

Variations

1. Three-Team Kickball.

2. Three-Team Base Football.

3. Three-Team Home Run or Out—Softball. Play Home Run or Out—Softball using three teams rather than two teams. Bat the ball off a batting tee or bat a pitched ball.

4. Three-Team Home Run or Out—Kickball.

5. Three-Team Home Run or Out—Base Football.

BASEBALL—USING 10-INCH OR 9-INCH SOFTBALL

The game is the same as softball with the following exceptions:

Equipment

Ten-inch or 9-inch official softball, or 10-inch playground softball; gloves for fielding team; catcher's mask and chest protector.

Diamond

Seventy-five feet between bases and 55-foot pitching distance; or 65-foot bases and 48-foot pitching distance, depending on skill level of players.

Rules

Pitch overhand; base runners lead off bases (it is not necessary for base runners to have one foot on the base until the ball leaves the pitcher's hand).

BIBLIOGRAPHY—SECTION TWO

1. American Association for Health, Physical Education and Recreation. *Skills Test Manuals* ("Basketball" For Boys [1966], For Girls [1966]; "Football" [rev. ed., 1966]; "Softball" For Boys [1966], For Girls [1966]; "Volleyball" For Boys and Girls [1969]). 1201 Sixteenth St., N.W., Washington, D.C.: American Association for Health, Physical Education and Recreation.

2. American Association for Health, Physical Education and Recreation. *How We Do It Game Book,* rev. ed., 1201 Sixteenth Street, N.W., Washington, D.C.: American Association for Health, Physical Education and Recreation, 1964.

3. Broer, Marion R. *Efficiency of Human Movement,* 2nd ed., Philadelphia: W. B. Saunders Company, 1966.

4. Division for Girls and Women's Sports, American Association for Health, Physical Education, and Recreation. *Official Basketball Guide, Official Soccer–Speedball Guide, Official Softball Guide, Official Track and Field Guide, Official Volleyball Guide, Recreational Games and Sports,* 1201 Sixteenth Street, N.W., Washington 6, D.C.: American Association for Health, Physical Education and Recreation.

5. Doherty, J. Kenneth. *Modern Track and Field,* 2nd ed., Englewood Cliffs, New Jersey: Prentice-Hall, Inc., 1963.

6. Gough, Frances. "Track and Field" (unpublished manuscript), Cerritos College, Norwalk, California.

7. Men's Official Sport Guides: *Official Basketball Rules,* National Federation of State High School Athletic Associations, 7 South Dearborn Street, Chicago 3, Illinois. *Official Soccer Guide,* National Collegiate Athletic Association, National Collegiate Athletic Bureau, New York. *Official Volleyball Rules,* United States Volleyball Association, USVBA Printer, Box 109, Berne, Indiana.

8. Meyer, Margaret H., and Marguerite M. Schwarz. *Team Sports for Girls and Women,* 4th ed., Philadelphia: W. B. Saunders Company, 1965.

9. Mortensen, Jess, and John M. Cooper. *Track and Field for the Coach and Athlete,* Englewood Cliffs, New Jersey: Prentice-Hall, Inc., 1959.

10. New York Physical Fitness Tests. Physical Education Bureau, State Education Department, Albany, New York.

11. Santa Monica City Schools. *Physical Education Activities for Fourth Grade,* Santa Monica, California, 1952. (Basic rules of Pin Kickball.)

12. Los Angeles City Schools. *Physical Education Teaching Guide, Grades Three, Four, Five, Six,* Division of Instructional Services, publication No. 537, 1961.

13. Welch, J. Edmund, ed. *How to Play and Teach Volleyball,* rev. ed., New York: Association Press, 1969.

AUDIO-VISUAL MATERIALS—SECTION TWO

CHARTS

14. Division for Girls and Women's Sports
    Technique Charts: "Basketball"; "Softball"; "Speedball"; "Volleyball."
    Polly Cartoons (12 charts) Humorous Bulletin Board Charts—to introduce
    various sport seasons. Rev. 1968.

FILMS

15. Aims Instructional Media Services, Inc.
    P. O. Box 1010, Hollywood, California, 90028.
    Physical Education Basic Skills—in slow motion.
    "Softball—Tumbling—Soccer"
    "Football—Basketball—Apparatus"
    Technical Advisor: Dr. James Harrison

    May be used as instructional films for children at the beginning and middle
    of each unit.
    16 mm color/silent. Sale/preview—individually or in sets. 8 mm—Sale.
    Films available for rental from regional sources.

ADDITIONAL SOURCES OF MATERIALS

16. American Association for Health, Physical Education, and Recreation
    1201 Sixteenth Street, N.W., Washington, 6, D.C.
    (Publications list available without charge.)
17. Division for Girls and Women's Sports Guides
    1201 Sixteenth Street, N.W., Washington 6, D.C.
    (Includes recommended audio-visual material.)
18. The Athletic Institute, Merchandise Mart, Room 805, Chicago, Illinois.
    (Visual aids include books, motion pictures, slide films, pamphlets, and hand-
    books. Catalogue published annually; available without charge.)

DANCE: EXPLORATION AND CREATIVITY

FIG. 10.1. Streamers add enjoyment.

"There once was a magical musical note who had the power to change himself anyway at all. He could be very loud or very quiet, very bouncy or very very slow. He could even sound like a big bass drum anytime he wanted. The magical musical note would like to share his power with you. What will you do?"

The intrigue of magic is sufficient in itself to introduce movement in response to rhythm. A percussion instrument of any description is all else that is needed to stimulate children to explore the infinite possibilities in rhythm patterns and to create unique combinations of rhythm and movement. Older children enjoy the challenge of developing syncopated rhythms and synchronized movements as an additional dimension.

The dramatization of stories through dance is yet another kind of creative movement inherently satisfying for children. This kind of reverbalization through movement increases comprehension of story lines on the one hand, and encourages individual interpretation of meaning on the other. Creative writing by students provides excellent sources for such stories or poems that are then enacted through movement. Children are wonderfully uninhibited; they *are* what they imagine, they do not pretend.

Education is increasingly aware of the place and value of creative rhythmic activities in the learning process. Such experiences not only provide a means of developing creativity, control, and skill, but also afford opportunities of enlarging concepts, experiencing social behavior patterns, and participating in group activities. The activities are also important in that they give ample opportunity for individual response as well as the experience of working with a partner or in small or large groups. Each individual reaction is a contributing part of an overall concept.

The activities in "Movement Exploration," Chapter 1, give each child complete freedom to move in his own way at his own tempo. As he moves, he increases his repertory of movement. The activities described in this chapter go beyond those in Chapter 1 by providing a guiding beat, which changes the focus slightly. Respond-ing to rhythm contributes to ease of movement and a smoother flow of motion. This is valuable to all children, but particularly for the clumsy, awkward, or self-conscious child.

In this presentation, activities of Chapter 1 are repeated and expanded, and auditory cues have been added. There is a wide selection of accompaniment available. Voice, clapping, and tapping may be used from the start. Percussion instruments provide auditory discrimination from the gross sounds of the drums and wood blocks to the finer tones of the claves and finger cymbals. Another group of instruments gives a different sound, such as the rubbing together of sand blocks and the scratching of the guiro. There are instruments to shake such as bells, tambourines, and shakers. Many subtle variations in sounds for fine auditory discrimination can be made by putting different materials in the shakers, such as beans, macaroni, rice, gravel, and shot. Percussion instruments are most practical: inexpensive and easy to make; transported easily, used any place; and anyone can play them. (See list of "Percussion Instruments" at end of the chapter.)

A piano may provide a very strong guiding beat along with all the variations in tempo, levels, force, intensity, accent, and mood. Piano music may also guide children to identify the qualities of movement from smooth and sustained, to jerky and mechanical ones.

Records provide a wealth of material that can take children from the beginning stages of responding to basic rhythms to the heights of creativity. While records are used mostly indoors, the music may be taped for outdoor use.

The Bibliography lists references to material by many authorities in the area of dance and creative activity. Each author may have a slightly different approach, but all are working toward the same goals. A review of the literature is strongly recommended.

PURPOSES

The purposes of this area are essentially the same as for Chapter 1, "Movement Exploration," with greater emphasis on two factors: response to a rhythmic beat, an auditory stimulus; and creativity.

This program is intended to accomplish the following:

—to explore and to experiment with the infinite possibilities of movement in response to rhythm;

—to encourage creative responses to various rhythmic stimuli;

—to increase skill in balance, coordination, and rhythm, as they enhance the quality of movement;

—to explore different ways of expressing thoughts and feelings through movement;

—to provide opportunities for originality and elaboration of ideas in response to songs, poems, and stories;

—to enhance social interaction through small and large group cooperation.

PRESENTATION OF MATERIAL[1]

To be effective the creative dance program must be thought of in terms of children and their experiences. It should have broad aspects and may be related to other fields of creative effort such as art, music, and literature. Although the basic thinking for the program will have to be done by the teacher, planning is a cooperative activity and affords excellent opportunities for children and teacher to work together.

As in other areas, the initial lessons should include familiar things that children can perform easily. With encouragement for variety, such activities as walking in different ways or moving at different levels set the stage for more abstract creations at increasingly advanced levels. It should be stressed that failure is nonexistent in this kind of program, and that only the degree of freedom in movement determines the amount of success possible. What children create may not be new to the world, but if it is new to them, it is an exciting and satisfying experience.

[1]Due to the wide variation in abilities and interest, no attempt was made to provide a suggested Grade Placement Chart. When well motivated and taught, the simplest activities are satisfying and fun at any grade level.

There are *many* ways of presenting material. The following pages enumerate but a few in several categories. Questions are suggested that may help to inspire children to improve their performances. Response to various stimuli provides many interesting and exciting activities.

With the wide variation in the ability of children to be creative, the evaluation is not of quality of performance as judged by the adult. Rather the evaluation is of the involvement, satisfaction, and enjoyment of the child. From the various types of experiences, the child may eventually be guided to evaluate his own performance in terms of quality. A child with keen imagination is rich indeed. Time spent in developing imagination and exposing creativity is time well spent.

RESPONSE TO RHYTHM

There are numerous ways of assisting the children to increase skill in responding to rhythm.

PROGRESSION

Use of voice, clapping hands, tapping foot, nodding head, swaying body.

Use of percussion instruments, accenting the basic beat.

Use of music along with voice and/or percussions to accent the beat.

Use of music with strong basic beat.

Use of music with more orchestration.

WITHIN A LESSON

1. Motivation—use verbal cues and visual aids.

2. Listen to the music, then all clap to the accompaniment, tap foot, move hands or body.

3. Experiment and explore possibilities for movement. Discuss and pose questions such as, "Could you . . . ?" or "What other ways . . . ?" "Who can . . . ?"

4. When working on basic patterns, the teacher may use verbal cues such as "Skip and skip . . . ," clap hands, or use percussion instruments to accent the basic beat, or the teacher may participate beside or near a child having difficulty. Some of the children may use the percussion instruments or clap the rhythm while the others participate, then exchange roles. Two or

more children may demonstrate the basic pattern while the teacher emphasizes the main points.

5. For boys, if needed, stress using smaller steps for better balance and control.

CREATIVITY

According to the research, as stated by E. Paul Torrance, a number of abilities are involved in creative thinking.

The abilities involved are sensitivity to problems, fluency (the ability to produce a large number of ideas), flexibility (the ability to produce a variety of ideas or use a variety of approaches), originality (the ability to produce ideas that are off the beaten track), elaboration (the ability to fill in the details), and redefinition (the ability to define or perceive in a way different from the usual, established, or intended way, etc.). (19)

As stated previously, the teacher should guide but not dictate when presenting creative activity. The following suggestions provide guidelines for class work:

1. Discuss the activity; provide visual aids.
2. Provide word pictures.
3. Encourage listening to the accompaniment.
4. Allow time to explore and experiment.
5. Encourage the children and recognize even small gains.
6. After participating, discuss the activity and then repeat it.
7. Have several children who are doing the activity *differently* show *their* way. Encourage the unique.
8. After individual participation, repeat the activity with a partner or in a small group.
9. Provide a variety of experiences.

CONTROL OF GROUP

The activities are conducted in an informal atmosphere and rigid control is not expected. However, adequate control for effective teaching and ability to regain attention quickly after activity are needed.

1. Provide a signal to "stop, look and listen," or to sit down and listen. The signal may be given on a percussion instrument; it may be a verbal cue or when the music stops. Stress "freezing" and then sitting down quietly.
2. Have children develop an awareness of space. If they forget to maintain adequate spacing, stop and have them respace. Review activities for "Spatial Awareness," Chapter 1.
3. Separate children who have difficulty when near each other.
4. Stand near a child who has difficulty with self-control.
5. Have one-half and then the other half of the group participate, especially when performing locomotor activities in a limited area. Children not participating in the activity may clap to the rhythm or use percussion instruments.

LESSON GUIDE

There are many different ways to present the various rhythmic activities. The following pattern gives one approach. The teacher will do the basic planning and have the lesson develop through a series of questions and discussions; at other times the subject and planning may result from the activities of the children. In any case, care should be taken that the lesson is based on definite objectives and includes a variety of experiences and activities.

These lessons should include (1) locomotor movements; (2) movement activities in place, or combinations of 1 and 2; (3) a period of relaxation, during which the children may discuss the activities and hear suggestions, listen to music, or plan for the conclusion of the lesson; (4) conclusion or culmination: an interesting and enjoyable way to end the lesson and to reinforce previous learnings. This pattern is not a fixed one; parts may be interchanged to fit the needs of the children and for the development of the ideas.

Within each lesson there should be provision for repetition: for better understanding, more creativity, increased accuracy in response to the rhythm, less noise with the feet, larger movements when appropriate, or reinforcement of learning. An activity may be repeated per se, or it may be performed in different ways: first as an individual and then with a partner or small group; first to the accompaniment of a percussion instrument (strong beat) and then to a record or piano music; or first with verbal cues and then without any cues.

EXAMPLE OF LESSON

LESSON BASED ON MOVEMENT EXPERIENCES VARIATIONS IN DIRECTIONS

Specific purposes

Recognizing and understanding change of directions.

Responding in movement to various directions.

Using directions in pattern form.

Motivational and guide material

In how many different directions can you go? Can your feet go in those directions? Can you go in different directions without bumping into anyone? Find your own space and we will try. Listen to the drum. (Drum: *even* rhythm.)

Did your feet walk or skip all the time? Can you go in different directions and have your feet do different things? Listen to this rhythm. . . . (Repeat with *uneven* rhythm.) What was the difference? Can you go in a different direction each time the drum tells you to go in the new direction? Listen! (Drum: *even* rhythm. Accent the first beat of each series of 8.) How do you know when to change? Let's try it.

Listen to this rhythm and we will do it again. (Drum: *uneven* rhythm. Accent 8's.) Can you move in different ways if your feet stay in one spot? Can you move up high and down low? To one side and then the other? Continue in one direction while I shake the tambourine, then change directions each time I stop.

Relaxation: How can you be a big circle and get smaller and smaller until you are a tiny one? It would be nice to be all relaxed and rest in the little circle. Check some children for relaxation (Record: "Time to Rest"—J-3. See Accompaniment.)

Evaluation: How many different direc-

tions did you find you could go?" Could you show us? (Select several children to demonstrate.)

Conclusion: Let's listen and clap softly to this music, accenting the first beat in each phrase. (Record: "Walk with Direction Change"—C.) Can you go in a different direction each time the *music* tells you to change directions, sometimes moving your feet and sometimes only your body?

Now that you know the music, try it again. You will probably think of other things to do.

INTRODUCTORY EXPERIENCES IN MOVEMENT

Movement plays a major part in the lives of children. It is a language for them, a means of expression, and therefore it is important for them to discover and experience many ways of moving in order to give expression to thoughts, ideas, and feelings. By experimenting, by doing, they learn to direct simple movements and to make new combinations. In other words, they begin to gain control of their bodies, their instruments of expression.

The activities may first be done in the form of experimentation, using fundamental body movements and then progressing to more complex combinations. By guiding questions the teacher can lead the children into making suggestions for exploring and trying out all types of movement combinations.

As children are highly imaginative and dramatic, it is only natural that ideas will often guide movements. The child is interested in being things at this period: a jet, a toy, a whale. The dramatization may be initiated from the feeling of the movement or from the mood of the moment. A slow walk may become that of an elephant or bear; a stretch may lead a group into being cats or elevators or fountains.

Another way to enlarge the experiencing of activities is to discover other activities having the same quality of movement. A brisk walk could lead to imitating a parade horse, a band leader, or popcorn.

Lessons centering around movement exploration are enjoyed by all ages when the activities are based upon or are developed from their needs, levels, and abilities. The activities may vary from the simple combinations of the primary age to complex and exciting experiences developed by the more mature children.

BASIC MOVEMENT PATTERNS

See description of movement patterns in Chapter 1, "Efficient Movement."

LOCOMOTOR PATTERNS (MOVING BASE)

Rhythmic Notations.

Even rhythm (one sound)

Usually ²⁄₄ or ⁴⁄₄ meter.
Example: ²⁄₄ meter

	♩	♩
Walk	step	step
	Left	Right
Leap	leap	leap
	L	R
Hop	hop	hop
(on one foot)	L	L
Jump	jump	jump
(on both feet)	L-R	L-R
Run	run run	run run
(double time)	L R	L R

Uneven rhythm (two sounds)

Usually ⁶⁄₈ or ²⁄₄ meter.
Example: ²⁄₄ meter

	♩. ♪	♩. ♪
Gallop	gal-lop	gal-lop
	step cl	step close
Slide	slide &	slide &
	step cl	step close
Skip	skip &	skip &
	step h	step hop
	L L	R R

NONLOCOMOTOR PATTERNS (STATIONARY BASE: LYING, SITTING, KNEELING, STANDING)

Bend-Stretch; Push-Pull; Swing-Sway. Turn, Twist—Rotate.

ACTIVITIES USING NONLOCOMOTOR PATTERNS

Streamers add enjoyment. (See Fig. 10.1.) For suggested activities, see Chapter 1, "Body Control," "Nonlocomotor Patterns," No. 8.

BEND—STRETCH (FLEXION AND EXTENSION)

1. Lying on back (variations of Angels in the Snow). (13) Starting with hands at sides, raise arms overhead keeping them in contact with the floor all the way. Identify arm position ¼ way up (upside-down V); ½ way up (Check each child's kinesthetic perception of this position in space; are the arms straight out shoulder height, or high or low); ¾ way up (like a V); all the way up and clap hands. Return to sides and clap sides. (Identify positions as arms are lowered.)

    a. Jerky movements, like a rusty robot. Stop ¼, ½, and ¾ way up and overhead. (Using xylophone—move up the scale note by note; wood block or claves—a single hit for each jerky movement.)

    b. Make three stops while raising arms. Stop at upside-down V position; stop at shoulder height; stop at V position overhead; clap hands overhead. Repeat movement, lowering hands to sides. Shake tambourine, then strike it for hand clap.)

    c. Sustained movement—move steadily without stopping. How slowly can you raise your arms and keep moving them all the time? Stretch as high as you can and then completely relax. (Shake tambourine, then strike it to signal relaxation.)

Move arms up (or down) as long as you can hear the sound of the gong. (Strike gong once.)

How fast can you raise your arms? How fast can you lower them? (Sweep up or down the xylophone or the keys of piano.)

2. On knees. How far down your side can you reach without turning your body? Boys, let your hand follow the seam down the side of your pants leg; now bend toward the other side. How far across the top of your head can you reach with one arm without turning your body? You are between two large pieces of window glass and can only move to the side. Can you put one leg out straight to the side and bend toward it? Now reach way overhead with your other hand.

3. Standing. How tall can you be? Can you pull up inside and be taller? How small can you be? Can you fold down

inside and be very small? What could you be when you are coming up? What could you be when you are going down? How far can you reach without moving your feet? How far and in how many different directions can you reach? How long a straight line can you make with both hands together? With one hand? How fast can you shoot up? Collapse? What are you when you shoot up quickly? (Missile.) What are you when you collapse? (Punctured balloon.) How slowly can you raise up, moving all the time? How slowly can you go down, slow motion? What could you be when raising up slowly? (Growing.) What could you be when you go down slowly? (Melting ice cream cone, tire losing air.) How would a great big balloon go if the air started to go out? Let's blow up our balloons and see what happens.

How tall can you be if you bounce up? Bounce from the inside: bounce—bounce; or jump—bounce—jump—bounce.

Accompaniment

Jerky, quick, or explosive movement.
Percussion: Staccato, sharp. Strike wood block or tambourine; sweep up or down the keys of the xylophone or piano.
Records.[2] Records for hopping, jumping, or ball bouncing; D-12, "Jack-in-the-Box"; K-8, *The Little Puppet.*
Folk Dance: Jump Jim Jo.

Accompaniment

Sustained.
Percussion: Move up and down keys of piano or xylophone; shake tambourine; strike gong.
Records: D-4, Sun and Growing Plants; D-5, Teetering; D-12, "Oil Wells"; H, Spiraling; J-5, Mr. Snowman.

PUSH-PULL (AGAINST RESISTANCE, REAL OR IMAGINARY)

1. Sitting—working with a partner. What different ways can you work (1) together, (2) providing *some* resistance for partner?
2. On knees—as an individual.
3. Standing—as an individual or with a partner; sawing wood; pushing or pulling a heavy object.

[2]References to records refer to "Accompaniment, List of Records."

Percussion: Sand blocks; drum with wire brush; coconut shells (rub together); shakers; gourds, or guiro (scraping).
Records: A; D-7, Tugs and Liner, Rowboat; B-3, F-1, Elephant.

PROJECT (THROW FORCEFULLY)

Ballistic action; projecting with force like a missile.
Mechanics of throwing a ball overhand.
Jump and reach—for height.
Missile or rocket take-off.
Team sports: basketball—chest pass; football—punt or forward pass for distance.
(May develop a team game in pantomime, or a Cavalcade of Sports in Tableaux.)
Percussion: One or two percussion instruments. For preparation of the action start the countdown with "Three—two—one—go!" Accent "Go!" for the explosive forward or upward movement. May use one percussion instrument for the countdown and another for the strong explosive movement on "Go!"
Record: B-3, Jackknife; D-12, Jack-in-the-Box.

STRIKE (PERCUSSIVE)

Striking an imaginary object; batting a ball.
Driving stakes of tent (circus tent, camping tent); cutting down trees (Westward Movement, Christmas trees); blacksmith (Westward Movement); carnival (striking the lever that sends the weight up to ring the bell).
Percussion: Cymbals; triangle; wood block; tambourine; drum.
Records: "Anvil Chorus"; music for giants; B-3; C, Big Run; H.

SWING (PENDULAR)

Experiment with various bases.
Experiment with various groupings: individual, partners, threes.
Kneeling: Pendular swing—one arm, both arms in unison, arms not in unison, arms in opposition; arm circles—one arm, both arms.
Standing: Pendular swing—arms, legs, and trunk (bells, clocks); underhand pattern when throwing.

Call: "Swing and swing and. . . ." (Call "and" for change in direction.) Add streamers—one in each hand.

"Reach and reach and. . . ." (Stress large movements.)

Percussion: Shake, then hold tambourine momentarily for change in direction; strike a percussion instrument in uneven rhythm.

Records: A; Clocks, Trapeze Performers B-1; C; G-2; H; The Swing J-3.

SWAY-ROCK (ARCLIKE PATTERN)

Experiment with various bases (for balance).

Prone lying, with arms overhead: raise feet and arms slightly off floor, rock side to side. Call, "Rock and rock and. . . ."

Sitting: "V" Sit—rocking, rowboats, buoys.

On knees: arms overhead, swaying trees.

Standing: sailboats, rocking horse, sawing wood.

Percussion: Sand blocks; drums and wire brush; gourds; shakers; metronome.

Records: Clocks B-1; B-3; H; "Bell Buoy Song" K-10.

TURN, TWIST, ROTATE

Turn like a weather vane; twist like a strong wind; rotate the body as in batting a ball; rotate the forearm as if turning a handle.

Experiment with various bases.

Turn slowly—sustained movement; turn using momentum—fast movement.

What are you as you turn slowly? Fast?

Percussion: Sustained or staccato.

Records: B-3; Wind D-4; Waves D-7; The Wind J-1; "Steam Shovel Song" K-9; L-105.

ACTIVITIES USING LOCOMOTOR PATTERNS

Note: See "Locomotor Patterns," Chapter 1.

EXPLORE VARIOUS WAYS OF MOVING

1. In how many different ways can you move and keep in time to this even rhythm? (All move in the same general direction within a large area in scattered formation, or move from one line or area to another.) Discuss and then explore the ways expressed by various children.

   a. Use different percussion instruments such as drums, wood blocks, claves.

   b. Use records or piano music.

2. Who can move and keep in time to this uneven rhythm?

   a. Use percussion instruments.

   b. Use records or piano music.

EXPLORE ONE PATTERN

1. Walk. March like a soldier; toe out like a duck; toe in like a pigeon; toe straight ahead and walk tall like boys and girls. Can you think of any other ways to walk? (In circus parade, tiptoe walk, mechanical walk, giant walk, crooked walk, animal walks.)

Percussion: Drum, claves, wood block.

Records: Walk; March; Toy Parade; Circus Parade; Walking Straight and Tall J-1.

2. Run. Light run; vigorous run, like a truck or airplane. Others?

Percussion: Wood block, claves.

Records: Run; Birds; Ponies.

3. Leap. Over puddles of water, like a deer or gazelle. Others?

Percussion: Wood block, drum (not too heavy a beat).

Records: Leap; Combinations of run and leap; Frogs D-3.

4. Jump or Hop. Bouncing ball, kangaroo, jump rope, hopscotch. Others?

Percussion: Wood block, claves.

Records: Jump; hop; jump rope; hopscotch; bouncing ball; frogs; kangaroos.

5. Slide or Gallop. Slide—move to the side; slide to the side, change directions; gallop—move forward; gallop lightly like a small pony. Others?

Percussion: Coconut shells, wood blocks, claves, Chinese or Korean temple block.

Records: Slide; gallop; ponies; cowboys; gallop and change lead foot with the phrasing 8-8-4-4-2-2-2-2. Slide making half-turns, continue in the same direction.

6. Skip. Skip high; skip quietly; skip to school.

Percussion: Wood block, claves.

Records: Skips; "Skipping We Go" J-2; A Visit To My Little Friend K-3; Beach Ball L107.

CHANGE FROM ONE PATTERN TO ANOTHER

How smoothly can you change from one way of moving to another? Call changes.

Listen carefully and change with the music. Have children listen and respond without the calls.

This time try different ways of using your arms. (For balance; for height; leading with body while dragging arms; arms leading and pulling body; one arm leading and one following.)

Percussion: Drum, wood block, claves.

Records: Combinations: B-1; C; D-1, 2, 3, 5; H; K-2, 3; and L.

EXPLORE VARIATIONS

(See "Body Control," "Variations," Chapter 1.)

In one activity period, a variation may be presented through the use of percussion instruments; the same variation may be reinforced through experiences to the accompaniment of a piano or the use of records. For intermediate grade children, folk dances that repeat the variation may be used.

VARIATIONS IN DIRECTIONS (FORWARD, BACKWARD, TO SIDE, CIRCLE, DIAGONALS)

Accent by clapping louder and/or stamping on *first* beat of a phrase.

Percussion: Take 7 beats and hold on 8; take 15 beats and hold on 16; start new direction on 1, after the hold.

Accent and change directions on the first beat of 16 counts; of 8 counts; of 4 counts.

Change directions *and* locomotor pattern at the beginning of each phrase.

Make geometric patterns accenting each change in direction. Change locomotor pattern with the change of direction.

Records: Clap and accent the first beat of a phrase (16 beats). Take activity and change directions at the beginning of each long phrase (16). Repeat all with phrases of 8 beats, 4 beats. Combine phrases such as 8's and 4's.

Walk with Direction Change (7 beats and hold), C.

Use "Combinations" as in B-1 and D-2. Change directions with the change in locomotor pattern.

See "Example of Lesson" stressing variations in directions.

Use Folk Dances such as: Glow Worm, Shoo Fly, and Green Sleeves.

VARIATIONS IN LEVELS
(LOW, HIGH, AND IN BETWEEN)

Participate as individuals. Participate with a partner: in unison, in opposition. Participate in groups of three (or in small groups): in unison; in opposition (2 against 1); on three levels; changing levels.

Percussions: Xylophone (and piano). Follow the ascending and descending notes. Use finger cymbals or small bells, and cymbals or larger bells. Move on a high plane, on toes, in response to the lighter tones; move on a lower plane in response to the cymbals or larger bells.

Records: Merry-go-round; airplanes and jets; teeters; swings; spiraling; up-down; balloons.

VARIATIONS IN TEMPO (SLOW, NORMAL, FAST)

What things move slowly? (Snails, turtles, older people, elephants, slow-motion pictures, tug-boats and liners.)

What things move fast? (Bees, birds, speedboats, fire engines, airplanes, rockets.)

What things move at a normal pace? (Boys and girls.)

What things go slowly then fast then slowly? (Trains, merry-go-rounds, jets and airplanes, cars.)

Percussions: Listen carefully and move as the drum tells you to move. (Provide variations in speed. Provide an even rhythm first and then an uneven rhythm.)

Use sand blocks. Start slowly as a train, increase speed, then gradually decrease speed. Work as an individual, with a partner, in a small group working together as one train.

Records: Use records that provide appropriate accompaniment for experiences that dramatize the children's ideas for things that move slowly, fast, or in between; and things that accelerate—A.

Use Folk Dances such as: *Noriu Miego*, RCA Victor LPM 1624; *Fjäskern*, Viking 200; *Gustaf's Skoal*, Windsor A-7S2.

VARIATIONS IN FORCE OF MOVEMENT
(STRONG-WEAK; HEAVY-LIGHT)

Stamping walk—normal walk.
Flatfooted run—tiptoe run.
Cut down a tree—chop off the branches.
Be giants—dwarfs.
Row a boat or paddle a canoe upstream-downstream.
Work against an imaginary force pushing-pulling-repelling.
Be wagon wheels rolling over a hard, level surface—through sand, water, uphill.
Percussions: Drum, sand blocks; various types of gourds; xylophone (alternating up and down or working up gradually and sliding down).
Records: Clocks (medium, large, small, naughty—tempo and force), B-1; Heavy and light walk, small light run, big gallop, C; Five Little Ponies—"Work Horse," D-1; My Playful Scarf, K-1; L-103.

VARIATIONS IN INTENSITY (LOUD-SOFT)

Percussion: Drum-claves; cymbals-finger cymbals; gong-triangle.
Records: Heavy-quiet, A; Ponies-galloping horses, B-1 #2; Jump, strike—floating, spiraling, H; Brave Hunter, "weather," L-105.

ACCENT

Metrical Accent: Accent on the first beat of a measure. Accent the first beat with a louder clap when clapping, heavier step than normal when walking. In what other ways can you accent?
Accent the beginning of a phrase—long phrase (16 beats); short phrase (4 beats); in between (8 beats).
Accent the beginning of each measure of 2 beats, 3 beats, 4 beats.
Percussion: Use various percussion instruments appropriate to the locomotor pattern such as: drums and wood blocks for a walk; claves for a run; coconut shells for a gallop; and sand blocks for a slide. See "Indian Dance Steps and Patterns."
Records: Walk with Direction Change, Jump Series, Waltz—accented 3's (walk, slow run) C; Skater's Waltz.
Use Folk Dances such as: Seven Jumps, Virginia Reel.

Rhythmical Accent: Accent on other than first beat.
Who can accent the third beat in each group of 4 beats?

$$/ \underline{\ } \underline{\ } \overset{,}{\underline{\ }} \underline{\ } / \underline{\ } \underline{\ } \overset{,}{\underline{\ }} \underline{\ } /$$
$$\ \ 1\ \ 2\ \ 3\ \ 4 \quad 1\ \ 2\ \ 3\ \ 4$$

Who can accent the third and the fifth beats of 6 beats?

$$/ \underline{\ } \underline{\ } \overset{,}{\underline{\ }} \underline{\ } \overset{,}{\underline{\ }} \underline{\ } / \underline{\ } \underline{\ } \overset{,}{\underline{\ }} \underline{\ } \overset{,}{\underline{\ }} \underline{\ } /$$
$$\ \ 1\ 2\ 3\ 4\ 5\ 6 \quad 1\ 2\ 3\ 4\ 5\ 6$$

VARIATIONS IN MOOD

Sad, happy, tired, gay, proud, funny, quiet, vigorous.
What can you do to show that you are happy? Sad? We show how we feel by the expression on our faces and the way in which we move. There are many things we do that show other people how we feel. (3) See what you can do to show your feelings.
Records: B-2; C; G-1; G-2; H; Play Activities J-1 to 5; K-1; L-104, may use streamers.

DRAMATIZATIONS

Animals and Birds: B-1, 4; D-1, 3, 4, 22; K-6, 7; L-102, 103.
Circus Animals, Performers, Ringmaster, Merry-Go-Round: B-1, 4; D-1, 3, 12; J-2; K-6, 7; L 102.
Game Activities: Bouncing balls: Jumps; E; contemporary music. Deep-Sea Fishing: D-7. Hopscotch: Music for jumping; hopping. Jump rope: E; contemporary music. Playground apparatus: D-5, J-3. Pogo stick: Music for jumping. Riding a Bicycle: D-14.
Harbor: Boats D-7; Sea Life D-22; What the Lighthouse Sees K-10; At the Beach L 108.
Marches: Patriotic Marches; Yankee Doodle, Windsor A7S1; B-2, 4; D-11; Circus Parades B-1; Mechanical Soldiers B-1; Parade of Toys J-5, K-5; Parade of the Wooden Soldiers.
Mechanical Things: A; B-1; B-3; D-12, 14; J-5.
Music for Dramatization: C; E; L 102–108. See "Holidays and Special Days."
Relaxation: A; J 1–5; soft music.

FIG. 10.2. Integrating physical education with activities in the classroom. (Developed by Miss Dixie Rogers, formerly of Peabody School, Santa Barbara, California.)

Seasons: Spring, D-4; Winter, J-5, L 103, 105, and Skater's Waltz.

Transportation: Airplanes: A; B-1; D-3. Boats: D-7; K-10; L 105. Bicycles: D-14. Bus: Song Books. Ponies and Horses: Gallop, Trot, D-1; J-1; L 103. Train: D-6; J-4; K-6; L 107.

Westward Movement: B-4.

Holidays and Special Days: B-2. In addition, Halloween: B-1; D-15; H; J-3. Thanksgiving: See "Indian Dance Steps and Patterns." Christmas: D-14; J-5; K-5; L-107; Jingle Bells, Folk Dancer MH 1111.

EXPERIENCES IN MOVEMENT— BASED ON A THEME (16, 17)

Lessons based on themes or stories are means of affording rich experiences in creative rhythmic activities. They give opportunity for a variety of movements and, executed by each child in his own way, satisfy each one's imagination and desire for dramatic action.

The activities in this type of lesson revolve around a central theme. The theme may be related to a social studies unit such as home, community, or a specific culture. The activities may center around a holiday such as Thanksgiving or Christmas, a special day like Halloween, or the seasons. The theme may come from a story book or it may cover a special event such as the circus. The lessons may be separate ones, or a series could be planned around the central theme. Children of primary grades especially enjoy this type of activity.

Using a circus theme (Fig. 10.2), the children had visited a circus and then developed an art project. Later they fashioned their own circus, taking the parts of animals, clowns, and a ringmaster.

SUGGESTIONS FOR THEME LESSONS

SINGLE RECORDS WITH COMPLETE THEME LESSONS

B-1 *Circus* (Fig. 10.2), Clocks; B-2, *Holiday Rhythms.*

D-1 "Five Little Ponies"; D-4, Garden

Varieties; D-7, *Boat Rhythms;* D-11, *Fire! Fire!;* D-14, *Christmas Rhythms;* D-15, *Halloween Rhythms.*

J-1 *The Farm;* J-2, *Night Time;* J-3, *Our Playground;* J-3, Halloween; J-4, *A Train Story;* J-5, *The Toy Shop.*

K-1 to K-10.

L-102 to L-108.

ADDITIONAL THEME LESSONS

Animals of the Farm, the Circus, the Zoo, or the Jungle; Transportation; A Day at School; The Harbor; A Trip to the Shore; Holidays and Special Days; Seasons; Stories such as Jack the Giant Killer.

EXAMPLE OF THEME LESSON

BOAT THEME

Record: Boat Rhythms, D–7.

Specific purposes

To increase skill in responding to variations in speed of movement.

To put ideas into movement.

Motivational and guide material

We have been studying about boats. Can you be different kinds of boats? What kind of boats go very fast? (Speed Boat)

Some large boats go very slowly. I wonder why? (Have heavy loads; pushing or pulling barges; pushing big ships; ferrying trains.) Can you be a big boat with a heavy load? (Tugs and Liners)

What kind of boats did the Indians have? How do you make canoes go through the water? Let's see if you can paddle your canoe upstream? Now can you go downstream? (Rowboat)

Let's get into a rowboat. Do you paddle a rowboat? Can you get upstream in your rowboat? You will have to pull hard.

Relaxation: It would be fun to sit on the deck of a boat and watch the waves and the sky. Let's try it. (Buoys)

Evaluation: What was the difference between going upstream and downstream? (Had to work hard going upstream; went slowly upstream and fast downstream.)

How many of you have seen a sailboat? Can you tell us about them? (May use visual aids.) What is the difference between a sailboat and a rowboat?

Conclusion: We will take a boat trip.

We will row out to the sailboat; get ready to set sail; sail our boat; then get into our rowboat again and come back to shore. Find your own space and we will be ready to go on our trip. (Call the change from rowboat to sailboat.)

Evaluate, and then repeat the activity without calling the change. Children may work with a partner.

EXPERIENCES IN MOVEMENT— BASED ON RESPONSE TO VARIOUS STIMULI

RHYTHMIC PATTERNS
(Includes listening skills and sequencing)

Rhythmic patterns have always had meaning and appeal for children and therefore provide another area for experiencing activity. One device for creating a rhythmic design is through the use of a leader, who claps a pattern that is then echoed by the children. This response can then be translated into movement.

Initially the pattern may be very simple and have movement in one direction; subsequent experiences may involve variations of direction, level, and intensity.

Children enjoy clapping the rhythm of words, particularly if their own names are involved. There are numerous possibilities of word combinations as a basis for activity: special days, name of school, chants, and verses.

LEAD AND FOLLOW

1. Teacher claps a rhythmic pattern. For example:

Beat: /——— ——— ——— ———/
Pattern: /——— ——— — — ———/

- a. Children repeat the pattern by clapping hands.
- b. Variations in clapping.
  1. Clap hands and knees: *hands hands knees knees hands.* (See pattern.)
  2. Sitting on floor, clap hands and floor.
  3. Children work out other variations, such as overhead, to side.
- c. Repeat rhythm with feet, hands and feet, or head. (Monkey Song, K-6)

d. Some (or all) children repeat rhythm on percussion instruments.
e. Some children repeat the rhythm on percussion instruments, others in activity.

2. One *child* claps a rhythm; class responds in various ways.

3. Partners or small groups.
   a. One child gives the rhythm; others in group respond in various ways.
   b. Work out a problem repeating a rhythm of their choice. (May be rhythm of name of child, school, community, or holiday. See "Rhythmic Pattern of Words.")
   c. One child creates a movement and partner repeats the movement. Exchange roles. *Record: Train to the Zoo,* "Monkey Song," K-6.
   d. One child creates a movement, partner repeats the movement and adds one. Original partner (or next player) repeats the two movements and adds one. Continue until one player misses, then start again.
   e. Work out a problem or routine (may be similar in nature to that seen in tap dancing, one dancer then the other performs).

SOUNDS[3]

Experiences in movement may be initiated through the use of various sounds. Percussion instruments lend themselves to many variations. Records of sounds are available. The children themselves may develop sounds through hand-clapping or moving the feet in various ways. Verbal sounds may also be used to simulate such things as trains, planes, or animals.

The procedure may be reversed by creating a movement, then developing appropriate sound effects. Upper grade children might enjoy working in partners or small groups to develop their ideas.

PERCUSSIONS

Gong: Strike hard. Start a movement and continue as long as you hear the sound.

[3]Contributed by Miss Carol Clark, Consultant in Physical Education, Los Angeles County Schools, Los Angeles, California.

RHYTHMIC PATTERN OF WORDS (16, 17)

1. Name patterns:
   ¾ Meter

   | Beat: | ′_____ _____ _____′_____ _____ _____′ |
   | Pattern: | ′_____ _____ _____′_____′ |

Name:	Mar	–	jor	–	ie		Brown
Activity:	step		hop		hop		jump

   ⅔ Meter

   | Beat: | ′_____ _____′_____ _____′ |
   | Pattern: | ′_____ _____′___ ___ ___′ |

Name:	Bob	by	Mer-ri-weath-er
Activity:	leap	leap	run run run run

2. Holidays and Special Days
   ⅔ Meter

   | Beat: | ′_____ _____′_____ _____′ |
   | Pattern: | ′____ ___ ___ __′_____ _____′ |

Words:	Hap – py birth – day Mar – y
Activity:	skip and skip and step jump

   (Later add ½ turn on the jump.)

   ⁶⁄₈ Meter

   | Beat: | ′__ __ __ __ __ __′__ __ __ __ __ __′ |
   | Pattern: | ′_____ ___ ___ __′_____ _____′ |

Words:	Mer – ry	Christ-mas	Hap-py New	Year
Activity:	Skip	and	skip and	run run run	step

Tambourine: Shake tambourine and then give a final hit. Start a movement and continue until the final hit.

Drum: Provide variations in pattern, accent, tempo, and intensity.

Sand blocks: Scrape together.

Bells: Shake; shake in uneven rhythm.

Finger cymbals or claves for light sounds; large cymbals or drum for heavy sounds.

RECORDS

Select appropriate sounds for developmental level of children. Selection may integrate with special day or season.

OTHER SOUNDS

A bouncing ball: Contact once or twice, then allow to bounce down to a roll; ball bouncing low—high.

Airplane taking off—landing.

Missile take-off.

Halloween sounds; Christmas sounds; farm sounds; sounds at the zoo; sounds in a clock shop; "Things Which Accelerate" (A).

What other sounds are fun?

ART

PICTURES SUGGESTING ACTIVITY

Drawings and paintings may be brought to the classroom and discussed as works of art. They may also be discussed and used as the bases for creative activity.

The pictures and stories in Fig. 10.3 are examples of integrating subject areas. The teacher read the Thanksgiving story to the children.[4] The children then told the story in their own words to the teacher, who wrote the words on reading charts. (There were five charts, and each was a chapter in their Thanksgiving Book.) During the art period each child drew a picture as suggested by the story on the chart. After the drawings were completed, the children selected the picture they thought best suited their book. With this background of knowledge and interest, the children used the charts and pictures for creative activity in dance. Possible outcomes using Fig. 10.3A: building and painting the ship, loading the boat, hoist-

[4]Mrs. Althea Sexton, formerly of Adams Elementary School, Santa Barbara, California.

ing the sails, pulling up the anchor, swabbing the deck, being the wind, being the ship, landing on shore. Possible outcomes using Fig. 10.3B: chopping or sawing the trees and cutting off the branches, carrying the logs to the building site, building a home, planting the corn, hunting for turkeys, hoisting the flag.

COLOR

Children may respond in activity to the colors and word pictures as expressed by O'Neill and illustrated by Weisgard. (12)

Children may also respond in activity to the colors or the feeling of various works of art. How does this picture make you feel? Feelings may be brought out by contrast, such as the blues of Monet with the reds and oranges of Van Gogh. The records *Colors* (F–I) and *Balloons* (L-104) include color and word pictures as a basis for activity.

DESIGN OR PATTERN

Children may respond to the design or pattern in works of art. They may respond to the design of their own art work through such media as finger painting or chalk and charcoal drawings. Through these designs, a mood and a pattern for moving may be developed.

The book by Elizabeth Waterman, which may be found in some libraries, contains excellent material in this area. (21)

MUSIC

Moving freely in response to music is one of the goals of creative activity in dance. Some children have a great deal of natural ability in movement and can enjoy such activity from the outset. Others need the opportunity to explore movement through the many approaches to dance in order to gain a movement vocabulary from which to draw and to realize their creative potential. The experiencing of various moods of music through movement is an important means of putting inner feelings, tensions, fears, and joys into outward form. It is a way to learn to appreciate music, as compositions take on new meaning through doing. Listening to recordings or musical selections is an excellent means for relaxation and music appreciation.

The men made a boat which they named the Mayflower. The boat was ninety feet long and twenty four feet wide so the Pilgrims were crowded on their trip over a rough ocean. They landed at Plymouth Rock.

FIG. 10.3A. Thanksgiving Book, Chapter 2.

The Pilgrims were busy cutting down trees and building houses. When the Pilgrims became friends with the Indians the Indians taught the Pilgrims how to plant corn.

FIG. 10.3B. Thanksgiving Book, Chapter 3.

Again, the selection of the material depends upon the age level, needs, interests, and abilities. Examples of records that may be used include: *Music for Rhythmic Dramatization* (C); *Dance Rhythms* (E); *Listen Move and Dance* (G–1); *Dance a Story*, side two—music only (L).

The children may work out movement in response to the various themes that recur in orchestral arrangements. During the music period the various themes would be presented and discussed. During the physical education period, groups of children would create the movement. For example, an upper grade class could work out quite an elaborate circus using the record album *Animals and Circus* (B-4) of the Bowmar Orchestral Library. The entire class could work on all the acts and then select specific groups to refine and perform the various parts. An upper grade class studying Westward Movement might enjoy selecting certain parts of the record

album *American Scenes* (B-4) of the same series.

REALIA

Realia, such as shown in Figs. 10.4A and B, provides interest and stimulation for creative activity. After observing the marionettes, the children were eager to express their ideas of movement as marionettes (K–8, L–106).

In a kindergarten, a toy monkey on a string resulted in the poem "Jocko on a String." The children enjoyed re-creating the antics of the monkey.

Here comes Jocko prancing—
  My monkey on a string—
While I pull him up, up, up,
  This is what I sing:
"Climb up, Jocko, climb, climb, climb,
  Climb up to the sky,
And watch the big round silver moon
  Go sailing, sailing by."

FIG. 10.4A. A marionette provides motivation for movement. (Courtesy Mrs. Helen Molles, Bellflower Unified School District, Bellflower, California.)

FIG. 10.4B. Moving like a marionette.

Then I make his string so snap!
  My, it's fun to see
Jocko, who has climbed so high
  Come tumbling back to me![5]

Other examples of Realia: Jack-in-the-box; slinky toys; mechanical toys; battery-operated toys; bouncing balls; rag dolls.

ACTIVITY SONGS AND POEMS (16, 17)

The rhythm of song and verse has been exciting to children since earliest days. The rhythmic patterns, melodies, and word content of these forms offer rich opportunities for creative activities. Singing songs and saying verses and rhymes are important to children; they like to repeat known rhythms and are interested in learning new ones. Children often make up their own chants, songs, and verses to accompany their activities or to tell of an experience. A poem can become a group activity, a folk song may be developed into a folk dance, and a nursery rhyme may be a drama with a well-planned plot.

Throughout the music books and related albums of records are songs that may be learned during music period, then repeated in creative activity during the physical education period. In the same manner, poems may be read and discussed for understanding and appreciation and then repeated with dance activity added. This procedure enriches the children's background in the areas of music, literature, and physical education.

The following criteria may be used when selecting Activity Songs and Poems:

1. Is there *movement* throughout the composition?

2. Do the words suggest movement to the children?

3. Is the content within the children's experience?

4. Is the theme suitable as to content, age level, and ability?

5. Is the suggested activity satisfying to the children?

[5]Reproduced from *Childcraft* with permission. Copyright © 1939 by the Quarrie Corporation. All rights reserved. (10)

In selecting and presenting the material, there should be more than the written word expressing activity: a gallop should feel or sound like a gallop; tiptoeing is usually read softly; and a wind may murmur through the trees or it may be stormy.

EXAMPLES OF ACTIVITY POEMS

RAG DOLL (10)

I'm a floppy, floppy Rag Doll
  Drooping in my chair.
My rag head rolls from side to side;
  It shakes my woolly hair.

My floppy arms are loose and limp.
  My body's limp. That's why
I droop until I'm just so limp,
  You hardly know it's I.

THE WIND AND THE LEAVES (10)

Leaves are floating all around,
  They make a carpet on the ground.
When, swish! The wind comes whirling by,
  And sends them dancing to the sky.

In poems in which the amount of time for dramatization is short, additional time may be allowed by providing 4 to 8 beats between lines.

BASIC GUIDE FOR A LESSON—USING ACTIVITY SONGS AND POEMS

DISCUSSION (MOTIVATION)

Sing the song or listen to the music or poem. Discuss the material. Use visual aids to provide a basis for understanding and for activity. Clarify difficult words. "After the child understands the idea, sing or say the words again while he plans how he can tell the idea through movement. Allow time for thinking and organization and give help by hints or occasional suggestions." (16) Percussion instruments may be used to add interest to the activity.

ACTIVITY

Children participate while the teacher guides them in responding to the rhythm through the use of voice or percussion instruments or by clapping. At the end of the activity he asks questions to stimulate more creativity, to encourage the use of larger movements, or to stress a more accurate response to the rhythm. Children may clap the rhythm and accent the phrases. The activity is then repeated for greater quality, satisfaction, and enjoyment.

RELAXATION, EVALUATION, PLANNING FOR CONCLUSION

The children may rest while evaluating and make suggestions. Three or more children may show *their* ideas (different ways of doing it).

CONCLUSION

The song or poem may be repeated, with the children trying different ideas or building upon previous ones. They may work with partners or be divided into various sized groups. After time for planning, the song or poem is repeated for the conclusion. End the period by recognizing improvement, giving encouragement, and possibly making suggestions for future activity.

CHORIC VERSE

The rhythm and the ideas for movement may be provided through Choric Verse. Individual children or groups develop the ideas for activity to accompany the reading.

Square dances may be called in Choric Verse. The class members exchange roles as callers and as dancers. The following plan for Texas Star is an example.

TEXAS STAR—CHORIC VERSE

INTRODUCTION AND ENDING

All:	All jump up and never come down
	Swing your honey round and round, 'til the
	Hollow of your foot makes a hole in the ground.
loud	Promenade, boys, promenade. _____
softer	Promenade, boys, promenade. _____
softer	Promenade, boys, promenade. _____
Clap	Clap Clap Clap Clap
	Clap Clap Clap Clap

FIGURE

Girls:	Girls to the center, and back so far,
Boys:	Boys to the center, with a right-hand star.
One Boy:	Form that star with the right hands crossed,
(Beats to complete call)	____ ____ ____ ____
Another Boy:	Back with the left and don't get lost.
	____ ____ ____ ____
All:	Pass your girl and take the next.
	____ ____ ____ ____
One Girl:	Girls swing in and the boys swing out,
	Turn that Texas Star about.
	____ ____ ____ ____
	____ ____ ____ ____
One Boy:	Boys swing in and girls swing out,
	Again you turn the star about.
	____ ____ ____ ____
	____ ____ ____ ____
One Boy: and One Girl:	Break and swing the girl around,
	Promenade around the town.
	____ ____ ____ ____
	____ ____ ____ ____

All: Dos-a-dos your corner girl,
Back to your own and give her a whirl.

——— ——— ——— ———
——— ——— ——— ———

CREATE A NEW DANCE—FOLK FORM

As a culmination of the folk dance unit, children may work out their own dance. The children select a folk song or some other music which they have learned and discussed during music period. In this way they are familiar with the meter, phrasing, and repetition. (A $\frac{2}{4}$ meter to which children may respond with an even or uneven rhythm allows for many variations.)

Children are divided into groups and select a starting formation for their dance (double circle with partners facing counterclockwise; double circle with two couples facing for progression; single circle with or without partners; or line formation). Rhythm for practice may be provided on a percussion instrument by the teacher or one member of each group. Later have all groups practice to the music. Dances created by the children may be used for programs.

INDIAN DANCE STEPS AND PATTERNS

Children love the rhythms and patterns of Indian dances and enjoy working out their own activities. This is quite appropriate since much of Indian dancing is the individual's response to the rhythm rather than set patterns.[6]

The Indian dances evolved out of the various aspects of everyday life, for example: religion—the evil spirit in conflict with the good spirit in the Apache Devil Dance; prayers to the rain god in the Hopi Snake Dance and the Zuni Rain Dance; worship of the sun god in the Sioux Sun Dance; hunting—Buffalo Dance; useful animal—Horse-Tail Dance; powerful spirit—Eagle Dance; celebration—Harvest Dance; health—Karok Brush Dance (ill

[6]For references for traditional steps and dances, see Bibliography.

person in center of circle of dancers); skill—Hoop Dance.

Indian dancers may carry a rattle or shaker, or may carry a small branch of a tree or part of a bush (Karok Brush Dance). In some of the dances, bells are worn. (Bells may be sewn on elastic bands and worn around the ankles, below the knee, around the wrists, or sewn on tape to wear down the side of the leg.)

Formations: Dances are performed in a serpentine or follow-the-leader formation; in a line or in circles; sometimes with a partner.

Arm Positions: Mason states that the most common positions of the arms are at the sides or held in front of chest.

The commonest use of the arms among the Indians is merely to allow them to hang naturally at the sides, fully relaxed. The only movement they make are the reflex motions that follow naturally upon the foot and body action. The hands, too, are kept open, and hang naturally. When allowed to hang in this way the arms contribute to the feeling of complete relaxation one often gets in watching some Indians dance." The hands may be held in front of the chest *"perhaps separated a few inches and moving in reflex fashion, perhaps with the fingers loosely joined, or perhaps with both hands fingering some small object that is being carried. The elbows hang close to the sides, the arms and hands completely relaxed. (23)*

Developing the dance steps:
1. Explore various ways of using a step: contact the floor with only the toes, or the toe and then the heel, or the heel and then the toe. Using the toe or contacting the floor with the entire foot, use a shuffle or a push step forward; use a pull or a drag step back.
2. Combine a step with one or more hops on one foot, or with one or more taps with the other foot (tap: not taking body weight on the foot).

3. Try variations with jumps—both feet.

4. Experiment with running: high knees in front or kicking heels up in back, a trotting step.

5. Move in various directions: forward, backward, to the side, turning in place, turning in own circle.

6. Move to the side with a step-close. Bend knees with body and arms relaxed (4 counts: step, bounce, close, bounce).

Providing the rhythm. Start with a drum:

1. Give a two-beat, accenting the first beat.

2. Give a two-beat with the first beat soft and the second beat accented.

3. Give a four-beat, accenting the first beat.

4. Use dance rattles, shakers, bells. May be used by dancers or by children not dancing.

RECORDS

1. *Indian Dance; Drum Beats:* Phoebe James, AED-10 (D-10).

2. *Indian Dance,* (Prayer for Rain): Folkraft F-1192.

3. Indian Harvest Dance: *Holiday Rhythms* (B-2).

4. *Dances of the North American Indians:* Folkways Records FD-6510.

ACCOMPANIMENT

LIST OF RECORDS

A. Ruth White, with Carol Clark
Rhythms Productions
Adventures in Rhythms, Vol. 1.
Locomotor Patterns
Swing, Move in Squares, Circles, Change Directions,
Heavy, Springy, Strange, Stiff, Quiet, Gliding, Long Legged Things
Trains, Motorcycles, Jets—things which accelerate
Machines—mechanical objects
Listening

B. Bowmar Records
B₁ *Rhythm Time #1*
Basic Rhythms; Combinations
Mechanical Rhythms, includes clocks
Circus: Parade, Merry-Go-Round, Ani-
mals and Performers
Rhythm Time #2
Basic Rhythms; Combinations
Dramatizations: Animals, Birds, Trees
B₂ *Holiday Rhythms,* Album
Going Home from School. Halloween; Thanksgiving: Indian Harvest Dance; Birthday; Christmas; Valentine's Day; Patriotic Marches; Easter; May Day.
B₃ *Music for Physical Fitness,* LP Record
Excellent music for creative activities. (Possible activities added.)
Side One:
1. Steam Engine (Variations in tempo); 2. Treadmill Turn (trot); 3. Lariat (cowboy); 4. Jumping Jack (march); 5. Skin Diver (mechanical things, Halloween); 6. Dervish Jump (twist, rock, strike); 7. Bobble (syncopated, juggler); 8. Jack Knife (twist and turn, project).
Side Two:
1. Airplane (circles); 2. Tortoise and Hare (change in tempo); 3. Twister (twist, swing, rock, mechanical things); 4. Elephant (force); 5. Egg Beater (swing, rock); 6. Scissors (creative dance); 7. Windmill (twist, circles, wagon wheels); 8. Woodchopper (work with partner: chop in unison, alternately).
B₄ *Bowmar Orchestral Library*
To integrate with music appreciation. Recordings with full orchestra; Theme Charts to reinforce music learning and understanding; suggestions for the teachers.
51. *Animals and Circus.*
54. *Marches*—11 different marches.
61. *American Scenes.* (Integrate with study of United States—upper grades.) Grofe, "Grand Canyon Suite"; Grofe, "Mississippi Suite."

C. Florence Bassett—Cora Mae Chesnut, A Bassett-Chesnut Production
Rhythmic Activities—Vol. 1
Basic Movement Patterns and Combinations with excellent variations in tempo and force.
Polka (or skip), Waltz (accented 3's), Music for Rhythmic Dramatizations.

D. Phoebe James Productions
Elementary Rhythms. Single Records AED1 to AED24.

1. *Ponies; Work Horse; Animals*
2. *Free Rhythms; Combined Free Rhythms* (changes within the band —listening skills)
3. *Animal Rhythms* (dramatizations); *Airplane* (variations in tempo and levels)
4. *Garden Varieties:* Bees, Butterflies, Small and Large Birds (may use streamers); Wind, Rain Sun, Growing Plants
5. *Fundamental Rhythms* (changes within bands)
   Interpretive Rhythms (includes concept of up and down)
6. *Train Rhythms* (variations in tempo; up and down)
7. *Boat Rhythms* (movement patterns with variations in tempo and force)
10. *An Indian Dance; Drum Beats* (creative activities)
11. *Fire! Fire!* (Theme Lesson)
    A March
12. *Favorite Action Songs* (locomotor patterns)
    Favorite Action Songs: Merry-go-Round; "Jack-in-the-Box"; Oil Wells (up and down)
14. *Christmas Rhythms* (includes mechanical rhythms)
15. *Halloween Rhythms* (creative activities)
22. *Sea Life Rhythms:* Seaweed; Crabs; Sea Anemone; Octopus; Sea Horse; Fish

E. Ruth Evans, *Childhood Rhythms* Series II, Album
Combination Rhythms: Up and Down (straight line, jerky);
Round and Round (curved lines; smooth); Fast and Slow.
Bouncing Ball Rhythms: (sitting; repeat kneeling; repeat standing; bounce ball in front, on right side, on left side; experiment with turning and moving about);
Combinations (sequencing)
Jump Rope Rhythms (hoops and jump ropes)
Interpretive Rhythms: Elevators; Clocks; Jumping Jack (variations in directions)
Dance Rhythms

F. Educational Activities, Inc.
Activity Records, Inc.
F_1 *Learning Basic Skills Through Music*
Hap Palmer Music. ARLP 514
"Numbers, colors, the alphabet and body awareness. . . ." Listening skills.
Contemporary music, enjoyed by children; change of pace.
For chorus: (1) clap, (2) tap, (3) nod, (4) combinations or other ways.
F_2 *Learning Basic Skills Through Music—Building Vocabulary*
Hap Palmer Music. ARLP 521
Contemporary music. Includes locomotor patterns; variations in directions, levels; concepts of over, under, around.
F_3 *Modern Rhythm Band Tunes*
Hap Palmer Music. AR 523.
Excellent music for listening, and for combining work with percussion instruments and activity.

G_1 Capitol Records
Listen, Move and Dance, Vol. 1
"A variety of exciting sounds, instrumental and electronic, especially created for movement work. . . ."
Music for creative activities, especially appropriate for intermediate and upper grade children.
G_2 Hoctor Records
Music for Special Children, Compiled and Directed by Elizabeth Polk, HLP-4074.
Suggestions for a variety of movements, dramatizations, and the use of accessories such as scarves, streamers, ropes and hoops; contemporary and traditional music.

H. Wayne State University, Detroit, Michigan, Audio-Visual Materials Consultant Bureau.
Music For Movement, Vol. I
Includes suggested dance activities.
Variety of movement patterns with excellent variations in tempo, direction, force, and mood.

J. Elizabeth Sehon and Emma Lou O'Brien
Rhythm-Time Records, P. O. Box 1106, Santa Barbara, California 93102.
Each album presents a complete Theme Lesson that includes locomotor and

nonlocomotor patterns, time for relaxation, and a conclusion. Each album also includes two play activities. All the activities are narrated to the accompaniment of organ music, and then the music is repeated without the narration.

Album 1. *The Farm* (Theme Lesson). "Walking Straight and Tall"; "The Wind." (Play activities.)

Album 2. *Night Time.* "Merry-go-round"; "Skipping We Go."

Album 3. *Our Playground.* "Raindrops"; "Halloween."

Album 4. *A Train Story.* "The Cowboy"; "Joyous Bells."

Album 5. *The Toy Shop.* "Mr. Snowman"; "Santa's Sleigh."

K. Activity Songs or Theme Lessons
Children's Record Guild (CRG) and Young People's Records (YPR)

1. *My Playful Scarf*—YPR-10012
   Use real or imaginary scarves.
   Cloud, Cowboy, Waves, Sailor, Dolly, King, Pirate, Butterfly.

2. *Nothing To Do*—YPR-10012
   Locomotor patterns; clap, tap, rock, spin (balance)

3. *A Visit to My Little Friend*—YPR-10005
   Locomotor patterns; "Thumbs keep moving." Repeat and add fingers, hands, arms, feet, head (coordination, body awareness). Gallop.

4. *Creepy . . . The Crawly Caterpillar*—YPR-10005
   Life cycle (balance, body awareness).
   Variations in tempo, levels, mood.

5. *The Merry Toy Shop*—YPR-10005
   Variety of toys including a Toy Parade.

6. *Train To The Zoo*—CRG-1001
   Dramatizations: Train, animals, birds.

7. *Let's Play Zoo*—YPR-802
   Dramatizations: Animals.

8. *The Little Puppet*—CRG 1060
   Contrasts: jerky, stiff movements of marionettes with relaxed movements of floppy rag dolls.
   For motivation, see Fig. 10.4

9. *Building a City*—YPR-10014
   Steam shovel, wheelbarrow, carpenter, painter, steam roller.

10. *What the Lighthouse Sees*—YPR-10014
    Tugboat, Speedboat, Ferryboat, Bell Buoy.

L. Paul and Ann Barlin
Dance a Story, RCA Victor, LE 102 to 108.
Excellent for creative activity. One side of record includes music and narration, a complete story. Reverse side presents music only. Album includes story book with the narration. This book comes with exquisite color characterizations of children in movement. Each album includes a wide variety of activities. Teachers may find that using one or two sections of a record at one time may be appropriate for the attention span of primary children.

102. *Noah's Ark*
     Build the ark; animal dramatizations.

103. *The Magic Mountain*
     Horses, birds, trees, leaves; wind, snowballs, snowman, puddle, and stream.

104. *Balloons*
     Colors; play with balloon; become a balloon.

105. *The Brave Hunter*
     Weather: variations in tempo, levels, intensity, mood; Paddling, hunting, soaring like an eagle.

106. *Flappy and Floppy*
     Marionettes with strings attached: elbows, hands, back, head, knee and feet.
     Contrasts: action—relaxation.
     For motivation, see Fig. 10.4.

107. *The Toy Tree*
     Beach ball (skip); Pogo stick (jump); Puppy (relaxation); "V" Sit (balance); Jack-in-the-Box; Train.

108. *At the Beach*
     Sitting in the sand (body awareness).
     Walk tall, run, crab walk, octopus, waves.

FIG. 10.5A & B.
Percussion instruments
to buy.

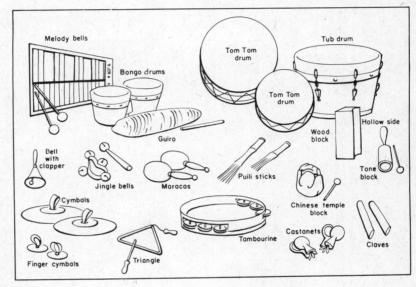

Melody bells
Bongo drums
Tom Tom drum
Tub drum
Guiro
Bell with clapper
Jingle bells
Maracas
Puili sticks
Wood block
Hollow side
Tone block
Cymbals
Chinese temple block
Finger cymbals
Triangle
Tambourine
Castanets
Claves

PERCUSSION INSTRUMENTS

(Figs. 10.5A, 10.5B; 10.6A, 10.6B[7] Record
F–3)

INSTRUMENTS TO STRIKE

Drums

Tom-tom drum.
Tub drum—various sizes.
To make—pickle barrel with top
covered.
Dance drum—large single-head drum,
tunable.
Bongo drums.
Decorated coffee cans with plastic
covers—one-, two- and three-pound
cans; bottom end open, bottom end
closed.
Beater—lamb's wool beater.
To make—cork float or sponge-
rubber ball on a stick; gauze or other
soft material to cover end of stick.

Tambourine
Recommend purchase of a good quality
tambourine.

Wood block and wood striker
Hollow on two sides.

Tone block and wood striker
Cylinder with handle.

Claves—rosewood (clä′vās)
To make—wood doweling 8 × 1 inches;
broom handle.

[7]Courtesy of Mrs. Mildred Jamieson, formerly
General Consultant, Elementary Music, Santa Barbara City Schools, Santa Barbara, California.

FIG. 10.6A & B.
Percussion instruments
to make.

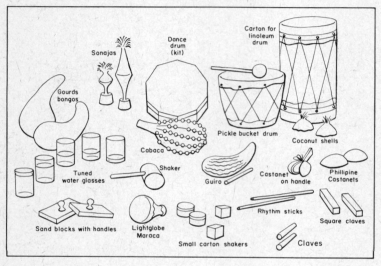

Rhythm sticks
To make—doweling 12 × ½ inches.

Castanets
Spanish castanets.
Castanet on handle.

Coconut shells
Philippine castanets
Polished coconut shells—strike tops together.

Temple blocks
Chinese or Korean temple blocks.

Gong
Recommend school purchase of a gong of good quality.

Cymbals
Cymbals—pair with metal striker.
Finger cymbals.

Triangle
With holder and metal striker.

Xylophone
Chromatic scale of wood, and striker.

Ipu (Ē′-poo)
Gourd.

Bongo gourds
To slap. Various sizes for various tones.

Puili sticks (Poo-e′-le)
Hawaiian bamboo.

INSTRUMENTS TO RUB TOGETHER OR SCRATCH

Sand blocks
Blocks of wood with sandpaper mounted on one side. May add handles.

Guiro (Wee′-ro)
Notched gourd with tongue depressor scraper.

INSTRUMENTS TO SHAKE

Bells

Jingle bells. Sleighbells, mounted on stick, sewn on web; sewn on elastic to wear on wrist, ankle or below knee. Bell with clapper.

Melody Bells (chromatic scale of metal) and striker.

Jingle clogs

Jingles mounted on wooden handle.

Tambourine

Shakers

Recommend making one with heavy sound and one with light sound. Use containers with beans, macaroni, rice, gravel, or shot. Cover with construction paper or paint the container. Provide various designs.

Small cartons.
Tomato sauce can with handle.
Coconut shell with handle.
Sonaja—Mexican rattles.
Chocolo (Chō'-cō-lō)—tennis ball can or long metal tube with shot or seeds. Hold in two hands, chest high, and shake it back and forth toward ends or roll the shot around in it.

Gourds

Maracas.
Cabaca (Kä-bä'-kä)—large gourd with string of wooden beads hung loosely on gourd.

PIANO MUSIC

Andrews, Gladys. *Creative Rhythmic Movement for Children,* New York: Prentice-Hall, Inc., 1954.

Daniels, Elva S. *Creative Rhythms For Your Class,* Dansville, N.Y.: F. A. Owen Publishing Co., 1965.

Evans, Ruth. *40 Basic Rhythms for Children,* Putnam, Connecticut: U.S. Textbook Company, 1958.

LaSalle, Dorothy. *Rhythms and Dances for Elementary Schools,* rev. ed., New York: The Ronald Press, 1951.

Renstrom, Moiselle. *Rhythm Fun for Little Folks,* 975 South West Temple St., Salt Lake City, Utah: Pioneer Music Press, 1944.

Saffran, Rosanna B. *First Book of Creative Rhythms,* New York: Holt, Rinehart and Winston Inc., 1963.

BIBLIOGRAPHY

1. Anderson, Harold L., editor. *Creativity and Its Cultivation,* New York: Harper & Row, Publishers, 1959. Fifteen contributors.

2. Andrews, Gladys. *Creative Rhythmic Movement for Children,* New York: Prentice-Hall, Inc., 1954.

3. Borten, Helen. *Do You Move as I Do?,* New York: Abelard-Schuman, 1963.

4. Clark, Carol E. *Rhythmic Activities for the Classroom,* Dansville, New York: The Instructor Publications, Inc., 1969.

5. Cole, Natalie Robinson. *The Arts in the Classroom,* New York: The John Day Company, 1940.

6. Detroit Public Schools. *Exploration of Basic Movements in Physical Education,* The Board of Education of the City of Detroit, Publication 4-322 TCH, 1960.

7. Halsey, Elizabeth, and Lorena Porter. *Physical Education for Children,* rev. ed., New York: Holt, Rinehart and Winston, 1963, Chapters 10 and 11.

8. "Dance for Children," *Impulses,* 1957. Annual of Contemporary Dance, Impulse Publications, 160 Palo Alto Avenue, San Francisco 14, California. Sixteen contributors from United States and Europe.

9. Latchaw, Marjorie, and Jean Pyatt. *A Pocket Guide of Dance Activities,* Englewood Cliffs, New Jersey: Prentice-Hall, Inc., 1958.

10. Leonard, Edith, and Dorothy Van Deman. *Say It and Play It,* Walter H. Baker Company, 100 Summer Street, Boston 10, Massachusetts, 1950. Copyright 1950, by Harper & Row, Publishers, Inc.

11. Murray, Ruth Lovell. *Dance in Elementary Education, a Program for Boys and Girls,* 2nd ed., New York: Harper & Row, Publishers, 1963.

12. O'Neill, Mary. *Hailstones and Halibut Bones, Adventures in Color,* Garden City, New York: Doubleday and Company, Inc., 1961. Illustrated by Leonard Weisgard.

13. Adapted from D. H. Radler with Newell C. Kephart. *Success Through Play,* New York: Harper & Row, Publishers, 1960, pp. 71–75. Copyright © 1960 by Harper & Row, Publishers.

14. Saffran, Rosanna B. *First Book of Creative Rhythms,* New York: Holt, Rinehart and Winston, Inc., 1963.

15. Schlein, Miriam. *Shapes,* New York: William R. Scott, Inc., 1952.

16. Sehon, Elizabeth L., and Emma Lou O'Brien. *Rhythms in Elementary Education,* New York: The Ronald Press Company, 1951. (Available in libraries.)

17. Sehon, Elizabeth, Marian Anderson, Winifred W. Hodgins, and Gladys R. Van Fossen. *Physical Education Methods for Elementary Schools,* 2nd ed., Philadelphia: W. B. Saunders Company, 1953, Chapter 8. (Available in libraries.)

18. Simon, Mina and Howard. *If You Were an Eel, How Would You Feel?,* Chicago: Follett Publishing Company, 1963.

19. Torrance, E. Paul. *Creativity: What Research Says to the Teacher,* No. 28 of series, Department of Classroom Teachers, American Educational Research Association of the National Education Association, 1963. Reprinted by permission of the National Education Association.

20. Torrance, E. Paul. "Seven Guides to Creativity," *Journal of Health, Physical Education and Recreation* 36:26, 27, 68 (April 1965) No. 4.

21. Waterman, Elizabeth. *The Rhythm Book,* New York: A. S. Barnes and Company, Inc., 1937. (Available in libraries.)

INDIAN DANCE

22. Hunt, W. Ben. *Indian Crafts and Lore,* New York: Golden Press, 1954. (In color. Includes pronunciation of Indian names; how to make dance costumes, drums and tom-toms; descriptions of dance steps and dances; suggestions for presentation.)

23. Mason, Bernard S. *Dances and Stories of the American Indian,* New York: The Ronald Press, 1944. (Includes an excellent presentation of steps, body movements, and moods; has large collection of dances, and a section on "staging the dances.")

24. Squires, John L., and Robert E. McLean. *American Indian Dances, Steps, Rhythms, Costumes and Interpretation,* New York: The Ronald Press Company, 1963 (Book is well illustrated.)

AUDIO-VISUAL MATERIALS

FILM

S-L Film Productions
Learning Through Movement
Paul and Ann Barlin
(See "Audio-Visual Materials—Section One")

CHAPTER 11
DANCE: TRADITIONAL AND CONTEMPORARY

FOLK SINGING GAMES

FOLK DANCES AND CIRCLE MIXERS

SQUARE DANCES

BIBLIOGRAPHY

FIG. 11.1. Tinikling—Bamboo Pole Dance: Creating patterns at various levels of difficulty.

The objectives of maximum participation and activity are certainly met in the dance program. Except for some of the square dances, everyone is in motion almost constantly. Dance contributes particularly to leg strength, endurance, and coordination, and provides opportunity for positive social contact, especially at the upper grade levels. Once basic steps are learned, there develops a certain freedom of movement and grace that is lovely to see. The children lose themselves in the music, experimenting with style and, on occasion, adding embellishments.

Included in this chapter are folk dances from many lands. These dances may be integrated into various study units. Special demonstration programs may be given an international flavor by selecting dances from this list. Children find it exciting to embark on a "dance journey" around the world, first planning an itinerary and then preparing appropriate dances, perhaps with authentic costumes. See "Dances Around the World."

The study of the Westward movement in the United States provides an opportunity to include many folk and square dances in the unit of instruction. Titles of some of the dances typify their origin: Virginia Reel; Texas Star; Oklahoma Mixer; Teton Mountain Stomp. Some square dances have regional histories that may be useful in studies of particular areas.

The folk singing games are especially appealing to children in the primary grades, perhaps because the words are also the directions for the dances. Once the song is learned, children can provide their own accompaniment. These singing games are important forerunners to the previously mentioned folk and square dances in that they provide various experiences in formations, spatial relationships, and social relationships. Positive experiences at this level will help to maintain interest in ensuing years.

The notations following each listing in the folk dance sections of the chapter are included to show the *formation* of the dance (e.g., 1's, 2's—mixers). This will facilitate planning and selection and may help to avoid the pitfall of choosing several different formations for one dance period, which can be time-consuming. The second notation (e.g., B-3; F-13) refers to the record list in this chapter. These records were selected on the basis of suitability to grade level, phrasing and tempo of music, and tonal quality. These factors can have an important bearing in children's acceptance of the dance program, and should be considered carefully when purchasing records for school use. Directions for the dances are included with most of the records. For the few exceptions, directions are provided in Section G.

In summary, dances are placed on the Suggested Grade Placement Chart on the basis of: (1) Progression—dances are in approximate order of difficulty. (2) Interest—dances are assigned to the grade levels at which they seem *most* appropriate. (3) Formation—dances of like formation (1's, 3's, 2 lines) are grouped together in order to alleviate change of formation within one period. (4) Integration—dances appropriate to particular social studies units influenced the grade placement of some of the dances.

PURPOSES

The activities in this chapter are designed to reinforce and elaborate upon those presented in Chapter 10, "Dance: Exploration and Creativity." However, more structure is apparent in the predetermined steps and patterns of the various folk and square dances. The purposes are:

—to utilize the developing abilities of balance, coordination, and rhythmic response in a structured setting;

—to increase auditory perception by listening and responding accurately to the guiding beat, phrasing, and mood of the music;

—to learn, and be able to recall, the sequences of steps in the various dances;

—to enhance social interaction through small and large group cooperation.

—to increase appreciation for the cultures of many countries through the study of their dances, costumes, customs, and festivals.

COMMONLY USED ABBREVIATIONS

CW   — clockwise
CCW — counterclockwise
LOD   — line of direction
RLOD — reverse line of direction
Ct   — count
ft   — foot
st   — step
R   — right
L   — left
B   — boy
M   — man
G   — girl
W   — woman
opp   — opposite
meas — measure
fwd   — forward
bkwd — backward
diag   — diagonally

FOLK SINGING GAMES (FIG. 11.2)

There has been a good deal of modernization of folk singing game material of late, which is fortunate for children and teachers alike. However, there are many traditional singing games that would be difficult to improve upon, except perhaps in orchestration. This is being done by a number of recording companies, many of which are noted in this section.

To be successful, a folk singing game must be within the realm of children's imaginations, and within their concepts of acceptable subject matter. If either of these factors is missing, the lesson will be found lacking, and probably frustrating as well.

The formations for singing games presented during one period should be as nearly alike as possible to avoid confusion and to make the most of available time. Once the children are in position, have them sit to listen to the music, and then clap the rhythm. Discuss the *meter* of the rhythm, whether even (hop, jump, walk) or uneven (gallop, slide, skip), the *tempo*, and the *mood*. As the children perform the dance, recognize skillful movement and encourage those who need assistance. If the quality of performance is not up to standard, have the children discuss ways of improving, and then repeat the activity.

The order of presentation of singing games is important to the success of the lesson. Begin with an activity that the children know and enjoy. The second selection should include some new activity to which the children would first listen, then walk through, and then dance. The final selection might be a review of material presented during the previous period. On certain days, including Choice Days, the activities would be all review.

For more enjoyment and greater variety, call out a different locomotor pattern for each verse in such Singing Games as Looby Loo and Did You Ever See a Lassie —cue the call, "Skip" or "Tiptoe" or "Gallop." Have the children move in scattered (informal) formation to give

FIG. 11.2. Adding the final polish for the Folk Dance Festival.

greater freedom of movement, and reinforce adequate spatial relations—maintain "own space" throughout the dance.

Once children become acquainted with various patterns of movement to music, have them create a dance to some favorite song or music. This spontaneous activity is often very successful, and gives the children a feeling of great importance in having done it all on their own.

RECORD REFERENCES: FOLK SINGING GAMES—KINDERGARTEN, GRADES 1 AND 2

Happy Times, Educational Dance Recordings. Arranged and sung by Dick Kraus. Sixteen Folk Singing Games.
Excellent music, good directions, and a variety of activities.

Singing Games, RCA Victor, Album E-87. No words on records; directions with album.
Twenty-one Folk Singing Games.

Multi-Purpose Singing Games. Activity Records, EALP-510 by Henry "Buzz" Glass. Educational Activities, Inc.
Good variety of activities in six Singing Games.

Singing Games from Many Lands, Rhythm Productions, CC 606.
Good music, easy to read directions. Eight Singing Games.

First Folk Dances, RCA Victor LPM-1625, Grades 1–3.
Twelve Singing Games. Excellent for primary grades.

Folk Dances for Fun, RCA Victor LPM-1624. Grades 2–6. See Record References: Folk Dances and Circle Mixers, B-2.

Christmas Folk Singing Game:
"Here We Go 'Round the Christmas Tree"
Music: "Here We Go 'Round the Mulberry Bush." *Singing Games* RCA Victor, Album E-87.
Formation: Scattered formation with one child in the center.
Action: Before starting to sing the verse, have the child in the center of the circle

say what present he would like for Christmas. Teacher then names a locomotor pattern. During the verse, the children move in the locomotor pattern called; during the chorus dramatize the present.

Verse:

"Here we go 'round the Christmas tree . . ."
"What would you like Santa to bring . . ."

Chorus:

"I would like (roll-er skates, roll-er skates, roll-er skates). I would like (roll-er skates) so early Christmas morning."

FOLK DANCES AND CIRCLE MIXERS

It is very difficult to recommend grade placement for folk dances since so much depends upon previous instruction and knowledge of basic steps. It is possible to use the placement chart as a plan of progression, and, once the skill level of the class is ascertained, to select a series of increasingly difficult dances appropriate to that level.

Children's reaction to folk dance is always interesting and certainly varied. Those who have had continuous instruction through the grades show a genuine enjoyment; those with only occasional exposure are less inclined to be enthusiastic, and will require a great deal of motivation. Most children will respond to the challenge of dance if the initial period includes easily mastered steps, and perhaps a simple but intriguing pattern. Once they realize that dance is not drudgery, the program has been launched successfully, and time is the only limiting factor in its progress.

When presenting a folk dance for the first time, have the children listen to the music. They may clap the rhythm and accent the beginning of each phrase. Teach the new step or most difficult sections of the dance first, using a starting signal and conducting a walk through. If the new step continues to be difficult, have the class stand in lines while the teacher, his back to the class, explains and demonstrates the step. This procedure is especially helpful in teaching cross steps such as the grapevine. Once learned, the class may return to dance formation for further instruction. It may be well for the teacher to demonstrate a pattern with a partner in the formation of the dance for greater clarity of direction.

When the music is added, cues are given on one or two beats preceding the change, as on 7 and 8 or on 15 and 16. It is important that the tempo of the music to be used is approximated in final walk-through. Continue to cue changes until the pattern of the dance is fairly well established and dancers can make transitions smoothly. Finally the dance is their own to perform without calls or cues.

The selection of dances for one period could include, first, a familiar dance that is enjoyable for the children; second, a new dance involving one or two new steps or patterns; and third, a review of a dance taught in the preceding lesson. A favorite dance at the beginning will help to set a positive mood for the period, and will make the children more receptive to further instruction. A review dance at the close of the period will leave them with a feeling of accomplishment and a desire to expand their repertory as rapidly as possible. If the period is short, a new dance may take the entire period. As a rule of thumb, a dance that cannot be taught within a class period is probably too difficult.

As a culmination for a unit on Folk Dance, or at the end of the semester or year, the children may "Create a New Dance—Folk Form" as presented in Chapter 10.

RECORD REFERENCES: FOLK DANCES AND CIRCLE MIXERS, A-G

Note: Directions for each dance are on the record jacket or are enclosed with the records as listed (for exceptions, the directions are presented in section G).
A. Happy Hour Records, Windsor Records, School Series.
   Excellent series.

A-1 A-7S1. Grades 3, 4.
Shoo Fly (2's).
   Phrasing and change in directions.
Seven Steps I (2's—mixer). Germany. Change in directions.
Yankee Doodle (3's—mixer), March.
El Molino (Circle La Raspa) (1's-2's), Mexico. Variations in tempo. See notation, *La Raspa,* B-3.

A-2 A-7S2. Grades 4–6.
Bingo II (2's—mixer).
   Grand R and L.
   Simplified version, G-1.
Gustaf's Skoal (Sq. Form), Sweden. Variations in tempo.
   Stealing: Extra boys, girls or couples may "steal" a place (step into a place) while dancers are skipping through the arches.
La Costilla (2's—2 lines), Mexico.
Hitch Hiker I (2's—mixer).
   Simplified version: Meas. 7-8 Dos-à-dos *own* partner; *then* move one place to the *left.*

A-3 A-7S3. Grades 4–6.
Circassian Circle (2's—mixer), England.
Pop Goes the Weasel (4's, 2's progress). (3's pop center person forward.) Good for phrasing.
Red River Valley (6's, 3's progress).
   Stress joining hands *as* dancers move to form the star.
Teton Mountain Stomp (2's—mixer).
   Stress: (1) stamp without taking weight on foot; (2) when changing from banjo to side-car position, boys *remain* on inside circle.

A-4 A-7S4. Grades 5–8.
Sicilian Circle (4's, 2's progress). With calls.
Chihuahua (2's—2 lines), Mexico. Skip.
All-American Promenade (2's—mixer). Stress moving forward and then backward, all in same direction.
Dance of the Bells (2's). Accented 3's, waltz rhythm.
B. *World of Folk Dances,* RCA Victor Albums, Michael Herman's Folk Dance Orchestra.

B-1 *First Folk Dances,* RCA Victor LPM-1625. Grades 1–3.

FOLK DANCES AND CIRCLE MIXERS

SUGGESTED GRADE PLACEMENT CHART[a]

	2	3	4	5	6	7–8
SECOND GRADE						
Hokey Pokey (1's) D-1	x	x	•			
Chimes of Dunkirk (2's—Mixer) D-1; B-2; C-3	x	•				
Frère Jacques (2's) C-3	x	x				
Hansel and Gretel (2's) D-1; B-2	x	x				
Shoemaker's Dance (2's) B-2	x	x	•			
Turn Around Me (2's) B-2	x	x	•			
Hopp Mor Annika (2's—Mixer) B-2	x	x	x			
THIRD GRADE						
Kinderpolka (2's—Mixer) B-1		x	•			
Jingle Bells I (2's—Mixer) G-2	–	x	•			
Yankee Doodle (3's) A-1	–	x				
Pop Goes the Weasel (3's) A-3, B-3	–	x	•			
El Molino (1's, 2's) A-1		x	•			
Circle *La Raspa*						
Seven Steps (2's—Mixer) A-1		x	x			
Bingo I (2's—Mixer) Simplified G-1		x	x			
Shoo Fly (2's) A-1		x	x	•		
Indian Dance Steps—Creative, see Ch. 10	–	x	•	•		
Seven Jumps (1's) B-3	–	x	x	•	•	
Fjäskern (2's) F-7		x	x	x	x	•
FOURTH GRADE						
Glow Worm (2's—Mixer) B-3; F-13		–	x	•		
Apat, Apat (2's—Mixer) F-11		–	x	•	•	
La Raspa (2's) B-3; C-4; F-13. Creative			x	x	x	•
Noriu Miego (4's) B-2			x	•		
Hitch Hiker (2's—Mixer) D-1; A-2			x	•		
Patty Cake Polka (2's—Mixer) C-1			x	x	x	x
Jingle Bells II (2's—Mixer) G-2			x	x	x	x
Galopede (2 lines; 6 couples) F-1, English Reel			x	•		
Canadian Lancers (2 lines; 4 couples) C-3,						
Canadian Reel			x	•		
Virginia Reel (2 lines; 4 to 6 couples) F-2;						
B-3; C-1, American Reel			x	x	•	•
Green Sleeves (4's) B-2			x	x	x	•
Maple Leaf Stomp (2's—Mixer) C-3			x	x		
Prairie Circle (2's—Mixer) C-3			x	x		
FIFTH GRADE—UNITED STATES AND CANADA						
See Albums E-1 and C-3						
Indian Dance Steps—Creative, see Ch. 10	–	x	•	•		
Virginia Reel (review) F-2			x	x	•	•
Oklahoma Mixer (2's) F-12				x	x	•
Red River Valley (3's) A-3				x	x	•
Teton Mountain Stomp (2's) A-3				x	x	•
Tennessee Wig-Walk (2's—Mixer) G-5				–	x	x
All-American Promenade (2's—Mixer) A-4				x	x	x
Jingle Bells II; III. G-2			x	x	x	x

SUGGESTED GRADE PLACEMENT CHART (Continued)

Square dance steps or formation	2	3	4	5	6	7–8
Gustaf's Skoal (Sq. Form) A-2				x	x	•
Puttjenter (Sq. Form) F-4				x	•	
Bingo II (Sq. Form) A-2; B-3				x	•	
Oh, Susanna (Sq. Form) B-3				x	•	
Irish Washerwoman (Sq. Form) B-3, no calls—create own				x	x	x
Brighton Mixer (2's) F-3				x	•	
Circassian Circle (2's—Mixer) A-3				x	•	
Sicilian Circle (4's—2's prog.) A-4				x	x	x
Oh, Johnny (2's—Mixer) C-1				x	x	x
Schottische (2's) C-1				x	x	x
See Traditional Folk Dance Steps						
Circle Schottische (2's—Mixer) G-3				x	x	x
Chestnut Tree (2's) B-3; F-13				x	x	
Schottische (2's or 4's) Creative Contemporary music				x	x	x

SIXTH, SEVENTH, AND EIGHTH GRADES

	2	3	4	5	6	7–8
United States mixers F–22						
Jiffy Mixer (2's) F-5				–	x	x
Hitch Hiker II (2's—Mixer) G-4						
(Record: Tennessee Saturday Night)				–	x	x
Tennessee Wig-Walk (2's—Mixer) G–5				–	x	x
Around the world C-2 to C-5						
Tant Hessie (2's) F-6				–	x	x
La Costilla (2's—2 lines) A-2			–	x	x	
Chihuahua (2's—2 lines) A-4					x	x
El Llanero (2's—2 lines) C-2					x	x
Hukilau (1's) C-5					x	x
Heeia (1's or 2's—with Puili Sticks) F-23					x	x
Songs and Dances of the Maori, F-24					x	x
Apat, Apat (2's—Mixer) F-11		–	x	•	•	
Tinikling Philippine Pole Dance (1's—2's) F-16)				–	x	x
Tanko Bushi (1's) F-17					x	
Hora (Hava Nagila) (1's) B-3				–	x	x
Cherkassiya (1's) B-3					x	x
Troika (3's—Mixer) F-14					x	x
Korobushka (2's—Mixer) F-14					x	x
Two step and polka (2's) C-1; F-12						
See Traditional Folk Dance Steps						
Klumpakojis (Wooden Shoes) (2's—Mixer) B-2				–	x	x
Doudlebska Polka (2's—Mixer) F-15					x	x
Oslo Waltz (2's—Mixer) F-15					x	x
Buzz's Mixer (2's—Mixer) F-21					x	x

– = May introduce activity   x = Depth in instruction   • = May continue activity
[a]Record References: Folk Dances and Circle Mixers, A to G.

B-2 *Folk Dances for Fun*, RCA Victor LPM-1624. Grades 2–6.

Green Sleeves (4's—2 couples), England. Walk.

Phrasing: clap and accent phrases in relation to steps—16, 8–8, 4–4–4–4.

"Chimes of Dunkirk" (2's—mixer) French-Belgian.

"Shoemaker's Dance" (2's), Denmark. Singing Game.

"Hansel and Gretel" (2's), Germany. Singing Game.

Hopp Mor Annika I, II (2's—mixer), Sweden.

I. Skip 16; walk 16; clap; slide with partner.

II. Substitute two-step or polka for slide.

Ten Pretty Girls (2–10 in line).

Noriu Miego (4's), Lithuania. Bleking with variations in tempo.

Klumpakojis (Wooden Shoes) (2's—mixer). Lithuania. Walk, two-step.

Cshebogar (the "Beetle") (2's), Hungary.

Crested Hen (3's), Denmark. Step-hop.

Turn Around Me (2's), Czechoslovakia.

Klappdans (2's—mixer), Sweden. Polka or two-step.

B-3 *All-Purpose Folk Dances*, RCA Victor LPM-1623, Grades 3–8.

Seven Jumps (1's) Denmark.

At the end of each figure, stand quickly and join hands quickly on the extra note (3rd note) in order to be ready to start the repetition of the step-hop on the first beat. Originally a dance performed by boys and men, good motivation.

Bingo II (2's—mixer), Scotland, America. Grand R and L.

Simplified version, G-1.

La Raspa (2's), Mexico. Bleking.

"What other steps could you use when turning with your partner?" (Two-step, polka, buzz step, Mexican dance steps.)

Glow Worm (2's—mixer).

Phrasing and change of direction: accent and clap 4's and 8's.

Virginia Reel (2 lines—6 couples). Two times through music for 6 couples. Simplified version, F-2.

Pop Goes the Weasel I (3's); II (4's); III (Sq. Form).

See A-3.

Chestnut Tree (2's), England. Schottische.

Sisken (2's), Denmark. Accented 3's or waltz.

Hora (Hava Nagila) (1's) Israel.

Cherkassiya (1's), Israel. Grapevine; various figures.

Calls on record, *Cherkassiya*, Israel Records, LP-7.

Present grapevine with all children in lines facing one direction, teacher with back to group.

Oh, Susanna (2's—mixer or circle of 8, Sq. Form).

Place 8 couples in one circle and return to own partner on Grand R and L.

Irish Washerwoman (Sq. Form). Square dance steps. No calls.

C. Bowmar Records—Albums

C-1 *American Folk Dances*, Album 5. Grades 4–6. Calls by Bob Van Antwerp. Excellent album.

Captain Jinks (Sq. Form).

Sicilian Circle (4's, 2's progress).

Patty Cake Polka (2's—mixer).

Oh, Johnny (2's—mixer). For smooth changing of partners, boys dos-à-dos R shoulders, then move *diagonally backward* toward the center of the circle *without turning around*.

Schottische (2's), military schottische. Schottische with instructions.

Good music for dances using schottische, or schottische rhythm such as Oklahoma Mixer.

Polka (2's), polka with instructions.

Virginia Reel (2 lines—4 to 6 couples).

Varsovienne ("Put Your Little Foot") (2's), mazurka with instructions.

C-2 *Latin American Folk Dances*, Album 6. Grades 6–8.

Eight dances including:

El Llanero (2 lines of 2's), national

dance of Venezuela (Bowmar 006-3 for single record).

Accented 3's; step-brush-step; stamp.

C-3 *Canadian Folk Dances*, Album.
Grades 2–6. Calls on records.
Prairie Circle (2's—mixer).
Frère Jacques (2's).
Maple Leaf Stomp (2's—mixer).
Carding the Wool (Sq. Form), Quebec.
Les Carillons de Dunkerque ("Chimes of Dunkerque") (2's—mixer).
Canadian Lancers (2 lines—4 couples).

C-4 *Mexican Folk Dances*
Six dances including:
La Raspa (2's)
La Bamba (2's)
Chihuahua (2 lines)

C-5 *Dances of Hawaii*. Ancient and modern.
Note: Authentic and beautiful music performed by South Sea Islanders. Directions and background information in accompanying booklet.
Nine dances including:
Hukilau

D. Activity Records, Inc.

D-1 Basic Concepts Through Dance—Body Image, EALP-601 Arden Jervey; Dorothy Carr.
Dances are simplified and each is repeated three times: slow, medium, and regular tempo. Verbal instruction and cues are given on record bands at slow and medium tempos; music only on regular tempo.
Hokey Pokey (1's)
Hansel and Gretel (2's) Germany
Chimes of Dunkirk (2's) French-Belgium
Hitch Hiker (2's)

E. Rhythms Productions. Good music, directions easy to follow.

E-1 *Folk Dances of North America,* cc 608.
Note: Combine with study of United States, Canada, and Alaska.

Brown-Eyed Mary (2's—mixer), United States, Middle West.
Jolly Is the Miller (2's—mixer), United States, folk singing game. Skip or two-step.
Dixie (2's), Southern United States.
Polly Wolly Doodle (2's—mixer), United States, West Virginia.
Miner's Polka (2's—mixer), United States, Alaska. Polka.
Branle à Six (2 lines—3 couples), French-Canadian.
Oxford Minuet (2's—mixer), United States (Colonial Period).
La Varsoviana (2's), American dance of European derivation.
(Colonial Period, Westward Movement.)

F. Single Records—Upper Grades
1. Galopede (2 lines—6 couples) English, Folkraft 1331.
2. Virginia Reel (2 lines) Folkraft 1249. Side A simplified, without reel; side B with reel.
3. Brighton Mixer (4's, 2's prog.) Folkraft F-1250.
4. *Puttjenter* (Sq. Form) Germany, Folk Dancer MH 1049. Use before teaching regular Grand R and L. In this dance girls only grand R and L; then boys only grand R and L.
5. Jiffy Mixer (2's), Windsor 4684.
6. *Tant Hessie* (2's) Folkraft 337–006.
7. *Fjäskern* (2's) Sweden. Aqua Record, V200.
Increased tempo with each repetition of the dance.
8. Hitch Hiker II (2's—Mixer).
Record: "Tennessee Saturday Night," Decca 9-46292. Directions G-4.
9. Tennessee Wig-Walk (2's—Mixer). Decca 9-28846. Directions G-5.
10. Jingle Bells (2's—Mixer). Folk Dancer MH 1111. Directions G-2.
11. *Apat, Apat* (2's—Mixer), Philippine. Folk Dancer MH 2031.
12. Schottische (2's—Mixer) MacGregor 5003 (Oklahoma Mixer).
Heel and Toe Polka (2's—Mixer) (Patty Cake Polka).
13. Chestnut Tree (2's) England. RCA Victor EPA-4139. Schottische.

FIG. 11.3. Maypole Dance.

La Raspa (2's) Mexico. See notation *La Raspa*, B-3.

Glow Worm (2's—Mixer).

14. *Troika* (3's) Russia. Folk Dancer MH 1059, Accented run.

Korobushka (2's—Mixer), Russia. Schottische.

15. *Doudlebska Polka* (2's—Mixer). Czechoslovakia. Folk Dancer MH 3016. Two step, polka.

Simplified: Double circle facing CCW. Link elbow with partner for steps 1 and 2. At end of dance, girls without partners step back until a boy without a partner comes along.

Oslo Waltz (2's—Mixer) Scottish-American. Accented 3's or waltz.

16. *Tinikling* (1's—2's) Philippine Pole Dance (Fig. 11.1). Folk Dancer MH 2033; RCA Victor EPA-4126.

Children may develop own routine as individuals or as partners. Good dance for program. Progression: Use 2 individual jump ropes on ground; use Chinese jump rope, ankle high (Fig. 2.52); use moving poles.

Neapolitan Tarantella (2's) Italy.

17. *Tanko Bushi* (1's) Japan. Folk Dancer MH 2010. (Coal miners' dance.)

18. Maypole Dance (2's), English. RCA Victor EPA-4132 (Fig. 11.3). A colorful dance suitable for a May Festival. Tether ball pole and streamers may be used.

Minuet (2's) Colonial Period.

Sellenger's Round (2's) England.

Gathering Peascods (2's) England.

19. "Donegal Round" (2's) Ireland. Folkraft 1425. Grand R and L, 7's and 3's.

20. Road To The Isles (2's) Scotland. Folkraft 1095.

21. Buzz's Mixer (2's—Mixer) Windsor 4637. Two-step.

22. Square Dance Associates. Honor Your Partner, Album 6. Walk through instructions and music by Ed Durlacher. (Couple mixers—fun for 7th and 8th graders.)

Patty Cake Polka Mixer.

Rochester Schottische.

Tandem Rochester Schottische.

Five Foot Two Mixer.

Narcissus.

Paul Jones Mixer.

23. *Heeia* (1's or 2's with puili sticks) Hawaii. Folkraft 1123.

24. Songs and Dances of the Maori. Salem XE 3003 (Fig. 13.1).

Song of the Seven Canoes.

G. *Directions for Folk Dances*

Note: This section includes directions for dances for which directions are not included with record. This section also presents variations of selected dances.

G-1 *Bingo I*

Record: Windsor A-7S2.

Step: Walk, skip. Meter: $\frac{4}{4}$.

Formation: Partners in double circle

facing CCW. Boys on inside circle, partners' inside hands joined.

Directions:

I. Skip—16.

II. Walk—16: (End facing partner.)

III. Clap.

B—Clap knees (1); clap hands together (2); clap both hands with partner (3).

I—Repeat as in B.

N—Repeat.

G—Repeat.

O—Clap knees, link R elbow with partner, walk once around and end facing CCW.

Repeat dance.

Mixer: Dancers in double circle, boys face CCW, girls CW. (Not necessary to identify partners.)

I. Skip 16.

II. Walk 16. (End facing a partner—if no partner, find one.)

III. Clap—same.

On "O" clap knees, link R elbow with partner, walk once around and end with boy facing CCW, girl CW.

Repeat dance.

G-2 *Jingle Bells* I (2's)

Record: Folk Dancer MH 1111.

Steps: Gallop, clapping, walk.

Meter: $\frac{2}{4}$.

Formation: Double circle, partners facing CCW with boys on the inside circle. Join both hands in promenade (skater's) position—R hand on top.

I. Verse: Gallop.

Gallop forward with R foot forward 7 gallops and a step—8 counts.

Gallop forward with L foot forward, 7 gallops and a step—8 counts.

Repeat galloping: R foot forward—8, L foot forward—8 counts. End facing partner.

Note: Change lead foot after the *step* on 8.

II. Chorus: Clapping, link R elbows, circle once and progress.

Clap hands together 3 times:

"Jin—gle—bells."

Clap both hands of partner 3 times: "Jin—gle—bells."

Clap hands together 3 times: "Jin—gle—all."

Clap knees once: "(the) way."

Link R elbow with partner. Walk once around partner and back to place—8 counts.

Repeat chorus and end facing forward.

Repeat dance.

Note: For mixer link R elbow with partner, walk once around, and move to new partner one place to L (boys move CCW, girls CW)—8 counts. Repeat chorus and move one more time.

Jingle Bells II (2's—mixer)

Record: Folk Dancer MH 1111.

Steps: Heel-toe, slides, clapping, walk. Meter: $\frac{2}{4}$.

Formation: Double circle with partners facing, boys on inside circle.

Directions: Similar to Patty Cake Polka, except both sections are repeated. See pattern for clapping, Jingle Bells I.

I. Heel-toe, heel-toe, 3 slides and step.

Boys start with L foot, girls with R. Place heel out to the side (count 1), place toe beside other foot (count 2), repeat (1, 2). Take 3 slides and a step moving CCW—4 counts.

Repeat back to place with boys starting with R foot, girls with L. (Start with the foot that is toward the direction each person will move.)

Repeat from the beginning.

II. Same as in Jingle Bells I.

Jingle Bells III (3's—mixer)

Record: Folk Dancer MH 1111.

Steps: Gallop, skip, clapping, walk or two-step. Meter: $\frac{2}{4}$.

Formation: In triple circle facing CCW, boy between two girls or girl between two boys, hands joined. Number the dancers: outside person No. 1, center person No. 2, inside person No. 3.

Directions:

I. Gallop; skip under arch.

Gallop with R foot forward, 7 gallops and a step—8 counts.

Gallop with L foot forward, 7 gallops and a step—8 counts.

Outside person goes under arch made by raised arms of numbers 2 and 3; center person follows and turns under own L arm—8 skips (No. 3 skips in place).

Inside person goes under arch made by Nos. 1 and 2; center person follows and turns under own R arm—8 skips (No. 1 skips in place).

II. Clapping; link elbows and walk around partner; progress.

Nos. 1 and 2 face. Clap and turn as in Jingle Bells I.

Nos. 2 and 3 face. Clap, then link L elbows and walk once around partner; center person then walks forward CCW to next group.

Repeat dance.

G-3 *Circle Schottische, Scandinavian*

Record: *Schottische,* MacGregor 400; Folk Dances: Bowmar Album 5.

Steps: Schottische, step-hop. Meter: $\frac{4}{4}$.

Formation: Single circle, partners.

Directions:

I. Meas 1–2: Schottische right, schottische left.

Moving to R—step R, step L, step R, hop R—4 counts.

Moving to L—step L, step R, step L, hop L—4 counts.

Meas 3–4: Step-hop in place.

Step R, hop R, step L, hop L— 4. Repeat.

Meas 5–8: Schottische right, schottische left, step-hop in place.

Repeat action of meas 1–4, ending facing partner.

II. Meas 9–10: Schottische right, schottische left.

Face partner. Starting R, move to own R, one schottische—step, step, step, hop—4 counts.

Starting L, move to own L back to place, one schottische—step,

step, step, hop—4 counts.

Meas 11–12: Link R elbows and step-hop once around partner. Go once around only with 4 step-hops (8 counts).

End facing partner in single circle.

Meas 13–14: Schottische R, schottische L (to new partner).

Schottische to R (same as action in meas 9–10).

Schottische to L, going *behind* original partner and facing new partner.

Meas 15–16: Step-hop around new partner.

Link R elbow with new partner. Step-hop once around new partner and finish facing the center of circle with girl on boy's R.

G-4 *Hitch Hiker II*

Record: *"Tennessee Saturday Night"* —Decca 9-46292.

(Variation of directions—*Windsor Record A-7S2.*)

Basic Steps: Chug and hitch, dos-à-dos, promenade. Meter: $\frac{2}{4}$.

Formation: Double circle, partners facing, boys on inside circle.

Directions:

I. Meas 1–4: Chug and hitch R.

Chug bkwd away from partner. (Chug is a short pull of both feet.) At same time clap own hands once. Call, "Chug." Repeat, "Chug." Jerk R thumb over R shoulder, turning R foot out with heel on floor.

Call, "Right."

Repeat the thumb and foot movement, "Right."

Meas 5–8: Chug and hitch L.

Repeat action for meas 1–4, using L thumb and L foot.

Meas 9–12: Chug and hitch with both.

Repeat action for meas 1–4, using both thumbs and both feet.

II. Meas 13–16: Dos-à-dos your partner.

Dos-à-dos partner R shoulders and finish in promenade position facing CCW—8 counts.

Meas 17–32: Promenade and progress.

Promenade with partner—8 counts.

Boys move up one person (girls take small steps waiting for new partner) and promenade new partner—8 counts. Finish facing partner.

Repeat dance.

G-5 *Tennessee Wig-Walk* (Origin Unknown)

Record: Decca 9-28846.

Steps: Point forward, side; grapevine; walk. Meter: $\frac{4}{4}$.

Formation: Partners facing, single circle formation. Boys face CCW, girls CW. Partners place R palms together at shoulder height.

Directions:

I. Point forward, side; step back, side, in front.

Point L foot forward (1–2), point L foot to side (3–4), step L in back of R (1), step R to side (2), step *onto* L in front of R (3 and hold). (Rhythm—slow, slow, quick, quick, quick.) With L palms together, repeat with R foot. Point R foot forward (1–2), side (3–4), step back R (1), to side L (2), step *onto* R in front of L (3 and hold).

II. Strutting Walk.

Place R palms together and walk around partner. Step: slow (1–2), slow (3–4); quick (1), quick (2), quick (3), hold (4)—8 counts.

Repeat step while progressing to next partner. Boys advance CCW and girls CW—8 counts.

Repeat dance.

Teaching suggestions

1. To teach the first step, place children in a V formation, with partners across from each other in the V. Teacher stands at the top (open end) of the V with back to group. Explain and demonstrate the step. Practice, then lead into circle formation for dance.

2. At end of grapevine in part I stress that weight is on L foot (in order to repeat the step pointing R foot forward).

DANCES AROUND THE WORLD[1] (FIG. 11.4)

Note: Dances of each country are in approximate order of difficulty.

NORTH AMERICA (EXCEPT UNITED STATES)

Canada

Canadian Folk Dances (Album) C-3

Branle à Six (6's—2 sets of 3's) E-1

MEXICO

Reference: Duggan et al., Folk Dances of *United States and Mexico.*

El Molino (1's, 2's) A-1

La Raspa (2's) B-3; C-4; F-13

La Costilla (2 lines) A-2

Chihuahua (2 lines—6 couples) A-4; C-4

Mexican Folk Dances (Album) C–4

LATIN AMERICA

Latin American Folk Dances (Bowmar Album) C-2

El Llanero (2 lines)

Tamborito (2's)

Palapala (2's)

Fado Blanquita (2's)

BRITISH ISLES

Reference: *Duggan et al., Folk Dances of the British Isles.*

England

Galopede (2 lines—6 couples) F-1

Green Sleeves (4's) B-2.

Circassian Circle (2's—mixer) A-3.

Cumberland Square Eight (Square Form) Folkcraft 1241.

Chestnut Tree (2's) B-3; F-13

Maypole Dance (2's) F-18

Sellenger's Round (2's) F-18

Gathering Peascods (2's) F-18

Ireland

Donegal Round (2's) F-19

Scotland

Road to the Isles (2's) F-20

Oslo Waltz (2's—mixer) F-15

[1]For record numbers, see "Record References: Folk Dances and Circle Mixers." For book references, see Bibliography.

FIG. 11.4. Costumes add interest and color to the study of dances around the world.

SCANDINAVIAN COUNTRIES

Reference: Duggan et al., *Folk Dances of Scandinavia.*

Denmark
"Dance of Greeting" (2's) B-1
"Shoemaker's Dance" (2's) B-2
Seven Jumps (1's) B-3
Crested Hen (3's) B-2

Sweden
Hopp Mor Annika (2's—mixer) B-2
Gustaf's Skoal (Square Form) A-2
Klappdans (2's—mixer) B-2

EUROPEAN COUNTRIES

Czechoslovakia
Turn Around Me (2's) B-2
Doudlebska (Polka) (2's—mixer) F-15

France
"Chimes of Dunkirk" (2's) B-2; French-Belgian
Branle à Six (6's—3's mixer) E-1

Germany
Kinderpolka (2's—mixer) B-1
Seven Steps—(2's—mixer) A-1
Puttjenter (Square Form) F-4

Hungary
Cshebogar (2's) B-2

Italy

Neapolitan Tarantella (2's) F-16

Spain; Portugal
Fado Blanquita (2's) C-2

ASIA

Israel
Hora (1's) B-3
Cherkassiya (1's) B-3

Japan
Tanko Bushi (Coal Miners' Dance) F-17

PACIFIC ISLANDS

Hawaiian Islands
Dances of Hawaii (Album) C-5
   Hukilau (1's)
   Kona Kai Opua I Ka Lai (2's), Kalaau Dance (Stick Dance)
Heeia (2's) (with puili sticks) F-23 (See Fig. 11.4—with drums for accompaniment.)

NEW ZEALAND (AND HAWAII)

Maori Stick Game (1–4's). Lummi Sticks, American version. (See Fig. 5.4.) Kits available.
Maori Poi Ball Game (1's) F–24 (See Fig. 13.1.) Kits available. For direc-

tions for making Poi Balls, see Appendix.

Philippines
  Apat, Apat (Four by Four) (4's) F-11
  Tinikling (Pole Dance) (1's, 2's) F-16
  (See Fig. 11.1.)

SOVIET REPUBLICS

Lithuania
  Noriu Miego (4's) B-2
  Klumpakojis (Wooden Shoes) (2's—mixer) B-2
Russia
  Troika (3's—mixer) F-14
  Korobushka (2's—mixer) F-14

AFRICA

South Africa
  Tant Hessie (2's—mixer) F-6

FORMATIONS FOR DANCES

Single Circle Without Partners (1's)
Single Circle with Partners (2's)
  Boy's partner is always on his R.
Double Circle Facing CCW. (2's) Boys on inside circle and girls on outside circle, on boys' R.
Double Circle with Partners Facing. (2's) Boy on inside circle facing partner on outside circle.
Fours in Double Circle, Couples Facing. (4's—2's progress) (Fig.11.5) One couple faces CCW with girl on R, opposite couple faces CW with *girl on R.* Couples may progress forward around circle.

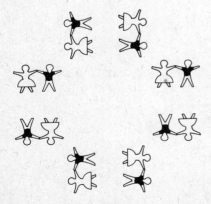

FIG. 11.5. Fours in double circle, couples facing.

Threes in Triple Circle. (3's) Usually a boy in the center with a girl on each side; may have a girl in the center with a boy on either side.
Sixes with Threes Facing. (6's—3's progress) (Fig. 11.6) One set of 3's face CCW; opposite set of 3's face CW. Threes may progress forward around circle.

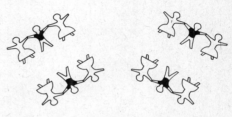

FIG. 11.6. Sixes, with 3's facing.

Eights with Fours Facing. (8's—4's progress) One set of 4's, two couples, face CCW; opposite set of 4's face CW. Fours may progress forward around circle.
Two Lines, Facing Forward—reel or longways formation. (2 lines—4 to 8 couples) Face toward music with boys in one line in single file formation, and girls across from partners in another line in single file formation. Girls are on boys' R.
Two Lines with Partners Facing—reel or longways formation. (2 lines—4 to 8 couples) (Fig. 11.7) Face toward music with boys in one line in single file formation, and girls across from partners in another line in single file formation. Girls are on boys' R. Turn and face partner. Lines should be about 6 to 8 feet apart; children in each line should be more than double elbow distance apart.
Square Dance Formation—square formation. (Fig. 11.8)
  One couple on each side of square with back to a wall.
  Girl stands beside and on the R side of the boy.
  Couple with back to music is couple

one. Couples 2, 3, and 4 number off counterclockwise. Couple 1 is head couple; couples 1 and 3 are head couples; couples 2 and 4 are side couples.

FIG. 11.7. Two lines, with partners facing.

FIG. 11.8. Square Dance formation.

TRADITIONAL FOLK DANCE STEPS

RHYTHMIC NOTATION AND PRESENTATION

Schottische: $\frac{4}{4}$ meter, even rhythm.

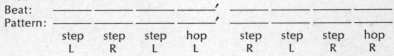

Beat:								
Pattern:								
	step	step	step	hop	step	step	step	hop
	L	R	L	L	R	L	R	R

Presentation

1. Clap the rhythm, accenting the first beat.

2. Take 3 walking steps, then raise knee on 4.

Call: "One, two, three, knee up; one, two, three, knee up."

Or "Step, step step, knee up; step step, step, knee up."

Continue.

3. Take 3 walking steps, then hop (knee up).

Call: "One, two, three, hop; one, two, three, hop."

Continue.

Variation

Step-hop, step-hop.

Try: "Step, knee up; step, knee up; step, knee up; step, knee up."

Then go into: "Step, hop; step, hop; step, hop; step, hop."

Usual Combination of steps

Two schottische steps followed by four step-hops.

Step, step, step, hop/ step, step, step, hop.

Step, hop, step, hop/ step, hop, step, hop.

Common difficulty

Attempting to leap from one foot onto the other, rather than taking the step and hop on same foot.

Two-Step: $\frac{2}{4}$ meter; usually performed in uneven rhythm.

Beat:					
Pattern:					
	step	*close*	step	step	*close*	step
	L	R	L	R	L	R

Presentation

1. Clap the rhythm, accenting the first beat.

2. Children face CCW in a single circle: step R to the outside (of circle), step to-gether L, step R to the outside. Repeat toward the center of the circle: step in L, step together R, step in L.

Call: "Out, together, out; in, together, in."

Continue in uneven rhythm.

3. With partners in double circle facing CCW, boys on inside circle and girls on outside. Join inside hands, *then* face partner. Boy starts with L foot, girl with R.

Step, close, step (pivot on last step to face outward).

Step, close, step (pivot on last step to face inward).

Call: *"Face to face; back to back."* Call in uneven rhythm: long, short, long; long, short, long.

4. Decrease the amount of turn or pivot and children should be two-stepping forward.

Common difficulty

Failure to transfer weight on each step. In practice of No. 2, children *have* to change weight in order to take the last step out from the circle (or into the circle). With inside hands joined as in No. 3, there is only one direction in which to turn.

Polka: $\frac{2}{4}$ meter; uneven rhythm with an up-and-down quality.

Beat: ——————— ——————— ' ——————— ———————
Pattern: —————— – —————— – ' —————— – —————— –

step close step hop   step close step hop
L   R   L   L   R   L   R   R

Presentation

1. Clap the rhythm accenting the first beat.

2. Repeat No. 3 as presented for two-step, adding a hop on the pivot: step, close, step, hop; step, close, step, hop. If there is a pickup note in the music, start with a hop on the pickup note, but *step* on the downbeat. Call:

"Face to face and' back to back and . . ."

—————— – —— —— —————— – —— –
L   R   L   L   R   L   R   R

With a pickup note, call: "And face

to face and back to back and . . ."

In many dances the polka may be done turning face to face and back to back with a partner. However, the amount of turn or pivot may be decreased and the polka step performed facing forward.

3. Dance position (Grades 7 and 8). In order to move around the floor more easily, the boy may alternate small and large steps. Take one polka with small steps while turning almost in place; then take the next polka with large steps while turning. Alternate between the small-step and long-step polkas.

Waltz: $\frac{3}{4}$ meter, even rhythm with a very smooth quality.

Beat: ——————— ——————— ———————,' ——————— ——————— ———————
Pattern: —————— —————— —————— ,' —————— —————— ——————

step   step   *close*   step   step   *close*
L   R   L   R   L   R

Presentation

1. Clap the rhythm, accenting the first beat.

2. Walk the rhythm, and dip slightly on first beat of each measure.

3. Walk the rhythm, and dip and clap hands on first beat.

4. Children in lines with elbows linked.
   a. Present the "box waltz." Teacher stands with back to lines of children.
      Box: Step forward L, to the side R, together L.

Step back R, to the side L, together R (Fig. 11.9).
      Call: *"Forward,* side, close; *back,* side, close."
   b. Move forward. On second half of box, step *forward* R.
   c. Alternate positions in lines, boys face forward and girls face backward with elbows linked. Boy starts forward with L foot, girl starts backward with R foot.

5. Girl steps in front of boy and partners face. Place hands on partner's shoulders.

Boys start forward with L foot, girls start backward with R foot.

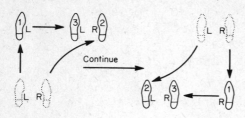

FIG. 11.9. Box Waltz.

6. Present the turn. Each child has own space and all face one wall, teacher in front with back toward the group.

    a. Turn using four complete box steps for one turn. Point L foot toward L wall and step onto L foot. Complete one box facing L wall, 6 counts. Repeat, turning to back wall, other side wall, and back to starting position. Continue. Repeat turning to the right. Start with R foot.

    b. Turn using two complete box steps for one turn. Point L foot toward L wall and step onto L foot, step to the side R, close L. Point R foot toward back wall while stepping *back* onto R foot, step to the side L, close R (completing one box and facing back wall). Repeat, continuing to L and finishing in starting position.

Common Difficulties

1. Failure to transfer weight with each step. Practice No. 2 and No. 3, checking that each step is forward and that weight is transferred on each step. Practice the box. Stress stepping onto L foot on third count (together), then stepping back onto R foot on second half of box.

2. Using a two-step pattern—step, together, step—instead of the waltz pattern—step, step, together.
Call: "Step, step, *close;* step, step, *close.*"

SQUARE DANCES

The first step in the presentation of square dance should be an orientation of the couples to their relative positions in the square. The head couple always stands with their backs to the music; couple no. 2 is to the right of couple no. 1, couple no. 3 across the square, and couple no. 4 to the left. Have the couples raise their hands as their numbers are called to be sure the positions are known. (Fig. 11.8)

The next step involves the introduction of basic calls and identification of *partner* and *corner.* Have the children walk through basic calls first without music, and then using a record. The teacher may find it necessary to take the place of one of the dancers to demonstrate the proper procedure. When the couples can execute the patterns smoothly, introduce dances which include the calls.

The first several dances should be fairly simple, with several repetitions of the same calls. As experience is gained, include more difficult dances by adding a new call each time. It will probably be necessary to walk through the new call before attempting to dance it.

When the children are sufficiently prepared, introduce a record that is new to the class and have them perform the dance as directed by the caller. They will welcome the challenge, and will be justly proud to learn they *can* square dance "on their own."

If studying a unit on the United States, include such square dances as Marchin' Thru Georgia, Arkansas Traveler, and Texas Star.

For added interest, use square dance music without calls. Divide into groups of nine or ten children, and have them create their own dances with their own caller. (While practicing, one child may accent a 4 beat on a wood block or pair of claves.) For additional challenge have the children divide into two groups: one group chants the square dance calls in Choric Verse; the other group performs the dance. See Chapter 10, "Choric Verse" (Texas Star). These suggestions have been used very successfully for programs.

PARTS OF A SQUARE DANCE CALL

Introduction. A warm-up that may include such calls as "Honor your partner," "Honor your corner," "Circle L," "Circle R," "Swing and promenade."

Figure. The main part of the call.

Break. The filler usually called after second couple has been active. Such calls may be included as "Dos-à-dos corner, dos-à-dos partner"; "All around your left-hand lady, seesaw your pretty little taw"; or "Allemande L, grand R and L, meet your partner and promenade home."

Ending. The conclusion, which may include an "Allemande L, grand R and L, meet your partner and promenade home."

HINTS FOR SQUARE DANCING

1. Square set with each couple with back to a wall. Couple standing with back to music is head couple.

2. Keep square formation small (dancers will not have to run). To square the set, stand beside partner and reach to corner of square with outside hand.

3. During promenade, keep set very small. Couples should be evenly spaced, making a good wheel with even spokes. The girl walks beside the boy, not slightly ahead of or behind him.

4. Take *small* steps. Use a smooth shuffle step. Imagine carrying a glass of water on the head without spilling a drop.

5. Explain and demonstrate new material with one set. Take one person's place in first couple. Difficult material may be presented in the classroom, with common difficulties pointed out and correct procedures stressed.

6. Dancers return to "home" position and wait for the next call if they get confused.

7. When introducing square dancing, write B (boy) and G (girl) in chalk on floor with proper spacing. Have each boy stand on a letter B; have each girl stand on a letter G.

8. To join hands in the circle, have boys raise hands to shoulder height, palms up, to form a shelf; girls place hands on top.

BASIC SQUARE DANCE CALLS

1. *Honor Partner.* Step back on one foot and bow (incline head). Girls hold out skirts. Boys may place back of hands on hip pockets.

2. *Shuffle.* Walk without raising feet clear of floor. Weight is on balls of feet. Take small steps in time to the music.

3. *Swing.*

   a. Two-hand swing. Join both hands and walk around partner CW.

   b. Upper-arm grasp. Stand *beside* partner with R hips together. Bend elbows and grasp the back of the arms of partner above the elbow. Use walk around or buzz step. Bend at the waist and lean away from partner as you swing.

   c. Waist grasp. Stand *beside* partner with R hips together. Put R arm around partner's waist and extend L arm up and out to the side. Use buzz step. Bend at the waist and lean away from partner as you swing.

   d. Buzz swing. Keep weight over R foot with L foot placed *behind* R. Use a push step around partner, or a very smooth gallop.

   e. Stress: (1) Keep swing smooth, do not go up and down. (2) Stand *beside* partner keeping R hips together, do not face partner. (3) Boy must return girl to his R side at the completion of a swing in order to be in correct position for following figure.

4. *Circle left and circle right.* Join hands and circle left, CW, unless otherwise directed, then reverse direction. Boys hold hands shoulder high with palms up; girls place hands on top.

5. *Forward and Back.* Move forward 3 steps and close (4 counts) and move back to place 3 steps and close (4 counts).

6. *Dos-à-dos.* Two persons facing. Walk forward, pass right shoulders, step sideward to the right, and then walk *backward* to place, usually done in 8 steps.

7. *Allemande Right.* Face partner (or other designated person). Join R hands, walk once around partner and return to place.

8. *Allemande Left.* All dancers face their corners (or other designated person). Join L hands, walk once around corner and return to place. Drop corner's hand and face partner. Call "L hands" as corners advance, until figure is learned. Allemande left is usually followed by a grand R and L.

9. *Grand Right and Left.* Face partner. Give R hand to partner and pass by, meeting next person. Continue in same direction, giving L hand to next, R to next, alternating hands while progressing around the circle or square. When introducing the call, have boys stand in place and girls weave in and out around the circle and back to partner. Then have girls stand still and boys weave. Then have both boys and girls progress in grand right and left until they meet their partners on opposite side of circle or square. Girls then turn and promenade back to place with partners. (*Puttjenter* provides a good introduction to grand R and L.)

    a. "Fancy" way of meeting partner. As partners meet and join R hands, they lift R hands and the girl turns under the arch (toward center of square) making a 1½ turn. Partners *continue to walk* CCW as girl turns under and as partners join L hands to promenade. (Girl turns and progresses as she turns.) Stress that she walks *forward* under the arch and turns once *and a half* around as she walks.

    b. "Fancy" ending at home position. From promenade position, partners raise joined R hands. Girl walks forward under the arch, and moves on around toward her R and faces her partner. Partners step back, dip away from each other with R hands still joined, then pull up to position in square. If time, partners swing once or twice around.

10. *Promenade.* Couples join R hands (shake hands), join L hands under R, and progress CCW around circle with girl on the R (skaters' position).

11. *Balance Partner.* Partners give right hands to each other and pull away in a suspended balance. Folk dance balance: Step forward R, together L, step R in place; step back L, together R, step L in place. It is usually done with quick, short steps in an uneven rhythm (R–L–R, long—short—long).

Simplified: Step forward and then rock back, or step forward R and close L, then step back L and close R. May balance to the side. New England style balance: step swing, step swing.

12. *Chassé* (or sashay). Sliding Step.

13. *Courtesy or Wheel Turn* (back grasp). Girl joins L hand with boy's L hand and places her R hand on her R hip with palm facing out. Boy reaches behind girl and takes her R hand in his R hand and walks *backward* as he guides girl forward once around. (Boy stands *beside* girl as they turn.)

14. *Right and Left Through.* Two couples face. Couples move forward and touch R hands with person directly opposite, as they pass through the couple. Finish with a courtesy turn. May repeat figure to return to place.

When introducing the figure, have couples take or touch R hands as they pass. Later they may walk through and pass R shoulders automatically, without touching hands.

15. *Ladies Chain.* Two couples face. Girls walk forward, join R hands, and cross over to opposite boy. Each girl offers her L hand to opposite boy and finishes with a courtesy turn. May repeat the figure to return to place.

16. *Ladies Grand Chain.* Square formation. Perform the same as ladies chain except that all girls extend R hands for a R-hand star to go halfway around circle to opposite boy for a courtesy turn. May repeat the figure to return to place.

17. *All Around that Left-Hand Lady.* Boy walks behind and around corner girl, and back to place. Girl steps forward, then backward as boy passes around her. (Boy walks forward all the way; it is not a dos-à-dos.)

Seesaw your pretty little taw. Boy completes a figure 8 by walking behind and around partner, and back to place. Girl again moves forward and backward as he passes around her. This figure is often followed by an allemande L and grand R and L.

RECORD REFERENCES: SQUARE DANCES, K-N

K.   Educational Dance Recordings, Inc.

K-1 *Square Dance Fair*, S.Q.1. Caller Dick Kraus (Basic Square Dancing).
     Side A (Excellent introductory material with instructions and practice.)
          Square Dance Formation
          All Circle—Swing—Promenade (Recommend a smooth shuffle walk rather than a skip.)
          Do-si-do
          Grand R and L
          Review of Steps and a Practice Square Dance
     Side B (Excellent material for introducing allemande L and other basic calls. Includes instructions and practice.)
          Allemande L
          Divide the Ring
          The Star
          Ladies Chain
          "Square Dance Fair"—Practice Square Dance

K-2 *Promenade and Do-si-do*, S.Q.2.
     Eight easy Square Dances, good second album.
          Duck for the Oyster, no allemande L.
          Buffalo Gals, no allemande L
          Around That Couple, Through That Couple, no allemande L
          Nellie Bly, no allemande L
          Star by the Right
          Red River Valley
          Divide the Ring
          Marching Through Georgia
          Turkey in the Straw (music only)

K-2A *Promenade Home*, S.Q.2A. Caller Dick Kraus.
     Eight easy Square Dances, includes allemande L.
          Take a Little Peek

Life on the Ocean Wave
Bell Bottom Trousers
Split Your Corners
Nellie Gray
Irish Washerwoman
Butterfly Whirl
Form an Arch
Pigtown Fling (music only)

K-3 *Square Dance Swing*, S.Q.3. Caller Dick Kraus.
     Eight moderately difficult Square Dances.
          When the Bloom Is on the Sage
          Uptown and Downtown
          Gents' Elbow Swing
          Pop Goes the Weasel
          Divide the Ring and Tunnel Through
          Pass the Left-Hand Lady Under
          Just Because
          Birdie in the Cage
          Ragtime Annie (music only)

K-4 *Square Dance Fun-Fest*, S.Q.4. Caller Dick Kraus.
     Eight Intermediate Square Dances.
          Lady 'Round the Lady
          Texas Star
          Swing Like Thunder
          Dip and Dive
          Coming 'Round the Mountain
          Chase the Rabbit, Chase the Squirrel
          Hurry, Hurry, Hurry
          Arkansas Traveler
          Rakes of Mallow (music only)
          Good 4's and 8's.

L.   RCA Victor, *Let's Square Dance*. Calls by Richard Kraus.

L-1 Album No. 1
     Good beginning album, no allemande L.
          Shoo Fly (Circle dance)
          Duck for the Oyster
          Red River Valley
          Girls to the Center
          Take a Little Peek
          Divide the Ring
          Hinkey Dinkey Parlez-Vous
          The Noble Duke of York (2 lines)
          Little Brown Jug (music only)

L-2   Album No. 2
Good second album, includes alle-
mande L.
Skating Away
Life on the Ocean Wave
Swing at the Wall
Nellie Gray
Form an Arch
Uptown and Downtown
Double Sashay
Bow Belinda
Angleworm Wiggle (music
only)

M.   MacGregor Records, *"Jonesy" Square
Dances*. Calls by Fenton "Jonesy"
Jones.

M-1   Album No. 7
Moderately difficult Square Dances
include:
Wabash Cannon Ball
Jingle Bells
Excellent for Christmas
Oh, Susanna
Oh, Johnny (circle or square
formation)
See notation, Folk Dances
C-1.
Solomon Levi (not difficult).
Start each figure with active
couple standing back to

back. Stress: Boys always
pass on *outside* of girls.

M-2   Album No. 4
Intermediate Square Dances in-
clude:
Hinkey Dinkey Parlez Vous
Marchin' Thru Georgia
Pistol-Packin' Mama
Pop Goes the Weasel
Hot Time in the Old Town
Tonight (Fig. 11.10)
(May allemande *R* with part-
ner rather than R-hand
lady.)

M-3   Album No. 8
Intermediate to advanced Square
Dances include:
Old Fashioned Girl
Red River Valley
Mañana
You Call Everybody Darling

N.   Single Records
1. *Cumberland Square*. England.
Folkraft 1241. Calls by Frank
Kaltman, (beginning Square
Dance).
2. *Texas Star*. Folkraft 1256. Calls
by Frank Kaltman.

FIG. 11.10. Allemande left with the lady on your left. "Hey!"

A and E Rag. Without calls.

3. *Mañana Square. Fun-n-Frolic* K 703. Calls by Henry Knight. Similar to Solomon Levi (beginning Square Dance). *Teton Mountain Stomp* (2's— mixer)

Texas Star Fun. *Hokey Pokey* (1's or 2's).

4. *My Pretty Girl.* Windsor 7412. Sundowners' Band, calls by Bruce Johnson *Marching Through Georgia* (intermediate to advanced).

BIBLIOGRAPHY

1. Duggan, Anne Schley, Jeanette Schlottmann, and Abbie Rutledge. *Folk Dances of the British Isles; Folk Dances of European Countries; Folk Dances of Scandanavia;* and *Folk Dances of the United States and Mexico,* New York: The Ronald Press Company, 1948. (Includes geographical, historical, and sociological backgrounds, and costumes and festivals; also includes music.) *Folk Dances of the United States and Mexico* in print—other references available in libraries.
2. Folk Dance Federation of California, Inc. *Folk Dances from Near and Far,* Vol. A-1 and Vol. A-2, 150 Powell Street, Room 302, San Francisco, California, 1962.
3. Harris, Jane A., Anne Pittman, and Marlys S. Waller. *Dance a While,* rev. ed., Minneapolis: Burgess Publishing Company, 1968. (For seventh grade and up.)
4. Kraus, Richard. *Folk Dancing, a Guide for Schools, Colleges, and Recreation Groups,* New York: The Macmillan Company, 1962. (Includes dance directions, record references, background material, and teaching suggestions.)
5. Kraus, Richard. *A Pocket Guide of Folk and Square Dances and Singing Games for the Elementary School,* Englewood Cliffs, New Jersey: Prentice-Hall, Inc., 1966.
6. Kraus, Richard G. *Square Dances of Today and How to Teach and Call Them,* New York: The Ronald Press, 1950. (Includes music.)
7. Latchaw, Marjorie, and Jean Pyatt. *A Pocket Guide of Dance Activities,* Englewood Cliffs, New Jersey: Prentice-Hall, Inc., 1958. (Includes single-note melody line of music.)
8. Stuart, Frances R., and John S. Ludlam. *Rhythmic Activities,* Series I and Series II, Burgess Publishing Company, 426 South Sixth Street, Minneapolis 15, Minnesota, 1963. (Card files) (Includes single-note melody line and chord symbols.)
9. Vick, Marie, and Rosann McLaughlin Cox. *A Collection of Dances for Children,* Minneapolis: Burgess Publishing Company, 1970. (Card file. A collection of dances for children—kindergarten through junior high school.)

COSTUMES

1. Duggan Series. See Bibliography 1.
2. Haire, Frances Hamilton. *The Folk Costume Book,* New York: A. S. Barnes & Company, 1926. (Available in libraries.)
3. Rhythm Production: *Folk Dance Costumes of Europe* and *Folk Dance Costumes of Latin America,* Rhythm Production, 6201 Santa Maria Boulevard, Los Angeles, 38, California. (Contains map, flags, and costumes.)

BEHIND-THE-SCENES PLANNING

The material in Part II is concerned with the theory behind play. Chapter 12 is a broad discussion of the "Purpose of Play." It would be well to refer to this chapter occasionally throughout the year to maintain direction in the course of planning the program.

The chapter entitled "The Cast" is concerned with the teacher who conducts the activity program, the other members of the school staff who may be of assistance, and, of greatest importance, the child. Included here is a presentation of the characteristics of children and the implications for an effective, developmental course of instruction. The implementation is to be found in "Developing the Program," Chapter 14, which presents methods of achieving balance and variety in meeting the needs of children. Competition is discussed as a natural outgrowth of the games program. Special emphasis is placed on attitudes and conduct in competition, as well as recommendations for the many opportunities to compete that are appropriate to elementary school children. Arrangements for tournaments are presented, with suggestions for organization.

The facilities and equipment necessary to conduct the program are presented in the Appendix. Attention is directed to recommended equipment for the different grade levels. This is an important consideration in the success of the program. Suggestions for integrating physical education with other subject areas and a selection of Seasonal and Holiday Activities are included in the Appendix.

FIG. 12.1. Totally involved in developing something uniquely their own.

In play, a child is totally involved: he moves, he thinks, and he feels. (19) In so doing he learns to control himself and objects in the environment, to work with and against gravity, to move in and through space. In self-directed play the child creates situations for himself that challenge his ability to cope with his environment: he builds things to climb through or jump off; he stacks things; he sets up targets; he strikes at objects with implements. His play becomes socialized as he seeks out others for cooperative or competitive activity.

A purposeful activity program in the school setting continues these challenges, appropriate to the abilities of each child, to broaden and deepen his understanding of movement. As a result his movement potential, or capacity for efficient movement, is more likely to be realized.

DEVELOPMENT THROUGH ACTIVITY (2, 44)

Physical education is concerned with child development through activity. According to Breckenridge and Vincent, "Development is achieved through the processes of growth (change in size), maturation (qualitative change not induced by learning) and learning (change through experience)." (11) *Play With A Purpose* is a planned program of physical education that creates a dynamic relationship between the individual and his environment, specifically designed to provide challenges according to growth stages and ability levels.

The learning process may be part of a highly formalized instructional situation or the casual interchange between two children during recreational play. The learning of the rules of a game or the steps in a dance require application on the part of the individual; the development and refinement of strategy demand even greater involvement.

There is a vast range of individual differences in the performance of physical activities. The child, parents, and the teacher need to understand and appreciate the reasons for these differences. Natural abil-

ity, interests of parents, previous instruction and participation, and closeness to facilities in terms of residence are but a few. In addition, the impact of heredity, body build, and health status upon performance should be understood. Rate of growth is sometimes a cause for concern among children; it should be stressed that

it is normal for a boy to start his preadolescent spurt as early as age 10½ or as late as 17. It is normal for a girl to start her preadolescent spurt as early as 9 or as late as 14. Level of maturity has a great influence on how an individual feels, thinks, and how he performs. Maturity is a key word in physical education interests and abilities, especially in upper elementary school grades. Although each child is normal and follows his own built-in timetable of maturity, he may not meet the statistical averages for his group. (30)

However, through understanding, interest, and continued effort, the slow maturer often catches up with, and may surpass, the early maturer in the performance of motor skills.

According to Richard Harsh one factor in individual differences often overlooked concerns the concept that children (and adults) vary in their threshold or sensitivity to stimulation as well as in the kind and intensity of their reaction to such stimulation. (21) One individual may react in a slow, deliberate way while another may be quick and explosive in his response. At the same time either individual may react in quite a different way to a stimulus, depending on the importance or value of the act to the individual.

Another factor with which Dr. Harsh is concerned is the amount of available energy that children have to expend. This may be related to such things as diet, assimilation of food, rest patterns, growth, and maturation. One child may become fatigued rapidly during activity on the playground and then exhibit behavior problems, while another child may have an abundance of energy and be able to enjoy the entire activity period.

In a broad discussion of individual differences, Singer (41) identifies several variables that influence performance. These include form, level of aspiration, fatigue, and level of skill. A performer will incorporate a new movement pattern into his own movement style, which is governed by age, experience, physical characteristics, and personality. The degree of skill developed is determined by his desire to achieve, based upon realistic expectations. The tolerance of fatigue will affect the rate of achievement in a given learning situation. The level of skill, which may be quickly determined by the experienced teacher, determines the kind of instruction to be presented. Each of these variables must be considered for each individual if effective learning is to take place.

In an article on "Tailor Your Teaching to Individualized Instruction," Dr. Madeline Hunter makes the following comments.

Individualized instruction is no one way of conducting education. It is the process of custom-tailoring instruction so it fits a particular learner. An individualized program is not necessarily different for each learner, but must be appropriate for each. It is based on the premise that there is no one best way for all learners, but that there are best ways for each learner, which may be different from those for another learner. (24)

In order to assist teachers in individualizing instruction in physical education, material in the activity chapters is presented in order of difficulty. Children need success in simple movement patterns and ball skills before being confronted with the more complex ones. In addition some children need to spend a greater length of time on certain patterns or skills in a variety of interesting and challenging ways in order to be able to perform them automatically. Such repetitions are provided throughout the text.

In the activity program there are unlimited opportunities to experiment; to explore and to discover the various possibilities in solving problems; or to create new and different ways of achieving goals. According to E. Paul Torrance, a number of abilities are involved in creative thinking:

. . . fluency—the ability to produce a large number of ideas;

flexibility—the ability to produce a variety of ideas or use a variety of approaches;

originality—the ability to produce ideas that are off the beaten track;

elaboration—the ability to fill in the details;

redefinition—the ability to define or perceive in a way different from the usual, established, or intended way. . . . ' (46)[1]

It is intriguing to observe children totally involved in working out a problem as individuals, or as part of a group, gaining new insights while developing something that is uniquely their own.

"Purposes" have been established along with the various activities in Section I. These are presented to identify the intent of the particular area of instruction and should be considered in the development of program objectives. The material that follows offers a broader discussion of the purpose of play.

POSITIVE SELF-CONCEPT

The degree of skill that a child demonstrates throughout the school years has bearing upon his self-concept. He needs to feel "I can." (Fig. 12.2) With this self-confidence comes greater acceptance and appreciation of others, and of the performance of others. This may well be followed by the child's acceptance by others and a satisfying relationship *with* his peers. Thus, a child's degree of skill has influence upon his social position. This is especially true of boys; to a lesser degree it is true of girls.

This concept is reiterated by Richard Harsh.

. . . Self-concept does have a very special relationship to how anyone will participate. . . . The experiences which we have had in the past tend to mold and be the feedback to us of what the body image is.

There may also be a disparity between the actual self-image and the image seen by others. On account of variations in maturity, the slow-developer may continue to hold a poor self-image long after the

[1]See articles on creativity by E. Paul Torrance in *Selected Readings in Movement Education* by Robert T. Sweeney (44).

FIG. 12.2. Play has many forms and many satisfactions.

condition has passed. A poor self-concept may be based on the child's unrealistic goals or standards of achievement, as set by himself or by his parents. (21) According to Gladys Gardner Jenkins,

Competition in which the child consistently loses is poor preparation for life in a competitive world. The ability to take real competition comes slowly. It is built upon self-respect and self-confidence in some area. . . . Occasional failure balanced by success is not harmful but to be expected; continuous failure can destroy a child's picture of himself as an acceptable person. (26)

To paraphrase, a better self-concept may be developed by changing what may be changed, accepting what cannot be changed, and knowing the difference. Self-concept has a strong influence on a child's achievement.

MOTOR SKILLS

The logic and importance of learning motor skills at the elementary school level is substantiated in a statement by John E. Anderson, formerly Director of the Insti-

tute of Child Development and Welfare, University of Minnesota. He stated that by the age of 12 the child has 92 percent of his gross bodily coordination, 83 percent of the finer eye-hand coordination, and 86 percent of similar coordination as determined by the aiming test. Of the two speed factors, the child of 12 has 90 percent of his reaction time, the speed with which the individual can react to a signal, and 85 percent of his serial speed, the rate at which he can make serial or successive movements as in tapping. His percentage of physical strength lies somewhere between 30 and 50 percent of his potential, depending on the measures used. Superior performance can be expected only in late adolescence or early adult life primarily because of the tremendous increase in strength that comes in the adolescent period. This gain is particularly true of the male. (5) Since these factors are in the process of great increase during the elementary school years, this is a logical time for concentrated instruction in the development of motor skills and learning to move efficiently.

According to Radler and Kephart,

Children develop "readinesses" of all kinds by piling one simple skill atop another. Each skill is acquired by a combination of natural maturation on one hand and learning on the other. (39)

Physical readiness is increased through planned progressions of activities commensurate with maturation.

In a related discussion of readiness it is pointed out that children may have a much earlier stage of "readiness" for instruction than previously thought possible. Witness the introduction of science and math into the primary grades. In further explanation, Lawther states,

In the attempts to understand the young child's learning and to foster it or improve its rate, four points stand out from the various observational and experimental studies. They are: (1) what seems to be a very slow rate of progress in primary or sensory-motor learning; (2) the need to automatize each activity before it can be integrated with another activity for a higher stage of learning; (3) the great number of experiences (the quantity of experience) necessary for primary learnings; and (4) the importance of motor experience—manipulating and exploring—as a means to learn intellectually as well as physically. (29)

The importance of instruction in basic movement patterns is also pointed out by Singer:

Many students have trouble learning motor skills because of a lack of experience with basic movement patterns in childhood. Ease in learning new skills will depend to a large extent on these many varied previous experiences. There are indications that even in later years familiarization with simple motor patterns facilitates the learning of more complex skills, e.g., those involved in sports. . . . Therefore, learners who have not had the opportunity to play and develop the simple motor skills associated with childhood are handicapped in later, more complex undertakings. (42)

SAFETY HABITS

Safety consciousness in physical education is developed by stressing and following safe practices during instruction and guided play. Instruction in safety is an integral part of the program. Each child not only should be made aware of hazards and unsafe practices, but should understand the need and be motivated to follow such practices at *all* times. He should be aware not only of his own safety but also of the safety of others.

Some of the skills in physical education are safety skills. Whether one dodges to avoid being tagged or to avoid being hit by an oncoming object such as a ball, bicycle, or car, the basic skill is the same. Learning how to land like a spring or how to fall and roll like a ball may well prevent broken arms or legs or even concussions. The development of such factors as balance and coordination ranks high in the prevention of accidents. Understanding the need for progression and recognizing one's own limitations will help the individual child to work within his own capabilities.

OPTIMUM LEVEL OF HEALTH AND FITNESS

A complete physical examination should be required of every child who enters school and be repeated periodically throughout the school years. Without professional evaluation an organic disability or physical weakness may be undetected and may result in a critical situation which might otherwise have been avoided. Vision and hearing tests should be included in the examination to forestall and correct problems. However, vision tests involving more than 20/20 vision are needed. A child may pass such a test but still have difficulty functioning adequately in the classroom or on the playground. Far-point near-point accommodation in vision is another important area for assessment. This accommodation refers to the ability to focus upon distant or close objects, and to shift focus from one to the other without difficulty. Examples of such accommodation include chalkboard/desk activities, or playground activities in which the focus is first on a batter or a person throwing or kicking a ball, and then on the oncoming ball. Difficulties in auditory perception may also show up in the activity program when a child has trouble responding to a given rhythm, or to verbal directions. A child deserves to have all his faculties in the best possible working order to gain maximum benefit from his educational experiences. Children having irremediable health handicaps require special consideration in program planning.

Children need a great deal of activity for natural growth and development. Strenuous activity increases organic development: heart efficiency, improved circulation and respiration. Endurance improves the capacity for strenuous activity in work or in play, increases the interest and ability to participate, and improves the capacity to recover quickly after such activity. An interesting and satisfying program also provides motivation for expending greater energy and becoming more deeply involved in improving one's level of performance.

Strenuous activity, commensurate with the child's development, is an essential part of the program throughout the year; and each child needs to understand and practice progression in the gradual increase in *distance, speed,* and *repetitions.* The knowledges gained and the practices established in the school years in *developing* fitness should carry over to the adult years. As an adult *maintaining* fitness appropriate to the individual is of prime importance.

The many opportunities for integrating health units with the activity program are often overlooked. Throughout the program, opportunities arise in which the need for good health practices may be readily observed. The relationships between good performance in activity and proper habits of eating and sleeping should be stressed, along with an understanding of the need for proper amounts of activity and rest for optimum physical efficiency. Better health practices should result from motivation and instruction in correct body alignment when sitting, standing, and walking as well as in activities. Finally, a child with a healthy body has a certain margin of safety in case of emergency due to illness, accident, or unusual stress; and a greater chance for total involvement in the physical education program.

RECREATIONAL SKILLS AND INTERESTS

One makes an effort to participate in things he enjoys. If a child is interested and gains satisfaction in the physical education program, he will make a greater effort and be more likely to participate during out-of-school hours.

The physical education instructional and guided play period provides valuable instruction in skills and affords opportunities for developing good attitudes, but the amount of time for participation is all too limited. Additional time in activity is needed by boys and girls in the growing years. The child who receives a good play program today has a greater appreciation of sports and dance activities and is better prepared to be a participant and spectator. He is also more apt to make wise choices in his leisure-time activities today and tomorrow.

It is important that the school program, from kindergarten to eighth grade, be a balanced program of activities. The educational objectives of this period include the development of skills and various opportunities to explore *many* areas in order to have a basis for making intelligent decisions for specialization at the secondary level or as an adult. Overemphasis in one area such as physical fitness or any one sport may result in a dislike for continued participation in activity.

Knowledge of skills, rules, and strategy will increase a child's appreciation of a sport as a spectator as well as a participant. Under good leadership, assuming the role of a team captain, umpire, or referee will also contribute to better understanding when playing or observing.

The need to develop continuing recreational interests and skills during childhood is evident in the adult world. The increased amount of leisure time, lessened amount of energy expended in work, and improved physical conditions all lend themselves to participation in some form of activity as adults. From this participation comes renewed vigor, a more efficient physiological system, and constructive outlets for energy —all aiding the maintenance of a sound balance of mental and physical heatlh.

FIG. 12.3. Play today—recreation tomorrow.

The play of today becomes the recreation of tomorrow. (Fig. 12.3) There is continuing value in participation in recreation programs throughout adulthood. Success in play as a child perpetuates the desire for activity as an adult. The release of tension, maintenance of fitness, and enjoyable use of leisure time are all beneficial objectives of a good recreation program. From the point of view of the participant, however, the ever-constant motivating force is the satisfaction that comes from his recreational experiences.

PHYSICAL EDUCATION PROGRAMS (4)

A concept that is appearing with more and more frequency in the literature is *movement education.* (3, 4) According to Lorena Porter,

The term movement education is used to refer to that part of the physical education program which emphasizes helping the child to learn about his unique movement behavior. Its advocates believe that as the child learns to understand and control the many ways in which his body may move, he is better able to direct the actions of his body, the control of which results in increased confidence in work and play. We refer to this greater understanding and control as body management. (36)

This type of program is most generally conducted through a problem-solving approach, in which the child is encouraged to seek his own solutions to various movement problems. Cognitive processes are involved in the selection or rejection of alternatives; as a result the child is led to greater understanding of the infinite possibilities in movement. (3, 44) This approach is stressed in the basic chapters of the text: Chapter 1 on movement skills; Chapter 6, ball skills; and Chapter 10, dance. With the activities throughout the text appearing in order of difficulty, various approaches may be used; the instructor determines the most effective way for his given situation.

There are many programs concerned with sensorimotor and perceptual-motor development. (1, 2, 9, 27, 33) These programs rely strongly upon principles of human growth and development and try to fill the gaps in each child's foundation for learning. According to Newell C. Kephart,

We are interested in a sort of motor generalization by which the repertory of movements, whatever they may be, available to the child

are used for the purpose of gathering information around him.

Many children find the motor learning required for a learning pattern difficult. As a result, they stop with a motor skill. They require additional help and additional learning experiences to continue this motor learning until a level is reached which will permit the use of movement, not only for specific purposes, but for the more generalized purpose of information gathering. It becomes the responsibility of the public schools to offer this aid and to help the child expand his motor learning. (27)

Research in sensorimotor and perceptual-motor development has provided guidelines for activity throughout the revision of the text, especially in Chapters 1, 5, 6, and 10.

Whatever the name, Physical Education, Movement Education, Body Management, or Play with a Purpose, the main objective is to meet the individual needs of each child. There are a great number of experimental programs attempting to fill this need at the present time. It is essential to continue and expand such programs along with action research to learn more about children: common patterns and individual differences, how they develop and how they learn, and what determines values. If there is to be a "modern physical education" as there is a "modern math," the change should start at the beginning with preschool, kindergarten, and primary children—the "sensory-perceptual-motor" years. Then let experimentation and research continue to open up better approaches, appropriate challenges, and greater involvement as the child finds ever

greater meaning in his educational experiences.

The concern of every educator is not only the top few in any classification, but also the great majority who fall in the other ranks. If society is to advance, it will do so only with consistent effort in raising the standards of performance at all levels. Strength, vigor, and health are but three requisites for progress. These must be inculcated in our children if tomorrow's leaders are to assume their inherited tasks. The responsibility of every physical educator, whether he be classroom teacher or specialist, is to be sure each of his charges has the opportunity to develop to the highest level of which he is capable.

SUMMARY

Play has many purposes: neuromuscular maturity; motoric and physiological development; social interaction; self-realization. Play as a basis for cognitive development is noted by Espenschade and Eckert: "There is widespread recognition today of the essential role of early motor experiences as a basis for perceptual and, subsequently, symbolic generalization." (17)

Athletic prowess alone is not sufficient justification for physical education programs. The broader purposes, as listed, must be reflected in the design of such programs to insure that each individual has the opportunity to develop to the highest level of which he is capable. Then it can truly be said that physical education has an important contribution to make in the total developmental process through which children come to know themselves.

BIBLIOGRAPHY

1. American Association for Health, Physical Education, and Recreation. *Perceptual-Motor Foundations: A Multidisciplinary Concern*, Proceedings of the Perceptual-Motor Symposium, May 8–10, 1968, 1201 Sixteenth Street, N.W., Washington, D.C.: American Association for Health, Physical Education, and Recreation, 1969.
2. American Association for Health, Physical Education, and Recreation. *Promising Practices in Elementary School Physical Education*. Report of the Conference for Teachers and Supervisors of Elementary School Physical Education,

October 2–5, 1968, 1201 Sixteenth Street, N.W., Washington, D.C.: American Association for Health, Physical Education, and Recreation, 1969.

3. *Ibid.,* pp. 58–64.

4. *Ibid.,* pp. 106–115.

5. Anderson, John E. "Growth and Development Today," in *Social Changes and Sports,* American Association for Health, Physical Education, and Recreation, 1201 Sixteenth Street, N.W., Washington 6, D.C., 1959, pp. 40, 41.

6. Association for Childhood Education International. *Physical Education for Children's Healthful Living,* Bulletin No. 23-A, eleven contributors, Washington, D.C.: Association for Childhood Education International, 1968.

7. Ayres, A. Jean. "Deficits in Sensory Integration in Educationally Handicapped Children," *Journal of Learning Disabilities* 2:3 (March 1969), pp. 160–168.

8. Ayres, A. Jean. "The Development of Perceptual-Motor Abilities: A Theoretical Basis for Treatment of Dysfunction," *American Journal of Occupational Therapy* 17:221–223 (1963).

9. Ayres, A. Jean. "Patterns of Perceptual-Motor Dysfunction in Children: A Factor Analytic Study," *Perceptual and Motor Skills.* Monograph Supplement 1-V20, Montana State University, Missoula, Montana: Southern Universities Press, 1965, pp. 335–368.

10. Ayres, A. Jean. "Tactile Functions—Their Relation to Hyperactive and Perceptual Motor Behavior," *The American Journal of Occupational Therapy* 17:6–11 (January-February 1964).

11. Breckenridge, Marian E., and E. Lee Vincent. *Child Development,* 5th ed., Philadelphia: W. B. Saunders Company, 1965, p. 6.

12. Broer, Marion R. *Efficiency of Human Movement.* Philadelphia: W. B. Saunders Company, 1966, pp. 25–32.

13. Bruner, Jerome Seymour. *The Process of Education,* Cambridge, Mass.: Harvard University Press, 1960.

14. Bruner, Jerome Seymour. *Toward a Theory of Instruction,* Cambridge, Mass.: Belknap Press of Harvard University, 1966.

15. Combs, Arthur W., and Donald Snygg. *Individual Behavior, a Perceptual Approach to Behavior,* New York: Harper & Row, Publishers, 1959, pp. 223–225.

16. Combs, Arthur W., Chairman, 1962 Yearbook Committee. *Perceiving, Behaving, Becoming, A New Focus for Education,* 1201 Sixteenth St., N.W., Washington 6, D.C.: Association for Supervision and Curriculum Development, 1962, p. 18.

17. Espenschade, Anna S., and Helen M. Eckert. *Motor Development,* Columbus, Ohio: Charles E. Merrill Books, Inc., 1967, p. 102.

18. Fleishman, Edwin A. "Individual Differences and Motor Learning," *Learning and Individual Differences,* Robert M. Gagné, ed., Columbus, Ohio: Charles E. Merrill Books, Inc., 1967, Chapter 8, pp. 165–191.

19. Halsey, Elizabeth and Lorena Porter. *Physical Education for Children,* New York: Holt, Rinehart and Winston, 1963, p. 16.

20. Haring, Norris G., and Jeanne Marie Stables. "The Effect of Gross Motor Development on Visual Perception and Eye-Hand Coordination," *Physical Therapy* 46:129–135 (February 1966).

21. Harsh, Richard. "The Relationship of Physical Development to Human Behavior," *California Journal for Instructional Improvement* 4–6:12–17 (December 1963).

22. Holt, John Caldwell. *How Children Fail,* New York: Pitman Publishing Co., 1964.

23. Humphrey, James H., Edwina Jones, and Martha J. Haverstick, eds., *Readings in Physical Education,* Palo Alto, California: The National Press, 1960.

24. Hunter, Madeline C. "Tailor Your Teaching to Individualized Instruction," *Instructor* 79:53–63 (March 1970).

25. Hunter, Madeline C. "The Role of Physical Education in Child Development and Learning," *Journal of Health, Physical Education, Recreation* 39:56–58 (May 1968).

26. Jenkins, Gladys Gardner. "These are Your Children," *Journal of Health, Physical Education and Recreation,* 1201 Sixteenth Street, N.W., Washington, D.C.: American Association for Health, Physical Education and Recreation, 37:34–37 (November-December 1966).

27. Kephart, Newell C. "Perceptual-Motor Aspects of Learning Disabilities," *Exceptional Children* 30:204 (December 1964).

28. Kephart, Newell C. *The Slow Learner in the Classroom,* Columbus Ohio: Charles E. Merrill Books, Inc., 1960.

29. Lawther, John D. *The Learning of Physical Skills,* Englewood Cliffs, New Jersey: Prentice-Hall, Inc., 1968, p. 22.

30. Metheny, Eleanor, Professor of Education and Physical Education, University of Southern California, Los Angeles, California, Lecture.

31. Metheny, Eleanor. *Movement and Meaning,* New York: McGraw-Hill Book Co., 1968.

32. Oxendine, Joseph B. *Psychology of Motor Learning,* New York: Appleton-Century-Crofts, 1968.

33. Philbrick, Barbara. "Selected Readings on Perceptual-Motor Learnings," *Journal of Health, Physical Education, Recreation* 39:34–36 (February 1968).

34. Piaget, Jean. *The Child's Conception of Space,* New York: W. W. Norton, 1967.

35. Piaget, Jean. *The Origins of Intelligence in Children,* New York: International Universities Press, 1952.

36. Porter, Lorena. *Movement Education for Children, A New Direction in Elementary School Physical Education,* Planned in cooperation with the American Association for Health, Physical Education, and Recreation, 1201 Sixteenth Street, N.W., Washington, D.C.: American Association of Elementary-Kindergarten-Nursery Educators, 1969, p. 5.

37. Quest, Monograph II, Spring Issue, April 1964. "The Art and Science of Human Movement," The National Association for Physical Education of College Women and the National College Physical Education Association for Men.

38. Leonard, George. *Education and Ecstasy,* New York: Delacorte Press, 1968.

39. Radler, D. H. with Newell C. Kephart. *Success Through Play,* New York: Harper & Row, Publishers, 1960, p. 11.

40. Sapora, Allen V., and Elmer Mitchell. Chapter 5, "Definitions and Characteristics of Play and Recreation," in *The Theory of Play and Recreation,* 3rd ed., New York: The Ronald Press Company, 1961, pp. 113–128.

41. Singer, Robert N. *Motor Learning and Human Performance,* New York: The Macmillan Company, 1968, pp. 117–127.

42. *Ibid.,* p. 126.

43. Skubic, Vera, and Marian Anderson. "The Interrelationship of Perceptual-Motor Achievement, Academic Achievement and Intelligence of Fourth Grade Children," *Journal of Learning Disabilities* 3:413–420 (August 1970).

44. Sweeney, Robert T., ed. *Selected Readings in Movement Education,* Reading, Massachusetts: Addison-Wesley Publishing Company, 1970.

45. Thompson, Richard F. *Foundations of Physiological Psychology.* New York: Harper & Row, Publishers, 1967.

46. Torrance, E. Paul. *Creativity: What Research Says to the Teacher,* No. 28 of series, Department of Classroom Teachers, American Educational Research Association of the National Education Association, 1963. Reprinted by permission of the National Education Association.

CHAPTER *13*
THE CAST

FIG. 13.1. A cooperative venture in the study of music and games of another culture.

The most ideal instruction imaginable would be to no avail if either of two components were missing: the teachers who administer it or the children who assimilate it. The discussion within this chapter is concerned with these two very important groups, their relationship in an activity program, their roles in *Play with a Purpose*.

THE LEADERS

LEADERS WITHIN THE SCHOOL

THE TEACHER

A teacher is many things in the eyes of children: taskmaster, friend, parent, all-knowing or possessed of a single-track purpose. Whatever his appearance, he has a most awesome responsibility to stimulate and guide young minds, leading them to a self-perpetuating and never-ending desire for knowledge.

His program is based upon the children's needs and abilities; his enthusiasm and interest are reflected by them. If he has a particular area of interest, his students will reflect this, too. His conviction of the value of subject matter will carry over to the class, and he will incorporate many different teaching methods in order to reach all his students. He will attempt to maintain a comfortable atmosphere conducive to exploration and creativity, while maintaining a charge of curiosity.

A teacher sets the example of fairness and good sportsmanship, exhibiting a genuine respect for each child and expecting the same from each. He helps the asocial child to interpret poor behavior, encouraging and guiding him to improve his attitude and demeanor. Treating all his students with firm kindness and kind firmness, the teacher avoids situations in which he or a child might lose face. His sense of humor is valuable in such instances and is appreciated by the class.

Knowledge of skills in many areas is basic to a teacher's preparation. He will expect students to perform within certain standards in each of the areas. He will utilize proficient students as demonstrators to heighten motivation within the class. He will help them to help themselves by guiding instruction rather than dominating it.

A teacher refreshes and renews his own knowledge in many areas by drawing from consultants or resource persons. He attends workshops and in-service training classes to gather new ideas and to keep abreast of current developments. He discusses ideas with other teachers and offers to put on demonstrations of particularly successful lessons.

Through enthusiasm, interest, knowledge of skills, a sincere appreciation of each child, and a real desire for a fine program, the teacher makes a significant contribution to the total development of each child.

THE CLASSROOM TEACHER

The classroom teacher who conducts his own activity program is in the favorable position of intimately knowing his students' abilities. Because he is aware of the personalities within the class, he is able to plan an effective developmental program. Because he is cognizant of patterns of growth and development, he knows how to complement these patterns through specific units of instruction in physical activity.

A balanced program of activities is planned to give his students every opportunity for the development and enjoyment of physical prowess. The teacher is in the best position to judge the most appropriate scheduling of his activity period in conjunction with his other instructional units. Since the time allotment for each of these units is so critical, he must organize each segment in the most efficient manner and transfer from one to the next with a minimum of waste motion. The classroom teacher may enjoy demonstrating new skills for the class, or he may elect a student to perform as directions are given.

If, for some reason, the classroom teacher feels himself to be unsuited to the role of "games teacher," there are several alternatives available to assure his students the best possible instruction. These will be discussed in the ensuing paragraphs.

THE EXCHANGE TEACHER

A teacher with strong talents in the areas of music or art may make arrangements to exchange classes with another teacher who enjoys conducting the physical activity program. Similarly, two teachers may combine their classes for instruction, one conducting the dance program while the other presents team sports and related skills. When upper grade boys and girls are separated in some of the sports activities, the man teacher usually takes the boys and the woman teacher the girls. However, the man teacher should sometimes take the girls for instruction in skills and to coach the activities.

The students benefit from teacher exchange and seem to enjoy the departure from classroom routine. Certainly, the teachers are more comfortable teaching in areas in which they have the greatest preparation and interest.

THE SPECIAL TEACHER OF PHYSICAL EDUCATION

As the title implies, this teacher has specialized training in physical education. Increasing numbers of such specialists are being employed in the schools.

Because of his training in such areas as the physiology of exercise, growth and development, and skill progression, the special teacher has a distinct advantage in conducting an efficient, balanced activity program. He is quick to ascertain the reasons for difficulty in a particular skill, and can provide coaching hints that assure success. Physical fitness is of concern to the specialist. By assessing the fitness level of each child, he can recommend activities that strengthen poorly developed muscles, and help instill a pride in good physical development.

The main purpose of a special teacher is to present skill instruction in depth. Games are then intoduced in which these specific skills are utilized, avoiding the drudgery of just "skill drill." By building skills one atop another, children are able to perform with greater proficiency and certainly with greater eagerness.

It must be remembered that not all children will greet with joyful enthusiasm the announcement of a forthcoming soft-ball, basketball, or touch football game. Some may admit privately that they don't know how to play very well, but publicly they can't very well go against the vote of the class leaders. However, given an opportunity to develop the necessary skills, they too will enter wholeheartedly into competition.

Ideally, there should be a special teacher of physical education in every elementary school. Children are capable of absorbing and retaining a great deal more subject matter than was previously thought possible; they are also capable of much greater skill development. The special teacher has the training and materials to capitalize on such potential, with the added advantage of having to prepare in depth in only one subject area.

If it is not feasible to place a special teacher in each school, other alternatives are available that are also in harmony with the objectives of the program. One such alternative is to establish a rotating schedule in which the specialist is assigned to two or three schools, arranging to meet with each class once or twice each week. The classroom teacher is then provided with the information to carry on activities for the remainder of the week. This schedule, while not so desirable as having a resident specialist, does provide stimulation to both students and teachers, promotes a better program, and makes available excellent in-service training.

TEAM TEACHING

Classroom teachers may prefer to conduct their activity program through team teaching.

The program is divided into areas equal to the number of teachers participating. Each teacher then makes preparation, in depth, in his particular area. All classes involved have physical education at the same time; each class reports to the assigned teacher for a unit of instruction for a given period of time. Three teachers may divide activities into the three sections of the book with each teacher covering one section: "Movement Skills," "Ball Skills," and "Dance." If more teachers are involved, the responsibility for Section One may be divided: material appearing in Chapters 1, 3, 4 may be covered by one instructor, while material in Chapter 2 would be handled by another. To divide Section II, one teacher may be responsible for ball skills and small group games, while another covers team games. Several of the advantages of such a program are readily apparent: variety, preparation in only one area for each teacher, improved instruction.

It will be necessary to have a chairman who will oversee such a program, making out schedules, assisting teachers in planning their units, and generally providing the impetus to make team teaching a success.

THE PRINCIPAL

Responsibility for facilities and equipment lies primarily with the principal. He is concerned with providing a safe playground with necessary areas for a good physical education program. He should enlist the aid of a physical education consultant or supervisor at city, county, or state level in selecting and evaluating equipment. He can sometimes turn to service groups or parent organizations for help in purchasing special equipment such as record players, records, and tumbling mats. In some cases he must establish a schedule of play areas to avoid overcrowding or reduce distractions to adjacent classrooms.

The principal may be consulted by the classroom teacher in planning and conducting the activity program. He may aid in the dance program by helping in the planning and, if needed, by working with the classroom teacher in presenting dances. Some principals are keenly interested in sports and enjoy demonstrating new skills or otherwise taking part in special events.

A principal's greatest contribution to the physical education program is his enthusiasm for and interest in it. When this attitude is present, the means will be found to make a most successful and rewarding program.

THE CUSTODIAN

Maintaining a safe, clean physical environment is the primary task of the custodian. Added to this responsibility may be the care and repair of playground equipment. The custodian is vitally interested in children and the functions of the schools, and, with proper notice, may be enlisted to prepare a room for dance or a playfield for a tournament.

The custodian appreciates consideration from faculty and students in making requests against an already busy schedule. Requests for unusual services are routed through the principal.

The custodian is a resource person in his own right in that he can often locate equipment when all others have failed to do so. He is a friendly, helpful person, a most valuable member of the school staff.

LEADERS OUTSIDE THE SCHOOL

SUPERVISORS AND CONSULTANTS

As in other areas of education, consultants and supervisors in physical education generally work directly with the teachers through workshops and in-service training sessions. They may be called upon to assist with the ordering of equipment and supplies, with the selection and placement of apparatus, or with the preparation of a new school site and the layout of facilities. They are excellent resource persons in the planning of special events such as track meets, folk festivals, or fitness days. These specialists may have responsibility for, or may assist in, the formulation of physical education curriculum guides.

Supervisors and consultants are able to furnish up-to-date information regarding the most effective types of programs, developed through research. They can also help direct team teaching programs.

If the services of a physical education supervisor are not available, a general elementary supervisor or consultant may be called upon for special help. Teachers requesting administrative assistance are respected for their desire to improve and enrich their programs.

PHYSICAL EDUCATION SPECIALISTS—SECONDARY SCHOOLS

When other help is not immediately available, secondary level teachers may be called upon to assist in the planning and implementation of the elementary school program. They might lead in-service training classes in the interpretation and understanding of a sound activity program. It is possible that such teachers might spend part of their time working at the elementary level, conducting demonstration lessons. They might also serve as curriculum consultants, working with committees of elementary school teachers.

PHYSICAL EDUCATION SPECIALISTS— COLLEGES AND UNIVERSITIES

The most important service provided by the college specialist is the presentation of workshops or lecture-demonstrations. These may occur after school on minimum days, or Saturdays; or they could be incorporated in the teachers' preschool institutes. The university specialist may also be called upon to assist with curriculum planning, school site planning, layout of facilities, and selection of equipment.

THE CHILDREN

If a fourth grade teacher were asked to describe the most typical characteristics of his grade level, he might respond, "Talkative, eager, restless—but this class is a little different." Sometime during the course of his description a qualifying statement appears, since he recognizes the futility of attempting to compartmentalize children. To be sure, there are *general* characteristics that emerge from the infinite individual patterns; these are the convenient hooks upon which classifications are hung.

It is recognized that not all children of a particular grade level will answer a given description; nonetheless, all children will pass through the various developmental periods at some time. The experienced teacher accounts for such individual differences in program planning.

The charts on the following pages describe the natural evolution of motor skill development. There will be a continuing need to present instruction in these and other skills as the child demonstrates his readiness for them.

A child's social and emotional maturity has great bearing on his performance. From extremely individualistic types of play, he progresses through small group organization to team activities. He begins to appreciate group cooperation and endeavor and accepts his role as a member of such a group. In making this transition, he learns to accept the similarities and differences between himself and his peers. He also learns to accept success and defeat realistically, without berating or gloating.

During the intermediate and upper grade years, children need particular guidance in understanding their changing selves. Sudden inability to perform well in a given activity can be very perplexing to a child who has always learned and performed easily. Sudden increase in height and/or weight, which disrupts the self-image, demands readjustment and relearning of bodily control.

The whole process of growth is a wonderful and exciting, if somewhat problematical adventure. When children are properly prepared for it, and have guidance through it, they will meet its various stages with the same eagerness and enthusiasm they show for all new and challenging experiences.

THUMBNAIL SKETCHES

The following material presents thumbnail sketches of the various grade levels. They were gathered from classroom teachers and are offered as lively word portraits, dedicated to the wonderful spirit of youth. At the risk of generalizing too broadly, it is felt that these are fair descriptions. A more detailed analysis of "What To Do" and "Why?" follows the sketches.

LOWER PRIMARY LEVEL

Kindergartners are "playful puppies," wide-eyed and eager, imaginative, creative.

First graders are wiggle-worms, "I"-centered, and enthusiastic. They like to fidget, fight, and be first.

UPPER PRIMARY LEVEL

Second graders are more independent, larger versions of first graders, carry tales, are ready for anything.

Third graders are easily distracted, like routine, like to be helpful, work well in groups, prefer playing with own sex, like to "run now—listen later."

INTERMEDIATE LEVEL

Fourth graders are talkative, eager, more concerned with playing than with skill development, argumentative, concerned with fairness—usually in the other person.

Fifth graders have a strong group feeling, like self-direction and responsibility, often do not lose gracefully.

Sixth graders desire good skill development, are becoming sophisticated and imitative of older brothers and sisters, fight verbally with the opposite sex; girls are generally more mature than boys.

UPPER GRADE LEVEL

Seventh graders are saying good-bye to their babyhood, eager to conform to their peers, often "too tall or too small or too fat or too slim."

Eighth graders are "in-betweeners," trying on many coats and satisfied with none, want to be treated as responsible adults—sometimes—self-conscious and unsure of themselves.

WHAT TO DO AND WHY

LOWER PRIMARY GRADES: KINDERGARTEN AND FIRST

"Who can?" "I can!"

WHAT TO DO: THE PROGRAM	WHY
Movement exploration	
Stress activities for body awareness and body control.	Provides a foundation for all movement patterns. Height and weight increase steadily. Need to develop gross body coordinations.
Provide activities to increase awareness of space.	Needs to be comfortable in own space and in surrounding space.
Provide individual activities.	Want to be active and not wait in line. May progress at own speed without fear of failure.
Evaluate movement skills.	Need to identify children who have a difficult time with balance and coordination, in order to provide an appropriate program of instruction.
Elementary games	
Provide running games.	Love to run, to chase and be chased, and to be active. Provides further reinforcement of spatial relations and movement skills.
Check evidences of holding back or trying to be tagged in order to be IT.	Are egocentric, love to be IT.
Avoid long lines and circle games with only two to four children active as the major part of a lesson. (This type of circle game may be used as a change of pace.)	Do not like to wait a long time for a turn. Cannot and should not have to wait; love to be active.

Stunts, small equipment, and apparatus

Provide instruction on the activities in stunts, with small equipment and apparatus. Be alert to recognize children being apprehensive.

Provide supervised opportunities to participate in the activities.

Love to climb, swing, hang, and balance —when ready. Need many opportunities to adjust to a changing center of gravity.

Need to develop balance and coordination —contributes to success in school. Increase self-confidence. Love to show what they can do—"Watch me." Want adult approval.

Posture activities and general health

Be alert to poor posture habits. Integrate instruction in posture with many types of activities.

Observe children carefully—some may not be up to usual level of activity.

Need to grow "right" from the start; difficult to change poor habits.

Susceptible to disease. Onset of illness may be evidenced first in activity. Children returning to school after an illness may not be up to par physically.

Ball skills

Provide sufficient equipment for individual participation. Encourage parallel play.

Provide instruction in basic skills using beanbags and various sizes and types of balls.

Need time to explore, be creative, and learn by doing. Need to develop eye-hand and eye-foot coordination.

Need instruction and practice in basic skills of rolling, bouncing, throwing, kicking, and catching. Anxious and eager to have instruction. Need to develop good habits from the start; difficult to change poor ones.

Dance—exploration and creativity

Provide dance activities in which children may explore movement, move freely, and create own movement experiences.

Provide opportunities to work with another person and in a small group.

Provide creative activities. Accept each child's offering. Be attuned to the child's world.

Guide sometimes, never dominate. Encourage the unique.

Provide singing games. Vary the locomotor skills appropriate to the meter. Whenever possible, have children move freely.

Love to move as an individual—"I can." Have wonderful imaginations. Have complete empathy, do not pretend—"I am."

Need experiences working with others.

Creative activities provide unlimited opportunities for the use of the imagination; tremendous outlet for emotions.

Need guidance in exploring movement in order to enlarge movement vocabulary, but should be encouraged to be creative.

Love rhythmic activities. Feel secure in a circle. Participate as an individual, with a partner, or as part of a large group. Activity slightly more structured than movement exploration, but can still be creative.

General comments

Show genuine enthusiasm, encourage effort, recognize improvement, give deserved praise.	Need and want encouragement, recognition, and approval of teacher, adult approval. Adult reaction to achievement is learned early.
Give instruction in skills.	Success is basic to security.
Provide repetition.	There is security in familiar things.
Provide progression.	There is faster learning and greater success in things which are not entirely new; a new element is a challenge.
Provide individual activities.	Are egocentric. Need many turns.
Provide activities for small and for large groups.	Need to learn to share and to work with others.
Change leaders frequently.	Love to be the leader—"*I* am first."
Praise children for specific actions of fair play and sportsmanship.	Need to have a basis for understanding, little background of constructive experience. Play activities provide a laboratory for action; learning is not involved with words alone.
Stress consideration of others, including safety practices.	Need to be aware of not only own safety but the safety of others.
Have boys and girls play together.	Have approximately the same skill level. Need experience of playing together.
Change activities during a period. Organize activities quickly. Present new material quickly. Explain and at *same time* demonstrate new games and dances. Provide activities with few rules. Provide frequent turns.	Have short attention span—"What next?"
Provide a change of pace in activities.	May tire, but recover quickly.
Provide opportunities for relaxation.	Can become overstimulated; may tire; may be tense.
Include a variety of activities.	*Each* child needs success.

UPPER PRIMARY GRADES: SECOND AND THIRD

"I can *do* it!"

WHAT TO DO: THE PROGRAM	**WHY**
Continue exploration and instruction in skills and activities noted for lower primary grades, but at a progressively more difficult level.	Movement is more refined. Ball handling skills increase. Need continued success and continued challenge in activities.
Movement exploration	
Enlarge upon basic patterns and concepts.	Need to be challenged. May be capable of more than thought possible.
Provide time to explore movement.	Love to be active and need time to experiment.
Evaluate movement skills.	Need to identify children who lack ability to motor plan, in order to provide an appropriate program.

Elementary games

Provide running and tag games.

Are egocentric and have a need for "I" games; still want to be IT and have equal turns. Enjoy learning the skills involved in running and tag games. Love the challenge of relays.

Reinforce movement patterns through relays.

Stunts, small equipment, and apparatus

Provide exploration and instruction in the activities and supervise performance.

Need activity which involves balance, flexibility, coordination, and strength. Love the challenge and satisfaction of doing stunts, working with small equipment, and performing on apparatus. Increase in ability to support own weight. Enjoy individual activities.

Posture activities

Provide motivation, instruction, and activities to promote interest and good habits in posture.

Need the interest and understanding to help insure good body alignment; are increasing in height.

Dramatize some of the activities.

Enjoy learning through dramatizations.

Ball skills

Provide exploration and instruction in rolling, bouncing, throwing, catching, and kicking the ball. Provide participation in individual, partner, and small group games including station teaching.

Increase eye-hand and eye-foot coordination. Need to progress at own rate.

Provide ample equipment.

Need turns to develop skills.

Provide simple team games with few rules.

Are developing a group feeling. Want to play the games of older brothers and sisters. Capable of learning some of the skills and rules of team games.

Dance

Provide opportunities for creative activities, folk singing games and folk dances.

Need to increase skills in rhythmic activities. Need continued experiences in various types of dance activities. Teacher may have to be more selective in the area of creative dance in grade 3.

General comments

Show genuine enthusiasm, encourage effort, recognize improvement, give deserved praise.

Need encouragement, recognition and teacher-adult approval.

Provide individual activities.

Need participation and practice without undue pressure for success or fear of failure.

Provide challenges.

Enjoy challenges of all sorts; "Who can?" is good motivation.

When presenting new material, give only rules necessary to start the game; add other rules as situations occur.

Have short attention span. Need the situations to understand rules.

Include a variety of activities.

Each child needs success.

INTERMEDIATE GRADES: FOURTH TO SIXTH

"We did it!"

WHAT TO DO: THE PROGRAM

Provide a great deal of activity.

WHY

Need activity for muscular and organic development; steady increase in height and weight with a rapid growth spurt for some children.

Period of excellent health.

Provide strenuous activities but gear to child's level.

Provide more involved activities, activities with more challenge.

Have greater capacity for reasoning; need to be challenged. Have longer attention span.

Movement exploration and physical performance tests

Provide movement exploration.

To increase skill in efficient use of the body.

Provide individual and small group activities.

Evaluate movement skills through Performance Tests.

To increase in skill at own rate of speed.

Enjoy competing against own scores and comparing scores with peers—good motivation.

Recognize amount of improvement.

Provides good motivation for the lesser skilled—satisfaction gained from improvement.

Stunts, small equipment, and apparatus

Provide stunts, tumbling, and activities on small equipment and apparatus. Provide motivation and challenging activities in these areas.

To increase balance, coordination, flexibility, and strength. Children may tend to neglect these types of activities at intermediate level.

Elementary games

Provide relays and other running activities.

Need to increase skills of running, dodging (agility), and the ability to stop and to start quickly. (These skills are basic to team games such as basketball and touch football, as well as individual and dual games such as tennis and badminton.) Less mature children may enjoy more success in this area than in ball games.

Provides daring for children.

Provides strenuous developmental activities; increases physical fitness—strength and endurance.

Provide games which involve finesse and strategy.

Develops basic movement skills; involves planning and teamwork.

Developmental and posture activities

Provide motivation and instruction for good posture habits. Check posture habits of standing, walking, and sitting; identify problems.

Provide developmental activities.

May regress due to rapid growth spurt.
Boys may get careless.
Tall girls may stoop and become round-shouldered in an attempt to cover up signs of maturing early.
Develop muscle strength in order to maintain good body alignment, especially for early maturers.

Sport units

Provide instruction and practice in skills in game situations: relays, small group games, and modified team games. Have children create small group games using appropriate sport skills.

Provide progression in skills.

Provide opportunities to experiment with and explore the various skills. Teach acceptance and understanding of individual abilities and potential.

Are capable and interested in developing skills of team sports but often prefer playing *the* game. Have wide range in ability due mainly to maturity level and interest. Need activities with many turns and with automatic rotation.
Skill is aquired by building from known to unknown.
Are capable of developing skills. Correlation between enjoyment of activity and ability to perform the skills; ability in games and self-image; level of skill and social status, especially among boys. Need to be accepted by peers; want peer approval. Need to be comfortable in organized activities or will not want to participate. The poorly skilled child is often not accepted and many times not wanted. (Everyone needs to be needed.) Peer acceptance gradually supersedes adult approval. May be the only area (or one of few) in which some children have success.

Provide repetition and provide good progression.

There is security in the familiar; learning is faster with good progression and the experiences are more satisfying. There is more time for activity if experience is not entirely new.

Provide team games.

There are strong group loyalties; children *need* to belong. There is great interest in competitive sports, especially among boys.

Use various methods in choosing teams. Avoid choosing in front of peers.
Provide numerous opportunities for leadership.

Tremendous emotional upset from always being chosen last.
Want to take on leadership roles and are capable of assuming positions of responsibility. Learning to lead *and* to follow aids in social growth. Some children need to move up a ladder of progressively more difficult roles. Satisfying experiences are basic to the desire to lead.

In some cases of disagreement, take a quick vote to settle the problem.

Encourage and demand good attitudes; stress the appreciation of peers, with such comments as "Nice try," "That's better."

Assist the overaggressive, the "bully," the "ball hog," the immature, and the misfit to reinterpret their outlooks or positions.

Learn to apply democratic principles in game situations.

Peer approval surpasses adult approval. Are outspoken. Self-image based largely on responses of others to self. If responses are poor, child is emotionally upset and may resort to undesirable social reactions along with no effort in activity. Emotional disturbance affects ability to use intelligence effectively. If responses from others are encouraging, the results are usually positive—better attitudes, greater effort, with resulting satisfaction and acceptance. Children need to develop self-confidence. Receptive to the formation of attitudes—attitudes which may be with them for life. Children are in "plastic stage."

Through reinterpretation of the situation, child may be more willing to help rather than hinder; if immature, more willing to accept his present position; if unskilled, more open for help from better skilled players.

Dance—exploration and creativity

Provide such activities, but on a more advanced or sophisticated level. Explore movement based on such subjects as sport skills; things mechanical; and orchestral themes, along with activities based on social studies units.

Need to have continuing experiences in learning to move efficiently. Activities should be based on interests and level of maturity.

Dance—traditional and contemporary

Review locomotor skills. Learn folk dance steps and square dance calls.

Provide dance activities: folk dance, circle mixers, and square dances.

Provide mixers in dance, using various methods of providing partners for the "starting line-up."

Increase skill in responding to rhythm.

Increase understanding and appreciation of people of many cultures. Integrate activity with social studies unit.

Boys may feel they have to protest against dance; they may not want to show preferences among the girls.

General comments

Include class leaders in program planning.

Have children assist in some of the program planning.

Have discussions explaining maturity and preadolescent growth spurt.

Leaders have strong influence on attitudes of class members.

Enjoy activities in which they have a part in the planning.

May confuse statistical averages with being "different." Need to understand own timetable of maturity.

Provide coeducational activities.	Need the experience and benefits of working together. Some girls should have the opportunity to compete against the skill level of boys in some games.
Provide activities in which boys and girls play separately.	Due to differences in skill level and aggressiveness, team games such as basketball, touch football, soccer, and speedball should be played separately for greater safety and interest.
Provide motivation and encourage activity for upper sixth grade girls.	Want to learn, but other things may interest them more.
Provide a variety of activities.	*Each* child needs to succeed.
Provide a strong recreational program.	Provides more opportunities to develop skills and participate in activity.

UPPER GRADES: SEVENTH AND EIGHTH

"Let's do it."

WHAT TO DO: THE PROGRAM	WHY
Sport units	
Provide team sports.	Enjoy the participation and challenge of team sports. Capable of performing more difficult skills, learning more rules, and developing strategy in the games. There is further increase in length of attention span. Need to be identified with a group.
Provide instruction in skills through relays and drills, small group games, skill tests, and modified team games.	Need coaching and many turns in order to develop the skills and strategy of team sports. Wide range in height, weight, and in level of skill.
Encourage, motivate, and provide understanding in each individual's level of skill.	Due to rapid growth period, some may regress in skills; peers may pass someone who previously was better. A child may experience loss in status.
Provide a wide variety of activities.	Need time for exploring and for gaining experience in many activities as a basis for selection later.
Individual and dual activities	
Provide individual and dual activities such as tennis, paddle tennis, deck tennis, badminton, and swimming.	Enjoy individual and dual activities. Are capable of developing more difficult skills. Need to explore many skills and activities.
Developmental and posture activities	
Provide strenuous developmental activities commensurate with maturity.	Need strenuous activity for muscular development for physical efficiency, period of rapid growth. Need muscular strength to maintain good body alignment.

Recognize lack of interest in activity due to genuine fatigue.

Rapid growth drains energy.

Be alert to poor posture.

May express state of health or reveal attitudes. May slump due to rapid growth, and lack of muscular strength.

Stress and motivate good posture.

Increase in interest in personal appearance —boys and girls.

Dance
Continue experiences in dance.

Assist through "awkward age." Improve movement skills. Awkwardness mainly due to rapid growth and developing social self-consciousness.

Provide mixers in dance with automatic assignment of partners.

Have wide range in skills in dance and in maturity—very self-conscious.

General comments
Discuss maturity and rapid growth spurt.

Need to understand own growth pattern and appreciate the growth pattern of others. Have wide variation in levels of maturity and growth patterns.

Motivate, encourage, and provide opportunity for lots of participation.

May become discouraged with performance in skills as compared with previous experiences.

Be alert to the stage of physical development of "the large boy."

Permanent injury may result from "the large boy" being the bottom of a pyramid or even trying to support his *own* weight on his hands and wrists. Should not participate in combatives or activities such as tackle football during this period of growth.

Hero worship is evident.

Set an example of fairness, sportsmanship, and good habits of posture.

Provide many, many opportunities for leadership.

Are capable and intensely interested in assuming responsibility and roles of leadership. Need opportunities to learn the responsibilities of a follower. Need to learn to play both roles with composure. Are anxious to become adult. Want to become self-directive and break away from adult control.

Provide more activities with boys and girls in separate groups.

Sex differences are more apparent. Boys are developing more strength than girls and have a greater interest in seasonal sports.

Provide coeducational activities.

Need opportunity to participate together in appropriate recreational activities.

Provide a strong intramural program. Provide opportunities to participate in Sports Days.

Need more time for activity than provided in the physical education period; need more time to participate in a variety of team, individual and dual games. Need more opportunities to develop skills learned in physical education period. Need to belong. Enjoy the participation and the competition.

SUMMARY

The teacher's role in education is all-important; his knowledge of children and knowledge of skills will affect the quality of education. Since the teaching of physical education requires rather specialized skills, it is best taught by the specialist—or introduced by the specialist and carried on by the classroom teacher. The practice of team teaching can be very effective.

The physical education program needs the combined effort of teachers, principals, custodians, supervisors, and consultants. When needed, specialists at the secondary and college levels may contribute to the program.

Children pass through the same stages of growth and development, but at varying rates of speed. Individual differences due to maturity, previous experience, and ethnic background increase the need for a variety of activities. At the same time, general characteristics of children at various grade levels provide guidelines for the selection of activities.

The physical education program provides a laboratory in which good attitudes, acceptance of self and others, and an appreciation for fitness may be developed. Understanding and friendly relationships with the teacher are paramount in this development.

BIBLIOGRAPHY

1. American Association for Health, Physical Education, and Recreation, Physical Education Division. *This Is Physical Education,* 1201 Sixteenth Street, N.W., Washington, D.C.: American Association for Health, Physical Education, and Recreation, 1965.
2. Anderson, John E. "Growth and Development Today," in *Social Changes and Sports,* American Association for Health, Physical Education, and Recreation, 1201 Sixteenth Street, N.W., Washington 6, D.C., 1959, pp. 35–66.
3. Breckenridge, Marian E., and E. Lee Vincent. *Child Development,* 5th ed., Philadelphia: W. B. Saunders Company, 1965.
4. Cratty, Bryant J. *Perceptual and Motor Development in Infants and Children,* New York: The Macmillan Company, 1970.
5. English, Horace B. *Dynamics of Child Development,* New York: Holt, Rinehart and Winston, Inc., 1961.
6. Fait, Hollis F. *Physical Education for the Elementary School Child: Experiences in Movement,* 2nd ed., Philadelphia: W. B. Saunders Company, 1971, pp. 30–58.
7. Halsey, Elizabeth, and Lorena Porter. *Physical Education for Children,* rev. ed., New York: Holt, Rinehart and Winston, Inc., 1963, pp. 15–47.
8. Lee, J. Murray, and Doris May Lee. *The Child and His Development,* New York: Appleton-Century-Crofts, Inc., 1958.
9. McCandless, Boyd R. *Children and Adolescence, Behavior and Development,* 2nd ed. New York: Holt, Rinehart and Winston, Inc., 1967.
10. Mussen, Paul Henry, John Janeway Conger, Jerome Kagan. *Child Development and Personality,* 3rd ed., New York: Harper & Row, Publishers, 1969.
11. Rarick, G. Lawrence. *Motor Development During Infancy and Childhood,* Madison, Wisconsin: College Printing and Typing Co., Inc., 1961.

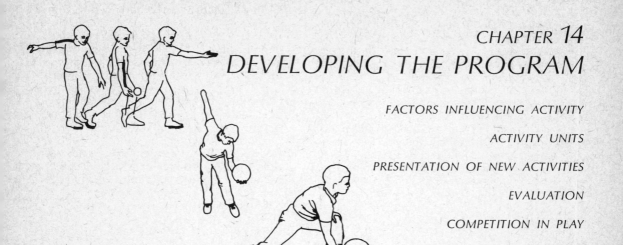

CHAPTER 14
DEVELOPING THE PROGRAM

FIG. 14.1. Teaching for transfer: What can you see that is similar in these skills? (Opaque projector enlargements of skills—underhand pattern, Chapters 6 and 8.)

The three sections of activities in the first part of the text are based on movement skills, ball skills, and dance skills, respectively. The sections may be thought of as a mountain with three peaks. The peaks gradually rise out of a common base. The children are carefully guided up the slopes. The ascent is fun if the trail is not too steep and if time to enjoy the excitement of reaching each plateau is provided. On the other hand, the fun on the ascent is dulled by inactivity and needless delays. Careful planning and directing are essential for a successful and enjoyable trip.

FACTORS INFLUENCING ACTIVITY

LENGTH AND CONTENT OF CLASS PERIOD

From surveys it would appear that physical education periods at elementary school level run from about 20 to 40 minutes a day to 30 to 40 minutes three times a week. How much of this time is spent in actual activity? What is included in the allotted time?

1. Does it include a recess period?
2. Does it start when children begin to put away books, papers, and other supplies from the previous period, or does it start after everything is put away?
3. Does it include the time needed to return to the classroom or does it end on the play area?
4. Does it include two passing times, going out and coming back to the room, or one passing time?
5. Is it at the end of the day, with time taken out to pick up sweaters, books, and lunchboxes in order to reach a bus on time?
6. Does it start when the bell rings after recess or when the children are lined up at the play area; or do the children return to the classroom before going out for physical education?
7. How much preparation time is spent in the classroom?
8. How many times do the children line up within one period? How many changes in organization are made during one period?

Some 20-minute physical education periods have little over 10 minutes for activity. A class that precedes recess has the following advantages: there is opportunity to give initial instructions in the classroom; the children are less keyed up than after recess; and there is only one passing time. A 30-minute period not including dressing time or a recess period is recommended as a minimum amount of time for daily instruction and guided play at the intermediate and upper grade levels. A daily 20- to 25-minute period may be allotted to primary grades.

DRESSING FOR ACTIVITY

It is agreed that greater enjoyment and benefit are derived from activity when one is properly dressed. In some schools children do suit up in gym clothes for activity at elementary level. Where facilities are not available and the time allotted to physical education is short, children may not be able to change clothes. In these schools the practice of girls wearing shorts under their skirts every day can be established. The girls may remove their skirts in the recess before the physical education period. Sometimes specific days are established for wearing shorts.

When participating indoors in Movement Exploration and Creative Activities, the freedom of bare feet and the resulting sensory input enhances the activity. Tennis shoes are of course the second choice.

Shoes without laces or straps, boots, tight-fitting clothes, narrow skirts, and "best" clothes limit activity a great deal. Through discussions with the children on the basis of safety and enjoyment, and through parent conferences, notes to parents, and PTA discussions, many difficulties concerning dress may be overcome.

ORGANIZATION FOR GAMES

1. Dismiss from seats by groups. Dismiss by tables, rows, teams, girls-boys, or other group method rather than having the entire class rush to the door at one time.
2. By established teams.

a. For games: Dismiss one team to a specific goal line and another to an adjacent side line; dismiss one team to the first base line and the other team to the third base line. For review games, the captains assign positions and players go to the positions *as soon as assigned*. For new games, the teacher places the players in correct playing positions.

b. For relays: Team captains lead own teams to positions for relays. They space themselves and allow a safe distance between relay lines for playing. (Two teams may leave classroom at a time.)

c. Have established positions on play area for warm-ups or initial instruction. Dismiss children by groups to go to prearranged positions.

3. Without established teams.

a. Unmarked circle—primary grades. Teacher leads double line of players into a small circle; all face center of circle and join hands; drop hands and move back one, two, or three steps. Stand in middle of "own space." (Joining hands while going into circle often results in pulling.)

b. Marked circle. From two-line formation, merge into one line when circle is reached and follow the leader around marked circle; or have everyone go to the circle and stand on it facing center. Take more than double elbow distance apart and stand in middle of "own space."

c. One goal. From two-line formation, merge into one line as goal line is reached and follow the leader down the line; or have everyone go to the line and stand on it. Face running area and take more than double elbow or double arm distance apart. Stand in middle of "own space."

d. Two goals. From two-line *partner* formation, the lines separate; one line of players follow the leader down one line, other group down opposite line. (Lines will be even if children start with partners.)

e. Relay lines.

(1) With children in two-line formation, check spacing between children, and then have them merge into one single line. For six-relay lines, mark six leader positions by number with chalk (or place six cardboard numbers, beanbags, or other markers for leader positions). Send first six players to position at each mark and have them face correct direction. Count off next six players and have them walk to respective lines *as they are counted*. Continue until all are placed. (If lines are not even, note which lines are short one player. Have two winning teams, the winner of the short lines and the winner of the other lines.)

(2) Know number of children in class and divide by number of relay lines needed. Count off appropriate number of children and place them in the first line, second line. Continue until all are placed. (Note players who do not play well together and place in different groups.) Try to make lines as near equal in skills as possible.

f. Small groups.

Use reading groups occasionally; or use groups by tables, rows, teams, or by teacher arrangement. One player in each group may be responsible for taking out, setting up, and returning equipment.

ORGANIZATION FOR DANCE

1. Boys line up at the door, then girls line up on *right* side of boys (girls are always to the right in dance). Lead into auditorium. Be sure that leaders lead into circle formation *counterclockwise*, boys on inside circle.

2. In auditorium.
   a. Boys make a circle, girls step in behind a "starting" partner.
   b. Girls make a circle then face CCW. Boys step beside a "starting" partner, on inside circle.
   c. Boys make a circle facing CCW, girls make a circle outside of boys and face CW. Walk while music plays. When music stops, stand beside nearest partner and both face CCW.
3. Square dancing.
   a. Boys line up at the door, then girls line up on boys' right. Lead into auditorium. Count off by four couples and assign space for making each square. Occasionally in sixth, seventh, and eighth grades, line up according to height. Have tall boys and girls at head of line one time, short ones at the head another time. Count off by four couples for each square.
   b. Select four boys to make a square, then select four girls to step in as partners. Continue until entire class is placed. Reverse the procedure occasionally by placing the girls first.
4. Latter part of sixth grade and in seventh and eighth grades: boy learns to ask a girl to be his partner; girl learns to accept the invitation graciously.
5. Dances for threes.
   a. Have one-third of the children make a circle and then face CCW. Assign two children to each circle player.
   b. If ratio of boys and girls is two to one, have the "1" group make a circle and then face CCW; have the "2" group take a place on either side of the circle players.

TIME-MOTION STUDY

Adaptations of rules can increase the efficient use of time available for activity. Reducing the number of times a team changes position saves time and speeds up a game. In Home Run or Out, for example, the rule that allows all the members of a team to bat before exchanging sides, rather than changing after three outs may be used. In the same game, throwing the ball around the bases each time the ball is hit provides more activity for the fielding team than regular softball or kickball. The use of a batting tee in softball negates the demand for accurate pitching and provides more turns at bat for more players.

The efficiency of organization and the supply of equipment have great effect upon the amount of activity available to each child. Teachers may be interested in giving the "stop watch test," in the form of a time-motion study. Note the time the period starts, how long it takes to get into actual activity, and when the period ends. Select one child, or, with two stop watches, select two children to observe. Start the watch each time the child being checked is moving during actual participation in the activity (other than such activity as walking to position). Stop the watch when he is not moving. The following are some interesting figures from "20-minute" periods. Some of the activities were organized for the purpose of checking.

1. Circle games with two children active. Seven seconds to run around the circle, 4 turns = 28 seconds of activity.
Recommendation: Use after great activity for a short time to provide a change of pace. Plan more than one circle.
2. Beginning of volleyball season while learning rules, one class and one game. One second to hit the ball, 2 turns = 2 seconds.
Recommendations: Five minutes or more in Keep It Up for each team on own side of net at beginning of period. Conduct two games at one time. Provide small group activities to develop skills.
3. Softball.
   a. Class divided into two teams. (Note: It takes 14 to 17 seconds to run the bases. This is the amount of time in activity if the child gets a turn at bat and if he makes a run.) Pitchers and catchers averaged 33.5 turns in handling the ball; infielders and outfielders averaged .75 turns. Out of the 36 players in the game, 11 players

did not have a turn to bat, 20 players did not handle the ball, and 7 players neither batted nor handled the ball.

   b. Work-up. (Batters limited to maximum of two runs, see directions for Work-up.)

     (1) Girls' Work-up using batting tee—17 players. Once and a half around the entire group for turns in batting; fielding chances averaged 7.58.

     (2) Boys' Work-up using a pitcher —17 players. Once around for turns in batting; fielding turns averaged 10.94.

Note: All children had at least one turn at bat; all but one handled the ball.

Recommendations: Plan at least two games, or plan one game with other children in small group activities. Use the batting tee, especially at the beginning of the season. Play adequate amount of Work-up, Home Run or Out, Three Team variation, and small group activities.

  4. Apparatus.

   a. Half the class on horizontal ladder for instruction and evaluation; half the class in Kickball Work-up. Activity time checked for two children on horizontal ladder—46 and 48 seconds, respectively.

   b. Same organization the following day with the other group, but activity added for children working on horizontal ladder. After being checked, each child climbed up and down the ladder of a slide two times, traveled around circular rings (reinforcement of instruction on horizontal ladder), then ran to a certain point and back again to wait for next turn on horizontal ladder; activity time—over 6 minutes (and willing to wait for next turn).

FACILITIES AND EQUIPMENT

Note: See Appendix for list of equipment and recommendations for facilities.

Two of the basic ingredients of a successful activity program are equipment and play areas. While the cost of supplying either may seem excessive at the outset, the net results in terms of active children and satisfied teachers more than justify the outlay.

It is not good practice educationally to provide a ratio of one ball to every 15 to 25 children if learning is to take place. Since it may not be feasible to equip each classroom with 10 to 15 assorted playground balls, the solution lies in preparing a central supply of equipment that all teachers may share *in addition to* the several balls that are assigned to each room.

If necessary, the new equipment that is held in reserve for classroom replacement could serve this purpose very well, and would not increase the equipment budget to any great extent.

Suggestions are presented for the most efficient use of outdoor play areas. Location of courts and apparatus may have an effect on the amount of use either is given during class or recess periods. Consideration must also be given to the number of effective teaching stations there are available at any one time in scheduling activity periods.

Special attention should be given to the section on surfaces for playgrounds and under apparatus. Especially for the latter, safe materials must be used to keep injuries at an absolute minimum, and to inspire confidence among children against being hurt even though they might slip or fall.

A well-planned playground and well-chosen equipment will promote purposeful and enjoyable activity.

CONSIDERATION OF SAFETY

Safety is the concern of the instructor at all times. Each of the activity chapters includes essential safe practices inherent in the activity. In addition it is important to follow logical progressions that prepare children for increasingly more difficult skills or combinations of skills. A review of "Safety" in Chapter 3 in terms of the play area and organization of games is also recommended.

One of the purposes in activity chapters has been to have each child aware not only of his own safety but the safety of others. This should become a habit at *all* times. Proper dress for an activity as well as proper shoes in terms of the play surface is of major concern.

The instructor has to be on the alert constantly for the unexpected. He should cultivate the habit of positioning himself in the direction of the group as a whole. In this way, along with frequent visual sweeps of the entire class, the instructor is able to become aware of and to stop unsafe situations before accidents occur.

Accidents can happen in any program. First of all it is necessary to take precautions for the health and safety of the children. In addition the cause, as well as the follow-up of an accident, may be considered *negligence*. Negligence is a key word in the case of an accident.

Each school district, as a rule, has a stated policy regarding the procedure in case of accidents. This generally includes the amount of first aid that can be administered, necessary steps in securing professional help, if indicated, and the procedure for reporting the incident. School nurses are often available to treat injuries and recommend additional action. Each teacher should certainly be familiar with recommended first-aid practices.

It is the responsibility of every teacher to become acquainted with the policies of his district, and to file an appropriate report of any accidents *before leaving the building for the day.*

It is also a *must* to carry personal liability.

ACTIVITY UNITS

Two or three consecutive days in one type of activity allow for better motivation and progression than random selection of activities. It is easier for the teacher to plan the program and to evaluate progress when covering one unit. With such a pattern the children understand the relationships within the activities and learn more quickly. Blocks of time may be as little as two consecutive days for activities such as dance or primary games, or as much as six or eight weeks, three days a week, in one seasonal sport unit for intermediate and upper grades.

A block of time may be planned for developing a skill such as dodging. The first day, elements of dodging could be stressed through movement exploration; experimenting with sliding to one side, to the other side, forward and back; running with quick change of direction; traveling through an obstacle course; working on peripheral vision and awareness of surrounding space.

The next day, Slalom and Dodging Relays and/or tests of coordination and balance could be covered. Finally, dodging would be used in such elementary games as Touchdown, Red Rover, or Capture the Flag. At intermediate and upper grade levels these experiences would be of particular value in conjunction with a field ball or basketball unit.

For Station Teaching the children may be divided into groups at *different* stations such as jump rope, small equipment, No. 6 and No. 7 balls, and target games. The teacher may instruct one group while children create their own activities in other groups. The groups rotate after a given period of time, and each receives instruction in new skills and related safety measures. Sometimes the teacher may rotate with one poorly skilled group and coach the various activities, or he may move from group to group as needed. (See "Station Teaching" in Chapters 2 and 6.) One or two days may be given over to scramble-choice days in which children move from one station to another at will. Guidelines for conduct should be discussed and established before going to the play area.

When conducted out-of-doors, instruction on playground apparatus or in tumbling may be given one group by the teacher while the other children play a familiar game in an adjacent area.

Physical fitness is a year-round objective. It is accomplished mainly through participation in vigorous developmental activities of all kinds that increase circulation, respiration, and heart power, activities that result in increased endurance and strength. This means strong personal involvement, not merely going through the motions. Some activities contribute more in one way than another; thus a variety of activities is needed. Apparatus contributes a great deal to shoulder strength, while game activities contribute more to leg strength. For intermediate and upper grade levels, running games and strenuous team games, developmental exercises, and stunts and tumbling are planned to increase strength and endurance, coordination and balance, and flexibility. At primary level, movement exploration, running games, and stunts and tumbling contribute to physical fitness, along with dramatized exercises. Good static and dynamic posture are stressed during participation.

Testing and test scores add motivation and interest to the program. Increased interest may result from discussing the relationships of the tests with other phases of the program. As a general rule children are able to make better scores each time. However, failure to do so may be due to a bad day, an individual's current position on the ladder of maturity, or lack of motivation.

In a sport unit, the first half of the given block of time would stress instruction and experimentation in skills, rules, and strategy through individual and small group activities. In Station Teaching the children may enjoy creating a drill or game using appropriate skills. Some team games could also be introduced during this block of time. During the last half of the unit the greater emphasis would be on the playing of team games while the small group activities would take a lesser role. Scores on skill tests may be recorded toward the beginning of the sport unit and again toward the end, for comparison of an individual's scores—check his own improvement. The unit may end with a round robin tournament within the class and/or between classes. During the unit, rotation of players is stressed; for the tournament, players are placed in the best positions for the benefit of the team.

For added motivation and interest, the sport units may follow the general time schedule of the seasonal sport as played in the high schools, colleges, and universities. For greater participation and enjoyment, the children may well be playing modified team games based on their abilities but involving skills, rules, and strategy of the seasonal sport.

PRESENTATION OF NEW ACTIVITIES

Much of the rationale and methodology for the activities appear in the introductions to the various chapters in Section One. The following material enlarges upon the introductions of selected chapters.

ELEMENTARY GAMES

Probably the greatest fault in presenting new material is too much verbalization. With limited time and short attention span, it is necessary to explain and, at the same time, demonstrate. The exceptions would include creative activities and problem-solving situations.

When presenting new circle games the teacher may sometimes be IT first, explaining and at the same time demonstrating—even in slow motion. A walk-through also helps the children to understand the game more quickly. Safety rules should be thoroughly understood by the children in the initial presentation, and as situations arise during the game.

For Line Games with children spread out over a large area, it is sometimes beneficial to diagram a new game on the blackboard before leaving the classroom. This will increase the amount of actual playing time on the playground. Line Games may also be introduced by having literally a "walk-through" in a foreshortened area. Here, too, safety rules should be stressed. (For presenting relays, see Chapter 3.)

Since the attention span of primary grade children is often of short duration, planning at least two games during a period is highly successful. One might be a new game; others may be review to reinforce learning or "just for fun."

The names of new games and dances may be placed on a chart and used for

FIG. 14.2. Choice Day. (Courtesy Mrs. Hazel Gridley, Harding Elementary School, Santa Barbara, California.)

selection of activities on "Choice Days" as shown in Fig. 14.2.

BALL SKILLS FOR TEAM GAMES

The skill may be explained and demonstrated in the classroom or on the play area, the teacher having a ball in hand. The teacher may turn his back toward the group for better orientation to the skill. Left-handed players are checked for correct adjustments. The class may then go through the mechanics of the movement while the teacher checks and stresses the *main* points. These points are then reviewed when referred to during the activity. Whether indoors or out, the explanation and demonstration should be brief, not too wordy. Some days only one or two aspects of the skill will be mentioned, especially in review after common difficulties have been noted.

The presentation of the skill may be done first as a whole, then divided into parts: grip on the ball, starting position, execution including the follow-through. It may then be reviewed as a whole. If the teacher is not proficient in the skill, he may not release the ball or he may have a well-skilled student demonstrate while main points are stressed. The teacher's ability to analyze, to recognize poor performance and give appropriate coaching hints is more important than his having a high level of skill. Common difficulties encountered in the performance of the skills and coaching hints are included in the text along with the descriptions and illustrations.

Give the initial presentation of the skill, then allow time for practice and experimentation. Stress main points rather than detail. Allow children time to work out some of the problems. Evaluate main points and repeat practice. Add a game situation in the form of experimentation as an individual, with a partner, in relay, or small group games.

RELAYS AND SMALL GROUP GAMES

With children in their relay lines, use one of the center teams to demonstrate *as* the relay is being explained (some of the adjacent lines of players may sit down in order for all players to see the action). The teacher may step in as the leader when demonstrating. Go through the relay, stressing performance of the skill and adherence to the rules. Have the demonstration team continue practice while equipment is being distributed to the other relay lines. Practice for a given period of time, evaluate, and then repeat the practice or start the game situation. Play for accuracy or for speed, whichever is appropriate in terms of the skill. For example, bowling the ball at a target would be for accuracy rather than speed, while a basketball chest pass would be played for speed after adequate time has been allowed for practice.

TEAM GAMES

The initial introduction to the game may be given in the classroom with a diagram on the blackboard or by using a small blackboard on the play area. (In activities such as Zigzag Basketball, the explanation and demonstration may be given in a small area as for a small group game.)

1. Discuss the *name* of the game and something interesting or challenging about the game (short and to the point).

2. Diagram the *play area and position of players* on blackboard.

3. Using the diagram, point out the *object of the game* and *scoring*.

4. Using the diagram as much as possible, give *only the rules and safety necessary to start the game.* Limit the amount of time spent in the classroom. (May answer one or two questions only. Other questions will probably be answered as a result of the walk-through on the play area.)

5. Dismiss the group by teams to line up at the play area. Designate appropriate goal lines, side lines, or base lines upon which each team should stand. (Placing players is easier for the teacher or a captain if players are on a line.)

6. On the play area. Place players in correct playing positions (a batting team or a team which is "up" may go directly to the batting position).

7. Conduct a short walk-through, one player having a turn *as rules are being explained;* or have a short play period during which basic rules are clarified.

8. Play the game and present additional rules as the game situation gives basis for understanding each new rule. At the same time, keep the game moving without too much interruption so that the initial experience is fun.

9. Evaluate the play as teams exchange sides or at other appropriate times during the activity. Evaluation may come at end of period to set up purposes for the review of the game the following day.

FOLK SINGING GAMES; FOLK DANCES AND CIRCLE MIXERS

The initial introduction to the dance may be presented in the classroom. A new formation, such as sets of fours or groups of threes, may be shown. Unusual turns or other anticipated difficulties may be presented and correct procedures stressed. The teacher may prefer to do this at the dance area. (Better attention of the group is sometimes gained *and* maintained by having the children sit while the teacher demonstrates with or without a partner.)

1. Write the name of the dance on the blackboard and present something interesting and challenging about the dance, including nationality and, if possible, background material.

2. Listen to the music, clap or tap the rhythm. Accent the first beat of appropriate phrases (are changes on 4's, 8's, 16's?). If control of group is difficult, may need to start with activity immediately.

3. May do the basic step with the music while accenting the phrases, but without regard to changes of directions or a change of step. May teach a difficult part of the dance first.

4. First step or first group of steps.

(Groups of steps which fit together are presented at one time.)

    a. Explain *and at the same time* demonstrate the first step or group of steps.

    b. Walk through the step with the children without the music. Give a starting signal such as "Ready [*pause*] and . . ." Call the steps with the walk-through, thus providing a substitute for the beat of the music. (If step is very simple, call with the music.)

    c. Repeat the step with the music. Time "starting signal" with introduction on record. Call or cue as needed. (Cues precede the action.)

5. Second step or second group of steps.

    a. Repeat procedure as in No. 4.

    b. Put steps one and two together with music. Cue the transition from first to second step.

6. Continue until dance is completed.

    a. Take entire dance with music and cue the transitions.

    b. Take entire dance with music without cues.

Note: Repeat dance two or three times through the music, then evaluate if needed. Repeat the walk-through of difficult parts and clear up any difficulties as needed. Repeat dance again with music.

On the first review of a dance, the preceding procedure may be followed, but at a faster pace. Whether the dance is reviewed the next day or a week or more later will affect amount of retention.

SQUARE DANCES

The procedure is much the same as for folk dancing. Square dances may be divided into parts: (1) introduction, (2) figure, (3) break and ending. If the introduction is not new, the class may start with the figure.

EVALUATION

EVALUATION THROUGH DISCUSSIONS

A review of one or more aspects of the day's activities, and setting future goals, are the concern of the evaluation period. This could include: a review of difficulties encountered in a skill and how to meet them; rules of an activity that were not understood or not followed; the further development of ideas relating to a problem at hand.

Activity is exciting and fun, and evaluation should not be a matter of routine. The amount of evaluation and the specific time for conducting it depend on many things: the need, the time available, and the amount of activity the children have had. After strenuous activity, time for evaluation may also provide time for needed rest. If the class period has been limited in time and the children had a good experience, congratulations by the teacher may keep the tenor of the class at a high level and may be all that is needed. One way to evaluate is to look at the faces of the children as they leave the play area.

Certain times *during* the activity may be more appropriate for evaluation than at the end of a period. Opportunity for evaluation may be provided before repeating a line or circle game, ball game or relay, or when teams exchange sides in a team game. Such evaluation has greater impact if held during the play situation. However, time may be wasted if the children are gathered in from the widespread area of a game except in cases of safety, flagrant infractions of rules, or the frequent breaking of a basic rule.

During evaluations, names of players having difficulty are not used. The evaluation is kept at a high level for the benefit of all. Normally, evaluations are kept to a brief period. Occasionally more time may be needed to solve a problem. More time is also needed to evaluate a unit that has been completed and to initiate plans for a new one.

EVALUATION THROUGH THE APPRAISAL OF SKILLS

Suggestions for evaluating individual performance in skills are provided throughout the text. However, evaluation is not an end in itself, but a means for determining where children are at the moment and the direction future experiences should take.

For activities in Chapter 1, "Movement Exploration," a chart for checking children "Who Can," may be made. Selected test items are written across the top of the chart, items such as Crane Stand; The Top; Side Leap; Backward Run; Sliding (to right, to left); Jump; Hop; Skip. A check is made on the chart if a child is able to perform the activity. The children who need additional instruction may then be organized into ability groupings for appropriate experiences.

Such a chart may be used with activities in Chapter 2, "Stunts and Tumbling"; "Small Equipment"; and "Apparatus," as well as Chapter 6, "Ball Skills and Activities." After checking the children, ability groupings may be organized for participation at appropriate "stations" where individual and small group exploration and instruction may take place. If a child has difficulty in tracking and catching a ball, the administration of visual tests, in addition to the Snellen Test, could identify visual problems.

Chapter 4, "Body Alignment and Developmental Exercises," includes Physical Performance Tests. Instruction and informal observation of fitness skills should be included as part of the Developmental Exercises, followed by administration of the Performance Tests. The "Track and Field Events" in Chapter 9 also provide opportunities for evaluating individual performance.

Skills related to sport units, Chapters 7 through 9, include Skill Tests. These chapters also present relays and small group activities that provide many opportunities for participation, evaluation, and instruction in needed activities.

In "Dance," skills in basic movement patterns such as jump, hop, skip, and slide (to right and to left) may be evaluated with stress on an accurate response to rhythm. The teacher may start with percussion instruments, pick up the natural rhythm of the children, and stress a smooth, regular response. Later evaluation may employ records for accompaniment during which time a child's performance is evaluated in terms of his response to various tempos. The chart suggested for evaluating activities in Chapter 1 may be used for listing these results as well. A contrasting color in check marks may simplify the recording. Such evaluation may indicate skill or, in some cases, the lack of auditory perception. A further check on auditory skills may reveal a dysfunction of which teachers and parents might have been unaware.

Evaluation in Folk and Square Dance may be in terms of skills and accurate response to the beat in the Traditional Folk Dance Steps of the schottische, two step, and polka as well as basic calls in square dance (maintaining a smooth, even rhythm). In addition a check may be made on an individual's ability to make smooth transitions from one step to the next. Capability in recall of sequence in steps in enjoyable Folk Dances, Circle Mixers, and Square Dances may also be evaluated.

SUMMARY

One of the most effective forms of evaluation is the day-to-day awareness of the interest, involvement, and performance of each child as a basis for program planning. Some programs are run on an "experiencing activity" basis. The effective teacher is constantly evaluating subjectively and objectively the progress of each child, and planning future experiences which will enhance each child's development.

COMPETITION IN PLAY

INDIVIDUAL DIFFERENCES IN COMPETITION

The word "competition" means different things to different people. If past experiences were usually successful, the word "competition" evokes excitement and pleasure; with a background of failure, the opposite response is observed.

Many times competition is used by teachers to increase achievement. This works very well, especially on an individual basis. However, English made the following observation:

Unfortunately, competition usually works best in the very pupils who need it least. Hank, who is already full of "the old fighting spirit," rises to the challenge and becomes even more aggressive, while meek little Billy withdraws psychologically, if not physically, from the contest. Furthermore, competition acts as a spur to learn for those who already have made the most progress and who would continue to progress without the added incentive. The child who finds a particular kind of learning difficult is very likely to believe that there is no use in competing. A group appeal to competitiveness works on the wrong people. (5)

There is a wide range of individual differences in terms of competition. It might be theorized that the less aggressive and less skilled children in play activities will progress faster with encouragement in individual and small group activities rather than in competitive team games.

In "These Are Your Children" (6) Dr. Gladys Gardner Jenkins made the following statement:

For many years we have been burdened with the cliché that we live in a competitive world and our children must, at any cost to themselves, get used to competition. In part, this is certainly true, but the statement does not take into account two very important considerations. It is only in childhood, particularly during school days, that children are expected to compete with no chance of ever winning. Yet the essence and challenge of competition is that you may have a chance to win. Even in a golf tournament handicaps are given to try to meet inequities in experience and skill. On the other hand, in the classroom and on the playground the skillful are too often pitted against those of less physical or mental ability or opportunity.

Secondly, a child must experience a degree of success before he can take competition in stride. He must have some self-confidence. Competition in which the child consistently loses is poor preparation for life in a competitive world. The ability to take real competition comes slowly. It is built upon self-respect and self-confidence in some area.

In the schools at primary level the emphasis should be on *cooperation, success,*

and increased skills. In order to lay a foundation for competition, children must have *self*-respect, *self*-confidence, respect for *others,* and a "*chance to win.*"

As evidenced by many situations, the trend of "*pushing* things down" seems to be a pattern in our culture. Competition on a national level is being provided for 5- and 6-year-olds.

Elementary school children do not *need* to travel outside the community or small district for suitable competition.

According to Anderson,

It is very easy to create such a highly competitive group atmosphere that positive harm rather than benefit may come to children. Two types of unfortunate results appear. First, the selection of only the best players for the games and activities; and second, the building of a value system which puts winning at any cost ahead of other phases of the program. Child development people feel that, in a good program, every child will have some opportunity to participate, and that the children who need participation the most, rather than those who need it the least, should be given more opportunity for practice and more instruction and guidance. In practice, we often reverse this principle by giving the best instruction to the outstanding performer who needs it the least. We should recognize clearly that we do this, not to benefit the outstanding performer, but because society places a very high value upon his particular skill; in other words, we are responding to a social demand rather than a need of the person. (2)

In intermediate and upper grade levels appropriate competition in physical education provides excellent motivation for activity and for the development of skills. Under good leadership, competition in games provides a laboratory in which the child may learn to adjust to winning and losing, and develop positive attitudes as a participant and as a future spectator.

TYPES OF COMPETITION

COMPETITION WITHIN THE CLASS

At primary level, the activities are usually on an individual basis: movement exploration; stunts, small equipment, and apparatus; elementary games; and simple ball games. The child is competing against himself and receives individual encouragement, or he may be competing against another individual. The activities can be easily continued during the recess and noon periods as well as during the out-of-school hours.

At intermediate and upper grade levels, the children are interested in team games as well as individual and dual activities.

INTRAMURAL—COMPETITION WITHIN THE SCHOOL

Physical education periods; Noon Leagues; Afterschool Programs.

EXTRAMURAL—COMPETITION OUTSIDE THE SCHOOL

Play days

Although the term "Play Day" may sometimes be used as a general term, strictly speaking it means competition between teams made up of players from more than one school. The emphasis is on getting acquainted and on the social values, along with competition. Play Days may well be used to acquaint children with a new environment when moving from one school level to the next.

Sports days

On Sports Days children play on their own school teams, and more than one team from each school competes. There may be as many as six or eight teams from a school. The teams may represent grade levels or may be divided according to skill level. The emphasis is on providing competition for many children.

Field days

Field Days are similar to Sports Days, but include basically individual activities: track and field events, performance tests, relays, and novelty events.

Telegraphic meets

Individual activities are covered in Telegraphic Meets. The events are conducted on each school's own area. Results are tabulated and the scores compared with the scores of the other schools. Such meets have many of the advantages of Sports Days. This type of competition is especially

appropriate for rural schools and where travel distances are great.

Varsity competition

Varsity competition is the term used when one team representing the "best" in one school or area plays against one team representing the "best" from another school or area. The number participating are few, the time and money spent are great in comparison with the number participating.

Such a varsity program is not recommended below the ninth grade due to the amount of coaching time, the facilities tied up, the trips and money involved for the few; the "overinvolvement" of some parents; and the varied difficulties and pressures associated with any kind of varsity competition.

TOURNAMENTS

Tournaments are used as a culmination of a unit of instruction, as a test of skill, and as a reward for diligent effort in improving skill. There are three basic types: Round Robin, Elimination, and Ladder or Pyramid Tournaments.

ROUND ROBIN TOURNAMENT

The main advantages of this type of tournament are: (1) every team plays every other team; (2) all teams play the same number of games, no team is eliminated; and (3) a truer winner is determined than in other type tournaments. A percentage system of games won, lost, or tied may be worked out as for major leagues in professional sports. The disadvantage of this type of tournament is that it may take too long a time to complete if many teams are involved. However, a large entry list may be divided into two leagues, with winners of each league meeting for a play-off. For example, 8 teams would have to play 28 games in one Round Robin Tournament, but 2 leagues of 4 teams would involve only 6 games each plus a final game between winners, a total of 13 games.

A simple way to set up the games is presented in the following example.

Round 1	Round 2	Round 3	Round 4	Round 5
1–6	1–5	1–4	1–3	1–2
2–5	6–4	5–3	4–2	3–6
3–4	2–3	6–2	5–6	4–5

Throughout the schedule, team No. 1 remains in the same position and the others rotate one place, counterclockwise. Fifteen games are scheduled in a Round Robin Tournament for six teams. If the number of teams is uneven, one number would represent a "bye," indicating that no game is played.

The most frequent use for Round Robin Tournaments is found in the physical education program during and/or at the end of a sport unit. If the class is divided into four teams, three days would be required for the tournament. However, in softball two consecutive days may be needed to play a sufficient number of innings for one game; thus the same tournament in softball would take six days.

Round 1	Round 2	Round 3
1–4	1–3	1–2
2–3	4–2	3–4

If the class is divided into three teams, three rounds would also be needed.

1–Bye	1–3	1–2
2–3	Bye–2	3–Bye

When boys in one class are divided into two teams, as in field ball or touch football, the winner of the tournament has to win two out of three scheduled games. At the same time the girls would compete in a two-out-of-three game schedule in a team game of their choice.

ELIMINATION TOURNAMENT (FIG. 14.3)

The advantage of an Elimination Tournament is that it will accommodate a large number of teams in a short length of time. The main disadvantage is that some teams are eliminated after playing only two games.

To arrange this tournament, teams are placed in brackets with two, four, or eight teams in each division. If the number of

teams is not a power of 2, it is necessary to have "byes." The diagram in Fig. 14.3 shows four games, A-B-C-D, and eight teams, teams 1–8, in the first round of play. The winner of each game in this Championship Flight moves to the right until a final winner is determined. Each team that loses is dropped directly down to the Consolation Flight. The winner of each of these games is then moved to the right until a final winner of the Consolation Flight is determined.

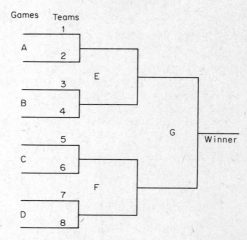

Championship flight

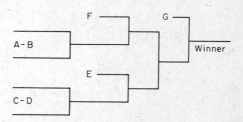

Consolation flight

FIG. 14.3. Elimination Tournament.

In this type of tournament the final games are more interesting if the teams are seeded as in tennis matches. In the eight-team bracket the strongest team, insofar as it is possible to judge, would be placed as team 1, the second strongest as team 5.

In seeding a third and fourth team, the third team would be team 7 and the fourth would be team 3. The advantage of seeding is that the best teams are more liable to meet in the final rounds.

LADDER AND PYRAMID TOURNAMENTS

These tournaments are most usable in the after-school and summer programs in individual and dual sports, such as tetherball, paddle tennis, and table tennis. Such a tournament is continuous, and, if properly motivated, places the players fairly well in order of ability. No player is eliminated. The disadvantage is that the tournament is never really finished unless a date is set for its ending. However, a terminal date should be set. A Ladder Tournament may be followed by an Elimination Tournament. Players would be seeded on the basis of the results of the Ladder Tournament.

In a Ladder Tournament, players draw

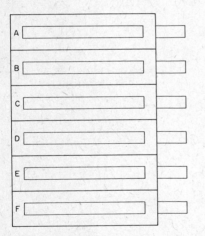

FIG. 14.4. Ladder Tournament.

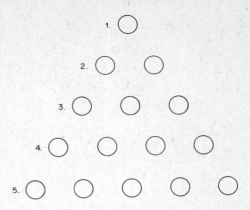

FIG. 14.5. Pyramid Tournament.

for original places. (Fig. 14.4) A player may challenge any one of the three players directly above him. That is, E may challenge B, C, or D, but not A. (Challenges may be limited to two players above if desired.) If E wins, his name card changes places with that of the player he defeated. If he loses, he cannot challenge the same player again until at least one other match has been played. Challenges must be accepted and played in the order they are received, and should therefore be posted to avoid misunderstandings. A student manager may be elected or appointed to conduct the tournament.

Pyramid Tournaments are much the same as Ladder Tournaments, except that the players may challenge only those in the rank above them. (Fig. 14.5) That is, players in rank 5 may challenge players in rank 4, those in rank 4 may challenge players in rank 3, and so on up the pyramid. Only those in rank 2 may challenge player No. 1. Names of the players may be placed on small round disks with metal rims and hung on a board.

BIBLIOGRAPHY

1. American Association for Health, Physical Education, and Recreation. *Essentials of a Quality Elementary School Physical Education Program*, 1969; *Intramurals for Elementary School Children*, 1964; *Intramurals for Junior High School*, 1964. 1201 Sixteenth Street, N.W., Washington 6, D.C.: American Association for Health, Physical Education, and Recreation.
2. Anderson, John E. "Growth and Development Today," *Social Changes and*

Sports, 1201 Sixteenth Street, N.W., Washington 6, D.C.: American Association for Health, Physical Education, and Recreation, 1959, pp. 35–53.

3. Andrews, Gladys, Jeannette Saurborn, and Elsa Schneider. *Physical Education for Today's Boys and Girls,* Boston: Allyn and Bacon, Inc., 1960.

4. Division for Girls and Women's Sports and the Division of Men's Athletics, Joint National Conference. *Values in Sports,* 1201 16th Street, N.W., Washington 6, D.C.: American Association for Health, Physical Education, and Recreation, 1963.

5. English, Horace B. *Dynamics of Child Development,* New York: Holt, Rinehart and Winston, Inc., 1961, p. 220.

6. Jenkins, Gladys Gardner. "These Are Your Children," *Journal of Health, Physical Education, Recreation* 37:34–37 (November-December 1966).

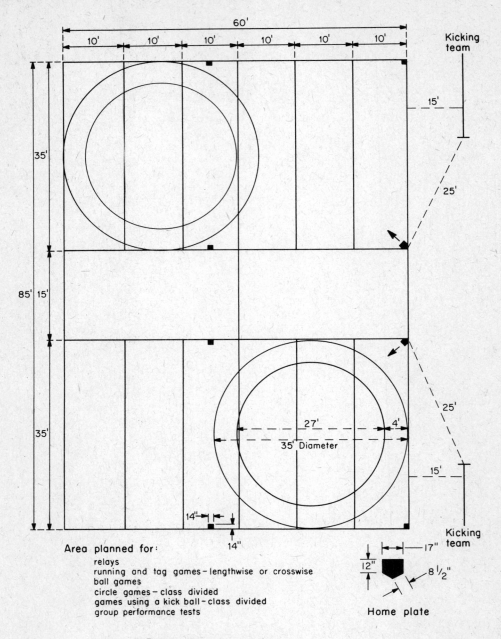

Area planned for:
relays
running and tag games–lengthwise or crosswise
ball games
circle games–class divided
games using a kick ball–class divided
group performance tests

Home plate

Multipurpose area—primary grades.

EQUIPMENT AND SUPPLIES

SCHOOL EQUIPMENT USED BY ALL GRADES

GENERAL EQUIPMENT

Record player—3 speeds (33–45–78), variable speed (fast-slow), loudspeaker, and microphone. (Variable speed is a *must*. Records may be played at a slower than normal speed for initial learning, then repeated at a faster tempo.) Battery-operated record players are available for use outdoors. (An outdoor electrical outlet may also be provided.)

Piano.

Library of records.

Library of resource books.

Pump—with pressure gauge. Table model. A pressure gauge is essential to avoid overinflating the balls, making them too "live" and causing deterioration; or underinflating, which results in poor rebound.

Chart—to specify correct pounds of pressure for each type ball.

Stopwatches.

Metal tapes.
50 or 100 feet; 8 or 10 feet.

String—100 feet—guide for marking lines.

Agricultural *gypsum*—for lines on turf. Agricultural gypsum is sometimes erroneously called lime. Lime is injurious to the eyes.

Field marker—dry marker for gypsum, 20-pound capacity. Field markers vary widely in price; check durability.

Traffic paint and marker—for lines on blacktop.[1] White and yellow traffic paint.

Yellow traffic paint—to mark apparatus for safety.

Ball marking equipment. White traffic paint; marking pen set.

Milk cartons or plastic containers—15 in a box. For relays, targets, bases, and play area markers. (Cartons or containers are slightly weighted with sand or gravel, easy to knock over with a bowled ball. Milk cartons may be covered with contact or construction paper.) Traffic cones may be used.

[1]Such equipment may be purchased by the district for use by several schools.

Plastic eyeglass protectors for basketball and soccer.

Belts and flags for Flag Football—optional.

Sacks for carrying balls—plastic mesh, canvas, or burlap.

SACKS OF BALLS (IN CENTRALLY LOCATED PLACE)

Kickballs—4 to 6: grades 1 to 6, deluxe utility No. 8 kickball; grades 7 and 8, soccer-kickball.

Footballs—4 to 6: grades 4 to 6, Nos. 6 and 7 footballs; grades 7 and 8, No. 7, youth, or regulation size.

Basketballs—4 to 6: grades 4–6, junior or intermediate basketball; grades 7 and 8, intermediate or regulation size.

Playground or utility balls, No. 8½—4 to 6 for primary grade activities and for upper grade volleyball and dodge ball type games.

Volleyballs—4 to 6, grades 5 to 8.

Playground or utility balls, No. 6 and 7—2 sacks with 16 to 20 in each sack (*small* mesh plastic sacks or plastic barrels).

12-inch soft softballs, playground softballs—8 to 15 for regular play.

12-inch super-soft softballs—6 to 10, grades 3 to 5 for learning to throw and catch.

12-inch regulation softballs—6 to 10, for boys in grades 7 and 8.

9-inch or 10-inch softballs, playground softballs—6 to 8, for boys in grades 5 and 6; official 9- or 10-inch softball for boys in grades 7 and 8.

SOFTBALL EQUIPMENT (IN ADDITION TO SOFTBALLS)

Softball home plate—one for each diamond. Official size with beveled edges, all rubber.

Outdoor: Home plate with spikes, set securely into the ground and with beveled edges slanting downward. Throw-down home plate with beveled edges.

Indoor: Suction design home plate with beveled edges.

Softball bases—set of 3 for each diamond.

Outdoor. Throw-down bases, 14-inch or 15-inch square. Bases not fastened to ground.

Indoor: Suction design rubber bases, 14-inch square.

Softball bats—28 to 32 inches long. Solid plastic or wood.
Batting tee—2 (of sturdy construction). (See Fig. 9.1.)
Softball catchers' masks—one for each softball diamond.
Mitts and gloves—grades 7 and 8.
Chest protector—grades 6 to 8.

TRACK AND FIELD EQUIPMENT

Batons or substitutes (ruler without metal edge; 1 inch × 1 foot dowel or cardboard tube; chalk eraser).
Chalk; chalkboard—2 feet × 5 feet; chalk eraser.
High jump standards; bamboo crossbars.
Low hurdles.
Markers: stakes or coat hangers with streamers on top, or weighted milk cartons.
Metal tape (8–10 feet) or 2 yardsticks.
Rake.
Starting blocks (optional).
100-foot steel tape.
Stakes—5 feet high.
Starting gun or board.
Stopwatch.
Take-off board.
Yarn—for finish of dashes and relays.

SMALL EQUIPMENT (FIGS. 2.46 AND 6.2)

Yarnballs—10 to 15 in a box.
Fleece Balls—No. 3—1 dozen.
Plastic Balls—hollow. Softball size; baseball size.
Sponge rubber balls.
Tennis balls—may use discards from Tennis Clubs or secondary schools.
Beanbags—one for each child.
Scoops—gallon and ½ gallon sizes—12.
Deck tennis rings—quoits.
Plywood bats—4 to 12.
Paddle tennis paddles (available with holes in paddle for less wind resistance).
Rebound Net (Pitch-back)—1.
Small Rebound Net (held in hands) 1 or 2.
Launcher—2 to 4.
Jump Ropes—No. 10 sash cord.
  Long ropes, 15 feet—6 ropes.
  Individual ropes—1 to a child.
  Stretch Rope—1.
Scooter Boards—8 (Approximately 17 inches long and 14 inches wide with

Shepard casters—good quality is more economical).
Barrels, lined with carpet or foam rubber —2.
Boxes.
Incline Mat, foam—1 (36 or 48 × 72 × 16 inches).
Incline Board—1.
Ladder—1 (7 to 10 feet).
Sawhorses—1 foot, 2 feet.
Hoops—minimum of 1 for 2 children.
White Sidewalls of Tires, sets of 3.
Airplane tires—4.
Wands, Sticks—8.
Balance Beam—Walking Board—2 inches × 4 inches × 6 to 8 feet—1.
  Graduated Balance Beam—2 inches to ½ inch—1. See Construction of Equipment.
Square Balance Board—4.
Stilts, plastic—4 pair.
Bounce Board—(Jumping Board)—1.

PRIMARY GRADE CLASSROOM EQUIPMENT[2]

Suggested quantity of balls assumes additional number available in a centrally located place.
Yarn balls, fleece balls, newspaper balls.
Playground balls—utility balls—light rubber balls.
  No. 6 and 7—at least 4 in classroom.
  No. 8½—at least 2 in classroom.
  No. 10—1 or 2 in kindergarten and grade 1.
  No. 13—1 in kindergarten.
  No. 16—1 in kindergarten (optional).
Kickballs—deluxe utility balls (heavier than utility balls) No. 8—2 in classroom.
Milk cartons—for relays, targets, bases.
Beanbags—one for each child.
Sponges (minimum size 1 × 3 × 5 inches —4 to 6. Available in various colors and sizes.
Jump ropes—No. 10 sash cord.
  Long ropes, 10 feet—2 ropes.
  Individual ropes 6½ feet—4 to 6.

INTERMEDIATE AND UPPER GRADE CLASSROOM EQUIPMENT

Suggested quantity of balls assumes addi-

[2]Includes only a few suggestions for kindergarten.

tional equipment available in a centrally located place.

A minimum of two balls for each sport unit in each classroom: kickballs (soccer-kickballs grades 7 and 8); footballs; basketballs; No. 8½ utility balls (volley-balls grades 5 to 8); 12-inch softballs, bats. (Footballs, softballs, and bats should be issued for the specific season.)

Small equipment could include: long jump ropes; individual jump ropes; milk cartons or plastic containers; beanbags; yarnballs; various sizes of sponges for indoor games; pinnies, T-shirts, or color bands to identify players on same team.

CONSTRUCTION OF SELECTED EQUIPMENT (FIGS. 2.46 AND 6.2)

Free and inexpensive equipment can increase the participation of all the children. Following are some suggestions for such equipment:

Balance Beams. (1) A 2 × 4-inch beam 6 to 8 feet in length is placed in support blocks at each end. Recesses in the support blocks accommodate the beam in a secure fit for both the 2- and the 4-inch surfaces.

Triple Balance Beam. (2) Three—8-foot balance beams of 3 different widths: 2½ inches, 1½ inches, ½ inch. Mark off each beam in feet. Mark the 2½-inch beam from 1 to 8; 1½-inch beam 9 to 16; and ½-inch beam 17 to 24. Beams may be mounted or recessed on support blocks individually or as a set of 3. If used individually place the supports as explained in the directions for number (1). As a set, the support blocks may be 3½ × 3½ inches by 30 inches in length. Use 3 support blocks, one in the center and one near each end of the balance beams. Allow 9½ to 10 inches between beams, and anchor or fit them securely.

Barrels. Large packing barrels lined with sponge rubber or carpeting.

Beanbags. 4 × 4-inch squares. Use heavy material such as denim and about ½ cup of beans.

Hoops. Use flexible plastic pipe along with straight couplings to join the ends.

For primary grades, 9-foot lengths of ½-inch pipe with ½-inch couplings are appropriate. For intermediate grades, 10-foot lengths may be used. In addition, 14-foot lengths of ¾-inch pipe with ¾-inch couplings present additional challenges to use as an individual, with partners, or in small groups—especially for children in grades 4 to 6.

The plastic pipe comes in 100-foot rolls, scored in one foot lengths. Heat the pipe by holding the spot to be cut under hot running water. Cut a straight edge with a sharp knife. Push the ends of the cut pipe over the ends of the coupling. To add color, place strips of masking tape on opposite sides of the hoop.

Jump Ropes (individual). Use No 10 sash cord. For measurement, have a child stand with both feet on rope with rope extending to armpits. Measure from armpit to floor to armpit. Tape ends of rope in different colors for different lengths such as: red, 6½ feet; white, 7½ feet; blue, 8½ feet.

Milk Carton Markers. One-half yard of contact paper covers three quart size milk cartons with flat tops. Three is the number needed for each group in slalom races and for bowling. Place a small amount of sand in the carton to make it heavy enough to withstand the wind, but light enough to be knocked over as a target. Cover the tops of the cartons. Fifteen such targets are appropriate for class use. (Fig. 2.46)

Newspaper ball. Crumple one double page of newspaper into a ball. Wrap once or twice around with masking tape. To make a "sticky" ball, wrap once around with sticky side of tape out.

Poi Balls. (See Fig. 13.1.) "How to Make Poi Balls" by Sara A. Brito, student in Dorothy Carol's sixth grade class, Wilson Elementary School, Santa Barbara, California.

First of all if you want to make them the original Maori colors you'll need two yards each of red, black, and white thick yarn. Besides that you need two pieces of plastic wrap, 16 pieces of tissue paper or paper towels, and two pieces of string each about 8½ inches long.

With the 3 pieces of yarn you tie a knot at

the end and make a braid about 22 inches long. Then tie another knot and cut the yarn. Bunch up one half of the paper in a round ball, stick the end of the braid in the center of the ball, and put it all into the plastic wrap. After you do that, pull up the wrap as tightly as you can and tie it with the string very tight! Now you've got yourself a poi ball. Now just make the other one.

Scoops. Use gallon and ½ gallon sizes of plastic bleach or soap bottles—with handles. With the handle of the bottle facing upward, cut off the large end and half of the handle side of the bottle. Round off the cut edge. The size of ball used depends on the size of the scoop. Various sizes and weights add challenge and interest. (Such bottles are discarded in quantities at Laundromats.)

Wands (Sticks). ½-inch and ¾-inch hardwood dowling in 3-foot lengths.

Yarn Balls. Equipment: 4 ounces of soft jumbo yarn (or equivalent substitute), 2 pieces of cardboard (back of 8½ × 11-inch tablet or shirtbox weight), a child's shoelace soaked in water (or a heavy piece of string), and a razor blade.

Draw concentric circles on the cardboard: outside circle with 8-inch diameter; center circle with 3-inch diameter. Place the 2 pieces of cardboard together and cut out the two 8-inch circles. Then cut a straight slit into the middle of the 8-inch circles and cut the center hole, 3-inch diameter, making the pattern look like a doughnut.

Roll the yarn into balls, which are small enough to pass through the center hole. Place one cardboard pattern over the other with slits on opposite sides. Wrap the yarn around the outside edge of the pieces of cardboard and through the center hole, gradually covering the cardboard patterns. (Keep yarn at center hole compact in order to wrap in a straight rather than diagonal line.) Continue wrapping several layers until yarn is gone.

Work your fingers through the yarn at the outer edge of the circle until you contact the edges of the two pieces of cardboard. Holding the wrapped yarn through center hole in one hand, cut the yarn around the outer rim with a razor blade.

Take the wet shoelace and slip it down between the two pieces of cardboard and encircle the cut yarn. Pull tightly and tie the ends. Remove the cardboard from the yarn. Cut off long ends of shoelace and trim ball—if necessary. (As shoelace dries, it tightens.)

For small yarn ball use 6-inch diameter for outer circle, and 2¼-inch center hole, with 2 ounces of yarn. (Jumbo yarn is timesaving.)

SOURCES OF SPECIAL EQUIPMENT

Automobile Accessory Sales Companies
    White sidewalls for tires—12, 13, 14, 15 inches in diameter

Ball-Boy Company, Inc.
26 Milburn St., Bronxville, New York 10708
    Plywood Paddles

Creative Ideas Co.
5328 W. 142nd Place, Hawthorne, Calif. 90250.
    Launchers
    Small Rebound Net (held in hands)
    Tooties—substitute for beanbags

California Correctional Industries
1020 12th Street, Sacramento, Calif. 95814
    Educational Toys and Teaching Aids:
    Balance Beams—6 feet long
    Ladder—7 feet
    Sawhorses, 12, 18, 24 inches
    Clown—wooden target

Community Playthings
Rifton, New York 12471
    Square Balance Boards, 16 × 16 inches, rubber covered

Cosom Corporation
6030 Wayzata Boulevard, Minneapolis, Minn. 55416
    All plastic softball bat, regulation size and weight, 30- and 32-inch bats

Developmental Design
P.O. Box 55, Carpinteria, California 93013
    Scooter boards (18½ inches × 15 inches) and balance equipment
    Catalogue available

Lee, Mildred R. and H. Severin
31 Winona Avenue, Lincoln Park, New Jersey 07035
Yarn Balls—Variety of colors

Oregon Worsted Company
8300 S. E. McLoughlin Boulevard, Portland, Oregon 97202
Fleece Balls—No. 3 for general play

Perception Development Research Associates
P. O. Box 936, La Porte, Texas, 77571
Jumping Board—Fiber Glassed Board, 6 feet long, 6 inches high, 16 inches wide

Port-a-Pit
P. O. Box C, Temple City, Calif. 91780
Incline Mats—Foam
"Skill Development Equipment" of foam
Large, heavy-duty inflated balls

Physical Education Supply Assoc., Inc.
P. O. Box 292, Trumbull, Conn., 06611
Stretch Rope

Plumbing Supply Companies
Flexible plastic pipe—100 foot lengths: ½ inch and ¾ inch in diameter for hoops.
Straight couplings ½ inch and ¾ inch.

Sears Roebuck Company
Plastic stilts (with plastic ropes)—3½ inches high

Twinson Company
433 La Prenda Road, Los Altos, California:
Bamboo Hop (Tinikling); Lummi Sticks; Poi-Poi (Maori ball game). Complete kits are available with instructional album, instruction sheets, and equipment.
The album and instruction sheets may be purchased separately

Wolters and Company
6644 South Buttonwillow, Reedley, California 93654
Plastic Ball Bags—small mesh
Indoor–outdoor Throw-down Bases

Manufacturers of the Stegel (or similar equipment)
Austin C. Lent
1561 Minert Road, Concord, California 94521

The Lind Climber Company (Lind Climber)
807 Reba Place, Evanston, Illinois 60202

Patterson Williams Manufacturing Company
P. O. Box 502
Santa Clara, California 95052

FACILITIES

INDOOR

GYMNASIUM

Some elementary schools are fortunate in having a gymnasium. However, such facilities are not the rule and are seldom provided in areas where it is possible to conduct the activity program out-of-doors most of the year.

A gymnasium should provide the following facilities and storage areas:

1. Dressing and shower facilities.
2. Two basketball courts, or one basketball court with two or four additional basketball goals.
3. Two or more volleyball courts. Sleeves, guide wire attachments, or other provisions for the net standards.
4. Gymnastic apparatus such as horizontal bars, climbing ropes, traveling rings, wall stall bars, and pegboards.
5. Storage for equipment such as mats, benches, balance beams, and apparatus.
6. Storage for supplies such as balls, beanbags, and markers. See list of recommended equipment and supplies.
7. Area for the care, marking, and repair of equipment, including a table or shelf for table model pump with pressure gauge.
8. Storage for record player, records, books, and percussion instruments. (Record player and percussion instruments may be placed on carts with rubber wheels.)
9. Convenient electrical outlets for record player where player is free from floor vibrations which affect the needle.
10. Convenient output channels for two microphones.

MULTIPURPOSE ROOM—AUDITORIUM—CAFETORIUM

The multipurpose room or auditorium in an elementary school is used for many activities. When the cafeteria is combined with an auditorium, it is sometimes called a "cafetorium." Folding-in-wall tables are usually installed for cafeteria use. In terms of physical education, the multipurpose room or auditorium serves as an indoor play space and an area for conducting dance activities. The regular use would be for a single class. Maximum use would be to combine two classes.

Floor: Surface that remains smooth and resilient through constant use and one that is easily cleaned; nonscuff and nonslip. Constructed so that the needle of the record player is not affected by vibrations of the floor when used for dances.

Windows: May need guards to prevent breakage. Good ventilation system is of added importance if games and dances are to be conducted in the multipurpose room.

Acoustics and lighting conditions: Acoustics good for voice and for the sound system of the phonograph.

Lights: Medium to high intensity, without glare.

Loudspeakers: Installed to suit the acoustics of the room. Amplifier unit located convenient to the stage, and equipped with input channels for two microphones and a record player.

Record player: Provisions for connecting the record player to the built-in public address system. Electrical outlets located so that the record player can be placed on the main floor near the stage. (This makes it possible for the teacher to conduct a dance class on the main floor or practice for programs on the stage, and at the same time have the record player close at hand.)

Storage space: Adequate space for equipment used in the multipurpose room. See equipment recommended for a gymnasium.

Storage for the phonograph provided near the front of the room so that it can be quickly and easily set in place for use.

Mechanics of moving chairs and equipment: Arrange so that the floor may be cleared in a minimum amount of time; doors of the storage room should be large enough to accommodate dollies for the chairs.

Time schedule of activities: A regular schedule for the multipurpose room or auditorium should be set up at the beginning of the year in order for the custodian to have the room ready for activity, and to encourage the teachers to use the area.

OUTDOOR FACILITIES AND TEACHING AREAS

In planning outdoor facilities, the courts and fields should be arranged in terms of "teaching areas." A "teaching area" is the minimum amount of space that a teacher needs to conduct activities for one class (or one group the size of a class) and keep each child reasonably active. The class may be divided into two groups, one for instruction and one for supervised play; divided into two groups for guided play or tournaments; or divided into small groups.

If areas are limited, classes having physical education at the same period may rotate sport units.

The following teaching areas may be provided.

MULTIPURPOSE AREA (ON TURF WITH PERMANENT LINES; ON BLACKTOP WITH MARKED LINES; SEE OPENING PAGE OF APPENDIX)

LARGE FIELD AREA (TURF)

SMALL FIELD (TURF) AND AN ADJACENT AREA (TURF OR BLACKTOP)

TWO OR MORE BASKETBALL COURTS (PREFERABLY SIDE BY SIDE)

TWO OR MORE VOLLEYBALL COURTS (PREFERABLY SIDE BY SIDE)

Provide for attachment of net at 3-foot height for Paddle Tennis.

TWO OR MORE DIAMONDS (WITH MOVABLE BACKSTOPS ON TURF; PERMANENT BACKSTOPS ON BLACKTOP)

ONE DIAMOND AND AN ADJACENT AREA

APPARATUS AND AN ADJACENT AREA

HANDBALL WALL (DOUBLE FACED; USED IN CONJUNCTION WITH ANOTHER AREA)

TETHERBALL SETS
(POLE, SLEEVE, CORD, ATTACHMENTS, BALL)

PLAYGROUND APPARATUS

Activity on apparatus is extremely important at both the primary and upper grade levels. At primary level, apparatus provides individual activity for the child, activity in which he may gain personal satisfaction and can progress at his own rate of speed. He loves to climb, swing, travel, hang by hands or knees, slide, and balance. In our urban and suburban areas, the child has little opportunity to participate in these activities in a natural setting. At upper grade level, apparatus provides one of the best opportunities to develop shoulder strength.

Accidents on apparatus are usually the result of using the equipment incorrectly. Safety precautions are given at the end of the descriptions of the activities for each piece of apparatus in Chapter 2. Apparatus may be used without injury for a long period of time and for thousands of child-hours of enjoyment. One or two accidents may result in the removal of the same piece of apparatus. The best safeguards against accidents on apparatus are *good instruction* and *constant supervision,* along with proper ground covering. Teaching how to land if one falls is an integral part of the instruction.

For greater ease in supervision and instruction, apparatus should be located adjacent to the play areas for the various grade levels. For safety, the apparatus should not be in line with game areas so that children run into the apparatus area in their play or when retrieving a ball. Also for safety, the apparatus should be purchased and *installed* at the appropriate height for the children involved. The use of apparatus beyond their abilities may result in accidents.

RECOMMENDED TYPES OF APPARATUS

Kindergarten

Jungle gym or geodesic dome.[3]
Low turning bar, 3 feet in height.

[3]Carefully check distance child must drop from center or highest point and install at appropriate height.

Parazontal bars.
Balance beam (placed parallel and close to fence).
Sandbox.
Optional: swings with rubber or canvas seats.

Primary level

Jungle gym—preferably with a center pole; or Geodesic dome.
Horizontal ladder, 5 feet to 5 feet 6 inches in height. (If length of ladder permits two children to use it at one time, paint the halfway mark of ladder yellow. The second child waits until first child reaches the center of the ladder before starting.)
Traveling rings, 5 feet in height with starting ring at 4 feet.
Low turning bar, 3 feet in height.

Intermediate grades

Horizontal ladder, 6 feet 6 inches to 7 feet in height. (Paint the halfway mark of ladder yellow. Second child waits until first child reaches the center.)
Traveling rings—circular or straight, 6 feet 6 inches in height, with starting ring 5 feet 6 inches in height, 6 feet apart.
Horizontal bars—graduated heights.
Graduated bars for wide range of height.

TYPES OF APPARATUS NOT RECOMMENDED

Teeters (use comparatively large amount of space and provide little activity), giant strides, merry-go-rounds, and other such apparatus that moves.
If slides have been installed, the fourth step should be painted yellow. A second child waits below the yellow step until first child starts down the slide.

SURFACES OF PLAY AREAS

Playground surfaces are important to consider in order to provide for safe, efficient play areas.

It is impossible to have one playground surface that is best for all types of games and for all conceivable uses. The main types of surfacing used for play areas are blacktop, turf, and natural or stabilized soil. Surfaces to be used under playground apparatus are presented separately.

BLACKTOP

Blacktop refers to the all-weather macadam-type surfaces. Authorities agree that a major part of an elementary playground surfacing should be blacktop. It is an all-weather surface. With proper drainage it may be used immediately after wet weather. (Some districts require a "flood" test before accepting the project.)

Lines can be permanently marked and the maintenance of the lines is negligible.

TURF

Some grass areas should be provided on *all* playgrounds.

Fewer abrasions result on turf than on blacktop. It is also more resilient and better adapted to activities in which children are liable to fall or tumble.

NATURAL OR STABILIZED SOIL

The least desirable surface for playgrounds is natural or stabilized soil. Natural wear causes a constant problem of holes that are serious safety hazards; it is abrasive and results in a more serious abrasion than one received on blacktop. If this type of surface is used, it should have a good drainage system and be maintained free of hazards. An effective method of soil stabilization should also be established.

SURFACES UNDER APPARATUS

The foremost concern of administrators, teachers, parents, and children is safety on and *under* the apparatus. The safety factors on the various pieces of apparatus are covered in the sections devoted to them, but proper surfacing is imperative for all apparatus. Matting should be placed under all pieces of equipment in the gymnasium or multipurpose room, and can vary from tumbling mats to a commercially made sponge-rubber-type material fitted for the contact area under and around the equipment. Permanent outdoor apparatus involves a different problem. Following is a list of recommended surface coverings available.

PERMANENT RUBBER MATTING (FIG. 2.59)

Several companies manufacture the rubber matting. This is installed on top of asphalt or cement. It is the safest surfacing although rather expensive. It is guaranteed by the manufacturers for at least ten years. Upkeep is negligible for this type of surfacing. Schools in which this material is being used have found it to be economical in the long run. It is highly recommended.

SAND AND SHAVINGS

This covering combines the best features of sand and shavings. Sand keeps the shavings from packing, allows for better drainage, and helps keep the shavings from blowing away. Shavings provide some "give" for safer landing, unless packed down.

SHAVINGS OR SIMILAR MATERIAL

This covering is used, but needs proper subsurfacing and drainage.

Problems involved: cannot be used in extremely windy areas; must be replaced frequently; packs and remains damp after wet weather.

SAND (FIG. 2.58)

Sand is relatively inexpensive and is adequate as long as there is proper drainage and a proper cover base is provided beneath the sand to keep it from settling into the ground.

Problems involved: Children playing with and "piling" sand; sand carried into classroom in cuffs and on shoes; sand getting so compact it offers little or no resilience; neighborhood cats and dogs.

CONCLUSION

Safety precautions listed with each piece of apparatus should be stressed by the teacher and carefully observed by the children. Most accidents on apparatus result from failure to follow safe practices. Teaching safety and how to land are important parts of the instructional program. The best safeguards against accidents are *good instruction* and *constant supervision,* along with a safe surface covering under each piece of apparatus. Permanent rubber matting provides the safest surface, and is the most economical in the long run.

INTEGRATED ACTIVITIES

Greater knowledge, understanding, and appreciation may be achieved by crossing over the lines of subject areas. It is possible to heighten interest in a particular unit by expanding the boundaries of study. Allocated time for two or more subject areas may be combined to provide for the evolvement and refinement of ideas.

There are many subjects in the primary curriculum that can be carried quite naturally into the physical education program. The study and re-enactment of a popular story, of the growth of an insect from larva to adult, of the actions of animals, are a few of the many possibilities.

Social studies and physical education are readily combined in the upper grades to include the study of and participation in authentic games and dances of various cultures.

Laws of physical science may be better understood by the child when related to the flight of a ball or to the application of force to an object.

There is a natural interdependence between health and physical education. Through the use of health texts it is possible to increase understanding of physical performance, growth, and structure.

Music, art, and physical education may be termed related fields with similar goals. Through music children learn to sing, to listen, to move, to be creative, and to use musical instruments, including percussion instruments. Through these experiences the child gains success and enjoyment and learns to work with others. In art the child learns to express himself through various media. In physical education the child learns to express himself through movement. There are many opportunities to correlate the activities in these fields of creative experience.

It is hoped that the following information will help to guide and stimulate thinking in regard to the many significant possibilities for integration of physical education with other subject areas. Chapter references are made to material within the text which implement the suggestions made here.

ART (Chapter 10)

1. Pictures suggesting activity.
2. Color, as a motivating device.
3. Design or pattern as a basis for movement.

Example: Finger painting. Follow the pattern with one arm. How large a pattern can you make? Follow the pattern with both arms; with one foot. Can you move and make your pattern on the floor? Can you repeat your pattern using different locomotor movements; using variations in tempo?

4. Playground activity as a basis for an art lesson.

HEALTH

1. Knowledge of physical examinations: kinds of examinations and importance of each in terms of the activity program.
2. Recognition of safe practices; establishment of habits for safety.
3. Understanding the importance of nutrition, rest and play.
   a. Effect of nutrition on performance.
   b. Effect of rest on performance.
   c. Understanding the impact of illness on the body and the need for a sufficient period of recuperation.
   d. Need for play and recreation.
   e. Assessment of individual practices.[4]
4. Knowledge of the structure and function of the body.
   a. Functions of the joints (range of movement).
   b. Implications for activity.
   c. Understanding the structure of muscles and how they function.
   d. Understanding posture and the relationship to health (Chapter 4).
      (1) Causes of poor posture.
      (2) Effects of poor posture.
      (3) Common posture faults.
      (4) Evaluation of posture.
      (5) Procedures for improving posture.

[4]Marjorie Latchaw and Camille Brown. *The Evaluation Process in Health Education, Physical Education, and Recreation*, Englewood Cliffs, New Jersey: Prentice-Hall, Inc., 1962, Chapter 4.

(6) Knowledge of exercises for improving posture.

(7) Mechanics of static and dynamic posture.

(8) Re-evaluation of posture.

5. Knowledge of the circulatory, respiratory, and nervous systems (use school texts, Health Series).

   a. Understanding the body.

     (1) Effects of activity.

     (2) Effects of stress.

     (3) Effects of strength and endurance on work and play.

   b. Assessment of individual status, including fitness as measured by tests of strength and endurance.[5]

     (1) Tests of Strength. (See Chapter 4, "Physical Performance Tests.")

       a. Curl-down (abdominal strength).

       b. Standing broad jump (leg strength).

       c. Sustained chin hold (shoulder strength).

       d. Pull-ups; Push-ups (shoulder strength).

       e. Grip strength test.[6]

     (2) Tests of Endurance.

       a. The Michigan Pulse Rate Test.[6]

       b. The Larson Cardiovascular Respiratory Rating Scale.[6]

       c. Squat thrust—30 seconds. See Chapter 4, "Developmental Exercises."

       d. Jog-run (440 yards), "Physical Performance Test."

6. Study of growth and development and effect on performance.

   a. Body size and proportions.[6]

   b. Varying rates of maturity. See Chapter 12.

   c. Level of performance.

     (1) Physical performance tests (Chapter 4).

     (2) Skill tests

       (a) Chapters 7, 8, and 9.

       (b) Development of other skill test items for current sport unit.

[5] *Ibid.*, Chapter 3.
[6] *Ibid.*

LANGUAGE ARTS

1. Describe and illustrate a game activity.

2. Listen to the directions and perform the activity. Examples: The activities in Chapter 5; "Stunts," Chapter 2.

3. Write or give an oral report on a sporting event.

4. Write or give an oral report on folk dances, festivals, costumes, and customs of a specific country or era (Colonial Times, Westward Movement, Contemporary). See Bibliography at end of Chapter 11 for references.

5. Write a paper on how you feel in physical education; interests in physical education; values of physical education.

6. Write a paper in terms of the health unit.

7. For spelling, include words used in the activity program.

8. Include spelling words from the following list of commonly misspelled words.

accompaniment	excellent	refereeing
admonition	explanation	repetition
appendix	extension	retrieve
athletic	forward	rhythm
barely	handling	sashay
boundary	hazard	seeded (players)
captain	inning	shiny
chassé	involve	shuttle
cymbals	lie (down)	soccer (ball)
diagram	locomotor	steps
discipline	loser	straight
dos-à-dos	maracas	strategy
(back to back)	planned	tagged
equipment	receive	throwing
excel	referee	xylophone

9. Develop reading charts around game and dance activities.

10. Use "Activity Poems" and "Choric Verse" as a basis for activity (Chapter 10).

11. Read and interpret the rules of a game for the class.

12. Read about a sport skill and present it to the class (Chapters 6 through 9).

13. Conduct research in the area of folk dance. (See Bibliography, Chapter 11.)

14. Encourage the reading of books and articles on sports and sports personalities.

15. Develop a vocabulary of sports terms.

MATHEMATICS

FREE MOVEMENT

1. Using body, make figures 0 to 9: lying on back or side; with weight on one or both feet. Use partner to make 10's.

2. Make geometric designs such as circles, squares, rectangles, triangles, and diamond shapes. Move in such patterns using various locomotor skills. Create geometric designs using arm(s), leg(s), or entire body (Chapter 1).

ELEMENTARY GAMES

1. At the end of the game, count the number of children on each team. Which team has the greater number?

2. Specific games (Chapter 3): Number Change; Find a Number; Steal the Bacon (see "Teaching Hints").

RELAYS

1. Equal number of players on each team (equivalent sets).

2. Specific relays: Number Relay; Three-Way Relay.

TARGET ACTIVITIES

1. Use pins or markers as targets. How many can you hit?

2. Use targets with point value. How many points can you make?

3. Establish a given number of trials. How many hits (or baskets) can you make? What is the ratio?

TEAM GAMES

1. Keep score; call out cumulative score.

2. Work out batting averages. Divide the number of hits by the number of times at bat. (Batting 1.000 means getting a hit every time at bat.)

3. Compute team average. Divide the number of wins by the number of games played. Compute professional team or player averages.

TRACK AND FIELD

1. Measurement of performance in inches: long jump, high jump. Convert inches to feet and inches.

2. Measurement of performance in feet and inches: softball throw; triple jump. Convert feet and inches into yards.

PHYSICAL PERFORMANCE TESTS

1. Determine class average in test scores.

2. Compare class scores with state and national norms.

3. Draw line graph of individual's performance scores in terms of state or national percentiles.

PLAY AREAS

1. Establish dimensions for various game activities: basketball or volleyball courts; play fields; softball diamonds; circle games.

2. Mark the lines for such games.

MUSIC (Chapter 10)

1. Music suggesting activity. Combine the music and physical education class periods. Ascertain the true essence of the music. Move to the music. Suggest and discuss problems which could result in better understanding and performance.

2. Activity songs. Learn the songs in the music period; then add the movement in the activity period.

3. Create a new dance—folk form. As a culmination of a folk dance unit, divide children into groups and have them create their own dances. The music may be discussed during the music period in terms of form, with particular reference to phrasing and repetition, tempo, mood, and dynamics.

4. Use of percussion instruments. Familiarize the children with the instruments and give instruction and practice in using them. Children may then provide accompaniment for activity.

5. Finger paint while listening to music. Use the finger paintings as a guide for movement.

SCIENCE

BIOLOGY

1. Dramatizations of animal, birds, and insect life. (See Chapter 10.)

2. Study and dramatization of stages of insect life.

ELEMENTS

1. Wind, rain, sun, heat, and cold.
2. Effect of the elements on growing plants.
3. Shadow pictures, Chapter 1.

PHYSICAL LAWS

Note: A reference appropriate for intermediate and upper grade children is a book by George Barr: *Here's Why: Science in Sports,* Scholastics Book Services, Division of Scholastic Magazines Inc., New York, New York, 1965. A second supplementary reference for children is a book by Earl Ubell and Arline Strong: *The World of Push and Pull,* New York: Atheneum, 1964.

1. Equilibrium (balance), Chapter 1.
2. Gravity, Chapter 1.
3. Friction, Chapter 1.
4. Momentum (motion), Chapter 6.
5. Force, Chapter 6.
6. Levers, Chapter 6.
7. Projectiles, Chapter 6, Chapter 8, Figs. 8.3–8.6.
8. Trajectory, Chapter 8, Fig. 8.8.
9. Analysis of motor skills in relation to physical laws.[7]

SOCIAL STUDIES

LOWER PRIMARY GRADES

Some of the classroom activities may revolve around such areas as the home, school, and community. Creative rhythms and game activities that reflect the studies in the classroom may be used. For creative rhythms see Chapter 10, "Experiences Based on a Theme." Certain elementary games from Chapter 3 may be played, or the names of the games may be adapted for use. Examples: Fire Engine (Shore Patrol); Bird Catcher (Animal Catcher, Fish Catcher); and Flowers and Wind.

UPPER PRIMARY GRADES

The units for this grade level may include activities in terms of the expanded community and primitive cultures. Here again creative rhythms may be used effectively to broaden the possibilities for increasing concepts. Chapter 10 presents creative rhythms, including "Experiences Based on a Theme," and a section on Indian Dance Steps and Patterns. The book, *Games and Sports the World Around,*[8] presents games of North American Indians. Elementary games such as Cowboys and Indians may also be included in the program.

INTERMEDIATE AND UPPER GRADES

Further depth in the units of study is experienced at this level, with the possibility of including the home state, United States (Colonial Times, Westward Movement, and United States today), North American Continent, Latin-American countries, Western Hemisphere, Eastern Hemisphere, or the world.

Increased understanding of the culture of any country may be realized through study of native games and dances. An extensive list and description of such games, including some background material of the country, may be found in *Games and Sports the World Around,* and *ICHPER Book of Worldwide Games and Dances.* See Bibliography, Section One (30), (32).

Folk dances of the countries enrich the instructional program and reflect certain aspects of the culture. Related material would include knowledges of folk costumes, customs, rituals, and festivals. See the list of "Dances Around the World," and the Bibliography, Chapter 11.

A unit of study of a country might include a recording of the language (either spoken or in music), a sample of the food, native games and dances in appropriate costume, and information on the history and development of the country. Such a broad undertaking should certainly spark the interest of children, and create greater understanding among world neighbors.

[7]Marion R. Broer. *Efficiency of Human Movement,* 2nd ed., Philadelphia: W. B. Saunders Company, 1966.

[8]Sarah Ethridge Hunt. *Games and Sports the World Around,* 3rd ed., New York: The Ronald Press Company, 1964.

SEASONAL AND HOLIDAY ACTIVITIES[9]

HALLOWEEN

GAMES

Halloween Witch (Red, White, and Blue), Ch. 3.

Black Cats and Pumpkins (Blue and White), Ch. 3.

Ghosts and Goblins (Blue and White), Ch. 3.

Pumpkin Blackboard Relay (Blackboard Relays), Ch. 5.

DANCES

See "Holiday, Special Days" (Dramatizations), Ch. 10.

THANKSGIVING

GAMES

Poor Turkey (Poor Pussycat), Ch. 5.

Turkey in the Pen (Bear in the Trap), Ch. 3.

DANCES

Indian Dances (Indian Dance Steps and Patterns), Ch. 10.

Early American Dances.

CHRISTMAS

GAMES

Merry Christmas (Cut the Pie), Ch. 3.

Red and Green (Blue and White), Ch. 3.

Christmas Tree, Blackboard Relay (Blackboard Relays), Ch. 5.

DANCES

See "Holidays, Special Days" (Dramatizations), Ch. 10.

"Here We Go 'Round the Christmas Tree" (Record References, Folk Singing Games), Ch. 11.

Jingle Bells, Circle Mixers (Record Reference G-2), Ch. 11.

Jingle Bells, Square Dance (Record Reference, M-1), Ch. 11.

[9]Games are variations of the ones in parentheses.

NEW YEAR

GAME

Happy New Year (Cut the Pie), Ch. 3.

ST. PATRICK'S DAY

GAME

Green and White (Blue and White), Ch. 3.

DANCE

Donegal Round (Record Reference, F-19), Ch. 11.

EASTER

GAMES

Easter Bunny, Ch. 3.

Happy Easter (Cut the Pie), Ch. 3.

Peter Rabbit (Fire Engine), Ch. 3.

Easter Basket (Red, White, and Blue), Ch. 3.

Jack Rabbit Relay, Ch. 3.

Rabbit Jump, Stunt, Ch. 2.

Easter Bunny, Blackboard Relay (Blackboard Relays), Ch. 5.

Bunny Target (Station Teaching, Color Target), Ch. 6.

DANCES

See "Holidays, Special Days" (Dramatizations), Ch. 10.

MAY DAY

DANCES

Maypole Dance (Record Reference, F-18), Ch. 11.

Sellenger's Round (Record Reference, F-18), Ch. 11.

FOURTH OF JULY; FLAG DAY; PRESIDENTS' BIRTHDAYS

GAME

Red, White, and Blue, Ch. 3.

DANCES

All–American Promenade (Record Reference, A-4 A-7S4), Ch. 11.

Patriotic March (Accompaniment, G-2), Ch. 10.

INDEX

INDEX